CHESAPEAKE BAY CRUISING GUIDE — VOLUME I, UPPER BAY

Susquehanna River to Patuxent River and Little Choptank River

by Tom Neale
Edited by Julius M. Wilensky

all photos, sketch charts and diagrams are by the author
unless otherwise indicated

Copyright© by Tom Neale
published 1996 by Wescott Cove Publishing Company
Box 130, Stamford, CT 06904
All Rights reserved
*No part of this book may be reproduced in any form
without written permission of the publisher*

1st Edition—1996

Library of Congress Card 96-60629
ISBN No. 0-918752-22-1
San No. 210-5810

TABLE OF CONTENTS

EDITOR'S PREFACE

So much has been written about Chesapeake Bay, but it never has had the benefit of a complete cruising guide, such as we have published for other areas. I've cruised the Bay four times in my own boat, sailing down from Stamford, and enjoyed several cruises aboard friend's boats. It's a fabulous cruising ground with variety enough to please anyone. Annapolis and Baltimore should not be missed, but there are hundreds of precious gunkholes and delightful rivers and complexes of rivers to explore.

Wescott Cove wanted to publish this guide long ago but we had to find a qualified author who knew the Bay and was willing to do the complete exploration. Tom Neale is the dedicated sailor who has undertaken this massive assignment. Tom has lived on the Bay nearly all his life. He's an inverterate cuiser in other areas as well, has the navigational skills required, and has honed his writing skills writing many articles for boating magazines and newspapers. I see his byline everywhere, and recently, a byline for Melanie and Carolyn, his two delightful teen-age live-aboard daughters!

Tom Neale has lived aboard with his wife Mel and the two girls on his modified Gulfstar 47 *Chez Nous* for over 16 years. Prior to that, they lived part-time aboard other boats. For the first five years of life aboard *Chez Nous*, Tom maintained the shoreside law practice which he began in 1970. His practice included admirality and product liability law.

Both Tom and his wife Mel were raised on the shores of Chesapeake Bay. He owned a boat since he was nine years old when he "began to seriously explore the Chesapeake." The whole family has been at it now for many years. They winter in the Bahamas, and know every nook and cranny of the way south, but much of their time is spent on the Bay. Tom is a life member of BASRA, the Bahamas Air-Sea Rescue Service. Mel is a fine arts painter and a commercial artist.

She did all the artwork on the charts and made the sketch charts in this book and has also been involved with picking up information and proof reading.

To pick up the current information for this book, Tom Neale revisited every harbor and anchorage described, including shallow creeks and bays with as little as 2½ feet depth at MLW. Where *Chez Nous* couldn't go, he used his well-equipped 12-foot dinghy which includes a hand-held Magellan GPS, a lead line, a sounding pole, an electronic recording depth-finder, a hand bearing compass, and his dictating machine. His recording depth-finder shows bottom contours and depths to within one-tenth of a foot. Tom is a trained observer, and Wescott Cove is proud to present his very thorough work to you.

Though great pains have been taken by experienced navigators to make this book as accurate as possible, the author and publisher cannot be responsible for any errors. Many parts of the Chesapeake Bay are subject to shoaling because of the great tributary rivers that flow into the Bay, changing contours and depths in the rivers and near their mouths. We strongly advice cruising skippers to have a full set of the latest NOS charts aboard, and to pay attention to courses and markers. Our charts are not to be used for any navigation, only as s supplement to the NOS charts.

We know that there will be changes in buoyage, and changes ashore. Tom Neale would appreciate your writing to tell him of whatever you see different from what is described, or if you know of any gunkhole that he missed. This will help improve the next edition. Please write to the author at the publisher's address on the title page.

We have enjoyed working with Tom Neale and Mel and visiting Melanie and Carolyn. His work is indispensable. Don't cruise Cheaspeake Bay without it!

Chez Nous crew. From left, Mel, Melanie, Carolyn, Tom Neale

AUTHOR'S INTRODUCTION

Cruising Chesapeake Bay is like exploring the Garden of Eden, with no limit on choices. The only difficult part is to decide what you want to pluck and when.

Do you like cosmopolitan museums, exquisite restaurants, and unequalled shopping, or do you like deserted anchorages where deer drink along the shoreline and trees and marsh grass whisper at night? Do you want to cruise where history happened or do you want to anchor among modern skyscrapers? Would you rather swim in fresh water in tree-shaded streams, or in ocean water off sandy beaches? Do you like boisterous sails beyond sight of land, or quiet puttering between meandering green banks? It is all here.

The Chesapeake is the largest estuary in the United States. It is around 170 miles long, and estimates of its shorelines and those of its tributaries range from 3,000 to 8,000 miles, depending on what is included. For most of the length of the Chesapeake, there are two shores, sometimes thought of as dintinct countries by old timers. These are the western shore, (or "the rest of the United States") and The Eastern Shore down the long Delmarva Peninsula that separates the Bay from the Atlantic. For years, the only practical way of crossing between the two was by boat. The '50s and '60s brought the Chesapeake Bay Bridge near Annapolis and the Chesapeake Bay Bridge Tunnel between Cape Charles and Cape Henry. These hurtled "modern times" at the Eastern Shore at 55 miles per hour across thin ribbons of tar and concrete, but the "Shore" is still much quieter and more rural than the "mainland" side, and even today the name is capitalized because of its dintinct identity. As you cruise up and down the Bay, it will be helpful to remember the difference.

I began cruising the Bay at age nine. In the past 42 years I have done so continuously. This book, however, is the result of the combined effort of my family. Mel and I married in 1968 and very soon had a 27-foot sailboat with which to explore. She had already been cruising the Bay with her family for most of her life. Our two daughters, Melanie and Carolyn,

have been with us on every trip since their birth, because we have all lived on a motorsailor for the last 16 years. The exploration trips, the photography, the writing, have all involved the entire family. We hope you will enjoy it as much as we have.

Julius Wilensky needs no introduction by me or anyone else, known as he is, throughout the world, as a cruiser among cruisers, and the father of the cruising guide book. We are honored to have him edit and publish this book and grateful for his help throughout. I must share one little experience which says so much.

During the October 1992 Annapolis Sailboat Show, Julius drove down to Annapolis from his home in Stamford, Connecticut. He arrived on a Friday, met with people from New Zealand to discuss his guide book in the works on that area, saw the show, and stayed in Annapolis that night. The next morning, at around 7 a.m., he was knocking on our hull where we were tied at Kent Narrows on the Eastern Shore. We then spent the entire day exploring different creeks in the Chester River in my 12-foot dinghy. That evening, Julius celebrated his 76th birthday with us, aboard the *Chez Nous*, and then said that he had to "get back." We tried to prevail upon him to stay aboard for the night, it being after 9 p.m., and knowing of the rigorous schedule he had experienced for the last two days. "It's a long drive back to Annapolis," we insisted.

"Oh, I'm not going back to Annapolis, I'm going home," was his reply. "I've got a lot to do to get ready for my cruise in New Zealand." He drove that night back to Stamford. Next morning I noticed that he had left his foul weather gear aboard. I decided to wait until late in the morning to call him for a shipping address, thinking that he would be exhausted from the trip back. When I called at 10 a.m., Mrs. Wilensky answered the phone. "Oh, he's not in. He got up long ago and is out sailing. It's a beautiful day here."

Tom Neale

Photo by Mel Neale

Tom and Julius at Kent Narrows departing on exploration in *Chez Nous'* tender

CHARTS, SKETCHES, MAPS, AND DIAGRAMS IN THIS BOOK

Photo by Julius M. Wilensky

Chez Nous at Kent Narrows

LIST OF CHARTS, PUBLICATIONS, SOURCES

National Oceanic and Atmospheric Administration, National Ocean Survey Charts and other publications, including current prices and where to buy them.

We cannot urge you strongly enough to cruise this lovely bay with a full set of up-to-date NOS charts. The charts in this book are designed to help you enjoy your cruise and to ease finding your way afloat and ashore, but they are not to be used for navigation. They are intended to supplement the NOS charts, not supplant them.

Publication	Price
U.S. Nautical Chart Catalog No. 1	Free
U.S. Coast Pilot No. 3 — Sandy Hook to Cape Henry	$20.00
(new editions published every two years)	
Tide Tables for the East Coast of North and South America	$12.00
Tidal Current Tables for the East Coast	$10.00
Marine Weather Services Charts MSC-3 — Manasquan, NJ to Cape Hatteras, NC	$8.00

All of the publications above, and all of the charts below can also be purchased by mail from the Distribution Branch (N/CG33) National Ocean Service, Riverdale, MD 20737-1199. Orders must be accompanied by a check or money order payable to NOS, Dept. of Commerce. Telephone orders can be placed by calling (301) 436-6990. Visa and Mastercards are accepted for 'phone orders.

US Coast Guard Light List Volume II. $28.75
    This is for sale by the Superintendent of Documents, Washington, DC 20402

NOS CHARTS

CHART NO.	DESCRIPTION	SCALE
12277	Chesapeake & Delaware Canal	1:20,000
12273	Sandy Point to Susquehanna River	1:80,000
12274	Head of Chesapeake Bay	1:40,000
12281	Baltimore Harbor	1:15,000
12278	Approaches to Baltimore Harbor	1:40,000
	Rock Hall Harbor	1:10,000
12282	Severn & Magothy Rivers	1:25,000
12283	Annapolis Harbor	1:10,000
12272	Chester River	1:40,000
	Kent Island Narrows, Rock Hall Harbor	1:10,000
12268	Choptank River — Cambridge to Greensboro	1:40,000
12270	Chesapeake Bay — Eastern Bay and South River	1:40,000
	Selby Bay	1:10,000
12266	Choptank River and Herring Bay	1:40,000
	Cambridge	1:10,000
12263	Cove Point to Sandy Point	1:80,000
12284	Patuxent River — Solomons Island & Vicinity	1:10,000
12264	Chesapeake Bay — Patuxent River & Vicinity	1:40,000

Prices for all these charts are $14.00 each.
There are hundreds of NOS Authorized Nautical Chart Agents all over USA. Names and addresses are listed in the U.S. Nautical Chart catalog, above. We are showing addresses of those agents located in the area covered by this book. This will help you if you are stuck for a chart while cruising.

Authorized Nautical Chart Agents in the Area Covered by this book are:

Annapolis
Boaters World, 4335-A Forest Dr., (301) 953-9611
C Plath North American Div., 222 Severn Ave., (301) 263-6700
Coast Navigation, 116 Legion Ave., (301) 268-3120
Fawcett Boat Supplies, Inc., 110 Compromise St. (301) 267-8681
Viking Boat Supplies, 320 6th St., (301) 268-8000
West Marine Products, Bay Ridge Plaza, 115 Hillsmere Dr., (410) 268-0129

Baltimore
Boat/US Marine Center, 6863 Loch Raven Blvd., (301) 296-0457
Maryland Nautical Sales Inc., 1400 E. Clement Street (410) 752-4268

Cambridge	R D Boat Supply Inc., Rt. 50, (301) 228-0674
Chesapeake City	Schaefers Market & Marina, 208 Bank St., (301) 885-2204
Chestertown	Worton Creek Marina Inc., 23145 Buck Neck Rd., (301) 778-3282
Grasonville	C&C Charters Ltd., Mears Point Marina, (301) 827-7888
Havre de Grace	Tidewater-Havre de Grace, Foot of Bourbon St., (301) 939-0950
Oxford	Crockett Bros. Boatyard Inc., 202 Bank St., (301) 226-5113
Rock Hall	Sailing Emporium Inc., Green Ln., (301) 778-1342
Solomons	Calvert Marina, Patuxent River, (301) 326-4251
	Zahnisers Inc., 246 C St., (301) 326-2166

**Crowded sailboat heeled at the dock at the Annapolis Sailboat Show,
largest in the Northeast USA**

HOW THIS BOOK IS ORGANIZED

Harbors are described in sequence as though you were cruising from the Susquehanna River south. After Havre de Grace, Tom Neale covers North East River, the Chesapeake and Delaware Canal, and the Elk River. These are all at the extreme northern part of the Bay. Then Tom takes you to the Sassafras River on the Eastern Shore. The book then goes south along the Eastern Shore and its many tributaries all the way to Little Choptank River.

Following this, we go back to the western shore, starting at the Bush and Gunpowder Rivers, and proceeding south to Baltimore and Annapolis, ending at the Patuxent River. Volume II will pick up where this book leaves off, to be published next year.

Chapter I has a great deal of miscellaneous general information about Chesapeake Bay. Much of this is known to local Bay sailors, but please review it anyway.

Included are large scale reproduction of NOS Chart excerpts marked to indicate additional navigational information, course lines where appropriate, and exact locations of marine facilities and points of interests ashore. There are several original sketches and diagrams, and we have included street maps of some towns. Many people find these maps and charts good guides to places of interest ashore, and they are so intended. The charts in this book are not intended for navigational use. We recommend that you carry the latest editions of NOS charts, listed in the front of this book (see Table of Contents).

We have included a big folded chart printed both sides in the pocket inside the back cover. This shows the entire area covered by Volume I, and is numbered to indicate coverage in each chapter. This is valuable for planning your cruise, for laying courses, and for orientation. We have also included regional charts for each chapter, showing the area covered in that chapter. Some of these cover more than one chapter. The text has chart references that tell you what chart to look at with reference to the text. All these regional charts are on a scale of 1:80,000. A complete list of charts in this book follows the Author's Introduction.

Appendix I, Books and Music is not only a bibliography, but describes some Chesapeake Bay music that the Neale family enjoys.

Appendix II, Festivals tell you when and where they occur. Try to catch one or more during your cruise.

Appendix III, History gives you an overview. Much history is woven into the text.

Appendix IV, Position Fixes. These are all in the text and on the charts, but this appendix can be handy as you make longer passages.

Appendix V, U.S. Coast Guard Stations of the Upper Bay.

Appendix VI, Some Helpful 'Phone Numbers.

Appendix VII, Major Lights and Markers. These also are all in the text and on the charts, but this appendix can be handy on longer passages.

Appendix VIII, Tidal Differences and Other Constants.

Appendix IX, Charter Listing.

A place name index follows these appendices. Following the index are tidal current charts, one for each of the 12 hours in a tidal cycle.

Chesapeake Bay Bridge (William P. Lane, Jr. Bridge) looking west.
Yes, there are twin spans

11

CHAPTER 1

GOOD THINGS TO KNOW ABOUT CRUSING CHESAPEAKE BAY

NAVIGATION TIPS

One of the many joys of Bay Crusing is that it is relatively forgiving for many of the types of navigational errors that could be very serious elsewhere. As an example, most of the bottom is either soft mud or sand, the few rocky areas are well charted. Ususally if you go aground, it is merely a matter of backing or kedging off, perhaps waiting for the tide. This makes exploration for gunkholes much less risky. But complacency can ruin any good cruise and is never a good idea on or near the water. Here are a few special concerns.

Keep track of where you are, noting landmarks or buoys as you pass them by. Not only will this be of general help in normal navigation, it will be important if visibility becomes obscured in rain or fog, and may be critical if you suddenly find that you need assistance. Always use your own independent good judgement and prudent seamanship in deciding what the facts are in any given situation. Aids to navigation are frequently changed in the Bay, both as to characteristics and location. Also, with the large areas of heavy population, it is not unusual for the shoreline and structures or landmarks thereon to change significantly.

Commercial Boats

Remember that the Bay is used by many vessels and that, even in the most idyllic of circumstance, knowledge of and adherence to the Rules of the Road are important. Many of the other vessels are huge freighters, tankers, or tugs with barges. They have very limited maneuverability, they require a lot of room, sometimes miles, to stop or change course (if they can), and even a close passing can be dangerous because of prop wash and suction. The larger ships usually stay in the main deep water channels, while we can usually sail outside those channels. If it is safe to do so in your area of navigation, it may be wise to avoid those channels. Note however, that you are more likely to run into crab pots or pound nets if you are in no marked channel.

Tugs will often have a tow, sometimes on a long hawser. Failure to recognize this and passing astern of a tug with a barge behind will probably be a fatal mistake. At night be especially watchful of this. We have seen barges that were not adequately lit to be easily seen by a craft low in the water.

Many commercial fishing vessels trawl long nets in the Bay. Probably the ones that you will most often encounter are the Menhaden fleets. At this time, these are not allowed to fish in the Maryland waters, but if you are coming up to the northern Bay through the lower Bay, you should watch for them. Many of these are stationed in Reedville, just below the Potomac on the western shore, but they range far and wide. Often a plane will be seen spotting the fish, and when a school is found, these boats will swoop in. When they reach the school, they will launch smaller "purse boats" to spread out a huge net around the school, and then encircle the school, ultimately closing the net around it so that they can be brought on board. These and other commercial fishermen can understandably become upset if the school that can make their day's pay gets away because one of "we cruisers" decides to insist on some notion of right of way and forces them to head off.

Fish Traps

Throughout the Bay, there are long rows of stakes driven into the bottom with nets spread between. These are commonly called "pound nets." At one end there will be a circular arrangement of stakes. As fish swim along the bottom, they encounter the line of net, and head instinctively for deeper water. It is therefore at the deeper end of the set that you will find the circular stakes which support the circular nets with a funnel entrance where the fish are trapped. These nets can be both a hazard and a help. Often they are not lit at night, and if you sail or motor into them, you will probably become seriously snagged in the netting, possibly holed by a stake. They are not supposed to be in the marked channels. The watermen who fish these nets will probably be more upset than you if you run one down, because their repair involves a great deal of expense, time and hard labor. I have asked several why don't they always use some type of lighting, and the most universal reply is something along the lines— "It doesn't make any difference, the danged fools run them down anyway, when they see a light they always want to come over and look." Some do use lights, but the markings are unreliable and varied. The bottom line is that if you see one, do not pass between the stakes, there will probably be heavy netting just below the surface. And if you are out at night, stick carefully to the marked channels. One good thing about these, from the navigator's viewpoint, is that you will generally be able to assume that the deeper water is at the end with the circular stakes, the line running to the shallow.

In other areas, such as the Sassafras, you will see floats coming out in a line perpendicular to the shore. These usually support netting called "fykes." These are used to catch catfish and other varieties. The principle of these is somewhat similar to pound nets, and it is important to not run between floats. You will in all probability snag a net. Usually these are too close to the shoreline to concern you in your main boat, but if you are skirting the shore in a dinghy or small motorboat you should be aware of them. They sometimes look like crab pots floats which you can go between because they are not connected. These fykes are connected and you should never pass between them.

You should always be on the watch for gill nets. These are nets strung between two floats. The nets catch fish by the gills as they swim through, and they are set out both commercially and by individuals for private consumption. They may be deep enough for your boat to pass over, or shallow enough to ensnare you. It is wise to avoid passing between gill net floats. Often they are similar in appearance to some crab pot floats, but they are supposed to have stakes attached to them, at least several feet tall, with flags or other warning symbols.

Crab Pots

One of the most irritating navigational hazards on the Bay are the thousands and thousands of crab pot floats to be found seemingly everywhere. Actually, they are usually not in the deep channels, almost never in the big ship channels. A crab pot is a square trap made of wire similar to (and it sometimes is) chicken wire with a bait section full of the juiciest of rotten meats, and a funnel for the crab to enter. The crab is then trapped inside. The trap has a strong line connected to a float to enable the crabber to find it and pull it up. The floats are usually anything from a styrofoam shape not much larger than a jumbo paper cup, to plastic bleach and soap jugs, to orange floats with sticks through the middle, specifically made for the purpose. You don't usually see too many of these because of the expense. Generally they use whatever is the cheapest and easiest to get. Sometimes the colors are blue, black, or other shades difficult to distinguish from the water.

Watermen tend these pots, usually at least once a day, pulling them up, emptying and rebaiting them, and dropping them down again. Since the crabber's boat normally remains running slowly during the operation to avoid delays, an individual crabber's pots will often be in a line. But with the great number of crabbers, sometime the pots are so numerous that you could almost step from float to float. Keep sharp watch for these. If you snag their line you can damage your prop or cutlass bearing, and if you snag them on your underbody while sailing, you will probably have to dive down to free them.

You will probably incur the unpleasant thoughts of the crabber who will have spent a great deal of money on the rig. I just keep reminding myself that these people are making a living for their families, they have been doing this for a long time on the Bay, they are harvesting crabs which many of us love to eat, their work is very hard, and their pay is scant. There are established "crab lines" which are politically decreed boundaries (usually marked by orange and white floats) beyond which crabbers cannot put their pots.

There are also clam lines and oyster lines where those operations are not allowed. These "lines" are usually marked by small floating white buoys with the words "crab line" or "clam line" written on the sides, almost impossible to read until you are very close. They are subject to change for various reasons, including political reasons, and are not noted on our charts. We have observed numerous instances where crab pots floats were over the lines.

Following Courses

All position fixes should be considered as approximate. When possible, these are normally taken from the "Light List" Vol. II published by the U.S. DOT, US Coast Guard. Even positions in government publications are usually noted as approximate. When needed, we have also taken coordinates derived from a Magellan GPS. Since our government has been deliberately obscuring GPS signals from time to time to supposedly thwart hostile position fixes by enemies, GPS cannot always be relied upon to be as accurate as its capabilities allow. The new differential GPS technology was not fully operational when these fixes were taken. In any event, I found that whenever I checked a GPS reading with a Light List reading, they usually coincided within a hundredth of a decimal point. I spoke with people in the industry about it and their answer was, perhaps, when I was taking my readings, the government was not tampering with the signals in that area. I have noted that Loran and GPS fixes are often less reliable around Annapolis, perhaps because of all the

towers and radio actively associated with the U.S. Navy facilities there. In any event, always assume that positions, and therefore, course runs between positions, are approximate.

Where a course line is given from one navigational aid to another, you normally should not go right up to that aid to begin your run. Often the aids are actually placed in shallow water. You should look at the chart, and begin your run at an appropriate distance into the channel. Remember also, that winds and currents will often set you from one side to another while running a course line, thus moving you into shallow water without your being aware until too late. Avoid this by checking for wind and current, and by taking bearings fore and aft as you run the course, compensating for lateral movement.

Aids to Navigation

Aids to navigation are changed frequently in Chesapeake Bay. It is an area of high use navigation, it is patrolled and checked often, and lately, there has been a general revamping of the aids in the area. Always use your independent observation and prudent judgement.

You will see many private aids to navigation. Some of these are quite elaborate, carefully maintained, regulated, and reliable. Others are no more than stakes in the mud or small styrofoam floats put out by whoever lives up the creek. Long established private aids are sometimes noted on the NOS charts, but even this does not ensure that the entity responsible for their maintainance is still there and doing the job. These present a dilemma for any navigator. While they can be very helpful, they can also be quite misleading. Often as conditions change, their markers are not changed. Sometimes a new stake will be pushed into the mud, with the old one still remaining. Sometimes private floats will drag off and be left where they are for a while because people are busy and everybody in the neighborhood knows the channel anyway. I have described private markers that I think will be helpful, that appeared to be correctly placed at the time, and that I believe would be maintained reliably. But with the exception of the private aids maintained by large established concerns such as successful marinas, reliance upon private aids should be observed with great caution.

When you encounter private aids, look first to see if they make sense with regard to what the chart and your observations show. If local boats are in the area, see if they are following them. Look also to see if they appear to be fresh. A new stick in the mud or a clean white styrofoam float is more likely to be in place than an obviously old one. If possible, ask somebody about the floats; most people in the Bay will be helpful and friendly. Never take them for granted and proceed with care.

Shoaling

There are some areas where the shifting of shoals is much more likely than others. Almost any time you are entering a creek or river mouth with a channel through shallows that are exposed to a long fetch, you should expect shoaling to occur and proceed with the assumption that things have changed since the last chartings, soundings, and markings. Whenever there is sand or mud to wash around and whenever there are waves to do it, it will happen. An excellent example of this is the northern side of Kent Narrows. We have tried to note some of these as we noticed them in our reporting, but there will be others.

Wrecks and Obstructions

Chesapeake Bay has been subjected to the march of "civilization" since the Europeans first began their encroachments in the seventeenth century. Since then, boats have been sinking, piers have been built and crumbled with age, mooring pilings have been driven and disappeared with the ages, buildings have covered the shores and fallen into the shallows with time, ships have been bombed in experimentation and practice, and even wars have been fought. Despite it all, this is still one of the finest places to cruise, but remnants of our incursions remain throughout the waters, and the charts constantly remind us.

The problem is that many of these "wrecks" and "obstructions reported" are no longer there, and have not been for some time. I have spent hours on occasion trying to track some of them down, to finally learn that they are simply not there anymore and that no one around them has ever seen them. Others are, and are dangerous. Another problem is that often where they occur, the creek or cove is narrow and the symbol covers the entire cove or channel when actually the "wreck" is just a few old ribs up in the marsh on the shore or in about a foot of water. Another problem is that, owning only one tender and with one spare propeller budget, I have been reluctant to go into wreck or obstruction areas to see if they are just below the surface when they clearly were not showing above the surface. Therefore, if I see them, or find what I think to be remnants on my recording depth finder, or if I have been able to find someone locally who knows that they are there as charted, I will tell you. If I don't see them, I tell you this, and simply suggest that you beware.

In many cases you will find that these are noted in front of active marinas. As a general rule, you can usually assume that the marina has either removed these or marked them if they are still there. In many cases you will see the wreck symbol up in an otherwise perfect cove. Often this means that generations ago, a boat was left there to die on the shore. Check along the marsh to see if this is not the case. There are some areas where there has been a great deal of industrial waterfront use and development over the years, and you should be especially careful to avoid these symbols in these areas. A prime example is some of the areas in Baltimore (not the inner harbor) as noted in the text.

Power Lines, Above and Below

Because of the abundance of civilization around the shores, there are power lines throughout the Bay. Some are stretched overhead, some are laid or buried along the bottom. In either case, tangling with one can be fatal. Not only can it ensnare your anchor or entangle and crash your mast, it can allow huge voltages of electricity to shoot throughout the boat causing electrocution.

The charts generally denote cable areas. In these areas, there is usually a sign on the shore at each end of an underwater cable, so that you can know where it is. However, we have noticed places where there were no signs or they were obscured. The best rule to follow is to **never** put the anchor down without first checking the chart (latest updated NOS chart) and then the shore to be sure you are safe. You will be checking the chart anyway to learn the contours of the bottom and to see if there is any information as to type of bottom. If there are signs, anchor well away from any line between them. If there is a designated underwater cable area and you cannot find signs, anchor outside of that area unless you have a certain local knowledge that nothing is there. Al-

ways assume that you might drag in a blow, and give yourself enough room to do this without snagging a cable.

Overhead power lines are also a serious danger. We are all accustomed to seeing power and telephone poles, and accustomed to proceeding under them as we travel ashore. If you are in a sailboat or any boat with high protrusions such as outriggers, you should never take clearance for granted. First, look up (sometimes a difficult habit to get into) to see if there are wires, and then check the charts for clearance. Never try a close call. Often wires sag for various reasons, and even a close passing could allow current to jump.

Overhead lines are not only a threat crossing rivers and streams. A surprising number of people have been killed or injured while launching or trailing sailboats when they passed under a line too low for the mast. Always remember to look up as well as around when you have a mast or other tall protrusion.

Bridges

Fortunately there are not as many bridges to deal with in Chesapeake cruising as there are in other areas. When you do encounter one that must be opened for your passages, the sound signal is one long and one short on your horn. Most bridges stand by on Channel 13 VHF, and that is the best way to communicate with them. You will then know whether they can respond, and they can advise you of any problems.

The vertical clearance of each bridge is supposed to be posted by a sign on that bridge. It is also noted on the charts, but these do not always reflect recent changes. We have attempted to note these as of our last visit, but beware that they may now be different.

Often bridges have schedules and restrictions. These change frequently, but we have attempted to describe these as they existed at the time of our last visit. Restrictions of schedules are usually posted on a sign on the bridge, but often the signs are obscured by weathering or have writing that is too small to read until you are too close for safety. Check ahead, or call on 13 VHF.

Duck Blinds

Duck blinds are essentially small sheds or shacks on pilings frequently out in the water, or along the shore. These pilings are often slender pine trunks, and the sheds in season may be partially camouflaged with pine branches fastened about the walls. They are built to hide the hunter who sits inside, usually on cold winter mornings, with shotgun in hand waiting for ducks or geese to pass by close enough to shoot. They dot the shoreline and are sometimes noted on charts, but are rather unreliable for navigational purposes. This is because they are usually put up in a flimsy fashion, with no thought in mind for navigation, and they are maintained only if hunters want to hunt here (if at all), as opposed to somewhere else, next year. Some few are solidly built, but this is not the rule. Therefore, whenever you see reference to one, treat it with great skepticism. When you do see a duck blind or the obvious remnants of one, you can be fairly certain that it is in shallow water. Custom usually has them built on shoals extending off the shore (often off points) just before the water deepens. Therefore, if there is no other clue, this clue might be helpful as to where the shoal ends. Do not anchor near one in the hunting season. Shooting starts with first light, and sometimes goes on all day. Ducks and geese swim and fly along the water.

River Navigation

Among the many pleasures of Chesapeake Bay are rivers and creeks which seem to wind forever into countryside of fields and woods. These are often not marked, or if so, only with an occasional aid to show a particularly troublesome shoal. Landmarks for the underwater configurations are obscure at best. Therefore, to enjoy this aspect of Bay cruising, it is helpful to learn a few of the tricks of river navigation. These will not be applicable to all situations, and none are fool proof, but they should be helpful.

As you head up or down a river, try to envision what the water is and has been doing to the bottom over the years as it flows along. This can help you to guess where the deepest part may be. For example, if you see a point of land ahead and a cove opposite, you may assume that there is a shoal extending off that point, that the water as it passes around that point has been deflected some away from it, and probably cut the deeper channel around the point into the curve of the cove on the opposite side. You will also know, however, that as it was deflected and cutting the channel into the opposite bank, it perhaps toppled some trees into the river, and you would not want to pass too close to the shores of that cove opposite the point.

If your river or stream is intersected by a side stream, look for a bar which will probably have built off the entrance to the side stream into your channel. This is particularly so if the side stream has a significant flow of current.

If the river widens significantly, slow down and assume that it may shallow significantly. Narrow banks often mean deeper channels because the water has to cut deep to get through, but if the water's passage is very wide, it may be just spreading out with no really deep channel. Often when you approach these spots there are no natural clues as to where the channel is, but usually local people will have placed stakes here. If there are pound nets, you can generally assume that the circled stakes are toward the deeper water, and if there are crab pot floats and you cannot see the pots, you will generally know that there is at least enough water to cover them (generally around 2 feet, depending on who built the trap). Often a string of crab pots close to a shore will mark an area of drop off, so that you will not want to pass inshore of the line, but, again, there is no guarantee.

Always watch the surface of the water for signs of what is going on below. For example, a very shallow area may appear flat and motionless as compared to a deeper area. An upwelling of water may indicate an obstruction or shoal down below. Eddies in the current could mean the same thing, or simply a change in the channel bed far below.

At any time that you are far upstream, and especially if the shores around or above are wooded, beware of stumps, not only along the shore, but also floating along or stuck at the bottom of the channel. Sometimes a large tree will fall in and start down stream and stick on the bottom leaving only some swirls in the surface, or perhaps a snag sticking up to mark its presence. If you see a snag, always assume that it is connected to something else below the surface. If you see any changes in the surface movement, assume that something is causing it.

Anytime you see stakes in the water, try to figure out what they mean. They may just be marking oyster beds or something else that has no relevance to navigation, they may, however, be marking shoals or obstructions. Generally, if they are close to the shore, pass outside of them, if they are in the middle, approach cautiously.

Anchor Lights

Because of the heavy amount of commercial and pleasure traffic, it is always important to see that you are operating with the proper lighting configuration, and that they are working. It is always important to burn an anchor light. There are many deserted creeks and coves where you would never expect anyone to see any anchor light until around 4 a.m., a workboat, with a sleepy waterman just beginning his day, heads out from a little slip up in the woods and doesn't know you are there. Even in so-called "designated anchorages," if someone can't see you and hits you, there may be substantial civil liability on your part and, conceivably, you could find yourself uninsured because you had not exercised proper care.

Middleton Tavern, Annapolis

COMMUNICATIONS

VHF

VHF radios can be the curse of a pleasant sail, with the frequent abuses of some boaters and the constant traffic. Many people leave them off because they are out there trying to get away from it all and enjoy the peace and quiet that only the water can bring. However, the VHF can be very important in keeping you from danger, or saving other lives. As abnoxious as it can sometimes be, it should be left on Channel 16. This is really the only way to hear warnings as to approaching storms, potentially dangerous shipping traffic, stuck bridges, damaged or destroyed aids to navigation, and Maydays. In areas of heavy concentration or commercial traffic, or whenever you are approaching the scene of commercial maneuvering, it is very helpful to have a second standby on VHF 13. This is the working channel for commercial ships and tugs. Areas such as the C and D Canal and its approaches, the Patapsco and its approaches, and the large shipping channel are particularly critical.

Ships and tugs normally use and stand by on Channel 13. This is a low power (one watt) frequency. Your radio will probably only transmit on low power when you are using this frequency. In areas of heavy commercial traffic, or if you are approaching ships maneuvering, it is very helpful to stand by on this channel also. You may get information that you need regarding the other ship's movement much more quickly this way. Some radios have a dual watch function, which you may wish to use in these circumstances so that you can stand by on both 13 and 16, or you may wish to use your handheld to standby on 13, while the main set is tuned to 16. The handheld should usually receive any relevant traffic on 13 since that traffic should be close due to the reduced output of the frequency. Channel 13 is also normally used by bridges. It is usually much more effective to call a bridge on Channel 13 to arrange for an opening. That way you can be sure he is reponding, and he can alert you to any potential problems or restriction.

Many people cruising the Bay use either the VHF radio or, more and more frequently, a cellular phone for communications. The VHF is the most practical way to communicate from boat to boat.

There are strict rules for use of the VHF. Adherence to the rules for VHF use is important not only because the FCC monitors transmissions and has the power to and does levy fines for misuse; it is also important because many people use the frequencies daily, and without the rules none of us would have the opportunity to get through. Often the messages being passed are critical to health and safety, often they are critical to the movement of the vessels. The law requires that you have aboard and be familiar with the rules for the operation of your radio. These rules and procedures may prove important to you if you ever need assistance or need to have critical communications, or if others in your vicinity do. You are also required to have your FCC operating license posted aboard. You should also be familiar with the operation of your set. You should also be certain that at least one other person on your boat is familiar with the operation of the set. Your life may depend on it.

First, notice that your VHF has a high or low power setting. Whenever you are able to conduct routine conversations on low power, you should do so. If you know that you will be talking to a vessel nearby, you can be pretty sure that lower power will suffice. This means that the radius of your transmission is much smaller and therefore more people may use the same frequency.

Your radio will probably have an international and US setting. When in the Bay, you should have it on the US setting. Some frequencies will be different and not work for you if you do not have it on this setting.

Normally Channel 16 is for standby, and distress calls and calling only. This is the channel where you are expected to stand by, listening. Here is where you will hear weather warnings, special navigational warnings or alerts from the Coast Guard or other vessels, and this is where you will normally hear calls to your vessel. Channel 9 is now being used as a calling channel, and some people and marinas are now standing by on there; however you may miss warnings or alerts if you only stand by here. Normally most marinas now stand by on Channel 16. If we have information that a certain marina stands by on another channel, we try to report it when we describe that marina.

If you ever have communications with the Coast Guard, they will probably ask you to switch to Channel 22A or one of the other frequencies designated exclusively for their use. Hopefully, you will have less interruptions. If you must call **Mayday**, remember that it is supposed to be used only for health and personal safety situations. Call **Mayday, Mayday, Mayday,** state the name of your vessel and its call sign, give your location, and a very brief statement of your distress. For other help, just call the Coast Guard and advise them of your problem after they take you to their working channel.

In most cases if you are calling another vessel, such as a friend on a cruise with you, there are certain channels to which you must switch for conversation. Call the other vessel on 16 (unless you know he is standing by on another channel) and then switch to one of the talking channels. These are 68, 69, 71, 72, and 78A at this time. Conversations should be brief and to the point. Other people may be waiting to use the frequency with important communications.

You may also contact marinas or other shore stations by calling them on 16, 9, or some other channel where they stand by. Unless you have information that they standby elsewhere, try them on 16 first. Normally marinas are only licensed to talk on certain communications channels, so try to follow their suggestion as to the frequency to which you will shift.

It is also relatively simple to make telephone calls from your boat with VHF. There are several marine telephone companies active around the shores of the Bay. The one that you will use will depend primarily on your location at the time you wish to make a call. The channels for these telephone stations are 24, 25, 26, 27, and 28. At this time, the operator in Baltimore uses 25 and 26, Cambridge uses 28, Prince Frederick uses 27, and Point Lookout uses 26. Listen first to be sure that there is no other traffic already in progress, and then call for the Marine Operator on the channel which you believe to be within your location. If they don't answer, try other channels. If you haven't registered with the system, they may require that you make it a collect call. Ask your local telephone service for information about registering. At this time they are not accepting credit card calls, and you certainly would not want to give out your number over the air anyway.

If someone wishes to call you, he may do so through the marine operator for your area. If he doesn't know what your area is, he should try the operator for the area where he thinks you are, and if that doesn't work, try others. He should know the name of your boat, for that is how you will be contacted through the VHF. He should obtain the latest information about how to contact the stations from his telephone operator. The maritime operator will call you on Channel 16, and ask that you switch to his working channel. They have high towers and can transmit farther than you, therefore, you may hear them although they do not hear your answer if you are too far away. Often, if you hear the marine operator calling you, even if you are too far away for that operator to hear you, if you answer anyway, the operator within your area will pick you up and be able to transfer the call.

Cellular

Cellular phones are being used more and more in the Bay. At this time there is controversy regarding what company has the better coverage in which locations. If you wish to use cellular, you should research for the latest information at the time. Cellular does not replace the VHF in many respects. These include the fact that you cannot call another boat with it unless they also have a phone and you know the number, you will also not receive Coast Guard alerts or storm alerts, you will not hear traffic announcements from other vessels, and other vessels will not be able to hail you without knowledge of your number. Therefore, as bothersome as it may be at times, it is still important to standby on Channel 16 VHF. Communications are changing rapidly, but that is the way it is now.

GOING AGROUND

Going aground can be a temporary inconvenience or a serious problem, depending upon the circumstances. It occurs frequently in the Bay with cruisers, probably because there are so many of us out there, the Bay is so conducive to exploring and gunkholing, and the waters are muddy. The best advice is to try to stay off the bottom. Usually this is not too difficult if you are paying close attention. Always give leeward buoys and shoals a wide berth, and assume that shoals extend beyond the buoys that mark their tips. If a grounding happens to you and the tide is falling or the wind is blowing you into shallower water, quick action is needed to avoid a long wait for the sea to rise, or for an expensive tow.

Most of the Bay's bottom is mud or sand, and therefore grounding probably won't do much initial damage unless you hit one of the bad spots (rocks in some areas of the Patapsco or the Susquehanna, for example) or unless you are a power boat and hit hard with your running gear. If the sea is pounding you, damage will be more likely to occur.

If immediate backing off doesn't help, one of the simplest and most effective methods available for the average cruising boat, including boats in the 40-foot long range, is to have one or more people quickly get off into the dinghy which you may be towing. It is amazing what the removal of a little weight will do to your buoyancy, and often an inch or two will float you. This could be a dangerous course of action if those involved are not nimble and experienced seamen, and it should be done with great caution and not in rough seas. Also, sometimes shifting weight forward will tip the boat sufficiently to enable you to back off. On a sailboat, shifting weight to one side, putting up a main to heel the boat (if the wind is right for this) or even having some able person swing out on the boom may tip the boat enough to raise the keel the necessary inch or two. If these fail, take out an anchor with your dinghy,

setting it off your beam in a line perpendicular to your boat, running the rode up to your bow, and winching in on it, hopefully to pull your bow out and off. Take soundings to determine where the deep water is. Then set your kedging anchor in the deep water. We have also frequently been able to simply push on the bow with a dinghy with outboard, swinging the bow around to deep water.

Any of this can be dangerous if not done carefully and with due regard for all circumstances, but often quick action such as this can avoid a call for help (frequently it will be commercial and expensive) or pounding and damage if the wind rises.

CHESAPEAKE BAY WEATHER

Bermuda Highs

A primary consideration for any cruise is weather. The dog days of summer (usually early to mid-July through mid-September) often bring many periods of flat calm winds, very humid hot days and nights, punctuated by violent thunderstorms with dangerous winds and lightning. Often during the summer months, dense high pressure systems will settle off the eastern seaboard. These can affect the weather for weeks, causing extreme heat and humidity, stagnant air with little or no wind, and haze. These are frequently called "Bermuda Highs."

Thunderstorms

Chesapeake Bay thunderstorms should be taken very seriously. They come up rapidly, usually from the southwest, west, or northwest, they often contain damaging hail and deadly cloud to earth lightning, with strong winds. The storm and winds seldom last long, but they can be quiet serious. The winds are usually from the west or northwest and may come up very quickly, sometimes gusting to hurricane force. Because of the sudden nature of the wind shifts and the fact that the wind may go from nothing to over 70 miles per hour very suddenly, most experienced sailors take in their sails and motor into the approaching storm if they are caught out. A knockdown could easily occur in these conditions, even with fully reefed sail. The weather stations on VHF radio usually issue watches and warnings, and the Coast Guard will also issue weather bulletins on Channel 16 when these storms are approaching. However, you should always keep a weather eye. Hot, humid conditions are most likely to produce these monsters, particularly if a front is approaching. Usually the sky to the west will begin to gray, sometimes becoming dull blue or copper in color. High towering cumulus clouds should always be watched. Often, on these days when the storms are most likely to occur, there is so much haze in the air that you can't see the changes to westward. In these conditions, it is particularly important to listen for thunder, observe the sky closely, and check the weather stations. If such a storm threatens, seek a safe anchorage or marina and prepare for strong gusty winds.

Tornadoes and water spouts also occasionally occur in the Bay area, particularly associated with severe violent thunderstorms and the systems that produce these storms. Any time that there is a violent thunderstorm watch, and anytime you observe the conditions that create these storms, be also on a lookout for these twisters. If you see one, report it to the Coast Guard, not only to alert others, but to alert them to your position and situation. Also, if you have not had the time to get in and are still on the water, take evasive action. Do not try to keep up your sail.

We are all familiar with cold fronts; we know that they can bring sudden shifts of very strong wind and preceeding thunderstorms. Usually, we relax after they have blown through, knowing that there will probably be at least several days of cool, comfortable, stable weather. However, we have noticed over the years instances of waterspouts occurring up to a day after the passage of a strong front when the Bay waters are warm. These can be quiet surprising and, of course, dangerous. These are apparently caused by reactions between the cool air and the warm water with moist warm air at its surface. Enjoy these post frontal days, but do not automatically assume that no violent weather can occur and heed any sky and cloud warnings.

Fog

Fortunately, fog is not very common, although at times it can be a very serious problem, usually in the fall. Most often, it will be associated with warm moist air over cold water. Fog is usually predicted over VHF weather, and visibility can quickly become totally obscured. Pay attention to the weather, and listen to the VHF. Fortunately, it seldom occurs on the crisp fall days for which the Bay is so well known and on which most people like to travel. Dense haze can not only make it difficult to sight approaching thunderstorms, but also obliterate the shoreline and aids to navigation until you are quite close. This makes navigation tricky, causing many people without radar and GPS (or loran) to become lost. This sort of haze can sometimes occur on hot muggy days, particularly when there has been a dense high pressure system dominating the weather. These conditions can, even on a sunny day, cause you to be totally out of sight of land even in areas where the shore seems very close on very clear days.

Hurricanes

Hurricanes are of great concern on Chesapeake Bay, as is true of other areas. Storms have swept up the Bay in full fury, leaving incredible destruction. Numerous landmarks around the Bay were either formed or demolished by these storms. Fortunately, the Bay in recent years has been spared the bad ones. Many times, as they move up the east coast, they seemed to become ensnared by the land of Cape Hatteras, spending the bulk of their energy down there, visiting the Bay with milder remnants. Don't become complacent because we never know what these monsters are going to do until they do it.

Editor's note: Hurricane tracking has become accurate recently. If you're tuned into weather reports, you'll get plenty of advance notice.

Chesapeake Bay is full of very good "hurricane holes." The criteria for a good hole will vary with the type of storm you are expecting, the type of boat you have, your draft, and whether you plan to tie up or anchor.

You will want a landlocked area, because of the customarily reversing winds as the storm passes over. It also helps to have high land around you, the higher the better. It is also important to get as far from the ocean as possible. Frequently the areas of most violence and with the greatest likelihood for tornadoes is near the landfall. There are many deep and long rivers with innumerable coves running up into the western shore.

Storm surge can be a serious problem, particularly if you have chosen to tie up. In the upper Bay, you are more likely to get a tremendously high tide rather than the wave-like surge often experienced along the coast. The height of the tide will depend on the wind direction and strength, and other factors

such as whether the storm is coinciding with a full or new moon. VHF radio will issue regular Hurricane Bulletins, giving late developing information on this and other concerns.

The ideal hurricane hole will vary with different boats. We have noticed that recommended holes are usually the first to fill up and therefore often dangerous with overcrowding. All it takes is a few protruding docks to ruin an otherwise good spot. If you are expecting a blow, look at our harbor ratings for protection, look at the charts, and read our descriptions of the area to help you decide what is good for you in your situation and time. Do not wait for the storm to begin before you find your spot. Start looking and settling at least a day or two before the expected hurricane landfall. Preparing for a hurricane takes a lot of work and time.

In choosing your spot, check the type of bottom. We have found that thick mud, preferably mud and gray clay, holds best in the Bay. Mud and sand with a Danforth (trademark) anchor is our next favorite. Others will have their own preferences. It is usually better to put in two anchors because the winds will shift 180° if the storm passes right over. Many people will place two anchors against the first expected direction (usually easterly or some quadrant thereof) because that will generally be the strongest wind. Then they place a third to hold after the windshift with the storm passage. There are many areas where you can tie off to the trees, and this is what many people do.

Observe piers, pilings, or other structures on the shore that could cause damage if you drag. Anchor in a place where if you drag in the time of maximum wind, you will drag into a forgiving bank rather than a bunch of broken pilings.

Once you are secured to the bottom or shore, remove or tightly tie down everything that is on your deck that could come loose. Always take down rolled furling around your headstay, and the main also unless it is inside the mast. If you have a leak around a window or port that you haven't gotten around to fixing, cover it with duct tape. If you don't, the driving rain will flood in.

As you settle to wait for the verdict, you may want to help others coming into the anchorage, if they need and want it. No matter how well you have prepared, if your neighbor does a poor job and drags into you or your lines, you may be no better off than he.

Weather Reports

For 24-hour weather which will include special alerts and sometimes tide information, turn to the weather stations on your VHF radio. In the upper Bay, the working frequencies are found on Channels 1, 2, and 3 depending on where you are and atmosphereic conditions. We have also found a small portable TV to be worth its cost and inconvenience just for the purpose of getting the weather maps on the evening or morning news. Most places in the upper Bay will get reception, at least good enough for this purpose, from one station or another.

Nothing beats knowledgeable observation with your eyes and feelings, and the use of a barometer. I would strongly suggest having a good quality working barometer and learning how to use it.

FLYING INSECTS AND NETTLES

Insects

With summer weather, there will be more problems from mosquitoes, particularly for those of us seeking the quiet anchorages among tree and marsh lined shores for which the Bay is so well-known.

Mosquitoes are always a problem in the warm months. The best way to handle them is to have screens on your hatches and portholes. Nothing can take the place of these. It also helps to avoid the areas where they are most likely to breed. These are generally places where there is flat stagnant water. This, of course, includes most of the Bay. As a rule, the farther you are from marsh or marsh shoreline, and the more breeze you have, the fewer the bites. Close wooded or marshy coves in hot season will always bring these pests. They will be the worst just as light is failing, engaging in a feeding frenzy upon whomever they can find.

You should also have a repellent spray aboard, particularly if you don't want to spend a beautiful evening cowering below behind screens.

Gnats and "no-see-ums" are also encountered mostly in the evening on quiet warm nights where there is marsh and wood around. Some varieties of these creatures are so small that they can come through most screens, necessitating no-see-um netting; but we seldom encounter this kind on the Bay. Usually spray and normal screening will help.

Editor's Note: We spray our companion way and hatches before we retire to our bunks and use Skin so Soft or Cutters on our persons. That keeps them away.

Flies can be a problem anywhere, even far out in the Bay. An interesting phenomenon related to the weather is the onslaught of flies on a southwester or just before a significant cold front. If you are planning a glorious sail in a southwester, prepare to use your screens, because this very frequently brings an incredible number of flys from the western shore, regardless of how far in the Bay you may be. We make the most of the situation by shooting them with fly swatter guns. Whoever gets the biggest pile wins! If a cold front is imminent in the fall, they will be desperately attempting to get below, as if they know that the changing temperatures will soon end their lives and they want to get into the warmth and to where they can engage in some fine last meals. Again screens are the ultimate answer.

Stinging Nettles

Many consider stinging nettles to be the greatest nemeses of the Bay. Without going into the wealth of scientific detail that is available, suffice it to say that they hurt, they are seldom if ever to be found in the far upper Bay where there is fresh water, and they usually abound around mid-June until early September, depending on rainfall and temperatures. They are "jellyfish" in character, some having long red tentacles and some having white or clear tentacles. Some types do not sting at all. Most people believe that meat tenderizer helps the sting. *Editor's note: This works for me! I have used river mud caked on. Don't swim when you see them.*

In certain times and places, you will see nettles everywhere. They can also be so numerous that they can clog up the water intake of small diesels. This is particularly true of water-cooled generators. They will also quickly clog up water-cooled air conditioners. Therefore, it is a good idea to install a long and wide strainer on the hull outside the water intake if you plan to run a generator or air conditioning. If you must swim, there are nets hung from round floats which you can tie to your stern, forming a small but protected pool. I always wear tight-fitting long johns. The nettles usually don't get through, but your face, neck, hands and feet are exposed.

Oyster Shells and Other Sharp Objects

Whenever you are swimming or wading, take care where you put your feet until you know what is there. The Bay is famous for its oysters, but these creatures can have sharp edges that make dirty cuts if you step on them. Usually they are in a "bed" and these can be in water that is wading deep. If you step on one and jump in pain, you will probably land on more, lacerating both feet. Beware also of other sharp objects around areas of civilization. Thoughtless people can throw a bottle overboard that will lie in wait for years until you step on it.

Best Times to Cruise

Editor's Note: I like to swim and have done this daily on my Chesapeake Bay cruises in July north of Annapolis, without ever being stung by sea nettles. There is so much fresh water coming into the northern part of Chesapeake Bay from the Susquehanna River and other tributaries, that sea nettles do not thrive there. If they come at all, they'll come later than south of the Bay Bridge.

The best times to cruise are spring and fall. Usually cruising is great from early May to mid-June, and from mid-September to early November. A spectacular bonus in the late fall will be the turning of the leaves, and in the crisp cold mornings, the geese will fly in formation overhead calling you to follow them south. Wind will often be easterly, particularly with the afternoon onshore sea breezes on the lower Bay. Cold fronts usually bring a day or so of preceding southwesterlies, then northwesterlies sometimes clocking around to the northeast. The north-south fetch in the Bay is quite long and the seas can get very rough with these winds. The summer months will have the most stinging nettles, the most bugs, many days of flat, hot, humid calm, and the worst thunderstorms.

SEA CONDITIONS

Chesapeake Bay can be very rough, uncomfortable, and even a dangerous place to be when the wind is from a long fetch. Much of it is relatively shallow, and therefore the seas are notoriously short, steep chop that can be merciless. If the wind is off the land, as it often is, the opportunities for brisk but comfortable sails are endless. But beware the northerlies and southerlies that can build tremendous seas from either direction with the vast fetch to work from.

Areas of strong and/or conflicting current can make the worst waves. These are often found off broad points of land (Wolftrap Light in the lower Bay is a good example) and off the mouths of large rivers (such as the Patuxent or Chester). One of the worst areas is the large body of open water off the Potomac in the lower Bay.

One of the great things about the Bay is that if it ever gets too rough, there are almost always places to duck in and wait it out, either at anchor or at a nice marina.

CURRENT AND TIDES

Compared to many other cruising areas, Chesapeake Bay is mild-mannered in these categories. Tides range from around 1½ to 2½ feet, and currents are seldom more than 1½ to 2 knots. But there can be significant departures from the norm relating to wind and weather, moon phase, and location. For example, we have found currents close to 3 knots at the bridge in Kent Narrows during peak flow.

Phases of the moon affect both the heights of the tide and therefore, the currents. Full moon and new moon will bring the greatest extremes between highs and lows. Since there is more water moving during these times, there will be more current. This doesn't have much impact on most Chesapeake cruising, but if you choose a time of full moon to go hard aground, don't wait until the next day to get off!

The times of high and low tide throughout the Bay are found in "The Tide Tables for the East Coast of North and South America Including Greenland," (published by the U.S. Department of Commerce, NOAA). But they can be obtained readily in advertising handouts at many marinas and fishing centers around the Bay. These consist of cards or pamphlets with the information for the relevant section of the Bay for the month or season. Most people pick up one of these from their marina or a related business before departure for a cruise. Low and high tide times for various locations are also given on the VHF weather stations. The tide tables change each year, and they also vary significantly from point to point. Therefore, we suggest that you pick up one of the handouts for the area where you plan to cruise before you leave. They will usually be for the month or season and show times for the upriver and upcreek areas that are more relevant to your cruise.

A base high and low tides for much of the southeast north Atlantic is that of Sewell's Point at the lower end of the Bay. Tides for the upper Bay, however, are reported for Baltimore Harbor. Tides for different locations are given in hours and minutes before or after low and high tides there. Differences can be considerable, particularly as you move up the tributaries. We include Appendix VIII a list of constant tide differences obtained from the "Tide Tables for the East Coast of North and South America" published by the U.S. Department of Commerce, the National Oceanic and Atmospheric Administration. They use Baltimore as a base, except for those of the C&D Canal which use Reedy Point as a base.

The time of high and low time doesn't correspond with the time of zero current. The current flow will stop and change at different times in relation to the tide peaks, and this will vary with the wind and moon. The "Tidal Current Tables, Atlantic Coast of North America" will give the norms expected, but don't rely on this completely. Predicting when the current will reverse flow while going up or down the Bay or a long river, such as the Chester, can be important to a slow moving sail or motor boat. For these reasons, we recommend a copy of this book aboard.

We have included tidal current charts which will give a reasonable idea of what to expect. This chart, unlike tide tables, does not change yearly. These charts are in the back of this book, following the index.

There are some areas in the upper Bay where winds have more effects than in others. Kent Narrows immediately comes to mind. A strong and a long norther can make it seem as though the tide is not coming in. The far northern section is also particularly susceptible to a strong norther. Areas such as the Sassafras River and the Elk River are two good examples. Obviously, a strong southerly for several days can pile the water up in these areas, causing tides to be higher than normal.

ANCHORING

Without getting into the eternal debate as to which anchor is best, we have always had both a CQR (Trademark) and a Danforth (Trademark) as our working anchors in the Bay, and have found that one or the other almost always works.

We use long lengths of heavy chain with both. Our anchor rode is ⅜" BBB chain. Chain will not be cut by pieces of glass or junk on the bottom, where rope will. Also, the weight of the chain will help to set any type of anchor, causing the pull to be more parallel to the bottom rather than up and down which will tend to pull the anchor out of the bottom rather than dig it in. A lot of heavy chain is absolutely critical in areas where the mud is very soft. Some bottoms are so soft that nothing will work, but long chain to drag through the mud, helping the hook to dig in, sometimes will save the situation with this type of bottom. We use at least 5:1 scope, all chain.

In the many years that I have been anchoring in the Chesapeake Bay up and down the east coast, and in the Bahamas, I have learned to rate bottoms in my log. I often examine the materials on my hook when I pull it up and note the holding it gave me. Gray clay mixed with mud is five star. This may be buried under loose black or reddish mud which will not hold. But once you get either a plow or Danforth type into the gray stuff, you've got it made. When the hook comes up in the morning, the flukes will be caked with gray mud-clay and you will probably have to scrape it off in globs. It's no fun, but neither is dragging. From this type, the quality of mud deteriorates with its thickness. There are many places where the mud is so loose that almost nothing will hold despite the amount of chain and backing down. Generally, if the stuff is clinging to your flukes and showing some consistency, you can probably get a good bite. If you run your finger through it and the mud immediately closes over the mark, plan to be up if the wind blows or the current changes.

Sand can also be good for holding, but not always. Some sand is too hard even for a Danforth type to easily dig in, although often this type will work in hard sand when a plow type won't.

Grass is seldom good. Worse, it can be very misleading. Any anchor may bite hard at first, but in a blow the roots will often give, a few at a time, until suddenly the last ones break and you are sailing downwind with a clump of weeds. Fortunately, there is not much grass in most Chesapeake anchorages. If grass is the only thing around, try a kedge type (sometimes called "Herreshoff type" or "yachtsman's") which may dig deeply enough through the grass to stay. Obviously, rock is also poor, although fortunately there is not much of this in the Chesapeake either. A kedge anchor may hang onto a ledge or corner, but then maybe not when the wind or current changes.

Bottom mixtures are common. Shell and mud is found in many areas. Unless shells are broken up, they often provide a hard surface that most hooks readily can't penetrate or, if deep, will result in a mixture that will only hold for a light pull. Shells also occasionally catch on the points of the anchor making it impossible to set. However, many small or broken shells evenly mixed in mud can make good holding. Sand and mud is generally a good mixture, very heavy concentrates of sand often requiring a Danforth type.

There are several ways to find what may be down there when you can't see. We have found that concave lead weights used to sound and take bottom samplings are not very helpful for anchoring purposes. The best way is to dig up some bottom with your anchor and check it. No one wants to do this on purpose, although it is what often happens when you drag on the first try. If you don't want to do this, first look at the charts. They sometimes give cryptic clues such as "stk" or "hrd." (NOAA charts have abbreviation guides that may indicate a different code than that actually used.) This occasionally helps, but only take it as a very general advice.

Look also along the shores for clues. Often, for example, many shells on the bank will indicate shell below. If the banks are marsh held in mud, with a fair current to keep the bottom free from mush, there may be good mud below. Quiet coves surrounded by beautiful forest often hold slime bottoms caused from years of siltation and decay with little cleansing current. Chesapeake Bay has many such areas. Sandy beaches ashore with a gently sloping bottom indicated on the chart often mean sand out where you wish to anchor.

If someone is already in the anchorage, it might be helpful to ask him what he noticed when he set his hook. He may have dragged and had to pull it up and therefore may know quite a bit. Sometimes a small grappling hook dragged along the bottom will bring up enough to let you know what it is like.

Time spent in anchoring properly could save you from a miserable night, property damage, and personal injury. Remember that the wind and weather can change. For example, if you are expecting a front or thunder squalls, be sure that your anchor is set from the direction of the anticipated strong wind, unless you are already experiencing strong winds from another direction. Also, anticipate where you will swing when the wind shifts. If it is into a bank, or into another boat or over his anchor rode, re-position yourself.

When the hook goes down, it is important to be at the bow to feel and listen to what happens as you fall back. If the bottom is hard with shells, you can usually hear the chain rattle as it drags across, and feel the vibration with your hand or foot. The ground tackle will often lightly vibrate as it slides across hard sand. I like to hang over and put my bare foot on the chain before it contacts the roller. If the anchor seems to hold but jerks out, there may be grass, a deep shell mixture, or marginal mud. When it just smoothly and quietly slides on back with the boat, it is probably floating through loose slimy mud.

If your anchor does hold after backing, don't stop there, particularly if you expect any weather. Continue backing down with slowly increasing RPMs until you are sure. Then a few jerks with the motor should really tell the story. To do this, wait in neutral until the line hangs slack, then back up, allowing the line to straighten. Drift back into neutral just before it goes tight to avoid shock to your drive train. If your boat jerks a little when the line taughtens and the stern swings around straight behind, you are probably in for the night.

Once you dig in, you can relax, enjoy the evening, and hope that your neighbor upwind has done as well.

TRAILER SAILING

Trailer sailing is great anywhere on the Bay. Pick your spot and go. Good launching ramps are almost everywhere and most of them are hard surfaced with ample parking. Some are free, some charge fees that do not generally exceed more than five to seven dollars. Some good publications are the "Chesapeake Bay and River Public Access Guide" copyrighted in 1989 by the State of Virginia; the "Boating Almanac" Volume 4, published each year by the Peter Geis of the Boating Almanac Co. Inc; and the magazine, "Fishing in Maryland" published annually by FIM Publishing. Most counties have publicly maintained ramps. When planning a trip you may wish to call the department of recreation for the county where you wish to launch. They will provide you with a list of ramps and fees, if any. We describe launching ramps in the sections covering the area where we found them.

**Schooner *Bill of Rights* in Baltimore Inner Harbor
before Great Chesapeake Bay Schooner Race**

Chesapeake Trail

Editor's note: For years, I have been a member of the Maine Island Trail Association, P.O. Box C, Rockland, ME 04841. They have obtained permission for use of all or portions of some of Maine's numerous islands, and incorporated those that are public. The Maine Island Trail is a 325-mile long waterway extending from Casco Bay to Machais Bay. The trail winds its way along the coast over protected saltwater rivers and quiet bays, around capes, and among islands. Along the route, public and private islands are available to members or to the public for overnight camping or picnicking in a wilderness setting. Members join work parties to clean beaches, clear trails and meadows, and they sponsor cruises for kayaks, or for small boats, or canoes. They have a newsletter and issue an annual guide book. Recreation and conservation are not mutually exclusive!

What has this got to do with the Chesapeake Bay? Well what would you think of a similar Chesapeake Trail? One is being developed by a group of kayakers who are exploring the Eastern Shore looking for potential campsites and other landings. They plan to set up an organization and a formal water trail.

Meanwhile, Tom Neale has included in this book waterfront campsites, launching ramps, and all public and private facilities for small boats as well as large boats, for power boats as well as sailboats. We pride ourselves in bringing you a complete work, useful to all watercraft from canoes to large yachts.

Other marine trails being developed at this time include those on Lake Superior, the Connecticut River, and Puget Sound. The Puget Sound one is well along, named the Cascadia Marine Trail, Washington Water Trails Association, 4649 Sunnyside Ave. N. Room 345, Seattle, WA 98103. Their trail will extend from Olympia 140 miles north to the Canadian border.

Another group is planning a British Columbia Marine Trail, to connect with the Cascadia Trail and extend 550 miles north to Prince Rupert.

Other Maine Trails being developed include the Kennebec River Trail which will extend from Moosehead Lake to Popham Beach in Phillipsburg.

Native Trails, P.O. Box 240 Waldbora, ME 04572, has visited and plans to open water trails formerly used by Native Americans, fur trappers, woodsmen and settlers. One 40-mile route is a challenge for canoeists and kaykers, starting from Damariscotta, going to Damariscotta Lake, then a portage to Pemaquid Pond, then following the Pemaquid River to Johns Bay, through the gut at South Bristol, and back up the Damariscotta River to the starting point. They have also completed exploration for the Eastern Maine Canoe Trail, 130 miles of rivers and lakes between Vanceboro on the Canadian border to Passadumkeag on the Penobscot River. This includes 7 miles of portages!

STINGRAYS

Captain John Smith's encounter with the stingray on what is now called Stingray Point (just to the south of the Rappahannock) left him in such pain that he reportedly ordered his men to dig his grave. Fortunately, he survived. These graceful creatures are still to be found in the Bay, and occasionally you will see them swimming along with the tips of their two wings breaking the surface. They will look like two sharks swimming side by side in perfect unison. I have never heard of them bothering swimmers. They do sometimes like to settle on the sand in the warm waters, and if you step on one, as apparently the captain did, they will sting with their barb.

PROVISIONING FOR A CRUISE

Planning a cruise usually includes a great deal of provisioning. But one of the features of the Bay is that you may prefer not to do that much provisioning so that you can take advantage of the many special restaurants, festivals, and shopping opportunities that abound around the shores. Unless you plan to avoid civilization as much as possible, you should plan to go ashore and sample restaurants here and there. You can plan your cruise so that you can find some sort of a market or restaurant every evening, if that is what you want. What you bring and how much you bring will depend on your preferences and the type of boat and storage you have. If you do not have refrigeration, you will find ice in almost all of the marinas.

CLOTHING AND SUN PROTECTION

In the summer season, you should be safe with light clothing, but in the fall or spring, the temperatures can range from very warm to very cold, and you should be prepared. Swim wear may be all you need for much of the cruise, even if you don't go into the water. Sunglasses and clothing to protect you from the sun are very important, as is foul weather gear. Most restaurants around the Bay shores expect boating clientele and understand that fine clothing and cruising do not always mix well. You will find excellent restaurants which are quite happy to have you without jackets and ties.

You should also bring items such as sun tan lotion, meat tenderizer for stinging nettles, and bug spray. *Editor's note: I wear broad brimmed hats, old long sleeve shirts, and long pants when not swimming. You'd be surprised how much tan I get.*

FISHING

Whether it is trolling, bottom fishing, or crabbing, the Chesapeake Bay has bountiful fishing. Both Maryland and Virginia now require fishing licenses, but they are readily obtained from many fishing centers and marinas on the shore. Fishing laws and rules change from year to year depending on depletion of the species and other factors. When you get your license, you can obtain a set of the current rules. When you plan your cruise, if you wish to do any fishing, pick up pamphlets on the current rules from most marinas or fishing shops.

You can bottom fish with gear ranging from a line on a spool to elaborate casting equipment. Many pleasant hours can be spent just fishing off the bottom with blood worms or crab parts on a hook. Spot, bass, perch, sea trout, cobia, flounder (along the bottom), and catfish will be some of your rewards.

Bluefish run in the spring and make great trolling game. They fight hard and, if you find a school in a feeding frenzy, they may give you an exciting time. These fish have a stronger taste than some others, but most love them. *Editor's note: To get rid of the strong oily taste, clean them promptly, and make a deep "V" cut along the dorsal fin, discarding all the brown meat. You'll be rewarded with elegant eating—fresh caught blues. They do not freeze well. Eat them when you catch them.*

In the fall there is usually a brief season for Rockfish. These are among the tastier fish in the Bay, but have been rare lately, thus there is a limit each year on what you can take.

There are numerous good fishing publications relevant to the Chesapeake. One which we found to be particularly helpful is a magazine entitled "Fishing in Maryland" published annually by FIM Publishing and sold in most fishing shops. This has fishing tips, hot spots, regulation updates, launching ramps, and much other valuable information. We recommend it if you are at all serious about fishing. At this time, it sells for around $7 and includes charts with fishing spots, identification charts for game fish, launching ramps, and much other very helpful information. Most marinas and boating stores up and down the Bay will have other fishing information, much of it free.

CRABBING

Crabbing is, and long has been, the classical pastime of the Bay as well as a major part of its seafood industry. It is the Blue Crab we are talking about, the Callinectes Sapidus (beautiful swimmer). They exist up and down the east coast, in the Bahamas, and in many other places, but a true believer will tell you that there is nothing that can compare to the Chesapeake Bay Blue Crab. When you visit the lower Bay, you will surely not miss the Crisfield Crab Derby in September where there are many events to celebrate this celebrity, including parades, crab races of most serious attendance, and crab picking contests with a high purse and much honor. Anyone cruising the Bay should read and have along the book "Beautiful Swimmers" written by William W. Warner and published by Little, Brown, and Co. This is a beautiful book about the Blue Crab, and also about the Bay itself.

You can tell a female from a male by the apron on the underside. A male has a pointed arrow-like apron, the female's is rounded. An adult male is usually called a "jimmy" crab, and a young female is called a "sally," while an adult female is called a "sook." When the sook is ready to release her fertilized eggs, you will see an orange or orange-brown spongy mass of the eggs protruding from the underside of the apron. Some people then call her a "busted sook" or a "sponge crab."

How to Catch Crabs

If you are going on a cruise, you should certainly be prepared to do a little crabbing. And if you are too sophisticated to handle a little rotten meat and some ornery critters, it would be a great pastime for your kids. All it takes is a string with a weight, a crab net, and a chicken neck (or some other peice of meat, preferably not too fresh). Tie the meat onto one end of the string and hang it overboard, letting it come to rest on or just above the bottom. When a crab comes calling, you will feel the string beginning to tug, and sometimes stream out as the crab tries to swim away with its feast. Then begin to gently pull the string in. If you jerk or go too fast, he will know that something is wrong and swim off. When he gets near the surface, you will be able to see him hanging onto the meat.

This will be the time that you will be glad you left your net nearby because, without disturbing the crab happily munching below, you must get the net and dip him up. Dipping him up is not as easy as it seems. You can't just splash the net into the water and hope to be fast enough. You won't be. Instead, slip the net silently into the water, moving it slowly up behind the crab. When you think you are close enough (but not too close because it will scare him), swoop the net in under him and pull him up.

You think that's fun? More is to come, for now it can get really sporting. It obviously doesn't do much good to stand there with a crab in a net. You have to get him into the bucket so that you can go back for more. Now some crabs will oblige nicely, but others are quiet ornery. Perhaps you will be able to just turn your net upside down over the bucket and he will just drop in. But more likely, he will hang on for dear life to leave you to shake and shake. You might try reaching into the now tangled mess of crab and net and pull him out by the backfin, but beware. You might also continue to shake, and eventually he will drop free, but never over the bucket. It will be over your toes, most likely. And a mad blue crab is a creature to be reckoned with. If he isn't already holding onto a piece of your flesh with agonizing tenacity, he will back into a corner where you can't get behind him and raise his claws before his face with a clicking and clattering leaving no doubt of his intentions should he get the slightest chance!

How to Cook Crabs

I've seen people crabbing with dozens of these creatures walking around in the bilge and hiding in the corners. You always have to face the music, though, and corral the critter without getting wounded, if you want to cook him. When you have enough, put them still alive in a large pan, pour in a can of beer, sprinkle very liberally with Old Bay Seasoning (TM), and steam until their shells are red (about 20 minutes). Let them cool, spread some newspaper, and start picking and eating.

They may get a bit lively when you begin to cook. Sometimes it is best to put a weighted top on to prevent them from climbing out and escaping into the galley. It does sound unkind to cook them alive, but that's the way it is done and is an assurance of freshness. Most people that we know would not eat a crab cooked already dead.

Crab picking is one of the Bay's finest arts, but fewer people seem to know how as each year goes by. Often machines are used today, resulting in grossly inferior picking (I don't care what they say). You can tell when a person who isn't qualified does it by the number of shells mixed in. At the Crisfield Crab Derby on Labor day weekend, some of the world's best crab pickers compete for serious prizes. We don't claim their prowess, but suggest a few tips.

Steam them first, as described above. When they are cool enough, lift the apron and put your thumb under the top shell to lift off that top shell from the back edge toward the face. It all comes off in one piece, the shell and the apron. Then use your fingers to clean out the dead man and remove the gills. The dead man is the yucky yellowish "stuff" and white sacs that is in the depression underneath the top shell in the middle. It should not be eaten. The gills, which are under the shell on each side, are long, grayish white, slender, and pointed. Break off the legs at their joint with the crab body and set aside. Break the crab in half by holding a side in each hand. Now, either using your fingers or a small knife, break or cut into the shell and remove the white meat from each compartment. The biggest compartment contains a backfin meat, the choice cut of the crab. Serious crab pickers use a knife to do this, but it is more fun with your fingers. You can lick them afterwards. The large claws can be opened with nut crackers or mallets. If you get good at it and can get the claw meat out in one piece still attached to the small pincer of the claws, you can use these as crab finger hors d'oeuvres dipped in cocktail sauce. Break open the small legs and suck or pull the meat out. You can eat the crab meat while you are cleaning them or save it to make into crab cakes or whatever.

Our Priceless Crab Cake Recipe

Our favorite crab cake recipe is something heretobefore never released to other mortals and worth many, many times the price of this book. The ingredients: one pound of carefully picked crab meat (backfin is best), one egg, chopped onions to taste, chopped fresh parsley to taste, a dash of Worcestershire, a heaping tablespoon full of Dukes Homemade Mayonnaise (TM), a teaspoon of Grey Poupon Mustard (TM), bread or cracker (saltines preferable) crumbs (enough to hold mixture together), Old Bay Seasoning (TM) used liberally to taste. Mix all ingredients. Make into patties or cakes; this makes 6 to 8 cakes. Fry till lightly brown in butter or oil.

Crab Pots

Many people also cruise with a crab pot aboard. If you don't mind the clutter (and mess sometimes), these are great to have if you intend to stay anchored for a day or so in one spot. Sometimes, just leaving them in overnight will bring enough for a feast. Just bait them up with meat and put them over. While just about any meat (preferably not overly fresh) will do, we notice that the most professional crabbers use fish (menhaden are popular) and eels.

Trot Lines

In the upper waters of the Bay, you will often see one or two people in a boat slowly working down a line, pulling it aboard carefully, and netting, hopefully crab after crab. This is called "trot lining." The line has numerous shorter lengths attached along its length, with bait tied on. This is laid out in a likely place, with an anchored float at each end. The crabber works from one end to the other, and then over again. It is important not to cut between a trot liner and his floats. If you jiggle his line, all the crabs may drop off. This method of crabbing is particularly popular on the eastern shore.

Soft Shell Crabs

Now comes the part about the best crabs of all—soft shell crabs. Periodically throughout the crab's life, he must shed his hard shell in order to grow. He will usually pick a quiet, hopefully safe place to shed. Often this will be in the grassy shallows, sometimes on the side of a piling, perhaps in your marina under your slip. Then begins a laborious shedding process where he slowly "busts" out, splitting at first along the back side and then working free a little at a time. The whole process takes hours, during which the crab is very vulnerable, not only to natural prey but also to people. "Peelers" are considered to be excellent fishing bait and that is what the crab is during the time when he still wears his old shell with the soft one in place underneath. Experienced hands can tell, by looking, whether the crab has a new shell. It is also during

this time that enterprising souls like to capture the crab and put it into a shedding float or pen. More on that below.

Eventually the crab completely sheds his old shell, at which point he is totally exhausted and almost immobile for a few hours while he is regaining strength and his soft shell is beginning to harden. Right after he comes out is the best time to find him, and eat him. This is, in the opinion of many people, the Bay's finest delicacy. Broiled, sauteed, fried, in sandwiches, almost any way but raw. You can find crabs peeling at just about any time during the summer, but periods of full and new moon seem to be the best. Once the soft crab is captured, if he is immediately killed and cleaned, his shell will, of course, remain soft. You can also chill them in a refrigerator or ice box and they will remain alive for days, with very little hardening. As they harden, they are called "paper shells" and are less and less desirable.

If you want to watch the entire process, visit one of the commercial shedding pens scattered around the Bay. For example, one of these is at Cantler's Restaurant on Mill Creek off Whitehall Bay. Another is Queen Anne's Marina on the west side of Kent Island, across the Bay from (east of) Thomas Point Light. Here, the operators collect the crabs before they begin to shed, and put them into a series of boxes, floats, or "pens" where they very carefully maintain an even and easy flow of natural Bay water. They then watch the crabs continuously, moving them from pen to pen according to the stage of their shedding. This is because crabs are cannibalistic, and will sometimes attack weaker crab during the process.

The shedding business requires hard work and constant attention, including all through the night to be sure that the new softies are removed from the hard pen before they are eaten and before they begin to get hard. If there is someone around who has the time to point out the different stages and explain the process, it will be well worth the visit.

Soft shell crabs should be cleaned while they are alive for freshness. With a sharp knife cut off the apron and the face. Then lift the top shell on each side and cut out the gills. Next, insert the knife into the hole left by the face and cut out the dead man. When you have removed all of the dead man, they are ready to cook. The top shell is left on.

To cook a soft shell crab, dip him in a mixture of egg and milk seasoned with hot sauce [Tabasco (TM) or Crystal (TM)] then dip in bread crumbs or cracker crumbs, or flour, seasoned liberally with Old Bay Seasoning (TM) to taste. Now fry in very hot oil until golden brown. Drain the fried crab on a paper towel. *Editor's note: It's easy to make friends during your Chesapeake Bay cruise. On my first cruise during the 50's, someone in a neighbor's boat in Patapsco River taught us how to catch crabs, and we had a lot of fun. Later, on that same cruise, we were invited to a Chesapeake Bay Crab Feast. It's similar to our New England clambakes that feature clams and lobsters, but they feature crabs and oysters. If you get invited, go.*

OYSTERS

The Chesapeake oyster has been eaten both as a staple and as a delicacy for thousands of years. Along with Blue Crab, it is probably one of the most well known examples of Bay seafood. In recent times, the population has suffered seriously from excessive human consumption, and an oyster disease called MSX which doesn't hurt people but ruins the oysters.

They are taken by tonging, dredging (pronounced "drudging") and now even by diving. Tonging is done by watermen standing in their low-sided boats in the shallows. They have long-handled two-sided rakes or tonging tools, and you will see them working the handles and moving the apparatus up and down before pulling it up hopefully with a good catch.

In some areas, this is now done by machinery and an engine requiring much less strength and covering much more territory over a day's time. This equipment is called the "patent tong" because it was patented by an enterprising blacksmith from the Solomons Island area. One of the most fascinating of the Bay's traditions is the dredging done by the skipjack fleet. Here, great dredges are pulled over the oyster beds by these beautiful vessels under sail.

Recently we have begun to notice divers with scuba gear. Whether this method will be successful is yet to be told. With the murkiness of the waters, the divers can only feel for oysters, and the cold waters of the season certainly make the job very unappealing to most.

You will see oysters growing in the shallows all around the Bay. They like to adhere to hard surfaces, especially other oyster shells. They cannot survive in soft silty bottom because they will suffocate in the mud. Occasionally, you will see buy boats, loaded to the gunnels with shells, steaming up or down the Bay. These will be washed over the side with high pressure hose in a chosen area, hopefully to serve as a good anchoring bed for a new generation. Often areas where you will find oysters are now posted by the authorities who fear pollution, and it is forbidden to take oysters. In Virginia, many oyster beds are "owned" and considered private to oystering even though they are underneath the water.

Many a cruiser has picked up a few in the shallows, but at their own risk. While we used to buy them from the boats fresh out of the water and eat them then and there, dripping over the side, many people feel reluctant to eat them at all now because of fear of various sorts of pollution. But a cold fresh oyster with a little horseradish has been a favorite delicacy for a long time. The traditional time to eat oysters has only been in the months with an "R." The reasons for this were the fact that because of the effects of reproduction on their bodies, they were better in those months, because before referigeration they were less likely to be spoiled in the cold months, and because it is generally thought that the colder water makes them safer. This custom still prevails today, and few Chesapeake Bay residents will eat oysters from these waters at other times. One of the festivals celebrating the arrival of the season, the Oyster Festival in Urbana on the Rappahannock, is always held on the first weekend in November, because the season usually starts then in Virginia, traditional lore being that the waters get colder later down there because it is farther south. *Editor's note: I've sampled oysters from many seas, and I rate Chesapeake Bay oysters very high. Because of all the fresh water flowing into the Bay, Chesapeake Bay oysters have less iodide content.*

CLAMS

There are hard and soft shell clams in the Bay. The soft shells are long with a shell that you can easily break. They have long siphons. They are usually taken with hand tongs or rakes, or hydraulic equipment. Many favor them, but many prefer the hard shells because they tend to have less silt inside. These are usually taken with hand tongs or rakes, or "patent tongs." The hard shelled clams are generally referred to as "littlenicks" (little necks), cherrystones, and chowders,

Crab Shed, Knapps Narrows

depending on size from very small on up. The chowders can be large and rather tough, but still good for chowder.

You will see people tonging and dredging for clams in a manner similar to oystering, but with a slightly different equipment. A favorite weekend pastime for many is to go out in the shallows where clams are known to be living, walk around towing your boat or a basket in an inner tube behind you, feeling for them with your toes, and then eating them raw or steamed on the beach in the evening. Again, if you do this, be sure that this is not in a posted or private area. Many prefer to cook or steam clams or to roast oysters rather than eat them raw because they feel that it helps to kill bacteria that may be present.

CHESAPEAKE BAY SEAFOOD

The Bay has been a huge supplier of seafood since its earliest civilization. Far before that, the Indian nations along the shores used the Bay as a major source of food. There are oyster shell mounds scattered about the shores that have been dated back to thousands of years B.C. When Captain John Smith was stung by a sting ray on what is now Stingray Point in the lower Bay, he was actually spearing fish in the shallows with his sword. While visiting Herring Bay in the upper regions, he found the fish to be so plentiful, that he tried to catch them with a frying pan.

In recent years, our consumption of Bay seafood and various ecological problems, some caused by man and others by natural processes, have depleted the resources. Oysters and Rockfish, have been felt to be dangerously under-populated and severe restriction on the taking of them have been enforced. *Editor's note: Rockfish are called Striped Bass in New England and other places.* You will still see commercial vessels fishing, clamming, oystering, and crabbing wherever you go on the Bay. Also, scattered liberally on the shores will be retail and wholesale seafood houses where you can buy the catch fresh. Both Maryland and Virginia actively attempt to regulate the seafood industry, trying to balance the needs of nature with those of civilization, sometimes with obvious success and sometimes not.

Restaurants around the Bay specialize in seafood, and you should certainly give it all a try. In the section on fishing we mentioned a few of the different varieties. Here we will discuss a few more, which most people buy rather than catch themselves.

CHESAPEAKE BAY BOATS

Chesapeake Bay is noted for many unique boats that have served its citizens over the generations and for the seamen who build and work from them. Many of the ancient boats are still around today, not only in the museums, but also on the water, in use. Your cruise will be much more meaningful when you recognize them out on the water, and you should seek them out and absorb their lines and traditions in the many places they may be found.

One of the best places to begin learning is at The Chesapeake Bay Maritime Museum in St. Michaels, where authentic examples of most of them will be found either on land or in the water. There is also a huge shop here where actual restoration and rebuilding by craftsmen skilled in the Bay boatbuilding arts can be watched from a balcony above the work

area. There are also educational displays and excellent resource material available here. The Calvert Marine Museum in Solomons Island is another excellent place to learn about Bay craft.

At the Inner Harbor of Baltimore, you will find several authentic examples in regular attendance, and others frequently visit and are often open for touring. The *Pride of Baltimore II*, a Baltimore Clipper replica, is seen at the city docks when she is not sailing around the Bay or to foreign countries. There are many good resource books available. These include "Chesapeake Bay Sailing Craft" and "This Was the Chesapeake" both written by Robert H. Burgess and published by Tidewater Publishers, and "Steam Packets on the Chesapeake" by Alexander Crosby Brown, also published by Tidewater Publishers. Don't be surprised to see tall sets of sails on the horizon, as though the past were sailing over the curve of the earth to meet you.

Log Canoes

One example of boats unique to the Bay is the Log Canoe; some, over a hundred years old, are still raced on the Miles River. These are actually built by fastening together several logs, and are beautiful and graceful, if not a bit tender under sail. Frequently, these race off the entrance to St. Michaels up and down the Miles. The Miles River Yacht Club in Long Haul Creek is famous for sponsoring many of these races. Anchor off the side on a windy race and enjoy the show. The Chesapeake Bay Maritime Museum will usually know when they are going to race.

Skipjacks and Other Work Boats

Skipjacks, large broad beamed sailing craft with clipper bows and graceful sterns are still working today, dredging for oysters under sail. They have no motors for propulsion and are propelled, if not sailing, by a yawl boat pushing astern. You can tour the skipjack *Minnie V* in Baltimore, the *Stanley Norman* in Annapolis, and others in the Chesapeake Bay Maritime Museum in St. Michaels and other locations around the Bay. They also proudly race, sometimes just amongst themselves romping in the chop over the shallows, or in organized events such as the one at Sandy Point usually in late October and in the Deal Island races in September. But there are also the Bugeyes, the Pungies, the Rams, and many other types of sailing vessels developed to serve a specific use, usually for the seafood industry but sometimes for cargo.

Baltimore Clippers

Among the more well known Bay craft are the fast and famous schooners called Baltimore Clippers. These were developed in the years prior to the War of 1812, and were used with great success for privateering during that war. President James Madison offered letters of Marque and Reprisal to many of the clipper captains, giving them an opportunity to show off their ships to the benefit of their own pocketbooks and the detriment of the British. They were slender and quite fast, and sank and captured many British ships. These vessels gained the admiration of the British to the extent that they sent a delegation over after the war to attempt to learn how they were built. Needless to say, they did not find willing teachers. One of the most well-known of these ships is the *Pride of Baltimore II*, operated as a public trust for educational purposes and to serve as an ambassador. Often you will find her at the Inner Harbor city docks; sometimes she is open to the public. The original *Pride of Baltimore* was lost in a sudden and severe storm at sea some years ago. A mast stands in memory to the vessel and her crew on the banks of the Inner Harbor.

Chesapeake Bay Deadrise

The proud but humble Chesapeake Bay Deadrise is seen every day in many forms throughout the Bay tonging oysters, dredging for crabs, or tending nets, buying catch to haul to the markets, spreading seed oyster, even hauling cargo. They may be anywhere from 16 to 18 feet to over 100 feet long. Usually today, the smaller ones used for crab potting, tonging, and pound netting have small pilot houses forward, with a stick on the starboard side for steering as well as a wheel forward. The larger ones, sometimes referred to as "buy boats" because many of them used to buy the catch out on the water, will usually have the house on the stern. The term "deadrise" refers to the form and manner of construction of her bow and underbody. Its lines are distinct, beautiful, graceful, and very seaworthy. I grew up on the Chesapeake knowing the Deadrise as a boat with a particular flair at the bow and aft, but others in some parts of the Bay use the term less genericaly. There are various forms that the Deadrise may take. The stern, in particular, varies considerably, depending mostly upon where the boat was built. The fame of the boat has spread far beyond the Bay. We have even seen some of these in the Bahamas serving well as fishing and freight craft, despite their aging timbers. For years there was a freighter plying the Bahamian water that we heard on the radio calling itself the *Yoki Meeko*. We finally learned that this was a Chesapeake Bay Deadrise brought down the coast for inter-island freight runs, and that what we were hearing was actually the *Yeocomico* with a Bahamian twist.

CHESAPEAKE WATERMEN

Although many may say that they are a dying breed, you will see the watermen everywhere, tonging for oysters, tending nets, running trot lines (a method of crabbing found mostly on the upper eastern shore), setting and pulling crab pots, raking for clams, and just going and coming in general. The Chesapeake is one of the major seafood producing waters of the world. These people work hard, it is their living, and we should respect that as we cruise and perhaps find a crab pot or pound net in the way.

There are several books available about the watermen. One of these is entitled "Working the Chesapeake" by Mark E. Jacoby, a University of Maryland publication. You should be sure to buy and savor the book "The Watermen of the Chesapeake Bay" by John H. Whitehead, III. Its photographs and quotes from the Bay's watermen say it all.

Their work is incredibly difficult. In the hottest, most humid days of summer, they are out on the water bending over lines to pull in pots or nets. When the line comes in, they are usually full of stinging nettles and the wind blows the strands into faces and eyes. In the bitter cold, they are out tonging or "drudging." Many of their boats have blocks of wood or copper sheathing to protect the prows from the ice. Most of them love their boats which are usually well cared for despite the fact that they generally look like what they are—hard living work boats. Often their transoms are varnished mahogany, sometimes they are a graceful drake tail. Their names are usually family names of mothers or wives, or the "*Three Sons*" or the "*Five Daughters*," or personal statements like "*Island Pride*."

The watermen don't make much money and there is always someone new on the block to tell them what they can

Spat (a small oyster) displayed at Chesapeake Bay Maritime Museum,
St. Michaels, for kids to play on and learn from

and what they can't do. People ashore can't understand the principle that some people had just rather take care of themselves than having everyone else do it for them, or at least tell them how to do it. But they survive, and I can't help but believe that they'll continue to do so. I have spent more than a few days, trying it myself when I was younger, and more recently going out with a good friend, now 81, who has been doing it since the age of seven. His name is Captain Wilson Rowe, of Gwynns Island, in the lower Bay just south of the Piankatank River. His boat is the 43-year old "Linda R," named after his first grand-daughter. Most of his latter life he spent pulling the nets by himself "cause I'm the onliest one around dang fool enough to work this hard."

But lately other islanders, good people, have been going out with him. And they help in the winter when he boils and tars his nets in the backyard behind the garden. And they help in the spring when he has to trudge out into the pine woods to cut new stakes. And they help pushing them into the mud to hold the nets strong against the storms; standing on the washboard, two or three of them, their hands on the stake, saying, "come on now, me an you" before each shove into the mud. Every birthday for many years, Cap'n Wilson has insisted on going out to fish alone. Today, his 81st, he took along Cap'n Ralph to help. Cap'n Wilson said it all one day, as we were heading out the river watching the light of the new morning spread around the waters. The glow in the east got brighter and brighter until finally the very first rim of the sun peaked over the horizon.

"Look at that, Cap'n Tom, look at that man," he said jubilantly. "They'll never stop that, Cap'n Tom, never in this world. That's one thing all them gol danged fools in Washington can't mess up Cap'n Tom, they can't take that away from us, they never will."

CRUISE ITINERARIES FOR THE NORTHERN CHESAPEAKE

To suggest a one, two, or three week cruise of the upper Chesapeake Bay is like suggesting that you attend a very fine banquet, the finest in the land, and then lightly sample only a few of the courses. The best that you can hope to do in such a short time is to hit a few of the many high spots, and whet your appetite for more. But it will be the finest sampling you have ever had. If you have already enjoyed some Bay cruising, you may prefer to pick one of the areas and spend time delving deeply into the various pleasures that it offers. However, if you are beginning to explore this lifetime cruising area, you may find the following cruise suggestions helpful. They were written with the thought of providing an overview of the many different types of areas and cruising experiences possible. You may then, in later cruises, want to concentrate on favorite areas, patterning each cruise to your preferences at the time. Never let this or any other guide limit your choices or exploration. After all, one of the great features of the Bay is that it is easy enough and user friendly enough for you to quickly become your own expert on the places that you enjoy most.

I have often met frustrated and disappointed cruisers because they missed parts of some suggested itinerary. That is not what cruising is about. Do what you can comfortably, and have fun. Therefore, we will give general suggestions with latitude as to length of stay and nearby explorations. If any point is to be made here, it is to try all of the places at one

time or another. Each is special in its own way. Have a general idea of what you want to do with your time. The fold-out chart inside the back cover of this book will help with that.

I have seen cruising suggestions which remind me of bus stop tours where you maintain a schedule, hitting another destination every day. This is not the way to cruise. Many cruises are ruined by this type of philosophy, and the Bay is certainly better appreciated and enjoyed by the cruising philosophy of doing what you feel like doing when you feel like doing it, (with regard for the weather), and feeling free to throw all schedules aside. Don't go to a different spot every day. Smell the roses; you will never find them so fragrant as the nooks and crannies, towns and villages, creeks and rivers of Chesapeake Bay. Therefore, these suggestions will be general in nature, with plenty of room for your own tailoring. Details of the areas suggested will be found in the text of this Guide.

The destinations in these cruises are intended to be within an easy day's reach for most sailboats. If you are in a power boat, you will have more time to relax when you arrive, or you may want to explore an extra creek, cove, or village. We have also "stuffed" the calendar with these cruises to give some options. For example, you may wish to emphasize marinas and restaurants instead of quiet gunkholes, or your boat may be fast enough to get to more places in less time.

While approximate mileages will be given, this can be somewhat misleading. For example, a trip from the Patuxent to the Choptank in a northeaster could take many hours longer than the same trip in a calm or with favoring winds. Also, your draft may allow you to take many shortcuts. For example, if you are in Eastern Bay and wish to go to the Chester River, a draft of only 4 feet should allow you to pass through Kent Narrows. Check the latest as to shoaling. There will probably be new dredging of the northern entrance soon. This saves you a day's trip up the Bay, under the Bay Bridges, around Love Point, and into the Chester River. This will be required if your draft won't allow you to pass through the northern entrance to the Narrows.

A few general considerations may help. The areas of high civilization and haute culture are nicely disbursed among areas of quiet tree-surrounded anchorages. Many prefer to enjoy a few days of nature on the hook, and then a few days living it up in an area with restaurants and shore side attractions. While geography is the major consideration here, weather is also important. For example, if it is summer and you are expecting tomorrow to be a day of oppressive heat and humidity with evening thunderstorms and a cool front, you may wish to be tied up tomorrow enjoying museums and restaurants, air conditioning and swimming pools. When the front blows through tomorrow night, you will be at a marina and not worrying about dragging anchor. The next few days may be crisp and cool and much better for gunkholing.

Most prefer cruising during spring and fall for reasons discussed in the section on weather in Chapter 1. If you are to cruise during the hot days of summer, you may wish to spend most of your time in the northernmost part of the Bay, concentrating upon the areas of Susquehanna, Northeast, Sassafras Rivers, and the upper creeks such as Still Pond, Fairlee, and Worton. The weather itself won't be noticeably cooler, but in these areas, the water is generally fresh and there are few if any stinging nettles. Thus you can jump in to cool off in a fresh water paradise anytime you want.

Remember also that festivals abound in the Bay, at all

times, but mostly in the fall. You should consider these and try to plan around the ones that you may wish to attend. Appendix II of this guide describes festivals and provides a representative list by month. The guide also gives phone numbers for various local agencies within the descriptions of the various areas. These agencies can give updated information about the festivals.

Believe it or not, a good Maryland Bay area road map may be of some use. Various maps are published by public and private entities. These will facilitate any overland trips, help you to identify counties that you may wish to visit thus facilitating calls to Chambers of Commerce.

If your cruise is to be during the months of June through mid-September, and you plan to be in stinging nettle waters (see the section in Chapter 1), you may wish to invest in one of the floating pools designed to let you soak without stings. These are essentially fine meshed nets hung from large circular floats, similar to huge inner tubes. You may also wish to bring along a pair of long johns or body stockings. Although they look somewhat weird to the uninformed, they can greatly diminish the number of nettles' stings.

We must assume a starting point. You may be coming through the C & D Canal, you may be coming up from the south, or beginning from any of the creeks around the shores of the northern Bay. Since the middle of the northern Bay is usually within one day's journey from either end, and because there are many charter boat businesses in this area, we will assume the Annapolis, Rock Hall, or Kent Narrows areas as a beginning point. You will see that we suggest the Chesapeake Bay Maritime Museum of St. Michaels as an early destination for all cruises. This is because you can learn much of the Bay and its culture here, thus making the rest of your cruise more meaningful. The Calvert Marine Museum at Solomons also offers a similar experience and many fine displays, although it is not as large. You will also note that we suggest that each cruise end with Baltimore's Inner Harbor. This is because this is such an excellent place to celebrate your cruise with a "grand finale." If, you wish to spend your last nights in seclusion, visit the Inner Harbor earlier, and pick one of the quieter spots mentioned for your last night.

A THREE WEEK CRUISE OF THE UPPER BAY

Within the first day or two of any cruise, I would recommend that you visit the Chesapeake Bay Maritime Museum at St. Michaels, Maryland, on the Miles River which empties into the broad Eastern Bay of the Eastern Shore. Although there is enough within this museum to consume several days, within one very full day you will be able to get a very interesting and helpful education about the Bay, its history, traditions, boats, people, problems and beauty. This will make the rest of your cruise much more meaningful and give a very helpful perspective to all that you see and experience. You can tie or anchor here. I would suggest joining the museum. This will enable you to tie up at the museum docks for a reasonable fee, giving easy access to all the displays.

Since most will be starting their cruise from some area of civilization and probably looking forward to quiet nights and anchorage, I hesitated to suggest this busy village as a first stop. The village is quaint and pretty, and there are many quiet rivers nearby for a retreat after you have visited the museum or just before. One of the most idyllic gunkholes of the entire Bay will be found only 1 or 2 hours away for most

boats, in the Wye East River in Dividing Creek. St. Michaels to Dividing Creek is approximately 8 NM. This is a tree-surrounded cove on an island, most of which is park, thus protected from encroachments of civilization. Here you can get your first taste of how nice Chesapeake gunkholing can be. If this cove is too crowded for you, Chapter 10 of this guide describing the Wye River, suggests many more which may be less crowded.

From the Miles River and Eastern Bay, you would probably enjoy a nice long sail heading down to the Choptank. In Dun Cove on Harris Creek, you will find a very pleasant anchorage with field, trees and marsh around. Dividing Creek to Dun Cove is approximately 37 NM around (to the west of) Poplar Island. If you can go through the Poplar Island Narrows and through Knapps Narrows, the distance will only be approximately 22 NM.

From here, a very long dinghy ride, or a day's excursion by your main boat, can take you to Dogwood Harbor on Tilghman Island to see the working Skipjacks that are usually to be found moored in large numbers there. From here, you could spend months going up the Tred Avon and the Choptank. The village of Oxford and the interesting and inviting town of Cambridge both offer marinas, restaurants, and other civilization opportunities. Far up the Choptank, Denton is scarce on marina facilities but long on pleasant Maryland Eastern Shore small town hospitality.

After a day or so enjoying the Choptank, a visit to Little Choptank will take you even farther from areas of dense civilization, anchoring behind Casson Point in Hudson Creek of the Little Choptank. Dun Cove to Casson Point is approximately 17.5 NM. There is a nice but small beach, and an opportunity to explore the next day any of other creeks of the River that you find interesting in this guide.

From the Little Choptank, crossing to the Patuxent offers the interesting village of Solomons Island with some nice restaurants, and many quiet pretty creeks just up the river, above the Bridge. Casson Point to St. Leonard Creek is approximately 30 NM. St. Leonard Creek of the Patuxent has many special quiet anchorages, and the south seas theme resort of White Sands. Next, a visit to Solomons Island will bring you to civilization anchorages or marinas and several restaurants such as the Lighthouse Inn. St. Leonard Creek to Solomons is approximately 6 NM. The village is quaint and nice. Visit the museum here.

Leaving the Patuxent, head back north up the western shore of the Bay. As you pass up the western shore, you should take note of the Herrington Bay area. Solomons to Herrington Bay is approximately 36 NM. Herrington Harbor South has excellent resort facilities and restaurant, and good repair shops. This is a great marina to visit at any time, but it is often a very convenient spot to duck in if weather changes as you transit this long fetch. This is also a great spot to meet members of your family who are jealous because they are not along. They can stay in the cottages a few minutes walk from your pier. They will have a nice beach and pool, and day sails in the Bay are easy from this location.

Consider trying next an anchorage, again in a seamingly remote area, in the Rhode River, among the islands. Herrington Bay to Rhode River is approximately 21 NM. Don't visit this anchorage on weekends unless you love a crowd. If you have a shallow draft boat, you can get well up into Sellman Creek, for near-wilderness surroundings. After this, a very short trip up the West River to the quaint village of Galesville will offer several nice restaurants that you can visit from anchor or marina, and a great country store with take out food.

If you are ready for some high civilization, you may wish to bypass the West River this trip and head on to Annapolis. Rhode River to Annapolis is approximately 16 NM. Spa Creek and surrounding area has an immense number of boating shops, both repair and purchase. This is one of the best places to shop around for anticipated boat projects, improvements, new additions, or even new boats. There are also a very large number of excellent restaurants within walking distance of the water.

From Annapolis, take the long trip up beyond the Chesapeake Bay Bridges and explore the very northernmost areas. I would first begin this area by a side trip up the Chester River. Anchor overnight in one of its many perfect creeks such as those found on the Corsica River or Langford Creek on the Chester River. Annapolis to Chester River in the vicinity of the Corsica and Langford Creek is approximately 28 NM. This classic Chesapeake river can take you into the very heart of Eastern Shore old Maryland countryside. If you have the speed and/or time, travel upstream to enjoy river cruising, with the rich reward of Chestertown at the end of the run. Chestertown from Corsica-Langford area is approximately 12 NM. You will need a lay day at Chestertown to enjoy what it has to offer, walks through historical tree-shaded streets, fine shopping, dining, and historical tours.

Chestertown to Rock Hall is approximately 29 NM. Rock Hall is another good place to stop for some good restaurants, good marinas, as well as a beautiful and protected anchorage in nearby Swan Creek. This is another place to shop and visit another very special small Chesapeake village dedicated to the Bay and those who love it. If you are not ready yet for even this much civilization, there are many creeks on the Eastern Shore for your next anchorages, including Worton and Still Pond Creeks. Rock Hall to Still Pond is approximately 20 NM. In each of these you can find lonely and pretty spots, with a smattering here and there of some civilization. Note that you will only want to visit Still Pond in settled easterly weather unless your draft (no more than 5 feet) will allow you to go up into the creek itself.

After gunkholing in one or more of the above creeks, cross back over the Bay, heading up to its far northwestern corner and visit Havre de Grace. Still Pond to Havre de Grace is approximately 17 NM. Anchor or dock, and then arrange a trip up the Susquehanna with its towering cliffs and upstream rapids. It would be worthwhile to charter a small fishing skiff with a guide to take you up into this area. You'll get a true feeling of the nature of the river that is known as the Mother of the Bay.

Crossing back again to the Eastern Shore, plan to spend a day or two in the beautiful Sassafras River with its many pristine anchorages and good swimming. Havre de Grace to Sassafras is approximately 15 NM. Georgetown upstream, offers marinas and restaurants but you would never know that these amenities, or any such civilization, is there until you round the bend just before.

I always suggest that friends end a cruise of the Upper Bay with a "grande finale" by visiting the Inner Harbor of Baltimore. Sassafras to Inner Harbor is approximately 40 NM. Consider stopping in Stony Creek to shorten the trip and allow your arrival in the morning to get the most for your dollar in the harbor. Sassafras to Stony Creek is approximately 30 NM. If you have over indulged yourself with anchorages among woods and marsh and field, you can here over indulge yourself with the very finest that high civilization has to offer.

This includes museums, restaurants, historical sights, shopping, and a constant carnival of cultural, ethnic, and maritime shows both in the amphitheater and on the water.

A TWO WEEK CRUISE

It seems that most fellow cruisers that we encounter on the Bay are either out for a weekend or a two week cruise. After spending around two days getting to and experiencing the Chesapeake Bay Maritime Museum at St. Michaels, head down to Casson Point on the Little Choptank for a peaceful first evening away from civilization in a beautiful anchorage.

Then run up one of the creeks in this river. St. Michaels to Casson Point is approximately 36 NM. We love Beckwith Creek just upstream from Cherry Island. Casson Point to Beckwith Creek is approximately 3 NM. This will be another nearly all natural anchorage. From here, a trip across the Chesapeake to Herring Bay and Herrington Harbor South and its excellent marina and restaurant may be in order. Beckwith Creek to Herrington Harbor is approximately 28 NM. After Herring Bay, an easy few hours will bring you to another perfectly beautiful anchorage in Harness Creek in South River.

Herrington Harbor to Harness Creek is approximately 17 NM. You may want to stay here for more than a day, but not on the weekend when it is very crowded. If you are here on a weekend and the crowd is bad in the first most popular anchorage just inside the entrance, go up the creek to the second spot mentioned off the park docks around the point. This is usually less busy. From the South River, it is but a short run around Thomas Point into the Severn. Harness Creek to first Severn River Bridge is approximately 13 NM.

Don't stop in Annapolis yet. Proceed up the Severn and pick any of the beautiful creeks to anchor there among tall wooded hills with nice homes interspersed among the trees. Chapter 17 describes them all. Then head back down the Severn and stop at Annapolis, planning to arrive early to get the most from the town. Walk around, shop, dine.

After Annapolis, head up the Bay to the Corsica River on the Chester and spend a night at anchor. Annapolis to Corsica River is approximately 21 NM.

After the Chester, try the long trip up to Still Pond. Corsica to Still Pond is approximately 34 NM. If the weather is settled and you are not expecting any westerlies, the anchorage outside in the Bay will be beautiful. If you wish, proceed into the narrow cut, past the Coast Guard station, and anchor inside this beautiful creek. I wouldn't recommend going in here with more than 5 feet of draft. Probably a day here will be enough, and you will be ready to move on to the Sassafras.

In the Sassafras are many prime anchorages, all of which are described in Chapter 6. Still Pond to Sassafras is approximately 10 NM. If you want civilization, go up to Georgetown where there are several good marinas and restaurants. You can also moor or anchor here, and walk around and dine out.

After the Sassafras, head on over to Havre de Grace for the unique delights of this special town where the Susquehanna, the Mother of the Bay, meets her daughter. Sassafras River to Havre de Grace is approximately 15 NM. It would be nice to rent a small boat with a guide to go upriver to the rapids, but unless you want to skip other stops, it may be best to save this for next year when you take your three week cruise.

From Havre de Grace it is a long trip down to the Patapsco, but usually an easy one, unless the winds happen to be blowing from the wrong direction. Watch the shoals, stay in the deep water, and out of the firing ranges. The trip may be too long for you to comfortably get all the way up to Baltimore Inner Harbor and settled down. If so, anchor in one of the creeks at the entrance to the Patapsco. We prefer Stony Creek. Havre de Grace to Stony Creek is approximately 44 NM. Check for the bridge schedule. If this does not coincide with your schedule, try Rock Creek.

The next day, head for Baltimore Inner Harbor, bright and early. Stony Creek to Inner Harbor is approximately 9 NM. If you get there early enough, there may still be time for a special morning coffee at one of the coffee shops. After satiating yourself here and rewarding yourself for all those nights on the hook with only the natural pleasures of the Bay, head home.

After the St. Michaels Chesapeake Bay Maritime Museum, head across the Bay into the Rhode River for a beautiful anchorage among the islands there. St. Michaels to Rhode River approximately is 22 NM. Then sail up to Annapolis for restaurants, shopping, and sightseeing ashore. Rhode River to Annapolis is approximately 12 NM. After Annapolis, head up the Bay to anchor in Sillery Bay in the Magothy River. Annapolis to Sillery Bay is approximately 15 NM. If you desire more protection, go into the cove on the north end of Gibson Island. Then either sail across the Bay up to Worton Creek for a beautiful anchorage there before your final destination, or sail directly for that final destination of the Inner Harbor of Baltimore. Sillery Bay to Worton Creek is approximately 23 NM. Worton Creek to Inner Harbor is approximately 28 NM, Sillery Bay to Inner Harbor is approximately 22 NM.

Calvert Cliffs, Patuxent River

Tidewater Marina, Havre de Grace

CHAPTER 2

SUSQUEHANNA

This is an absolute "must" place to go. It has among the very best shoreside interests (cultural, historical, entertainment, and commercial), access to these from the boat, nature and scenic interests, and Bay heritage. Anchoring is not the best, but certainly feasible. There are good marinas for small to very large boats, with good services.

MOTHER OF THE BAY

The Susquehanna River area is, without reservation, one of the finest in the Bay to visit and explore. The river is the mother of the Bay, 200 miles of its ancient channel now lying beneath the risen Bay waters.

Two million years ago, this area was covered by glaciers of the ice age. As the ice receded, the waters running off formed rivers, including what is now the Susquehanna. The movement of the ice changed the land dramatically, cutting, shaping, and depositing. As the ice melted, probably around 10,000 to 15,000 years ago, the oceans rose because of the great amounts of released water. The sea rose into the valley around the lower Susquehanna, submerging it beneath the waters that we now call Chesapeake Bay. This ancient river bed is now the deep channel running down the Bay. When you approach today's Susquehanna, you are approaching the earlier higher river. You have already sailed over its ancient lower banks.

Today the Susquehanna pours 24 billion gallons of fresh water each day into the Chesapeake, from its 440-mile meandering through valleys, mountains, farmland, and forests; beginning in Otsego Lake in New York. This is almost 50 percent of the total daily fresh water flow into the Bay. One of the most scenic parts of a Chesapeake cruise is the view into and up its valley as you head in from the Bay. The river at its mouth offers freshwater swimming, beaches ashore or out in the middle on the famous Susquehanna flats, it provides anchoring and protection, and one of the nicest and most boat friendly towns on the Bay. A very short distance up and within easy range of the cruiser, the river turns into a spectacular mountain-type flow with water swirling and riffling around and over huge boulders and ridges. Here is fresh water stream fishing at its best with native brook trout, small mouth bass, and giant muskellunge, channel catfish, redbreast sunfish, and walleye. Despite all of this and more, the area is not yet over populated by visiting boats and is a place where you constantly feel that you are welcome and appreciated.

APPROACH
Refer to Regional Chart #12273-A—"Head of the Bay."

The approach to the Susquehanna is not only beautiful, it is easy. From Fl G 4 sec. "5" and Fl R 2.5 sec. "6" (31) of the ship channel, which are between Grove Point (67) and Tur-

key Point (66), head on a course of 350°M to RG "A" (29) which marks the junction for the Susquehanna Channel (83) and the North East River Channel (64). On a misty day, this may be hard to pick up. We took GPS coordinates of 39°26.50'N by 76°02.10'W for this mark, and this is what the Light List shows. From there follow the buoys in. If you stray outside the channel, you will quickly find very shallow water and some rocks.

Refer to Chart #12274-B—"North east River entrance, Susquehanna River entrance, Susquehanna Flats.
The course to Fl 2.5 sec. G"1" (84) off Spesutie Island (85) in the Susquehanna approach channel will be 346°M.

Aberdeen Proving Grounds Restricted Area
Be mindful to stay out of the restricted area to your left (west). You may hear booming of the guns in the Aberdeen Proving Grounds (86) over there. Indeed, you can hear it all the way up into the Sassafras River (93). Don't be alarmed by any of this. The channel is well marked, easy to follow, well used, and has plenty of water even for the huge tugs that regularly make their way up river. If you need information regarding exploring any areas of which you are not certain, the military range safety office may be reached at (410) 278-2792.

Susquehanna Flats
All that vast body of water to your right (east) will be the Susquehanna Flats (63), a hugh shallow delta which is among the more famous natural areas of the Bay. Today you see local families anchoring their boats where the water is wading deep, spending hours swimming and playing in the fresh water over the hard sand bottom. There is fishing and crabbing. In the past, these areas were famous for hunting. There were fishing batteries, which were huge rafts big enough to hold shanties for men to live and sleep for days at a time. Fishing Galleys, with sometimes four sets of oars and a sweep astern, would ply the flats with their nets.

Hunters would come in sinkers for the ducks and geese. These were huge boxes with lids. The boxes would float just a few inches above the surface. When ducks landed, the men inside would throw open the lids and open fire. "Bushwacker" boats would bushwack the fowl, coming down on them to open fire. Then there were the "body boot" hunters in huge rubber boots up to their necks who would stand out in the cold waters holding their guns for hours waiting for the flocks. For a period, these hardy souls would stand on submerged steel folding tables about the size of card tables, which they would place down under the water. Stepping off the sides with the heavy body boots could mean a very difficult swim. Usually the hunting forays were accompanied by a larger boat used as a base with a warm stove, good food, and necessary portions of hunter's anti-freeze!

In those days, many hunters and fishermen would drink the fresh water of the river or upper Bay, I am told, rather

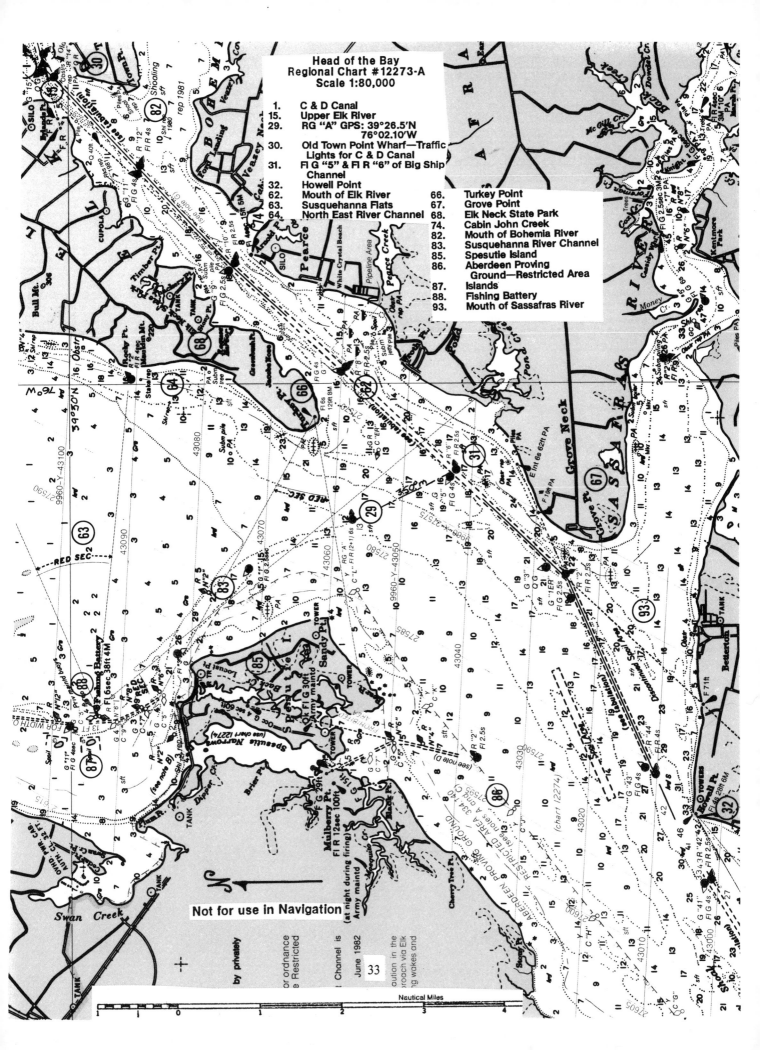

Head of the Bay
Regional Chart #12273-A
Scale 1:80,000

1. C & D Canal
15. Upper Elk River
29. RG "A" GPS: 39°26.5'N
    76°02.10'W
30. Old Town Point Wharf—Traffic
    Lights for C & D Canal
31. Fl G "5" & Fl R "6" of Big Ship
    Channel
32. Howell Point
62. Mouth of Elk River
63. Susquehanna Flats
64. North East River Channel

66. Turkey Point
67. Grove Point
68. Elk Neck State Park
74. Cabin John Creek
82. Mouth of Bohemia River
83. Susquehanna River Channel
85. Spesutie Island
86. Aberdeen Proving
    Ground—Restricted Area
87. Islands
88. Fishing Battery
93. Mouth of Sassafras River

Not for use in Navigation

June 1982

33

than carry drinking water. You can learn more about this history in the area museums and books on the subject. People in town can tell you plenty from their own experiences.

Following the channel in with Spesutie Island to left and the wide flats to right, you begin to see the spectacular beauty of the place. Ahead are islands **(87)**, with low green foliage that almost reminded us of some of the tropical cruising grounds that we have seen. The channel takes you up among them and as you pass by, you will probably see local boats up against their beaches, swimming and playing. To right are the huge open shallow waters of the flats and North East River. Ahead, tall tree-covered hills and cliffs rise over the river, giving the impression that you have left the Bay altogether and are heading for yet another beautiful area, perhaps in the Allegheny Mountains.

Fishing Battery

Among the islands surrounding you heading in, is the Fishing Battery **(88)** to right. It is marked on the chart. A small white lighthouse stands guard here, with a white structure alongside. A marked channel leads in for small boats. Bulkheading is inside. The island is wooded and looks intriguing as you pass by. Many years ago it was used as a large fishing center for the industry around the flats and northern Bay. Smaller steamers are reported to have come into its docks. Now it is a nice place to visit by dinghy.

HAVRE DE GRACE
Refer to Chart #12274-A—"Susquehanna River."

The town that begins to appear ahead and to left is Havre de Grace, MD **(89)**, one of the nicest places on the bay for the cruiser. It was incorporated in 1785 and named by General Lafayette, whose statue stands in town. It is only 30 miles northeast of Baltimore, but in a very different world. The citizens there are outgoing and friendly, and eager to make your stay pleasant and interesting. The Chamber of Commerce, (410) 939-3303, can provide historic and business information and maps, and also a schedule of cultural events and other assistance.

Marinas and Yacht Club

As you approach the town, the **Havre de Grace Municipal Boat Basin (70)** appears to left. A red-roofed office and sign identifies this protected basin with a marked entrance channel **(70)** just in from G "17" **(90)**. The controlling depth is 5 feet with recent dredging. This facility will take transients if there is vacancy among the 240 permanent slips. There is up to 50 amp service. They stand by on VHF 68. There is a pumpout, concrete ramp, gas and diesel, and a small snack bar. Bait is also available.

Passing more of the town to left, you will see **Penn's Beach Marina (64)**, catering mostly to smaller motor boats and fishing. They have a sign and are just before the tall two-story gray condos to left ahead. There are 110 slips with 15 amp electricity. The marina is in a basin which has a small opening. There is a very well-stocked fishing supply, bait and tackle store here, which also has light snack foods, ice, and other boating supplies. They have a 4-ton lift and rent boats of approximately 15 feet with 9.9 hp engines. Sometimes they can take small transient boats. There are two concrete ramps. You can get gas here, no diesel. Visa and MC are honored.

Next door and next up the river is the **Havre de Grace Marina at Log Pond (63)**. This is a bulkheaded basin in front of a

Decoy Carving Contest, Havre de Grace

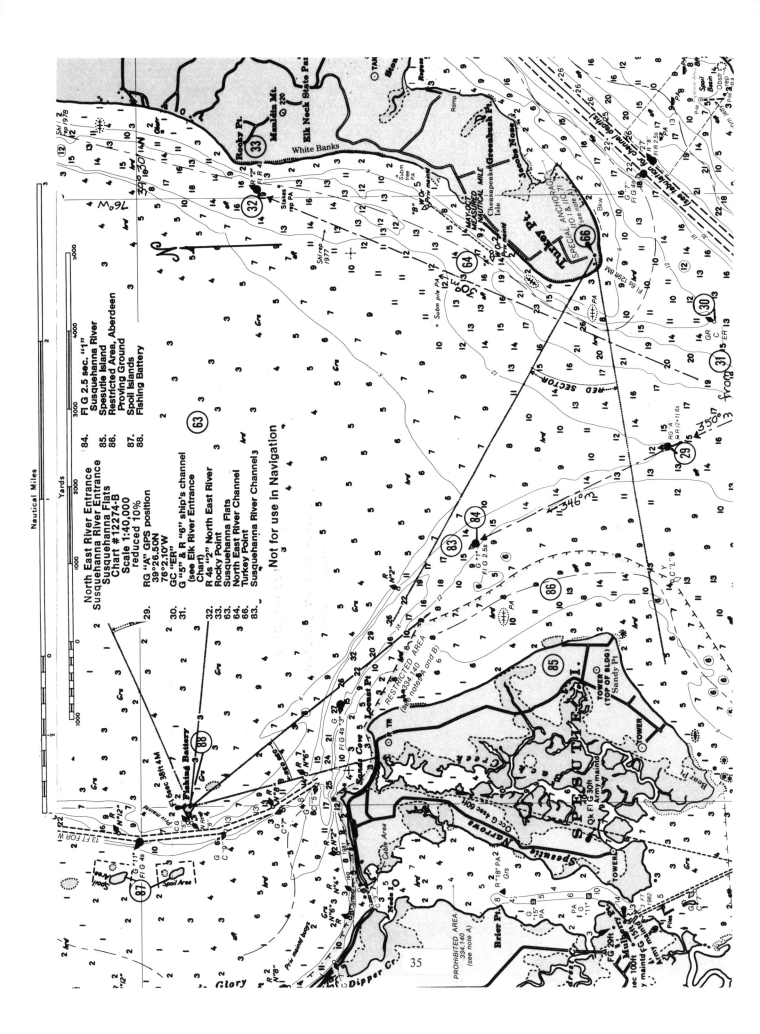

Nautical Miles

Yards

North East River Entrance
Susquehanna River Entrance
Susquehanna Flats
Chart #12274-B
Scale 1:40,000
reduced 10%

29. RG "A" GPS position
    39°26.50N
    76°2.10'W
30. GC "ER"
31. G "45" & R "46" ship's channel
    (see Elk River Entrance
    Chart)
32. R 4s "2" North East River
33. Rocky Point
63. Susquehanna Flats
64. North East River Channel
66. Turkey Point
83. Susquehanna River Channel

84. Fl G 2.5 sec. "1"
    Susquehanna River
85. Spesutie Island
86. Restricted Area, Aberdeen
    Proving Ground
87. Spoil Islands
88. Fishing Battery

Not for use in Navigation

S P E S U T I E I.

Page 35

large new condo complex. There is another Havre de Grace Marina **(60)** up the river on the other side of the bridge **(91)**, and these two are related. The second (original) unit is oriented primarily to repair work for its customers, the marina at Log Pond having none. This is a new facility with docks and 78 slips behind bulkheading. They do take transients with 10-foot depths reported. Their longest slip is 48 feet, but there may be room at the fuel face dock for a larger vessel. Electric service is available up to 50 amps. There is a laundromat, nice restroom and shower rooms. A pumpout is at the gas and diesel dock, just inside the entrance. Visa, MC, and Discover are accepted. Immediately to the right of the entrance channel, just inside of the bulkheaded marina area, are buoys marking obstructions **(63A)** which should be noted especially if you are coming in after dark. On the premises is the Havre de Grace Yacht Charter and Sailing Center **(63)** which offers lessons and charters.

Right next door is the **Tidewater Marina (61).** In my opinion, this is one of the finer marinas in the Bay, with an exceptionally friendly yet professional staff, a very well run and popular full service yard, and a loyal following of permanent slip holders. The marina is within two deep basins separated from the river by filled land, not mere wooden bulkheading. There are 162 slips and a concrete ramp. They welcome transients with docks up to 65 feet and electricity up to multiples of 30 amps. Larger vessels can tie up on the bulkhead outside. Boats of at least 8 feet draft can dock here. There are also moorings. The easily accessed gas and diesel dock has a pumpout. Visa and MC are honored here. One of the best stocked marine stores is just behind the fuel dock. This store sells NOS charts and various chart books, it maintains the Notice To Mariner updates, it has clothes, hardware, head repair kits, books, anchors, pumps, nuts and bolts, and much more. Their policy is to equal prices of the discount mail order businesses. They maintain some of these catalogues at the front door so that the customer can be sure of their deal. The repair facilities of Tidewater Marina include both 20 and 30 ton lifts and dry storage both inside and outside with a 25-foot forklift. They also have a "dry sail" operation for sailboaters who wish to keep their boats ashore, launching only to use them, and bringing them ashore at the end of the

day. There are nice showers and restrooms, and ice and beverages and similar items are sold here.

We see many marinas today which appear to be understaffed for cost reasons. Tidewater Marina is fully staffed, but so well managed that its fees are very competitive. They also sell new and used boats, with a well-stocked new boat showing facility of Hunters and Catalinas. Gary Pensel, the marina owner since its inception, has done much cruising with his wife and is also an avid fisherman who knows more than most about the Susquehanna above the bridges.

The Havre de Grace Yacht Club (61) makes its home on the Tidewater premises. Each Thursday for around 15 years they have held races for several classes beginning around 5 p.m. The start and finish line is right at the marina and everyone has a perfect on-the-line seat. There are serious and fun events.

Also on the Tidewater premises is Havre de Grace Sailing Services, Inc. **(62).** In business since 1978, this outfit charters sailboats and teaches several levels of sailing from windsurfing to summer sail camping, to coastal cruising. You can also rent bikes at the marina for town exploration.

At the premises of Tidewater Marina you will find Bay Yacht Transit, Inc. **(61)**, which has a large Mack Truck especially fitted to haul yachts of most sizes. The owner and operator, Joe Morgan, has considerable past experience with boats as manager of a boat yard, and owns and cruises his own sailboat.

The uppermost **Havre de Grace Marina (60)**, still on the west side of the river, is the one mentioned above as being related to the "Havre de Grace at Log Pond Marina." This is the original of these two facilities. It is above the first Susquehanna Bridge **(91)** which has an alleged vertical clearance of 52 feet and requires 24 hours notice to open. (The chart notes 52 feet clearance, but we noticed 49 on the board when we passed under, and the river was not unusually high.) This facility has moorings, and 55 slips with electricity up to 30 amps, but their primary transient business is at the Log Pond facility. Gas and diesel are sold and there is a marine store. Visa and MC are taken. They sell new and used boats and have a full service yard. They have a truck and trailer to do light boat hauling and have a dry sailing lift, as well as a regular lift.

Concord Point Light, Havre de Grace
(landing from Susquehanna River)

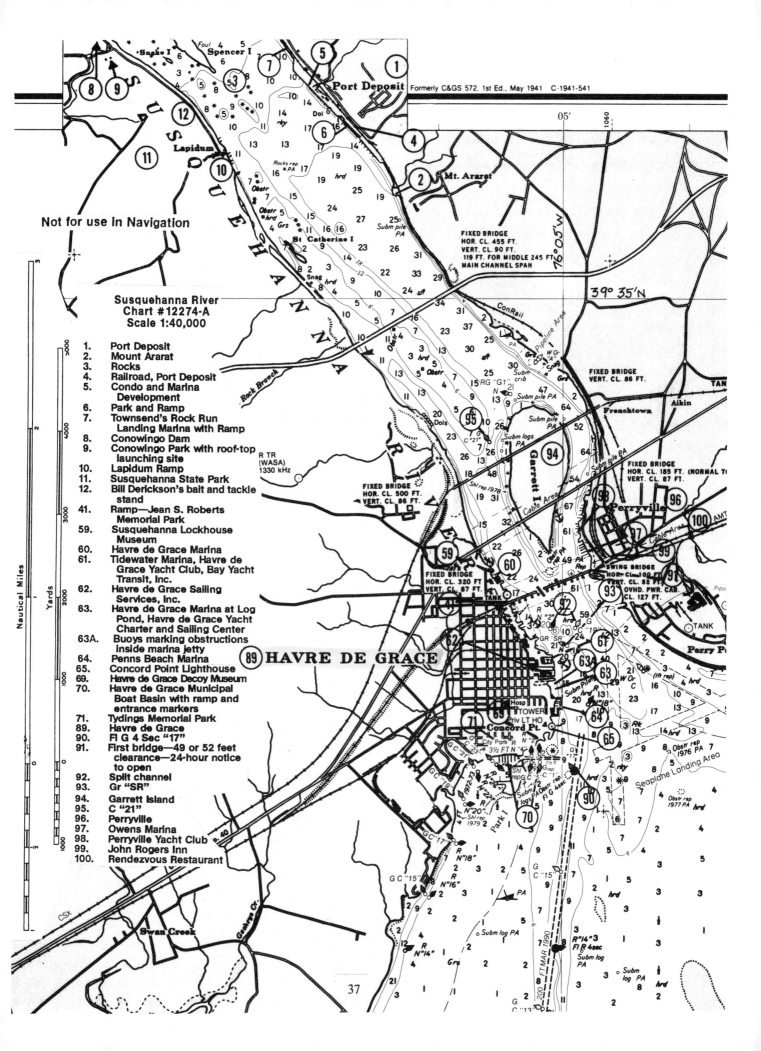

Not for use in Navigation

Port Deposit

Formerly C&GS 572, 1st Ed., May 1941   C-1941-541

Mt. Ararat

FIXED BRIDGE
HOR. CL. 455 FT.
VERT. CL. 90 FT.
119 FT. FOR MIDDLE 245 FT.
MAIN CHANNEL SPAN

39° 35′N

FIXED BRIDGE
VERT. CL. 86 FT.

Aikin

Frenchtown

FIXED BRIDGE
HOR. CL. 185 FT. (NORMAL T
VERT. CL. 87 FT.

Perryville

FIXED BRIDGE
HOR. CL. 500 FT.
VERT. CL. 86 FT.

R TR
(WASA)
1330 kHz

SWING BRIDGE
HOR. CL. 100 F
VERT. CL. 92 FT.
OVHD. PWR. CAB.
CL. 127 FT.

AMT

Perry P

FIXED BRIDGE
HOR. CL. 320 FT.
VERT. CL. 87 FT.

TANK

TANK

HAVRE DE GRACE

Hosp

TOWER

Priv LT HO

Concord Pt.

City Park
3½ FT N

Seaplane Landing Area

Obstr rep
1977 PA

Swan Creek

200 FT MAR 1990

FI R 4sec
Subm log
PA

Subm
log PA

Susquehanna River
Chart #12274-A
Scale 1:40,000

1. Port Deposit
2. Mount Ararat
3. Rocks
4. Railroad, Port Deposit
5. Condo and Marina
   Development
6. Park and Ramp
7. Townsend's Rock Run
   Landing Marina with Ramp
8. Conowingo Dam
9. Conowingo Park with roof-top
   launching site
10. Lapidum Ramp
11. Susquehanna State Park
12. Bill Derickson's bait and tackle
    stand
41. Ramp—Jean S. Roberts
    Memorial Park
59. Susquehanna Lockhouse
    Museum
60. Havre de Grace Marina
61. Tidewater Marina, Havre de
    Grace Yacht Club, Bay Yacht
    Transit, Inc.
62. Havre de Grace Sailing
    Services, Inc.
63. Havre de Grace Marina at Log
    Pond, Havre de Grace Yacht
    Charter and Sailing Center
63A. Buoys marking obstructions
     inside marina jetty
64. Penns Beach Marina
65. Concord Point Lighthouse
69. Havre de Grace Decoy Museum
70. Havre de Grace Municipal
    Boat Basin with ramp and
    entrance markers
71. Tydings Memorial Park
89. Havre de Grace
90. Fl G 4 Sec "17"
91. First bridge—49 or 52 feet
    clearance—24-hour notice
    to open
92. Split channel
93. Gr "SR"
94. Garrett Island
95. C "21"
96. Perryville
97. Owens Marina
98. Perryville Yacht Club
99. John Rogers Inn
100. Rendezvous Restaurant

Nautical Miles

Yards

37

Anchorage

If you don't want to tie up on your visit here, you can anchor off Tidewater Marina with the moored boats, or better, just around the point north from that marina. The holding is good in mud. There is current, and a south or southeast wind can bring a chop, but the second anchorage is much more protected as you get closer in to shore behind the point. I have read much about the bottom being too rocky to anchor here, but this just isn't so if you are in the right areas. Also, people anchor in 5 and 6 feet of water just up from the Lock House Museum (59), but this drops off very quickly. Many local people anchor between Garrett Island (94) and Perryville (96), close to the island in mud, but you have to do so carefully as the mud and sandy shallower bottom quickly becomes very deep and untenable.

Sightseeing

Up the hill from Havre de Grace Municipal Boat Basin (70), is Tydings Memorial Park (71) which occasionally has concerts and other activities. This park is within easy walking distance from several other marinas. Examples of activities here are a duck fair featuring whittling contests and duck and goose calling contests, a seafood festival, a children's art festival, and arts and crafts shows.

The next point of interest is Concord Point Light House (65), to your left, on the point of that name. This was erected in 1827, and the sign at its base advises that this is the oldest "continuously" operating lighthouse in the states. It was apparently here that one of the town's heros, John O'Neil, during the War of 1812, decided to fire a cannon on the fleet of Admiral Cockburn as he was passing by. Some say that the admiral had assumed (quite wrongly) that there was nothing worth noting ashore, but changed his mind when it became obvious that someone thought that there was something so worth defending. In any event, O'Neil fought very bravely, but Cockburn landed and torched some of the area. O'Neil was injured and captured and taken to the British Frigate *Maidstone,* but his daughter Matilda negotiated his release, winning the admiration of Admiral Cockburn who gave her a gold mounted snuff box as a token of his appreciation for her heroism. Later, the city of Philadelphia presented O'Neil with a sword in honor of his bravery. You can visit this lighthouse today and go inside on Saturdays and Sundays. There is a public dock for small boat landing and it is within easy walk of most of the town's marinas. Joe Guzzman, a local resident and historian, gives tours and slide presentations of the lighthouse and related history at various times. He may be reached through the Chamber of Commerce.

Near the lighthouse is the Havre de Grace Decoy Museum (69). Havre de Grace is considered by many to be the duck decoy capital of the world. There are decoy shops all over town, and this museum not only displays some of the best examples of this folk art, but also gives a fascinating insight into that part of our Chesapeake heritage.

Adjacent to the uppermost Havre de Grace Marina (60) upstream is the Susquehanna Lockhouse Museum (59) which displays artifacts related to the old barge canal that formerly bordered the west bank of the river connecting Havre de Grace with points upriver in a series of 28 locks lifting barges 233 feet. The heyday of this canal was around 1870. You can see a lock, the locktenders house, a canal swing bridge, as well as other historical items. A dock in front allows small boats to visit. The canal bed still exists along the river bank, often grown over and still with pockets of water.

HAVRE de GRACE
Street Map

1. Brass Beds and Antiques
2. A & J Travel, local tours
3. Bay City Market & Trustworthy Hardware
4. Preston's Stationary and Fax Service
5. Green's Pharmacy
6. Ice cream shop
7. Fortunato Brothers Pizza
8. Monograms and More T shirts etc.
9. Joseph's Department Store
10. Western Auto
11. Danny's Groceries (ABC and meat)
12. Riverside Antiques
13. Chat & Chew Restaurant & Bar
14. Robinhood Tavern
15. Amanda's Florist
16. Goll's Bakery
17. Misc. shops and businesses
18. Rochambeau Plaza
19. First Virginia Bank and Most Machine
20. Dentist
21. Carl's Carry out (will deliver)
22. Chiropractor
23. Bomboy's Homemade Candy
24. Professional buildings
25. Bloom's Ceramics (to sell and craft)
26. Library
27. Town Hall (restored playhouse 2d story, occasional plays)
28. General practitioner
29. City Pharmacy
30. Bank
31. Post Office
32. End of the Lane Antiques
33. Susquehanna Trading Co. (antiques and art)
34. Crazy Swede's Restaurant
35. Golden Vein Antiques
36. Van Cheeries Restaurant
37. Sun Cleaners
38. Starbird Cleaners
39. Country Flow Shop
40. Statue of LaFayette ("C'est La Havre")
41. City park and ramp
42. Tidewater Grille (full menu)
43. East Coast Divers, Sail Loft, Seaplane, antique, books, art
44. Mac Gregor's Tavern (full menu)
45. Tim's Tavern
46. Vigna Restaurant
47. Summer Place Antiques
48. Lyon's Rexall Pharmacy
49. "Quakers Live Comedy Club"
50. Hounds Tooth Pet Supplies
51. Graybar's Gems (also rocks, minerals fossils & gifts)
52. Spangler and Barrow fine jewelry
53. Sails & Rigging, Divers, Seaplane, Antiques, Books, Art, (same building as #43)
54. Dental Building
55. Robinhood Tavern
56. Park with paddle boats
57. Skelly Sailmakers
58. Park
59. Susquehanna Lockhouse Museum
60. Havre de Grace Marina
61. Tidewater Marina
62. Tidewater Marina Ship's Store & Havre de Grace Sailing Services
63. Havre de Grace Marina at Log Pond
64. Penn's Beach Marina
65. Concord Pt. Lighthouse
66. Havre de Grace Maritime Museum
67. John O'Neill Museum
68. Havre de Grace Decoy Museum
69. Bayou Hotel (condos and prof. offices)
70. Havre de Grace Yacht Basin (municipal marina and public ramp)
71. Millard E. Tydings Memorial Park
72. Harford Memorial Hospital
73. Vandiver Inn bed & breakfast and gourmet dinners
74. Spencer Silver Mansion, bed & breakfast

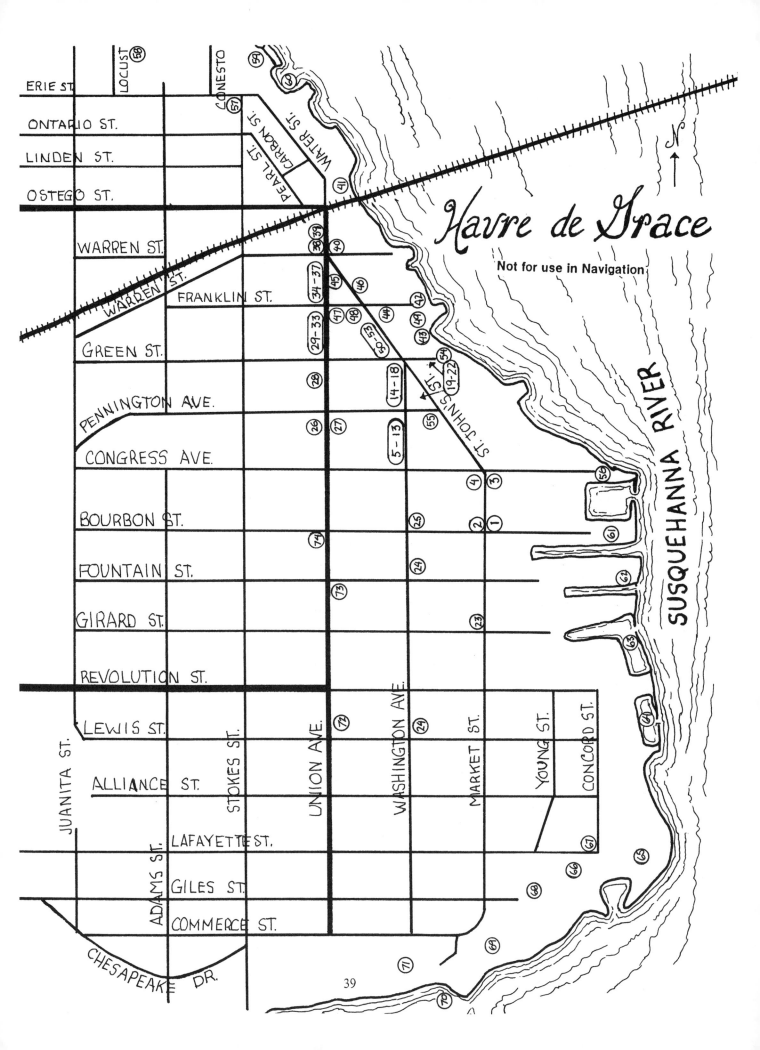

Havre de Grace

Not for use in Navigation

Town
Refer to—"Street Map of Havre de Grace."

Town exploration and shopping is one of the best points of this area. Tidewater Marina and the two marinas just down-river are in an excellent location for this. Within a few shady blocks walk, you can find just about anything that you need. I have seldom seen so much so close to the waterfront to which the cruiser can so easily walk from his marina or anchorage. Because of this, the walking map included here attempts to list most of the businesses within a reasonable walking distance of these three marinas, even though each is not de-scribed in this text. The omission of any establishment should not be construed negatively. For shopping, this town offers the completeness of a large mall, but the beauty, friendliness, and personal service of a very nice small town in the country on the Bay.

A very convenient place to begin a tour of Havre de Grace is at the entrance to Tidewater Marina. This address is "The Foot of Bourbon Street" (61). From here, a turn to right (north) on Market Street and a block's walk will get you to the "Bay City Market" (3), on the southeastern corner of Market Street and Congress Avenue. This market has complete gro-cery shopping, deli, salads and sandwiches and more. There are no alcoholic beverages sold. In the same building is a hard-ware store (3), and across the street on the southwestern cor-ner of Market Street and Congress Avenue is Preston's Busi-ness Supplies (4) with fax services. If you continue walking on, Market Street becomes St. John's Street. A few more blocks walk on this street will net you several light restau-rants and several full menu very nice restaurants such as Tidewater Grill (42) and Mac Gregor's Tavern (44). These are found by turning to your right (east) down Franklin Street where it intersects Market, around four blocks from Bourbon.

If you turn left (south) on Market Street you can walk to the lighthouse (65), the Decoy Museum (68), the Maritime Muse-um (66), the park (71) with concerts, all within seven blocks. On the way, you will pass one of the best chocolate shops (Bomboy's) (23) you will ever find. This is on the northwest corner of Girard and Market Street, around two blocks from your left turn. If you head straight up Bourbon Street (to the west) you will reach Washington Avenue in two blocks. To your left (south) down Washington will be rows of medical buildings (24) (a hospital (72) is nearby). To your right (north) up Washington will be the shopping "downtown" area with restaurants, pharmacies, a bakery, the five and dime, a cloth-ing store, shops, and more. If you were to continue straight up Bourbon Street three blocks from Tidewater, and turn right (north) onto Union Avenue, a couple of blocks farther north on Union would bring you to the library (26), city hall (27), and post office (31). After walking five blocks north on Union, you will see a small park with the statue of Lafayette (40). Here is the junction with St. John's Street. Turning right again and heading back in a southerly direction will bring you back to your point of origin.

Just before the railroad bridge (the first bridge) and just up-stream (northerly) from Tidewater Marina, is a park with fishing pier and paddle boat rental (56). Up stream from that, you will see a dock for small boats to tie up for dining at the Tidewater Grille (42), one of the very fine full menu restau-rants. Upstream farther, just under and beyond the railroad bridge, is the Jean S. Roberts Park with a public hard sur-faced ramp (41).

Havre de Grace is a place to treasure. Stay awhile to ex-plore the town and the upper Susquehanna. With the person-al amenities and conveniences ashore, the tradition of Bay living of the Susquehanna flats, the excitement of the Susq-uehanna, and the wonderfully friendly people, it can't be beat.

ABOVE HAVRE DE GRACE
Refer to Chart #12274-A—"Susquehanna River."

Many will tell you that you can't go upriver from Havre de Grace because of the rocks. Not so. You can take a deep draft boat up to Port Deposit. Tugs regularly do this. You can also make this exploration in a proper dinghy. Note the split channel (92) just below the first bridge off Havre de Grace. Gr "SR" (93) marks this because of a large flat rock in the vi-cinity which, when the water is low enough, could catch a boat of 6-foot draft.

Garrett Island (94) looms ahead as you pass under the first bridge. This large island used to be farmed, but now sits va-cant. Local people use its beaches on the Perryville side as places to swim and relax. You can get around the island on either side. Note that the channel to your left (western side of the island) is the one marked by Can "21" (95). This and oth-er buoys in the area may be removed for the winter season in the late fall in anticipation of ice. Most local boats going to Perryville (96) pass on the eastern side of the island, but to be safe, you may want to take the buoyed route upriver. From just before the first bridge on up, when they talk about shal-low water, they are usually talking about rocks. Carefully watch the chart.

Perryville

After coming through the first bridge, the Owen's Marina (97) is the first to the right in Perryville. There are approxi-mately 200 slips with electricity up to 30 amps, gas, ice, a laundromat, a concrete launching ramp, and light snacks and beverages, and limited repair and storage facilities. They plan to construct condos behind the marina.

A short distance up is the "Perryville Yacht Club" (98). This is actually a private marina with very friendly people, but has had this name for years. They are often filled with their per-manent slip holders, but will take transients if space is availa-ble. The water here is very deep. They can handle lengths up to 60 feet on the face dock, the electric is up to 30 amps at the 120 slips, and cable TV is available. They have gas, block and cube ice, a pumpout station, a concrete ramp and 20-ton lift with mechanics available. There are camp sites for trailers. A small grocery store selling fishing items is across the street, a laundromat is 2½ blocks away, and the post office is close. They rent 16-foot aluminum boats and 9.5 hp motors and jet skis. The John Rodgers Inn (99), the home of the founder of the U.S. Navy, is also within a few blocks, walking inland on the road from the marina.

Within Perryville is the Rendezvous Restaurant (100). This has an informal atmosphere with a fairly complete menu. They will pick you up by water taxi or van if you wish to dine there, even if you are in any of the spots in Havre de Grace. Call them on 16 or 09 VHF.

PORT DEPOSIT

The trip up from Perryville to Port Deposit (1) is straight-forward and scenic with its cliffs and the beginnings of a mountain-like river. The bridges have minimum clearances of 87 feet in the center channel sections. The cliff of Mt. Ararat (2) to right above the last (4th) bridge is spectacular.

Captain John Smith is said to have first explored this area in 1608. He could not travel much farther up the river because of the rocks (3), which will probably also stop you today. At that time, the Susquehanna Indians lived along the shores in the area.

At first there were ferries here, and the town gradually developed as a shipping port because of its location. This used to be the farthest point upstream to which ships could navigate from Chesapeake Bay, and it was the port of deposit for goods coming and going, thus its name. Even after shipping of lumber and other goods dwindled, the well-known granite quarries just above the town supplied a source of cargoes and other businesses for the area. Many granite buildings around the Bay today had their stone shipped from here. In 1828, an iron foundry was started. The town has lost its significance as a shipping center, and the iron foundry and several other major businesses that were once here have gone. But the town is so well preserved and so well represents a mid-nineteenth century industrial town that it (the whole town) was placed on the National Register of Historic Places in 1978. Today it is a very interesting place to visit. The Port Deposit Heritage Corporation publishes "A Walking Tour of Historic Port Deposit," which you will want to acquire when you land. Ask the friendly people at the Municipal Building on North Main Street for additional and up to date information.

Port Deposit is a small village squeezed between the high cliffs behind it and the river in front. A railway (4) goes the length of the town, along the river, and its single main street parallels that. The houses and commercial buildings back up to the cliff. In some cases they seem to climb right up the wall. There are several points of historical interest here, including Jacob's Ladder, a steep flight of wooden steps leading from the base of a cliff. Underway is an ambitious condominium and marina project (5) right on the shore. There is a park and hard-surfaced ramp (6) at the downstream (southern) side of town, with fishing dock and bait, tackle and snack shop across the street. On the other end of town is **Townsend's Rock Run Landing Marina (7)** with ramp and tackle and bait. There are slips for small boats up to 19 feet. They sell fishing licenses and are oriented to that business. A few miles by car from Port Deposit is the locally well known Union Hotel restaurant with candlelight dining.

RIVER ABOVE PORT DEPOSIT

Port Deposit is where you stop unless you really know the river and how to handle this type of water. I took a trip up from here in a 16-foot bass boat with someone who has been doing it all of his life, and we hit rock more times than I can remember. This is so expected, that often the local boats have pitchforks attached by brackets to the lower units of their outboards. But if you love fishing or would like to see the incredible beauty of this river, there are plenty of guides whose names and numbers you can get at most of the marinas and fishing establishments. There are also locally drawn maps of the river, but these will not keep you out of trouble if you don't have experience in this sort of water. This can be very dangerous to the inexperienced. Losing a prop is mild compared to having the bow sucked under in eddies when you have anchored and the water suddenly starts rising. Personally, I wouldn't have missed it.

Main Street, Port Deposit

41

This guide will not describe the river above Port Deposit, because it is not navigable as we normally use the word. But it is more than worth the trip with a guide, and there is great fishing. I will note a few highlights above Port Deposit, although our charts do not extend that far up. A short distance upstream the Conowingo Dam (8) backs up the river so that the folks in Philadelphia can turn on their lights. The flood gates have different openings. The schedule and expected water and current heights can be obtained by calling the dam authorities at (410) 457-2409. This is very important for anyone going upriver, because the river rises rapidly and the current picks up considerably when the gates are opened. Just below the dam on the southwestern side of the river is the Conowingo Park with a roof top launching site (no trailers) (9). The sign warns that flashing red lights and sounding si-

rens mean rising water level, and that you should seek high ground, watch anchors, and wear life jackets. Many people fish from the shore here. The generation facility of the dam can be toured. Below that, on the same side of the river, is the Lapidum Ramp (10), part of the Susquehanna State Park (11). This is a good concrete multiple ramp for trailer launching. There are numerous tackle and bait shops on the roads leading into the vicinity. Also, Bill Derickson, who has lived on the south bank just across from Port Deposit for over 55 years, operates a road and river side bait and tackle stand (12), with fresh vegetables and sandwiches and soft drinks. He has a river landing.

When you visit the area, engage a local guide with boat to take you up this river to the dam. It will be exciting, beautiful, and an impressive lesson in how the Bay began.

Conowingo Dam, Susquehanna River

CHAPTER 3

NORTH EAST RIVER

This is a pretty river, but not very easy for boats with over 4 feet draft. There are several nice marinas, but no really good anchorages. Two small towns offer some interest ashore, with a few restaurants. While there are some good marine stores at some of the marinas, serious grocery shopping and obtaining other supplies would be inconvenient compared to other areas.

•

Looking northward from the Bay, the North East River seems to be a vast plain of water leading up forever into the hills. Actually, much of this area of wide water is the Susquehanna Flats, which was described in Chapter 2. The North East River is rather shallow, particularly as you get up inside. Although it has a few nice marinas and many nice folks, I would not consider this as a good place to visit on your cruise if you draw more than 4 feet. I was repeatedly told by marina operators up the river that while they had water for 6 feet and more at their piers, it would be "very iffy" getting in from the Bay. If you don't want to deal with the vagaries of the channel, and if you have a fast tender, consider exploring this river in your tender from Havre de Grace.

ENTRANCE
Refer to Chart #12274-B—"North East River Entrance, Susquehanna River Entrance, Susquehanna Flats."

There are two ways into the North East River (64). The deeper and buoyed route is from between the junction buoys "RG A" (29) and "Gr C ER" (30) off Turkey Point (66). These are to the north of G "5" and R "6" (31) of the big ship channel in the Bay. From approximately half way between "RG A" and "Gr C ER," proceed 30°M toward Fl R 4 sec. "2" (32) off Rocky Point (33) in the North East River. This may take you over some water with depths as shallow as 10 feet. The Susquehanna Flats (63) shoal out from the west and it is important to watch the depth finder to be sure to stay off this shallow area. Once you have Fl R 4 sec. "2," proceed on into the river following the markers. At first your course is fairly close to the eastern shore of the river, but then the markers wander more to the middle as the water shallows.

Refer to Chart #12274-C—"Route from Havre de Grace to North East River."

The route from Havre de Grace (89) follows the shore, rounding Perry Point (34), swinging slightly into Furnace Bay (35), then rounding Carpenter Point (36). You must be careful with this route also not to stray too far out onto the flats. This route is not marked, and is advisable only for tenders and shallow draft boats. Portions of this area dry at low water and there are stumps. The line on the chart (37) follows the general route, but there will be no precise landmarks to identify, if you do it. It will be important to follow the chart, the general lines of the shore, and watch the depths. On either of these routes, you should study the chart, and remember that shoaling can occur because of the long fetch into the area from the open Bay to the south and southeast, and because of silting from the rivers.

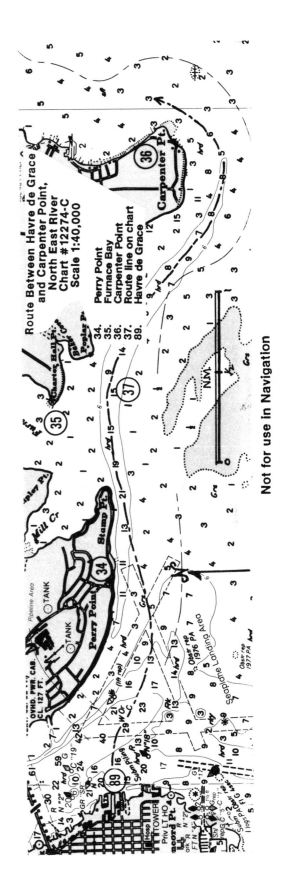

Route Between Havre de Grace and Carpenter Point, North East River Chart #12274-C Scale 1:40,000

34. Perry Point
35. Furnace Bay
36. Carpenter Point
37. Route line on chart
89. Havre de Grace

Not for use in Navigation

43

WESTERN SHORE OF NORTH EAST RIVER
Refer to Chart #12274-D—"Upper North East River."

Just inside of Carpenter Point, you will see some old bulkheading with docks for small boats. This is a part of Ponderosa Pines Camping Ground (38). There is a concrete ramp and fishing dock, and some slips within the bulkheading for trailer size boats.

Next up on the left is **Craft Haven Marina (39)**. They have a concrete ramp, some docks, gas and pre-mixed gas, propane and a dump station for Porta Potties. It is primarily a small boat facility and seasonal camp. There is a red drum to the right of its entrance, and a yellow and black sign to the left. Depth is 3 feet at the docks, and small transients are welcome if there is space. There is no electricity or water on the docks.

Farther up on the same side you will see Chestnut Point Marina (40) identified by a Shell sign and marked channel with stakes on each side. This facility is primarily for seasonal trailers and camping operations. They are not set up to take transients. There is a ramp for use of their campers.

Charlestown, MD (42)

The fourth facility on the west shore is the large and full service **Charlestown Marina (41)**. They reported depths at their facility of 7 to 8 feet, although as noted earlier, I would not recommend taking a boat of that draft into the river from the Bay. You can recognize the marina from the river by its purple sign with white writing and a Mobil sign over the boat house. There are 142 open docks and 125 covered, all surrounded by a bulkhead, transient slips but no moorings; electricity at up to 30 amps, gas, diesel, a large well-equipped marine store selling everything from paints and hardware to clothing. Mobil, MC, and Visa are accepted. We saw numerous motor yachts in the 50-foot range tied there. Charlestown Marina has a 25 and 50-ton lift and their large yard does general repair work, including a canvas and awning shop on the premises. A brokerage business is in the same building with the marine store.

Immediately south of Charlestown Marina is a public concrete ramp (49) and small park with landing.

From Charlestown Marina you can easily walk into town (42). A small village with some points of interest, Charlestown was incorporated in 1742. If you begin at the street (43) running into Charlestown Marina, a walk of several blocks shows most of the town. Walk straight back from the marina, and the town hall (44) will appear a little over a block up the street on your left. They will help you arrange a historical tour. At the corner here, turn right and walk a block or two. You will pass C J's Market (45) which also sells bait, and a few small restaurants (46). If you turn right again at the cemetery (47), putting it to your right as you head back to the water, you will pass Crustacean's (48) which advertises gourmet pizza and fresh seafood.

Charlestown's past was more active than the quiet town existing today. It was the county seat until that was moved in 1787. There was considerable shipping until a hurricane changed the channel in 1786, making Havre de Grace an easier port. In the War of 1812, as Admiral Cockburn was roaming the northern bay burning various villages, the citizens built a small-earthwork fort. A hard rain washed away the fort the night before the British were expected. Apparently the British did not do a great deal of damage to the village.

A very short distance up the river is **Pat's Marina (50)**. This is the fifth facility on the left. Depths are 2 to 5 feet at slips.

They have 86 slips up to 34 feet including some for transients, electricity up to 30 amps, no fuel, small marine supply store, engine repairs, and a 40-foot closed 25-ton lift to service their storage yard.

Close to Pat's Marina, farther upstream, is **Lee's Marina (51)**. You can't miss their large sign atop the building. They have 59 slips, welcome transients, 4-foot depth, two 30 amp plugs for each boat, ample voltage for air conditioners, block and cube ice, complete gas engine repairs, complete hull repairs, 20-ton lift, marine supply store, which also sells snacks and supplies and a hard surfaced launching ramp. The local Fire Rescue Boat is stationed at Lee's Marina. This is an attractive facility staffed by helpful, friendly people.

The last marina on the western shore of North East River is **Avalon Yacht Basin (53)**, nestled in a creek entrance. It has some covered sheds and open docks.

EASTERN SHORE OF NORTH EAST RIVER

Cara Cove (54) is the only place to consider for an anchorage, but it is shallow to around 5 feet and not well protected except from southeast to southwest. It appears on the chart well north from Turkey Point. The Elk Neck State Park (68) is described in Chapter 4. It's shown on **Chart 12274-C** in this chapter. The park also borders the North East River near its entrance here. There are beaches along the shore of the park in Cara Cove and down to the point.

On the east shore of the river, you will first notice **Shelter Cove Yacht Basin (55)**, just around Hance Point (56). There are also signs here for Jackson Marine Sales (57). The place is identified by its signs as well as a Phillips 66 sign on the breakwater. These are related facilities. Shelter Cove Yacht Basin is a large full-service marina with 170 open and 28 covered slips up to 60 feet, 5-foot depths, 30 or 50 amp electricity, phone hookups, gas, diesel fuel, block and cube ice, a very large marine and parts store, lifts up to 50 tons, and a boat brokerage on the premises. They are dealers for MerCruiser, Onan, Avon, Volvo Penta, Crusader, and Chrysler. Shelter Cove accepts Visa, MC, and Discover cards.

Bay Boat Works (58) is another full service marina, tucked farther into the little cove east of Hance Point. You'll see their Shell sign. They have 6-foot depth at the docks, but I didn't find 6 feet getting into their area. They have 129 slips including 12 covered, room for transients up to 50 feet, 50 moorings, electricity up to 50 amps, gas and diesel fuel, block and cube ice, marine store, complete engine repair, a 35-ton lift and a 60-ton marine railway. Bay Boat Works are dealers for Achilles inflatables and Cruise-n-Carry outboards. They sell windsurfers and give lessons. A bed and breakfast (59) with a swimming beach is adjacent, connected with the marina.

Leaving this cove, you will notice a high pier coming off the second point marked Hance Point Creek (60) on the chart. This pier has a floating dock in front of it, connected by a ramp and parallel to shore. This belongs to **Hance's Point Yacht Club (61)**. Ashore are several houses and a large yard, none of which can be seen from the river below. No large boats are kept at the dock, but there are numerous small boats moored off. There is also a launching ramp here.

North East Yacht Sales (62), farther up the river, does not offer fuel. It has a breakwater and boats moored off. They have a 60-ton lift and electricity up to 50 amps, 10 to 20 feet depths, but like the rest in the area, 5 feet would be the maximum depth I would feel comfortable coming in from the Bay.

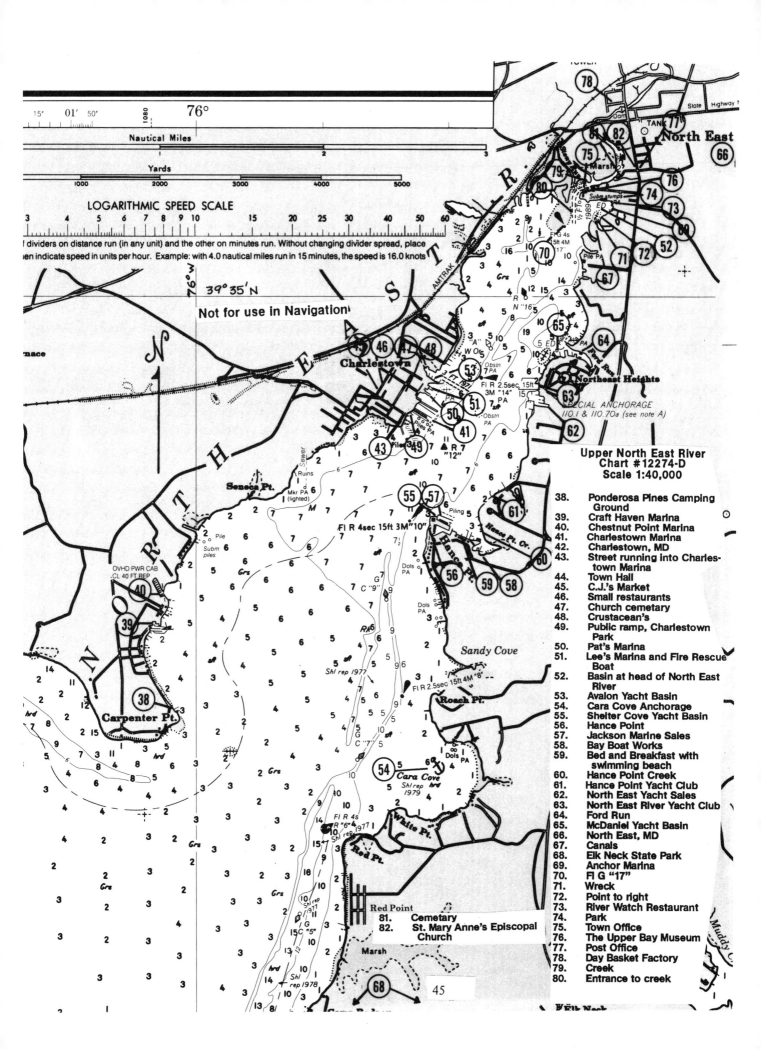

Not for use in Navigation

Upper North East River
Chart #12274-D
Scale 1:40,000

38.	Ponderosa Pines Camping Ground
39.	Craft Haven Marina
40.	Chestnut Point Marina
41.	Charlestown Marina
42.	Charlestown, MD
43.	Street running into Charlestown Marina
44.	Town Hall
45.	C.J.'s Market
46.	Small restaurants
47.	Church cemetary
48.	Crustacean's
49.	Public ramp, Charlestown Park
50.	Pat's Marina
51.	Lee's Marina and Fire Rescue Boat
52.	Basin at head of North East River
53.	Avalon Yacht Basin
54.	Cara Cove Anchorage
55.	Shelter Cove Yacht Basin
56.	Hance Point
57.	Jackson Marine Sales
58.	Bay Boat Works
59.	Bed and Breakfast with swimming beach
60.	Hance Point Creek
61.	Hance Point Yacht Club
62.	North East Yacht Sales
63.	North East River Yacht Club
64.	Ford Run
65.	McDaniel Yacht Basin
66.	North East, MD
67.	Canals
68.	Elk Neck State Park
69.	Anchor Marina
70.	Fl G "17"
71.	Wreck
72.	Point to right
73.	River Watch Restaurant
74.	Park
75.	Town Office
76.	The Upper Bay Museum
77.	Post Office
78.	Day Basket Factory
79.	Creek
80.	Entrance to creek

81.	Cemetary
82.	St. Mary Anne's Episcopal Church

45

They rent stretch limousines. Visa and MC are accepted.

Farther north is **North East River Yacht Club (63)**. They have nice docks and a large club house up on the hill. There is a small beach, moorings, and they honor other clubs. The restaurant is open Thursday through Sunday and on holidays. This is a well kept and friendly place. Like most yacht clubs, dock space is limited because of members' boats.

McDaniel Yacht Basin (65), on the south shore of Ford Run **(64)**, is a very large full-service marina, in business more than 50 years. You'll spot their facility easily from their two-story dockhouse with windows slanting outwards, at the fuel dock. They have more than 200 slips up to 60 feet, dry storage, electricity up to 50 amps, Shell gas and diesel fuel, laundromat, pumpout station, propeller repair shop, marine railway for boats up to 60 feet, two cranes up to 20 tons, travel lift up to 50 tons, swimming pool, and tennis courts. McDaniel Yacht Basin are dealers for Cruisair, MerCruiser, Kohler, Volvo Penta, and they sell new and used boats. They advertise that if they don't have the model you're interested in, they'll fly you to the boat manufacturer in their own plane. They have ample depth at their docks, but as we mentioned earlier in this chapter, it could be difficult to bring a boat in from the Bay if you draw more than 5 feet.

TOWN OF NORTH EAST

You think that you are at the town of North East **(66)** at the head of the river, as you begin to see private canals **(67)** to the right and a large, deep basin **(52)** to the left with a dry storage and launch area and restaurant. You aren't, and would have to walk from around one half mile to a mile to reach the area of shops and other facilities if you land in the basin. The dry storage facility is called **Anchor Marina (69)**. They don't regularly take transients.

The basin is very deep inside, and 6 feet can be taken from the channel to the deeper basin (assuming you have been able to get 6 feet up the river from the Bay). I found ample water for this, rounding the point from the channel after Fl G "17" **(70)**. A wreck **(71)** is noted on the chart, off the point. I ob-

served no markers for this and the basin is well used with the restaurant and marina. Stay off that point **(72)** to your right, heading into the middle of the basin.

A nice restaurant called River Watch **(73)** has opened here with both inside and outside dining. The menu is lighter outside. They will allow docking at the floating docks in front of the restaurant for restaurant patrons. We saw no electricity or water on these docks, although there were plans to add them. Motor yachts up to 60 feet use the restaurant docks. River Watch's docks are the closest for visiting the town of North East.

North East was established in 1658 and is about 28 miles southeast of Wilmington. On the Point a little over a block's walk from the docks is a park **(74)**, a town office **(75)**, and a local museum (The Upper Bay Museum) **(76)** which is usually open on Sundays and contains artifacts on fishing, hunting, and boating in the upper Bay. To get into the rest of town requires a longer walk of a half mile or more, depending on where you wish to go. In town you can find a post office **(77)**, medical offices (around 2 miles), small businesses and shops, and several restaurants. The Day Basket Factory **(78)**, founded in 1876, sells their hand woven white oak baskets.

There is an intriguing creek **(79)** winding back behind the town area, beginning behind the point with the park. We have read that there is only 2 feet or so inside, but found it to have consistent depths of 6 feet and more. The trick is getting in. We found 2 to 3 feet at the mouth **(80)** on a moderate low tide, with stumps on each side. However, numerous work boats up to 30 feet length regularly dock inside at the houses. This leads me to believe that there is a trick that I couldn't find for crossing the bar, other than wait for high tide. The creek is beautiful, with homes and docks to the right and lush green woods and marsh to the left. We went as far as a very old cemetery **(81)**, right to the water's edge. This is related to the St. Mary Anne's Episcopal Church **(82)**, established in 1706 as North Elk Parish. The building dates from 1742. Here we stopped when told by two fishermen that the creek continued on without much water. We saw no places for the public to land in this creek. It is not a closer access to town, but it is worth a dinghy trip to see the lush foliage on the left going up creek and the homes of watermen and boats on the right.

North East River Yacht CLub

CHAPTER 4

CHESAPEAKE & DELAWARE CANAL

This is a business-only safe passgeway between the Chesapeake and the Delaware Bay, but there is a jewel buried inside called Chesapeake City. There is an anchorage basin intended for temporary shelter and it is controlled by around 5 feet at low water. There are some marinas.

Editor's Note: I've sailed on Chesapeake Bay on friends' boats, but I've sailed there four times in my own boat from Long Island Sound. Though these were wonderful cruises and we had enjoyable stops en route in New Jersey, it's a long haul up Delaware Bay and River to the C & D Canal. This has never been any fun. We've encountered fog, rain, and always heavy commercial traffic bound for Wilmington, Philadelphia, Camden, Trenton and other upstream ports. Even if you leave Cape May at the crack of dawn, you'll only have favorable current for a little over 6 hours. When the current turns against you, progress is slow for a low-powered sailboat. We've never reached Reedy Island or the east entrance to the canal in daylight. This gets you to stopping places in the canal after dark. No problem, because the canal is very well lit and easy to follow, but when we finally dock at Chesapeake City or find anchorage, we're bushed from too long a day.

There are interim harbors on both the Delaware and New Jersey shores of Delaware Bay, but all of them are a long detour off the rhumb line from Cape May to the C & D Canal. None are anywhere near as pretty or as interesting as the lovely shore and myriad of beautiful harbors that greet you as you leave the Canal into Chesapeake Bay.

It's fun to explore Chesapeake Bay in your own boat, but Long Island Sound sailors should consider chartering. In recent years excellent charter fleets have grown in the Bay. Next time, that's what I'll do.

HISTORY

This canal was originally suggested in 1661 by Augustine Herman, a Dutch map maker and surveyor. However, it was not until early 1800s that a private company, the Chesapeake and Delaware Canal Company, undertook the project and connected the two bodies of water by hand labor. When completed in October 1829, the canal was 13 miles long and 10 feet deep. Constant erosion, higher maintenance costs and an increasing size of ships and traffic resulted in the canal being taken over by the Corps of Engineers in the 1920s, with a complete rebuild being completed in 1927. From this point on, the locks were no longer used. The canal was improved again in the 1940s. You can see a very interesting display of much of this history at the Canal Museum (23) (on the Chesapeake City chart in this chapter) at the eastern end of the anchorage basin and alongside the canal. This includes some of the original lock machinery, and what is said to be the largest and oldest steam engine, still on its original working foundation, to be found in the United States. The huge steam pistons remain preserved just where and as they were when in operation. This sits in an original lock house, converted to the mu-

seum, with a gigantic waterwheel that used to pump 1,200,000 gallons of water an hour for the lock before the entire canal was made sea level in the 1920s. There are picnic tables under the shade trees beside the building where you can watch the traffic pass. It is a fascinating small museum, well worth a visit. There is no admission charge. A public cement boat-launching ramp is next to the museum.

GENERAL NOTES ABOUT THE CANAL

Much has been written to instill fear and respect of the C & D Canal for cruisers. Actually it can be an interesting, easy, and painless passage, with the same prudent care and good seamanship that should be exercised normally. This passage not only takes you from the Bay to the Ocean (through Delaware Bay), it also takes you from one time and place to another. On the western side are the high wooded hills and quiet villages of Chesapeake Bay and a better, more gentle, older time and place; yet on the eastern side, just 15 miles away are the low lands of the Delaware and Jersey coast with modern industry, a nuclear plant, huge ships moored and moving up and down the river, and the salty tang of the worldwide sea. The shore changes slowly as you traverse this ditch, the low marshes and fields of the eastern end with their occasional residential areas yielding to the woods and hills of the other side. It is a necessary and safe passage between two waters. The only place to "hangout," unless you are a slip holder in a marina, is Chesapeake City.

Factors to remember are the current, the fact that huge ships regularly make this passage and that the passage was intended for business only, and that there isn't any Chesapeake-style quiet anchorage readily available. The current can be 2 knots, and up to 5, under certain circumstances such as strong winds and moon tides. Taking it with a fair tide is great, but remember that you may have to be very careful holding in place for traffic or the one opening bridge with the current pushing you. Many hours can pass with no large traffic in the canal, or it can be very busy.

When traffic does come, be assured that the pilots know a lot more than we do about what to do. I have seen much written about huge wakes from these ships, but the worst wakes I have experienced in here, by far, are those from pleasure motor yachts. Remember that the commercial vessels normally cannot yield to us, cannot change course or stop within short distances, and that we must very carefully give them right of way.

There are red and green traffic lights at each end of the canal, on Old Town Point Wharf at the western end and Reedy Point at the eastern end. Red generally means to stay out until traffic passes. If there is doubt, the canal authority monitors VHF 13, but this channel should not be used except for serious business. I would not consider taking this canal without standing by on Channel 13 as well as 16. This is where you usually first learn if there is traffic trouble ahead, and

47

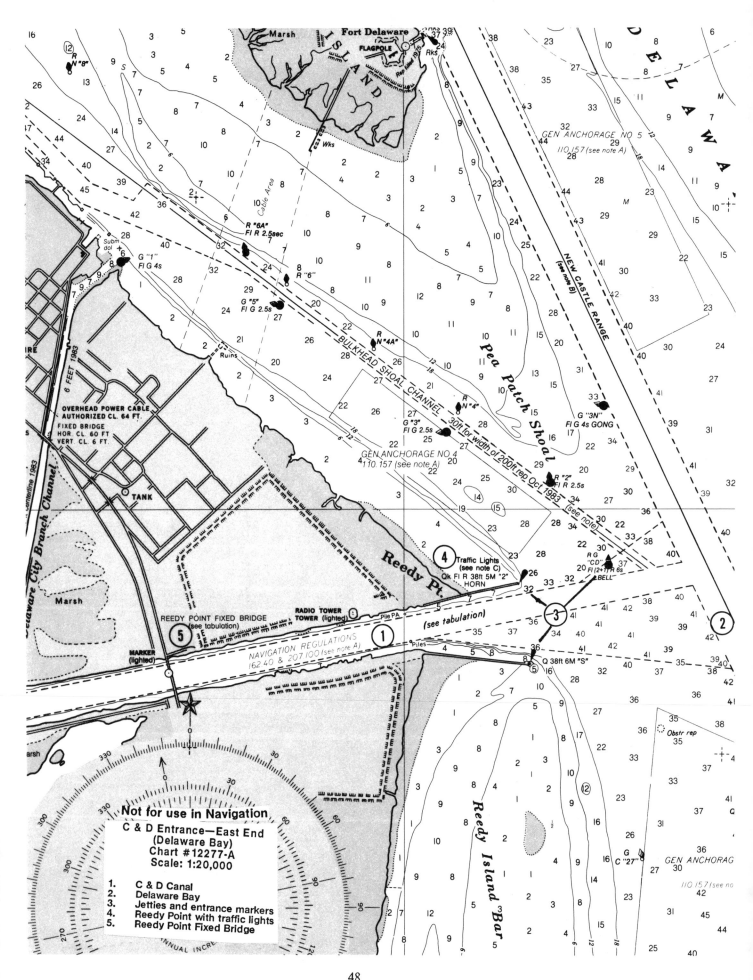

Not for use in Navigation

**C & D Entrance—East End
(Delaware Bay)
Chart #12277-A
Scale: 1:20,000**

1. C & D Canal
2. Delaware Bay
3. Jetties and entrance markers
4. Reedy Point with traffic lights
5. Reedy Point Fixed Bridge

48

where you will find the large ships standing by if you need to communicate.

Because of the nature of this waterway, there are specific rules for navigation of the C & D. Important information is found in "Title 33 of Navigation and Navigable Waters, Chapter II,—Corps of Engineers, Department of the Army; Part 207—Navigation Regulations for the C & D Canal." It is worthwhile reading these regulations. A few points are that "clearance for any vessel to enter or pass through any part of the waterway will be contingent on the vessel's having adequate personnel, machinery, and operative devices for safe navigation." Anchorage is not allowed except in the basin on the south side of the canal at Chesapeake City, and special permission must be obtained to stay more than 24 hours because of the limited space and need. "Transiting the canal by vessels under sail will not be permitted between Reedy Point and Welch Point." Motorsailing is seen here frequently.

The normal tidal range is 5.4 feet at the Delaware River end of the ditch, and around 2.6 feet at Chesapeake City. High water at the Delaware River usually occurs 2 hours later than at the Elk River end. Strong winds may vastly affect these tides and the ranges. The current in the canal changes direction approximately at the times of high and low tide at Chesapeake City. The flow is eastward during the period from low to high tide at Chesapeake City, and westward from high to low tide.

If you are coming in from the Delaware, remember that generally, the canal current is flowing westward during the first half of an ebbing current in the Delaware River; it is flowing eastward during the last half of an ebbing current in that river; it is flowing eastward during the first half of a flooding current in that river; and it is flowing westward during the last half of a flooding current in that river.

There is room to turn inside for most pleasure craft in an emergency, although you should check ahead (look at the light) and plan ahead so that this will not be necessary. There is not room for the huge ships to turn or do much maneuvering at all. There are five bridges inside, four are fixed with a reported 132 feet of vertical clearance for the lowest, and one is a railroad lift bridge and has only 45 feet reported vertical clearance while closed. It opens to proper horn signal or VHF call on 13. This bridge is the third one in if you are coming from the Delaware, and the third one in if you are coming from the Bay. It is a little over 5 NM east from Chesapeake City, and just under 6 NM west from the first bridge that you will pass under if coming in from the Delaware.

Normally boats with a fair tide, particularly if they have less maneuverability than you, will have the right of way at bridges. Without getting into the intricacies of the rules of the road, it is safe to say that pleasure craft are required to yield right of way to one of the big ships passing through. These ships are restricted in maneuverability, very deep draft, and should normally always be given the right of way. As always, be familiar with, and follow, the rules of the road. The actual ditch itself is around 12 miles long. It is well lit at night, but I would certainly recommend doing it in daylight because of possible confusion for those not thoroughly familiar with the

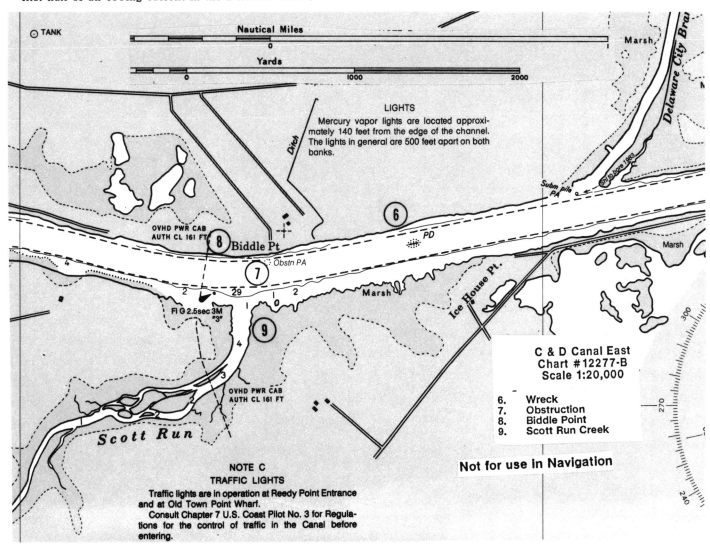

Not for use in Navigation

NOTE C
TRAFFIC LIGHTS
Traffic lights are in operation at Reedy Point Entrance and at Old Town Point Wharf.
Consult Chapter 7 U.S. Coast Pilot No. 3 for Regulations for the control of traffic in the Canal before entering.

C & D Canal East
Chart #12277-B
Scale 1:20,000

6. Wreck
7. Obstruction
8. Biddle Point
9. Scott Run Creek

passage and lights from other vessels. The buoys are red to your right from each end. As you enter from the Delaware Bay, they will be red to right all the way to Chesapeake City, where they will reverse. As you enter from the Bay side, they will be red to right all the way to Chesapeake City, where they will reverse.

APPROACH AND PASSAGE
Refer to Chart #12277-A—"C & D Entrance, East End."

Coming into the C & D Canal (1) from Delaware Bay (2) is simple. The river is somewhat "wide open" here, but the markers are close and easily seen, directing millions of tons of shipping traffic in every year. The jetties are obvious as is the marking (3). Check the traffic control light on Reedy Point (4) on the northern bank. You should see the first bridge (5), a fixed high rise, up inside the canal. The land on either side will be rather flat and unattractive at first, with small houses and other indicia of suburb civilization on the southern bank. As you move westward, the land will begin to have higher hills and more woods.

Refer to Chart #12277-B—"C & D Canal, East." PG49
Amazingly, a wreck (6) is indicated around 1 mile west of the first bridge, near the middle of the channel. I can't believe that it is there, but if it is, don't worry about it. The big guys

sure get over it with no problem. As to the obstruction (7) noted just a little farther westward on the northern bank, off Biddle Point (8), again I cannot believe that there is anything there that makes a navigational hazard now, although you certainly should not be hugging the banks but remain out in the channel. After passing under the first bridge, passing Scott Run Creek (9) on the southern bank, and rounding a bend (10), you will see the second bridge, St. Georges fixed bridge (11).

Refer to Chart #12277-C—"C & D East Central—St. Georges Fixed Bridge." PG51
Passing under this and rounding another long bend (12) will bring the Conrail lift bridge into sight.

Refer to Chart #12277-D—"East Central—Conrail lift bridge." PG50
This vertical lift bridge (13) has a 45-foot vertical clearance and you may need it opened. Plan ahead, especially if you have a tide pushing you. Give plenty of time with your signal. Shortly after this bridge, on your right (north bank) you will see the traffic lights (14) for the cut into Summit North Marina (15).

Summit North Marina
This first facility in the canal (around 7.7 miles from the Delaware River) is a brand new first-class, full-service mari-

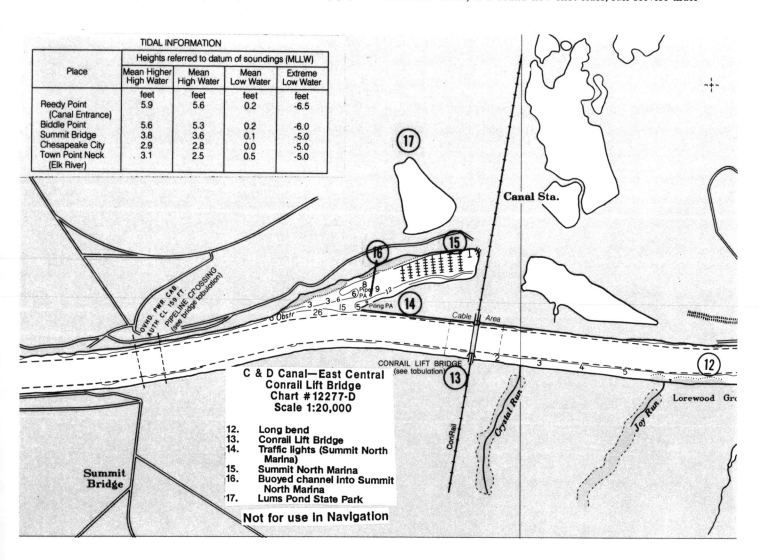

	TIDAL INFORMATION			
	Heights referred to datum of soundings (MLLW)			
Place	Mean Higher High Water	Mean High Water	Mean Low Water	Extreme Low Water
	feet	feet	feet	feet
Reedy Point (Canal Entrance)	5.9	5.6	0.2	-6.5
Biddle Point	5.6	5.3	0.2	-6.0
Summit Bridge	3.8	3.6	0.1	-5.0
Chesapeake City	2.9	2.8	0.0	-5.0
Town Point Neck (Elk River)	3.1	2.5	0.5	-5.0

C & D Canal—East Central
Conrail Lift Bridge
Chart #12277-D
Scale 1:20,000

12. Long bend
13. Conrail Lift Bridge
14. Traffic lights (Summit North Marina)
15. Summit North Marina
16. Buoyed channel into Summit North Marina
17. Lums Pond State Park

Not for use in Navigation

50

na offering permanent slips and transient. It is tucked up into a deep cove to your right heading west, which used to be a part of the old canal. The entrance is buoyed (16) and there is a sign announcing the marina. There are traffic lights controlling egress from this marina channel to avoid difficulty with large ship traffic. Controlling depth once in the marina channel, about half way to the docks, is 4½ feet. There is a tidal range of around 4 feet and there is considerably more depth at the docks. The marina is surrounded by woods, the docks with slips to 100 feet are floating and have cable and telephone, electricity ranges up to 250 volt 50 amp. There is a pool, marine store, 50-ton lift, new clean showers, gas and diesel, a high promenade boardwalk, foot paths through the woods, and a few minutes away is Lums Pond State Park (17). Restaurants and shopping are within 15 minutes by car.

Refer to Chart #12277-E—"C & D West Central." PG 53
If you pass the marina, you will next come to the Summit fixed bridge (18). More bends later you will see Chesapeake City ahead.

Refer to Chart #12277-F—"C & D West Central and Chesapeake City." PG 52
Chesapeake City (19) will be unmistakable with its high arched bridge (20) ahead, the canal pilot's station (21) and the long face docks of **Schaefer's Canal House Restaurant and Marina (22)** on the northern bank, and the Canal Museum

(23), Corps of Engineers buildings (24), and basin (25) on the southern bank. The pilots often embark and disembark at this location. This can be interesting to watch, but if you are doing so from your boat, be sure to keep clear of the pilot boats and ships. Also, be cautious of boats docking or leaving the marina and coming out of the basin.

Refer to Chart #12277-G—"C & D West Entrance, Back Creek." PG 54
Continuing on, the straight cut will gradually widen and turn into Back Creek (26), then open into the upper stretches of Elk River (27) with Welch Point (28) to your right, Harbor North Marina (29) soon to your left (on the southern bank) and eventually the western traffic lights on Old Town Point Wharf (30) to the left.

Entry From Chesapeake Bay
Refer to Chart #12277-H—"C & D West Entrance, Elk River." PG 55

If you enter from the Bay side, the well-buoyed entrance (31) will resemble another beautiful river through rolling hills of farmland and woods, until it gradually narrows and straightens into the canal section. As with the other end, the buoys are close and easily followed. You will move from the Elk River (27) into Back Creek (26), hardly realizing from the scenery that you are approaching the canal, unless a huge

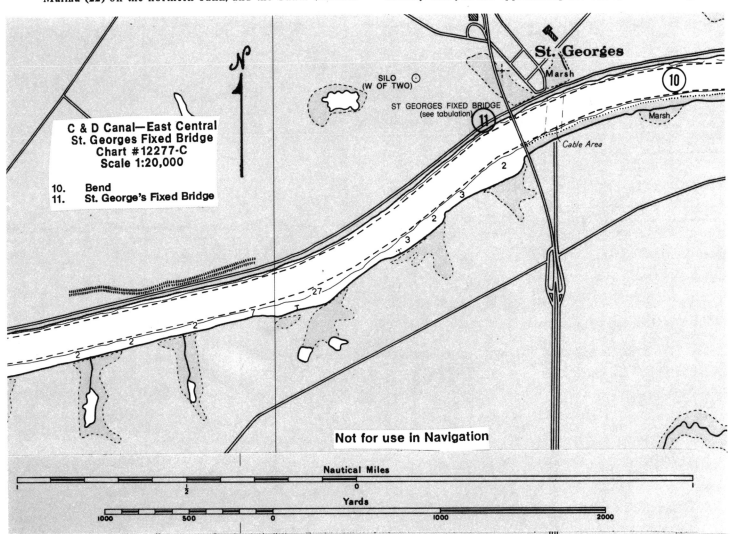

C & D Canal—East Central
St. Georges Fixed Bridge
Chart #12277-C
Scale 1:20,000

10. Bend
11. St. George's Fixed Bridge

Not for use in Navigation

Nautical Miles

Yards

Anchorage Basin at Chesapeake City

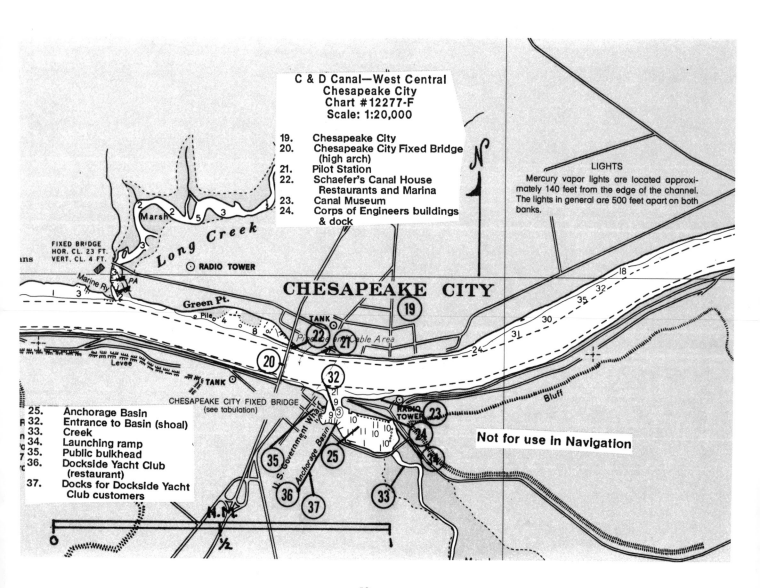

C & D Canal—West Central
Chesapeake City
Chart #12277-F
Scale: 1:20,000

19. Chesapeake City
20. Chesapeake City Fixed Bridge
    (high arch)
21. Pilot Station
22. Schaefer's Canal House
    Restaurants and Marina
23. Canal Museum
24. Corps of Engineers buildings
    & dock

LIGHTS

Mercury vapor lights are located approximately 140 feet from the edge of the channel. The lights in general are 500 feet apart on both banks.

CHESAPEAKE CITY

25. Anchorage Basin
32. Entrance to Basin (shoal)
33. Creek
34. Launching ramp
35. Public bulkhead
36. Dockside Yacht Club
    (restaurant)
37. Docks for Dockside Yacht
    Club customers

Not for use in Navigation

52

**Schaefer's Canal House Restaurant & Marina,
Cheapeake City, MD**

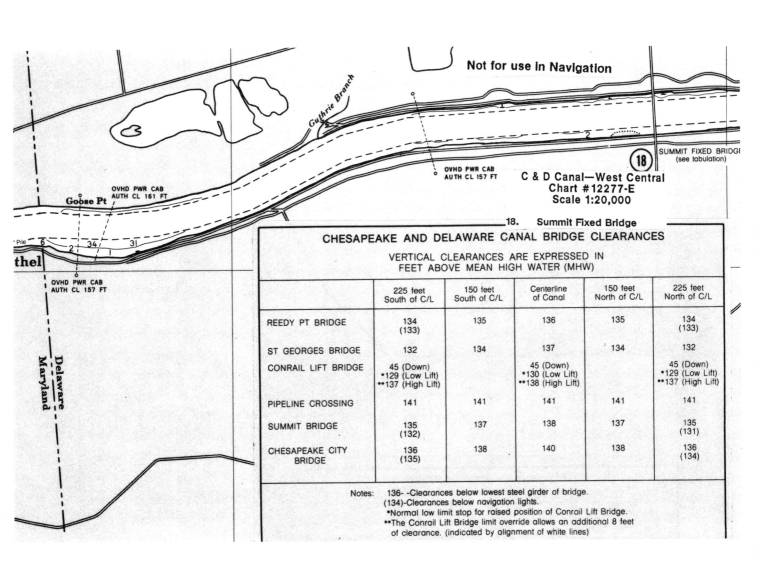

Not for use in Navigation

Guthrie Branch

OVHD PWR CAB
AUTH CL 157 FT

SUMMIT FIXED BRIDGE
(see tabulation)

(18)

**C & D Canal—West Central
Chart #12277-E
Scale 1:20,000**

OVHD PWR CAB
AUTH CL 161 FT

Goose Pt

Pile 6 34 31
2   34

thel

OVHD PWR CAB
AUTH CL 157 FT

Delaware
Maryland

18.   Summit Fixed Bridge

CHESAPEAKE AND DELAWARE CANAL BRIDGE CLEARANCES

VERTICAL CLEARANCES ARE EXPRESSED IN FEET ABOVE MEAN HIGH WATER (MHW)

	225 feet South of C/L	150 feet South of C/L	Centerline of Canal	150 feet North of C/L	225 feet North of C/L
REEDY PT BRIDGE	134 (133)	135	136	135	134 (133)
ST GEORGES BRIDGE	132	134	137	134	132
CONRAIL LIFT BRIDGE	45 (Down) *129 (Low Lift) **137 (High Lift)		45 (Down) *130 (Low Lift) **138 (High Lift)		45 (Down) *129 (Low Lift) **137 (High Lift)
PIPELINE CROSSING	141	141	141	141	141
SUMMIT BRIDGE	135 (132)	137	138	137	135 (131)
CHESAPEAKE CITY BRIDGE	136 (135)	138	140	138	136 (134)

Notes: 136- -Clearances below lowest steel girder of bridge.
(134)-Clearances below navigation lights.
*Normal low limit stop for raised position of Conrail Lift Bridge.
**The Conrail Lift Bridge limit override allows an additional 8 feet
of clearance. (indicated by alignment of white lines)

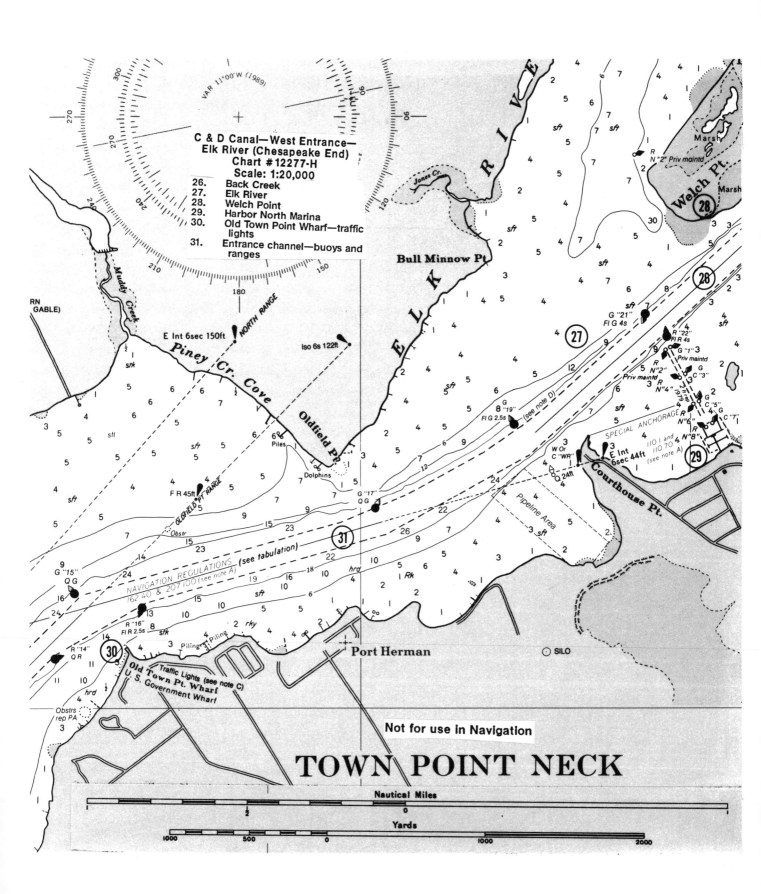

C & D Canal—West Entrance—
Elk River (Chesapeake End)
Chart #12277-H
Scale: 1:20,000

26. Back Creek
27. Elk River
28. Welch Point
29. Harbor North Marina
30. Old Town Point Wharf—traffic lights
31. Entrance channel—buoys and ranges

VAR 11°00'W (1989)

RN (GABLE)

Muddy Creek

Piney Cr. Cove

NORTH RANGE

E Int 6sec 150ft

Iso 6s 122ft

Oldfield Pt.

Piles

Dolphins

FR 45ft

OLDFIELD PT RANGE

Obstr

G "15"
QG

NAVIGATION REGULATIONS (see tabulation)
162 40 & 207 100 (see note A)

R "16"
Fl R 2.5s

R "14"
Q R

Piling Piling

Port Herman

Traffic Lights (see note C)
Old Town Pt. Wharf
U. S. Government Wharf

Obstrs
rep PA

Jones Cr.

ELK RIVER

Bull Minnow Pt.

G "17"
Q G

8 "19"
Fl G 2.5s

(see note D)

W Or
C "WR"

24ft

Pipeline Area

Courthouse Pt.

SILO

G "21"
Fl G 4s

R "22"
Fl R 4s

G "1"
Priv maintd

R N"2"
Priv maintd

R N"4"

C "3"
1979

G "5"

SPECIAL ANCHORAGE
110 1 and
110 70
(see note A)

E Int
6sec 44ft

R N"6"

C "7"

N"8"

Welch Pt.

Marsh

R N "2" Priv maintd

Marsh

28

28

27

31

29

30

Not for use in Navigation

TOWN POINT NECK

Nautical Miles

Yards

1000   500   0   1000   2000

54

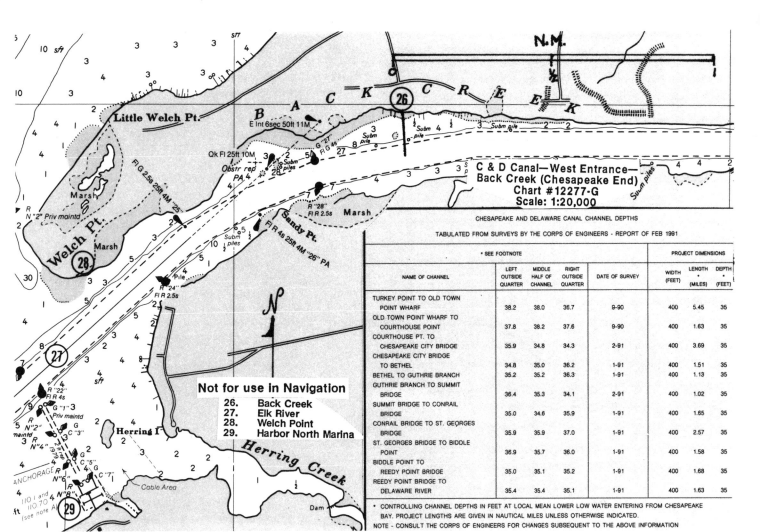

The image above contains the following labels and text:

N.M.

Little Welch Pt.

B A C K C R E E K

26

C R E E K

E Int 6sec 50ft 11M

Qk Fl 25ft 10M

Obstr rep
PA 4

G "27"
Fl G 4s

Subm
pile

27

Subm pile

Subm pile

Subm piles

C & D Canal—West Entrance—
Back Creek (Chesapeake End)
Chart #12277-G
Scale: 1:20,000

Fl G 2.5s 25ft 4M "25"

Marsh

R
N "2" Priv maintd

Welch Pt.

Marsh

28

Sandy Pt.

R "28"
Fl R 2.5s

Marsh

Fl R 4s 25ft 4M "26" PA

Subm piles

30

Pile

R "24"
Fl R 2.5s

N

27

sft

R "22"
Fl R 4s

R
N "2"
maintd

R
N "4"

G C "3"

Priv maintd

Herring I.

Not for use in Navigation
26.   Back Creek
27.   Elk River
28.   Welch Point
29.   Harbor North Marina

Herring Creek

G C "5"

ANCHORAGE R

N "6"

G C "7"

Cable Area

110 1 and
110 70
ft
(see note A)

N "8"

29

Dam

CHESAPEAKE AND DELAWARE CANAL CHANNEL DEPTHS

TABULATED FROM SURVEYS BY THE CORPS OF ENGINEERS - REPORT OF FEB 1991

| NAME OF CHANNEL | * SEE FOOTNOTE | | | | PROJECT DIMENSIONS | | |
	LEFT OUTSIDE QUARTER	MIDDLE HALF OF CHANNEL	RIGHT OUTSIDE QUARTER	DATE OF SURVEY	WIDTH (FEET)	LENGTH * (MILES)	DEPTH * (FEET)
TURKEY POINT TO OLD TOWN POINT WHARF	38.2	38.0	36.7	9-90	400	5.45	35
OLD TOWN POINT WHARF TO COURTHOUSE POINT	37.8	38.2	37.6	9-90	400	1.63	35
COURTHOUSE PT. TO CHESAPEAKE CITY BRIDGE	35.9	34.8	34.3	2-91	400	3.69	35
CHESAPEAKE CITY BRIDGE TO BETHEL	34.8	35.0	36.2	1-91	400	1.51	35
BETHEL TO GUTHRIE BRANCH	35.2	35.2	36.3	1-91	400	1.13	35
GUTHRIE BRANCH TO SUMMIT BRIDGE	36.4	35.3	34.1	2-91	400	1.02	35
SUMMIT BRIDGE TO CONRAIL BRIDGE	35.0	34.6	35.9	1-91	400	1.65	35
CONRAIL BRIDGE TO ST. GEORGES BRIDGE	35.9	35.9	37.0	1-91	400	2.57	35
ST. GEORGES BRIDGE TO BIDDLE POINT	36.9	35.7	36.0	1-91	400	1.58	35
BIDDLE POINT TO REEDY POINT BRIDGE	35.0	35.1	35.2	1-91	400	1.68	35
REEDY POINT BRIDGE TO DELAWARE RIVER	35.4	35.4	35.1	1-91	400	1.63	35

* CONTROLLING CHANNEL DEPTHS IN FEET AT LOCAL MEAN LOWER LOW WATER ENTERING FROM CHESAPEAKE BAY. PROJECT LENGTHS ARE GIVEN IN NAUTICAL MILES UNLESS OTHERWISE INDICATED.
NOTE - CONSULT THE CORPS OF ENGINEERS FOR CHANGES SUBSEQUENT TO THE ABOVE INFORMATION

ship, lumbering like a dinosaur in pastoral countryside, moves out from behind the hills. You will pass Harbor North Marina **(29)**, described in the section on the Elk River in this chapter. Back Creek will gently give way to a canal-like appearance as you approach Chesapeake City. This will soon come into view behind the arched bridge **(20)** **(on Chart #12277-F)**, which will be the first bridge of the passageway that you will encounter coming from the west.

CHESAPEAKE CITY
Refer to our—"Sketch Map of Chesapeake City."

The Anchorage Basin

Chesapeake City is around 3 miles east of Welch Point **(28)**. An anchorage basin **(25)** is maintained on the southern shore. However this regularly shoals despite dredging. Local people advise that the swift current coupled with the constant passage of large vessels simply pushes the mud up into that entrance. Corps of Engineers tugs regularly enter the basin and dock there, but they use the left side of the entrance going in. The current charts show 3 feet across the middle **(32)**. I found this to be accurate when I sounded with the best water to the left against the Corps docks **(24)** where I found around 5 feet at low water, a little less in spots. I was told that the entrance will be dredged again, soon. Once inside and over the

shoal area, the water is deeper, but a 6-foot draft boat could easily sit in the mud at low tide in much of the basin. There is current inside because of the creek **(33)**. If you draw more than 4 feet, I recommend you anchor on the Chesapeake Bay side, or tie at one of the marinas rather than rely on this basin at this time. Even though it is dredged more frequently than many other areas, it fills in again rather quickly.

There is a hard surfaced public launching ramp **(34)** in the far eastern corner. The bulkhead **(35)** at the west end of the basin, to your right as you enter, is considered open temporary public docking, but the water is shallow, down to 2 to 3 feet at low tide.

Within the basin, opposite the entrance, is the **Dockside Yacht Club (36)**. This is a restaurant with a very large menu and many specialties such as seafood, prime rib, and milk-fed veal. There is an upstairs area, and from both areas diners can view the basin or canal. The restaurant has docks **(37)** in front for its customers, although it does not consider itself to be primarily a "marina" business. There is electricity available at the docks, but no water, and there are no showers. While dining, the tie up is free, but there is a charge to stay overnight.

Chesapeake City Bridge

Unless you are shallow enough to comfortably enter and anchor in the basin, the only marina is at Schaefer's **(22)** across the canal. The bridge has a walk but the distance is much too long and fast moving traffic would make it dangerous. There are no water taxis across the canal, but if you are tied up at Schaefer's, a call to Hill Holidays Travel Agency (38) will get you a ride across the bridge. The phone is (410) 885-2797 or (800) 874-4558. If you want to tour the area, contact Wayne Hill of "Hill Holidays." His office is at 103 Bohemia Avenue, a little over a block from the basin bulkhead. It, as is typical of the area, is in a restored home which also contains a nice shop, the Victorian Lady (39), described below. This gentleman seems to know about all there is to know about the area. He also conducts tours of the local horse country. He advises that there are currently around 800 thoroughbreds within several miles of town. He also will take out charters on a deadrise which you will probably see against the public bulkhead (35).

Schaefer's Canal House Restaurant and Marina

Schaefer's (22), across the canal from the basin, has a long face dock to accommodate almost any size vessel. They have 30 transient slips available, with 110 and 220, up to 50 amps. The price posted last year was $1.35 per foot with electricity extra. They charge extra for water if you do not tie up overnight. They have gas and diesel fuel, block and cube ice, a ship's store which includes light groceries, a gift shop, a good restaurant overlooking the canal, and a pumpout station at the fuel dock. There's also a large separate banquet building and shoreside accommodations in restored Victorian homes.

Chesapeake City

Chesapeake City is mostly residential (40) on the northern side of the canal, while the southern side has a fascinating collection of historical restored homes and businesses (41). The mostly wood buildings are colorfully painted, often with shops in the homes. The overall area can be easily explored on foot. It purveys a sense of being in an early quaint seafaring village, successful in its endeavors of hard work and earnest values, and proud of its appearance.

A small park called Pell Gardens (42) overlooks the basin on the western end. During summer, there are regular musical events on the bandstand. It is not unusual to see local folks with picnics sitting under the trees watching the canal traffic. The Canal Creamery Ice Cream Shop (43) is adjacent to the park.

There are several nice restaurants on this side of the canal. Up the hill west of the basin, one block's walk across the park from the public bulkhead, is the Bayard House (44). This is a very fine restaurant with an elegant and historical atmosphere. It overlooks the canal from its hilltop with a splendid view. The Village Café (45) is a nice little restaurant specializing in home cooking and exhibiting the decor of the area. It is a short walk out Second Street. The Tap Room (46), on the corner of Second and Bohemia Avenue, offers seafood as a specialty. including crabs year round, and prides itself on Italian food, within a nice casual atmosphere of a tavern. The Kitchen Witch, LTD (47), specializes in baked goods and beverages such as espresso and hot chocolate which you can enjoy on the premises or take back to the boat.

There are numerous shops where you might obtain gifts or collectibles, or personal souvenir items. Canal Country Gifts (48) at 100 George Street, has many handcrafted items, including duck decoys, and many items made by local people. The Back Creek General Store (49) is located in a building constructed around 1861, at 100 Bohemia Avenue. It has been restored with some original shelving and glass cases. It specializes in crafts, gifts, and collectibles. The Mary-Go-Round (50), located at 200 Bohemia Avenue, also features these things and local craft. Reminisce (51), at 3rd and Bohemia Avenue, has collectibles of present times and the past. Fish Whistle Goods (52), at 3rd and Bohemia Avenue, is another shop offering a variety of collectibles including dinnerware and pottery. The Victorian Lady (39) is located in a 1915 restored home at 103 Bohemia Avenue and specializes in such items as jewelry, potpourris, collectibles, and gourmet foods of that era. Town Hall (53) is within a few minutes walk from the basin.

Canal Artworks (54), at 17 Bohemia Avenue, offers original artwork, often locally done. Sassafras Potter's Guild Gallery Shop (55), at 19A Bohemia Avenue, sells crafts and arts by local artists. Canal Lock Antiques (56), at 105 Bohemia, Black Swan Antiques (57), at 3rd and Bohemia, and the Antique Turtle (58), also at 3rd and Bohemia, as the names imply, specialize in antiques, many of local significance. A short walk up Bohemia Avenue, just past Second Street and on the right, is a small grocery store named Granny Kay's Mini Mart (59) with a selection of convenience groceries including frozen hamburger.

As might be expected, there are several very nice bed and breakfasts within walking distance of the water front. These include Inn at the Canal (60), and The Blue Max (61), which was built in 1844 and was used by Jack Hunter while he worked on this well-known book "The Blue Max."

Among festivals in the town is Holiday Happenings, which occurs in early November, and involves tours of decorated homes and bazaars, street musicians, and similar events. There is an antique show in May. Canal Day, usually near the end of June, features seafood, boat rides, games, historical displays, good eating, music, and fun.

Editor's Note: If you're coming from Cape May, Chesapeake City is a mandatory stop. Even if you don't have to stop there, I've found it most interesting. I've been pleased to observe the improvements in Schaefer's since the mid 50's when I first stopped there and swapped yarns around a pot-bellied stove on a cool evening. Chesapeake Bay watermen have much in common with watermen all over the world. They're among the most interesting people you'll meet on your Chesapeake Bay cruise.

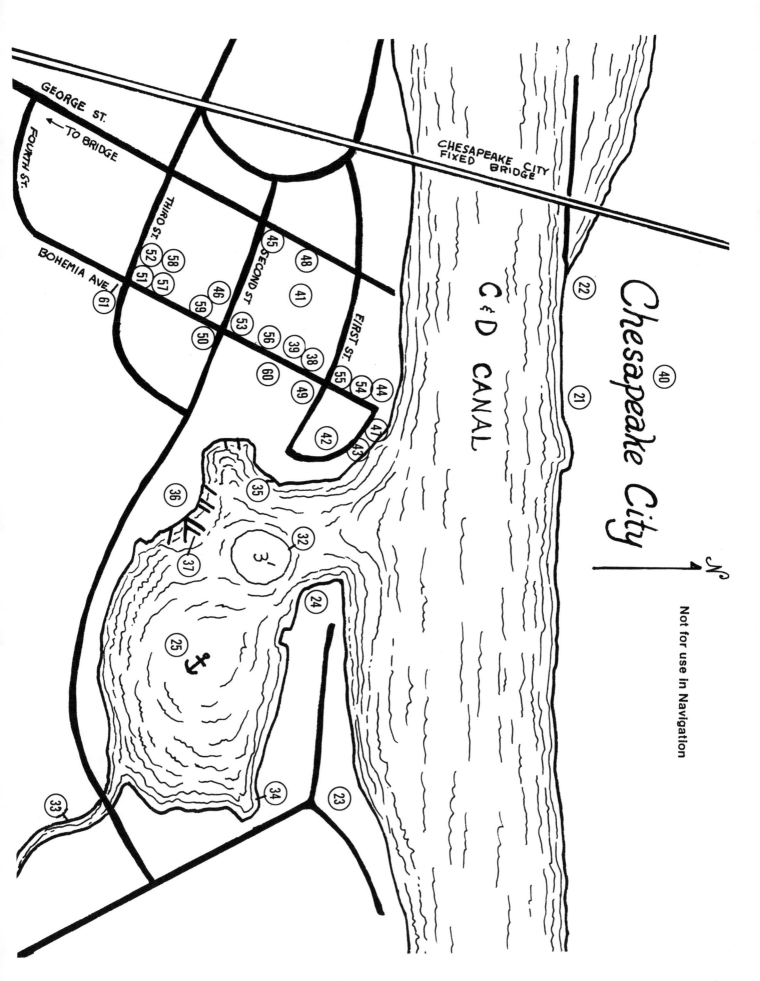

GEORGE ST.

←TO BRIDGE

FOURTH ST.

CHESAPEAKE CITY
FIXED BRIDGE

THIRD ST.

BOHEMIA AVE.

SECOND ST.

FIRST ST.

C & D CANAL

Chesapeake City

N

Not for use in Navigation

(22)

(40)

(21)

(48)

(45)

(52) (58)

(51) (57)

(61)

(41)

(46)

(59)

(53)

(50)

(56)

(39)

(60)

(38)

(49)

(55)

(54)

(44)

(47)

(43)

(42)

(35)

(36)

(32)

3'

(37)

(24)

(25)

(34)

(23)

(33)

CHAPTER 5

ELK RIVER

With the exception of the C & D Canal channel, most of this river is shallow for any boat with more than 5 feet of draft. It is in a rural area without many attractions ashore behind the marinas. There are several full-service marinas in the area if you draw no more than 5 feet. The Elk is pretty, but there are not any good protected anchorages unless you draw 4 feet or less and can go into Cabin John Creek.

Special Note About Tides

In this area of the Bay, tidal ranges can vary considerably, with unusual influences such as wind.

Refer to Chart #12274-E—"Mouth of the Elk River and Cabin John Creek."

This is true in all areas of the Bay, but Chart #12274-E for "Mouth of the Elk River and Cabin John Creek" notes a height range of, for example, Georgetown on the Sassafras, from 3 feet at mean higher high water to .4 feet at mean low water, and -5 feet at extreme low water. If there has been prolonged strong northerly wind, then expect depths considerably lower than those noted on the charts or here. In other sections of the Bay, a north wind may bring higher water. Local knowledge is always helpful on the effect of winds for the particular creeks or river which may interest you.

Entrance to Elk

Refer to Chart #12274-E—"Mouth of Elk River and Cabin John Creek."

Leaving the C & D Canal and entering the Elk River, the canal gradually becomes less harsh in its artificial lines until it is more like a large creek gradually widening into the Elk River. A feeling of relaxation and of entering into a better world settles over most travelers as the hills and pastoral shores of the Elk begin to slide by. This gradual change starts at Chesapeake City.

Although this guide starts from the north, the following entrance discussion will begin with the Elk as though entering from the Bay. Many will do it this way. It would be pretty difficult to miss the Elk as you are leaving the canal. Also, this guide as a rule will follow the rivers in from the mouth, and that format will begin here.

Raising the mouth of the Elk (62) from having come up the Bay can be an exciting and almost mystical experience. Looking north you see the broad open expanses of water that are the Susquehanna Flats (63) and the North East River (64). In the background are high hills, almost reminiscent of the foothills of the Alleghenies. In places, high cliffs sheer down to the waters edge. It seems as though you are approaching an entirely different and remote part of the world. Indeed, the area toward the Susquehanna on your left is one of the closest areas of the Bay for the Piedmont highlands. Then out of the distance, a huge container ship lumbers through the waters like a dinosaur from another place and time. The

ominous booms from the Aberdeen Proving Ground (65) rumble through the quiet air, a reminder of the mechanical world still around.

The well-known Turkey Point (66) is easily identified by a large white traditional lighthouse with a small square white building just to its left. It is on a high bluff with a cliff. The southern shore, at Grove Neck (67), has more houses than the wooded and higher north shore. Most of the tip of Turkey Point is the Elk Neck State Park (68). This very large area has hard surfaced ramps, shoreside fishing, swimming beaches, hiking, nature studies, picnic areas, and rest rooms and showers, camping and boat rental. There is a landing with dock and hard surfaced ramp (69) at Rogues Harbor (70) which also has hardware and ice, gas and snacks. You will see many moored boats in this vicinity on the north shore of the river. Some anchor here, but it has only limited protection and is exposed to wakes from large ships moving to and from the C & D Canal. Elk Neck State Park is primarily oriented to those visiting from the land. Phone (410) 287-5333.

To your right heading upriver you will notice Arnold Point (71). This is another example of changing scenery overtaking the charted landmarks. The NOS chart indicates a silo (72) here. It is still there, but hardly noticed with the sea of small houses and double wides (two-trailer houses put together) which now constitute a local private development with its ramp, beach and pool (73).

Cabin John Creek

Just northeast of Arnold Point is Cabin John Creek (74). This was originally known as "Captain Jones' Creek," but the name gradually changed over the centuries to the present form. If your draft permits, this could be a fair place to wait for a C & D passage. Looking in, there are high wooded bluffs to the right and lower wooded hills to left. A farm with cleared field down to the creek sits at what appears to be the head of the open creek (75). There is a beach on the southern shore. Following the middle, we found the entrance (77) to be slightly deeper than the chart shows, up to around 6 feet at moderate low, with around 5 feet just inside. The chart shows an obstruction (78) about half way up the creek. None is marked and I noticed local ski boats running in that vicinity, but it is still there. Past the little point to the right (79) where the chart shows a continuous 2 feet of depth, we found 5 feet of depth or slightly better (80). Several 30-foot or bigger sailing boats are privately docked at the end of that "2-foot" basin. If your draft is no more than 4 feet and you don't mind feeling your way in carefully, this could be a nice anchorage; protected and pretty. There is a buoyed ski area (81) in the basin at the end, which could be less than pleasant for those inclined to the quiet anchorage on the weekend. Beware of strong northwest winds that have a long fetch in this creek.

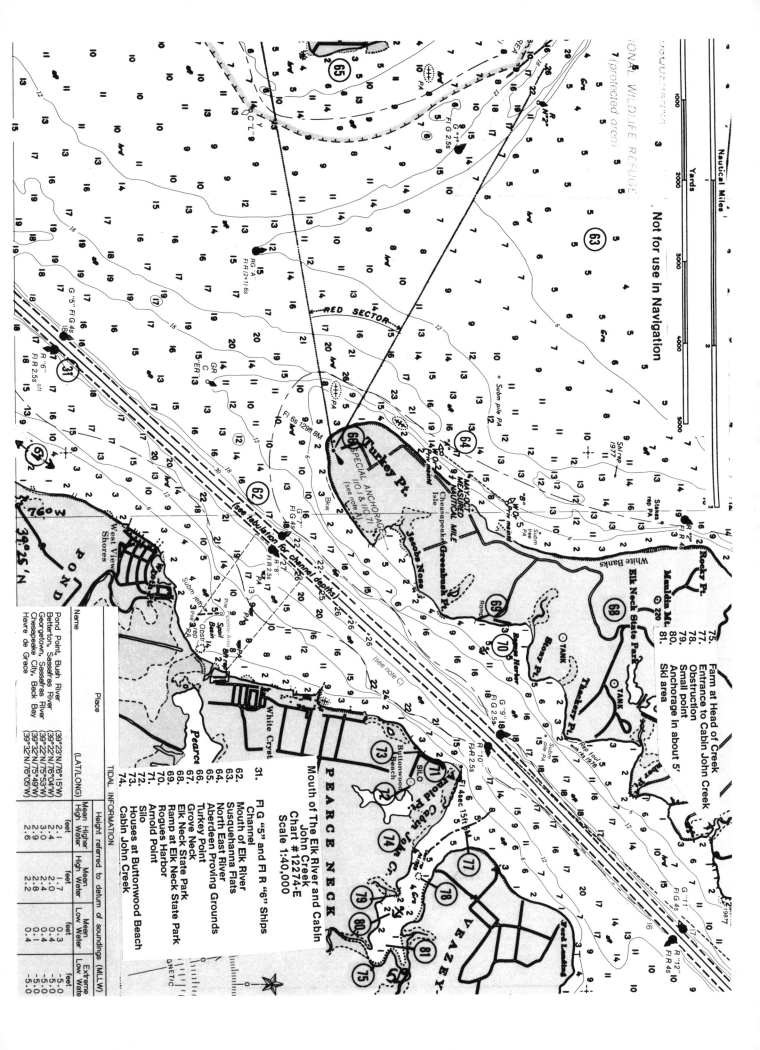

BOHEMIA RIVER
Refer to Chart #12274-F—"Bohemia River."

This river is shallow for boats drawing over 5 feet. Overnight anchoring is poor. There are some marinas and some repair facilities. The area is pretty, especially upriver if you can get over the shallower entrance. The shore behind the marinas is primarily rural.

The northern banks of the lower Bohemia River were first settled by Augustine Herman who was born in Prague in the Kingdom of Bohemia. He had traveled to New York in 1663 as an employee of the East India Company. In 1659, he was sent by New York's Governor Stuyvesant to confer with Maryland's Governor Calvert and he first saw these beautiful lands. Later, having disagreements with the Dutch of New York, Herman returned to the area and sought and was granted citizenship. He obtained much land here and built a large manor house, now destroyed. Herman was an engineer, and apparently the first person to seriously envision the C & D Canal.

Entrance Area

The Bohemia River (82) is shallow and wide until it reaches its bridge (83) where it narrows and becomes prettier with higher banks of wood and field. There is a substantial boating population among its marinas, but many cruisers pass it by except as an anchorage to await passage through the C & D Canal. Even for this use the area is not very popular for deeper draft boats. The wide mouth (82) is noted on the charts at generally 7 feet. However, I found it to be barely 6 feet in many places. This makes it prudent for boats of 5½ feet or better to anchor in the mouth, unless they wish to risk having to await tides. Anchoring in the mouth can be nice on hot summer evenings when you crave a breeze, but not much fun when the squalls with high northerly or westerly winds rip through. Also, pleasure boats from up the river seem to use the entire mouth as an entrance, depending upon their course, and fast boats and wakes can be bothersome. Close to the southern side of the entrance (84), off the unnamed cove just before Veasey Cove (85), there is thick mud bottom off the farm house (86), a reasonable anchorage if you draw over 5 feet. The traffic can still be heavy here, but the water is a little deeper (8 to 9 feet) than closer to Town Point (87), and there is better protection from the southwest to west.

Bohemia River is pretty at this anchorage, with hills, fields, and trees. To the north the mist-shrouded highlands of the Elk River reminded us of the foothills of the Blue Ridge Mountains. From this anchorage, it is difficult to imagine the C & D Canal up among the trees opening to the industrial world on the other side. But then an occasional ocean freighter looms like a behemoth down the channel through the trees and hills, as if from a small creek in the woods.

Veazey Cove (85), to right opposite Town Point, provides a popular anchorage for local and cruising vessels, with some fetch to the northeast to northwest. We found less water than the 6 feet indicated in Veazey Cove, 5 to 5½ feet.

Bohemia River to the Bridge

The river up from the mouth is also nice. Near the bridge, you enter a 6 MPH zone (88). Even on a busy hot Sunday afternoon with hundreds of boats out on this river, almost everyone was observing this zone. Many were enjoying the fresh water swimming on the beaches ashore, and others were motoring slowly, stopping to talk with friends in a relaxed and pleasant manner different from that seen on many other rivers. The Bohemia Bridge (83) has a vertical clearance of 30 feet.

Heading up the river, the first marina on the left is **Two Rivers Yacht Basin (89)**. You will notice many sailboats moored (90) off, the first such sight to left coming in. This is the beginning of an area of docks on that side. The controlling draft is 3 feet. The marina has 150 slips and some moorings. There is a 25-ton lift, dry storage facility, rest rooms with showers, pool, beach, pumpout, gas, and transient slips. Gulf, Visa, MC are accepted. Maximum boat length is 40 feet and 16-foot beam. The marina is in a very protected basin, with fuel dock and office to the left as you come in past the jetty (91) which is also to your left entering. This basin and jetty are noted on the NOS chart just east of Rich Point (92).

Next up the river, and still to the left, is **Bohemia Vista Yacht Basin (93)**. There is 5 feet at the entrance. There are 130 slips with electricity up to 50 amps. This is not in a basin, but the docks have bulkheading. There is a large work yard here, with rocks and dirt, extending some space back from the docks. They have moorings and transient slips, hull and mechanical work, including sandblasting, a 30-ton lift and 10-ton crane for engines and masts, a marine store, ice and beverages. Visa and MC are accepted.

Bohemia Bay Yacht Harbor (94) is third on the left going upriver. They are in a basin with dredged entrance, and show a conspicuous sign. There is a small decorative white lighthouse (96) on the jetty to the left of their entrance coming in. There is also a sign advising that this is the Northern Bay Maryland Police Headquarters (97). This is a relatively new marina, accomodating 5½ feet draft. The basin is quite large with nice motor yachts in the 40 to 45 foot range as well as sail. There are 168 open and 117 covered slips which are up to 65 feet with cable standard and telephone optional. Electric is up to 125/250 volt 50 amp. Both gas and diesel are sold and there is a pumpout station. Visa and MC are honored. There is a 40-ton open end travelift with some marine services and a ship's store. They have a small beach on the river.

There is a ramp close to and just to the south and upriver of the marina, but it is private. You will then see a series of beaches (98) where many local pleasure boaters anchor and swim. This continues on up the river.

Proceeding up the river, one has to really hunt and peck to find as much as 6 feet depth. Even boats with only 4 feet draft must be careful to avoid the shoal off Town Point (99). The only marker to help inside is flashing red "2" (100) off Long Point (1). This is difficult to spot on hazy summer days. My GPS derived lat-long for this was 39°28.54' by 75°53.18'. This was a point just inside (to the left of) the marker. In crisscrossing the entrance area looking from deeper water, I found that the bottom is very uneven with no clear deep water channel, and often less water than the chart shows. Once you get up to Long Point, the water gets much deeper, more consistent with charted depths.

The first marina to right is **Long Point Marina (2)**. There are moorings and slips. They take transients only if there is space available from permanent slips. The entrance was reported as 4½ to 5 feet, others say 3 feet. There is a store with snacks and some supplies, and a 25-ton lift. They have a pumpout and complete hull and engine repairs. They pump gas only and honor Visa, MC, and Mobil.

Next up and still to right is **Losten Marina (3)**, just to your left as you begin to turn into Scotchman Creek (4). This appears to be primarily oriented to trailer boats although there

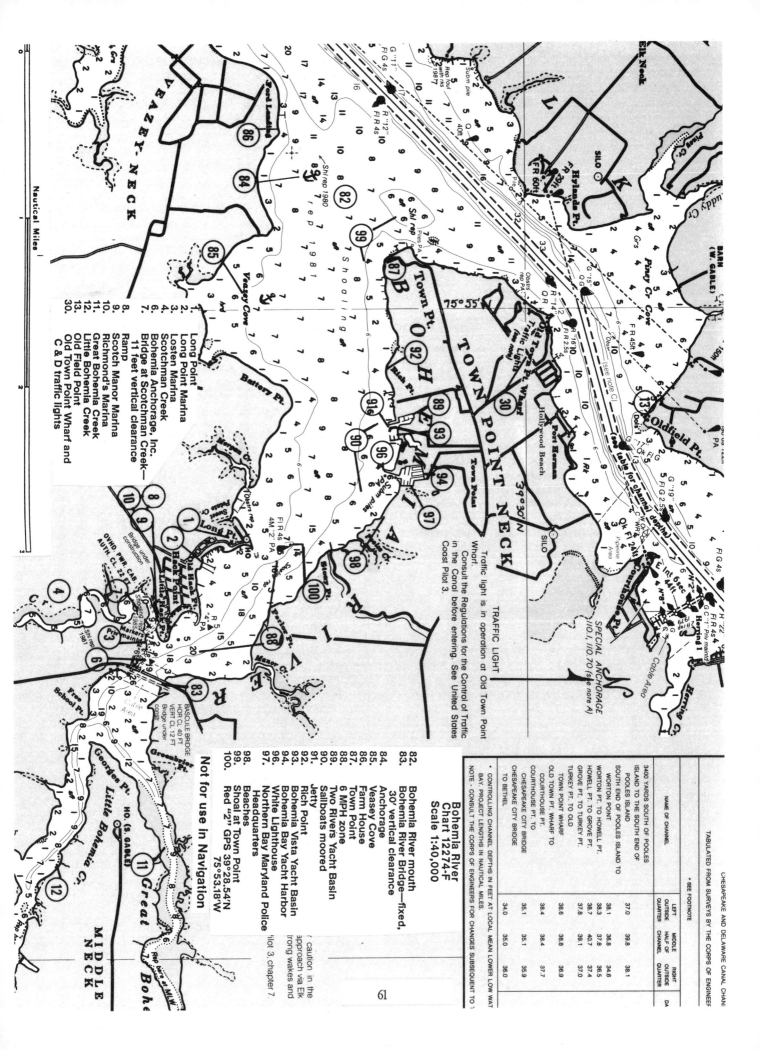

1. Long Point
2. Long Point Marina
3. Losten Marina
4. Scotchman Creek
6. Bohemia Anchorage, Inc.
7. Bridge at Scotchman Creek—
   11 feet vertical clearance
8. Ramp
9. Scotch Manor Marina
10. Richmond's Marina
11. Great Bohemia Creek
12. Little Bohemia Creek
13. Old Field Point
30. Old Town Point Wharf and
    C & D traffic lights

82. Bohemia River mouth
83. Bohemia River Bridge—fixed,
    30' vertical clearance
84. Anchorage
85. Veasey Cove
86. Farm House
87. Town Point
88. 6 MPH zone
89. Two Rivers Yacht Basin
90. Sailboats moored
91. Jetty
92. Rich Point
93. Bohemia Vista Yacht Basin
94. Bohemia Bay Yacht Harbor
96. White Lighthouse
97. Northern Bay Maryland Police
    Headquarters
98. Beaches
99. Shoal at Town Point
100. Red "2" GPS 39°28.54'N
     75°53.18'W

Bohemia River
Chart 12274-F
Scale 1:40,000

Not for use in Navigation

TRAFFIC LIGHT

Traffic light is in operation at Old Town Point Wharf. Consult the Regulations for the Control of Traffic in the Canal before entering. See United States Coast Pilot 3.

SPECIAL ANCHORAGE
110.1, 110.70 (see note A)

Nautical Miles

CHESAPEAKE AND DELAWARE CANAL CHANNEL
TABULATED FROM SURVEYS BY THE CORPS OF ENGINEERS

NAME OF CHANNEL	LEFT OUTSIDE QUARTER	MIDDLE HALF OF CHANNEL	RIGHT OUTSIDE QUARTER	DA
3400 YARDS SOUTH OF POOLES ISLAND TO THE SOUTH END OF POOLES ISLAND	37.0	39.8	38.1	
SOUTH END OF POOLES ISLAND TO WORTON POINT	38.1	38.8	34.6	
WORTON PT. TO HOWELL PT.	38.3	37.8	36.5	
HOWELL PT. TO GROVE PT.	38.7	37.4	37.4	
GROVE PT. TO TURKEY PT.	37.8	40.7	37.0	
TURKEY PT. TO OLD TOWN POINT WHARF	39.1	39.1	37.0	
OLD TOWN PT. WHARF TO COURTHOUSE PT.	38.6	38.8	36.9	
COURTHOUSE PT. TO CHESAPEAKE CITY BRIDGE	38.4	38.4	37.7	
CHESAPEAKE CITY BRIDGE TO BETHEL	35.1	35.1	35.9	
	34.0	35.0	36.0	

* SEE FOOTNOTE

· CONTROLLING CHANNEL DEPTHS IN FEET AT LOCAL MEAN LOWER LOW WATER
  BAY PROJECT LENGTHS IN NAUTICAL MILES.
  NOTE : CONSULT THE CORPS OF ENGINEERS FOR CHANGES SUBSEQUENT TO

are 54 slips with electricity at 15 amps and 6 feet depths. You may have some difficulty getting up the river that far carrying 6 feet. Losten Marina has a nice concrete ramp and dock, a marine store, snacks, heads and showers, and block and cube ice. There is a 15-ton closed end lift.

The last marina to right before the Bohemia bridge is the **Bohemia Anchorage, Inc. (6)**. This has a controlling depth of 4 feet. There were some covered sheds and there is a 20-ton lift with repairs available. There are 20 moorings and 36 slips with electricity up to 30 amps, a ramp, and gas.

Scotchman Creek and Upper Bohemia

If you go up Scotchman Creek **(4)**, you will find a low bridge **(7)** at its entrance with an 11-foot vertical clearance. Just above it is a ramp **(8)** and two marinas, all to your right. It is difficult to distinguish between the two marinas and private docks behind the homes lining the creek. They are **Scotch Manor Marina (9)** and **Richmond's Marina (10)**. These appear to be primarily oriented to trailer size motor boats and are popular locally. There is gas available here and some repairs and supplies. Transient space is usually available with electricity reported at 15 amps. The creek is beautiful beyond this area. A dinghy exploration or ramp launch here would certainly be worth the trouble. There is marsh, wood, and the feel of remoteness from civilization up the creek, but it is a creek which requires cautionary measures, and perhaps a spare prop. For smaller boats, these two marinas would be a great place to use as a base for exploring this creek.

Beyond the Bohemia bridge, the river divides into Great Bohemia Creek **(11)** and Little Bohemia Creek **(12)**. The area is pretty with trees and hills, but the channel is narrow, with 6 to 10 feet reported up into both branches. In this upriver area, pick your anchorage, it is all beautiful.

Back out in the Elk River after you pass the Bohemia River to the right (southeastern bank). You will then pass Old Town Point Wharf **(30)** with its canal traffic light on your right (southeastern bank), and then Old Field Point **(13)** on your left (north side).

UPPER ELK RIVER
Refer to Chart #12274-G—"Upper Elk River."

Your next choice is to go through the C & D Canal and its Back Creek **(14)** entrance, or veer to the left and explore the rather shallow upper Elk River **(15)**. Many local boats get into the upper Elk by passing close to Welch Point **(28)**, taking off from Fl G "21" **(16)** of the C & D channel. The chart shows a controlling depth of 7 feet meandering from that area southwest of Welch Point to the ship channel. It's best not to go in with over 3½ feet of draft, because it gets much shallower before you get anywhere inside. Local people do it, but I found the bottom to vary quite a bit despite the markings on the chart. There were no easily used ranges upon the shore, and the charted aids to navigation leave much to be desired for a boat with greater draft. As is true of much of this area, you are in a rural community here, and there is not much of interest behind the marinas.

For smaller boats who do venture in, **Triton Marine (17)** is the first to the left up the river. They have 220 slips, 89 and 100 octane gas, a concrete ramp, and jet ski rental. Visa and MC are accepted. Depths can be as low as 2 ½ feet, although I saw motor yachts in the 40-foot range in permanent slips. There is a 20-ton, 38-foot closed end travel lift as well as a 15-ton open ended lift, hull and engine repairs, marine store selling some hardware and fishing gear and bait, snacks, and block and cube ice.

Next up the river to the left is **Elk Point Marina (18)**. Sometimes the water is too shallow for the local small craft with permanent slips to get in or out. It was too shallow at low tide for my dinghy. They don't usually do a transient business. There is a nice big yard here on this point, and the slips were primarily filled with permanent smaller boats.

The first marina to the right heading in is **Mitchell's Marina (19)** with 98 slips. It has a buoyed channel with a range on the dock. There is a small lift and ramp. There were primarily small boats in the slips. They advertise brokerage and there is a marine store with block and cube ice and snacks.

Taylor's Marina (20) comes up next to the right with a large sign advising that it is full service, with engine and hull repair and marine store. There are 76 slips. The store behind the dock area has limited light groceries and block and cube ice. Depth here can get as low as 2½ feet. This marina is used primarily for smaller trailer-type local boats. The ramp is normally rented only during the week because of tight parking. They advertise brokerage and sales of MerCruiser and Cobra.

Locust Point Marina (21), on the point by that name, has piers, a concrete ramp, rest rooms, and nice piers for the hard ramp. There are 40 slips with a few available for transients.

The town of Elkton **(22)** is not readily accessible to the typical cruising boat. However, there is a "Marine Electronics Service" **(23)** in Elkton, phone (410) 398-0471. They do repairs on radar, Loran, VHF, depth sounders, autopilots, VCRs, stereros, TV sets, and other electronic items.

In the Elk River, but near the entrance to Back Creek and the C & D reach, is an active marina just in from Courthouse Point **(24)**. **Harbour North Marina (29)** has been in business for over 10 years. It has 150 slips and a well marked, if shallow, entrance channel **(25)** from the main channel. Depth can be as low as 3½ feet, sometimes as low as 3 feet. A call ahead on VHF is always worthwhile to get the latest depth information. Harbour North Marina has transient slips with 20 and 30 amps available. There are 150 slips, block and cube ice, gas, marine store, and they sell fishing licenses. Visa, MC, and Discover are accepted. They offer inside and outside dry storage with maintenance and repair work. There is a 20-ton open end lift and 4-ton forklift. **The Harbour North Yacht Club (26)** is located here. It has a brochure that advertises reasonable membership rates. There is also Burres Upholstery Company and "House Boat Charters" **(27)** (call (215) 622-6723) located on the premises.

Back out into the main stream of the Elk River, the well marked and deep big ship channel brings you into Back Creek and the C & D Canal.

62

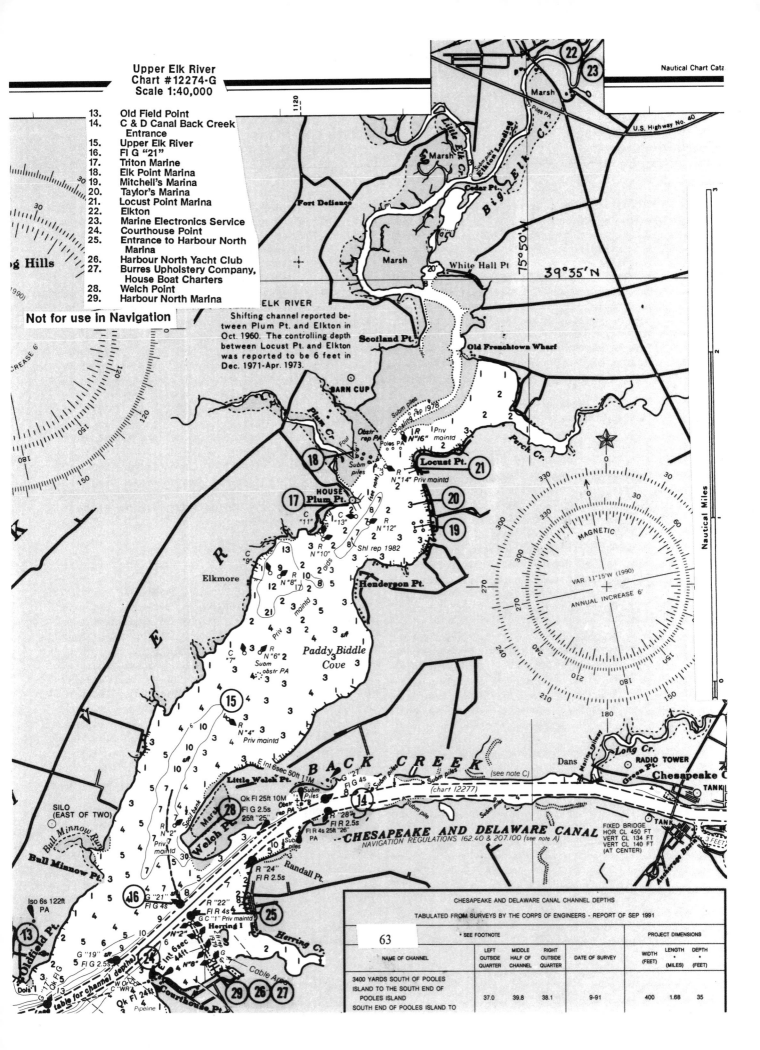

Upper Elk River
Chart #12274-G
Scale 1:40,000

Not for use in Navigation

Shifting channel reported between Plum Pt. and Elkton in Oct. 1960. The controlling depth between Locust Pt. and Elkton was reported to be 6 feet in Dec. 1971-Apr. 1973.

CHESAPEAKE AND DELAWARE CANAL
NAVIGATION REGULATIONS 162.40 & 207.100 (see note A)

FIXED BRIDGE
HOR CL 450 FT
VERT CL 134 FT
VERT CL 140 FT
(AT CENTER)

63

	CHESAPEAKE AND DELAWARE CANAL CHANNEL DEPTHS						
	TABULATED FROM SURVEYS BY THE CORPS OF ENGINEERS - REPORT OF SEP 1991						
	* SEE FOOTNOTE				PROJECT DIMENSIONS		
NAME OF CHANNEL	LEFT OUTSIDE QUARTER	MIDDLE HALF OF CHANNEL	RIGHT OUTSIDE QUARTER	DATE OF SURVEY	WIDTH (FEET)	LENGTH * (MILES)	DEPTH * (FEET)
3400 YARDS SOUTH OF POOLES ISLAND TO THE SOUTH END OF POOLES ISLAND	37.0	39.8	38.1	9-91	400	1.68	35
SOUTH END OF POOLES ISLAND TO							

CHAPTER 6

SASSAFRAS RIVER

The Sassafras River is one of the prettiest and most pleasant places to cruise in Chesapeake Bay. The high wooded hills along its shores are sparsely populated, the water runs deep well up the river past Georgetown, there are many beautiful anchoring coves with good protection and holding, the water is fresh and nettle-free, and there are some excellent marinas in the Georgetown area. There are not many restaurants or other attractions close to the shore, but those few are good and there are several shops and other points of interest.

Editor's Note: I found many Philadelphia sailors based at marinas in the Sassafras River. They know a good thing when they see it!

ENTRANCE
Refer to Chart #12274-I—"Western Sassafras."

Approaching the river from the south, you will see the hills and occasional mists of the Elk River and the enchanted Susquehanna Flats. Deep water lies close to Howell Point (32) with its 28-foot light and tower (33). In the contour south of Howell Point, you may notice the activity and masts of the Echo Hill Sailing Camp (34). As you continue on around the point and into the river, the civilization of Betterton (1) quickly appears to your right (south). Approaching from the north, the water will shoal quickly off Grove Point (67), occasionally to less than the 10 feet noted on the chart.

Coming into the river, the houses and beach of Betterton (1) appear to your right (south). Betterton is located on the site of a very early farm named "Fish Hall." When the first house was destroyed in the early part of the century, skulls were found under the floor boards. Some say that these had been put there by early inhabitants to ward off evil spirits. Betterton later became a very active resort community with people coming from far around to enjoy the beach here, and the Victorian era atmosphere. This died out, but the village is attempting to again become an attraction for swimming and boating.

Betterton rests on the hillside overlooking the river. It has a Kent County public concrete landing ramp (1A) (fee required) and bulkheaded small boat docks which can be reserved from the government. The docks do not have electricity and water and I didn't find much more than 4 feet inside the slips. These docks are quite exposed to northerly blows, or any blow except from the south right off the land. There is a nice roped-off swimming beach with lifeguard stand, a nice shower and restroom facility, and dumpster. To obtain information about docking and launching at this facility, call the Kent County Dept. of Parks and Recreation at (410) 778-1948. Charlie's Restaurant and Bar (1B) sits atop the hill about a block from the ramp. This is a full-service restaurant with casual dining overlooking the river.

Just a few minutes from the docks, at 115 Ericsson Avenue, is a nice bed and breakfast named Lantern Inn (1C). To reach this, walk up Main Street, which comes down to the docks. Then turn to your right onto Ericsson, about a quarter of a block from the river, and follow it until you reach the address. This bed and board would make a very convenient place to stay for those wishing to get off the boat for a night or two, or wishing to have guests visit but not sleep aboard. This home was built in 1904 and the hosts are knowledgeable in and helpful with the many activities that the surrounding area offers. These include crabbing and fishing, tennis, bicycling, windsurfing, nature walks, visits to area wildlife refuges, and antique shopping.

There is a condo development (1D) behind and upstream from the park. It has private docks with some lift-out slips on the shore just up from the public area. Provisioning is not conveniently available in Betterton, and the anchorage is exposed except from the south.

As you move up into the river, you will notice lines of floats coming out from close inshore in many places. These are markers for a type of netting for fishing called "Fykes," described in Chapter 1. Do not pass between the markers, or close to them. You may entangle them in your prop or keel, doing damage to both yourself and the hard working fishermen.

LLOYD CREEK

Just past Betterton, to your right (south) and inside the river, is Lloyd Creek (2). In settled weather there is a pretty anchorage (2) with 9 to 12 feet depth in the cove just outside of and north off the creek entrance. Very high wooded hills and a sheer cliff overlook you from the shore. This creek is very shallow inside, but great to explore by dinghy. The entrance to the creek is very difficult to see until you are right at it. Head to the face of the cliff (2B), and you will see it opening up as you get close. The water is 7 feet deep close to this cliff, and the actual entrance has even deeper water between the point (2C) and the cliff. Going in is a spectacular experience. The cliff sheers over you as you move along in a southwesterly direction toward the narrow opening. The current is very strong as you draw near, powerfully swirling past the wall. Because of this, care should be taken going in. It is necessary to have a motor powerful enough to control your dinghy in strong current. If you stay in the middle, you should avoid any of the rocks or shoals that are on the sides, but if you are not careful eddies, could set you aside. The beach on the point to your right (west) is private. As you pass it, a large and beautiful shallow bay opens up with little in the way of civilization. Just inside the opening, there is 8 feet depth, seemingly enough room for small cruisers to anchor, but the current would not make this advisable. The chart shows a shoal (2D) just inside and implies that a course along the spit in a north-northwesterly direction may get your dinghy farther inside. This did not work for me. I found the better depths by going straight on south until off the house to the left (east). This

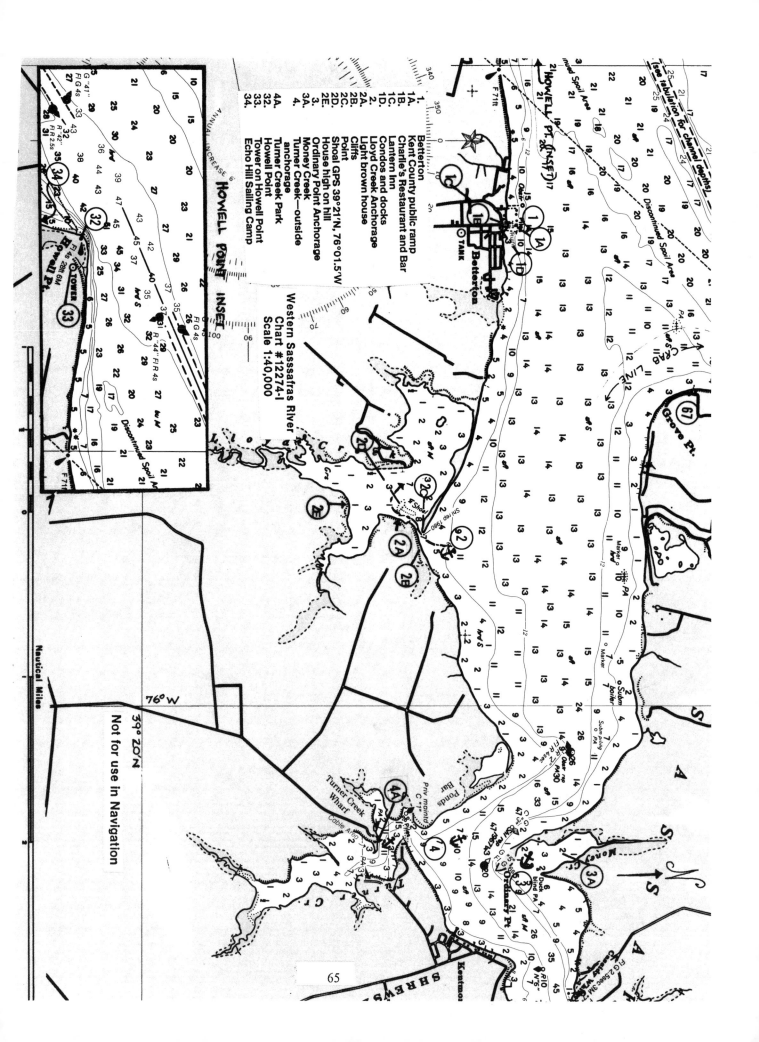

HOWELL POINT INSET

ANNUAL INCREASE 6'

Western Sassafras River
Chart #12274-1
Scale 1:40,000

1.   Betterton
1A.   Kent County public ramp
1B.   Charlie's Restaurant and Bar
1C.   Lantern Inn
1D.   Condos and docks
2.   Lloyd Creek Anchorage
2A.   Light brown house
2B.   Cliffs
2C.   Point
2D.   Shoal GPS 39°21'N, 76°01.5'W
2E.   House high on hill
3.   Ordinary Point Anchorage
3A.   Money Creek
4.   Turner Creek—outside
          anchorage
4A.   Turner Creek Park
32.   Howell Point
33.   Tower on Howell Point
34.   Echo Hill Sailing Camp

Nautical Miles

39°20'N

76°W

Not for use in Navigation

65

light brown house **(2A)** has a green wall around it with a dock. Ahead (south) across the bay, is a house high on a cleared hill **(2E)**. I headed to the westerly end of the cleared area in front of this house until the water in front of the brown house to my left (east) began to shoal. At this point, I headed to my right (westerly) in 4 feet of water. The shoal came off this brown house to an area in the vicinity of the GPS derived position of 39°21.00'N and 76°01.50'W. With the speed of the current, continuous shifting of this shoal area would not be surprising. Once past this shoal area, the bottom was more even, but still very shallow. This is for dinghies only. The bay and creek are beautiful, and coupled with the exciting entrance, are worth a look.

ORDINARY POINT

A short distance farther up river, and well out of the open water, is everybody's favorite anchorage at Ordinary Point **(3)**. The anchorage is around the point and in toward Money Creek **(3A)**. The point has a beach on its western side, the holding is good, and the land of the neck is low enough to allow breezes to blow in from the wider mouth of the river. There is more depth behind this point than the chart indicates. Paralleling the spit, you can carry 6 feet well inside. Moving off away from the spit to the northwest will bring shallower water. I found 6 feet up to the general area of the GPS derived position of 39°22.38'N and 75°58.70'W. As is true of much of the Sassafras, this is an ideal place to lie waiting for favorable conditions to head out through the C & D Canal.

TURNER CREEK
Refer also to our—"Sketch Chart of Turner Creek."

Turner Creek **(4)** opens up across from (south of) Ordinary Point. Many anchor in the cove off the mouth of the creek. There is good water and holding deep into the cove. The Columbia Sailing Association uses Turner Creek as a base. Work boats use the creek daily, and this could cause some early morning awakenings. The water is very deep just off the beach **(4B)** to your right (west) just before the shoal **(4C)** to your left (south). Local small sailboats sometimes anchor bow onto this beach with a stern anchor in deeper water. I have seen deer along this beach, especially in the still of the early morning or late evening.

The entrance to the creek looks more difficult on the chart than it actually is, although caution is required. A long bar **(4C)** does come off the eastern side of the entrance, well off that point and close to the western shore. A small locally placed green buoy **(4D)** marks the end of the shoal. There is well over 7 feet depth going in. The green marker is so far to the right (west) going in that many don't trust it, but the shoal that it marks is quite shallow. The piles **(4E)** noted on the chart are old dock pilings. They are there and generally visible, but are well to the right (west) of the channel. The chart makes it look very close, but it is better than you would expect, once you see the area.

Once clear of the green marker, the tendency is to round to your left (east) and head up into the creek. Don't. The shoal is wide and continues on well into the creek. Instead, favor the mud cliff on the right (west) side **(4F)** and head toward the park building of Turner Creek Park before you turn up into

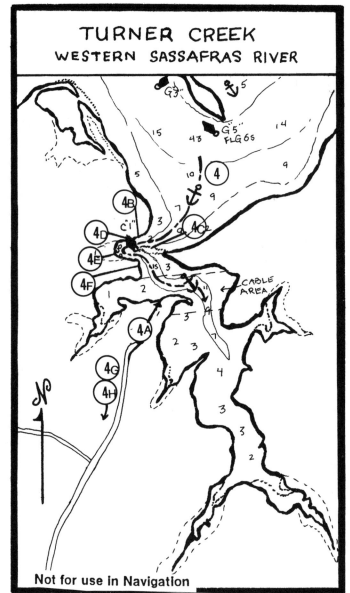

Not for use in Navigation

**Sketch Chart
Turner Creek—
Western Sassafras River**

4.	**Turner Creek—Outside Anchorage**
4A	**Turner Creek Park**
4B	**Beach—small boats anchor stern out & put bow to beach**
4C	**Long shoal from eastern shore**
4D.	**C"1"**
4E	**Piles on right side of channel going in**
4F	**Cliff on right**
4G	**Kent Museum**
4H	**"Knock's Folly"**

the creek. Turner Creek Park **(4A)** is recognized by a ramp, docks (generally used by work boats) and an old gray building at the water's edge. It will be just ahead of you as you begin to round the shoal. Once inside, the deep water is wide enough to anchor, and there are local sailboats docked and moored there. The creek shoals quickly as you move farther up from the basin in front of the park docks. The chart notes much of this as a buried cable area. Often catfish and eel floats are moored in the water just off the park dock. These

Betterton, Sassafras River

Turner Creek Park docks, Sassafras River

are large boxes which usually protrude only a few inches from the surface of the water. The watermen who use the park dock keep their catch fresh in those boxes until shipping. They can be difficult to see in poor light.

The park has a picnic area, ramp, restrooms (in basement of old building up the hill), trash cans, a volley ball area, and a pay phone. There are 56 acres of trails and fields and woods in this park. To obtain information about docking and launching at this facility, call the Kent County Dept. of Parks and Recreation at (410) 778-1948. Kent Museum (4G), is located on Route 448 to your left (west) just up from this landing as well as the colonial mansion known as Knock's Folly (4H), also to your left. The museum is only open on the first and third Saturday of the month from 10 a.m. to 4 p.m.

BACK CREEK
Refer to Chart #12274-H—"Eastern Sassafras River."

Back Creek (5) behind Knight Island (5B) (not really an island) is the next popular anchorage, but don't go in with more than 5 feet draft. The shoal extending well north-westerly out from the tip of Knight Island presents a problem. There appears to be more depth over the shoal than the 2 feet shown, but it still must be avoided. I found the shoal to end in the GPS derived position of 39°22.79'N and 75°56.87'W. Coming in, head northerly to the west of the old dock at the foot of the old weatherbeaten house (5A) on the shore to the north-northeast. Then round the tip of Knight Island as the water deepens to 10 feet or more. After this deep pocket, the bottom will begin to come up again, and the deeper area is quite narrow. Boats often anchor between and to the northeast of the area between the dock on the northern shore and the private dock (5C) inside the tip of Knight Island. The stakes and piles (5C) noted on the chart are apparently the remains of old docks. They are not related to navigation except that they should be avoided.

With all the other good anchorages in the area, this would not be worth the effort to me, unless I was in a boat drawing less than 4 feet. The area is pretty, with low fields and wooded hills. The structures on the northern shore are a part of Mount Harmon (5D), an old tobacco plantation with a lovely Georgian brick mansion and restored gardens. This is a National Trust house and can be seen by appointment. Its land address is Grove Neck Road, 4 miles west of Cecilton, and the phone is (410) 275-8819.

FREEMAN CREEK

Freeman Creek (6) is another pretty place to explore by dinghy, or anchor if you are blessed with a shallow draft boat. Inside are woods, marsh, field and some civilization. There is a small windmill (6A) to your right (west), in the yard of a home ashore. There is 5 feet depth just past this windmill. Farther in is a dock with white piles (6B) to your right (west), with lily pads on the opposite shore. The depth is just under 5 feet here.

WOODLAND CREEK

Passing Knight Island, the river sweeps under some beautiful high wooded bluffs to your left (north) with beaches at low tide. Many anchor (7) here, where you can hear the winds moan in the trees high overhead. The mud bottom is a little softer than many other locations in the river. Take extra care in setting the hook.

Across the river (south) and farther east is the cove entrance to Woodland Creek (8). With the feeling of more openness, this area does have some excellent clay-mud bottom for serious holding. The creek is shallow as the chart shows, but beautiful. Daffodil Island (8A) inside is very special, but an abandoned sunken houseboat mars its western shore. A little shack lies within its trees. You can anchor in 4 feet off the east and north side (8B), and the water is deeper than the chart implies for dinghy passage between the island and the mainland. Well up into the southern end of the creek in 1-foot depth, we found a 6 MPH speed buoy bobbing authoritatively to the trees and marsh grass!

GEORGETOWN

Coming abreast of Old Field Point (8C), the view opens to the Georgetown area, where route 213 crosses the Sassafras River by a drawbridge with 4-foot vertical clearance. This is within approximately 2 hours drive from Philadelphia, Baltimore, or Washington, D.C. There really isn't a "town" here, as most people consider the word. As one resident commented, "There's just a few houses on each side of the river, some boating and antique shops, and that's it behind the waterfront." This description should not belie the fact that this is a prime area for the cruiser to visit. Actually, the community on the north shore is called "Fredericktown," but most people, as will I here, refer to the entire area as "Georgetown." There is a 6 MPH buoy marked speed restriction here, there is room to anchor, there are moorings, several nice marinas and restaurants, and some excellent repair facilities. There is also a post office (22) within a few minutes' walk from the docks and there are points of historical interest. All of the marinas described here are within a few minutes' walk and/or launch trip to the post office, few shops, and restaurants.

Kitty Knight House

Georgetown was erected by act of the Assembly of Maryland in May 1736, and like many other locations in the vicinity, it was burned by Admiral Cockburn during the War of 1812. As he sailed up the river, he sent a message that he would leave the villagers alone if they did not attack, but then the local citizens opened fire from the woods along the shore. The Admiral then burned most of the buildings in the settlements. There was one notable exception.

The Kitty Knight House (9) standing today as a well-known restaurant and inn, was the home of a well-respected and staunch lady of that name. She was so determined in beating out the flames around her house that the Admiral, in admiration, ordered his troops to desist, and the home, as well as that of a neighbor, was saved. This proud building stands on the high hill on the southern shore up from the bridge. It has dining facilities in its historically restored area as well as a more modern dining room, and has an outdoor porch area with bar and spectacular view over Georgetown harbor. There is also very fine lodging in this inn.

Marinas

Georgetown Yacht Basin (GYB) (10) is the last marina to your right (south) before you reach the bridge. This is one of

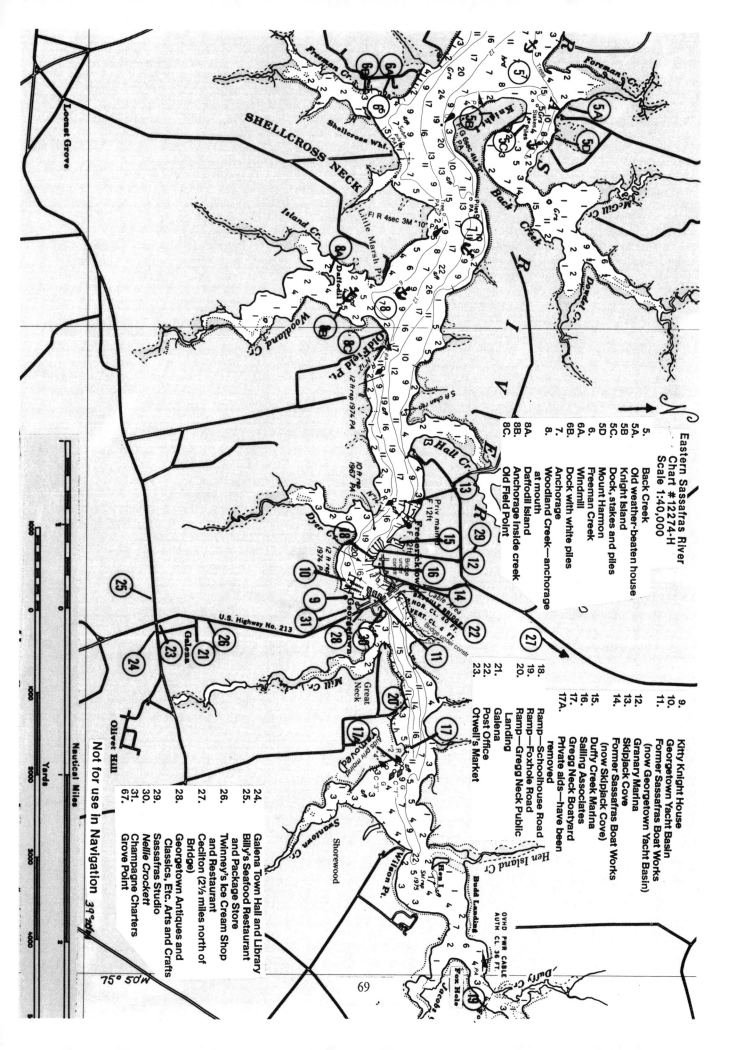

Eastern Sassafras River
Chart #12274-H
Scale 1:40,000

5. Back Creek
5A. Old weather-beaten house
5B. Knight Island
5C. Dock, stakes and piles
5D. Mount Harmon
6. Freeman Creek
6A. Windmill
6B. Dock with white piles
7. Anchorage
8. Woodland Creek—anchorage
at mouth
8A. Daffodil Island
8B. Anchorage inside creek
8C. Old Field Point

9. Kitty Knight House
10. Georgetown Yacht Basin
11. Former Sassafras Boat Works
(now Georgetown Yacht Basin)
12. Granary Marina
13. Skipjack Cove
14. Former Sassafras Boat Works
(now Skipjack Cove)
15. Duffy Creek Marina
16. Sailing Associates
17. Gregg Neck Boatyard
17A. Private aids—have been
removed
18. Ramp—Schoolhouse Road
19. Ramp—Foxhole Road
20. Ramp—Gregg Neck Public
Landing
21. Galena
22. Post Office
23. Otwell's Market

24. Galena Town Hall and Library
25. Billy's Seafood Restaurant
and Package Store
26. Twinney's Ice Cream Shop
and Restaurant
27. Cecilton (2½ miles north of
Bridge)
28. Georgetown Antiques and
Classics, Etc. Arts and Crafts
29. Sassafras Studio
30. Nellie Crockett
31. Champagne Charters
67. Grove Point

Not for use in Navigation

75° 50′W

39° 20′N

69

the finest and strongest full-service marinas on the Bay. They have purchased much of the property formerly belonging to the old Sassafras Boat Works (11), and the Granary Marina (12) across the river. This makes the GYB facilities even more attractive to the boater. Skipjack Cove (13), the first marina on the left (northern shore) as you approach, has been purchased by Westrec Properties, Inc. which also purchased a portion of the former Sassafras Boat Works (14) facilities. They also are working to expand.

Skipjack Cove (13) has docks and facilities with capacity for boats up to 175 feet and 10-foot draft. There are over 346 open slips and 21 covered, up to 100 amp electric up to 240 volts, and a pumpout facility at the gas and diesel fuel dock. Visa and MC are honored. This marina has 28 air conditioned bathrooms, each with its own private shower. There are several laundry units, cable TV and optional phone hook-up on the docks. It has 33 seasonal moorings to 50 feet and free launch shuttle to other harbor areas. There is a bar and deli with light fare, marine supplies, gifts, limited groceries, and block and cube ice. A swimming pool is near the deli and bar, and there is a great deal of yard area for children and events. Repair facilities on the premises have mechanics on duty. Their maximum haulout is 70 tons. Nautilus Yacht Sales brokerage is on the premises.

Heading up the river, Duffy Creek Marina (15) sits to the left, (northern shore) back in an enclosed cove. This facility is run completely by family members. There is 6 feet depth in its entrance and less inside. It does not sell diesel but sells 93 octane Gulf gas and has a pumpout. It honors MC, Visa, Amex and Discover. There are 130 slips with electricity up to 30 amps, the largest slip being 50 feet. Because of its controlling entrance depth and the somewhat tight quarters inside, many sailing vessels and single screw power boats 35 feet and over may have a difficult time maneuvering inside. It has a double concrete boat ramp, 25-ton lift, 130 slips from 17 feet to 65 feet, marine store, and are dealers for Volvo Penta, Crusader, Onan, and Kohler. The marine store is well-stocked and includes boating gear, parts, snack food, fishing gear, and block and cube ice. There is a swimming pool here. There is also a public ramp nearby at Schoolhouse Road (18).

Next, still to the left (the northern shore), is the Granary (12), the facility mentioned above. This large marina has a well known and popular restaurant by that name on the premises. It is upstairs and has a distinctive cedar roof. There is a light fare restaurant downstairs. As you might surmise, for many years in colonial times, a granary stood on this site. The marina has over 150 slips (the largest at 60 feet) with free dock space reserved for diners while eating. There is telephone hookup available on the docks, which can take vessels of over 100 feet alongside face docks. Dock electricity is available for up to 100 amps, 240 volts, in both single and three phase configuration. Visa, MC, and Discover are honored. Moorings are available. There is no fuel or repair here. These services are available at Georgetown Yacht Basin (GYB), the parent facility, across the river. There is a free launch service by the Granary and GYB for all points in the area. There is a Patagonia clothing store at the docks.

East of the Granary, still to the left, (on the north shore) is one of the prettiest marinas I have seen in the Bay. Sailing Associates (16), as the name implies, has many sailboats at its docks which run out perpendicular to the shore. A sign identifies the marina. This is a full-service marina with 80 slips up to 60 feet with electricity up to twin 30 amps. The shower and

bathrooms are air conditioned. There is a swimming pool nearly hidden by the carefully tended garden surrounding it. There are also moorings, a brokerage business, and they are dealers for Westerbeke, Volvo, Perkins, Yanmar, and Universal. Their complete yard work capabilities include rigging and swaging, furling systems, outboard motor service, refrigeration and electrical repairs, and haulouts up to 60 feet. They have been in business since 1964. You would hardly know that Sailing Associates is there, looking in from the river. Its docks appear as any other docks, but they lead back to a wooded shore. At first, some people think there is nothing back there behind the piers. As you walk down the dock toward shore, you pass first through marsh grasses with cattail, then trees, until suddenly appears a beautiful yard with tall trees, wood chip paths, picnic tables, and a beautiful old house. The house turns out to be the office of the marina, with the tastefully blended smaller houses serving as the shower area and work shops. Behind all this is a quiet storage and work area, where quality rules.

Across the river on the southern shore is one of the Bay's largest, finest, and most prestigious marinas. Georgetown Yacht Basin (10) has been in business for over 43 years and has a reputation of unsurpassed quality. The fuel dock has a "Facet" fuel filter system with filters over 6 feet tall for gas and diesel, reportedly making the fuel close to airport pure; yet the fuel price is very competitive. Visa, MC and Discover are accepted. GYB's docks can accommodate boats up to 200 feet long and depth of 15 feet. There is cable and telephone hookup available at some piers. Electricity is available up to 208/240 volts at 100 amps in both single and three-phase configuration. There are 186 open slips and 96 covered, propane and CNG, a pumpout, a pool, laundry, transportation (local and to the airports), bike loans, launch to other harbor areas, extremely well-stocked marine store with a full range of goods from nuts and bolts and serious parts to fine boating clothing, new air conditioned shower facilities, moorings, and a bar. Georgetown Yacht Basin's dock master, Dave Wright, has been there for around 15 years, and its manager, Phil Parrish, has been with the facility for around 30 years. Many of its skilled employees are veterans of over 15 years. GYB contains about as complete a repair facility as you will ever hope to find. It has 3 lifts, the largest being 110 tons with ability to haul boats up to 125 feet. This facility is capable of doing well any kind of work needed for sail or motor, large or small. It also has a towing and salvage service and propeller reconditioning. It carries most popular lines of equipment and engine parts and services, and they are dealers for Yanmar, MerCruiser, Caterpillar, Perkins, Volvo Penta, Onan, Cruisair, OMC, Westerbeke, Pathfinder, and Detroit Diesel and others. They have Awlgrip capabilities. The Kitty Knight House is just up the hill, and the Harbor View snack restaurant for lunch and drinks is just above the pool. Each year they have an old-fashioned pig roast as an expression of appreciation to their customers and friends. All in the related marinas that night are among the invited guests. Owner Ford Hall stands for hours at the end of the groaning tables, personally serving his guests in the finest of local traditions.

Champagne Charters (31) in Georgetown will charter a large motor yacht by the hour or longer. Their number is (410) 648-5411.

Launching Ramps at Georgetown

In addition to the commercial ramp at Duffy Creek Marina,

there are hard-surfaced public ramps on the north side of the river at Schoolhouse Road (18) in Fredericktown; Foxhole Road (19) on the south bank up beyond Jacobs Creek [permit required, phone (410) 778-1948] and Gregg Neck Public Landing (20) on the south bank just before Gregg Neck Boatyard.

Georgetown Ashore

There are only a few shops outside of the marinas. These include Georgetown Antiques (28) just on the south side of the bridge, and Glassics Etc. Arts and Crafts (28) a very short distance farther south. Sassafras Studio (29), gifts, art, and antiques is open part time and is two doors east of the Granary. There are several other shops apparently in homes, but I never could find anyone there. The bridge is easily crossed on foot, with a wide walk on its western side.

Galena

The closest grocery store is Otwell's Market (23) in Galena (21), around 1½ miles from the bridge, on the south shore. This small market has good grocery shopping and includes fresh meat, seafoods, and cheeses. There is a library and town hall (24) across from the grocery store and on down the street. If you turn right at the crossroads here, you will soon pass Billy's Seafood Restaurant (25) to your left and a package store (25). Galena also has other shops, a few restaurants, and a video rental. This could be a hot walk along the highway, but Georgetown Yacht Basin will lend bikes with side bags for the trip and the road has very wide paved shoulders. Walking in, you will be happy to pass Twinney's Ice Cream shop and restaurant (26) to your left near the cemetery and church (opposite side of the road).

North of the Bridge

If you go north at the bridge, you will find Cecilton (27) after around 2½ miles. I mention this because many around the area had the idea that it was much closer, when I asked its distance. This is hardly within walking distance for most folks.

The post office (22) is on the north side, up the hill on the road that crosses the bridge. It will be on your right as you walk away from the bridge. Walking along the street behind the waterfront on that side of the river, you will find a few antique shops within a block from the water. Just behind Sailing Associates is the home of a local waterman who fishes the river daily and sells fresh fish, eggs, and a few other such items.

Upriver

Just upriver of the bridge on the south side of the river lies the *Nellie Crockett* (30), a vintage deadrise buy boat. She is being lovingly restored by Ted Parrish, who lives with his wife in the old bridge house at the foot of the bridge. Ted has his master's license and runs huge commercial ships, but he loves the Bay and its boats. He can tell you things you would never know about these boats if he has the time, which is seldom, and it is a treat to see his efforts. Ted's father, Phil, manages the GYB, and if you can find him during one of the few moments when he is not caring for the facility's customers, you will find another very well-informed source of information about the area.

The bridge seems to end the hustle and bustle of this harbor, but the deep water of the river continues above the bridge for well over a mile, with shoal draft exploring for some distance on. There are wooded hills and creeks, with beautiful anchorages in many places, wherever your draft allows. There is more civilization along the shores, but it is still beautiful.

At Great Point, just at the river's corner with Swantown Creek, Gregg Neck Boatyard (17) offers transient slips when available, permanent dockage and moorings, brokerage, a 50-ton lift with full repair service or do-it-yourself, gas, diesel, pumpout, and a well-stocked marine store with many nuts and bolt-type marine hardware items that are often hard to find, snacks and drinks, and block and cube ice. Visa and MC are honored. There are 80 slips, 10 covered, the largest at 60 feet. Electricity up to 50 amps is available. The chart here shows four privately maintained buoys (17A) at the entrance to the creek. These were not there last year, and I understand that they will not be replaced. There are many moored boats in the vicinity.

Georgetown Yacht Basin, Sassafras River

HISTORY

It is reported that Captain John Smith first referred to this river as the "Tockwogh River" because of an Indian settlement that he found here. Apparently this word came from the name of a water weed called "Tuckahoe" which had a bulbous root of food value. According to Smith's journal, these Indians gave him a memorable feast when he first met them. The Calvert settlers who later spread into this area gave the river its present name.

The Sassafras has enjoyed a peaceful and serene history, with the exception of Rear Admiral Cockburn's raid in the War of 1812. With numerous sailors, 150 marines, and five cannon, he rowed up the river in small boats on May 5, 1813, two days after he had burned Havre de Grace. This is described in more detail in the section on Georgetown earlier in this chapter. Since then, much of the river banks have been part of large estates, thus slowing the building of houses and other development along the shore, preserving trees and natural surroundings.

Kitty Knight House, Georgetown Yacht Basin, Sassafras River

72

CHAPTER 7

STILL POND CREEK TO ROCK HALL, EASTERN SHORE

STILL POND CREEK AND CHURN CREEK

This is a beautiful and popular rural anchorage on the Eastern Shore in the northern Bay.

History

Most today think of the name of this beautiful area to be suggestive of the placid waters in the creek. Actually, the area was originally called "Steele's Pone." Steele was an early settler who owned land around the area. "Pone," in Elizabethan English, meant "favorite." This would indeed be the favorite of anyone who lived here. There is a village of that name, but boats visiting the anchorage do so to be away from civilization, surrounded by woods and pastoral scenery. The village area, is some distance away from the shore, not within walking distance. In 1908, the first women in Maryland to vote did so in Still Pond village.

Approach

Refer to Chart #12274-J—"Still Pond Approach and Anchorage." Pg. 75

Still Pond Creek (36) lies inside of the large "Still Pond" basin (37), which many think of as "the anchorage" when they come to the area, although the creek offers much better protection. The basin lies between Worton (30) and Howell Points (32). On a hazy day it can be difficult distinguishing the basin and its hidden creek from the rest of the shoreline when sailing up or down the Bay. Worton Point has a 99-foot light tower. North of it and inland are two silos behind Plum Point (39). Howell Point, farther north, has a tower (33) on its hill and a 28-foot flashing 4 second red marker on the point. Moving south from Howell Point, you will see the docks of a sailing camp (34) between that point and Meeks Point (41), and then the 100-foot tower (42) on Meeks Point.

A course of 212°M will take you from the Fl G "41"and the Fl R "42" (35) out in the big ship channel of the Bay into the center area of Still Pond Basin, passing somewhat close to the shallow water off Meeks Point. A course of 225°M will take you more to the middle area of the outside of the basin, and not so close to the point, but still in far enough so that you should be able to make out the lay of the land. On a misty day, the first course may make it easier to pick up the Still Pond Creek entrance buoy (43). If using 212°M, watch your depth finder and round out to the southwest direction if it begins to get too shallow for you. If approaching from the south, a course of 128°M will take you from Fl G "39" and Fl R "40" (44) out in the big ship channel of the Bay to the area of the first Still Pond Creek entrance marker, Fl R "2," up in the basin. In most weather, proceed into the Bay and you should not have any problem finding that marker. You only need to find this creek entrance marker if you wish to go into the creek. You can use Fl R "2" as a point of reference to enable you to anchor away from routes into the creek.

Coming into Still Pond Basin, tall cliffs greet you on the northern banks, with a small beach about half way in. The southern bank is also high, but with gentler slope, with woods, meadow, and sandy shore. Looking straight into the head of the basin you will see a beach which is actually part of a sandy spit (45) that can be mostly covered at high tide. Farther into the creek is a building, part of the Coast Guard station (46). In front of the spit and building will be the outside red marker for the creek, Fl R "2."

Anchorage

Many people prefer to anchor in this outside basin. In settled weather, this is a great place to be, with plenty of room and open space, nice breezes, and a great feeling of privacy except on the weekends. You can anchor out in the main part of the basin around the shores, or up in the little cove at the southern end between Kinnaird Point (47) and Rocky Point (48) at the entrance to Churn Creek (58). Here there will be a dock (49) coming out from the eastern shore, and high shore close in with trees. The chart shows submerged piles (50) out in the middle of this cove. I cannot find them. I have seen many boats anchoring in here but proceed with caution. It would not be wise to anchor in the approach to the channel into the creek. Be sure that you are always well lit at night.

Don't stay outside if there is any hint of a westerly, particularly a northwesterly. As is obvious from looking at the chart, this is no place to be then. This includes threat of the typical summer thunderstorm. These can blow viciously from the west or northwest for their duration, making the Still Pond Basin a very unsafe place to be. It is possible to get some shelter from the west by tucking up into the basin between Rocky Point (48) (there are rocks there) and Kinnaird Point. However, you never know whether one of these blows is going to be exactly from the west or northwest, and it certainly isn't worth taking the chance. In a southwesterly there is even better protection, but usually a southwesterly precedes a clocking to the west and northwest. The place to go is inside beautiful Still Pond Creek, if your draft allows.

The entrance to the creek looks chancy at first glance, and, indeed it is a place where you have to be right where you are supposed to be. However, it is very well marked. The Coast Guard Station is just inside behind the spit on the northern bank, and there is plenty of water to that point. Beyond here is where the entrance gets shallower, but this carefully is marked by private aids.

Channel Into Still Pond Creek

Now refer to Chart #12274-K—"Still Pond Creek and Churn Creek." Pg. 76

To make the entrance, first pick up Fl R "2" (43). The GPS derived approximate position is 39°20.20'N by 76°08.20'W. There can be some difficulty seeing the mark from far out on a misty day, but if you just came into the basin, head for the

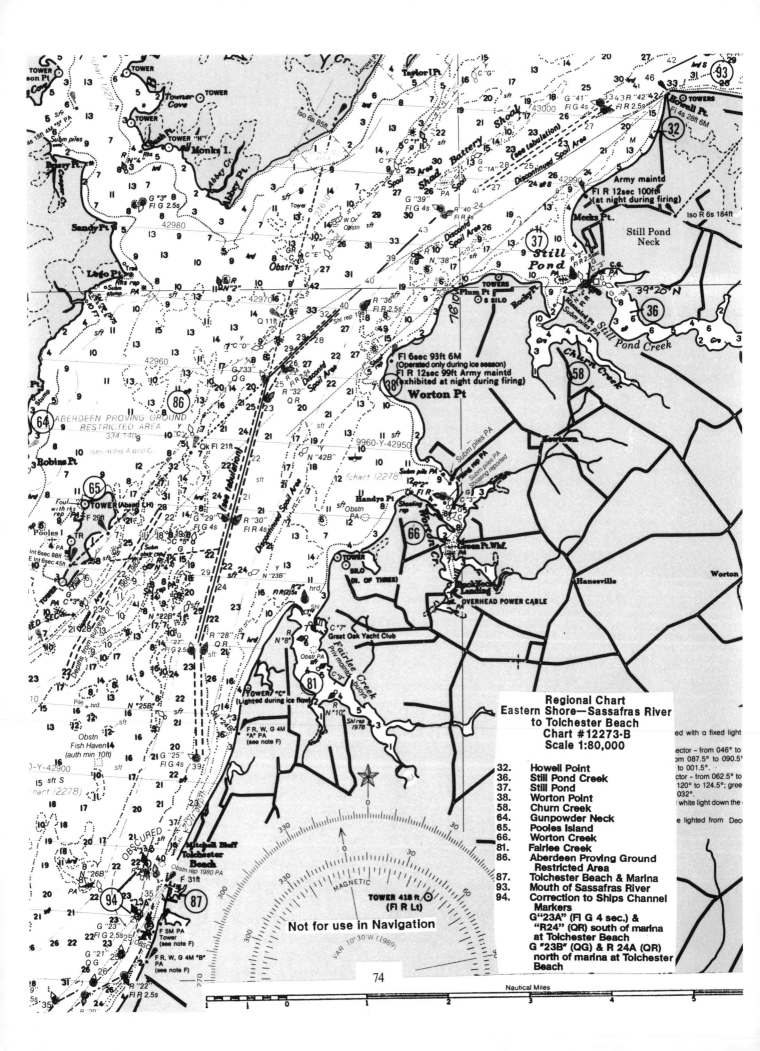

Regional Chart
Eastern Shore—Sassafras River
to Tolchester Beach
Chart #12273-B
Scale 1:80,000

32.	**Howell Point**
36.	**Still Pond Creek**
37.	**Still Pond**
38.	**Worton Point**
58.	**Churn Creek**
64.	**Gunpowder Neck**
65.	**Pooles Island**
66.	**Worton Creek**
81.	**Fairlee Creek**
86.	**Aberdeen Proving Ground Restricted Area**
87.	**Tolchester Beach & Marina**
93.	**Mouth of Sassafras River**
94.	**Correction to Ships Channel Markers**
	G"23A" (Fl G 4 sec.) & "R24" (QR) south of marina at Tolchester Beach
	G "23B" (QG) & R 24A (QR) north of marina at Tolchester Beach

Not for use in Navigation

74

Nautical Miles

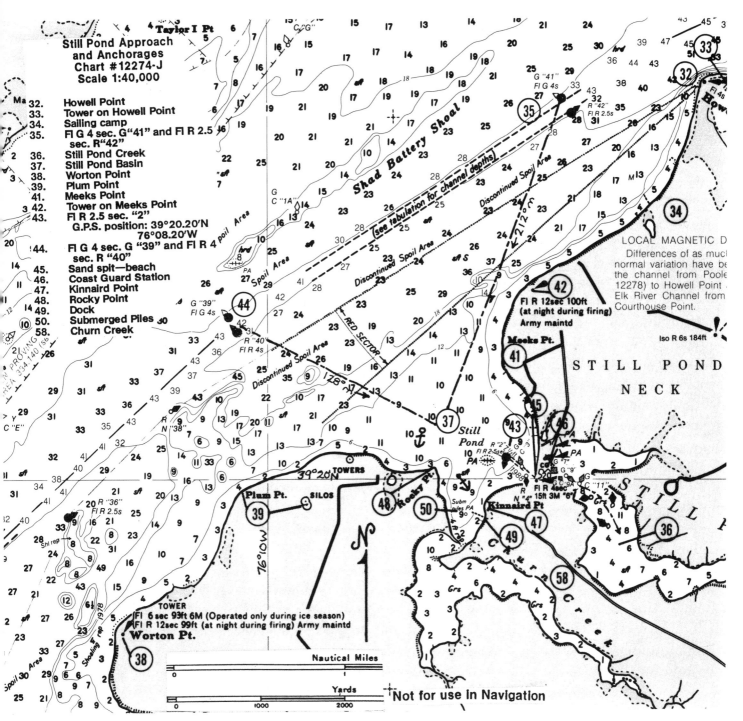

Still Pond Approach
and Anchorages
Chart #12274-J
Scale 1:40,000

32. Howell Point
33. Tower on Howell Point
34. Sailing camp
35. Fl G 4 sec. G"41" and Fl R 2.5 sec. R"42"
36. Still Pond Creek
37. Still Pond Basin
38. Worton Point
39. Plum Point
41. Meeks Point
42. Tower on Meeks Point
43. Fl R 2.5 sec. "2"
     G.P.S. position: 39°20.20'N
                          76°08.20'W
44. Fl G 4 sec. G "39" and Fl R 4 sec. R "40"
45. Sand spit—beach
46. Coast Guard Station
47. Kinnaird Point
48. Rocky Point
49. Dock
50. Submerged Piles
58. Churn Creek

Nautical Miles

Yards

Not for use in Navigation

Coast Guard building and its radio tower behind the sand spit. Depending on the tide, this spit will appear as beach in the middle. You will eventually see the marker. Refer also to the instructions for coming in at the beginning of this chapter. Normally, there should be no problem in sighting this marker. The wreck (40) will be avoided, if there is still any part of it there, by coming straight into the channel. I saw no part of any wreck.

Following the markers in takes you close to the spit, to your left (north). The water is deep here, and the current can be very swift because of the amount of water emptying or filling through such a narrow cut. As soon as you pass through the cut, you will see the Coast Guard station, with its docks and brick buildings, on your left (north), just behind G "7" (51). A sign on the spit announces its presence and warns, "No Wake." Continuing on past the station, the channel goes close to the southern shore. Follow the buoys closely. Looking ahead and to the east behind Fl R "6" (52), you will see impressive high cliffs up in the creek. Just beyond Fl R "6," a private bulkhead with gazebo and picnic area appear on the bank to the right. Nice homes, backing up into the woods, are on the banks to your right (south) as you continue on this narrow entrance channel.

Looking at the markers ahead, you may think that some have come adrift! G "9" (53) is very close to the right (southern) bank. So is the narrow channel, G "9A" (54) seems even closer to that wooded bank. Between these two markers, I found only 5 feet at low water. This was confirmed by local people. Past this hump, the water deepens to between 7 and 8 feet, and then gets deeper, as the chart shows, as the creek widens out. Ahead the creek opens into a beautiful scene with meadow, woods, and hills. It is yet another broad area to an-

75

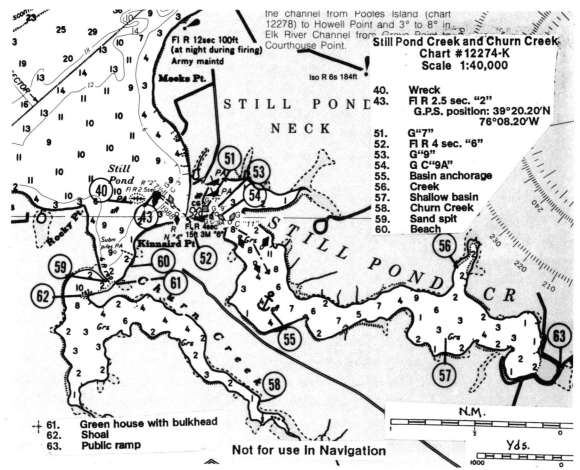

Not for use in Navigation

Still Pond Creek and Churn Creek
Chart #12274-K
Scale 1:40,000

40.	Wreck
43.	Fl R 2.5 sec. "2"
	G.P.S. position: 39°20.20'N 76°08.20'W
51.	G"7"
52.	Fl R 4 sec. "6"
53.	G"9"
54.	G C"9A"
55.	Basin anchorage
56.	Creek
57.	Shallow basin
58.	Churn Creek
59.	Sand spit
60.	Beach
61.	Green house with bulkhead
62.	Shoal
63.	Public ramp

chor where you find your favorite spot, as long as the water is deep enough for your boat.

I felt that the nicer area to anchor would be in the outer reaches of the creek, for example, in the basin (55) to your right (southern side). There you can still see a little of the Coast Guard Station, but it is less crowded ashore than farther in. Moving on into the creek, you will see more homes set back in the woods, and docks on the southern bank. Many will have boats moored off. As you explore farther back, you get to the vicinity of the creek to your left (56) (northern bank) and to the basin (57) across on the southern bank. To many, the area would seem less attractive as an anchorage because of the number of houses and docks on the shore, particularly the northern shore. There is a dirt public ramp (63) at the very head of Still Pond Creek. For information on the fee requirement, call (410) 778-1948 Kent County Department of Parks and Recreation.

Churn Creek

Churn Creek (58) is the very pretty creek which opens from the southeastern basin in Still Pond. It is separated from the open waters by a sand spit (59) around which a very narrow channel runs with a very strong current at normal flow. The entrance, indeed the creek itself, is very shallow and I would not want to take anything other than a dinghy inside, although the scenery and the adventure certainly make this a worthwhile small boat trip.

I found the best water by hugging the shore to my left (southeastern side) going in. The chart implies that there is deeper water on the northwestern side, but I found the deeper water to be on the southeastern side, where you will see a little beach (60). This entire approach area is very shallow. When I got to the spit, I kept to the middle. Between the spit and the

eastern bank I found 4 feet and better, with yet deeper water just inside. There is a green house with a bulkhead (61) right across from the spit, just south of the little spot of marsh.

As I left the bulkhead, I proceeded 50 to 75 feet, still favoring the left (southeastern side) before I started heading out to a shoal (62) that comes off the point ahead. I tried heading to my right (west-northwest) as soon as I got in, but this soon had my outboard bumping. The deeper water off the shoal is not as deep and wide as the chart implies, and doesn't last long. Soon it becomes very shallow again.

WORTON CREEK
Refer to Regional Chart #12273-B—"Eastern Shore Sassafras River to Tolchester Beach." PG. 74

This well-protected and pretty creek provides a limited but good anchorage with some friendly and helpful marinas ashore. It is in a very rural area of the Eastern Shore with woods and marsh surrounding. There is little to do ashore outside of the marinas and a restaurant. The marinas can take care of many needs and can order parts not available.

Across the Bay from Gunpowder Neck (64) and the northern tip of the Poole's Island (65), Worton Creek (66) opens with a wide mouth from a wide bay.

Refer also to Chart #12278-A—"Worton and Fairlee Creeks."

Heading easterly from about two-thirds of the way up between R "30" (67) and R "32" of the big ship channel in the bay, the entrance to Worton Creek normally becomes clear except in very poor visibility. Coming in north of Y N "42B" (69) helps to avoid the shallower water on the southern side

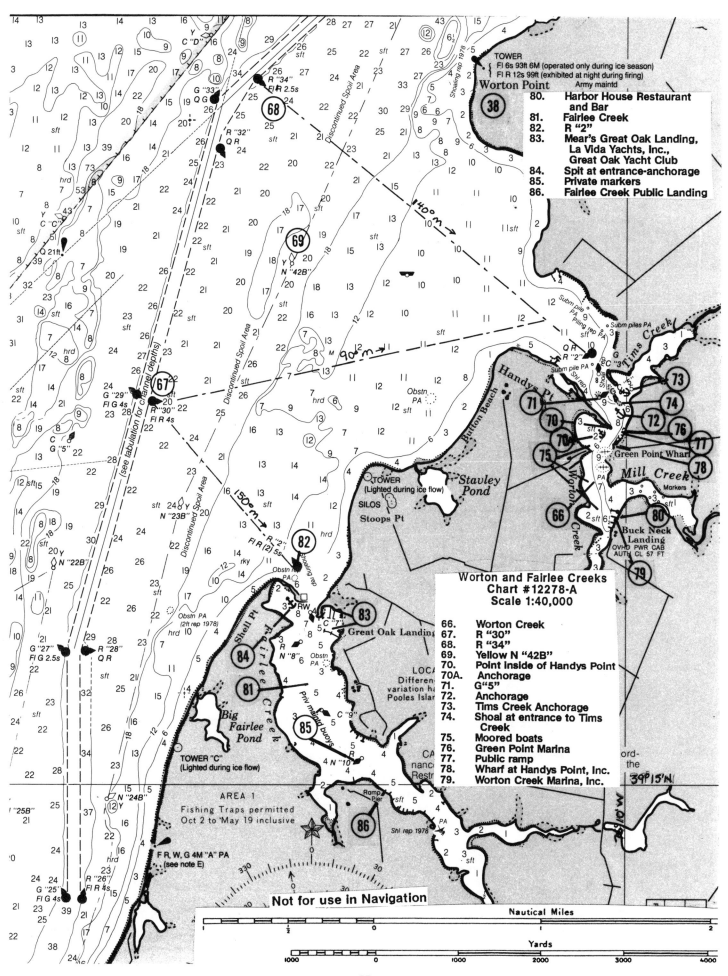

80. Harbor House Restaurant and Bar
81. Fairlee Creek
82. R "2"
83. Mear's Great Oak Landing, La Vida Yachts, Inc., Great Oak Yacht Club
84. Spit at entrance-anchorage
85. Private markers
86. Fairlee Creek Public Landing

Worton Point

TOWER
Fl 6s 93ft 6M (operated only during ice season)
Fl R 12s 99ft (exhibited at night during firing)
Army maintd

Worton and Fairlee Creeks
Chart #12278-A
Scale 1:40,000

66. Worton Creek
67. R "30"
68. R "34"
69. Yellow N "42B"
70. Point inside of Handys Point
70A. Anchorage
71. G "5"
72. Anchorage
73. Tims Creek Anchorage
74. Shoal at entrance to Tims Creek
75. Moored boats
76. Green Point Marina
77. Public ramp
78. Wharf at Handys Point, Inc.
79. Worton Creek Marina, Inc.

Great Oak Landing

TOWER "C"
(Lighted during ice flow)

Big Fairlee Pond

AREA 1
Fishing Traps permitted
Oct 2 to May 19 inclusive

F R, W, G 4M "A" PA
(see note E)

Not for use in Navigation

Nautical Miles

Yards

77

of the entrance bay. If you come in from R "34" (68), a course of 140°M should take you into the area where you will be able to easily see the entrance buoys. If you come in from R "30" (67), a course of 90°M should do the same.

Carefully follow the creek markers coming in. Many boats use the creek daily. The deep water is there, but like so many creeks, you do have to be where it is. The point to your right (70) on the western side, as you pass G "5" (71) has deep water up to the beach. Many like to swim off this point. The creek to your left on the eastern side (72) and off Tims Creek (73) provides a nice little anchorage basin for boats of shallow draft. Tims Creek, with its sandy bottom and wooded shores, is a nice place for a shallow draft vessel of no more than 3½ feet to enter and anchor, carefully feeling the way in. Note the shoal (74) coming out from the creek, which will be to your left or the northwest as you go into this little creek.

Many boats are moored (75) in Worton Creek in conjunction with the marinas. These don't leave as much room for anchoring as you might expect from looking at the chart because of the narrow area of deep water. Plenty of boats do anchor wherever they find room and enough depth, and it is nice. If there is enough depth and you're not obstructing access to a marina or the channel, it is a good place to "set her down." Slips and extra moorings are available from the marinas. This area is a few miles drive from Chestertown, MD. *Editor's note: I anchored with 4 feet draft behind the spit farther northwest than the anchor on the chart and walked across for great swimming on the outside. Feel your way in carefully. It's a great anchorage.*

The first marina to your left (on the eastern bank) coming in is **Green Point Marina (76).** They take up to 55-foot boats at the 57 slips and there are also moorings. Depths are 10 feet at their deepest docks. There is 30 amp electricity. This is a full service yard with hull and engine repair and a 15-ton lift. There is a small ship store. The marina sells gas and diesel, ice, and has a pumpout. Visa, MC and Discover are accepted. They don't sell tackle but do sell worms. They are dealers for Mercury Outboards, MerCruiser, Volvo Penta, and OMC stern drive. Adjacent south is a public concrete launching ramp (77). Call Kent County Parks and Recreation at (410) 778-1948 for fee information.

Next up the creek to the left (eastern bank) is the **Wharf at Handys Point, Inc. (78).** This is a facility with nice new docks with phone jacks, showers, a launch service, laundry, Texaco Starport gas and diesel with a pumpout. There are 55 slips, and 10 feet at their deepest docks, moorings, a 35-ton travelift, and general mechanical services. Transients up to 80 feet are welcome, with 50 amp electric available. This marina is well protected and in a pretty setting. Texaco, Visa, MC, and Amex are accepted.

The last facility in is **Worton Creek Marina, Inc. (79).** It is also on the east bank and farther up the creek with 6 feet controlling depth. They handle transients up to 80 feet with 50 amp service. The longest slip is 60 feet. There are 56 open and 24 closed slips, many moorings, gas and diesel fuel, pumpout, block and cube ice, and laundry. They accept most major credit cards. There is a 25-ton lift and 30-ton railway, general mechanics for hull and machinery repair, with subs available. They have a full Imron shop, paint shop, heated wet shed, and specialize in wood boat repair and painting. The ships store sells chart books, some foods and frozen meats and other groceries, marine hardware, tackle, and bait. They are dealers for Crusaders, Onan, and Westerbeke. An apartment is available for those who want to stay ashore.

On the hill overlooking the marina and creek is the Harbor House Restaurant and Bar (80), very popular locally. They feature Eastern Shore cuisine and accept MC and Discover. They are open from May 1 to October 31, serve dinner only, and are closed on Tuesday.

FAIRLEE CREEK
Refer to Chart #12278-A—"Worton and Fairlee Creeks."
PG. 77

This broad shallow creek has a very narrow entrance and is quite protected from the Bay, but the fetch inside could be more than what some people would find comfortable while anchoring. There is a large first class resort area and marina just inside the entrance and a public landing farther up.

Entering Fairlee Creek (81) will make you a true believer in following the buoys. The channel goes very close to the shore and until you are right on the opening, you may not believe it

View from "The Wharf" Marina towards the mouth of Worton Creek and Handys Point

is there! Look at the chart, and follow the markers precisely. There can be a fair amount of current in the cut. Don't allow yourself to be pushed aside. On holidays and weekends, the cut can be very busy, so proceed slowly. A heading of 150°M will take you from R "30" (67) in the big ship channel out in the Bay into the entrance area of Fairlee Creek where you should be able to easily see the first entrance buoy R"2" (82). From here follow the markers in.

You will immediately see **Mear's Great Oak Landing (83)**, a huge resort area, to your left (on the northern bank) when you enter. Controlling depth to the marina (not farther up the creek) is 8 feet. They can handle boats up to 90 feet with up to 50 amp electricity at their 347 slips. They sell gas, diesel, and have a pumpout. MC, Amex, and Visa are accepted. This huge resort has all that you would expect from such an area, including restaurant, live entertainment, tennis, golf, miniature golf, beach, lodging, pool, and more. There is also a 50-ton open end lift with repairs on the premises. LaVida Yachts, Inc. (83) makes its home here, with new sales, brokerage, a sailing school, and chartering. The ship's store is very well stocked, including package goods. The **Great Oak Yacht Club (83)** bases here also.

It is possible to anchor in Fairlee Creek, according to draft. Many like to anchor behind the protective entrance spit (84) where there is a beach, but the area can be very busy and the channel is close. There are private markers (85) as the chart shows, indicating the deeper waters. Boats drawing over 4 feet would probably not wish to go beyond the marina. Most who enter the creek from the Bay in cruising boats tend to go to the marina resort to enjoy all the things offered there. The areas of the creek with deep enough water for anchoring (except for boats of very shallow draft) are too open for the tastes of many anchorers.

The **Fairlee Creek Public Landing (86)** is farther up the creek where noted on the chart. There is a dock and concrete ramp.

TOLCHESTER BEACH
Refer to Chart #12278-B—"Tolchester Beach and Tolchester Marina."

This is a dredged basin in the Eastern Shore occupied by a very large, complete, marina with full service repair and maintenance, but not an anchorage area.

Tolchester Marina (87), is in a privately dredged basin for the marina and large repair facility. The docks and marina facility fill the basin. The area is rural, and there is little to do ashore. However, this is an important marina of refuge on the stretch between Fairlee Creek and Swan Point, and a place to go to get almost anything fixed or work done to the boat.

The big ship channel passes very close to the shore here. The jettied entrance to the basin opens east of that channel between buoys R "24" (88) and R "24 A" (88A). Enter the marked jettys (89) and tie at the fuel dock (90) for service unless you have other instructions. Depth at the entrance is around 6½ feet. Check on the VHF before entering if your draft is near that.

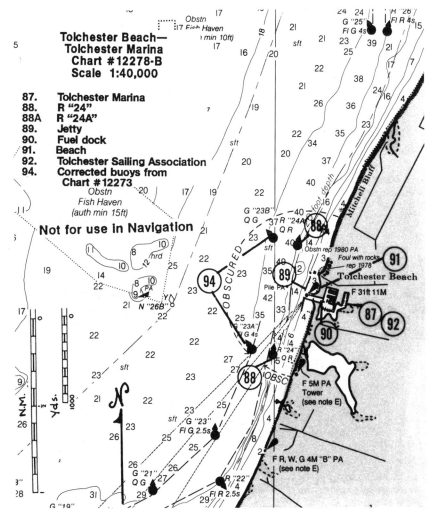

Tolchester Beach—
Tolchester Marina
Chart #12278-B
Scale 1:40,000

87. Tolchester Marina
88. R "24"
88A R "24A"
89. Jetty
90. Fuel dock
91. Beach
92. Tolchester Sailing Association
94. Corrected buoys from Chart #12273

Not for use in Navigation

Tolchester Marina can take 90 feet maximum LOA at the docks. There are 177 open slips and 86 covered slips. Electrical service ranges up to 220 volts at 50 amps. There is a nice beach (91) by the jetty, tennis court, and park-like hill overlooking the Bay. The Marina sells gas and diesel, block and cube ice, and has a laundromat and a pumpout. It accepts Visa and MC. There is a 50-ton lift capable of hauling up to 73 feet LOA, 30-ton crane, and a huge two-story parts department. They sell charts, fishing gear and bait, and light groceries. On the premises are a canvas shop, fiberglass shop, machine shop with varied welding, brokerage, and well known Bramble Engine Power Company that builds, refits, and re-builds engines. They are dealers for Detroit Diesel, Cummins, Caterpillar, Westerbeke, Perkins, Ford Diesel, Marine Power, Mann & Iveco, John Deere, Onan, Kohler, Universal, Volvo Penta, Northern Lights, Crusader, and they build boats to order from hulls. They also operate a towing service. The facility also specializes in rebuilding boats. There is a snack bar, and even a tennis court and private beach on the Bay. This is also the home of the Tolchester Sailing Association (92).

Tolchester Beach was a very popular resort beach in the earlier 1900s. There was the beach, a large hotel, an amusement area, and other resort facilities. Passenger steamships made regular runs from Baltimore and other ports. Three of these ships were named *"Tolchester."* One of these, built in 1878 as the *St. Johns*, was later named the *Tolchester* when she began service in 1933 carrying Baltimoreans across the Bay to the resort. Her career ultimately evolved into the life of a barge, carrying logs for the Chesapeake Corporation of West Point, Virginia. For many years you could see her sleek hull with welded over portlights, cutting through the waters of the Bay with logs piled where once stood her beautiful superstructure. Today, you can re-visit the Tolchester Resort Bandstand at the Chesapeake Bay Museum in St. Michaels. It was moved there as a reminder of that part of the Bay's history.

SWAN CREEK
Refer to Chart #12278-D— "Swan Creek, Rock Hall Approach."

Swan Creek provides an anchorage for those wishing to visit the town of Rock Hall (29) without tying up, it has several marinas, and it is a nice place to go as a destination anchorage. Although the creek is north of Rock Hall on the Eastern Shore, because of the bar, it is necessary to approach the town in order to approach the creek. Many people think of the creek when they think of the town.

Swan Creek has always looked forbidding to me on the chart with its charted notation of a 3½-foot shoal (31) in the approach and wrecks inside. But many boats in the northern Bay consider it to be an ideal anchorage, and there are some very well run and successful marinas inside. In fact, the shoal is not in the channel as is reported and the wrecks inside have been removed or marked. This is a great place to go, even with 6 feet of draft. I did find a shallow area close to the eastern shore near some docks (33), just before you get to the point (34), in the approximate location of the noted shoal. This is misleading, because as they are passing through a channel with docks on one side, people think that the deeper water will be near the docks. Stay off the docks on the eastern shore just before you get to the point. I suspect that soon, this hump will either be removed or marked. We saw no wrecks in the marked navigable area of the creek. The management of Haven Harbour Marina (35) way inside the Swan Creek, told me

that they had been careful to remove any wrecks that could be an obstruction, and that they had sounded and surveyed and dredged and cleared the bottom to assure access to their area of at least 6 feet at MLW. There are now private markers leading into Haven Harbour Marina. Call them if you have any questions or feel doubtful.

Anchor in Swan Creek wherever it strikes your fancy. Be careful to stay out of the channels and don't block any docks. I prefer the area above G "9" (36) as being more out of the way and protected. I would not anchor before this because of traffic. The area is very pretty, with wild marsh to your west, beautiful stream, marsh and woods to your north, and the attractive marinas to the south and southeast. It is somewhat unique in that you can feel as though you are in an almost secluded anchorage, yet there are so many marinas and other businesses nearby. On good weeekends, this is often a very crowded anchorage. There is all-around protection from weather, despite the appearance of openess to the south. Although the marinas on this creek are a bit far for many people to walk into Rock Hall, there is much to be had at the marinas themselves. This is the type of community with the type of people and businesses where transportation should not be a serious problem if you have a need. As long as it is not rough, you could always go around into Rock Hall Harbor by dinghy, if yours is fast enough to suit your schedule. On the eastern bank of the channel into the creek, you will see a beach, called Town Beach (38). This is 1¼ mile to the main section of the town.

As you head into Swan Creek, the first marina that you will pass on your right (east) (at R "6") will be **Gratitude Marina** (38) with 90 slips taking boats up to 45 feet. It is bulkheaded from the open waters of the Bay and there is 6 feet maximum depth at the docks. They do marine and engine repair and have a 45-foot 12-ton closed end lift and a 35-ton open end lift. Both gas and diesel are sold on the outside dock which also has a pumpout station. There is a swimming pool. Next door, to the south, is the Strawberry Factory Bed and Breakfast (39). This is a very old building that used to be a strawberry factory, but has been remodeled into a nice bed and breakfast right on the water.

Next in will be **Gratitude Yachting Center** (40) on the shore to your right (east) before you round the point. Here there are 38 slips with electricity up to 30 amps, heads, showers, and ice in this very popular, successful operation. Sailboats are chartered here as well as sold, and there is the Maryland School of Sailing and Seamanship. Gratitude has been the largest dealer of Ireland Packet Sailing Yachts for years, and now also sells nauticals and Kiries.

Nestled around the point is **Swan Creek Marina** (41) with numerous boats moored off its docks. There are 31 moorings, 8 feet at the docks, 110 slips with 30 to 50 amp electricity, block and cube ice. They have two yards in the cove east of the point, and offer full services marina and yard services, with 8 acres of dry storage, and a ship yard facility in one of the yards. This facility has been owned by the Mayne family for over 41 years. They offer full yard work, rigging work, which includes rigging surveys and repairs, including rod rigging. They also do refrigeration and air conditioning work, regular carpentry and woodworking, regular maintenance, welding (including stainless steel), and fiberglass repair and painting by the Lenox Company. They have a 40-ton lift and a spar shed. They will assist with car or bike transportation if available.

Around the next point is **Osprey Point Marina** (42), set well into the protected bay of Swan Creek that is called "The Ha-

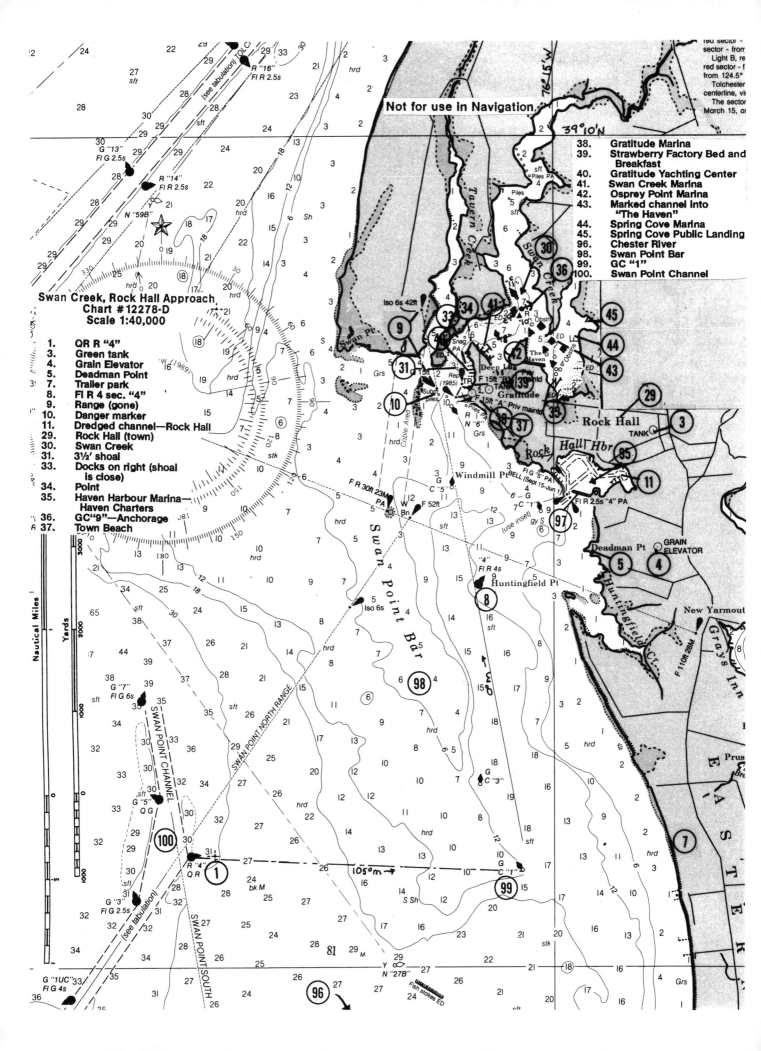

Not for use in Navigation

Swan Creek, Rock Hall Approach
Chart #12278-D
Scale 1:40,000

1. QR R "4"
3. Green tank
4. Grain Elevator
5. Deadman Point
7. Trailer park
8. Fl R 4 sec. "4"
9. Range (gone)
10. Danger marker
11. Dredged channel—Rock Hall
29. Rock Hall (town)
30. Swan Creek
31. 3½' shoal
33. Docks on right (shoal is close)
34. Point
35. Haven Harbour Marina— Haven Charters
36. GC"9"—Anchorage
37. Town Beach

38. Gratitude Marina
39. Strawberry Factory Bed and Breakfast
40. Gratitude Yachting Center
41. Swan Creek Marina
42. Osprey Point Marina
43. Marked channel into "The Haven"
44. Spring Cove Marina
45. Spring Cove Public Landing
96. Chester River
98. Swan Point Bar
99. GC "1"
100. Swan Point Channel

ven" locally. It is designed to blend harmoniously with its 30 acres of woodland park-type surroundings. Osprey Point Marina is associated with Gratitude Marina in Rock Hall. Gratitude Marina handles yard work and fueling. Osprey Point is like a country manor, totally for pleasure and relaxation in peaceful beautiful surroundings. Osprey Point Marina can take 6½ feet and can accommodate boats up to 75 feet at their docks. Transient rates last year were $1.50 per foot per night plus electricity, higher than typical rates I observed elsewhere. There is a pumpout. They have bikes for marina users, there is a nice pool with bath houses, and a club house which contains laundry and other facilities, and an excellent restaurant. Major cards are taken.

Deeper into The Haven lies the very large, impressive and state-of-the-art **Haven Harbour Marina (35)**. There are 217 slips which take boats up to 60 feet, with electricity up to 50 amps, moorings, a welcoming station with a gas and diesel dock with pumpout, which they offer for free to permanent slip holders. Visa and MC are accepted. They report a minimum of 6 feet available to their docks. They survey and dredge to maintain this, and have a marked channel **(43)**. A very nice ships store includes the "ditty bag," a specialty gift and clothing shop, and a well stocked parts store upstairs. It is amazingly well-stocked with many items that you would not expect to find anywhere except in the large municipal warehouse areas. Propane is also available. This store also sells NOS charts, in addition to the books. There is a dinghy dock for those wishing to use the store. There are 24 heads and 16 showers in separate rooms. Light groceries are available, as is block and cube ice and a laundry area. This marina will assist you with transportation and has bikes to rent, as well as a battery operated jitney. The Haven Charters **(35)** charter company operates from here, with boats from 27 to 40 feet. A marina yacht club is on the premises. There is a bandstand in the front as you enter from the road, and a barbecue and covered picnic area, and two pools. There are other entertainment areas such as TV, VCR, and lending library in the marina clubhouse, and shuffleboard and croquet.

Haven Harbour also has a very large and fully staffed repair yard, including a machine shop, woodwork shop, paint shop, fiberglass repair, sail repair, electronics work, and towing service. The lift is 25 ton. They are dealers for Cruiseair, Crusader, MerCruiser, Onan, Volvo Penta, and Yanmar. There is also a large shed capable of taking the travel lift and its load for inside work. The washdown water from this marina goes into a three-chambered 1500-gallon cistern for environmental protection. They recycle their oil and use it to heat their buildings in the wintertime.

The last marina around the shoreline in The Haven is the beautiful **Spring Cove Marina (44)** with 150 slips, electricity up to 30 amps, head, showers, a pumpout, and swimming pool. This marina has such natural landscape that from the water you only see docks, as though there were only fields and woods ashore. From the land, the marina has a beautiful entrance through marsh and woods. As the marina area opens before you, it is as though you were entering the yard of a large estate. You have the feeling here of docking your boat at a huge but exclusive park with grass, picnic areas, groves of shade trees, and lots of places for kids to play or grownups to walk, run, or just enjoy the outdoors in the country.

Farther around the cove, the cement ramp of Spring Cove Public Landing **(45)**, with dock, invites trailer boats to the area. Call (410) 778-1948 Kent County Department for Parks and Recreation for fee information.

ROCK HALL

Rock Hall is a waterman's town, strategically located on the Eastern Shore. It has made a concentrated and very successful effort to become a boater's haven. It has first rate marinas, a beautiful protected anchorage in Swan Creek, nice things to do ashore, and good supply and repair facilities.

Editor's note: I like Rock Hall for its excellent marine facilities and waterfront restaurants, but I have been cruising Chesapeake Bay long enough to remember how it was 40 years ago when the emphasis was more on commercial fishing and less on pleasure boating. I liked this picturesque port better then, but the people are still industrious, colorful, and welcome visitors. Go see it even if you don't need any marine supplies or repairs.

History

Rock Hall was founded in 1707 as the settlements on the shore of Kent Island, to the south of the Chester River, began to expand. The area now known as the Eastern Neck, between the Bay and the north bank of the Chester River, was a logical choice for additional settlements with its harbors and high lands. Rock Hall soon became a center of fishing and shipping, being a terminal on what is said to be the oldest turnpike in North America.

During the American Revolution, the town was a key shipping port. One of Rock Hall's citizens, Captain Lambert Wickes, was a major naval hero of that war. In April 1776, he took command of the *Reprisal* and began a campaign resulting in the brilliant captures of many British vessels. In the first engagement of the war between American and British naval vessels, he defeated the sloop of war *Shark* off Martinique. The confidence placed in this naval hero was clearly shown when he was chosen to take Benjamin Franklin to France to begin his very important duties as ambassador to the country. Leaving France with a small group of three vessels, he captured 18 British ships in the waters off Ireland in just seven days. When the 74-gun *HMS Burford* took chase, he ordered his fleet to disburse and drew the *Burford* away, as he jettisoned his cannon and anything else that he could spare to gain speed. As the *Burford* still closed, he had some of his main beams sawn up and tossed, thus finally becoming light enough to pull away. After a return trip to France, he sailed for home and his ship was lost in a gale off Newfoundland, taking with her all hands except the cook.

In March 1791, George Washington traveled here to board a ship, with a party so large that the town with all of its cheering citizens almost overflowed. After the Revolutionary War and the War of 1812, Rock Hall continued to be a shipping terminal and a base for a thriving seafood industry. As the catches diminished, so did the town's seafood business. There are still many boats heading out every day, and in the fall and winter, skipjacks often base here. But the area wisely turned to other maritime businesses and there are now many very fine marinas and supply and repair facilities for pleasure boating.

The Waters of Rock Hall

Refer to Regional Chart #12273-C at the beginning of Chapter 8 Pg 88 and

Chart #12278-D—"Swan Creek and Rock Hall Approach" in this chapter. Pg 91

Rock Hall **(95)** is hard to miss from the Bay, regardless of your approach. It sits to the north of the wide mouth of the

Chester River (96), with buildings and masts of boats behind two obvious jetties (97) protecting the harbor. It is necessary to clear Swan Point Bar (98), unless your draft is very shallow. Even if you only draw 3 feet, I would not recommend cutting this bar because it is uneven. Like any bar that was formerly a point of land, it may have obstructions. Heavy seas could mount up on the bar causing a boat to bottom out between the swells. Coming from the north, it should not be too difficult to pick up the outside Gr can "1" (99), because you will be following the very conspicuous Swan Point Channel (100) with all of its buoys and range. From R "4" (1) of that channel, a course of 105°M will take you to the vicinity south of Gr can "1," close enough to see it in mist. Note that on this course, you would be passing close to the end of Swan Point Bar with its 10- and 12-foot depths. You may want to round this, depending on your draft and sea conditions.

If you are coming from the Chester River or that area, a straight line from Love Point Light (2) to the green water tower (3) behind Rock Hall Harbor, will bring you close enough to the area of Gr can "1" to see it. [Don't confuse the water tower with the grain elevator (4) behind Deadman Point (5) or the other green water tower at Gratitude (6)]. It also helps to know that this Gr can "1" is off a trailer park (7) on the land to its east. You can see the trailers along the shore. From this marker, a course of due north will bring you in to the vicinity of Fl R "4" (8). The range (9), is no longer there, but there is a "Danger" marker (10) in the vicinity of where the first range marker was formerly located on the shoal. From R "4," the jetties are obvious, and you go between them into Rock Hall Harbor. The inset on the chart shows the dredged channels (11) inside. They are marked and should not be difficult to follow.

Inside Rock Hall Harbor
Refer to Chart #12278-C—"Rock Hall Harbor—Inset."

As you approach the jetties, you will get the idea that you are coming to a place of special significance to boating because of the masts and buildings appearing inside and the marine traffic. When you clear the jetty (97), you will see an area of many possibilities for a visit or a stay.

As soon as you come in, there will be an easy access fuel dock to your left (northwestern side) where it is convenient to get gas and diesel, as well as block and cube ice. This is **Windmill Point Marina and Motel (12)** with 120 open slips and 30 covered slips, the largest slip at 60 feet. Electricity at 110 and 220 volts is available, up to 50 amps. Depths are 7 feet. There is a Chevron sign on the dock. There is also a marine store, laundromat, and swimming pool. The five-unit motel has efficiency units, some of which overlook the Bay and the spectacular harbor. They accept Visa and MC. There are mechanics available. It is possible to charter sailing boats through this marina. They monitor Channels 68 and 16.

Next on your left (west) is **Cain's Wharf (13)** which has 28 slips, sells gas and diesel, and has electricity up to 30 amps. They also sell bait.

Ahead of you, as you are going up the left channel (the one on the northwestern side of the harbor), you will see the **Fin, Fur, and Feather Restaurant (14)**. It has a conspicuous sign in front, and a flashing red light on top for night identification. This is a great place to go for good food and fine local atmosphere, overlooking the harbor and serving the boaters and hunters for over 12 years. They cut steaks to order and prepare excellent seafood, much of which is off-loaded at the

docks as you watch, because they buy and sell seafood wholesale. There is an aquarium from which you can often pick what you wish to eat as it swims around. Another speciality of this house is roast turkey. They will come in a launch to pick you up at your slip in the harbor. If you are not tied up in the actual harbor but are at one of the nearby marinas in Swan Creek, they will come and get you by land if you phone 639-7454. There is dockage for patrons, with room for about eight boats. This is run by Buz Burke, a great person to talk about local hunting and fishing. If you bring him your goose or duck already picked and cleaned, and early enough in the afternoon, he will "cook it up" and serve it for you with a full meal in the finest of Eastern Shore fashions.

The **Pelorus Marina (15)** is to the right (east) of Fin, Fir, and Feather. This has 50 slips with the largest for vessels of 45 feet. They honor Visa and MC. Charter boats are available through this marina. There is a dockside pumpout and electricity up to 30 amps, propane, and block and cube ice. They also have a 15-ton open end lift. Depths are 6 feet. Mechanics, electricians, and sail repair are available here, with an indoor climate-controlled building for blister and other work.

The flat bulkhead area on the northern shore where the channel comes around to the southeast is the town landing (16). This is a busy dock where many local and other commercial boats unload and tie, often anchoring bow off with stern tied in "med moor" fashion. When passing by here, be

Rock Hall Harbor (Inset)
Chart #12278-C
Scale 1:10,000

12.	Windmill Point Marina & Motel
13.	Cain's Wharf
14.	Fin, Fur, and Feather Restaurant
15.	Pelorus Marina
16.	Town Dock
17.	Bay Harbor Restaurant
18.	Rock Hall Marine Railway
19.	Rock Hall Landing Marina
20.	Club Nautico
21.	Black Duck Inn Bed and Breakfast
23.	Waterman's Crab House Restaurant
24.	Sailing Emporium
25.	Obstruction
26.	Rock Hall Sailing Association
28.	Public Ramp
97.	Jetties

Not for use in Navigation

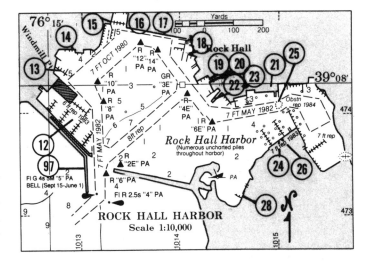

83

sure not to foul the anchor lines that may be stretched out away from the bows of these vessels. Behind this dock is the Bay Harbor Restaurant (17), across the parking lot. There is an upstairs deck overlooking the harbor, as well as a less casual dining room downstairs. They have a full menu and a carry-out menu, specializing in fresh seafood and prime rib.

To the east of the town docks to your right, you will see the **Rock Hall Marine Railway (18)**. There are 30 slips here, 4 feet depth and they can take a few transients up to 40 feet as space is available. Their slips are primarily for their permanent customers. There is a 55-foot railway, a 2-ton crane, a 20-ton closed end boat lift and a 15-ton open end lift, with full repair yard. They sell gas and have electricity up to 30 amps available at the docks. There is a full marine store with a good selection of "nuts and bolts" type of practical hardware that is often hard to find elsewhere. There is a head with showers, and ice is available. Visa is accepted.

The next marina as you head around the loop, is **Rock Hall Landing Marina (19)**. This 80-slip floating dock marina also has a high and dry storage. Electrical service up to 220 volts and 50 amps is available, as is a pumpout station and 7 to 9 feet depths. Thay can accomodate vessels up to 80 feet. Visa, MC, and Discover are accepted. They will rent small boats for local fishing, with a Club Nautico (20) operation on premises. Fishing gear is rented here, as are bikes. There is also a 12-room motel here, with other living rentals, such as condos, available. A swimming pool and barbecue area add to the attractions. There is also a bakery and ice cream parlor on site. Block and cube ice are sold. There are eight bathroom/shower combinations. A marine store is also on site, and an ice house is right next door, with ice in all shapes and sizes. The Black Duck Inn Bed and Breakfast (21) is on the water, just to the south of Rock Hall Landing.

Next to Rock Hall Marina is the well-known Waterman's Crab House Restaurant (23) with its dockside bar with pink roof and seafood specialities, which is right on the water, easily identified by its signs. This restaurant has 20 slips for its customers.

Ths Sailing Emporium (24) with 150 slips (taking boats up to 75 feet) and a full service yard, is at the eastern end of the harbor. The chart notes an obstruction (25) on your right just before you get to the basin, but none is there in the channel. The marina has controlling depths at 7 feet, gas and diesel fuel, CNG and propane, a pumpout station, block and cube ice, and electricity up to 30 amps. Visa and MC are accepted. In this huge facility you will also find a sailing school, a well-run and well-established sailboat charter service, yacht sales and brokerage, a full service yard, swimming pool with barbecue area and gazebo, and laundromat. There is a large marine store with clothing and gifts, some groceries including a few gourmet items, sports equipment, and also a well-stocked chandlery and parts department. The bathroom/showers are air conditioned. They have bicycles available to get into town and ride around. There is a 35-ton open end lift, and 15-ton crane. They are dealers for Awlgrip and Westerbeke. This marina offers courtesy transportation around town. The Rock Hall Sailing Association (26) is located on premises.

Almost completing the circle around shore, the county public cement ramp (28), with temporary docking and parking, provides good trailer boat access to this area. Check with Kent County for the latest as to fees. Phone (410) 778-1948.

Behind the waterfront of Rock Hall Harbor is a very nice town with more restaurants, sights to see, groceries, and shops.

Rock Hall Town
Refer to our Street Map—"Town of Rock Hall."

The Town of Rock Hall is surrounded by Eastern Shore countryside with woods and marsh abounding, and the Eastern Neck Wildlife Preserve a few miles drive away. Walking out from town, you can get the impression that you are far out in the country before you leave the town itself. The 1990 census counted 1584 souls here, many of whom are watermen, hunting and fishing guides, and decoy carvers.

Rock hall is a good spot for walking around as well as provisioning or getting parts and repairs. It is not laid out in a way conducive to a block by block walking description from the waterfront, so I will pick a few relevant spots to describe.

I found that almost universally the marinas said that they would be happy to assist their customers with transportation, and because things are somewhat spread out from the water, for shopping, I would suggest that you contact your marina to see first if they have what you need, and if not, to help you find and reach what you need.

The main area of town, with most of the non-marine businesses, is centered around Main Street generally between where it intersects with Chesapeake Avenue and where it crosses Rock Hall Avenue. From the town dock area, walk along Bayside Avenue in an easterly direction, then turn right at Hawthorne and follow the waterfront until Hawthorne intersects with Chesapeake Avenue. Then turn left and follow this avenue in an easterly direction until it intersects with Main. A left turn onto Main Street will bring you into the main business area of town. Most of these businesses will be from ½ mile to 1 mile away.

An IGA grocery store called "Bayfitters Food Store" offers a full line of groceries. This is at Rock Hall Avenue and North Main Street. Next door to the grocery store, you will

LEGEND FOR STREET MAP~PG 85
Town of Rock Hall

12.	Windmill Point/Northside Marina and Motel	47.	Coleman and Fithian Marine Construction
13.	Cain's Wharf (marina and seafood)	48.	Ebbtide Marine Service
		49.	Lenox Company (boat repair)
14.	Fin, Fur, and Feather Restaurant	50.	Rudisill Sailmakers/Bay Canvas
15.	Pelorus Marina (and charters)	51.	Big Electronics
16.	Town Dock	52.	Ships Store
17.	Bay Harbor Restaurant	53.	Rock Hall Clam and Oyster
18.	Rock Hall Marine Railway	54.	Rock Hall Ice
19.	Rock Hall Landing (marina boat charters and fishing charters)	55.	New Yarmouth Inn
		56.	Civic Center Park
20.	Club Nautico (at Rock Hall landing)	57.	Library, Rock Hall Museum, Town Office
21.	Black Duck Inn	58.	Post Office
23.	Waterman's Crab House, McJoiners Country Bakery, Rock Hall Bicycle Rental	59.	Waterman Statue
		60.	Mariner's Inn (motel)
		61.	Annie J's Seafood (retail)
24.	Sailing Emporium, Cat's Paw (gift shop and clothing), Charters	62.	Village Hardware and Garden Center
		63.	Dowling's Hardware
26.	Rock Hall Sailing Association	64.	Rock Hall Lumber
28.	Public Ramp	65.	Boulter's Launderette
35.	Haven Harbour Marina, Haven Charters	66.	Rock Hall Liquor
		67.	Shore Stop (groceries)
38.	Gratitude Marina	68.	Swan Point Inn (restaurant)
39.	Strawberry Factory	69.	Durding's Drug Store
40.	Gratitude Yachting Center, charter	70.	Bay Breeze Inn (Bed and Breakfast)
41.	Swan Creek Marina	71.	Bay Area Caterers (carry-out)
42.	Osprey Point Marina	72.	Bayfitters Food Store
44.	Spring Cove Marina	73.	Old Oars Inn
45.	Spring Cove Public Landing	74.	Pasta Plus
46.	Great River Yacht Charts	75.	Rock Hall Snack Bar
		76.	Lewis' Rainbows End
		77.	Harbor Wash (launderette)
		78.	Dentist (Dr. Charles Roth)
		79.	Maryland School of Sailing and Seamanship of Rock Hall

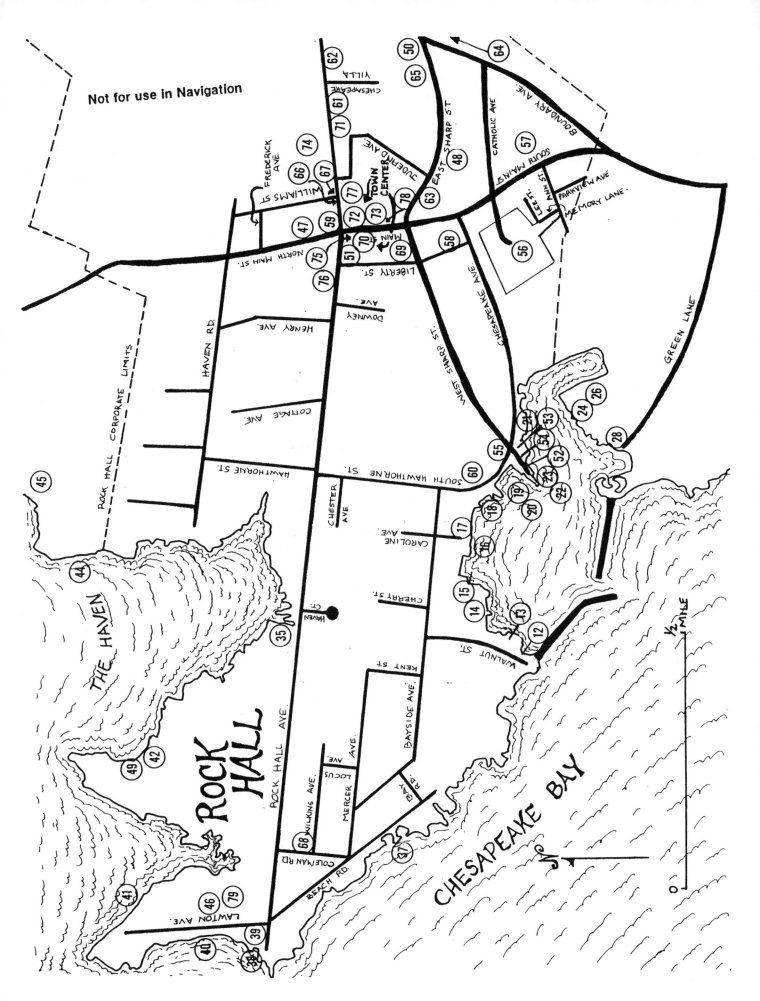

Not for use in Navigation

85

find a laundromat, called Harbor Wash (77), and there is a Boulters Launderette (65) at Boundary Avenue and E. Sharp Street. Both of these are roughly ¾ mile walk from the town dock. Across the street (Rock Hall Avenue) from this grocery store, and down about a block to the south (to your right facing away from the grocery store) you will find the Rock Hall Liquor (66) store. Also in this neighborhood, across the street and to your right (south) about half a block, is the Shore Stop (67), a convenience food store. Dowlings Hardware (63) is located at East Sharp Street near Main Street. Village Hardware and Garden Center (62), an ACE outlet, is on Rock Hall Avenue and Chesapeake Villa. Rock Hall Bicycle Rental (23) is found next to the Watermans Crab House (23) right at the waterfront. The Post Office (58) is around a ½ mile from the town docks, at Liberty Street between Sharp Street and Chesapeake Avenue. There is a dentist (78) on Main Street, a little over ½ a mile from the town dock. Durding's Drug Store (69), is located on N. Main Street near where it intersects with West Sharp, around ½-mile from the town docks. Durding's has prescriptions and over the counter items as well as an assortment of personal care and other things normally found in drug stores. This drug store also has an old fashioned ice cream soda fountain.

Rock Hall has several restaurants in town in addition to those right at the water's edge. The Lewis' Rainbow End Restaurant and Lounge (76) can be found at Route 20 (Rock Hall Avenue), with casual dining offering steaks, seafood, and prime rib. The Pasta Plus (74) has carry-outs as well as the informal restaurant specializing in pizza, stromboli, sandwiches, and dinner entrees. The Swan Point Inn (68) at Coleman Road and Wilkins Avenue, offers fine dining and lodging. This is around a block and a half from the beach, north of the jetties. Their house specialities are crab imperial, crab cakes, salmon, scampi, and crab bisque soup in a casual and intimate atmosphere. The Rock Hall Snack Bar (75) is on Rock Hall Avenue near Liberty Street in the main section of town. This features home-cooked breakfasts and light lunches, including carry-out service. A tradition in town, again in the main section, is the Old Oars Inn (73) on Main Street. This tavern and restaurant is located in one of the more unusual two-story buildings you will see around the Bay. As you face the building from the street, the forward end of the work boat sticks out of its wall to your right, and the after end of the boat protrudes from the wall to your left.

There are several retail seafood establishments in town. These include the Annie J. Seafood Company (61) offering crabs, shrimps, fish, salads, soups, platters and sandwiches as well as carry-outs. It is at the Rock Hall Avenue and Chesapeake Villa, a walk of close to a mile from the town docks.

Cain's Seafood (13) is at Walnut Street just up from Windmill Point Marina.

In addition to the bed-and-breakfasts, and marina accommodations mentioned, there are two motels near the water. These are the Mariner's Motel (60) at S. Hawthorne Avenue and Bayside Avenue, adjacent to the Rock Hall Landing Marina, and the new Yarmouth Inn (55) at Sharp Street Wharf around a block from the docks of that marina.

Throughout the harbor are various fishing vessels for day charters, and hunting and fishing guides. Any marina can recommend names and boats and assist you in contacting these people.

As would be expected, there are numerous boating-related businesses and services, not all of which are necessarily connected to marinas. Big Electronics (51) is on Rock Hall Avenue and Liberty Street, not much more than ½ mile from the town docks. Ebb Tide Marine Service and Sales (48), makes boat calls and does mechanical and electrical service. This is on East Sharp Street, a little over ½ mile walk, phone 639-2656. Rudisill Sailmakers (50) are at Boundary Avenue and Sharp Street, a walk of around 1 mile. Great River Yacht Charters (46) is located on Lawton Avenue. The Maryland School of Sailing and Seamanship of Rock Hall (79) is also on Lawton Avenue at Gratitude Yachting Center.

The Fourth of July weekend is a great time to come to town here. There is a parade, a seafood and local speciality cookout with food galore, a street dance, live music, great fireworks, and much more. One of our favorites is the annual waterman's docking contest. These people dock their work boats every day all year long, but in this contest there are points for how fast they are docked, how many pilings they touch, and other subtleties.

There are many places within a relative short driving distance from Rock Hall that make the area worth a visit in addition to other reasons. There is no regular public transportation service in the area, but I have been told that such is actively under consideration. It should not be any trouble to arrange a ride to wherever you might wish to go. Those who wish to see Chestertown but do not wish to take a long (and beautiful) trip up the Chester River, should consider stopping here in Rock Hall, only around 13 miles from that lovely town. Also, the Eastern Neck Wildlife Refuge is only around 6 miles away. With boardwalks over marsh and tide lands, paths, bird-watching stations, and many more educational experiences, this would be a great place to visit from Rock Hall. Their phone is (410) 639-7056. There are quite a few places of interest inland in Kent County, and the Chamber of Commerce Office for that county, which is located in Chestertown, will be of great help. Their number is (410) 778-0416. See Chapter 8 on Kent County and Chestertown.

Author Tom with Buzz (owner of Fin, Fur and Feather Restaurant) on tour of Rock Hall Harbor

CHAPTER 8

CHESTER RIVER

The Chester River offers miles of beautiful high banked river, protected anchorages, nice marinas, and historical Chestertown. *Editor's note: You could spend two weeks in this beautiful river and never repeat yourself. It's navigable all the way to Chestertown, and has many worthwhile tributaries. It's been one of the high spots of my Chesapeake Bay cruises. Tom has done us all a service exploring every nook and cranny. I accompanied him for a day to do a small portion of this exploration. I was impressed by Tom Neale's meticulous work, by his conscientiousness, and by his 12-ft. dinghy, equipped with a Magellan GPS and a depthfinder!*

ENTRANCE
Refer to Regional Chart #12273-C—"Eastern Shore—Tolchester Beach to Kent Island and Chester River." Pg 88

The Chester River (96) is an easy run from Baltimore just across the Bay, Annapolis, Eastern Bay (if your draft will let you through Kent Narrows), Middle River, and all of the rivers and marinas in the northern Bay. It is pretty hard to miss its mouth because it is just north of the Bay Bridge, and is very wide. There could be some confusion on misty or hazy days because there is so much space. Red Nun "2" (80) marks the end of the shoal off Love Point (81), and sighting it helps considerably in heading into the Chester. If you are leaving Baltimore, or are coming from that general direction, a course of 160°M will take you from the vicinity of the Flashing Red Bell "2BE" (82) to the vicinity of that Red Nun "2". "2BE"'s position is 39°08.9'N by 76°20.0'N by 76°16.4'W, which marks the eastern end of the eastern extension of the Brewerton Channel (83). The position of Red Nun "2" is 39°04.0'N by 76°16.4'W. Keep a good lookout for buoys enroute on the 160°M course. Their location will let you know if you're being set off your course. Love Point Light (2) provides another good reference. It also has a bell and is on a 35-foot skeleton structure. Its position is 39°03.4'N by 76°17.0'W. It is often easier to see, but the depth is only 7 to 8 feet at its structure, and it should not be taken close. Notice also that there is a series of markers just off the Chester River entrance for the North and South Swan Point ranges (100). These can be helpful in obtaining a reference, but also confusing if you don't recognize them for what they are. Looking off up to the northeast, the bulkheading, marinas, and town of Rock Hall (95) can be seen, as an additional orientation reference. Coming from the south is primarily a matter of rounding Love Point, which is hard to miss. This is the northern tip of Kent Island (84), it is relatively high, and as the chart indicates, a large barn-like structure (85) can be seen ashore to your west, before you get to the point.

LOWER CHESTER RIVER
Refer to Chart #12272-A—"Lower Chester River—West" pg 89
and
Chart #12272-B—"Lower Chester River—East." PG. 90

Heading up the river, particularly from a low sail or motorboat, on a hazy day, it is often difficult to pick up some of the next few markers. There is nothing particularly difficult about the run, just a bit vexing when trying to see these in all the spaces against the often high hill background. The following courses give routes and should not be substituted for your own careful observations and navigation. From just off Red Nun "2" (80), a course of 195°M will take you to the vicinity just off G "3" (86). From there, 160°M brings you to the area just off Fl R "6" (87). Next, 135°M runs to the area, just off Fl G "9" (88). Rounding Cedar (89) and Hail Points (90) to your north, it is not very difficult to pick up G"11" and Fl R "12" (91), but the next two courses up river can be difficult to find in poor visibility. From Fl R "12," you can utilize the range at Ringgold Point (92) to bring up R "14" (93) (on a course of 348°M) and a course of 45°M will bring you to the vicinity of R "16" (94). Before heading that far up river however, there are many areas you may wish to visit or explore first.

Refer to Chart #12272-A—"Lower Chester River—West." Pg 89
Obvious to all who enter the river is the large Castle Harbour Club Marina (95) complex. This is the first facility on your right (east), straight in southeast from Fl R "6." Just to its left (southeast) is a large horizontally red and white striped structure which looks like a light house but is actually a water tower (96) for the Queen's Landing Condominium (97) complex just under it. The letters QL are painted on the structure.

Castle Harbour is both a residential club and a marina. They maintain 6 feet in the entrance channel. There are 266 open slips and 44 covered. Electricity is available up to 50 amps and the docks can take boats up to 65 feet, possibly more if special arrangements are made for T docks. There is an olympic-sized pool just up from the docks, Jacuzzi and saunas, ship's store, nice bathrooms and a laundromat, gas and diesel. MC, Visa, and Discover are accepted. There is a local accredited Castle Harbour Yacht Club (98) using the premises. The Castle Marina Inn (99), offering waterfront dining has a full and very complete menu ranging from light fares to entrees up to around $19. There is often entertainment here on weekends and other special times.

Continuing into the river, the entrance to Kent Narrows (100) quickly becomes conspicuous on the southern shore. This entrance is described in Chapter 9. Note that the markers (1) into the narrows are green to right and red to left heading in from the Chester. They remain so all the way through the narrows.

WINCHESTER CREEK

I did not find much reason to go into this creek, from the cruiser's perspective, except for the nice restaurant and golfing range upstream, if you draw 3 feet and less.

Refer to #Chart 12272-B—"Lower Chester River-East." Pg 90
The entrance to Winchester Creek (2) is difficult to pick out,

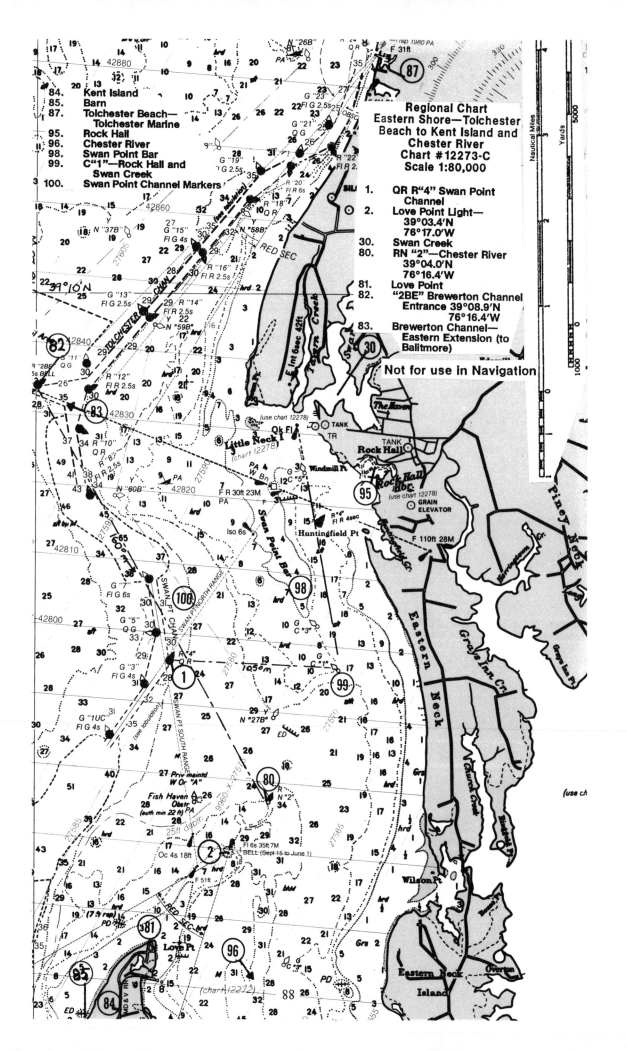

84. Kent Island
85. Barn
87. Tolchester Beach—
    Tolchester Marine
95. Rock Hall
96. Chester River
98. Swan Point Bar
99. C"1"—Rock Hall and
    Swan Creek
100. Swan Point Channel Markers

Regional Chart
Eastern Shore—Tolchester
Beach to Kent Island and
Chester River
Chart #12273-C
Scale 1:80,000

1. QR R"4" Swan Point
   Channel
2. Love Point Light—
   39°03.4'N
   76°17.0'W
30. Swan Creek
80. RN "2"—Chester River
    39°04.0'N
    76°16.4'W
81. Love Point
82. "2BE" Brewerton Channel
    Entrance 39°08.9'N
    76°16.4'W
83. Brewerton Channel—
    Eastern Extension (to
    Balitmore)

Not for use in Navigation

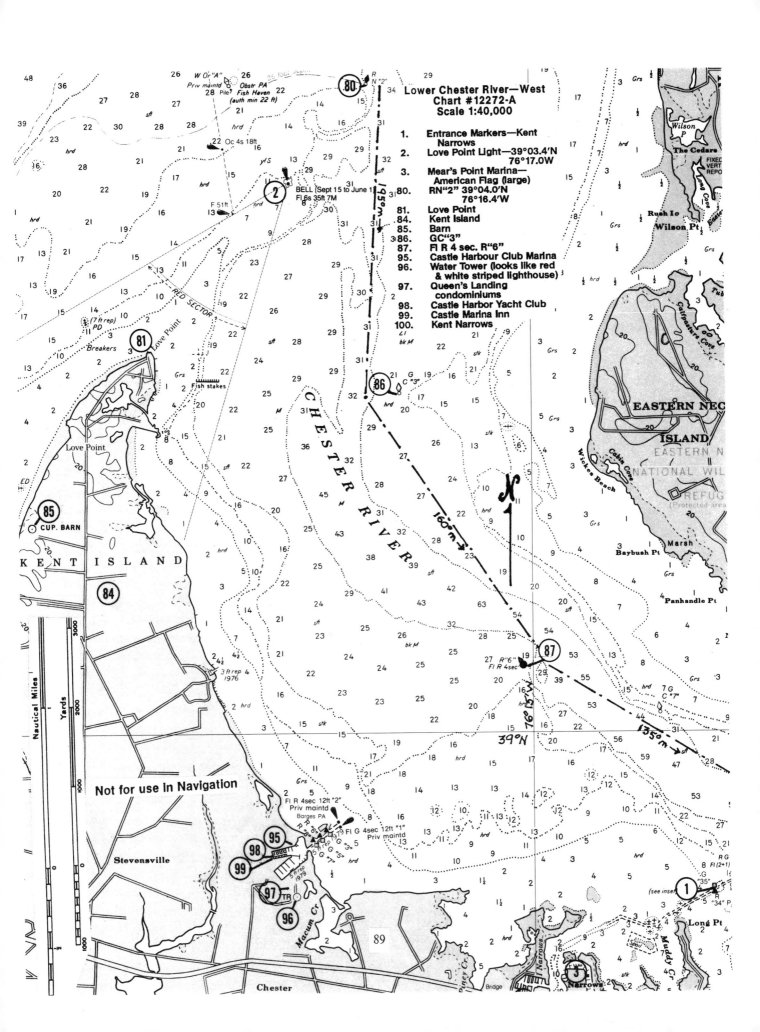

Lower Chester River—West
Chart #12272-A
Scale 1:40,000

1. Entrance Markers—Kent Narrows
2. Love Point Light—39°03.4'N 76°17.0W
3. Mear's Point Marina— American Flag (large)
80. RN"2" 39°04.0'N 76°16.4'W
81. Love Point
84. Kent Island
85. Barn
86. GC"3"
87. Fl R 4 sec. R"6"
95. Castle Harbour Club Marina
96. Water Tower (looks like red & white striped lighthouse)
97. Queen's Landing condominiums
98. Castle Harbor Yacht Club
99. Castle Marina Inn
100. Kent Narrows

CHESTER RIVER

KENT ISLAND

EASTERN NECK ISLAND

Not for use in Navigation

Stevensville

89

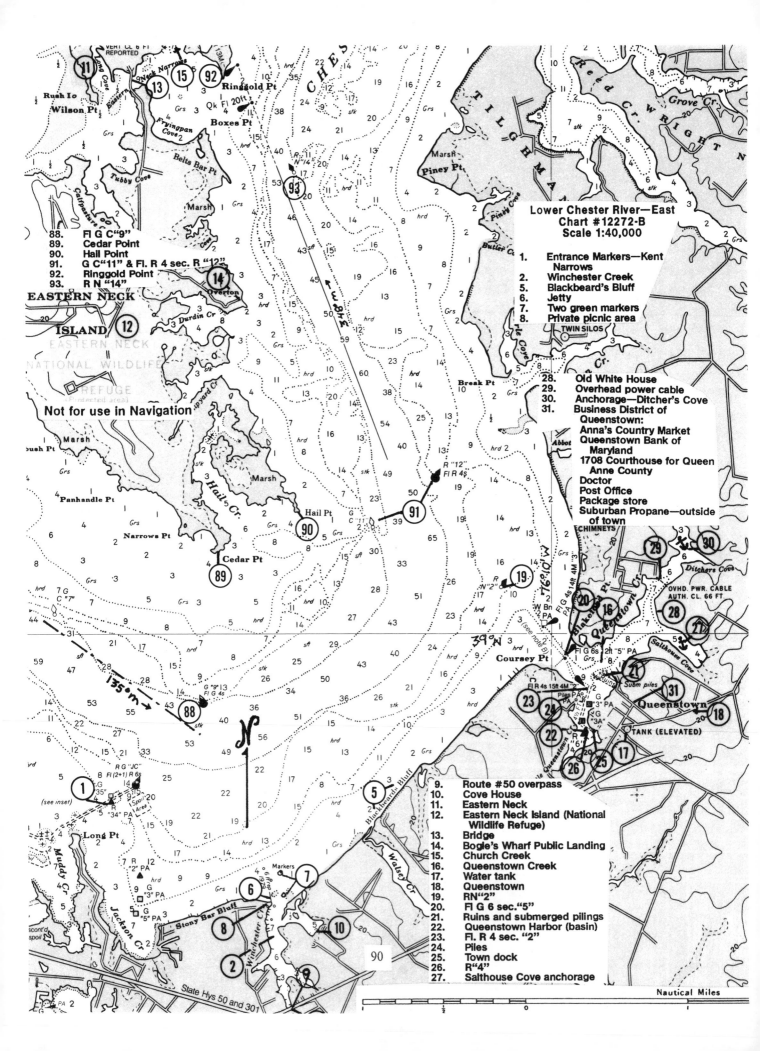

Not for use in Navigation

Lower Chester River—East
Chart #12272-B
Scale 1:40,000

1. Entrance Markers—Kent Narrows
2. Winchester Creek
5. Blackbeard's Bluff
6. Jetty
7. Two green markers
8. Private picnic area

28. Old White House
29. Overhead power cable
30. Anchorage—Ditcher's Cove
31. Business District of Queenstown:
Anna's Country Market
Queenstown Bank of Maryland
1708 Courthouse for Queen Anne County
Doctor
Post Office
Package store
Suburban Propane—outside of town

88. Fl G C"9"
89. Cedar Point
90. Hail Point
91. G C"11" & Fl. R 4 sec. R "12"
92. Ringgold Point
93. R N "14"

9. Route #50 overpass
10. Cove House
11. Eastern Neck
12. Eastern Neck Island (National Wildlife Refuge)
13. Bridge
14. Bogle's Wharf Public Landing
15. Church Creek
16. Queenstown Creek
17. Water tank
18. Queenstown
19. RN"2"
20. Fl G 6 sec."5"
21. Ruins and submerged pilings
22. Queenstown Harbor (basin)
23. Fl. R 4 sec. "2"
24. Piles
25. Town dock
26. R"4"
27. Salthouse Cove anchorage

EASTERN NECK
ISLAND
EASTERN NECK
NATIONAL WILDLIFE
REFUGE
(Protected area)

90

and is very shallow. The landmarks for Kent Island Narrows are on **Chart #12272-A**, [the large U.S. flag at Mears Point Marina **(3)**]. The entrance to Winchester Creek is between this landmark to the west, and the high hills called Blackbeards Bluff **(5)** to the east. Letting your gaze sweep the southern bank in an upriver (easterly) direction from Kent Narrows, you will see high density houses along the Chester River shoreline until your gaze gets to the creek. Here the houses will stop with the west bank of the creek. East of the creek, the Chester shoreline is wooded for some distance. The creek itself has a jetty **(6)** coming off the point of its western shore where this intersects the river. The jetty is apparently to stop shoaling, but has not been very successful. There are small privately maintained private markers to help coming in, but I found no more than 3 feet between the two green markers **(7)** and the jetty. Just as you pass the jetty, you will see a private picnic area **(8)** to your right.

This creek has a high density of private homes and docks, and is not very attractive as an anchorage. There are fewer homes on the eastern shore of the creek, but I would feel like I was anchoring in someone's backyard. You will see the overpass of Route 50 **(9)** as you approach the upper area of the creek, and the highway noise can be quite loud when you shut down your engine. The only real attraction is **Cove House (10)**, with its guest docks for restaurant patrons and a motel. There is also a nearby golf course. Boats with shallow enough draft would find this a very attractive place to have dinner, or to stay to meet friends or play golf. I hoped to find an area to anchor larger boats within dinghy distance of a restaurant, but did not find any with which I would feel comfortable. Anchoring outside the creek near its mouth in the Chester River would suffice if you trusted the weather, but this is exposed 180°.

EASTERN NECK NARROWS
Refer to Chart #12272-B Pg 40
and
Chart #12278-E—"Eastern Neck Island to Nichols Point."

This would be an intruiging dinghy trip with passage all the way through the shallow cut between Eastern Neck **(11)** and Eastern Neck Island **(12)**, passing under the little bridge **(13)**, (6-foot vertical clearance). It looks so intruiging that I spent well over an hour to find my way in and through. I should have paid more attention to all of the local boats watching me with some amusement and consternation! They kept signaling that there was no water anywhere, and I finally

had to admit to myself that they were right. If you have a trolling motor and don't mind rowing, this would make a great exploration trip, but there are no special routes. Just be prepared to bump and grind and enjoy it on half tide and rising.

Eastern Neck Island is a protected national wildlife refuge. Its 2,285 acres were set aside in 1962 by the U.S. Government. Its shores and marshes make great exploration area for nature lovers, with trails and observation areas. You may contact the park at (410) 639-7056. There are no cruising boat destinations on its shores. There is a **Bogle's Wharf Public Landing (14)** on the eastern side with a hard surfaced launching ramp, bathroom facilities, and a fishing pier. There is a small fee and the phone is (410) 778-4600.

Church Creek **(15)** is pretty and has ample depths, but its entrance is controlled by 1-foot depth at MLW, too shallow for most cruising boats.

QUEENSTOWN CREEK
Refer to Chart #12272-B—"Lower Chester River—East."
Pg 40

This is a pretty creek notable for the quaint village of Queenstown and some scenic anchorages, but rather tricky for boats with a draft of over 3½ feet.

The entrance to Queenstown Creek **(16)** is dredged and prone to shoaling. If you draw more than 3½ feet, go in only in calm weather and half tide and rising. The potential difficulty of the entrance is witnessed by the fact that the chart indicates that a depth of 6 feet is available with local knowledge. The channel is well used by local working boats, and by the time that you enter, it may have been redredged, but there has been constant shoaling at the entrance channel.

To spot the entrance area from the Chester, look for the entrance buoys, just upriver from the tall silver water tank **(17)** over Queenstown **(18)**. Head straight in from Red Nun "2" **(19)**, following the mark carefully. The channel is dredged through very shallow sand, and grounding in the exposed outer part could be a difficult experience. The point of land behind Fl Gr "5" **(20)** has a nice beach with marsh behind. There is also beach on the shore opposite this marker. The entrance presents beautiful scenery with woods and marsh, but houses can be seen ahead up in the creek. I did not see the extent of the ruins or the pilings **(21)** noted on the chart ahead of you to the southeast as you come in. I understand that there is still some debris here, and the area should be avoided. The buoys take you outside of this area.

Hydraulic clam dredge, Chester River

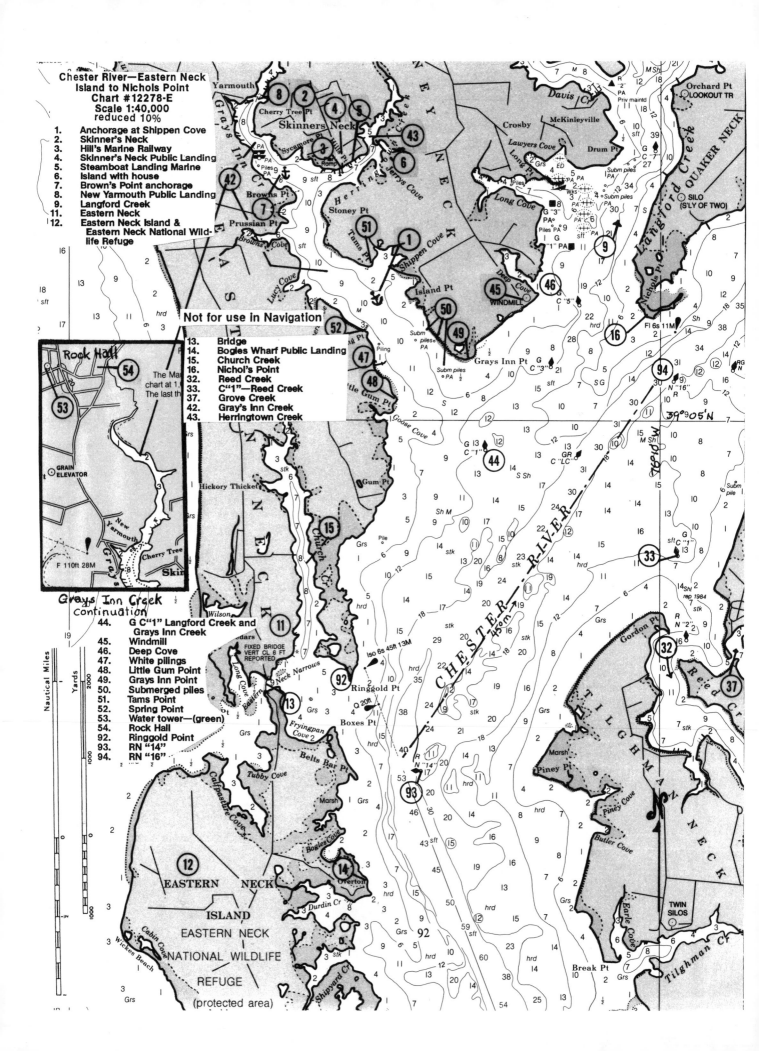

Chester River—Eastern Neck Island to Nichols Point
Chart #12278-E
Scale 1:40,000
reduced 10%

1. Anchorage at Shippen Cove
2. Skinner's Neck
3. Hill's Marine Railway
4. Skinner's Neck Public Landing
5. Steamboat Landing Marine
6. Island with house
7. Brown's Point anchorage
8. New Yarmouth Public Landing
9. Langford Creek
11. Eastern Neck
12. Eastern Neck Island &
    Eastern Neck National Wild-
    life Refuge

Not for use in Navigation

13. Bridge
14. Bogles Wharf Public Landing
15. Church Creek
16. Nichol's Point
32. Reed Creek
33. C "1"—Reed Creek
37. Grove Creek
42. Gray's Inn Creek
43. Herringtown Creek

44. G C "1" Langford Creek and
    Grays Inn Creek
45. Windmill
46. Deep Cove
47. White pilings
48. Little Gum Point
49. Grays Inn Point
50. Submerged piles
51. Tams Point
52. Spring Point
53. Water tower—(green)
54. Rock Hall
92. Ringgold Point
93. RN "14"
94. RN "16"

To go into Queenstown Harbor **(22)**, turn to the right (south) as you get to Fl R "2" **(23)**. There is a white boathouse and dock to your right (southerly) as you round the point. Piles **(24)** are indicated on the chart here, apparently the remains of an old dock. They do not extend into the channel. I could find no more than 5 feet of water between Fl R "2" and G "3." The channel is very narrow here, with the deepest water closer to the Fl R "2." From here the chart indicates 4½ feet, but this could be less in unusually low tides.

When I reached the basin, I was disappointed from the cruiser's perspective, because after all the work of getting in, the basin off the town dock was full of working boats and dredge equipment permanently moored on stakes, leaving little or no room to anchor. The town dock **(25)** has a sign allowing landing for a few hours, with no overnight docking, but there is often no space here because of daily activity. This landing is on the east side of the cove, just beyond R "4" **(26)** and is easily identifiable. From the landing, you can walk in to the "downtown" area of this small and pretty town. While there are not many high-tech boating attractions here, Queenstown offers a good example of what the shore used to be like before the "bridge boom" bought on by the construction of the Chesapeake Bay Bridge.

If you wish to visit Queenstown, proceed up Queenstown Creek as far as your draft allows in your large boat and come back to the town basin by dinghy. There are some beautiful anchorages up the creek, without the congestion and the bustle of the town dock area. The creek is mostly woods, marsh and field. Salthouse Cove **(27)** is a beautiful anchorage with depths of 4 to 5 feet. Here the view is of trees, marsh, and field all around with only one house in sight. This is an old white home **(28)** to the north with a chimney and white columns, nestled up in the woods. Farther up the creek stretches an overhead cable **(29)**, with a chart indicated vertical clearance of 66 feet. Don't take these clearances for granted, particularly where there is not much tall traffic, as is the case here. The cables often sag and sometimes for other reasons are not as high as they are supposed to be. The creek, off the mouth of Ditcher's Cove **(30)** and just north of there, offers a beautiful anchorage for those with shallow enough draft, generally 2 to 5 feet, depending on how far you wish to go in. You can position yourself where the only civilization visible is remnants of an old duck blind, with fields, marsh and trees all around.

Queenstown

The town dock, as noted earlier, is busy, mostly with commercial fishery activity. There is a dumpster here. The walk into the main area of the town is pleasant, through tree-shaded streets with old, pretty homes. The town's "Second Street" ends at the dock. To get to the main part of town, walk up Second Street, turn right at Charity Lane after walking one block, then walk about a block and a half to the stop sign at the highway. Look to your left and you will see a small area of establishments **(31)**. These include Anna's Country Market offering deli food, fresh cut meats, breakfasts, hot coffee, ice cream, block and cube ice, and a few groceries. Also in the same circle of establishments, you will find a Queenstown Bank of Maryland and the 1708 courthouse for Queen Anne's County. There is also a doctor's office, a Post Office, a package store, and various other businesses. Suburban Propane are on the outskirts of town, but they are not within easy walking, especially with full tanks. Their phone number is 758-1200.

REED AND GROVE CREEKS

Refer to Chart #12272-C—"Reed Creek, Grove Creek, Corsica River, Centreville."

Entry to Reed and Grove Creeks

The entrance to Reed Creek **(32)** is difficult at best. Once inside there are several nice anchorages, but if I drew over 4 feet, I would not risk entering since there are so many other nice anchorages with easier access.

The worst part coming in is from Can "1" **(33)** to R Nun "2" **(34)**. The 2-foot shoal **(35)** marked on your left (northeast) is wandering into the channel, and the shoal outside and off Gordon Point **(35A)** tapers so gradually into the channel that if you are rounding too much off the 2-foot shoal, it is very difficult to tell that you have gone too far to your right. I began with Can "1" approximately 75 feet off to my left (to the east) and started heading for R "2," putting it a little to the left of my bow. You will see a red house with gray rip-rap **(36)** on its shore to your left (on the northeastern shore) as you come past the worst of the 2-foot shoal which, as of last year, begins to recede off the point on your left just before that red house. Be careful because the shoals on each side will continuously change because of the fetches affecting them. I found that the R Nun "2" had apparently been moved since the last printing on the chart which shows it inside of the shoal off Gordon Point. It was on the very tip of that shoal, thus in a more appropriate position. But the channel is very narrow here, and R Nun "2" must be passed very close to your right to avoid the shoal on the other side. From here you can go on up into Reed Creek, or if in a shallow boat and looking for a really tight but snug anchorage, go into Grove Creek **(37)**.

Grove Creek

The entrance to Grove Creek is very narrow, and marked by private markers **(38)** nuns and can floats last year. We've noted their approximate positions on the chart. They are small, but easily seen. Follow them closely. At low tide the channel is so narrow that some of them lay over on their sides on the bare shoal. Do not go in with more than 3 feet draft and only at half tide and rising, although I saw boats of apparent deeper draft inside, but those folks do it all the time. As you head into the Grove Creek private markers, beware of the 1-foot shoal **(39)** to your left (northeast) just off R Nun "2," making it necessary to round a bit by heading on a south-southwesterly course as though you were proceeding on up into the main creek before heading to the private markers of Grove Creek. Inside Grove Creek, the water deepens and you are totally landlocked, but there are many houses with docks making this anything but a secluded anchorage.

Reed Creek

To continue on up into Reed Creek, the biggest problem will probably be in rounding the shoal marked by R Nun "2." Although the marker must be passed very closely to avoid the 1-foot shoal to your left, you must then continue on a little, rounding it a little more broadly before heading into the cove behind Gordon Point. After passing R Nun "2," look to your right (northwesterly) and you will see the tiny point **(40)** coming out just before the big basin. Having rounded R Nun "2," I then headed to just off this point to find deeper water. There is deep water, as the chart shows, close up to the tip of this point and the shore beyond it. From here on in, things get much easier. The shoal behind R Nun "2" and the shoal opposite it are clearly changing, and you may find things very different.

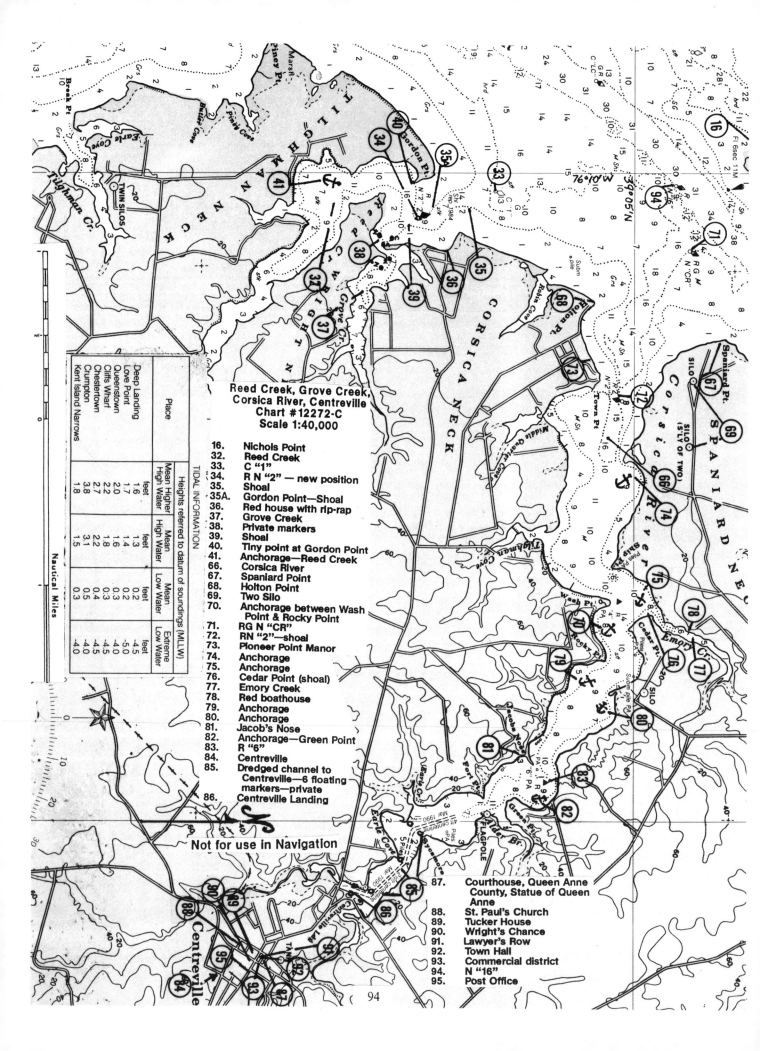

Reed Creek, Grove Creek,
Corsica River, Centreville
Chart #12272-C
Scale 1:40,000

TIDAL INFORMATION

Heights referred to datum of soundings (MLLW).

Place	Mean Higher High Water	Mean High Water	Mean Low Water	Extreme Low Water
	feet	feet	feet	feet
Deep Landing	1.6	1.3	0.2	-4.5
Love Point	1.7	1.4	0.2	-5.0
Queenstown	2.0	1.6	0.3	-4.0
Cliffs Wharf	2.2	1.8	0.3	-4.5
Chestertown	2.7	2.2	0.4	-4.5
Crumpton	3.8	3.1	0.5	-4.0
Kent Island Narrows	1.8	1.5	0.3	-4.0

Nautical Miles

Not for use in Navigation

94

The anchorage in the big cove (41) to your right (south) is broad with plenty of room and areas of good holding. There are several houses along the shores of this cove, but they are nice and there is enough room to anchor far enough off to have privacy. Seven feet is the controlling depth here, and for a while farther up, as the chart shows. Heading on up, Reed Creek becomes even prettier and you could anchor anywhere your draft allows. It gets prettier as you go farther up and water gets shallower, with field, woods, and marsh all around.

GRAYS INN CREEK AND HERRINGTOWN CREEK

Refer to Chart #12278-E—"Eastern Neck Island to Nichols Point." *Pg. 92*

Near the mouth these creeks are too open to the south-southeast to provide quiet anchorages. The shores upstream where there would be quieter anchorages are somewhat congested with private homes.

The approach to these two creeks can be somewhat difficult to discern from out in the Chester. This area of the Chester is very wide, and on a hazy day or when there are many boats fishing (not unusual), it is often difficult to identify creeks or marks. The first marker, G Can "1" (44) can be difficult to find from out in the river.

Heading up the Chester and to those creeks, you should notice the tall range markers off Ringgold Point (92). Shortly past these markers, the bay which opens in to these creeks becomes apparent. If you see the windmill (45) on your left (northwest) off the point of Deep Cove (46), you will have gone too far up river. From the river, in the vicinity of the creek entrance, if you look in the north-northwesterly direction, you will notice a line of white pilings (47) coming off the western shore of Grays Inn Creek (42), just in from Little Gum Point (48). Behind the pilings lies a white house with two stories. The westernmost section of the house has four white columns. This assists in recognizing the entrance area of the creeks. Also as you come up the river, you will see a green-domed water tower back behind the trees in this general vicinity. This will disappear as you reach Gr Can "1," but it

helps to bring you into the area. The dome is apparently the water tower (53), as marked on the chart, for Rock Hall (54) out on the Bay.

From G Can "1," I headed 332°M into the creek mouth to pass the shoal areas between Little Gum Point and Grays Inn Point (49). Note the submerged piles (50) charted in the shallow water off Grays Inn Point. On the east side across from the white dock, you will pass two clumps of trees with a sand bank in between them and a beach upstream of the two clumps. The point that you are now approaching ahead should be Tams Point (51). The stakes noted off the shore of Spring Point (52) are there and barely visible. For boats who like wider spaces, there is a beautiful anchorage off Shippen Cove (1) in 10 feet depth. However, this is exposed to a southeasterly blow. To help passing traffic avoid you, move over to the side as much as draft allows and be well lit at night. Moving up the creek, there is a low land to the east with trees, farmland, fields, and many woods on the western side with some beautiful stands of pine.

Skinners Neck (2) divides the creek into Grays Inn Creek to the north and Herringtown Creek to the northeast. Here are several facilities. The first is **Hill's Marine Railway (3)**, a small establishment catering to local work boats with a railway which can haul up to 40 feet at 15 tons and not much more than 4-foot draft. There is a Mobil Gas pump on the dock. No credit cards are taken. They do occasionally take transients with a depth of up to 6 feet. There are 30 slips, mostly used by local boats. Thirty amps is available, as is a head and cube ice.

Next upstream and into Herringtown Creek (43) to the northeast, the **Skinner's Neck Public Landing** offers a gravel ramp, some parking, and a municipal face dock which is usually used by local work boats. Overnight docking is not allowed.

Immediately up from that you will see **Steamboat Landing Marine (5)** which has a very complete small boat wood workshop in which they build and repair small wooden boats. There are also 25 slips here and they will take transients, if there is room, up to a depth of 7 feet. Thirty amps are available. A

Fuel dock, Steamboat Landing Marina, Herringtown Creek

large Texaco sign on the docks helps to identify this facility, but they do not take any credit cards.

Above this point, Herringtown Creek becomes fairly populated with houses and one gets the feeling of clutter. To your right, just after you round the point, there is an interesting little island (6), separated from the mainland by marsh and connected only by a corduroy road (road made from slabs of trees spread cross-ways across the path). The island has a very small and old two-story house. The story is that the land was given to a free slave after the War Between the States and that he built the tiny home and raised eight children there. The island and home are now used as a summer retreat by the owners who generate their own electricity.

Upper Grays Inn Creek has depths as indicated, and many houses and fields ashore. Just around Brown's Point (7), there is a nice anchorage in a cove that is actually better than would appear from the chart. The depths are good pretty close to the shore, certainly for a 4- to 5-foot draft boat. It shoals easily, so that you can feel your way to a comfortable distance from shore. Once anchored, you can look out to the east up Herringtown Creek and see the marinas in the distance, but immediately around you and on the shore of the cove are woods and field, with some farm houses in the distance of the Grays Inn Creek branch.

There is a public landing at New Yarmouth (8) with hard surface. It is possible to walk from this landing to Rock Hall, 1½ miles. Rock Hall is described in Chapter 7. Above the landing, the creek continues among houses and docks and fields until it seems to dissapear in a huge field with an ancient brick silo next to a barn. Only 1 to 2 feet depths are up there.

LANGFORD CREEK

Refer to Chart #12272-D—"Chester River—Gray's Inn Point to Quaker Neck Landing, Langford Creek, Comegys Bight."

This is a very large triburary of the Chester River, and has bountiful exploring opportunities, anchorages to suit most cruisers, and a few nice marinas.

Langford Creek (9) can also be rather difficult to identify amidst the hazy expanses of this part of the Chester. Once

you find Gr can "1" (8) (the same marker used as a reference point for entering Grays Inn Creek) things begin to fall into shape. It then helps to find the silo (10) and the tall fire lookout tower (11), both of which are up inside of the eastern shore of the creek. A good landmark for the western shore of the creek is the windmill (45), again inside the creek. The windmill is behind a barn with a light gray roof and red sides. Looking farther up into the creek, you can identify Drum Point (12) by its large brick house with a chimney on each end and, a small white house nestled on its eastern side. From Gr Can "1," a course of 50°M takes you to the vicinity of Gr Can "3" (13). Gr Can 5 (14) is next and very close. From here, 36°M takes you up to the vicinity of Gr Can "7" (15) but a straight line course on this route will put you over 7 feet of water in from Nichols Point (16). Therefore a little rounding to your left (westerly) may be necessary. *Editor's note: Once you have cleared the shallows off Nichols Point, the deepest water is off the east shore on this run between Green cans "5" and "7."*

Long Cove

The chart shows the entrance to this cove (17) (looks like a creek to me) to be studded with obstructions and a wreck. These were not obvious, but there are two marinas and a public ramp up the creek, the channel is marked, and if you carefully follow the markers, there should be no problem. I found 6 feet to be the controlling depth into the marinas, but the owner of one of the marinas advised that boats of 7 feet draft could be brought in on low tide, and he has been here most of his life. Before you get to the ramp, you will see the remains of an old oyster packing house (18) on your right (north). The building is no longer there, but the pier and jumble of red bricks remains.

Next to your right (north) is **Long Cove Public Landing (19)** which has a cement ramp, a bathroom, and some parking. A small fee or permit is required, as is true for all Kent County public ramps. Call Kent County at (410) 778-1948, for fee information. There is also a dock for fishing here.

The next facility, still on your right (north), is **Long Cove Marina (20)**. This is a very nice facility, run by Mort Deckleman who has been in the business all of his life. There are 100 slips with the largest at 50 feet but they can

Photo by Julius M. Wilensky

Long Cove Marina, Langford Creek, Chester River

96

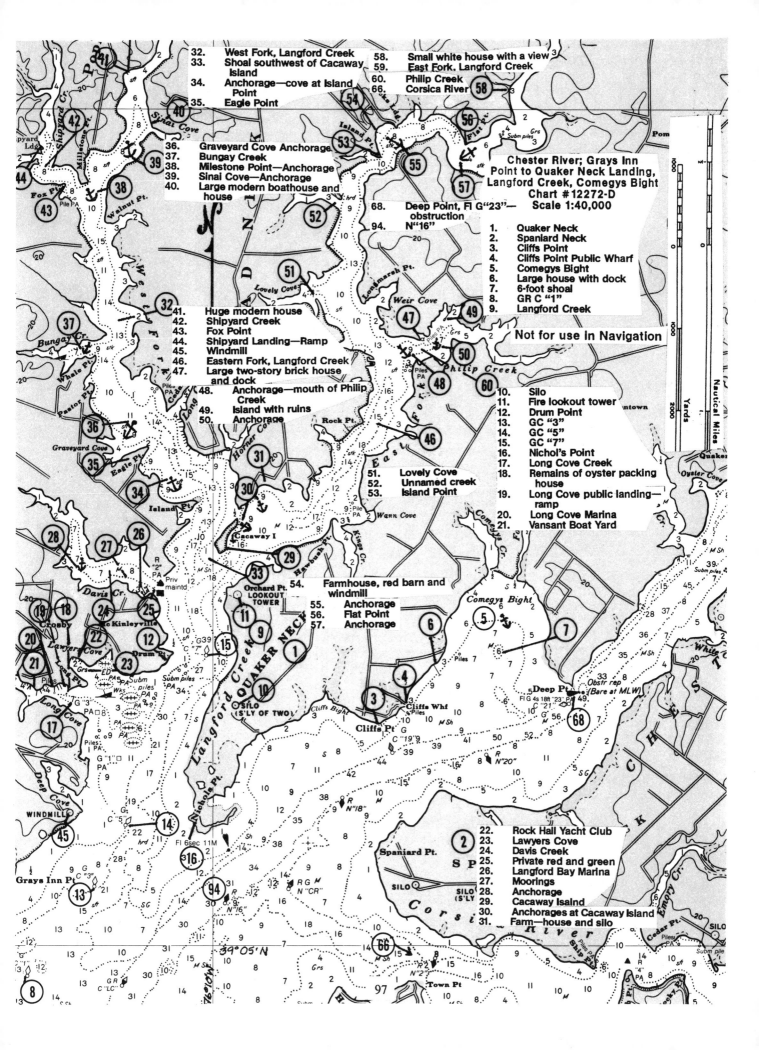

32. West Fork, Langford Creek
33. Shoal southwest of Cacaway Island
34. Anchorage—cove at Island Point
35. Eagle Point

58. Small white house with a view
59. East Fork, Langford Creek
60. Philip Creek
66. Corsica River

36. Graveyard Cove Anchorage
37. Bungay Creek
38. Milestone Point—Anchorage
39. Sinai Cove—Anchorage
40. Large modern boathouse and house

Chester River; Grays Inn Point to Quaker Neck Landing, Langford Creek, Comegys Bight
Chart #12272-D
Scale 1:40,000

1. Quaker Neck
2. Spaniard Neck
3. Cliffs Point
4. Cliffs Point Public Wharf
5. Comegys Bight
6. Large house with dock
7. 6-foot shoal
8. GR C "1"
9. Langford Creek

68. Deep Point, Fl G "23"—obstruction
94. N "16"

Not for use in Navigation

41. Huge modern house
42. Shipyard Creek
43. Fox Point
44. Shipyard Landing—Ramp
45. Windmill
46. Eastern Fork, Langford Creek
47. Large two-story brick house and dock
48. Anchorage—mouth of Philip Creek
49. Island with ruins
50. Anchorage

10. Silo
11. Fire lookout tower
12. Drum Point
13. GC "3"
14. GC "5"
15. GC "7"
16. Nichol's Point
17. Long Cove Creek
18. Remains of oyster packing house
19. Long Cove public landing—ramp
20. Long Cove Marina
21. Vansant Boat Yard

51. Lovely Cove
52. Unnamed creek
53. Island Point

54. Farmhouse, red barn and windmill
55. Anchorage
56. Flat Point
57. Anchorage

22. Rock Hall Yacht Club
23. Lawyers Cove
24. Davis Creek
25. Private red and green
26. Langford Bay Marina
27. Moorings
28. Anchorage
29. Cacaway Island
30. Anchorages at Cacaway Island
31. Farm—house and silo

accomodate boats up to 70 feet on face docks. Electricity up to 50 amps is available. There is a nice marine store with a good selection of hardware and block and cube ice. The bathrooms have several private units. There is a pumpout station. A marina yacht club is on the premises. Gas and diesel are sold, but credit cards were not taken last year. The owner advised that 7 to 8 feet of draft can be brought into the docks, but I would consult with him before I brought in any more than six. There is a large repair yard here, with a shed that is 100 feet wide and 80 feet deep and 36 feet tall, perfect for climate-controlled work. They have a 60-ton crane, a 70-ton and a 20-ton open end lift, barges, do complete repairs and also have a salvage and tow business. Propane is available nearby and they are only a few miles from Rock Hall, with its supplies and parts. There is also a large dry storage area.

The last marina up the creek, still to your right (north), is the **Vansant Boat Yard (21)**. This has 20 slips and some moorings off and upstream from the slips. There is a railway for 50 feet up to 20 tons. Fifteen amps are available at the slips. Farther up past this marina, the creek becomes very narrow and cluttered with moored boats.

The small building of **Rock Hall Yacht Club (22)** sits back from a very exposed small dock in shallow water up in Lawyers Cove (23). The facility is white with brick chimney and large windows. Because of the obstructions abundantly noted on the chart, do not venture in here without specific local instruction. I found a little more than 3 feet at the end of the dock. Several shallow draft boats are moored off the club.

Davis Creek

Heading farther north into Langford Creek brings you to Davis Creek (24) with a nice marina and anchorages. There is a set of privately maintained red and green markers (25) to aid in the entrance to this creek.

As soon as you round the point, you notice a large old white house on the point. Then **Langford Bay Marina (26)** comes into view with its attractive gray buildings. It has a very nice appearance, it is set within very pretty surroundings of eastern shore countryside, and it is locally owned and operated, having been in business for around 40 years. The docks and facilities are well maintained. There are 23 moorings (27) in protected waters up from docks and around 100 slips up to 50 feet long. Depths are from 5 to 7 feet, depending on location. Thirty amps are available at the docks. Chevron gas and diesel are sold, with Chevron, Visa, and MC honored. There is a very well-stocked marine hardware and parts store, with block and cube ice available. They sell charts, fishing gear and bait, as well as limited groceries. A retail seafood store is next door. You can rent bikes here for a nice ride in the country. There is a full service yard with a 2-ton crane and a 60-foot 40-ton lift, and two large boathouses for inside work in the water. They do much carpentry work as well as other types of marine work. There is a marina yacht club here. This area is also a few miles from Rock Hall with its supplies and facilities. They are dealers for Westerbeke, Volvo, and Ferkins.

The creek ends a short distance up from the marina, but there is a nice place to anchor (28), surrounded by field and wood, just upstream from the marina. This is a great place to rest awhile with the quietness and beauty of pastoral scenery, but also with the conveniences of the marina nearby.

Cacaway Island (29)

This pretty, uninhabited small island forms a popular anchoring spot, especially on its eastern side (30). There is only 2 feet depth between the island and the mainland, and it is fun to explore around the shores of the island in a dinghy. Cacaway Island is privately owned. The northern point next to the mainland has a beach, and there is a beach on the eastern shore in the cove. Anchoring on the eastern side, you will see less civilization ashore, although there are houses and farms. The cove up into the mainland above the northern point of the island, with 9 feet depth close up to the shore, is a nice anchorage. It is not quite as private as might be expected because it is dominated by a large farm facility, with house and silo (31). Many boats anchor in the cove on the eastern side of the island up close to the beach. Here, depths of around 10 feet carry well into the cove, with 4 feet of water within around 20 feet of the beach. Looking south you will notice the fire lookout station (11) on Orchard Point. There is also a two-story gray house with red roof just to the north of the tower, just behind a large dock.

West Fork of Langford Creek (32)

This is a nice area to explore, visiting a typical Eastern Shore river with forest, field, and farm. There are many places to anchor. Coming in, you will pass Cacaway Island to your right (east). Be careful to avoid the shoal (33) extending well out from the southwestern point of that island.

Following the river up, pick your favorite anchorage; a few suggestions follow. The cove behind Island Point (34) looks inviting on the chart, and is nice except for the many homes and docks directly across the creek from you. As you pass Eagle Point (35), you will see many more houses on the eastern bank than on the western. Graveyard Cove (36) behind Eagle Point, is another nice place to set the hook. Bungay Creek (37) is pretty, with a wreck visible up on shore. There is a white boathouse on the northern side of the creek, with farmland, trees, and marsh.

If you anchor off Milestone Point (38), you will find a pretty view up both branches and down the river, without too many houses in view. There is another pretty anchorage just before Sinai Cove (39). If you proceed farther, denser houses ashore will begin to impair your feeling of privacy. Just upstream from Sinai Cove is a large modern boathouse and house (40), and farther up the creek another huge modern house (41) sits on a hill on the western bank with much cleared land around it. Farther up, the creek becomes more scenic and woodsy, but here the depths are only a couple of feet.

Shipyard Creek

Entering this creek you will find many houses with docks on the western shore in the cove behind Fox Point (43). Because of this, I would feel uncomfortable anchoring here, although it is very well protected. Farther up is the Shipyard Landing (44), with a cement launching ramp and a dock. This is a Kent County fee ramp, call (410) 778-1948 for information on fees. The area off the landing, in 6 to 7 feet of water, makes a pretty area to anchor, but this can be busy with traffic from the landing. Farther up, the creek becomes very pretty with a feeling of deep woods, but is shallow and stumpy. This is a nice place to explore by dinghy.

Eastern Fork of Langford Creek (46)

Entering this branch, keep Cacaway Island on your left (to the west). This branch is deep and pretty, with much woods and farm land. There are many places to anchor. It is always nice to tuck up into one of the coves or side creeks, but there are also many places out in the river which would give more breeze on hot buggy evenings. A few suggestions follow.

In Philip Creek (60) there are two very nice places to anchor, one near the mouth and another farther in. Behind the first point on the north as you enter, there is a very large modern two-story brick house (47) which dominates the scenery. It has a dock in front of it in the vicinity of the "piles" indicated on the chart. There is another smaller house. Anchoring in the area marked 9 feet (48) gives a nice open feeling. Farther in, past the large house, the creek becomes prettier. The strange-looking landmark coming off a point on the northern shore appears as a little island (49), man-made and very old, perhaps a duck blind, with what was once a dock or causeway connecting it to the mainland. It now appears as part of nature, and the anchorage (50) between it and the little cove on the opposite shore is snug and very pretty, although I found depths in here to be around a foot less than reported on the chart. Note that the bottom is grass up from this point, making it difficult to hold with most anchors. If you draw more than 5½ feet, feel your way into this area carefully.

Lovely Cove (51) is as pretty as its name implies, but if you are looking for secluded anchorages, this cove doesn't quite fit the bill. There are homes on the southern shore, at least one permanent mooring inside, and docks coming out from the homes.

Next north, on the western shore, there is an unnamed creek (52) that looks like a boot, with 3 feet of depth indicated near its mouth. If you have a very shoal draft, this is a very pretty anchorage without too much civilization to impair the scenery.

Farther up the East Fork, there are more houses over all, but still some nice spots to stop. One such is just around Island Point (53). There is a red farmhouse and red barn (54) with windmill on the western bank, right up in the middle of the cove, with a white house on the eastern bank. I could see no dock where there is a broken line indicating such on the western bank in the cove, but the farmhouse is above this and there may be ruins below the water. In any event, this makes a very nice, quiet, pretty place to anchor (55). Farther up, off Flat Points (56), is another particularly scenic area. There are homes around, but they do not overpower the scenery. Just beyond Flat Point is a beautiful cove (57) for the very shallow drafted cruiser. Be careful of the submerged piles shown on the chart, and note that the area may contain less that the 3 feet indicated, especially closer in to the shore. There is a small white house (58) high up on a hill overlooking the cove and the creek, which meanders off northeasterly. This home has beautiful view, and certainly enhances the special feeling of quiet Eastern Shore beauty in this area.

Corsica River
Refer to Chart #12272-C— "Reed Creek, Grove Creek, Corsica River, Centreville." Pg. 94

This is one of the most popular rivers for anchoring and weekend cruising. It features many areas of wooded shorelines and a sparsely civilized character, coupled with nice coves and snug anchorages. Centreville, at the head of the river, offers some provisioning if you don't mind a lot of walking, but is not very conveniently reached by a large boat.

The entrance to the Corsica River (66) is easy enough to find, directly from across Nichols Point (16) and between Spaniard (67) and Holton Points (68). There are two silos (69) on Spaniard Point which help. Shoals meander out into

the Chester River from both sides of the entrance, and these may change in the exposed area as seas from storms and tides wash back and forth over the seasons.

While heading up the Chester River, you will pass R Nun "16" (94), and round it, passing between it and RG Nun "CR" (71). From a point around half way between these two buoys, 120°M will take you into the river to the vicinity of R Nun "2" (72) inside. Note that the shoals do meander out from the sides of the channel, and this course may need to be modified as you come in, depending on what you find with your depth finder. Boats with up to 7 feet of draft should not have much problem until they pass R Nun "2." Here the shoals reach out from each side, and we recently found only 7 feet (72) here at low water. You would think that with the great amount of water flowing into and out of the river with each tide, there would be a better naturally maintained channel here, but it doesn't seem to be the case. If you draw more than 6 feet, it would be best to squeeze through this shallow area on a rising tide.

As you pass into the mouth of the Corsica, you will see a huge mansion on the southern bank, called "Pioneer Point Manor" (73). This was built by John J. Raskob, who also built the Empire State Building. In more recent years, the Russians have used it as a retreat for their embassy personnel.

Once past R Nun "2," the going is much easier as the water deepens and widens. From here in, pick your favorite place and anchor. There is a pretty spot just past the spit on the northern bank (74). Though it is a little exposed, breezes are good here, and there is a nice beach on the spit. A house with dock looks down onto the anchorage.

The cove off the mouth of Emory Creek (75) is a beautiful place to spend the evening. When settling in, stay well off Cedar Point (76) to the east, because the shoal builds out from here. At low tide, it makes a nice beach. There are woods right down to the shore around the mouth of the creek, and fields back from the shore, but they are mostly concealed by the woods. In the fall, the geese will gently talk you to sleep as they discuss their day and the flight tomorrow.

Emory Creek (77) itself is a near perfect anchorage if your boat is shallow enough to get in. The entrance looks very constricted on the chart, but it is not as narrow as it may seem. I found depths to be as indicated on the chart. Just follow the chart in. The banks shoal up quickly, and you will know if you are moving too far to the left or right. Despite the depths, don't take a boat of more than 5 feet in here, because there is not much room in the deep water for turning around and maneuvering. Explore by dinghy first. Emory Creek is beautiful and very snug. You'll have a feeling of isolation, with deep woods all around. There is a quaint red boat house (78) on the second point in, on the western shore, but it seems to fit there.

Moving west, there are two more popular anchorages on either side of the Corsica River, in the cove (70) between Wash Point and Rocky Point, and in the cove opposite Rocky Point (80). You could also anchor west of Rocky Point. Up here, there are more houses ashore with docks and moorings, and you begin to sense a return to higher civilization. Many like to anchor just around Jacob's Nose (81) in the cove behind Green Point (82). This is not as pretty an anchorage area as those closer to the mouth because there is a large house on the northern shore dominating the scenery in the cove, and there are many houses across the river and tucked behind Jacob's Nose. If coming up the river this far, be sure to round R "6" (83) well to the north, since the shoal that it marks continues on a little beyond it. Except for very shallow boats, I would not recommend anchoring farther up river than this. Not only do the coves become shallow, the river becomes fairly congested as it approaches Centreville (84) with its narrow dredged entrance channel (85) and work boat traffic.

As you approach Centreville, you will notice that the channel is marked with small local floats (85) and the channel is narrow. It is dredged, and well used by many work boats, but they normally do not draw much more than 3 to 4 feet. The chart indicates 2½ feet centerline depth to the landing. I found around 3 feet. If your boat is of shallow enough draft to get up into this channel, you will find scarce room for anchoring off the town dock. If there is any room to tie up at all at this dock, it can not be for long because it is public and used by many. There is public asphalt launching ramp (86) here, with fees charged by the county as follows: $5/day in-state; $10/day out-of-state. Call (410) 758-0835 or (410) 778-4430. From the dock, a walk of a little under a mile will bring you to the compact center of this small, nicely preserved old town.

Centreville

Centreville (84) is not a boating town with those types of supplies or businesses. However you can get groceries, package goods, hardware items, and find many other conveniences such as a post office, restaurants, and historic scenery. As you will find in most places on the Shore, the folks are very nice.

Getting to town from the town docks looks a little discouraging as you land. The landing area ashore is dirt without much to see. You must cross this dirt area to Bridge Street, which crosses the bridge that you will have noticed just ahead of you as you come up the river (now more like a creek). Turn left on Bridge Street (don't cross the bridge) and walk in an easterly direction. After several blocks, it will become Chesterfield Avenue. Keep walking. You will pass a public school on your left. Very shortly after that, Broadway intersects Chesterfield. Turn left (north) on Broadway, and a few blocks more will have you into the center of Centreville. This downtown area encompass several blocks with such street names as "Lawyers Row," "Water Street," and "Liberty Street."

Here you will find what many consider to be the main attractions of the town. The historic courthouse (87) sits back on its green with a statue of Queen Anne, befitting the oldest courthouse in continuous use in the State of Maryland, since 1791. A few blocks away, St. Paul's Church (88) has a section dating back into the late 17th century, with communion silver dated 1717. There are numerous houses historically preserved. Two of these are Tucker House (89) and Wright's Chance (90), both located on Commerce Street. Lawyers Row is an interesting street from the past where attorneys hung their shingles a short walk across the street from the Court House. The town hall (92) is a traditional old building with a bell tower and clock.

There are typical commercial establishments (93) that you could expect in a small town. Of particular importance would be the hardware store at Broadway and Commerce across from the courthouse. A drugstore, post office (95), and grocery store are also in this area, as well as several small restaurants.

Chester River above the Corsica

Refer to Chart #12272-D—"Chester River; Grays Inn Point to Quaker Neck Landing, Langford Creek, Comegys Bight."

Pg. 97

The nature of the Chester changes considerably after you

pass between Quaker Neck (1) on the northern shore, and Spaniard Neck (2) on the southern shore. From expanses so wide that mouths of tributaries are hard to recognize, the river narrows between banks that are often high, and generally covered with woods and fields, sometimes protected by the marsh. The river is deep and easy up to Chestertown. If the wind favors the bends, this can make a beautiful sailing trip into the rolling countryside of the eastern shore. There are ample places to anchor off the channel. Most are exposed to whatever fetch the bend brings. Take your pick. A detailed description of the river from here to Chestertown and beyond would be quite redundant, with one beautiful scene after another each bend you round. There are navigational buoys to Chestertown where there is a bascule bridge with vertical clearance of 12 feet. The friendly bridge tender told me that the bridge opens on demand from 6 to 6 in season from April 1 to September 30. They stand by on Channel 13 and respond to proper horn signals. At other times or seasons, call 6 hours ahead of time at 1-800-787-9439 or at (410) 829-3008.

Immediately past Cliff's Point (3), which is just beyond Nichol's Point, you will notice Cliff's Point Public Wharf (4) on the northern shore. This is a permitted facility, with fees according to the latest county schedule, call (410) 778-1948 for fee information. The ramp is cement, and there is a dock with 2 to 3 feet at its end, I found the bottom to be uneven here. The dock is quite exposed and is not for overnight use.

Just beyond Cliff's Wharf is a large cove in the northern shore called Comegys Bight (5). This is considered by many to be an anchorage, but is certainly not much more so than any other open stretch of the river. As long as you do not mind some open water around you, this is a nice area for northwest to northeast winds. Southwest to southeast would be no fun at all. A very large three-story house (6) with long dock with white railings dominates the western bank, and other houses and docks frequent the shores farther in. The chart shows a 6-foot shoal (7) in the middle of the bight. This is not marked, but it shallows gradually and is not difficult to miss if you're paying attention and just go around in the middle. I favor approaching on the western side toward the large house. To avoid any remains of the pilings noted on the chart, just stay off the shore and well beyond the dock in that area.

To follow the Chester River up to Chestertown, follow basic river navigation common sense as well as the markers (see our notes on this subject in Chapter 1). Beware of the shoal and obstruction reported to bare at low water to the southeast of Deep Point (68) (the "Deep Point" at the southeast tip of Comegys Bight) and which is marked by Fl G "23."

Refer to Chart #12272-E—"Quaker Neck Landing to Chestertown."

Note the shoal east of the rounding point between Hollow Marsh Point and Fryingpan Point. If you go straight for G "35" (13), you may wind up aground, but if you round the point, taking into consideration Fl R "34," you should have no trouble.

There are two nice facilities relatively close to each other on the southern bank of the Chester River before you reach Chestertown. One is Kennersly Point Marina (8) in Southeast Creek (9), and the other is a nice bed and board with marina at Rolph's Wharf (10).

Southeast Creek (9) is very shallow with pretty woods and farm around its shores. Other than for exploration in a shallow draft boat, few cruisers would find much of interest here, except the very nice marina at Kennersley Point.

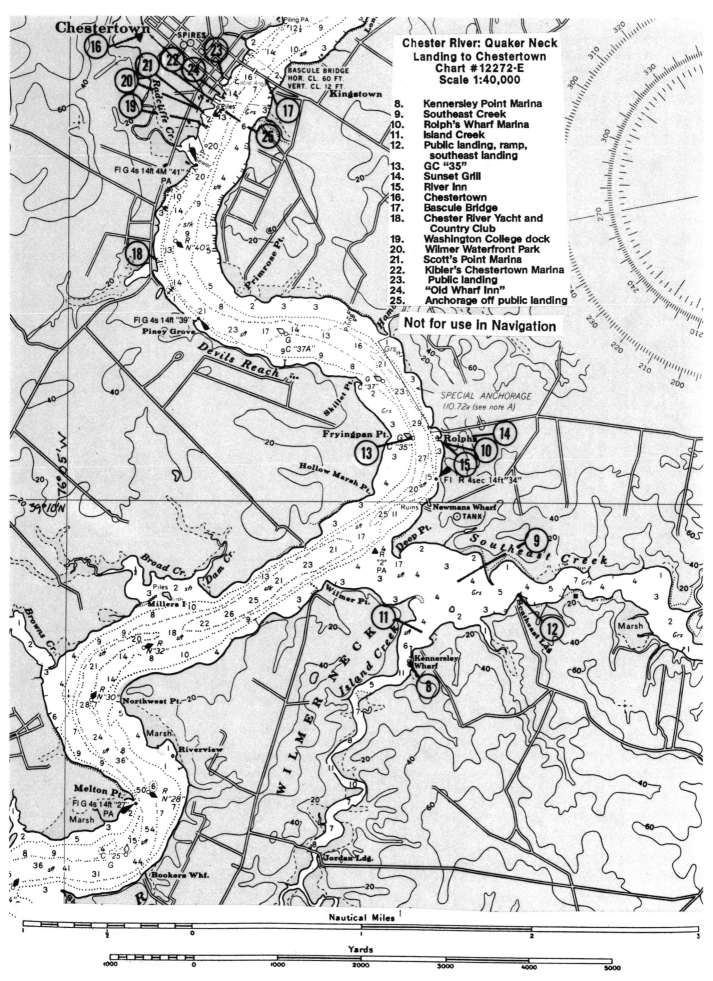

Chester River: Quaker Neck
Landing to Chestertown
Chart #12272-E
Scale 1:40,000

8. Kennersley Point Marina
9. Southeast Creek
10. Rolph's Wharf Marina
11. Island Creek
12. Public landing, ramp,
    southeast landing
13. GC "35"
14. Sunset Grill
15. River Inn
16. Chestertown
17. Bascule Bridge
18. Chester River Yacht and
    Country Club
19. Washington College dock
20. Wilmer Waterfront Park
21. Scott's Point Marina
22. Kibler's Chestertown Marina
23. Public landing
24. "Old Wharf Inn"
25. Anchorage off public landing

Not for use in Navigation

Nautical Miles

Yards

101

Kennersley Point Marina (8) is a very nice family run marina on a creek which runs beside an old farm. The proprietors live on the premises in a nice house off to the side. Its approach is very shallow however, passing through the wide and somewhat exposed mouth of Southeast Creek. The owners report 4 to 5 feet, but don't go in here without talking to them first to get the very latest information. Call them on VHF 16 or at (410) 758-2394. The chart indicates a controlling depth of 3 feet. The marinas try to keep markers set, but I have not indicated them on the chart, because there was some question as to where they would be at that time. However, they will be obvious.

Kennersley Point Marina is very attractive, with its slips along the southeastern shore of beautiful Island Creek (11), facing the wooded banks opposite. There are 50 slips with the longest at approximately 50 feet, but they can take transients up to 70 feet. The docks have electricity up to 50 amps. Gas is sold and they honor MC and Visa. There are seven moorings in the creek. There is a small marine store with a few convenience grocery store items, block and cube ice, and fishing gear and bait, a clean air conditioned head and showers, pumpout, and laundromat. The marina has a large area for dry winter storage and a 15-ton lift. A cement launching ramp is also on the premises.

Impressive to me is that Kennersley Point Marina is a very nice place for families, well out in the woods and country and away from the smog and bustle of the cities. There is a swimming pool, large yards for kids to run in, and various games such as horseshoes, badminton, a playground, and a barbecue area with covered picnic tables. There is a marina yacht club. The proprietors will cater for meals and parties on the boats or at the facilities. Bikes can be rented for a ride along the country roads, and the proprietors will assist with transportation to nearby Chestertown when a vehicle is available. There is also a rental unit with a fireplace and small kitchen on the premises which will sleep up to six people.

Farther west up Southeast Creek, on the southern shore, you will find a public landing at "Southeast Landing" (12). This has a dock and a plank ramp.

As you continue up the Chester River, Rolph's Wharf (10), on the site of an old steamship landing, offers an excellent opportunity for dining. You can tie up or anchor off. This is also a nice bed and breakfast in an 1830s Victorian home. This makes it an excellent place to meet friends who may not wish to stay aboard. The marina is across from Gr can "35" (13) on the eastern shore, around 2 miles downstream from Chestertown. Dockage is free while dining at the restaurant. Depths are up to 8 feet for dockage, with 40 slips taking lengths of up to 65 feet and offering electricity up to 50 amps. The docks are on the river banks, and in a very severe blow from offshore or up or down river will be exposed, although the river is not very wide here. This factor should be considered as you tie up, particularly if a typical summer storm is forecast with the usual strong west or northwest winds. Citgo gas is sold, and MC, Visa and Amex cards are honored as well. An 8-ton lift capable of taking boats up to 34 feet allows storage and launching. There is also a cement ramp. Bathrooms and showers are a short walk up the yard, as is a nice swimming pool. They sell live bait and block and cube ice. Rolph's Wharf will offer a loan vehicle, when available, for driving into Chestertown.

Their bed and breakfast offers three meals, in the Sunset Grill (14), and in the River Inn (15). They will also cater for special events on the premises or fix picnic lunches. On weekends and other special nights there is often live entertainment. A beach next to the docks presents one more attraction on this 6½-acre establishment.

CHESTERTOWN

This beautiful and historic town, on the west side of the Chester River offers nice walks down tree-covered lanes amidst historic surroundings. Good shopping and fine restaurants abound, but there are not many basic marine supplies. Unless you tie up in a marina, you will have to anchor out in the river. Although not very wide here, the river has considerable fetch in a northeasterly and southwesterly direction.

Chestertown Waterfront

As you approach Chestertown (16) around the river's bend at Devil's Reach, you will see the bridge (17) ahead with nice homes on the eastern bank across from town. Before Chestertown, the docks of the Chester River Yacht and Country Club (18) come into view to your left. A white sign arching over the end of the dock proclaims "CRYCC." The club house is back across the road that runs along the river here. This club features golfing as well as boating.

The next dock will be the landing belonging to Washington College (19). The college itself is back up behind the town, well away from the water, but uses this landing for water-related activities. This is a single dock perpendicular to the shore with a pavilion behind it and a brown building inshore. It is not for public use.

You will next see Wilmer Waterfront Park (20). This is a grassy area with benches and a pavilion. Often concerts are held here in the summer.

The next facility is the first of the two marinas in town, Scott's Point Marina (21). They are easily identified by the signs on their pier. They do not sell fuel. Depths are 10 feet on the outside piers and 6 feet on the inside. There are 36 slips with up to 30 amps available in some slips. No credit cards are taken. There is a head and shower, and block and cube ice. They will loan bikes if available, and they monitor Channels 78A and 16.

The marina immediately upriver is Kibler's Chestertown Marina (22). This is not to be confused with the public dock (23) which is closer to the bridge. The dock house for the marina is red stained wood. Depths are up to 13 feet on the outer docks. There are 54 slips with electricity up to 50 amps, with 110 and 220 volts. It is possible to tie up very long boats on the face piers. Chevron gas and diesel are sold with Visa, MC, and Chevron cards accepted. There is a helpful marine store on the premises selling marine hardware, block and cube ice, and fishing tackle. They have a pumpout station. Wet and dry storage is available, and there is a 20-ton closed end lift. There is a laundromat and there are showers and a head. On the premises you will find Williams Marine and Cabinetry (22), specializing in boat repair and woodworking. A cement ramp is available to the public for a small fee. This marina has been open since 1959 and you will find the people very helpful and this is a good marina to stop at while visiting Chestertown. It is within easy walking distance to most of the downtown area with its restaurants, shops, and sightseeing. Propane tanks are filled a few blocks away and car and bike rentals are convenient. A post office is only several blocks walk. The "Old Wharf Inn" (24) has a menu generally ranging from around 10 to 20 dollars. Dine here and watch the

Chestertown

17. Bridge
20. To Wilmer Park
21. To Scotts Point Marina
22. Kibler's Chestertown Marina & Williams Marina & Cabinetry
23. Public Landing
24. Old Wharf Inn
25. Anchorage
32. Chamber of Commerce— Town Hall
33. Library
34. Water Street—historic and residential area
35. Queen Street
36. "Customs House"
37. "Wide Hall"
38. "River House"
39. Houston Dockside Emporium
40. The General Store
41. Buck-Bacchus Store (circa. 1735)
42. Imperial Hotel and Restaurant and "Cellar at the Imperial" (crafts, art, jewelry, etc.)
45. Geddes Piper House— Historical Society of Kent County. (410) 778-3499
46. Feast of Reason
47. Stam Drug Company
48. Chestertown Pharmacy
49. Map of Chestertown, UPS, FedEx at Chesapeake Bank and Trust Co.
50. Monument Park
51. Kent County Court House
52. Town Park
53. Andy's
54. Farmer's market (on Saturdays)
55. Corsica Bookshop
56. Chestertown Art League (local original art)
57. Sutton's Towne Stationers
58. The Singletree—fine hand crafted gifts
59. White Swan Inn—18th century bed and breakfast inn serves afternoon tea
60. Royal Farms Store (convenience grocery store)
61. Billy's Blue Crabs and More (outdoor dining, steamed seafood)
62. Ironstone Café
63. Wilma's Kitchen (breakfast, sandwiches, ice cream etc.)
64. Dollar General Store
65. First United Methodist Church
66. Emmanual Protestant Episcopal Church
67. Kent and Queen Anne's Hospital
68. Washington College
69. Kent Plaza Shopping Center
70. Chestertown Fire Co.
71. Chestertown Police
72. Library
73. Post Office
74. Chesapeake Inns (administrative office for six country inns —1-800-787-Inns)

Not for use in Navigation

103

river roll by with the excitement of boat traffic approaching the marina or public landing.

The public landing (23) allows dinghy docking and tie up for limited stays, not overnight docking. It is north of Kibler's Marina, and is at the base of High Street, the main thoroughfare for your exploration ashore. Often boats anchor in the river directly off the landing (25), but beware of the cable area. The cable lies from the foot of Cannon Street to just south of the bridge where it joins the western bank of the river. When I visited last year, I saw no cable signs, and was told that they are awaiting surveying before placing the signs. Unless signs make the cable route clear when you visit, check with Kibler's Marina or someone else to be sure that you are not setting the hook in the wrong place.

Chestertown History

First called the "Port of Chester," this town was founded in 1706 under the auspices of Queen Anne for the express purpose of advancing trade in this area of Maryland. The streets were surveyed and planned by nine port commissioners on the 100-acre tract. This was a very strategic shipping area, the river winding deep into the countryside and easily navigable. Trade and shipping flourished. Chestertown was known in the days prior to the American Revolution to be a place of high living and fanciful extarvagance. In 1786, The Reverend Francis Asbury, a very famous traveling Methodist preacher, proclaimed it to be a "wicked place," referring to the fine and fast life then in progress in this prosperous port. The railroad and then highways made water transportation far less useful as time passed on and now the town no longer serves as a port

but is a cultural and beautiful reminder of the past.

Chestertown has long been a major center of historical interest on the Eastern Shore. George Washington College there is the tenth oldest college in the United States, founded in 1782. Some of the original construction money for this college was obtained by selling lottery tickets, and George Washington was reportedly responsible for the sale of some of these in Alexandria, Virginia. Indeed, the town square boasts not merely that "George Washington slept here," but that he visited there on at least eight known occasions. As would be imagined, there are many beautiful and old buildings and homes in the town, and the town itself has nicely preserved its heritage in the more recent development. A walk up High Street from the river is like a walk through history, with trees arching over the quiet street and old buildings, some with white columns, set back from the sidewalk.

Chestertown Ashore

Refer to our Sketch—"Street Map of Chestertown." Pg. 103

The downtown area within walking distance of the waterfront is full of shops, businesses, restaurants, and services, that you would expect to find in any small and prosperous town. The area Chamber of Commerce (32) is very active and within walking distance, on the northwest corner of Maple Avenue and Cross Street in the Town Hall. They have maps showing not only commercial establishments but also places of historical interest, phone (410) 778-0416. As you walk up High Street, you will even encounter a map of downtown (49) Chestertown on the side of the bank building at the corner of High and Cross Streets. You may also find helpful an early

High Street, Chestertown

visit to the Geddes Piper House (45) on the northwest side of Queen Street between High Street and Maple Avenue. This is the home of the Historical Society of Kent County, phone (410) 778-3499.

The first two streets back (northwesterly) from the river are primarily residential in nature, containing many historical homes. These are Water Street (34) and Queen Street (35). A turn to your right (northeast) at Water Street and a walk down the street along the river, circling up northwestward along Maple Avenue and then turning left (southwesterly) down Queen Street will give you a quick taste of the charm of the non-commercial area. The Kent County Chamber of Commerce publishes a walking tour map identifying all of the landmarks and giving a brief sketch about each. Examples of these homes are the Customs House (36), built around 1746 and near which the original Chestertown Tea Party occurred, "Wide Hall" (37) with Georgian architecture, built around 1770 by a very wealthy merchant and "River House" (38), built around 1784 and now owned by the Maryland Historical Trust.

If you want to head straight into town, walk northwesterly up High Street. This beautiful broad road is lined with trees and homes. The homes give way to businesses at Queen Street, but charm remains even in this section. On the corner of Queen and High Streets, you will see the Houston Dockside Emporium (39), selling marine and sporting clothing and other items of a nautical theme, no marine hardware. The Buck-Bacchus Store (circa 1735) (41) is nearby.

About half way between Queen Street and Court Street, you will find the very special Imperial Hotel (42) with its three stories of white-columned front, flags flying from the balconies, and quiet, opulent interior. The hotel was built in 1903 and was entirely remodeled in mid-1980s keeping Victorian style and decorations, blended with Eastern Shore craftsmanship. This renovation received the Restoration Project Award from the Maryland Trust for Historic Preservation. There are now 11 deluxe guest rooms and a parlor suite with one bedroom. Their restaurant is acclaimed to be one of the finest. Behind the main building there is a unique walled-in courtyard with benches among crepe myrtle, cherry laurel, Chesapeake holly, and oak. The old carriage house to the rear

of the grounds has been converted to a family suite with a cathedral ceiling living room. It also has a kitchen and dining area and there is a conference room on the floor below. This structure fronts on the courtyard.

If you are after some fine health and gourmet food, you will find on the northwestern side of the intersection of Queen and High streets, second from the corner, the Feast of Reason (46) offering gourmet health food to take with you or eat on the premises.

A little farther down the block, still on the southwestern side of the street (your left as you walk away from the water), The Stam Drug Company (47) sells prescriptions and fountain items, as well as all the general over the counter medicines, and other things such as sun glasses, suntan ointments, cosmetics, and toilet and personal articles that you would expect to find in most drugstores today. There is another pharmacy, the Chestertown Pharmacy (48), about two blocks farther up on the same side of the street. This also is well-stocked and contains most items that you would expect to find in a typical drugstore. Before you reach the end of the block, and still on the left (southwest) side of the street, stop and enjoy the White Swan Inn (59), an 18th century Bed and Breakfast and Inn which still serves afternoon tea. Walking up to High and Cross street intersection, you will find a Federal Express box and UPS next day air box outside of the Chesapeake Bank and Trust Company (49).

Looking across High Street to your right you will find Monument Park (50) with a World War II memorial and old cannons. Behind this is the old courthouse building (51) which stands at the original seat of Kent County when it was established in 1706. This is where George Washington has visited on at least eight known occasions. Across the street from the Town Park (52), and behind it to your right (northeast) is the town hall (32) which contains the Kent County Chamber of Commerce. A Farmer's Market (54) is held in season, weather permitting, in Town Park on Saturdays. If you need fresh provisioning, this would be the place to come.

Navigating even farther inland, still on the left side of High Street, you will come upon Andy's (53) on the fourth block up. This is a tavern and bar, featuring live entertainment such

Hotel Imperial, Chestertown

as folk music, blue grass, and other types. A Dollar General Store **(64)** is across from this. To reach this area you will have been heading uphill toward a very prominent steeple with a gold cross on top. This is the First United Methodist Church **(65)** with huge white columns in front. As you have passed up this street you will have passed many other nice shops and service businesses.

Walking around the area will bring many other delights. A left turn at High and Cross streets, and another left at Cannon Street will bring more restaurants and shops. Maple Avenue is more residential. There is a small grocery store **(60)** at the north corner of Cross Street and Maple Avenue, only a little over three blocks from the town dock.

There is a fairly large hospital for this area approximately a mile from the waterfront. This is the Kent and Queen Anne's Hospital **(67)**, (410) 778-3300. Travel up High Street, until you either reach Queen or Cross Streets. Turn to your right on either of these to reach Maple Avenue. Turn to your left (northwesterly direction) and follow Maple. When it intersects with Spring Avenue, it will bear off to your right (north-north-easterly) as Washington Ave. Continue following Washington Avenue away from the water. You will shortly see the signs to the hospital on the right side of the road.

Farther out Washington Avenue is George Washington College **(68)**. Farther still is a shopping center **(69)**, about 1½ miles from the water. Here there is grocery store, several restaurants including fast food, clothing and shoe stores, hardware, video rental, an optometrist, Radio Shack, a drugstore, a mailing and shipping service, a laundromat, and many other shops.

There are several interesting annual events in Chestertown. In late May the town re-enacts the Chestertown Tea Party. This is a major festival locally. On May 23, 1774, irate local colonists boarded the brigantine of the port tax collector and threw its cargo of tea into the Chester River. Townspeople dress as colonists and throw the tea over again each year. There are associated parades, contests, food booths, and other fun events. July features a fireworks show on the fourth, and a sailing regatta sponsored by the Chester River Yacht and Country Club. In mid-September there is a candlelight tour of the old homes, and there is another house tour during the Christmas season. Late October brings a Wildlife Show and Sale, featuring contests such as duck and goose calling and decoy carving, wildlife displays and ecological displays, music in the park, Eastern Shore wildlife art, special food booths, a town-wide wine and cheese tasting party, and much more. November brings an Arts and Crafts show.

KENT COUNTY

Chestertown today is still the county seat for Kent County, the smallest county in Maryland with 281 square miles. This county was settled in the 1600s, having been first visited by Captain John Smith during his explorations. Farming still makes a large part of the economy of this county, which has no heavy industry. Of course, seafood and hunting also play a significant role in the county, as does recreational boating. The county borders the Chesapeake and stretches between the Chester and Sassafras Rivers. Therefore it has some nice marinas including those on the northern tributaries of the Chester, those in Rock Hall, Worton Creek, Tolchester, Fairlee Creek, and Georgetown. There are many bed and breakfasts, historical sites, antiques and other items of interest throughout the county. The number for the Chambers of Commerce is (410) 778-0416.

The public ramps in the county have small fees. Call (410) 778-1948, the County Department of Parks and Recreation, for the location of the closest place to get a permit for the ramp which you wish to use. As is true in other countries, there is usually a nearby location at a sports store or similar place to pay the fee. These change, and the signs at the ramps do not always direct you where to go. This number will get the current necessary information.

Chester River Above Chestertown
Refer to Chart #12272-F—"Chester River—Chestertown to Travilah Wharf"   and
Chart #12272-G—"Chester River—Deep Landing to Kirby Landing."

Above the bascule bridge at Chestertown, the Chester River goes on and on, winding through some of the prettiest of Eastern Shore countryside, until it gets too shallow. The usual practices of river navigation, described in Chapter 1, generally apply in travelling up river. There are a few private markers to mark the very shallow water off Possum Point **(27)**, which would stop all but shallow draft boats. There is a fixed bridge at Crumpton **(28)** with 14 feet of vertical clearance. There are three ramps above the bridge, at Buckingham Wharf **(29)** (dirt), Deep Creek **(30)**, and Crumpton Creek **(31)**.

Photo by Julius M. Wilensky

Boathouse and private docks in Herrington town Creek (pg. 95)

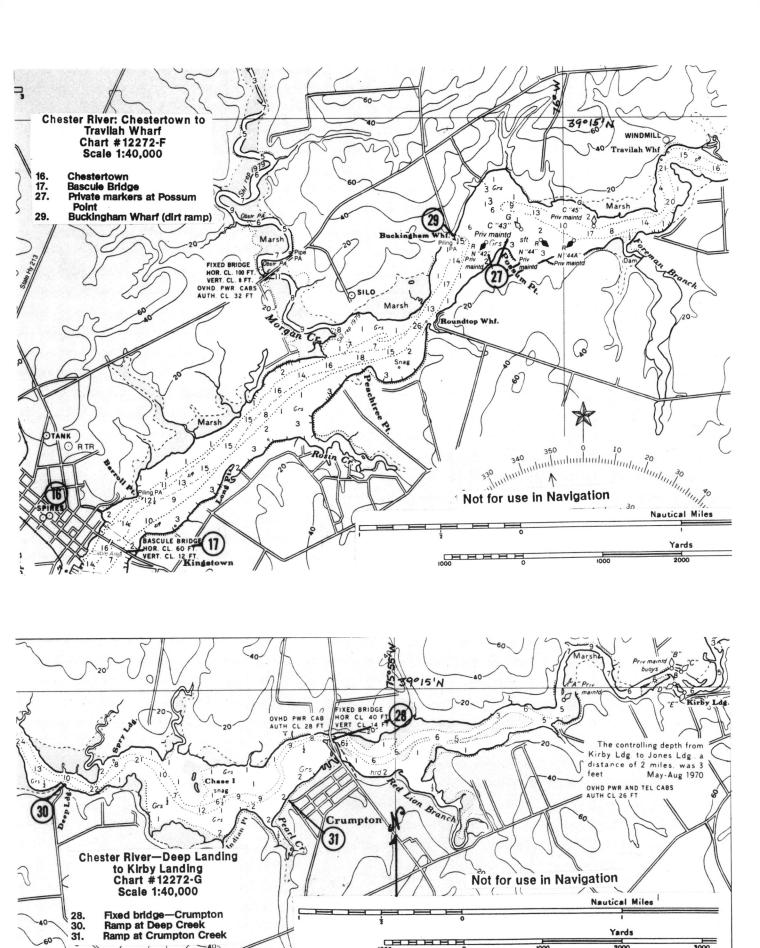

Chester River: Chestertown to Travilah Wharf
Chart #12272-F
Scale 1:40,000

16. Chestertown
17. Bascule Bridge
27. Private markers at Possum Point
29. Buckingham Wharf (dirt ramp)

Not for use in Navigation

Nautical Miles

Yards

Chester River—Deep Landing to Kirby Landing
Chart #12272-G
Scale 1:40,000

28. Fixed bridge—Crumpton
30. Ramp at Deep Creek
31. Ramp at Crumpton Creek

The controlling depth from Kirby Ldg. to Jones Ldg, a distance of 2 miles, was 3 feet May-Aug 1970

Not for use in Navigation

Nautical Miles

Yards

CHAPTER 9

KENT ISLAND NARROWS AND EASTERN BAY

KENT ISLAND NARROWS

This is an area of high density marinas, marine facilities, restaurants and shops. It is not known as a particularly good spot for anchoring or gunkholing, but on any good weekend, this is a very popular place to be.

Refer to Regional Chart #12270-A—"Kent Narrows, Kirwan Creek, Goodhands Creek."
Kent Island Narrows.(100) is a strategic link between the two beautiful cruising grounds of Eastern Bay (5) and the Chester River (2). It is also convenient to many other areas. It is only around 25 minutes drive from Annapolis, and just over an hour from Baltimore. It is central to many popular cruising areas. At around 7 knots, you can go to St. Michaels in a little over 2 hours, Oxford in around 5 hours, Annapolis in approximately 4 hours, the Wye River is close to 1½ hours, and the Baltimore Inner Harbor in less than 5 hours.

Approaches
Refer to Chart #12270-A—"Kent Narrows, Kirwan Creek, and Goodhands Creek"
and
Chart #12272-I—"Kent Narrows—Entrance from Chester River."

The southern approach is described later in this chapter in the section on Prospect Bay (6) (on **Chart #12272-H**) within the Eastern Bay section. Approaching from the north, pick up day beacons "34" and "35" (1) just inside the RG junction buoy "JC" (7) in the Chester River (2). With all of the congestion and activity, this is normally easy to find. The huge U.S. flag at Mears Point Marina (3) marks the vicinity and is usually clearly visible from the northern shore of the Chester River. You will also notice a conspicuous round red and white lighthouse (96) west of the entrance to the Narrows. This is actually a water tank behind and just to the east of the Castle Harbour Club (described in Chapter 8 on the Chester River).

This also serves as a reference point for picking up the Narrows markers. Note that the markers run from south to north, with red to right (9) going north all the way through and out into the Chester River. This means that entrance from the Chester River will have red to your left going in. Follow these markers closely. There is currently an effort locally to have the channel re-dredged to follow a more natural northwesterly course. This might lessen the degree of constant shoaling brought about by storms and wave action. Even if they do not change the dredged channel, it changes from time to time of its own accord. This should be kept in mind as you follow these markers. While 6 to 6½ feet can usually clear into the southern entrance and up to the last two marinas north of the bridge with no difficulty, I would feel reluctant taking more than 5 feet at this time through the northern entrance, and then at two-thirds tide and rising.

The tide can be significantly affected by strong winds. This should be considered if your draft is marginal. Northeastern winds will lower the water level, while southwestern winds will raise it. If in doubt, call local marinas on the VHF. They are acutely aware of the difficulties of the northern entrance. Mears Point Marina has very detailed soundings in the area.

Now Let's Enter Kent Island Narrows From The South
Refer to Chart #12272-H—"Kent Narrows." Pg. 111

As you near the Narrows, it is obvious that you are entering a busy area. Ahead are the two bridges. First is a bascule bridge (10) with vertical clearance of 18 feet. This has restricted openings every half hour in the summer. North of that is the new high rise bridge (8) of 65-foot clearance. Tide ranges considerably here, from 1½ foot to 3½ feet, approximately, depending on winds. Check the gauge before going through if there is any question. This bridge takes Routes 50 and 301 across the Narrows. This is a major highway, heading to the twin Chesapeake Bay Bridge and Annapolis, just a few minutes ride to the west, and Easton and the major Eastern Shore routes and destinations to the east.

Marshy Creek and Lippincot Marine
Passing Fl G 4 sec. "1" (11) to the left (west), you will see Marshy Creek (12) opening wide to the right (east). For boats of 5-foot draft or less, this is a decent anchorage (13). A shoal (14) comes off the point with the three-story gray condominiums (15) which is just to the north of Marshy Creek. It is best to follow the route in as privately marked (16) by Lippincott Marine (17). This begins at Red "2" (18) of the Kent Narrows Channel. Turn to right (easterly) around 50 feet before this aid and head to Green "1" of the private channel. When I last sounded the channel, I found there to be questionable water for 6 feet at low tide, but the bottom is mud. As described below, this whole area may be changing. Lippincott Marine is well run by responsible people, and I would call them if I had any questions about the creek entrance to their facility. There is up to 6 feet just beyond the entrance to the marina for anchoring, but this depth is spotty and I would not take more than 5 feet east of the marina channel. The channel is very busy up to the marina, and anchoring prior to that is not recommended.

Lippincott Marine (17) is a well established and very fine marina with full service boat yard, new and used boat sales, and a full charter line of sail and power. There are 200 slips up to 65 feet in length, with room for longer vessels on face docks. The marina tries to maintain a 7-foot entrance depth, and they keep the entrance channel marked. Call them in advance if you draw 6 feet or more draft. The docks have electricity to 50 amps. Block and cube ice are available, and they honor Visa and MC. There is a 250-boat dry storage area on the premises and the marina has speciality shops on most mechanical and hull work. The docks are within a mile of all the action, restaurants and shops of Kent Narrows, but are

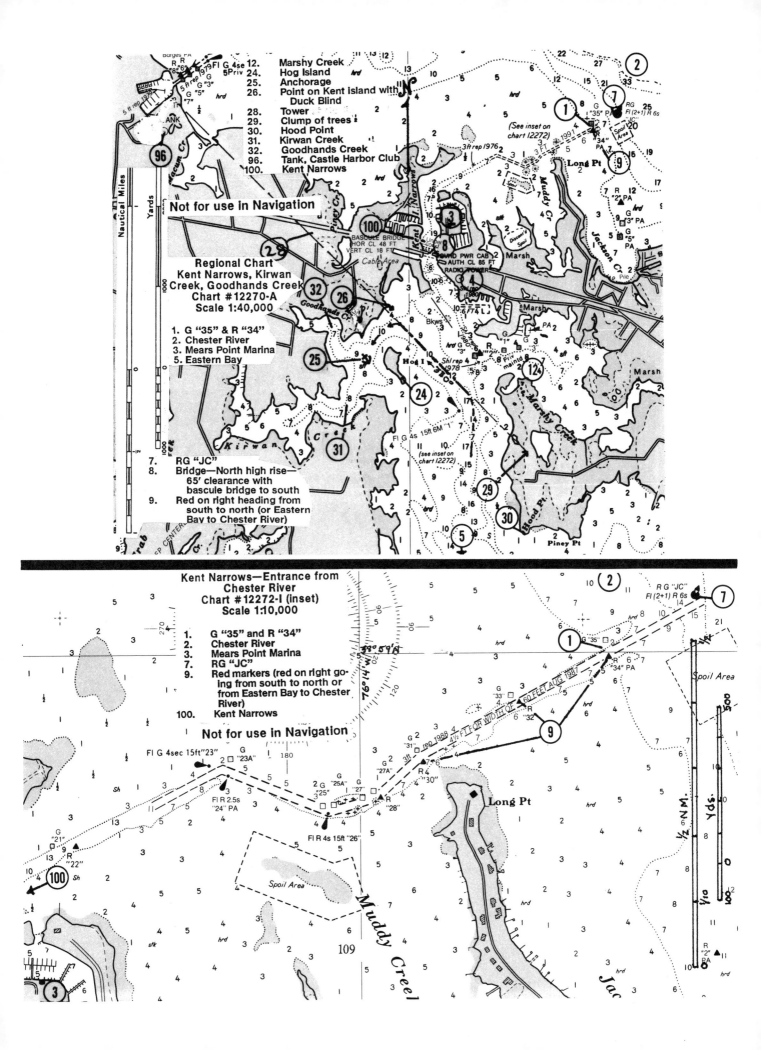

Not for use in Navigation

Regional Chart
Kent Narrows, Kirwan
Creek, Goodhands Creek
Chart #12270-A
Scale 1:40,000

1. G "35" & R "34"
2. Chester River
3. Mears Point Marina
5. Eastern Bay

7. RG "JC"
8. Bridge—North high rise—
   65' clearance with
   bascule bridge to south
9. Red on right heading from
   south to north (or Eastern
   Bay to Chester River)

12. Marshy Creek
24. Hog Island
25. Anchorage
26. Point on Kent Island with
    Duck Blind
28. Tower
29. Clump of trees
30. Hood Point
31. Kirwan Creek
32. Goodhands Creek
96. Tank, Castle Harbor Club
100. Kent Narrows

Kent Narrows—Entrance from
Chester River
Chart #12272-I (inset)
Scale 1:10,000

1. G "35" and R "34"
2. Chester River
3. Mears Point Marina
7. RG "JC"
9. Red markers (red on right going from south to north or
   from Eastern Bay to Chester
   River)
100. Kent Narrows

Not for use in Navigation

quiet at night and protected from weather by the creek mouth and a sea wall around the docks. They do not monitor VHF but can be telephoned at (401) 827-9300. They are authorized sales and service representatives for Northern Lights Generators and Cruisair A/C.

Proceeding into the Narrows channel, beware of a shoal (14) extending out from the point which is to the right (east of) of R "2." This is the point with the three-story gray condos mentioned above. It is best to favor the green side here between G "3" (19) and G "5" (20). The entire Narrows channel has very swift current, and is quite exposed to the south and southwest. Action is being taken by the local businesses to have the area dredged better, particularly on the north side. However, as is true of any such area, I would not be surprised at unexpected shoaling. A serious wash-through behind the breakwater (21) to the left (on the western side) is now developing. Where the chart shows 2 feet (22) and less between the northern end of the breakwater and the land, I found an area 6 feet deep and better. I noticed strong current flowing around this end of the breakwater. Also, the channel (23) around the north of Hog Island (24) is considerably shallower than indicated, not much more than 6 feet at low tide. All this could indicate that the Narrows is attempting to shift its channel at the southern end approach. There is little doubt that any such shift will be marked, but cautiously observe any markers as you proceed in, particularly if you carry more than 5 feet draft. Because this area joins the two large bodies of water, wind can play a very significant role on current and tide. As noted above, strong northeasterlies can keep the tide lower than normal for days, while a strong southwesterly can do the opposite.

Anchorage Behind Hog Island
Refer to Regional Chart #12270-A— "Kent Narrows, Kirwan Creek and Goodhands Creek." Pg. 109 Top

The area behind Hog Island (24) makes a snug, quiet, and pretty anchorage (25). This area is subject to shoaling. Although I took my 6-foot draft inside, I slid along the bottom at half tide. Don't go in with more than 5-foot draft.

As you proceed in behind the breakwater, note a duck blind (26) on the point of Kent Island to your right (north), opposite the north point of Hog Island. We found the deepest water between about ⅔ of the way toward the point to your north, favoring the northern side, off the north point of Hog Island. Heading in, we saw a tall antenna (28) far ahead behind the trees. Looking aft, we noticed a clump of trees (29) standing out on the rounded peninsula between Marshy Creek (12) and Hood Point (30) on the western side of the main channel. A course of 330°M, with the clump of trees on the stern and the antenna on the bow took us through the best water. But with the current changing through this area, as it seems to be, this could be different next week. Once in behind the island, the water becomes deeper to 7 and 8 feet and you can anchor behind the island or up Kirwan Creek (31) or Goodhands Creek (32). Throughout this anchorage and its entrance, depths are generally less than the chart shows, and changing.

Marine Facilities in Kent Narrows
Refer to Chart #12272-H— "Kent Narrows."

Continuing north in the main Kent Narrows Channel, Wells Cove (34) comes up to the right (east). The royal blue building on the jetty on your left (to the northeast) as you enter this cove is "The Jetty" (35). This is a popular bar and restaurant with light fare and an open Tiki-type bar out on the jetty. There is docking here for customers. There is often live entertainment on special nights. The dredged channel into Wells Cove then brings you to Kent Narrows Boat Yard (36), a small railway doing primarily hull repair, woodwork, and painting on local work boats. Three feet is the controlling depth here for hauling at low tide. This is the first (northwestern most) repair facility on the northeast shore of Wells Cove.

Next door is Scott Marine (37), just to the right of Kent Narrows Boat Yard (to the southeast of it). This is a marina and yard, identified by its large sign. Depth is 8 feet. There are 44 open slips and 36 covered with the largest at 55 feet, and up to 50 amps of electricity available. A pumpout, laundry, block and cube ice, bathroom and shower facilities, and spa are available. There is a 45-ton lift and 12-ton crane with general repair and maintenance on the premises. They honor MC and Visa. The dredged basin (38) with its entrance at the far southeastern corner of Wells Cove, with the gray condos ashore, is for boats belonging to the condo owners. This is the Oyster Cove development.

North of Wells Cove, the large buildings with docks on the point to the right of (east of) the main channel belong to the Harrison Yacht Sales (39), a sales and service facility. Harrison's has a 50-ton lift and does general repair. They are dealers for Carver and Searay. The southernmost (40) building is for commercial offloading of seafood.

Farther north, still to the east, are the three Fisherman's Inn facilities. These are actually a very nice "Fisherman's Inn Restaurant" (41), with entrees beginning at around $11; a turquoise painted retail seafood store (42); and a Crab Deck (43) restaurant, more casual than the larger restaurant, but with full fare with open area and bar on the water. Docking is available for customers in boats up to 50 feet, with 8 feet depths but no electric or water normally available for temporary tie-ups. There are 30 slips. You won't see the little pond (44) from the main channel. Docks and a jetty walk obscure the entrance, but it is there, and seen from the shore, adding to the atmosphere.

The Crab Deck often has live entertainment on weekends and special nights. The three businesses have been run by the Schulz family since the 30s. They are still actively involved, insuring the fine quality for which they have become known. The restaurant has a very fine collection of oyster plates, some antique 200 years old. Mrs Betty Schulz began collecting them many years ago, and still adds to the assortment when she finds something interesting. These include Wedgewood, Minton and Quimper, Haviland, Majolica, and others from France, England, Germany, Austria, and Japan. There are also some fascinating photographs showing the area in earlier years, and ship models including one of *The Pride of Baltimore* and the oyster sloop *J.T. Leonard*. Beer, soda, block and cube ice and food to go are available at the seafood store and Crab Deck. Visa, MC and Amex are honored.

Across the main highway from the Fisherman's Inn Restaurant stands the Comfort Inn (46), a motel with very noticeable red roofs seen clearly from the water. This motel has an indoor pool, whirlpool, exercise room, and sauna. Its rooms feature microwaves, refrigerators, and coffee makers. Some large suites have their own whirlpools. Most major credit cards are honored. There is no restaurant on the premises, but all of the ones mentioned in this Kent Narrows chapter are within walking distance.

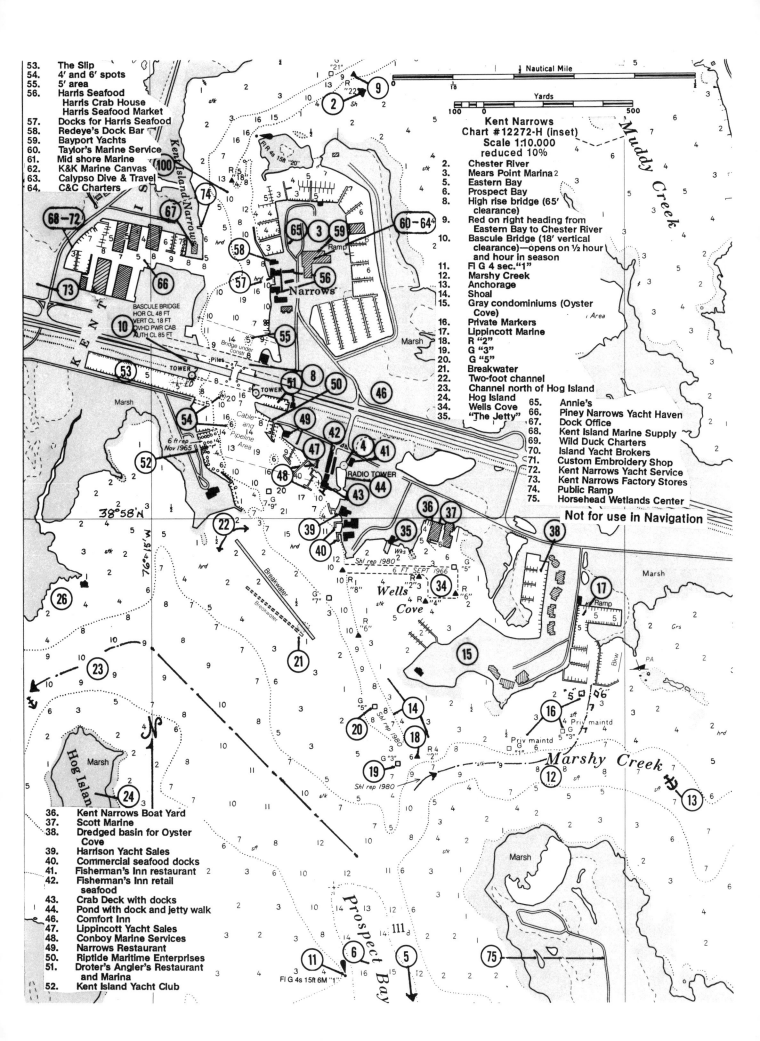

53. The Slip
54. 4' and 6' spots
55. 5' area
56. Harris Seafood
     Harris Crab House
     Harris Seafood Market
57. Docks for Harris Seafood
58. Redeye's Dock Bar
59. Bayport Yachts
60. Taylor's Marine Service
61. Mid shore Marine
62. K&K Marine Canvas
63. Calypso Dive & Travel
64. C&C Charters

Kent Narrows
Chart #12272-H (inset)
Scale 1:10,000
reduced 10%

2. Chester River
5. Eastern Bay
6. Prospect Bay
8. High rise bridge (65' clearance)
9. Red on right heading from Eastern Bay to Chester River
10. Bascule Bridge (18' vertical clearance)—opens on ½ hour and hour in season
11. Fl G 4 sec. "1"
12. Marshy Creek
13. Anchorage
14. Shoal
15. Gray condominiums (Oyster Cove)
16. Private Markers
17. Lippincott Marine
18. R "2"
19. G "3"
20. G "5"
21. Breakwater
22. Two-foot channel
23. Channel north of Hog Island
24. Hog Island
34. Wells Cove
35. "The Jetty"

65. Annie's
66. Piney Narrows Yacht Haven
67. Dock Office
68. Kent Island Marine Supply
69. Wild Duck Charters
70. Island Yacht Brokers
71. Custom Embroidery Shop
72. Kent Narrows Yacht Service
73. Kent Narrows Factory Stores
74. Public Ramp
75. Horsehead Wetlands Center

Not for use in Navigation

36. Kent Narrows Boat Yard
37. Scott Marine
38. Dredged basin for Oyster Cove
39. Harrison Yacht Sales
40. Commercial seafood docks
41. Fisherman's Inn restaurant
42. Fisherman's Inn retail seafood
43. Crab Deck with docks
44. Pond with dock and jetty walk
46. Comfort Inn
47. Lippincott Yacht Sales
48. Conboy Marine Services
49. Narrows Restaurant
50. Riptide Maritime Enterprises
51. Droter's Angler's Restaurant and Marina
52. Kent Island Yacht Club

The next two docks, also to the right (eastern side of the channel), belong to Lippincott Yacht Sales (47) and **Conboy Marine Services (48)**. Lippincott sells new and used boats and also does brokerage. The sales facility is at the front of the building, facing the road. Conboy's faces the water, with a conspicuous sign over the door of the large service building. This business is separate from the Lippincott Yacht Sales and is owned and operated by Joe Conboy, who for years was a builder of wooden and fiberglass motor and sailing yachts. Articles have been published about him in popular yachting magazines. He offers complete hull and mechanical services on the premises. There is a 50-ton travel lift here, and a 64-foot enclosed shop for work requiring climate control. Conboy Marine Services takes projects and boats of all sizes.

Next north to the right (east) is the very fine Narrows Restaurant **(49)**. This also has docks with deep water for customers with boats up to 50 feet, but no electric or water normally available for the temporary tie-ups. You can identify this restaurant by the big orange awning outside and a large fish sign on the dock. Entrees average $10 to $25 and Visa, MC, and Diners cards are honored.

Just south of the bridge on the east shore are more docks with an office and a sign proclaiming **"Riptide Maritime Enterprises" (50)**. There are slips and 14 feet depth at the face dock.

Behind Riptide, and immediately next to (still south of) the bridge, with 66 slips on the channel and into the small basin to your right (east), is **Droter's Anglers Restaurant and Marina (51)**. They sell gas and diesel, block and cube ice, have showers and do some repair work. There is a restaurant advertising home cooking and bar; dockage is free while dining. They take some transients with up to 38 feet maximum length with up to 12 feet depth at the outside docks. There is some electricity available at the docks up to 30 amps. They accept Visa and MC. At the little green house in back, you can rent bikes, get block and cube ice, get boat work done, including varnishing, and charter a 65-foot ketch for day trips, evening cruises, and other cruises. A boardwalk has been built along the eastern side of the Narrows. While most of it runs north of the bridge, you will see some of it along the shore near the, south of the bridge.

The only facility on the left (west) south of the bridges is the **Kent Island Yacht Club (52)**. These are friendly people who do have some facilities for members of visiting clubs. Depths up to the docks are 5 feet. There are 57 slips but only five normally held open for visitors. They sell block and cube ice and will stand by on Channel 16 if they are expecting someone. Electricity up to 50 amps is available. There is a pool and shower with restroom facilities. They do not take credit cards.

Just before going through the bridges, you will notice a small dredged cut to the left (west). This is called "The Slip" **(53)** locally and for many years has been a place for area watermen to tie their craft. It is interesting to visit this in the late afternoons and watch them come in. This is not a place for transient docking.

Passing through the bridge **(10)**, it is important to watch the current. As would be expected, this cut has about as strong a current as you would normally find on the Bay. If it is running with you and you have a single screw boat, you may wish to stay well back (south) of the bridge until it begins to open. Don't keep the bridge holding because often there is heavy vehicular traffic on the road. For boats with limited maneuverability, this can be a tight spot to hold with a fair

tide and many other boats circling. There is room for most boats to circle on both sides of the bridge, but the area can become very congested. The bridge tender normally stands by on 13 or 16 and can be very helpful. I could not find the 4- and 6-foot spots **(54)** on the south side of the bridge, although it is shallower here on the western side of the channel. The shallow area **(55)** marked on the northern side of the bridge to the eastern side of the channel is there, but I found at least 7 feet here at low tide. The northern side of the bridge is apt to become very congested with traffic very suddenly just before the bridge opens. This is because of the two busy marinas, the fuel docks, and the popular restaurants and bar are very close to the bridge. Often many boats will cast off just in time to make it through an opening. Boats with a fair tide pushing them toward the bridge will have the right of way going through the bridge over those boats holding on the other side against a tide that is opposing them. There are exceptions, such as if a tug and tow are involved and have even more limited maneuverability.

Passing through on to the north side, the Harris Seafood **(56)** concerns appear to the right (east). The first building is for commercial unloading, but next is the popular **Harris Crab House** restaurant, where you can get good steamed crabs and other seafood in a casual atmosphere with most entrees under $10 but ranging up to around $15. This has docks **(57)** for customers, up to 40 feet long. There is 15 amps electricity and water on some of these docks with depth of 7 feet in the slips and more at the face. Also here is the Harris Seafood Market, selling retail seafood.

Along the boardwalk are several shops selling souvenirs, ice cream, Tee shirts, and crafts.

Mears Point Marina Complex

Next north on the right (east) is the huge **Mears Point Marina (3)** Complex. As noted elsewhere, there are several Mears Marinas within VHF range. It is a good idea to specify the one thing you are calling. In this facility, you can find almost anything you want with many independent marine businesses on the premises. The marina itself is full service, including a large yard with independent contractors housed on the premises ready to serve most needs. The marina complex is easy to recognize because of its sign and because of a huge U.S. flag on a very tall pole which can be seen from far up and down the Chester River. Also it is the first marina on your left (east) as you come through the Narrows from the Chester River. There is 8 feet depth at the face docks. There are 600 slips, both open and covered, in the back basin. The minimum depth there is 6½ to 7 feet, depending on the slip and wind conditions. The wind can play a very critical role with the tides in this area. The marina keeps current information on depths and can give you very reliable docking information. The maximum slip is 60 feet, but longer boats can dock on outside face docks. There is up to 50 amp electrical service available. There is a large pool, very nice bathroom and shower facilities, a good laundry facility, pumpout, gas and diesel, and a marina **Kent Narrows Yacht Club.** The marina honors Visa and MC. Mears Point Marina reminded me of a huge maritime mall with its many marine businesses.

Taylor's Marine Service (60), a full service repair center, is also found on the Mears premises in the large building behind Redeye's. They are certified mechanics for MerCruiser, Volvo, Crusader, Pleasure Craft, Marine Power, Westerbeke, Onan, Velvet Drive, they have Cruisair sales and service, they are an application center for Interlux Gelshield, and they have a 35-

ton travel lift.

Also at Mears is **Mid Shore Marine (61)**. They are dealers for Volvo Penta, MerCruiser, Velvet Drive, PCM Marine Power, Onan, Crusader, Chrysler Marine, and Westerbeke. They have a marine supply store and certified mechanics specializing in repowering, stern drive, and transmission rebuilding. They take Visa and MC.

K&K Marine Canvas (62) at Mears does custom canvas fabrications, upholstery, cushions, bimini tops, and custom stainless steel frames. **Bayport Yachts (59)** is a brokerage firm with many listings, both on the premises and elsewhere. **Calypso Dive and Travel (63)** sells diving gear, instruction, and diving work.

Of special interest to those wishing to enjoy this area but may not have a boat here, **C&C Charters (64)** is headquarterd at Mears, operating a large fleet of bareboat and captained charter boats. This is a large, well established, and well run outfit which knows how to insure a good cruise. Boats range from a 28-foot sailboat to a 43-foot sailboat and a 41-foot trawler. Phone number for C&C is 1-800-773-SAIL.

Those familiar with dining in the Washington D.C. area will know of the excellent restaurant "Annie's" **(65)**, specializing in steaks and other fine food since 1948. There is now an "Annie's" at Mears, run by one of the family, and specializing in excellent steaks as well as its full, rounded menu including prime rib, seafood, chicken, and ribs. Entrees range from just under $10 to above $20. There is docking at the marina for customers of the restaurants while they dine.

At Mears Point Marina you may also buy used boats including repossessions, with quite a few always on the premises.

Redeye's Dock Bar

Throughout the northern bay, and even farther south, you will hear people talking about "Redeye's Dock Bar" **(58)**. It is one of the first things you will see as you come alongside Mears Point Marina. People travel for hours by car and boat just to be there. Its followers wear T-shirts, hats and other clothing with its logo. This is a little open bar on the dock right at the water's edge. Some would put it under the classification of "Tiki Bar" but it seems to have an ambiance of its own. A conspicuous sign on the roof proclaims the name.

An upstairs bar inside is also open, and tables are set up on the docks outside under the palm trees growing in large planters. Light fare is served with beer, mixed drinks, and soft drinks.

A small store immediately behind sells Redeye's memorabilia, block and cube ice, light groceries, boating supplies and clothing and other items such as sun glasses, sun tan lotion, and some hardware. A spoken policy here is for people to have fun and relax. The staff are great and help to convey a special atmosphere that is widely recognized. The name of the establishment comes from the past of Bob Wilson, the manager of this and other Mears marinas. He was formerly a fire-fighter and had great difficulty with irritation from smoke, earning the name "Redeye." He envisioned this bar and set it up, and his name stuck. You will sometimes find Bob here enjoying the crowds and seeing old friends.

Each Sunday Redeye's sponsors a bikini contest with participants from many areas. This is a male as well as a female competition. Videos are taken and played during other days. Each fall around the end of September, there is a grand finale with the winners from each week returning. This is one Sunday that most boats in the northern bay seem to be headed in the same direction. There are official photographers, video coverage, local DJ's spinning music and chatter, barbecue and charcoal pits with special vendors, waitresses walking among the crowd carrying coolers with beer, rows of gleaming Harleys and other bikes, and enough people to sink an island! Non-alcoholic beverages are given away free to help people to be safe, and anyone having too much to run his boat back

Crowd waiting for Bikini contest, Red Eye's Dock Bar, Mears Point Marine, Kent Narrows

to harbor is given free overnight dockage and encouraged to use it. This overnight dockage policy is in effect throughout the season at Redeye's. Also throughout the year, designated drivers are given free N/A drinks. Dockage is available for customers of the bar. On any weekend there may be rafts out from the dock, five to eight boats deep, sometimes all slick "go fast" type boats.

West Shore Facilities North of the Bridges

Across Kent Narrows (west side) from Mears is another large marina with most of its docks in the dredged basin behind the face and fuel docks. This is **Pineys Narrows Yacht Haven (66)**. It is full service and has a large yard with many private businesses within. There is a gray house **(67)** with brown roof on the face dock with the fuel pumps and a white sign with a pine tree and setting sun. There are 280 slips. Controlling depth is 6 feet to get in, with more depth at the fuel dock which sells gas and diesel. Block and cube ice is available. Electric service is available up to 50 amps. They take MC and Visa. This marina is across the water from most of the Kent Narrows restaurants, but they can arrange for water taxi service or a car taxi. There is a very well-stocked marine supply and parts store called the Kent Island Marine Supply **(68)**, a laundry, pool, pumpout, the Wild Duck Charter **(69)** service for motor and sail, and other shops including Island Yacht Brokers **(70)**, marine surveyors, an insurance broker, and a custom embroidery shop **(71)** with "while you wait" service. A large full service repair and maintenance shop called **Kent Narrows Yacht Services (72)** operates on the premises with 60-ton travel lift and yard.

The Kent Narrows Factory Stores **(73)** shopping mall is west across the road from the Piney Narrows Marina Complex. They have over 20 retail outlets advertising regular savings at 20 to 70 percent. Many of these sell imperfects at very low prices. The stores include clothing, luggage, leather, kitchen utensils, toys, shoes lingerie, sportswear, and fashion brand ladies and men's apparel and much more. This mall can be easily reached with a short walk from the marinas across the channel by crossing the old bascule bridge. Walk across the bridge carefully. Cars may not be accustomed to pedestrians on these bridges.

The last facility to the left (west) as you head to the Chester River is a public ramp **(74)** with two cement ramps, a dock, and large parking area. This is adjacent to and to the north of Pineys Narrows Marina but is not a part of that operation. The county launching ramps require permits for which fees are collected. Last year fees were $5 per day for in-state and $10 for out-of-state users. Permits are sold by the county and at various stores and locations, which change from time to time. Usually these stores are very close to the ramp, and often they sell fishing and other gear that you may need. There is usually a sign at each ramp advising the nearest store or location to pay the fee. For latest information call (410) 758-0835 or 778-4430.

QUEEN ANNE'S COUNTY

Kent Narrows is located in Queen Anne's County. There are additional points of interest here which are not within walking distance of these marinas, but which should be mentioned to give an overall view of what is easily available by a short drive from this popular marina center. Some of these are on or near other creeks, but many people prefer to visit them from Kent Narrows because of marinas and attractions

at Kent Narrows, and the relative ease of navigation into the Narrows as compared to some of these other shallower creeks. When attractions are near other creeks, this is also noted in descriptions of those creeks.

Supplies and Shopping

If you can get land transportation, there are good supply and shopping opportunities close to Kent Narrows.

None of these are within walking distance, but most of the marinas in the area are generally helpful with arranging transportation. Sometimes, if a car is available, this service will be at no cost or very inexpensively. You might not expect supply and services to be there because of the rural nature of the area. A shopping center is approximately 1.8 miles west of Kent Narrows bridges on Route 18 which parallels Route 50 immediately to its south (and which crosses the bascule bridge). This shopping center has a hardware store, a Safeway supermarket with pharmacy, a deli and seafood shop, a dentist, Radio Shack, book store, mailing and shipping service which also makes copies and sends faxes, a barber shop, several fast food restaurants, Chinese and Italian restaurants, dry cleaners, a physical therapy center, and a foot health center.

Nearby, on the corner of Route 8 and Dominion Road, Tri Gas and Oil fills propane and sells kerosene. Approximately ¾ miles to the west, you will find Marshy Creek Video and a package shop.

Around 1 mile farther out, Red Apple Plaza with its red roofs, has other restaurants, a supermarket, a marine electronics shop, phone (410) 643-6888, an oral surgery office, and a "Sportsman's Service Center" selling hunting and fishing equipment.

If you are interested in antiques, there is a multi-dealer antiques marketplace with quite a variety of finds. This is near Queenstown, phone (410) 827-6640. Next to this center is the Chesapeake Pottery Outlet. Both of these are at the area of the Chesapeake Village Shopping Mall which features designer labels, lingerie, toys, leather goods, crystal and china all at advertised savings of 20 to 75 percent off retail. This is a factory outlet type of mall with fine stores and stock. The mall phone number is (410) 827-8699. The area is about 10 minutes drive east from Kent Narrows at the intersection of Routes 50 and 301. People travel from the Western shore and even from Delaware to shop at these places. They cannot be accessed by boat, but ground transportation is usually not a problem.

Golf

Golfers will find at least three golf courses convenient to boats at Kent Narrows with a little ground transportation. Queenstown Harbor Golf Links is about 5 minutes drive away just off Route 301, and bordering the Chester River and Winchester Creek. It is next to the Cove House Restaurant and Motor Lodge. This restaurant is very nice both as to atmosphere and dining, and overlooks Winchester Creek. **Refer to Chart #12272-B in Chester River, Chapter 8.** They honor Visa, MC and Amex. In good weather you can dine outside overlooking the yard and creek. The creek is navigable to the restaurant for shallow draft boats. I found 3½ feet to be the controlling depth. There are 12 slips at the restaurant for customers, although this is not a regular marina and they do not offer water and electricity. On Sundays the Cove House offers a brunch, and at times you can take out lunch in the Elco. This is probably the closest golf course to Kent Narrows, as well as being accessible by water from the Chester. Call (410) 827-6611 for the golf course, or 827-6300 for the Cove House. Queenstown Golf Links are located a few minutes drive farther east. Blue Heron Golf Course has nine holes and it is in the Stevensville area of Kent Island, around 10 minutes drive to the west of Kent Narrows.

Launching Ramps, Airport, Busses, Visitors Center

Tourism is a substantial interest here. The public Bay Bridge Airport for small planes is on Route 8 near the Bay Bridge, phone (410) 643-4363. There is a public transportation system utilizing busses. Call (410) 758-0848 for schedules and routes. For general current information on what is interesting in the county, call the Visitors Center at (410) 827-4810. The county launching ramps require permits for which fees are collected. Last year fees were around $5 per day for in-state and $10 for out-of-state users. Permits are sold by the county and at various stores and locations, which change from time to time. Usually these stores are very close to the ramp, and often they sell fishing and other gear that you may need. There is usually a sign at each ramp advising the nearest store or location to pay the fee. For the latest information call (410) 758-0835 or 778-4430. These ramps, as well as many privately operated ramps, are mentioned in the description of the area where they are found.

Festivals

You may want to plan your visit to attend one of several annual festivals. In early June, there is a Waterman's Festival, sponsored in part by the seafood industry. This occurs at Kent Narrows and includes food, waterman contests such as boat docking and line handling, and many other events. In mid-June there is a Bay County Music Festival at Centreville with country, jazz, rock, and folk music. In late July to early August at Kent Narrows, there are fast powerboat races including hydroplanes. This event also has special food concessions

and related activities. Around the second week in August, the County Fair is held near Centreville. Centreville can be approached by water through the Corsica River (Chapter 8), but it may be just as convenient to arrange transportation from the Kent Narrows. This is billed as one of the longest-running agricultural fairs in Maryland, featuring food, jousting tournaments, (jousting is the state sport of Maryland, believe it or not) games, rides, the traditional cake and pie baking and eating contests, livestock shows, and all the other good things that go along with country fairs. In early October, the Rotrary Artisan Festival occurs with arts and crafts done in the show, at Centreville. Usually around the first weekend after Thanksgiving, Kent Narrows has a Christmas boat parade.

Sightseeing and Theater

There are numerous points of historical interest. The Christ Episcopal Church houses one of the oldest established congregations in the United States on Route 18 in Stevensville. St. Luke's Episcopal Church was built in 1732 for 140,000 pounds of tobacco, to be found on Route 213 (follow the sign) near Church Hill. The oldest Queen Anne's County business is the Old Wye Grist Mill on Route 662, in operation since 1671. It produced grain for Washington's Army in 1778 and still grinds by water power four times a year. This is not conveniently accessed by boat.

The Church Hill Theater in Church Hill, presents plays regularly. Again, this will require a car. Phone them at (410) 758-1331.

Horsehead Wetlands Center

The Wildfoul Trust of North America has established the Horsehead Wetlands Center (75) near Grasonville, which has over 300 acres of property. There is a visitor center with sea-

Annie's Restaurant, Mears Point Marine, Kent Narrows

sonal exhibits, trails, concealed blinds and towers, and a boardwalk. Their phone number is (410) 827-6694. You will see this protected area to your right (west) as you approach Kent Narrows from the south. It is the marshy point just before the Narrows. Unfortunately, they do not have the facilities for receiving visitors by boat, but this is just a few miles from the Kent Narrows by car.

History

Queen Anne's County has an interesting historical background. The county claims the first settlement in Maryland. This occured in August, 1629, when William Claiborne established a trading post on Kent Island. This grew to a full settlement by 1631. Claiborne was a Protestant merchant from the County of Kent in England. He was also a government official in the Virginia Colony. Maryland was being settled under the auspices of Lord Baltimore, a Roman Catholic. Leonard Calvert was their colonial leader. Their people at St. Mary's across the Bay saw the Kent Island settlement as a threat to their control of Maryland, and Lord Baltimore ordered them to proceed to control the settlement. Claiborne also saw the people across the waters as a threat to his operations.

For years there was a series of legal maneuvers and actual battles between the two groups of settlers. Claiborne built two forts on the island. At times each side sent parties to attack the other. In an early sortie, an invading party from Kent was defeated at St. Mary's and the captain executed. Later, it is told, Claiborne sent a party over to St. Mary's, captured the governor, brought him back to Kent, flogged him, and sent him home. The ownership of the island transferred back and forth between Virginia and Maryland colonists, eventually settling with the latter.

Before all this hubbub of the oncoming civilization, the island was inhabited by the Matapeake Ozininie Indians, who apparently treated the raucous Britishers with much more civility than they treated themselves. The only problems reported with the Indians came when occasionally war parties of Susquehannas from the north and Nanticokes from the south would attack some homes.

The county was named later after England's Queen Anne. Centreville's courthouse, built around 1791, is claimed to be the oldest continuously operating courthouse in Maryland. Centreville can be visited by water, as was described in Chapter 8 in the section on the Corsica River off the Chester River. The county remained, as did the rest of the Eastern Shore, apart from the bustle of the Annapolis and Baltimore area until the building of the Chesapeake Bay Bridge. Despite the fact that this gateway of "progress" opens onto this county's shores, it is still largely rural with mostly small businesses and many water-related concerns.

Today, county watermen harvest over 90 million pounds of seafood a year with a dockside value of over $45 million per year. Queen Anne's County towns are pretty, quaint, and nice places to visit.

KENT ISLAND BAY SHORE
Refer to Regional Chart #12263-A—"Eastern Bay—Western Section"   and
Chart #12270-B—"Kent Island Bayside, Cox Creek." Pg. 119

Kent Island (84) is a prime boating area on the Bay, as the Kent Island Narrows section of this chapter shows. There are also a few points of interest on the Chesapeake Bay shore of Kent Island. This shore is a diverse collection of a few marinas, all with good protection once you get inside, and one park.

Starting at the northern end of the shore, the large **Pier One Marina (77)** rests in a dredged basin immediately to the south of the eastern end of the Bay Bridge (76). The channel in from the Bay is marked with privately maintained aids. They are easy to see ½ NM off the shore west of the marina. A marina sign is visible from the Bay, and the well known Hemingway's Restaurant (79) has a large sign which is very conspicuous from the water, as an additional aid to identifying the marina. You will see the restaurant just to your left (north) as you come in. It features a full menu with a cocktail lounge. There is free docking for customers of the restaurants while dining.

Pier One Marina has 230 slips with the largest at 55 feet, and room for boats up to 80 feet available at face docks. Electricity up to 50 amps is available. There are 25- and 70-ton open end lifts with full service yard and dry storage for up to 200 boats. Both gas and diesel are sold. They honor Amoco, MC, Visa, and Amex. Block and cube ice are available. Private charters can be arranged through the marina. There are a pumpout, laundry and full bath and shower facilities, and a swimming pool. The channel (78) into this basin is dredged. They try to keep it 7 feet depth, but a call on VHF 16 to check before entering would be wise if you draw more than 5 feet because the entrance area is prone to shoaling. Lippincott Yacht Brokers (80) has an office and show boats on the premises and elsewhere. Also Midlantic Marine, Inc. (81), advertising new and used boats has an office here. This marina complex was undergoing large scale remodeling and improvement last year and other concerns will probably be opening soon.

Pier One, right at the foot of the bridge, is close to Rt. 50/301 (82) and the many businesses along the route. Many of these are described in the section on Kent Narrows (100) earlier in this chapter. Pier One is only around 10 minutes drive from there. Don't consider walking around to go to stores or other facilities outside the marina complex. Route 50/301 cannot be easily crossed on foot, and most of the facilities are not within easy walking distance. Don't even drive around here if you are not familiar with the area. The roads are very confusing with the main highway cross-overs, and rapid traffic. Often I would see a store and then drive for miles trying to find an exit to reach it. Ask the marina for help in transportation or in contacting the facilities. These services and shops include doctors, wrapping and shipping, a post office, hardware, grocery stores, drug stores, boat supply stores, dentists, and most of what you would expect in any small town.

Next of interest, moving south down the coast approximately 2 miles from the Bay Bridge, is the Matapeake Harbor of Refuge (83). It is easy to recognize from offshore because of the large red and white tower there (68). You will also see a large bulkhead which surrounds the basin. Within the basin area and ashore, are some large buildings (at the northern end of the basin) which are part of the repair facility of the U.S. Army Corps of Engineers (87) for their boats. This was formerly an important ferry landing for crossings to and from the western shore, before the days of the Chesapeake Bay Bridges. As mentioned in the section in this chapter, "Queen Anne's County," this island was originally the home of the Matapeake Indian tribe, thus the name of the nice facility ashore is "**Matapeake State Park**" (86). There is a modern concrete ramp (85) within the bulkhead basin, a fishing pier,

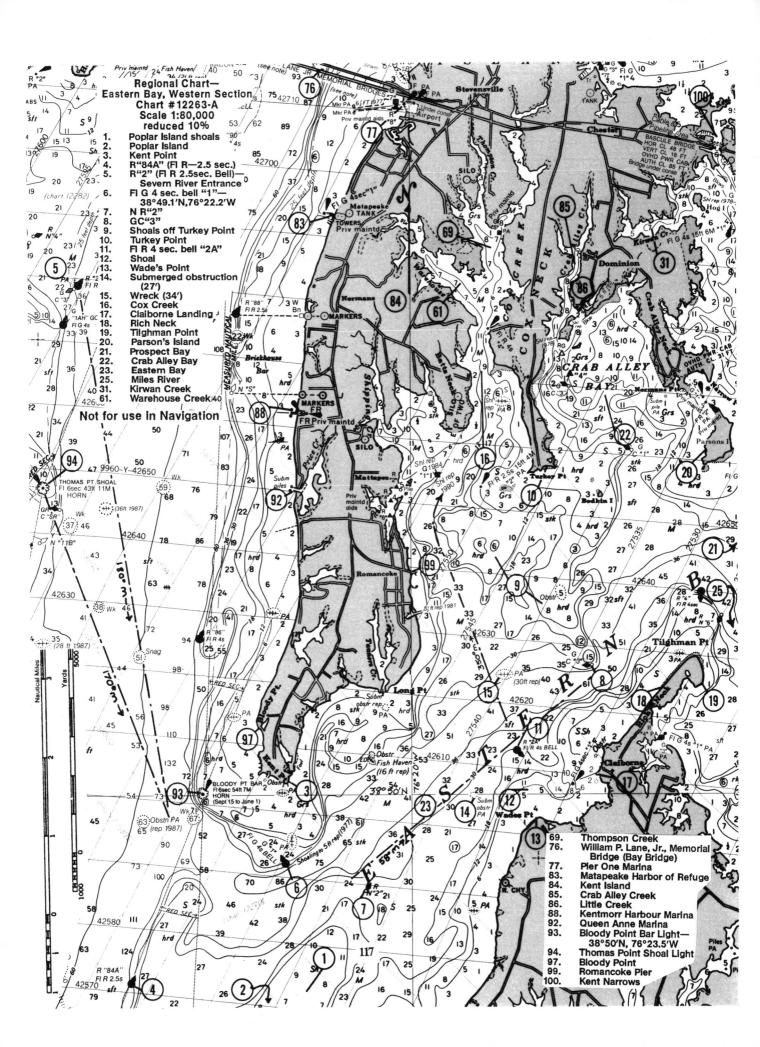

**Regional Chart—
Eastern Bay, Western Section
Chart #12263-A
Scale 1:80,000
reduced 10%**

1. Poplar Island shoals
2. Poplar Island
3. Kent Point
4. R"84A" (Fl R—2.5 sec.)
5. R"2" (Fl R 2.5sec. Bell)—
   Severn River Entrance
6. Fl G 4 sec. bell "1"—
   38°49.1'N,76°22.2'W
7. N R"2"
8. GC"3"
9. Shoals off Turkey Point
10. Turkey Point
11. Fl R 4 sec. bell "2A"
12. Shoal
13. Wade's Point
14. Submerged obstruction
    (27')
15. Wreck (34')
16. Cox Creek
17. Claiborne Landing
18. Rich Neck
19. Tilghman Point
20. Parson's Island
21. Prospect Bay
22. Crab Alley Bay
23. Eastern Bay
25. Miles River
31. Kirwan Creek
61. Warehouse Creek

Not for use in Navigation

69. Thompson Creek
76. William P. Lane, Jr., Memorial
    Bridge (Bay Bridge)
77. Pier One Marina
83. Matapeake Harbor of Refuge
84. Kent Island
85. Crab Alley Creek
86. Little Creek
88. Kentmorr Harbour Marina
92. Queen Anne Marina
93. Bloody Point Bar Light—
    38°50'N, 76°23.5'W
94. Thomas Point Shoal Light
97. Bloody Point
99. Romancoke Pier
100. Kent Narrows

117

head, and wooded picnic area.

Farther down, **Kentmorr Harbour Marina (88)** is noted on the chart. This is about 4.5 NM south of the Bay Bridge, has rock jetties coming out from the shore, and is just south of the marked measured nautical mile course **(89)** which is just south of Fl R "88" **(90)**. There are 62 slips with 36 covered and the largest slip is almost 50 feet. The piers have electricity up to 50 amps and gas and diesel is sold. There is a 30-ton closed and 40-ton open ended lift with service yard and dry storage. Head, showers, block and cube ice, and swimming pool are near the docks. There are charter fishing boats here that can be contacted through the marina, phone (410) 643-2445 and there is boat brokerage. Marina depth is 4½ to 5 feet. Call on VHF first if your draft is close to that. Don't enter this jettied channel on a strong onshore breeze without local familiarity. There is a hard-surfaced ramp here; gas and diesel are sold and Visa, MC and Shell credit cards are honored. A full menu casual restaurant is on the water, featuring also a cocktail bar. Dinners range from around $10 to $22, and there is no dockage while dining. Often on weekends and other special evenings, there is live entertainment.

Still farther south, just inside the entrance to Price Creek **(91)** can be found **Queen Anne's Marina (92)**. It can be recognized from outside by a green building with the large letters "QA" on top. It is roughly 4 NM north of Bloody Point Bar Light **(93)**, and 5 NM south of the Bay Bridge. It is also straight across from Thomas Point Light **(94)**. Controlling depth coming in is 4½ feet. The entrance to the creek is jettied, and marked by two poles with red and green reflectors **(95)**. This is yet another area where shoaling can be a real problem because of onshore winds and unprotected shore. There are 124 slips with 15 amps electricity and a 40-foot 18-ton closed end lift. They have heads, showers, gas, diesel fuel, some marine supplies, a fair selection of groceries and snacks, block and cube ice, and beverages, and a steel launching ramp. Fishing gear and bait are sold here, and charter fishing vessels can be contacted through the marina, as well as hunting guides. There is also a light menu restaurant with good home cooking, serving lunch and breakfast with most meals ranging from $3 to $7. The owner, Larry Hansel, told me that around 50 percent of the boats there belong to local fishermen, crabbers, eelers, and hunting guides.

Mr. Hansel operates a large soft crab shedding facility **(96)** here, which is interesting to see. This requires constant supervision and "nursing" in season, including getting up late in the night to see that the crabs which have just shed are removed from the pens before being eaten by the stronger ones. You can get soft crabs here as fresh and as good as they come.

Price Creek quickly becomes very shallow beyond the docks with little disturbing the natural beauty of its salt marshes and woods to the south and east of the marina. This seems to

be a great place for boats with shallow enough draft to get in, whose owners are interested in some serious local bay fishing without a lot of the hoopla of some other areas.

EASTERN BAY

Eastern Bay is an incredible cruising area of the Chesapeake. It is huge, and it has just about everything from wide open waters to beautiful protected anchorages, from high density high-tech marina areas to the best of Bay culture. In addition, it is a nice run from the highly populated areas around Annapolis on the Western shore. A cut through Kent Narrows, if you have the draft, puts you into the beautiful Chester River. A hop to the south around Poplar Island (or through the shallow Poplar Island Narrows) brings you to the Choptank.

Approach
Refer to Regional Chart #12263-A—"Eastern Bay—Western Section" Pg. 117 and Chart #12270-C—"Bloody Point Bar." Pg. 120

The approach into Eastern Bay **(23)** contains no mysteries or difficulties. It is wide open and well marked with ample depths. Some of the deepest water in the bay is to be found just to the west of Bloody Point **(97)** at 165 feet **(98)**. Stay well off Bloody Point. The bottom rises quite rapidly here from this depth, and it can be quite rough with an onshore wind.

I have talked to many historians and local people about the source of this name and have heard many stories, all with some doubt as to accuracy. Some say that it was named for the blood that flowed in altercations between the St. Mary's settlers and the settlement of William Claiborne as described in the section on Queen Anne's County in this chapter. Others say that the point was named because of shipwrecks, and others say that the name was associated with pirate activities and perhaps hangings.

With very deep draft vessels, it is better to favor the northern side as you move into Eastern Bay. The shoals **(1)** coming north off Poplar Island **(2)** are at least somewhat gradual, but can catch you if the width of the vista puts you off guard. These are shown on **Chart #12270-D—"Poplar Island."**

The only problem coming in occurs on misty days, not uncommon in the heat of the summer. Eastern Bay is so large that it can be a bit confusing as to just what is where inside. Though this can be disconcerting, things start to make sense as you close, and the bay is well-marked.

Coming in from the Chesapeake, look for Bloody Point Bar Light **(93)** and Poplar Island **(2)** to get an initial orientation. The light, a 54-foot circular brown structure appearing red-

Conboy Marine Service, Kent Narrows

118

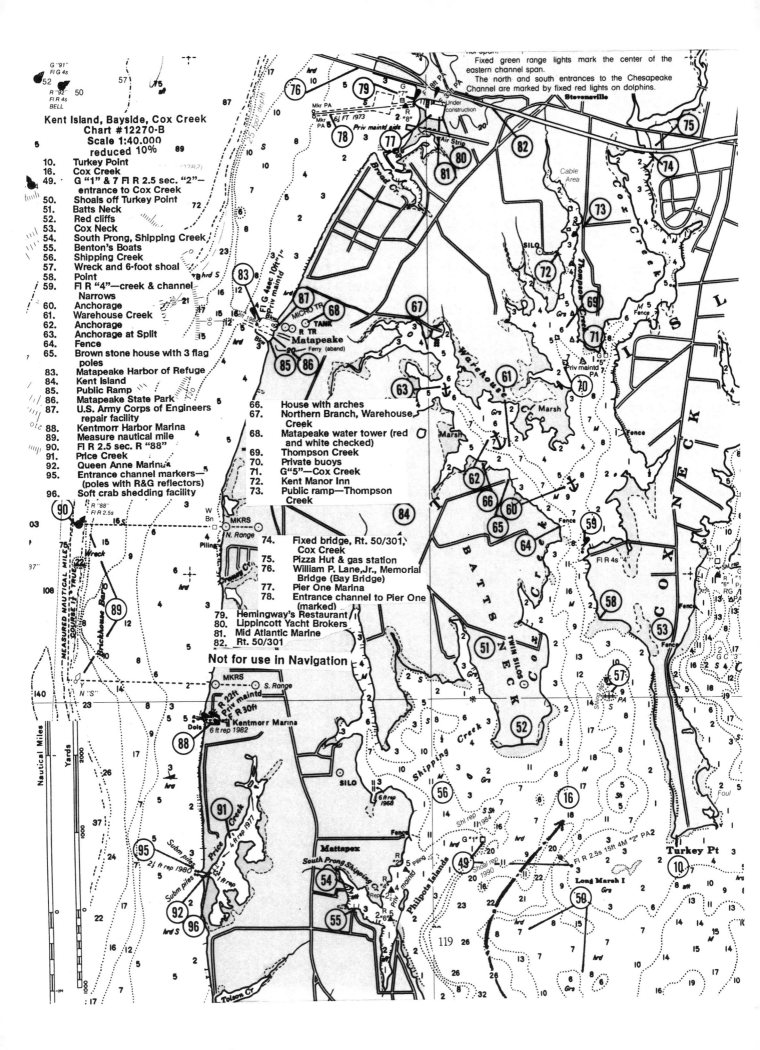

Kent Island, Bayside, Cox Creek
Chart #12270-B
Scale 1:40.000
reduced 10%

10. Turkey Point
16. Cox Creek
49. G "1" & 7 Fl R 2.5 sec. "2"— entrance to Cox Creek
50. Shoals off Turkey Point
51. Batts Neck
52. Red cliffs
53. Cox Neck
54. South Prong, Shipping Creek
55. Benton's Boats
56. Shipping Creek
57. Wreck and 6-foot shoal
58. Point
59. Fl R "4"—creek & channel Narrows
60. Anchorage
61. Warehouse Creek
62. Anchorage
63. Anchorage at Split
64. Fence
65. Brown stone house with 3 flag poles
83. Matapeake Harbor of Refuge
84. Kent Island
85. Public Ramp
86. Matapeake State Park
87. U.S. Army Corps of Engineers repair facility
88. Kentmorr Harbor Marina
89. Measure nautical mile
90. Fl R 2.5 sec. R "88"
91. Price Creek
92. Queen Anne Marina
95. Entrance channel markers— (poles with R&G reflectors)
96. Soft crab shedding facility

66. House with arches
67. Northern Branch, Warehouse Creek
68. Matapeake water tower (red and white checked)
69. Thompson Creek
70. Private buoys
71. G"5"—Cox Creek
72. Kent Manor Inn
73. Public ramp—Thompson Creek
74. Fixed bridge, Rt. 50/301, Cox Creek
75. Pizza Hut & gas station
76. William P. Lane, Jr., Memorial Bridge (Bay Bridge)
77. Pier One Marina
78. Entrance channel to Pier One (marked)
79. Hemingway's Restaurant
80. Lippincott Yacht Brokers
81. Mid Atlantic Marine
82. Rt. 50/301

Not for use in Navigation

Fixed green range lights mark the center of the eastern channel span.
The north and south entrances to the Chesapeake Channel are marked by fixed red lights on dolphins.

119

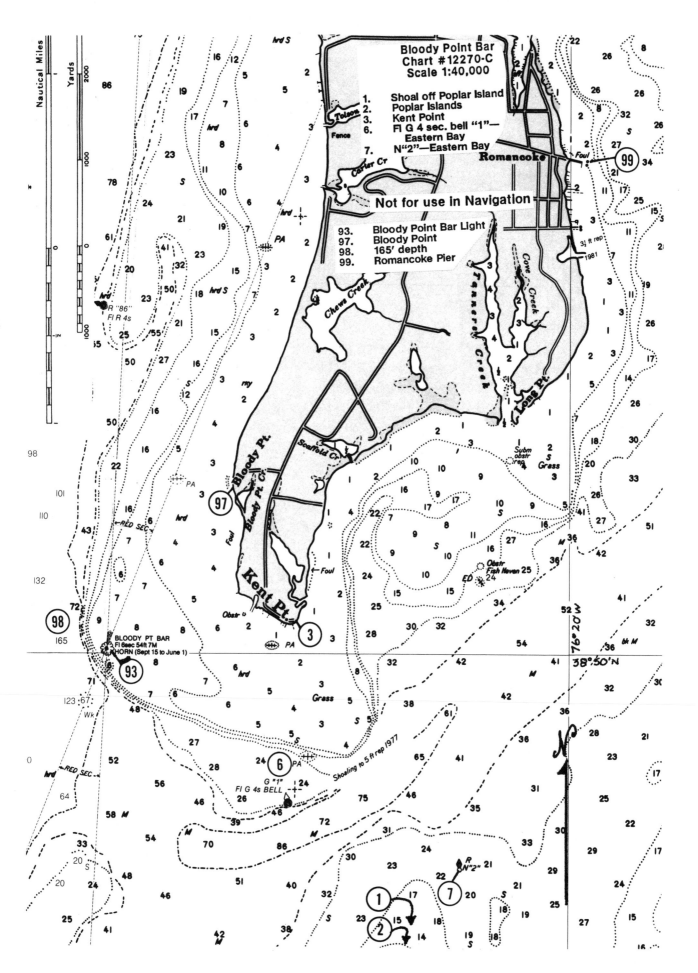

Bloody Point Bar
Chart #12270-C
Scale 1:40,000

1. Shoal off Poplar Island
2. Poplar Islands
3. Kent Point
6. Fl G 4 sec. bell "1"—
   Eastern Bay
7. N"2"—Eastern Bay

Not for use in Navigation

93. Bloody Point Bar Light
97. Bloody Point
98. 165' depth
99. Romancoke Pier

120

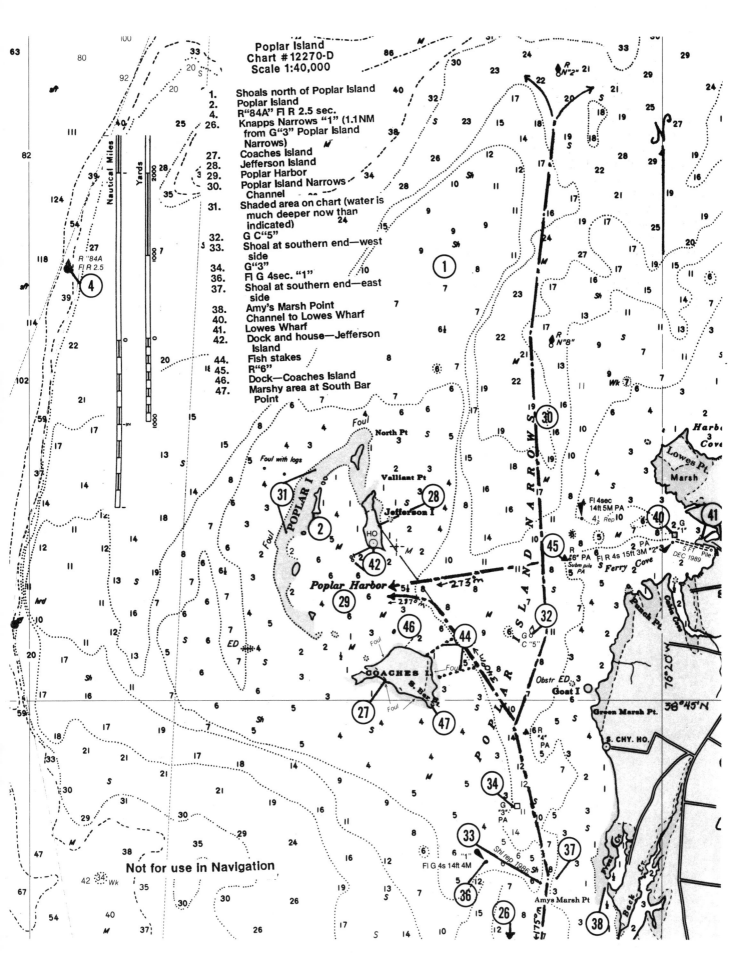

Poplar Island
Chart #12270-D
Scale 1:40,000

1. Shoals north of Poplar Island
2. Poplar Island
4. R"84A" Fl R 2.5 sec.
26. Knapps Narrows "1" (1.1 NM from G"3" Poplar Island Narrows)
27. Coaches Island
28. Jefferson Island
29. Poplar Harbor
30. Poplar Island Narrows Channel
31. Shaded area on chart (water is much deeper now than indicated)
32. G C"5"
33. Shoal at southern end—west side
34. G"3"
36. Fl G 4sec. "1"
37. Shoal at southern end—east side
38. Amy's Marsh Point
40. Channel to Lowes Wharf
41. Lowes Wharf
42. Dock and house—Jefferson Island
44. Fish stakes
45. R"6"
46. Dock—Coaches Island
47. Marshy area at South Bar Point

Not for use in Navigation

121

dish, on a cylindrical foundation, is easy to see against Kent Point (3). Its position is 38°50'N by 76°23.5'W, but don't go up to that. Poplar Island appears as a group of several islands, depending upon the state of the tide, the clarity of the air, and your relationship and distance from them. Sighting flashing red "84A" (4) also helps, particularly if you are coming in from the south.

Coming from the Annapolis area, a course of 180°M from Fl R "2" (the entrance buoy to the Severn River) (5) will take you to the vicinity off Bloody Point where you should be able to pick it up without getting too close. A course of 170°M will take you from Thomas Point Light (94) on the western shore to the vicinity of Bloody Point so that you can safely pick it up. Watch for wind or current setting you onto the shore. As you get closer in, it helps to sight Fl G bell G "1" (6) which is south of Kent Point. Its position is 38°49.1'N by 76°22.2'W. Passing Red Nun "2" (7), putting it to your right (south), will safely take you past the shoals off Poplar Islands. A course of 58°M will take you from a point just off this nun into the vicinity of G "3" (8), which you will want to put to your left (north) in order to avoid the shoals extending well southerly off Turkey Point (10). On this course, you will be passing very close to Fl R bell "2A" (11) marking the shoal (12) coming north off Wades Point (13). It is not necessary to pass close to this R "2A." I have never found nor talked with anyone who has had any problems with the submerged obstruction (14) reported in 27 feet of water off north of Wades Point or the wreck (15) reported in 34 feet of water south of the entrance to Cox Creek (16).

On the southern shore of Eastern Bay, inside Fl R bell "2A" you will notice markers and a dock against the shore of Claiborne. This is **Claiborne Landing (17)** with a public cement launching ramp, fishing pier, and restrooms. Many years ago, this was a resort area with a large hotel and ferry boat landing. On the western shore of Eastern Bay, northwest of Claiborne Landing, there is a park with a dock for fishing and crabbing, maintained by Queen Anne's County, called Romancoke Pier (99). This also has picnic area and restrooms. There is a $3 per person ($5 for out-of-state) charge for non-county residents.

As you move up into Eastern Bay, you will notice Rich Neck (18) and its Tilghman Point (19) (on the northeastern end of the neck) ahead on the southern shore. As you proceed into Eastern Bay, Tilghman Point stands out conspicuously ahead of you to the northeast, because of its tall trees that seem to stop abruptly over the water. The tree line ends so abruptly that, on many days from afar, the water appears to cut under the trees. This landmark can be of great help in obtaining a general orientation within Eastern Bay. Parson's Island (20), is on the other (northern) side of Eastern Bay and to the north-northeast of Tilghman Point. Crab Alley Bay (22), is on the western side of Parson's Island. Prospect Bay (21), which takes you to the entrance to Kent Narrows (100), begins on the east side of Parson's Island. The sharply dropping tree line of Tilghman Point will be of further help in obtaining bearings in other situations, including from inside the Miles River (25).

All of the above will seem silly if you make your approach on a crystal clear day. But if it is misty, hazy, or near dusk, it will help. Suggested compass courses are for general guidance and should be supplemented by your own observations, careful navigation, and readings. *Editor's note: These magnetic courses do not allow for current set, or drift due to waves. Keep track of where you are.*

Poplar Island
Refer to Chart #12270-D—"Poplar Island." P&121

This is a beautiful spot to explore by dinghy or visit by shallow draft boat in the daytime. It is not an anchorage or harbor.

Poplar Island (2) is not normally considered to be a part of Eastern Bay, but because of its proximity and significance in entrance navigation, we will describe it here. Actually, it can be conveniently accessed from Knapps Narrows (26) as well as Eastern Bay.

Poplar is really a set of islands, appearing as several depending upon your bearing and distance. These are generally locally referred to as "Poplar Islands," but Coaches Island (27) and Jefferson Island (28) are the main areas of land that you will see above high water. The chart still names the area in the center as Poplar Harbor (29). For all practical purposes it is almost totally exposed and you would not wish to anchor here except in very settled, flat calm weather. In addition to the exposure to the Bay, there is also constant traffic on weekends by people using Poplar Island Narrows (30).

The two smallest islands, including the one actually named "Poplar Island" are barely above water. The green shading on the chart (31) that implies very shallow water exposed at low tide is misleading. This ridge is too deep to afford any meaningful shelter from the west. However, the area is certainly worth a visit by small boat. It is open and clean, with water often so clear that you see the bottom quite well in 6 feet depth, even in the summertime. The bottom is mostly grass, and I noticed local youngsters fishing and crabbing here. It is a nice reminder of what the Bay used to be like before the influx of people.

Approaching the islands from Eastern Bay is a matter of following the markers in. The water is as reported on the chart, with plenty of wide depth up to Can G "5" (32). These narrows make a great short cut between Eastern Bay and Knapps Narrows, if you have the shallow draft and can pick your way among the shoals at the southern end. It is indeed about as bad as it looks on the chart at the southern end (33). I spent hours trying to find a clear and easy way to bring 5 to 6 feet through without feeling the bottom, and really was not able to. Five feet is controlling depth, but its not easily found. It is probably just as well, because any formula for getting through here is going to need reconsideration after every serious storm.

Most boats take a course of 175°M from just inside of (east of) Green "3" (34) down to the outside entrance marker G "1" of Knapps Narrows, rounding that marker well off and to the north and west of it. This run is approximately 1.1 NM. On this course, there still must be some guessing or local knowledge to round the shoal coming off (southeasterly of) Fl G "1" (36) and the shoal (37) coming off (west of) Amys Marsh Point (38). Fl G "1" is prominent, 14 feet with a heavy frame and a round wood structure at its base, but its placement so far west on the shoal makes it useless as an aid to navigation through the narrows.

At times there is a clam line (white floating buoys with those words written on them) along the shoal that is on the east side of the channel opposite Fl G "1." Do not rely conclusively on this however, as these are subject to being moved at any time. By constant criss-crossing, I found generally 6 feet available if you round correctly, but there is nothing to use as a range to assure this. Without someone leading me who knew the latest up to the minute information on the shoaling, I would not want to take more than 5 feet through here, and then on half tide and rising, never in strong onshore winds. Local boats take this short cut regularly, and if you have shallow draft, it should not be difficult to find someone to follow through.

On the eastern side of this narrows is a small dredged channel into the mainland and Lowes Wharf (41). The channel is marked (40), and inside you will see a large green building with bulkheading and some docks. When I last visited, this appeared to be not in use at the time. The docks were empty. This could make an emergency safe haven for shallow draft boat, but it is not particularly inviting nor of much interest to the cruiser. The place has potential, and may be developed further later, though protection is not good from the west.

Returning to the Poplar Islands, whose interest brought us here in the first place, Jefferson Island has a house (42) on it and some trees. It is not as large as Coaches Island which has more trees, some bulkheading, some rip-rap, a dock, and a little beach.

To enter this area between the islands, if coming from the south, from R "4" head toward the northern tip of Jefferson Island (28) at 340°M. Fish stakes (44) are normally on the northwestern side of Coaches Island, where marked on the chart. You can pass close to the end of these at 10 feet depth or better. This course will have you heading to the little house on the west side of the trees on Jefferson Island. I turned and headed 287°M just past the fish stakes and rounding toward the mid-point between the two islands, finding 5 feet up into the area designated as "Poplar Harbor." Coming from the north, I headed 273°M from R "6" (45) to find the best depths up into the "harbor" area.

An old dock (46) comes off Coaches Island, as noted on the chart by dashed lines. There is rock rip-rap behind the dock. I found 4 feet depth up to the outside end of the dock. A red and white horizontally striped marker was affixed to the end, but it appeared ready to fall into the water at the next gust. There is a stretch of marshy grass behind the rip-rap and trees behind this. The rip-rap has one small break where you could walk up a small beach to the grass and trees. As the rip-rap approaches the point at the southeast end of the island, it ends in marsh grass (47). The feeling here is one of isolation and windswept beauty.

Jefferson Island has a bulkhead around the house with a little beach and a long dock (42). This is not public.

Cox Creek

Cox Creek appears to be an interesting gunkholing creek from the chart, but actually it is not among the better ones because it is mostly open from the south and fairly congested. It stretches all the way up to and under Route 50/301. This brings it deep in to the heart of a very busy section of Kent Island.

Refer to Regional Chart #12263-A—"Eastern Bay, Western Section" Pg. 117 and
Chart #12270-B—"Kent Island, Bayside, Cox Creek." Pg. 119
It is an easy matter finding the entrance into Cox Creek (16). It looks huge, but if the weather is misty, you may find it difficult distinguishing the mouth from the rest of the northern part of Eastern Bay. A course of 350°M from Fl R bell "2A" (11) off (north of) Wades Point (13) will take you into the mouth where you should be able to pick up G "1" and Fl R "2" (49) inside. Favor the western side to avoid the shoals (50) off Turkey Point (10). Note that a straight course from Fl R bell "2A" to Fl R "2" at the mouth Cox Creek will take you

over very shallow water. It is for that reason that the course line goes into the center area of the mouth of this creek, somewhat to the west of Fl R "2" inside. Going in, Batts Neck (51) is prominent ahead to the north; it has reddish high cliffs (52) which will be facing you. As you continue on up the creek, the shore of Cox Neck (53) to your east will have houses, cliffs, and a combination of rip-rap and cement seawall. Most of this appears light gray. This neck is fairly high, with a flat appearance to the top.

Looking up into Shipping Creek (56) to the northwest, you will see over the end of the creek four double towers with connecting beams between each set. These look strangely out of place behind the trees and high hills. They are the towers for the Bay Bridge, although you would never expect it from the rest of your surroundings. This creek may appear at first to offer some good anchoring spots, but it is mostly exposed to southerlies and is also very built up ashore with many private docks and homes. South Prong Shipping Creek (54) with its narrow marked entrance also is crowded, shallow, and of little interest to the cruiser. Inside is Benton's Boats (55) with some slips used by smaller local boats.

Past Batts Neck the chart shows a wreck and 6-foot shoal (57) to the west. These are not marked but are well west of the channel going in, and are inside of the point (58) rounding out to the west from the narrow part of Cox Neck. The creek is wide with trees and houses on both sides, as well as farms. At Fl R "4" (59), the creek narrows considerably, but then opens out into a wide area and a nice spot to anchor (60) if you don't need to be tucked up into a tight cove. However, anchoring out in the middle at the junction here could put you in the midst of traffic.

Warehouse Creek (61), which wanders off to the west of this wide area, is pretty with some nice spots to anchor depending upon your draft. The scenery is nice with large houses, trees, field, and marsh. I did not see the fence (64) marked on the chart coming off the shore rounding into this creek. These fences are usually installed to keep livestock from wandering around the end of a field, seldom extend out into navigable waters, and are not always kept up as farming needs change.

There is an interesting very large two-story brownstone house (65), which looks very formal and austere, just around that point, on the south western shore of Warehouse Creek. The yard has three flag poles. A large boat house and large pier with dock house are in front of it. This home because of its size and structure, looks like a club or structure of similar public nature, but it is not, it is a private home. Another large home, one-story with conspicuous arches (66), graces the banks farther up on the same shore.

Upstream from this home, Warehouse Creek is very pretty for anchoring (62), with nice spots anywhere you might want to stop and your draft allows. The area where the creek splits (63) is very nice, but don't take more than 5 feet in. The scenery is woods and marsh with little clue of the bustle of Route 50 except for the four towers on the Bridge hovering over the trees to the northwest. The northern branch (67) of the split has more houses, and when you get up here you can also see the red and white checked water tower (68) at Matapeake (83). Therefore, from the viewpoint of finding the best scenery, I would not suggest anchoring farther up than this split, where we've noted on the chart.

Proceeding farther north up Cox Creek would not be of much interest to me if I were gunkholing or looking for very pretty places to explore. Thompson Creek (69) is marked by privately maintained buoys (70) which we've approximately marked on the chart. These may be changed and you should rely on your own observations here. The mouth of Thompson Creek, with the cove area to your left (west) is pretty, although there are many houses along the east side of the creek. The first appearance would suggest that this would be a good anchorage, but the congestion upstream with all the small boat traffic passing would change your mind quickly. The western side is mostly field, woods, and marsh with some houses seen in the background. The small markers continue up here past a well known local inn on the western bank, and up to and just beyond a public ramp on the eastern bank.

Kent Manor Inn (72) is a stately country mansion set amidst a rural countryside. There are 24 VIP guest rooms and a very fine restaurant. There are walking paths along the property's 1½ miles of waterfront, and 226 acres of farmland. Swimming, golf, volleyball, horseshoes, croquet and golf on the nearby Queenstown Harbor Golf Links are available. Their telephone is (410) 643-5757. There is a small dinghy dock on the water in front of the house. While passing, we saw a wedding in progress with a fast boat tied to this dock with all the markings, balloons, and decorations of a get-away boat for the newlyweds. This would be a good place to have friends to meet if you wanted to anchor nearby and have them stay in a convenient and luxurious spot ashore.

The public ramp at Thompson Creek (73) is run by Queen Anne's County and has fees as follows: $5 in-state, $10 out-of-state per day; phone: (410) 758-0835 or 778-4430. The ramp is black hard surface with limited parking area. There is also a small fishing dock and a portable bathroom. Just upstream from this ramp, the area is completely congested with workboats moored out on stakes, is very congested ashore, and becomes very shallow as the chart shows. Soon you will see Highway 301/50 (82) with cars zooming. This will probably want to make you turn around and flee back to the nicer world you just left down the creek.

Passing by the mouth of Thompson Creek and heading farther up Cox Creek does not bring much better in the way of cruising niceties. Above G "5" (71), the creek has many more houses, boat houses, and docks. The eastern shore of Cox Creek is very congested with houses and their docks. The western shore still has some woods and marsh. The creek passes under Route 50/301 with a low fixed bridge (74) of only 6-foot clearance at high water. Looking up to the highway and just to the east, you will notice a Pizza Hut and a gas station (75). There's no place to land, and the highway is too busy to cross.

Crab Alley Bay and Creek

Refer to Chart #12270-E—"Crab Alley Bay and Prospect Bay."

This is one of my favorite names on the Chesapeake. The area is also nice, but primarily from the standpoint of keeping your boat in a marina.

Heading farther into Eastern Bay, Crab Alley Bay (22) to the north opens up wide and is a little confusing. Approaching the mouth from the west, you must first pass the shoals (16) off Turkey Point (10) to your north, extending far out into the bay in a southerly direction. The small Bodkin Island (77) is in the middle of these shoals. Many people have said that this reminds them of a battleship, and they look for that profile while trying to get their bearings. If you get exactly the right bearing, have just the right amount of mist, and are not too far or too close, you might be able to squeeze a

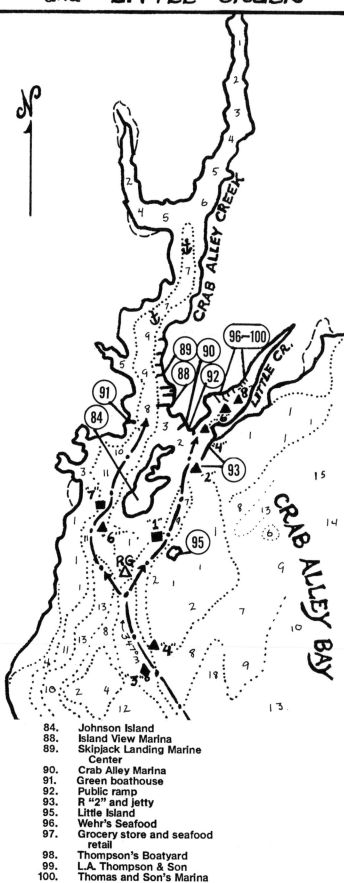

CRAB ALLEY CREEK
and LITTLE CREEK

84.	Johnson Island
88.	Island View Marina
89.	Skipjack Landing Marine Center
90.	Crab Alley Marina
91.	Green boathouse
92.	Public ramp
93.	R "2" and jetty
95.	Little Island
96.	Wehr's Seafood
97.	Grocery store and seafood retail
98.	Thompson's Boatyard
99.	L.A. Thompson & Son
100.	Thomas and Son's Marina

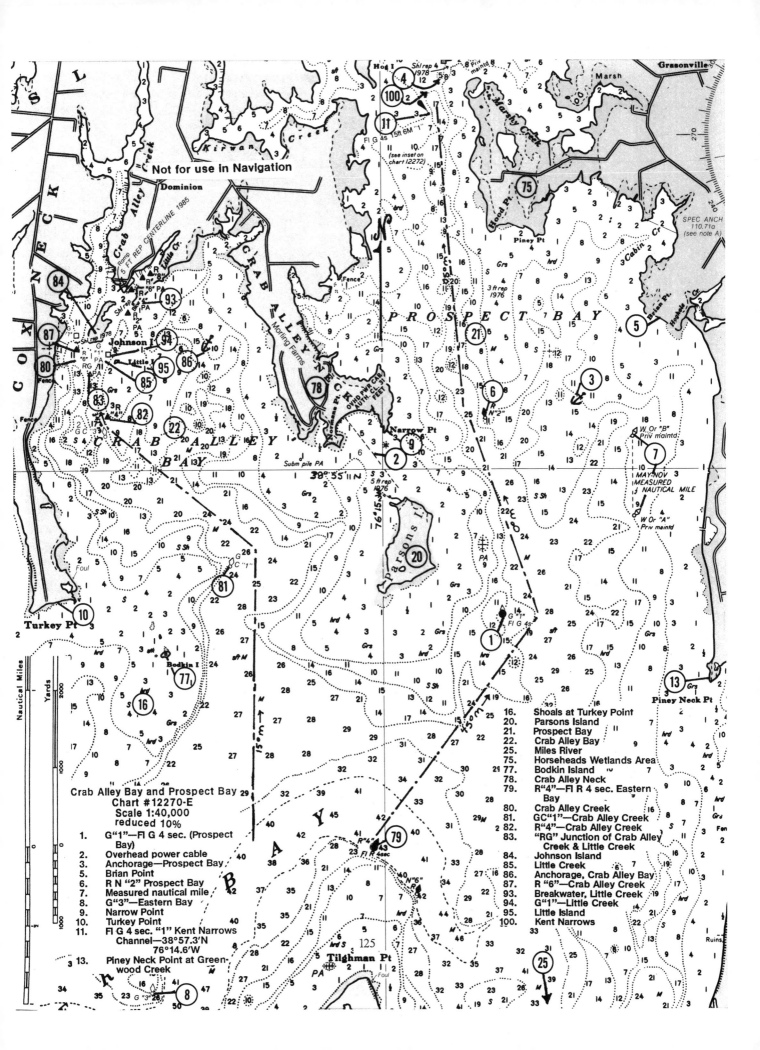

Not for use in Navigation

Crab Alley Bay and Prospect Bay
Chart #12270-E
Scale 1:40,000
reduced 10%

1. G"1"—Fl G 4 sec. (Prospect Bay)
2. Overhead power cable
3. Anchorage—Prospect Bay
5. Brian Point
6. R N "2" Prospect Bay
7. Measured nautical mile
8. G"3"—Eastern Bay
9. Narrow Point
10. Turkey Point
11. Fl G 4 sec. "1" Kent Narrows Channel—38°57.3'N 76°14.6'W
13. Piney Neck Point at Greenwood Creek

16. Shoals at Turkey Point
20. Parsons Island
21. Prospect Bay
22. Crab Alley Bay
25. Miles River
75. Horseheads Wetlands Area
77. Bodkin Island
78. Crab Alley Neck
79. R"4"—Fl R 4 sec. Eastern Bay
80. Crab Alley Creek
81. GC"1"—Crab Alley Creek
82. R"4"—Crab Alley Creek
83. "RG" Junction of Crab Alley Creek & Little Creek
84. Johnson Island
85. Little Creek
86. Anchorage, Crab Alley Bay
87. R "6"—Crab Alley Creek
93. Breakwater, Little Creek
94. G"1"—Little Creek
95. Little Island
100. Kent Narrows

125

battleship out of your imagination while looking at this island. In the meantime you will probably have run aground trying to conjure it up! Just look for a little island southeast of Turkey Point.

Rather than worrying so much about what Bodkin Island looks like, it makes better sense to head 15°M from a point approximately half way between G "3" (8) and Fl R "4" (79) of Eastern Bay. This should take you into Crab Alley Creek (80) and east of G "1" (81) marking its entrance. Watch for lateral movement from tides and wind so that you will not be set on the shoals coming off the two points. From R "4" (82), a bearing of 347°M goes to the vicinity of the "RG" junction buoy (83) at the southern tip of Johnson Island (84), and which notes the joining of the main channel of Crab Alley Creek with that of Little Creek (85).

Once you are inside the mouth of Crab Alley Creek, trying to sort things out ahead and to the north can be confusing. There is a tendency to look up between Johnson Island and the mainland when trying to find that junction buoy. The marinas appear between the island and the mainland, and that contributes to the confusing scene. Instead, look for the 347°M bearing.

To the right (east) of R "4," the northern bay of Crab Alley Bay welcomes as an anchorage (86). However, you must run well up into this area to feel secure, and then certainly not from southerlies. The bottom is very uneven and much of it is very hard sand which makes holding difficult. We have not been happy here the several times that we have tried it. However, there is, an enjoyable feeling of isolation and wide open space. After some of the "snugger" anchorages around, this may be refreshing. You will have the company of crabbers in their boats, and you should keep well lit at night.

Continuing into the upper reaches of Crab Alley, passing the "RG" junction buoy to your right (east), you will notice a brown house back in the trees on Johnson Island (84) as you pass R "6" (87). The area ahead to the north-northeast, on the tip of the mainland land that is to the north of Johnson Island, will seem crowded with marina docks and houses, but once you go ashore, you will find that it is more "country" than you would have expected. If you wish to anchor in Crab Alley Creek, proceed north up past the last marina. You will not be alone. There are many houses around, but it is a pretty area.

Refer to Sketch Chart—"Crab Alley Creek and Little Creek." Pg. 124

Island View Marina (88) is the first marina to the right (east) on the Crab Alley side of the peninsula after you pass the shallow cut north of Johnson Island. This full service marina has 40 slips, depth of up to 8 feet. They do not regularly do transient business, but it would be a nice place to stop if they have room. They have a lift available and do hull and mechanical work. They sell block and cube ice and do not take credit cards.

Skipjack Landing Marine Center (89) is the second on your right (east). This is full service, with a large Texaco sign on a large gray shop building facing the water. There are 80 slips with depths up to 8 feet. The longest slip is 40 feet but there is much greater length along face docks. Block and cube ice, marine hardware, and gasoline are available. Electricity up to 30 amps is available. There are two open end lifts at 25 and 35 tons, and a fork lift for boats up to 27 feet long for the dry storage facility. There is a full service yard, a marine store and they sell and service MerCruiser, Mercury. Volva Penta, PCM, and OMC. They also had new Apache, Sierra, and Kencraft boats for sale.

Right on the point of the mainland off Johnson Island, you will find **Eastern Bay Marina trading as Crab Alley Marina (90)**. There are 20 slips with a maximum length available at 40 feet and up to 30 amps of electricity. There are bathrooms only, no shower. Block and cube ice are available, as are fishing bait and crabbing bait and gear. The depth and approach can be quite shallow. Depths are from 2 to 6 feet at the docks. The best entrance is from Crab Alley Creek.

There is a green boathouse (91) on the western side of Crab Alley Creek. The route from that boathouse to the end of the piers of Crab Alley Marina at the tip of the point carries the best depth in. Don't try approaching Crab Alley Marina with any more than 3 feet depth at near high tide and rising, without discussing the latest soundings with them first. They will rent 14-foot skiffs with small outboards and fully stock and gear you for a day of fishing or crabbing. A cement ramp has a $5 fee. The marina hosts regular crab-catching contests, with the seasonal winner getting a dinner for two. There is also dry storage available, and a very nice, large yard with green grass and picnic tables. This is a great place to come by land and smaller boats to enjoy the Bay. They are in the process of building a launching lift designed especially for trailerable catamarans. This would be an ideal launching spot and great sailing area for this type of boat. Their phone number is (410) 643-7339.

There is a public ramp (92) immediately next to Crab Alley Marina, just around the point on its southeastern side. This is a modern cement ramp with parking lot. There are fees as follows: $5 in-state, $10 out-of-state per day. For more information, phone: (410) 758-0835 or 778-4430. From this ramp, most boats go out into Crab Alley Bay through Little Creek.

Little Creek

Little Creek is the little creek east of the bigger Crab Alley Creek. It offers no scenic anchorages and has no more than 4 to 5 feet depth up to its R "8." There is a ramp mentioned above, a commercial and retail seafood dock and store, and several small docking areas with some repair facilities mostly occupied by working boats.

Refer to Chart #12270-E—"Crab Alley Bay and Prospect Bay" Pg. 125 **and**
Our Sketch Chart—"Crab Alley Creek and Little Creek." Pg. 124

The approach to Little Creek (85) is the same as the approach to the junction buoy described above for Crab Alley Creek. The creek mouth is narrow and there can be difficulty in distinguishing it from the rest of Crab Alley Bay to the east of the little peninsula (93) which forms the eastern bank of the creek. A gray rock jetty, extending out southwesterly from that peninsula, on the east side of that Little Creek channel, makes it easier to understand this entrance as you approach. Green "1" (94) is south of the tip of Johnson Island, between that tip and Little Island (95) to its east. Little Island is very small, appears to be a spoil island, and has a duck blind. It is a help in locating G "1" if you are having trouble. Red "2" (93) is near and just off the tip of the jetty. From there, just follow the markers. All the concerns are on the west bank, and the creek will appear to be rather built up as you come in.

The first establishment is Wehr's Seafood (96). It is across from R "4" and has a Shell sign on its dock. They sell gas only, taking MC and Visa. Work boats land local seafood at the dock. This seafood and that from other areas is sold retail from the same building. They also sell block and cube ice in addition to bait.

Blue crab, properly held at base of backfin

Bikini contest at Red Eye's Dock Bar, Mears Point Marine, Kent Narrows

Next upstream from Wher's is a little seafood retail and grocery store (97), offering a small selection of some convenience groceries, including ice cream. There are a few locally used docks here, and the store faces the road behind it from the water. Farther up the creek are three facilities with some repair operations. They appear to be used primarily by local work boats. They are still on the western shore, and in the same area. Here the creek shallows with some work boats moored out. **Thompson's Boatyard (98)** has 24 slips with 15 amps electricity and a 45-foot 25-ton railway. They sell gas and do some engine and hull repairs and some boat building. **L.A. Thompson & Son (99)** has some service slips for its 35-ton railway, and they do hull and engine repair and boat some building. **Thomas and Son's Marine (100)** has a 10-ton 45-foot railway and 6 slips, also offering engine and hull repairs. These places might be a good place to check if you are in the vicinity and need some good basic repair work, welding or engine work.

Parson's Island

This is a large, high, and rather flat island which is farmed and has a home and farm buildings. Approaching as you come in from Chesapeake Bay, it sometimes appears as though it were a part of mainland from afar in misty conditions, but it will separate itself from its background as you get closer. The chart shows an overhead power cable (2) coming out to it from the mainland to its north, but this is not there. Local small boats regularly traverse about half way between the island and the mainland, with 2 to 3 feet depth at mean low tide. There are probably stumps near the shores and irregular spots, but it can save time for a shoal draft boat. Don't anchor in here because a buried power line runs from the mainland to the island in place of the old overhead line.

Prospect Bay

Refer to Chart #12270-E—"Crab Alley Bay and Prospect Bay." Pg. 125

This is the southern entrance to Kent Narrows. It is a large open area on the eastern side of Crab Alley Neck with no real anchorages, marinas, or shoreside attractions with convenient landings. The eastern shore of Prospect Bay, with the obvious exception of the Horsehead Wetlands area described in the section on Queen Anne's County in this chapter, has many private homes. The western shore is less populated. It is a pretty area, and a nice place to sail, but is usually honored only in passing as boats head to or from the Kent Narrows mecca.

In easterly and northeasterly weather we have anchored (3) in Prospect Bay (21) in the area southwest of Brian Point (5), heading easterly in from the Kent Narrows approach channel at Red Nun "2" (6). If you do this, be sure to move well out of the busy channel and keep well lit. The shallower area near the shore becomes hard sand requiring anchoring gear for that type of bottom. The buoys for the measured nautical-mile course (7) are helpful in getting your bearings for an anchorage, as well as checking your speed and distance equipment.

Refer to Chart #12270-A—"Kent Narrows" Pg. 109
and
Chart #12270-E—"Crab Alley Bay and Prospect Bay" for entrance. Pg. 125

Heading north toward Kent Narrows (100), follow the buoys. The course from Fl R "4" (79) (which is out in Eastern Bay and to the north of Tilghman Point) to the vicinity just east of Fl G "1" (1) (which is southeast of Parson's Island) is 45°M. The route from Fl G "1" to the vicinity just west of R "2" (6) (which is east of Narrow Point (9) on Crab Alley Neck) is about due north M.

The next stretch is a bit long between markers, especially considering that shoals meander out from the sides in the northern end of this well-traveled run. In poor visibility it can be difficult to see the other relevant channel marker Fl G "1" (11) which is well up into the Bay, serving as the outside southern marker for Kent Narrows Channel. The position of Fl G "1" is 38°57.3'N by 76°14.6'W. It is 15 feet tall. A course of 5°M takes you from the area to the west of R "2" to that Fl G "1," avoiding the shoals coming out from the side. It is best to pay close attention to the depth finder on this run and take note of your relation to the shorelines. Note that in the heading next to Kent Narrows, red is to your right (the eastern side) and remains so all the way through the Chester River.

The bridge and buildings of Kent Narrows will grow as you get closer. They are described in detail in the section on Kent Narrows early in this chapter as is the Narrows channel and vicinity.

Greenwood Creek

Refer to Chart #12270-F—"Entrance to Miles and Wye Rivers."

This small pretty creek has many residences and private docks thickly lining the shores, and is very difficult to enter if you draw more than 4 feet. It can be bad enough at that. For the serious gunkholer, it presents a challenge and nice places to anchor well out of any weather.

Entrance into Greenwood Creek (10) is hardly worth the effort unless you have friends inside, have local knowledge, or are fanatically determined to explore yet another nice Chesapeake Bay creek, no matter how difficult. Don't waste time reading the following entrance description unless you really want to go in here and love tortuous navigation (and reading). The channel is privately marked, but it is a classic example of areas in the Bay subject to constant shoaling and bottom changes because of exposure to wave action, and it is quite shallow and meandering in the first place. I spent hours trying to find a reliable way in for at least 4 feet of draft, and had difficulty even with the markers. I finally followed two boats whose owners lived on the creek inside. They were very helpful, but the course changes were so frequent that I barely had time to check the depth finder. Don't even think about entering if there is an onshore breeze of any significance. There is up to 8 and 9 feet depth once you get inside, and 6 feet well up into the creek, and I did find at least 4 feet in the marked entry channel, but it was at times difficult to locate.

The first trick of entering, depending on your draft and sensitivity to shallow water, is to avoid the 6-foot shoal (11) areas west of the middle of the neck leading out to Bennett Point (12). This area is part of a longer shoal, extending out from Piney Neck Point (13) to the area west of Bennett Point, obviously marking the shore and creek bed of times past. This shoal has rocky areas (14), and although the chart indicates nothing less than 6 feet here, if the water were rough and if I had anything approaching 6 feet draft I would make my approach along the original channel (15) inside that shoal. To do this, I took a course of 20°M from 600 to 700 yards off the small privately built lighthouse (16) structure on the tip of Bennett's Point to get to where I could better see the private creek entrance markers. This course also runs from

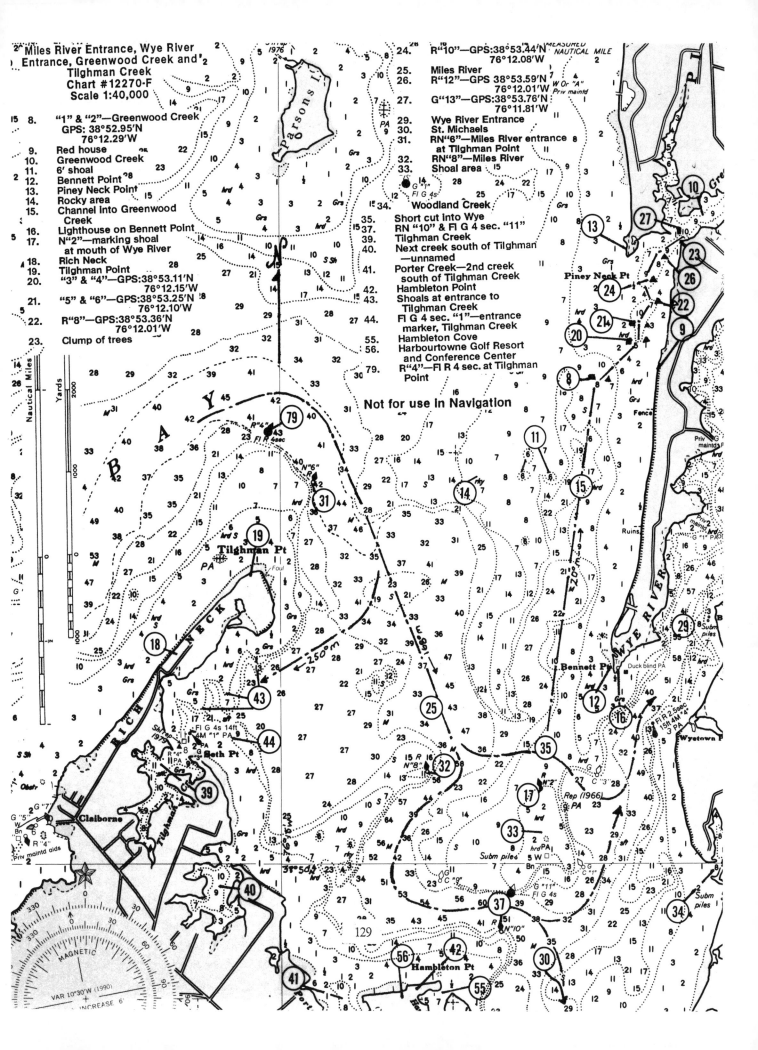

Miles River Entrance, Wye River
Entrance, Greenwood Creek and
Tilghman Creek
Chart #12270-F
Scale 1:40,000

8. "1" & "2"—Greenwood Creek
   GPS: 38°52.95'N
   76°12.29'W
9. Red house
10. Greenwood Creek
11. 6' shoal
12. Bennett Point
13. Piney Neck Point
14. Rocky area
15. Channel into Greenwood
    Creek
16. Lighthouse on Bennett Point
17. N"2"—marking shoal
    at mouth of Wye River
18. Rich Neck
19. Tilghman Point
20. "3" & "4"—GPS:38°53.11'N
    76°12.15'W
21. "5" & "6"—GPS:38°53.25'N
    76°12.10'W
22. R"8"—GPS:38°53.36'N
    76°12.01'W
23. Clump of trees

24. R"10"—GPS:38°53.44'N
    76°12.08'W
25. Miles River
26. R"12"—GPS:38°53.59'N
    76°12.01'W
27. G"13"—GPS:38°53.76'N
    76°11.81'W
29. Wye River Entrance
30. St. Michaels
31. RN"6"—Miles River entrance
    at Tilghman Point
32. RN"8"—Miles River
33. Shoal area
34. Woodland Creek
35. Short cut into Wye
37. RN "10" & Fl G 4 sec. "11"
39. Tilghman Creek
40. Next creek south of Tilghman
    —unnamed
41. Porter Creek—2nd creek
    south of Tilghman Creek
42. Hambleton Point
43. Shoals at entrance to
    Tilghman Creek
44. Fl G 4 sec. "1"—entrance
    marker, Tilghman Creek
55. Hambleton Cove
56. Harbourtowne Golf Resort
    and Conference Center
79. R"4"—Fl R 4 sec. at Tilghman
    Point

Not for use in Navigation

129

Red Nun "2" (17) south of Bennett Point, if you wish to use this marker as a reference.

Some of the Greenwood Creek channel markers were in haphazard condition, not surprising considering their exposure. Following them in by dinghy with plenty of time to study them, I still found them very confusing because they dogleg back and forth, sometimes so sharply that I had trouble determining which marker was the next set until I got up to it. I found them so confusing, that while I would normally just say to follow the markers, I have tried to give rough courses here with GPS derived fixes. The fixes are not to the markers themselves, but to a point off each marker where you should be for deep water. GPS fixes are not precisely accurate at this time because of government interference with the signals, and at best should only be used as general guidance. The first set, R "2" and G "1" (8) will be approximately west of the red house (9) with dark brown roof and bulkhead in front on the shore to the east. This house has one story for most of its face, but a second story on the portion behind a porch. There are two chimneys with a third structure that appears as a chimney.

I found no more than 4 feet of water between this first pair. The GPS derived position was 38°52.95'N, by 76°12.29'W.

The course to the second set of markers (3 and 4) (20) is 55°M. Between the second set (20), the GPS derived position is 38°53.11'N by 76°12.15'W.

The next course to markers 6 and 5 (21) is 25 °M. Their GPS derived position is 38°53.25'N by 76°12.10'W.

The next course, to R "8" (22), heads towards (but not to) the point ahead to your northeast with the clump of trees (23). This is 43°M. Its GPS position is 38°53.36'N by 76°12.01'W.

The course to R "10" (24) dogs back to your left, at 337°M. You are heading now generally toward Piney Neck Point (13), which separates the Greenwood Creek from Prospect Bay. The GPS derived position for R "10" is 38°53.44'N by 76°12.08'W.

Next you dogleg again back to your right on a course of 33°M to get to R "12" (26). This GPS derived position is 38°53.59'N by 76°12.01'W.

The last entrance marker is G "13" (27). The course to this is 55°M and very close to the point on your right ahead, marking the end of the shoal that extends far out from the point on the western shore of the creek. This GPS derived position is 38°53.76'N by 76°11.81'W. The width of the channel between this marker and the point of land to its east is not much more than 100 feet. It takes certain amount of faith to pass this green marker on its proper side [put it to your left (west) going in] because the channel is so close to the point while there is such a wide expanse of shallow water on the wrong side of the marker.

Editor's note: I have done a lot of exploring in channels like this, some with no markers. No trepidation, because I take my dink in first, and stay till I sort things out, then take my sailboat in. For a dink exploration of a shallow, strange channel, I take my leadline, a 6-foot oar (to get acquainted with the nature of the bottom if I can't see it), and a handbearing compass. I have a handheld Magellan GPS that has done good work, but I haven't used it in my dink yet. If there is a chart, I bring it and plot what I find. If there isn't one, I can make an accurate sketch taking soundings and bearings. So can you, if you'll spend the time. You must know the state of the tide while you're working, so that you can later reduce your soundings to MLW. If you've never done this, try it, you'll like it!

Tom has the best equipped dink I ever saw, with a calibrated depth sounder, a handbearing compass, and a handheld GPS. Tom has the buoys plotted for you, but take the dink in first to confirm that nothing has changed. I can hardly wait to try it!

Now that you are in, you will see houses everywhere. It is pretty, and you can go up as far as your draft allows. The main branch (10) to your right (northeast) contains more options and less congestion on the shore. The chart shows the depths. Anchoring here in serious weather should be particularly secure if not very private.

Eastern Bay Approach to Miles and Wye Rivers

Refer to Chart #12270-F—"Entrance to Miles and Wye Rivers" Pg.129   and
Regional Chart #12263-B—"Eastern Bay, Eastern Section, Miles and Wye Rivers," in Chapter 10. Pg. 133

A large percentage of boats cruising into Eastern Bay are heading for the Miles (25) and Wye Rivers (29), and the town of St. Michaels (30). A detailed description of the entrance into those two rivers is given in Chapter 10 on the Miles River. However, a few comments about this approach belong in any description of Eastern Bay.

As mentioned earlier in this chapter, Rich Neck (18) and its northeasternmost point, Tilghman Point (19), will be a prominent landmark as you head into Eastern Bay. Behind Rich Neck is the incredible area of the Miles and Wye Rivers. Passing around (to the east of) Tilghman Point introduces you to these waters. Be sure to put Fl R "4" (79) and R Nun "6" (31) to your right (southwest) as you round Tilghman Point. We often see boats taking them inside, but the water shoals up very quickly, the bottom is hard sand, and currents and wind can push you too far over before you know it. Once around this point, you will see the broad mouth of the Miles River ahead to the south, with the Wye and Wye East Rivers off to your left (east).

Private lighthouse at entrance to Wye River

CHAPTER 10

WYE RIVER AND MILES RIVER

The Miles River should be one of the highlights of a Chesapeake cruise. This is because of the unique Bay town of St. Michaels and its Chesapeake Bay Maritime Museum, and because of the beauty of the river and its anchorages. But you may wish to avoid weekends and holidays when the crowds are overwhelming.

Some people consider the Wye and the Wye East Rivers to be a tributary of the Miles River, and think of that as part of the beauty of cruising the Miles. The Wye Rivers empty into the lower waters of the Miles River. As you head into the Miles, you pass the Wye Rivers to your left (northeast). You can explore the Wye Rivers without going up into the Miles, although most do. The Wye Rivers are a different and complete cruising ground in their own right.

ENTRANCE TO MILES AND WYE RIVERS
Refer to Regional Chart #12263-B—"Eastern Bay—Eastern Section," Wye and Miles Rivers in this chapter; Pg 133
and
Chart #12270-F—"Miles River Entrance, Wye River Entrance, Greenwood Creek and Tilghman Creek" near the end of Chapter 9. Pg. 129

The entrance to the Miles (25) and Wye Rivers (29) is common. As described in the last section of the Eastern Bay Chapter 9, you gain the entrance area by rounding Fl R "4" (79) and R Nun "6" (31) which are just north-northeast of Tilghman Point (19). If not already familiar with the area, the scenery ahead may be a little confusing after you have rounded the point.

One of the things that you may notice as you come around into the Miles River is the small lighthouse (16) over on Bennett Point (12) in a direction of 136°M from R Nun "6." It is not really a working lighthouse. It is a privately built water tower and playhouse and has no official navigational significance. It does help you to get the lay of the land. If you wish to head into the Miles River, a course of 168°M should take you from the vicinity of R Nun "6" to the vicinity of R Nun "8" (32). From here on into the Miles River, the markers are closer together and not very difficult to find. It is important to note the shoal area (33) which will be to your east, to the west of the mouth of Woodland Creek (34), as you head on a southerly course into the Miles. Parts of this area are as shallow as 2 feet and less, as the chart shows. Because it is out in the open water, not where you would normally expect a large shoal to be, it traps many unwary boaters.

If you are proceeding into the Wye, you have the choice (if you have the draft) of either taking the short cut (35) through the deeper part of the shoal that extends southwesterly from Bennett Point (12); or going on to R Nun "10" in the Miles River and rounding back up northeasterly, passing that shoal to your left (west). This second route is certainly easier, deeper, safer, and thus preferable. For those in a hurry, the short cut

is made simply by going approximately halfway between R Nun "2" and Gr Can "3," both of which are south of Bennett Point. The chart shows 8 feet to be the minimum depth here. I have noticed 7 feet at times, although I can't swear that I was precisely in the right place. From the east of Gr Can "3," the course on up into the lower Wye is simple. Stay in the middle except where otherwise indicated by markers or other signs.

Before going farther into the Miles, it may be helpful to note that an interesting feature of the Miles River is that its deep water twists between some rather shallow shoals. A significant example is this shoal, just described, between N "2" and G "11" to the west of Woodland Creek. Another important example is the long Fairview Point (38) shoal extending well past the middle of the river. The width of the river in places and the beautiful scenery can deceive you into more relaxed navigation than is appropriate under the circumstances. The markers are clear and will keep you out of trouble, but it is important to concentrate on your course, the chart, and the plentiful markers in the Miles River.

TILGHMAN CREEK (39)

This creek at the mouth of the Miles River, has long been thought of as the ultimate in storm protection in these parts, and the anchorage to be coveted. It does offer good protection, with landlocked water and some high hills, but the scenery ashore is not special, if you are seeking sylvan coves. There are many homes ashore and docks. Also, the approach is subject to continued shifting and shoaling.

Refer to Chart #12270-F—"Miles River Entrance, Wye River Entrance" near the end of chapter 9. Pg. 129
When looking for the entrance to Tilghman Creek (39) from the Miles, the other two creeks (40) & (41) between Hambleton Point (42) and Rich Neck (18) can fool you unless you remember that they do not have markers, and Tilghman Creek is right behind (to the southeast of) Rich Neck which leads out to Tilghman Point (19). The chart clearly shows one of the problems on approaching. Shoals (43) finger out from the neck. These shoals shift and any approach must be with a close eye on the depth shoulder.

Refer to our Sketch Chart—"Tilghman Creek, Eastern Bay—Miles River." Pg. 132
I found that an approach of 250°M off the first marker (44) never got me into less that 7 feet, but remember that these shoals shift from both sides. It is not as difficult as would appear at the approach if you are careful. The worst problem is at the three markers at the entrance. It is necessary to round between the two outer green markers, Fl Gr "1" (44) and Gr "3" (45). A shoal comes out from the left between them. They are very close together, and a gradual rounding gets you past. However, between G "3" and R "4" there is more serious shoal-

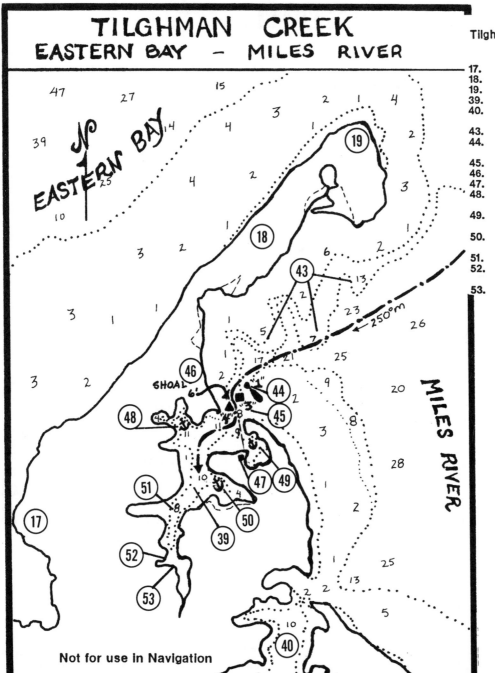

TILGHMAN CREEK
EASTERN BAY — MILES RIVER

Not for use in Navigation

ing and I could barely find 6 feet. I was told that this is growing worse. The shoal (46) behind R "4" continues beyond it in a southeasterly direction into the creek, so that once you are past, it is not wise to head straight into the middle of the creek. Instead, head for the two-story house (47) ahead on the point to the left (south) side of the creek. It will be on a bluff opposite you coming in. The bottom story is white and there are white dormers in the roof which forms the second story. Continue heading carefully toward that house until the bottom starts deepening. Soon you will be back in around 10 feet and can start up into the creek, leaving the house on its point to the left (east).

The first cove to the right (west) (48) has 10 feet depths, but is not very well protected from a northeasterly, and has houses and docks. The first cove to the left (east) (49) is much better protected and has 9 feet depth. There are also houses and docks here. Like the rest of the creek, it does not make a

very private anchorage. The second cove to left (east) (50) is a little prettier. It is possible to get into good protected waters, but the houses are on low land much of which has been cleared, and there is not very much privacy here. This cove grows very pretty near its head with marsh and woods, but it goes down to 2 or 3 feet, then shallower.

The depth carries up the rest of the creek pretty much as indicated on the chart, with only 8 feet depth (51). Anywhere in here would make an anchorage, but there are homes and docks ashore. As is so often seen, some homes have multiple docks, but these are not available to the public. Near the head of the western side there is an old railroad, with an old shed and docks and a high Gulf sign behind (52). This is on the right (west). Just upstream from the shed is a public dock (53) used by work boats. Beyond this, for all practical purposes, the creek ends.

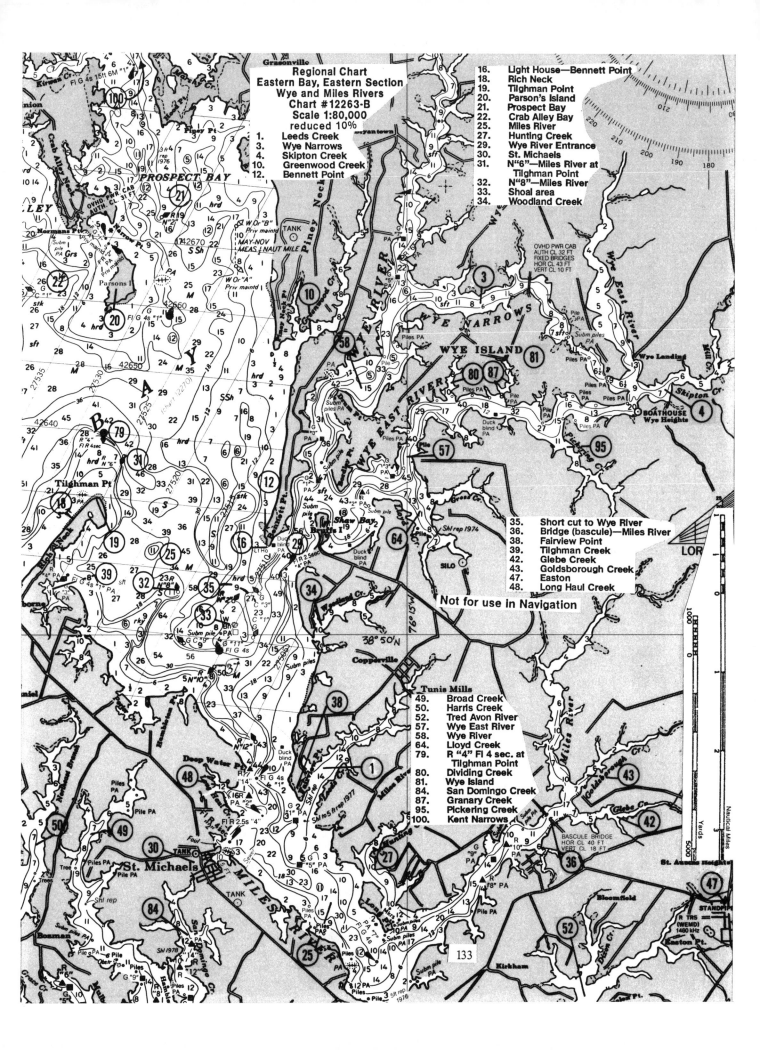

Regional Chart
Eastern Bay, Eastern Section
Wye and Miles Rivers
Chart #12263-B
Scale 1:80,000
reduced 10%

1. Leeds Creek
3. Wye Narrows
4. Skipton Creek
10. Greenwood Creek
12. Bennett Point

16. Light House—Bennett Point
18. Rich Neck
19. Tilghman Point
20. Parson's Island
21. Prospect Bay
22. Crab Alley Bay
25. Miles River
27. Hunting Creek
29. Wye River Entrance
30. St. Michaels
31. N"6"—Miles River at Tilghman Point
32. N"8"—Miles River
33. Shoal area
34. Woodland Creek

35. Short cut to Wye River
36. Bridge (bascule)—Miles River
38. Fairview Point
39. Tilghman Creek
42. Glebe Creek
43. Goldsborough Creek
47. Easton
48. Long Haul Creek

49. Broad Creek
50. Harris Creek
52. Tred Avon River
57. Wye East River
58. Wye River
64. Lloyd Creek
79. R "4" Fl 4 sec. at Tilghman Point
80. Dividing Creek
81. Wye Island
84. San Domingo Creek
87. Granary Creek
95. Pickering Creek
100. Kent Narrows

Not for use in Navigation

133

Continuing on into the Miles River, you will notice some single-story brown wood buildings of modern structure on Hambleton Point to your right (west). These immediately precede the very shallow entrance to Hambleton Cove (55) on the same shore. These buildings are a part of the Harbourtown Golf Resort and Conference Center (56). This is about 15 minutes drive from St. Michaels. The creek is of no real interest to the cruiser because of its shallow entrance, but the conference center does rent small paddle and sailboats from the mouth of the creek.

At this general area you must decide whether you wish to explore the beautiful and less civilized area of the Wye or Wye East River (29), or go up into the Miles (25) and St. Michaels (30). If you have recently come from a marina or town area, I suggest, that you next proceed on up into the Wye East River and enjoy the natural environment of that area. Then you will more enjoy the hustle and bustle and all the interests ashore of St. Michaels.

WYE AND WYE EAST RIVERS

This is certainly one of the prettiest areas of the Bay for anchoring and dinghy exploration, with innumerable perfect creeks and coves. The shore is mostly woods, field, and private homes, with no towns or marinas. St. Michaels is nearby on the Miles River. Once into the Wye, settle down to miles of incredibly beautiful shoreline, ideal anchorages, total protection, and some of the biggest blue crabs of the Bay.

Refer to Chart #12270-G—"Wye River, Wye East River, Wye Narrows."

What most cruisers consider to be the Wye (29) is actually two rivers, The Wye East River (57), and the Wye River (58). The Wye East has what most feel to be the most pleasant anchorages, although the Wye is also notable for its cruising. These two share a common mouth, and they are connected upstream by the Wye Narrows (3), which runs in a general east-west direction around the top of Wye Island (81), cutting that off from the rest of the mainland to its north. Let's first journey up the Wye East River, then head through the Wye Narrows to join the Wye River. Then we'll cruise the Wye River from its mouth northward, passing the narrows, and going up to its headwaters.

WYE EAST RIVER

For entrance use, Chart #12270-F near the end of Chapter 9.
PG. 129

The entrance into this river has been described at the beginning of this chapter. Once you are around the shoal south of Bennett Point and up into the wide and deep mouth, there is not much to be said about coming in to this or its sister river.

Shaw Bay

Refer to Chart #12270-G—"Wye River, Wye East River, Wye Narrows."

The first major anchorage is in Shaw Bay (59), to the east of Bruffs Point (60), which is to your east as you come in. As is clear from the chart, "T'aint no secret gettin' in." Round the point and anchor as you wish. On the weekends there are usually quite a few boats in here, many preferring the openness

Wye River, Wye East River	62A. Beach in anchorage
Wye Narrows	63. R "2" with shoal
Chart 12270-G	extending northward
Scale 1:40,000	64. Lloyd Creek
reduced 10%	65. Tall brown cliffs
1. Piles	66. Beach
2. Upper Wye East River	67. Shoal at entrance of
3. Wye Narrows	Lloyd Creek
4. Skipton Creek	68. Gross Creek
5. Boat house	69. Entrance shoal—3' MLW,
6. Anchorage—Skipton Creek	private green marker
7. Anchorages—Upper Wye	71. Anchorage—Gross Creek
East River	72. Shoal with duck blind
8. Wye Landing	73. Large brown house
9. Schnaitman's Boat Livery	(Wye House)
10. Greenwood Creek	77. Anchorage—Wye East River
11. Bridge—Wye Narrows	78. Anchorage Cove
12. Bennett Point	80. Dividing Creek
13. Anchorage—Wye Narrows	81. Wye Island
14. 3 small creeks	82. 2 ft. shoal—west bank—
15. Shoal with duck blind at	Dividing Creek
De Coursey Cove	83. Shoal, east bank,
16. Lighthouse—private	Dividing Creek
17. De Coursey Cove	84. Quarter Cove
19. Brick mansion	85. Brown boat house,
20. White mooring buoy—private	Quarter Cove
21. Shoal	86. Point on east bank of
22. Shoal marked by G "1"	Dividing Creek
23. Bordley Point	87. Granary Creek
24. Unnamed Cove—south of	88. Greenish, gray house
Drum Point	inside Granary Creek
25. Drum Point	89. Point on east side of
26. Anchorage	Granary Creek entrance
27. Bigwood Cove	90. T-shaped cove—Anchorage
29. Wye River Entrance	91. Unnamed creek
33. Grapevine Cove	92. Pilings
34. Grapevine Point	93. Dock and house inside creek
35. Upper Wye River	94. High Point
57. Wye East River	95. Pickering Creek
58. Wye River	96. Anchorage at the mouth of
59. Shaw Bay	Pickering Creek
60. Bruffs Point	97. "Tire Cove" Anchorage
61. Shoal—Shaw Bay	98. Anchorage farther up
62. Anchorage	Pickering Creek
	99. Anchorage in Wye East River
	100. Anchorage cove in Wye
	East River

of Shaw Bay to the narrower anchorages upstream which are likely to have less breeze. The shore is lined with forest and marsh and a few houses; the most notable of which is the large private estate on Bruffs Point. My only objection to this anchorage is that much of it is rather deep, often 18 or 19 feet, and I would prefer shallower anchorages so that I don't have to put out as much anchor rode and don't have to work so hard getting it all in. You can find shallower water here closer to the shore, but feel your way to this because it does shoal up fairly quickly in places. Note that the eastern side (61) of this bay is shallow well out from the shore, with 3-foot depths far enough out to ensnare the unwary. The soft bottom inside will hold well, but may require some extra work setting and backing down to get the hook in securely.

If Shaw Bay is too crowded for your comfort, and you don't want to proceed too far into the river, you may wish to anchor in the cove (62) up the river and to the northeast of Shaw Bay. There is a nice little beach (62A) on the small point protruding into that cove from its north-northeastern bank. Note that the shoal extends beyond R "2" (63) in a northerly direction. You should give this a wide berth.

Lloyd Creek

Fewer boats go up into Lloyd Creek (64) which also provides room to anchor and has pretty scenery. Heading into this creek, you get the feeling of more openness and less protection, but it is really not as open as Shaw Bay. Heading into

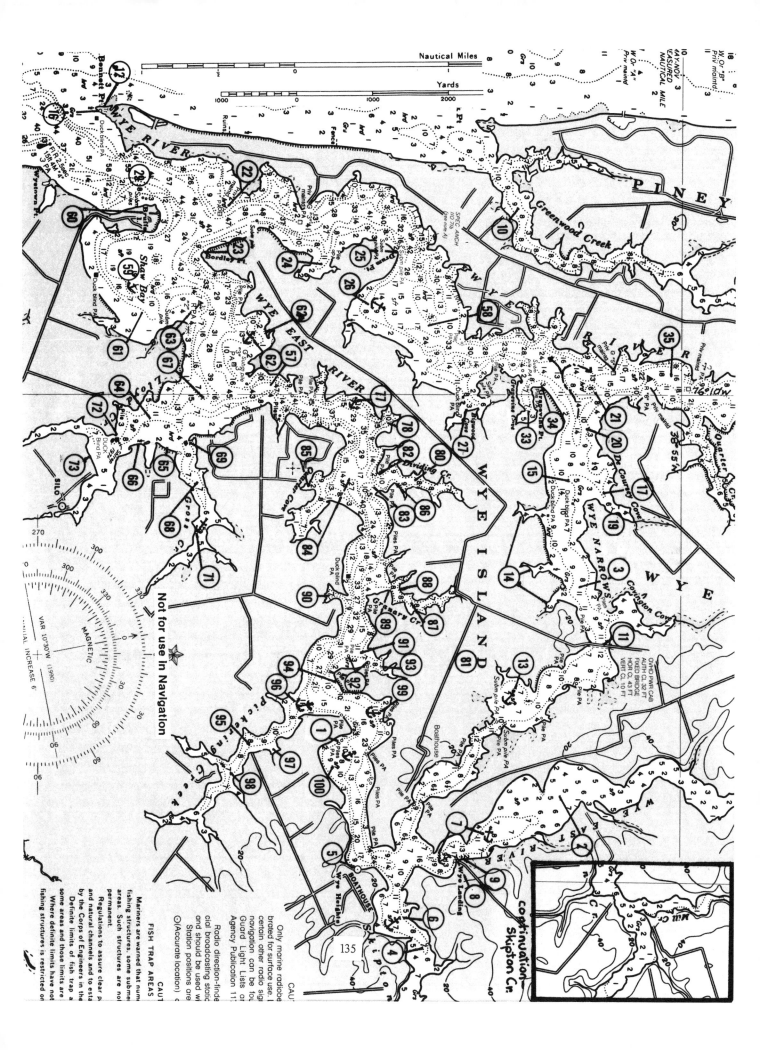

Not for use in Navigation

135

the creek, in a southeasterly direction, you will see ahead tall cliffs (65) of brown dirt. There will be a small beach (66) just to the south of the cliffs. If you draw 6 feet or more, beware of the shoal (67) charted at 7 feet depth coming out from the southwestern shore. Favor the northeastern side and watch the depth finder.

The main branch of Lloyd Creek, as it goes off to the south and southeast, also has nice scenery, some good anchorages, and makes a nice dinghy exploration area. The farther up you go, the shallower the water. If your boat is shallow enough, you should explore up as far as you can go. The shoal (72) reported off the point on the southwestern side of the creek is best handled by simply giving that point a wide berth and not taking more than 5 feet draft beyond that anyway. A duck blind helps to identify that point. Remember that duck blinds are often built on the shoals, near the edge of the shallow water, as is apparently the case here. Across from that point, you will see the beach (66) first noticed as you came into the outer reaches of Lloyd Creek.

A big brown house (73) sits on the blunt point separating the two upper branches of Lloyd Creek. As you go into the western branch, you will see a pretty, old white boat house alone on its eastern shore, solitary amidst beautiful trees and marsh. This western branch is the prettiest of the upper two branches. The eastern branch is shallower, and as you go into it, you see tennis courts and a big TV dish associated with the large brown house on the point. Anchoring here would have you close to the folks in the house. The creek is more secluded farther up, but there's only 2 to 3 feet depth up there.

Gross Creek

Gross Creek (68) is a great place for boats of 3 feet of draft or less. The creek is deeper than this inside, but the entrance shoal going across the mouth is 3 feet. There is a small privately placed green marker (69) off the little point to the north as you go into Gross Creek. It is hard to see—at first I thought it was a crab pot. Honor it going in. There are some homes inside but farther up, just before the Y, where indicated on the chart, there is a beautiful anchorage (71) surrounded by trees and marsh. There is also good protection here, but enough room to get a little breeze.

•

There are two or more good anchorages back out in the Wye East, in the cove opposite (to the northwest of) the point which is just to the west of Quarter Cove (84). One is a large open cove (77), the other is a smaller cove (78) at the northeast end of the larger area. There are woods along the shores, and some beach on the low shoreline. The smaller cove is very pretty and deep but very narrow. Because depths are 10 to 15 feet and the narrowness of the anchorage, you should use two anchors or a Bahamian moor.

Dividing Creek

Perhaps one of the most loved anchorages in the Bay is Dividing Creek (80), just upriver on the northern bank. It looks good on the chart, but is so much more attractive than a chart could ever hope to portray. It goes deep into the countryside, with shores surrounded by woods. Behind the woods are fields, but you hardly notice that. The fields assure that there will not be the sounds of cars, homes, and other vestiges of civilization. Here and there, small beaches dot the shoreline beneath the trees at low tide. In most places, trees come right down to hang over the water. Holding is generally good, although it is soft mud and requires some effort to get a good

set. Because of the isolation of the creek and because it goes into Wye Island (81) rather than the mainland, it is not unusual to see wild animals such as deer along the banks in the twilight and early morning.

The only two negatives about Dividing Creek are the crowds on weekends and the entrance which will be a little tricky to boats drawing more than 3 feet. The crowds can't be helped, although the magic serenity of this creek is so deep that it seems to absorb the civilization even when dozens of boats are anchored here. The entrance can be negotiated by paying attention to the chart and depth finder. There is a 2-foot shoal (82) coming off the west entrance bank, and it protrudes easterly toward another shallow shoal (83) coming off the eastern entrance bank. Looking at the chart, it appears difficult. Actually, most boats just go gently on in through the middle, backing off if necessary. Hundreds of boats do this without problem every year.

We also use a rough range which helps getting 6 feet draft into Dividing Creek. As you stand off Dividing Creek, still out on the Wye East River, look into Quarter Cove (84) on the opposite (southern) side of the creek. Inside this cove, on its south-western shore, you will see a boathouse (85) that is open at the bottom with a brown roof and brown sides. With that boathouse on your stern, head 007°M into Dividing Creek, heading to just off the point (86) that you will see jutting into the creek from its eastern side. Proceed carefully until you get into the cove on the eastern bank just before (to the south of) that point (86). Then begin turning to your left (west) into the deeper water beyond the 2-foot shoal coming out from the western bank. From here on, there is plenty of water as the chart indicates. Pick your favorite spot and enjoy.

Quarter Cove

If you find Dividing Creek to be too crowded, you may wish instead to go into Quarter Cove (84), on the opposite side of the river. This is not as pretty, but has more swinging room in the outer areas and usually more breezes. There are some houses along the shore, and the trees around the shore are not as thick as those in Dividing Creek, thus exposing more of the field and homes to view from the water. The woods are deeper near the head of the cove, with marsh along the water's edge. If you are going into the upper area, watch the chart and stay off the shoals indicated along the shore.

Grannary Creek

The next little creek upstream, also on the northern bank, is Grannary Creek (87). Like Dividing Creek, it has a shoal reaching out from each side of its entrance to snare the unwary. This creek isn't as pretty as some other creeks from the viewpoint of the gunkholing cruiser because of the houses, and other vestiges of civilization. But it is very protected, and would be a good storm anchorage for boats of 4 feet draft who can take advantage of the upper reaches, particularly if the other creeks nearby are crowded. Heading in, you will notice a greenish-gray, single-story modern house (88) on a grassy hill with a bulkhead before the house. This will be straight in front of you, in a northeasterly direction, as you go in. We headed in at 30°M, with the east end of that bulkhead on our bow until we were past the point to the east (89) which guards the entrance. We found 7 feet into the creek off this house, with gradual shoaling farther in. Passing the greenish-gray home, you will see additional homes to your left with field and some trees around the shore.

Yet another snug, and somewhat prettier anchorage, is the little T-shaped cove (90) on the opposite bank from Grannary Creek. I would not recommend it for boats of over 4 feet draft, but it is both pretty and snug. We entered by proceeding straight in the middle until we found a place to stop. Inside are very pretty woods and marsh. There is a dock on the eastern shore, and permanent mooring, but they didn't impair the beauty. A trailer was near the dock last year. This may be an omen of additional structures.

•

Proceeding on up the river, we next come to a small unnamed creek (91) on the northern bank with considerable shoal area noted around its mouth and a woodsy view inside. There are piles (92) on the eastern shore, where noted on the chart. Don't take in more than 3 feet draft, because the water is shallower than the chart shows. The chart is more accurate near the mouth of this creek, but this is wide open to the south. To get in past the shoals, we proceeded in the middle, carefully watching the depths, heading generally to the dock (93) noted on the chart, on the point to the north up in the creek. Behind this dock, a house stands up in the trees, hardly visible from the water. For most boats drawing 3 feet or less, the good anchorage would be behind the point with the dock and the house. This area is very beautiful and snug, with a feeling of deep forest and lush marsh around. However, any boat anchored here would be deceptively close to the home. You can still hardly see it from this anchorage behind the point, but it is there behind the trees and very close to the water. All concerned might feel some invasion of privacy if a boat was anchored in here.

Pickering Creek

As you pass above the creek, the high point (94) coming out from the northern bank points the way into Pickering Creek (95). The river bends around to the northeast here, with Pickering Creek meandering to the southeast. Cruising along without looking at the charts, you might become confused at this juncture, as to which is creek and which is river.

The creek has some very nice places to anchor, but it becomes more civilized and less pretty as you near its upper reaches. Therefore, most would want to choose an anchorage nearer the mouth. Navigation in this creek involves staying to the middle and staying off points and following the general

creek and river suggestions found in Chapter 1. Any time you go up the narrow forest creeks, there is a much larger likelihood of stumps and logs dragging along the bottom unseen. The anchorage inside the mouth (96) is very nice with woods around the high bluff across the river. Ironically, we privately named one of the prettiest anchorages "tire cove" (97) because it had a large dump of tires, sliding down the bank on its southern side. But the cove was so pretty, despite the tires, that we thought it to be a very special anchorage. However don't go in there with more than 3 feet draft. The predominant theme surrounding you here is deep woods and marsh, despite the tire intrusion.

Farther up the creek, on the southwestern side, there is another creek, the mouth of which makes another beautiful anchorage (98) with mostly woods and marsh.

•

After Pickering Creek, the next nice anchorage as you head upriver, still in a generally easterly direction, is just on the east side of the bluff (99) which pointed your way into Pickering. This anchorage may be too open for some people's standards, but it is very beautiful and gives a great feeling of privacy. The shore is mostly thick trees, with the high bluff to the west of the anchorage providing great protection from the west and northwest winds of cold fronts and thunderstorms. You can carry 9 to 10 feet depth very close to the shore here, and be well out of the channel.

If you like this neighborhood and the winds kicks up strong from the southwest to southeast, you might wish to try the cove just to the south (100) and across the river from the last spot. This is shallower, but OK for a boat of 7 feet draft. The piles (1) are as noted on the chart, apparently the remains of old docks. There is a feeling of privacy with few reminders of civilization.

•

The main channel of the river now takes you to a junction where you can continue up into the Wye East River (2), head around to Wye Narrows (3) and around the island, or up into Skipton Creek (4). You will notice your approach to this area by the wide waters and the large boathouse (5) noted on the chart on the southeast bank just before the junction.

Anchorage, Dividing Creek, Wye River

Skipton Creek

Skipton Creek (4) has a pretty anchorage (6) near its mouth, where we've indicated on the chart. There is a large estate on the southern bank, but it enhances the scenery. However, I found the water to be 6 feet, sometimes less, rather than the 7 feet reported on the chart. This cove is pretty, with some houses on the shore to your southeast. Don't go much farther up this creek except to explore by dinghy. It gets much narrower than the chart shows, and there are stumps, as would be expected. There are some houses as you go farther up the creek, but there is also a lot of forest, and surprisingly little field under cultivation. The creek becomes even shallower and prettier as you reach its head waters. If you have a fast enough dinghy, the anchorage cove here would be a great spot to stop for a few days, and explore first the upper reaches of this creek, and then the upper reaches of the Wye East. Too often, we tend to stay on our main boats when we anchor. Dinghy trips could add so much to your enjoyment and appreciation of the Bay and its tributaries.

Wye East River

The Wye East River (2), as just noted, would make another nice dinghy ride, but its width and relatively straight course can make it a bit rough if there is much wind blowing up or down the river. You can also anchor in the lower reaches (7), anywhere out in the middle where you feel comfortable with the depths, traffic, and surroundings. However, this area is busy with traffic because Wye Landing (8) is on the northeastern shore just north of the mouth, and just above (to the north of) this is Schnaitman's Boat Livery (9). The river quickly shallows above Wye Landing. You can anchor (7) in wide water, 6 to 7 feet deep just north of the landing. Few take their large boats farther upriver. However, you should take your dinghy farther up. Once you get past the wider reaches with their occasional homes and workboats, the rivers narrows and becomes almost wilderness in nature, with only an occasional field hardly noticeable back behind the trees. This area gives you a sense of deep and untouched forest and is well worth the trip. Beware of submerged logs and snags. Take your time and enjoy it.

Wye Landing (8) is a public landing with cement ramps, a dock, heads and a dumpster. **Schnaitman's (9)** is easily recognizable by the many small gray boats in front of the dock and small store ashore. They don't specialize in transient business, but have docks and many boats tied or moored out, ready to go if you wish to come in by car for a day's fishing or exploring by small boat. Most of his boats are around 16 feet long. He sells gas, fishing gear and bait, crab bait, soft drinks and snacks, block and cube ice, and both hard and soft crabs. Both Schnaitman's and the landing are around 4 miles from Wye Mills, a quaint old village with an ancient grinding mill.

WYE NARROWS
Refer to Chart #12270-G—"Wye River, Wye East River, Wye Narrows." Pg. 135

Heading in a northwesterly direction from the junction, you begin to realize your circumnavigation of Wye Island (81). The connecting body of water between the Wye River and the Wye East River is called Wye Narrows (3). Unfortunately, the bridge (11) connecting the island with the mainland and crossing these narrows near their middle does not open and has a vertical clearance of only 10 feet. Therefore, most who want to circumnavigate must do so by dinghy or power boat.

If you want to anchor closer to the bridge to further your exploration, there is a nice basin (13) from which you could launch dinghy trips around to the other side. I found slightly less than 7 feet in this basin. It is a wide and easy anchorage, but not as pretty as some of the others mentioned. As always, be sure to keep well lit at night.

Wye Island Natural Resources Management Area

Continuing on northwest to the bridge, you will find it to be of wooden pilings, and not very heavily traveled. It formerly served a much busier Wye Island, with enough farms and homes to warrant a small schoolhouse. However, the Stewards, who built the castle on Leeds Creek, tried to buy up this entire island, reportedly being insistent in their efforts to get the Eastern Shore natives to sell out. Now the island is principally utilized by the Wye Island Natural Resource Management Area, covering 2400 acres of the 2800-acre island. This area is owned by the Maryland Department of Natural Resources. There aren't provisions for boats to land here. Most people come in by road to walk the trails. Some of these trails cross virgin forest, and there is the 250-year old Wye Island Holly Tree. The endangered Delmarva Fox Squirrel has made a protected comeback here, and there are many other species. One of the many good points about this protected area from the viewpoint of the cruiser, is that it will help to preserve the area and its beautiful natural anchorages.

Bridge at Wye River Narrows, from mainland to Wye Island

De Coursey Cove

Passing through the bridge, you will notice that the shore on the mainland is low with much cultivation. The shore of the island is mostly woods and very pretty. There are three shallow creeks (14) on the island shore just to the west of the bridge. These go into deep woods and are great for dinghy exploration, but watch for submerged stumps and snags inside.

Just to the west of the westernmost creek, it will be important to avoid the long shoal (15) coming off the western point of De Coursey Cove (17). The chart notes a duck blind just before you reach the southernmost extrusion of this shoal, but never rely on the existence of duck blinds. Most are built to last only for a few seasons. It is best to favor the southern shore after you pass the last of these creeks.

De Coursey Cove (17) is not a favorite anchorage. It is tricky getting in, and it is built up with both old and newer structures. There is a large brick mansion (19) on the point, there are many docks coming out from the shore around the cove, and most cruisers would feel a lack of privacy here. West of the cove, on the northern bank, there was a white mooring buoy (20) last year. Don't let it confuse you.

As you approach the western end of Wye Narrows, you must decide whether to explore northward up the Wye River or head back down around Wye Island in a southerly course. I would certainly recommend an exploration trip up the Wye at some point. This river is much more built up than the Wye East, with a far greater sense of the intrusion of civilization; but there are still some very nice anchorages and great scenery.

There is a shallow spot (21) in the Wye River, just east of the end of Wye Narrows. Avoid this if you draw anything near its charted depth of 6 feet. It is not marked but it is easily avoided. Coming west out of the Narrows, just proceed along the south bank as though you were rounding to go south down the river, and proceed on out into the Wye until you are on the other (western) side. Then head northerly if you wish to head upriver, favoring the western side until you get past the mouth of the Narrows. The bottom shoals toward the 6-foot hump gradually enough to give you time to take evasive action if you are getting too close. We have drawn course lines for this junction to help you avoid this shoal.

WYE RIVER—SOUTHERN SECTION
Refer to Chart #12270-G—"Wye River, Wye East River, Wye Narrows." Pg. 135

As you head up into the Wye River (58), there are many houses and docks along the western shore, and you at once get the feeling that this is a civilized area. Indeed it is, but there are still some pretty coves and nice stretches to cruise. But as you first head in, the western shoreline has so many docks that it almost looks like a long marina! Note the long shoal (22) just to the northwest of Bordley Point (23) of Wye Island (81). The shoal is on the opposite side of the river, and is marked by a privately maintained green marker, G "1." Favoring Wye Island here keeps you in very deep water.

Very soon you will come upon a cove (24), just south of Drum Point (25), which at first glance looks as if it would make an anchorage. It is not really a good one, being open to the west, and with the cluttered shore of the other side in plain view. A very shallow draft boat of 1½ feet could tuck up into its very tip behind the little point for a very pretty anchorage.

Anchorage East of Drum Point

There is a much deeper anchorage in the cove just to the east (26) of Drum Point. This is broad and exposed to the northwest, but on most summer nights it would be very good because of the breezes. The shoreline in the cove is pretty, surrounding you with woods and marsh and some field, giving you a nice feeling of privacy and being "away from it all." The docks and houses on the opposite shore of the river are visible from here, but far enough away as to not intrude upon the anchorage.

Bigwood Cove

A very special treat awaits the shallow draft cruiser just upriver in Bigwood Cove (27). The southeast branch is one of the greatest little gunkholes anywhere around. It is only difficult getting in because it is so shallow. Don't try it with more than 2 feet of draft. Even with 2 feet, be prepared to bump some as you feel your way in, but it will be worth it. Enter the outer reaches of the cove by going down in the middle, avoiding the shoals coming out from both sides. The duck blind noted on the chart was in place last year although almost demolished from age and weather. I did not see the piles reported. The northeastern branch is not as pretty as the southeastern branch, but you may wish to poke your nose up into it for a look around before heading to the southeast. Heading into the southeastern branch, I found the shallowest water to be between the two points at the entrance to this branch, and I got through here by passing close to the point to my left (northeastern point), staying only around 25 feet off the shore. Once through this guardian shoal, the water deepened into around 5 feet and I was totally surrounded by deep woods wilderness, primitive and isolated with no vestiges of civilization. It is a place where you would go to stay for a few days, to allow your spirit to remember the way it used to be.

Grapevine Cove

Grapevine Cove (33), the next cove upstream and still on the eastern bank, is also pretty. It is not as nice as Bigwood, but deeper draft boats can enter. There is a pretty large osprey nest where indicated, west of Grapevine Point (34), but this may be gone when you get there. I did not see any of the submerged piling reported. As you will see on the chart, there is extensive shoaling at the mouth. I only found 4 feet controlling depth here instead of 8 feet charted. I found the best water (4 feet) by favoring the northern side (left side) going in. There is a beach on the northern point. After crossing the outer shoals, the water gets deeper. The cove winds on into Wye Island with deep woods, and marsh. You can barely see the houses on the western shore of the river, off in the distance. Go in carefully as far as your draft allows. The farther into the cove you get, the prettier you will find the scenery.

WYE RIVER—NORTHERN SECTION
Refer to Chart #12270-H—"Wye River, Northern Section." Pg. 140

Passing Grapevine Point (34), you will see to your right (east) Wye Narrows (3), described above. The Wye River (35) above here (north) is still crowded with homes and docks, but there are also some good anchorages. Normally, you might expect a river such as this is going to become wilder as it reaches its headwaters, but this river is going very close to the busy thoroughfare of Route 50 and the civilization associated with that.

After you pass Wye Narrows, if you look to your east, you will see a tower **(36)**, reminiscent of an ancient castle, up in the woods on the southern shore of the little un-named cove to your east. Closer inspection reveals it to be a private home, but it is quite intriguing if you spot it behind the trees while going by.

Quarter Creek

The next good anchorage, proceeding northerly up the river, is Quarter Creek **(37)** on the eastern shore. You have left Wye Island behind, and this creek has more farmland and homes on it, certainly no feeling of deep woods isolation. But it provides good shelter and is pretty. You can go well up into the countryside as your draft allows. Stay in the middle going in. We found the deeper water to be in the middle throughout. Don't go in with more than 6 feet draft.

Going north past Quarter Creek, you will find a relatively narrow passage with a wreck **(38)** marked on the western bank. This is in the shallower water. Be sure to stay in the deeper water in the midstream area between the two points here. Houses continue on both sides of the river, with their docks. Another good anchorage will be found in the small creek **(39)** on the eastern shore if your draft is no more than 3 feet. Up in the creek, once again, you are in woods and field. The houses on the opposite branch are difficult to see here, although there is a very large house **(40)** on the point at the southern entrance bank. A pretty beach **(41)** will be to the right (south) shortly after you enter the creek. The little creek opposite **(42)** this creek, (on the western shore) is very narrow and built up with many docks coming out from yards. It is not a good place to anchor.

Northern Part of Wye River

If you continue on up the river, you will not find many good anchorages unless you have a very shallow draft, 2 feet or less. It is possible to anchor out in the river, but there are still many homes on the shores, and the river could be busy. You will note that the chart notes "snags" **(43)** in places. I did not see these last year but most snags are not seen; they are fallen trees or limbs that have snagged in the bottom and wait to snag your boat. It is futile to plot them because by their very nature, they move about and drift along. Even if they are stuck solidly, they can break off easily or rot quickly. Any new storm can add more. These are a common occurrence in any river, as here. If you are going into the upper reaches, just remember that a snag could be down there. Watch the water for unusual eddies, and proceed slowly.

Before the split **(44)** there are many nice houses on the western bank, and mostly field on the eastern bank. The northeast fork **(45)** at the split makes a beautiful dinghy exploration creek, soon ending in marsh. The main branch **(46)** continues on amid field, woods, and still many homes, generally smaller than many of those downstream. Finally the banks become very marshy and you are in canoe country **(47)**.

MILES RIVER

Having cruised the Wye River, Now let's proceed up the Miles River, having already described its entrance near the beginning of this chapter.

Long Haul Creek

Refer to Chart 12270-I—"Miles River, St. Michaels, Leeds Creek, Hunting Creek, Long Haul Creek."

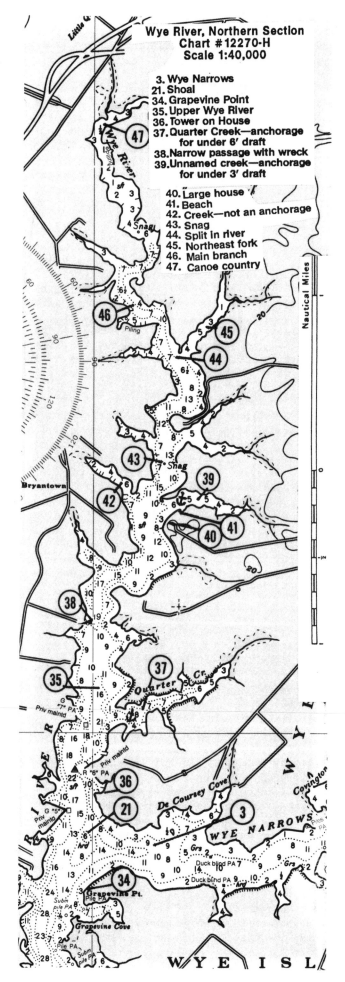

Wye River, Northern Section
Chart #12270-H
Scale 1:40,000

3. Wye Narrows
21. Shoal
34. Grapevine Point
35. Upper Wye River
36. Tower on House
37. Quarter Creek—anchorage for under 6' draft
38. Narrow passage with wreck
39. Unnamed creek—anchorage for under 3' draft
40. Large house
41. Beach
42. Creek—not an anchorage
43. Snag
44. Split in river
45. Northeast fork
46. Main branch
47. Canoe country

140

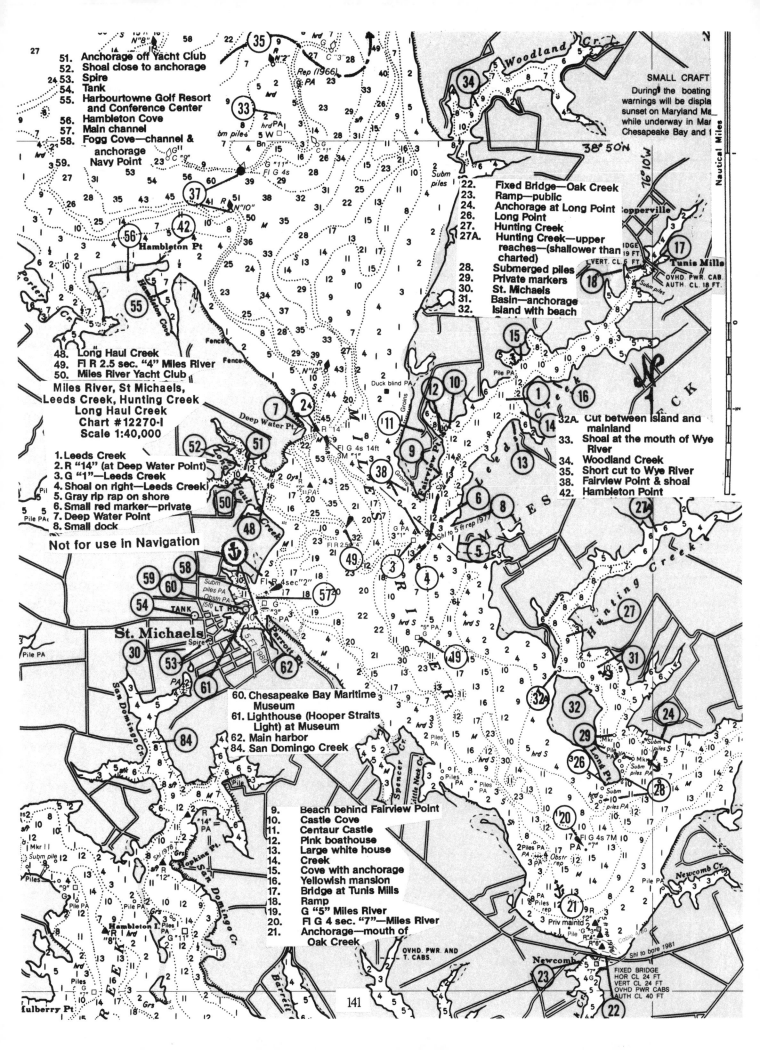

51. Anchorage off Yacht Club
52. Shoal close to anchorage
53. Spire
54. Tank
55. Harbourtowne Golf Resort and Conference Center
56. Hambleton Cove
57. Main channel
58. Fogg Cove—channel & anchorage
59. Navy Point

48. Long Haul Creek
49. Fl R 2.5 sec. "4" Miles River
50. Miles River Yacht Club

Miles River, St Michaels, Leeds Creek, Hunting Creek Long Haul Creek
Chart #12270-I
Scale 1:40,000

1. Leeds Creek
2. R "14" (at Deep Water Point)
3. G "1"—Leeds Creek
4. Shoal on right—Leeds Creek
5. Gray rip rap on shore
6. Small red marker—private
7. Deep Water Point
8. Small dock

Not for use in Navigation

60. Chesapeake Bay Maritime Museum
61. Lighthouse (Hooper Straits Light) at Museum
62. Main harbor
84. San Domingo Creek

9. Beach behind Fairview Point
10. Castle Cove
11. Centaur Castle
12. Pink boathouse
13. Large white house
14. Creek
15. Cove with anchorage
16. Yellowish mansion
17. Bridge at Tunis Mills
18. Ramp
19. G "5" Miles River
20. Fl G 4 sec. "7"—Miles River
21. Anchorage—mouth of Oak Creek

22. Fixed Bridge—Oak Creek
23. Ramp—public
24. Anchorage at Long Point
26. Long Point
27. Hunting Creek
27A. Hunting Creek—upper reaches—(shallower than charted)
28. Submerged piles
29. Private markers
30. St. Michaels
31. Basin—anchorage
32. Island with beach

32A. Cut between Island and mainland
33. Shoal at the mouth of Wye River
34. Woodland Creek
35. Short cut to Wye River
38. Fairview Point & shoal
42. Hambleton Point

SMALL CRAFT

During the boating warnings will be displa sunset on Maryland Ma while underway in Ma Chesapeake Bay and t

This nice creek is heavily populated, and is the home of the **Miles River Yacht Club**. Deep water goes into protected anchorages, but with many houses and docks ashore. Not all cruisers are allowed to use the yacht club, and the anchorage is limited because of other uses of the creek.

As the chart shows, head straight into Long Haul Creek (48) from Fl R "4" (49) out in the Miles River. The Miles River Yacht Club (50) will be conspicuous to your left (south) from well out in the river. Many boats anchor (51) off the club before the split in the creek. The shoal (52) coming southeasterly off the point at that split rises sharply from the bottom, is very shallow, and protrudes well into this anchorage as the chart indicates. It is also possible to anchor up either branch if you want to be among houses and docks. Both branches are much more protected.

The Miles River Yacht Club has 43 slips which can be used for transient purposes for members of the AYC or the CBYCA for boats up to 50 feet with twin 30 amp service available. There is a restaurant and sometimes live weekend entertainment. This has long been recognized as one of the finer clubs on the Bay. It is well known for its racing and bay boating heritage, included the famous and well attended log canoe racing events and the Maryland Governor's Cup races, usually around the last weekend in May. Call ahead for reservations. If you can't get into the dock, it is always a treat to anchor out to watch these exciting races.

ST. MICHAELS

The harbor and village of St. Michaels are steeped with history and preserved Chesapeake Bay watertown tradition. The area is a very busy tourist mecca for boaters and land travelers, with all of the related businesses that you might expect. Therefore, with some notable individual exceptions, while this is a "must" on any cruise, the area is not an area of major provisioning or major refitting projects. The harbor is usually very crowded, and prices often reflect the abundance of tourist business. The Chesapeake Bay Maritime Museum is located here. It is without doubt one of the finest institutions of its type on the Bay, and anyone cruising the Bay should visit this museum very early in the trip, spend a few days there, and reap the wealth of knowledge, Bay culture, and history that it offers.

The entrance to St. Michaels (30) is clearly marked, and easy to follow. Many people, on the first trip up the river, at first confuse the Miles River Yacht Club (50) up in Long Haul Creek (48) with the docks of St. Michaels. Looking in a westerly direction from far out in the Miles River as you are heading up that river, the two creeks can be a little confusing on the first visit. As long as you know that St. Michaels is to the left (south of) of the creek with the yacht club and that it has more buildings and boats, you will have no problem.

Heading toward the entrance, a tall church steeple (53) will pierce the sky over the town, slightly to your left. This is Christ Episcopal Church, originally founded in 1672. The impressive stone church is one of the many sights awaiting you and is a good landmark as you head in. There is also a water tank (54) ahead. Getting closer, you will notice small private buoys marking the main channel (57), in addition to the normal buoys maintained by the Coast Guard.

Heading off to the right (northwest) is a secondary channel into Fogg Cove (58), also marked by the small red and green floats, leading up into the anchorage and docks on the other

side of Navy Point (59) with the Chesapeake Bay Maritime Museum (60). The museum will be obvious with its collection of skipjacks, buy boats, other boats and buildings. A large white lighthouse (61) with green roof prominently sits on Navy Point. This was the Hooper Strait Lighthouse and is a museum exhibit, moved ashore. It is one of the early "screw pile" types. You are allowed to go inside to see what life aboard these structures was like and climb to the top. The main harbor (62) will be to the left (south) of the museum.

Anchorages and Marinas

Refer to our Sketch—"Map of St. Michaels Town and Harbor"

Both Fogg Cove and the main harbor have been recently dredged. Both make good anchorages (58) and (79), although they are open to the Miles River and can be very crowded, particularly on weekends. The grounds of the very exclusive Inn at Perry Cabin (96) can be seen up in Fogg Cove from the museum. As the chart shows (12270-I), the bottom in both anchorages allows a 6-foot draft boat to anchor fairly close to the shores, and deeper draft boats to anchor nearer the middle. I have noticed that the bottom is irregular in places. One irregular bottom area (63) is off the **Town Dock Marina (64)** (northwest of the docks) where there is slightly less than 6 feet coming out into the main harbor. This does not obstruct dockage at the marina. Another irregular bottom area is off (south of) the large T (65) dock of the museum in the inner harbor. The main harbor begins to shoal around a line between the outer docks of Higgins (67) and the Town Dock Restau-

IDENTS FOR MAP ON PG. 143

Sketch Map of St. Michaels— Town & Harbor		
9.	Justine's Ice Cream Parlor	
10.	Chesapeake Bay Outfitters— Crockett Brothers Ship's Store	
11.	Broken Rudder Sportswear	
12.	High's Ice Cream Store	
13.	Port of Call	
14.	208 Talbot	
15.	Big Al's	
16.	Evinrude Repairs	
17.	The Bakery	
18.	Acme Market	
19.	Carpenter Street Saloon	
20.	Hope's Hardware	
21.	Thrift drugs (Hudson's Pharmacy)	
22.	Christ Episcopal Church (1878)	
23.	St. Michaels Hardware	
24.	Post office	
25.	Maryland National Bank (MOST Machine)	
26.	St. Luke's Methodist Church (1871)	
27.	Library	
28.	Bay River Gourmet and Espresso Bar	
29.	St. Michaels Video and Photo Center	
30.	The Village Shoppe (package grocery and deli)	
31.	Evans Foundry	
32.	Family Practice Medical Center	
33.	Dentist	
34.	St. Mary's Square (museum)	
35.	Hell's Crossing	
36.	Laundromat	
58.	Fogg Cove —channel & anchorage	

60.	Chesapeake Bay Maritime Museum with dockage for members
61.	Hooper Strait Lighthouse display
63.	Shoal off Town Dock Marina
64.	St. Michaels Town Dock Marina
65.	Shoal southeast of T-Dock of Museum
67.	Higgins Yacht Yard
68.	Town Dock Restaurant
69.	Crab Claw Restaurant
70.	St. Michaels Harbor Inn & Marina
71.	Lighthouse Restaurant
72.	*Jayhawk* Charter
75.	St. Michaels Crab House and Bar
76.	Public ramps
77.	Town Docks
78.	Trovato Dock & *Footloose* Charter
79.	Anchorage—in front of Crab Claw
80.	Anchorage
81.	Parrott Point
82.	Anchorage outside of harbor
83.	Anchorage outside of harbor
84.	San Domingo Creek— dinghy landing at foot of Chew St.
85.	"Cannonball House"—1805
86.	*Patriot*
96.	Inn at Perry Cabin
97.	*Odyssey*
98.	Public dinghy dock
99.	Dinghy dock for museum members
100.	Muskrat Park

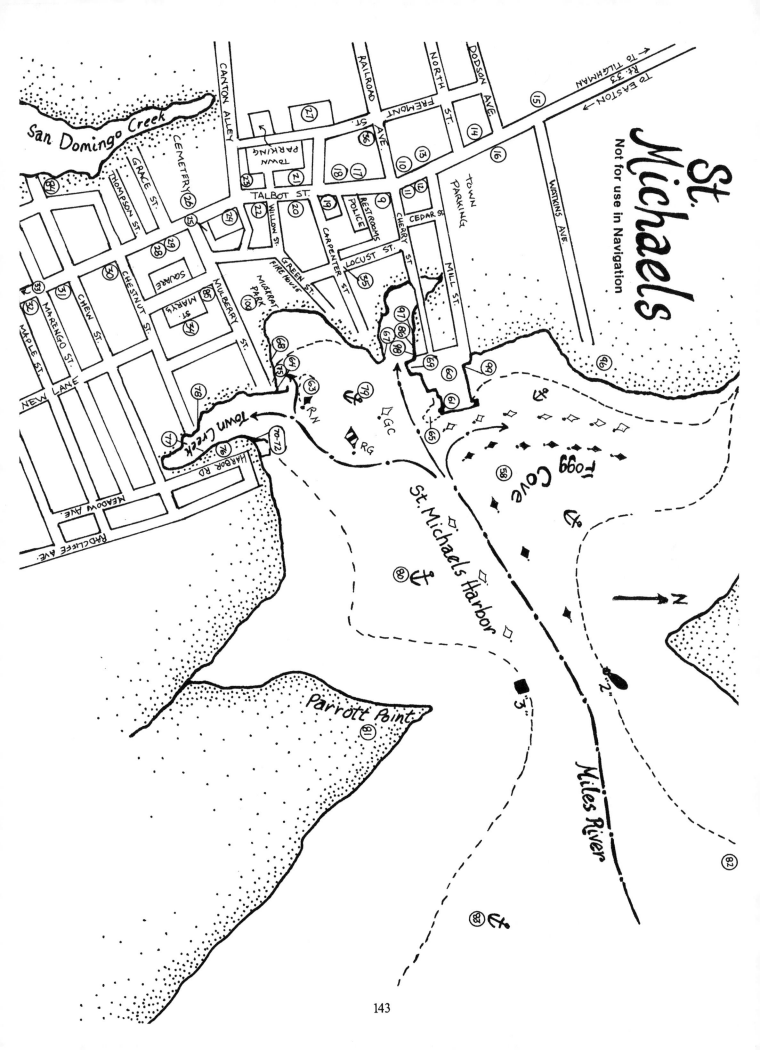

rant (68). There are three marinas in the harbor, in addition to the museum docks.

Coming into the harbor, the museum (60) with its working display boats will be to the right. There are bulkheads and piers on both sides of the point for members to dock. Often there will be tall sailing ships or other special boats tied alongside. Beside (immediately to the east of) the museum is very famous Crab Claw Restaurant (69). Crab boats come alongside and unload crabs, clams, and other catch onto the dock, where they can be steamed or cooked. You can sit on this dock amidst all of the activity to eat them, as fresh as they can be. An upstairs section is available with the same menu but less activity. The docks around the Crab Claw are for the customers. They do not normally stand by on the radio, but if you plan to eat there (and you should), if space is available, tie up in front or on the side of the building, not along the land bulkhead. Check to be sure that the place where you tie up is OK, since they sometimes expect certain work boats to come in to off-load.

Straight ahead to the southwest is **Higgins Yacht Yard (67)**, identifiable by its sign. This facility takes transients up to 60 feet lengths with drafts available up to 7 feet in some of its slips. Electricity ranging up to 30 amps is available, as are bathrooms and showers. There are 40 open slips and also some covered. With the 30-ton lift, they are a full service yard, specializing in fine wood work. Block and cube ice is available. Visa and MC are honored.

Directly to left (southeast) across from the museum and Crab Claw is the **St. Michaels Harbor Inn and Marina (70)** with its red-roofed gray buildings reaching in an "L" around and into the creek. The 60 slips can accomodate boats well over 100 feet, with 8-foot depth, and electricity up to 50 amps. There is a marine store which carries items from tackle and bait to clothing, as well as beverages, light snacks and block and cube ice. Daysailers, canoes, and paddle boats are available for rent, as well as bikes. There is a pool. The pumpout station is readily accessible. This is a full service Inn with the very nice Lighthouse Restaurant (71). The facility can provide full vacation services, with rooms containing refrigerators and wet bars, and complimentary transportation to Easton Airport. It could be a long walk to town, but there are water taxis which stand by on VHF 71 and 68 and can often be hailed. These taxis also serve anchored boats. St. Michaels Harbor Inn and Marina honors Visa, Amex, Diners, and MC. The *Jayhawk* (72), a 36-foot center cockpit sloop, charters from this marina. Their number is (410) 745-3599.

The dock manager of the Harbor Inn and Marina is Shelley Abbott, who not only is well known for her excellent assistance at the marina, but who is also a very popular singer. She specializes in familiar country and other hit songs as well as a repertoire of her own creations, usually quite humorous, about boating and Bay activities in the area. Shelley is an excellent entertainer, and if you are in the area, you should find out where she is playing, and go to see her. We have noticed that her audiences range from the elderly to the very young, all enjoying her talented singing and guitar playing, and sense of humor. Sometimes she performs in Muskrat Park (100) at the head (southwest end) of the harbor, and you can go in by dinghy or walk from your slip to hear her.

Town Creek

Town Creek opens next to the left (southeast), separating the Harbor Inn from the **St. Michaels Town Dock Marina (64)**.

This is the only facility in the harbor selling fuel, with both gas and diesel at competitive prices, and a pumpout. It can accomodate boats of over 100 feet. Some of the slips have shallower depths, but the courteous attendants will see that you get the depth you need. Electricity is available up to 50 amps. There is a marine store that sells clothing, chart books, memorabilia, block and cube ice, beverages and offers bike rentals. A swimming pool and two restaurants, the St. Michaels Crab House and Bar (75) and the Town Dock Restaurant (68), are on the premises. Signs identify the facilities, with the sign for the Crab House and Bar right behind the dockmaster's office and store. Town Dock Marina accepts Visa and MC.

Heading up the creek, your left (the east side), you will find two public ramps (76) just up from the Harbor Inn and Marina, and Town Docks (77) rented mostly to local watermen, and some private docks.

On the right (west side), about half way down the creek, a beautiful stand of pine trees in a yard behind a tall white house identifies a very nice docking facility (78). This looks like a small park, with its natural setting so different from the hubbub of the rest of the harbor. The house is actually the private home of Vince Trovato and his family, who own the docks. He also charters the *Footloose*, a 44-foot CSY, locally in season and in the Bahamas in the winter. The phone is (410) 745-3717. The quiet privacy of the yard and the cool whispering of pines provides a nice place to rest, but is close to the activity of the harbor, and within easy walking of the business section of town. Short term dockage is available, but not transient or overnight at this time because of pending zoning issues.

Other docks in this creek are private, and usually run from the yards of the private homes. We found 7 feet depth up to the pine trees on the right going in, but there is not much point in bringing your big boat up here unless you visit someone who lives here. Homes along this creek, as well as those surrounding the harbor, are private and their residents would resent strangers walking across their yards, tying up uninvited to their docks, and walking their pets on their yards.

Within the main harbor, many seem to think that the only anchorage is in front of the Crab Claw (79). Actually, you can also anchor off the mouth of the little creek (80) southwest of Parrot Point (81), where we found up to 10 feet well out of the channel. In addition, it is often nice to anchor outside in the river to either side of the entrance channel (82) and (83). Be sure that you are outside of the approach and remain well lit at night. This area (82) and (83) can become a bit rough on a brisk north, to east, to south breeze. However, we prefer it because the anchorages inside can be very crowded, particularly on any weekend or holiday, boats are often left unattended as the crew enjoys pleasures ashore. With the careless anchoring habits of only a few people, it doesn't take much wind to make a mess of the anchorage. The holding is reasonably good, but due care is required to set anchors.

If you don't want the hustle and bustle of this harbor but still wish to visit the town, San Domingo Creek, which you can enter from Broad Creek off the Choptank River, provides a nice quiet anchorage. The dinghy landing (84) for this is at the foot of Chew Street. The walk from this landing to the Museum on the other waterfront is around a mile. On this walk, you pass through much of the small downtown area and its shops, restaurants, and other points of interest.

History of St. Michaels

St. Michaels traces its history back to the early 1600s when

Chesapeake Bay Maritime Museum, St. Michaels

Crab Claw Restaurant, St. Michaels

records show that Captain William Claiborn, who settled Kent Island in 1631, traded here. It is named after St. Michael, the Archangel because of the Episcopal parish established there in 1677. The Miles River was originally called by the same name, but it is said that years of Eastern Shore pronunciation and perhaps a little Quaker influence eroded the name to "Miles."

Practically surrounded by water, and in an area of dense forests, the town quickly became a major shipbuilding center. As such, it was very important during the Revolutionary War and the War of 1812. Naturally, the British targeted the town during the War of 1812. The town now calls itself, "The town that fooled the British" because on the foggy night of the attack, the people hung lanterns high in the surrounding trees and blacked out the town. This tricked the British ships into firing into the trees, with only one cannon ball striking a home. It pierced the roof, rolled across the attic and down the stairs, past the lady then at home as she carried her baby in her arms. That house stands today and is known as "The Cannonball House" (85). St. Michaels claims that this was the first time in recorded history that a blackout was used as a military tactic.

After this war, the fortunes of the town gradually declined as Baltimore became the major shipping center for the area. St. Michaels did continue to build boats and harvest the bay's seafoods. The Crab Claw restaurant began as a seafood landing and processing house. Over the years, it began to feed tourists, and today it stands as a unique mixture of both. St. Michaels has attracted many tourists and retirees, so that it is now once again busy.

Chesapeake Bay Maritime Museum
Refer to our "Sketch Map of Chesapeake Bay Maritime Museum."

I suggest that you do two things as soon as you get your boat settled in St. Michaels. Join the Chesapeake Bay Maritime Museum (60), and take a ride on the tour boat *Patriot* (86) which docks next to the Crab Claw. The *Patriot* is not a part of the museum. Having reached a destination via their own boat, most people see little reason for hopping on a tour boat. However, a trip aboard the *Patriot* will make your stay in the area much more enjoyable. Captain Dave Etzel, of many years experience on these waters, will take you up the Miles River and give a fascinating background explanation of ecology of the area, interesting and historical points ashore, natural points of interest, and things to see and do in town. He keeps his wheel house door open and is delighted to answer individual questions, including those of cruisers who are interested in learning about and seeing additional creeks and nice anchorages. Bring along your chart or this book, and he will point out the places where you may wish to go. You do all of this from the safety of his boat, in air conditioned comfort below decks, or from the bird's eye perspective on the top deck, with a bar and snacks available. It is really nice to let someone else do the driving while you are enjoying the water and getting information to improve your visit and cruise.

The museum was founded in 1965 and covers 18 acres of land. It has 28 full time staff members and around 200 knowledgeable volunteers. It is a private, non-profit educational institution and receives no operating funds from state, local, or federal government. Exhibits are located in eight buildings and about the grounds and along the docks. They trace the Bay's geological, social, economic, and maritime history and development. There is also a 4,000 volume library open to members and researchers, by appointment. A museum store has relevant books, paintings, and prints, models, memorabilia, some clothing, collectibles, and many other articles.

One of the nicest things about this museum is that it is not just a collection of stale artifacts. It is a living museum, functioning daily before your eyes to restore and maintain Chesapeake Bay heritage and culture, with boat bulding and repair work, cruises, and hands-on displays. There is even a marine railway (87) on the premises, near the lighthouse, where they regularly haul vintage boats for restoration and repair. In one huge shed there is constant boat building or repair underway on traditional Bay vessels (88). Visitors can watch all of this from high above on a balcony that allows you to see in detail the fine craftsmanship of skilled people as they work.

The Hooper Strait Lighthouse (61) provides a fascinating look into the daily lives and workings of the old lighthouses. It is furnished and equipped as it was in its former days, from the beautiful fresnel lenses to the weighted clockwork machinery that rang the fog bell. The spiral stairwell leads to the top where a great view of the museum and harbor awaits.

Other displays include a "Bay of Chesapeake Building" (4) dedicated to different boats and the history of the Bay, with some beautiful models. There is the Point Lookout Bell Tower (90) standing near the lighthouse, which stood with its 1000-pound fog bell 100 years ago near the mouth of the Potomac River. A small boat shed (89) has a great collection of boats including an Indian dugout canoe, versions of log canoes used later after the European settlement, sailing vessels, and other boats. There is also a building dedicated to waterfowl (92) with a fascinating display of the duck and goose hunting era. This display includes many beautiful decoys and models, and the large guns which used to kill hundreds of fowl at a time. They include the punt gun and the eight-barrel battery gun, both of which are featured in Michener's "Chesapeake." Nearby, in a building called "The Corn Crib" (91), are some of the early boats used for hunting, including the sinkbox and bushwacker both described in some detail in Chapter 2 on Havre de Grace. A new display building (93) will feature the history of propulsion on the Bay with more than 50 steam and gas engines planned.

There are always floating exhibits (94), including a working skipjack and bugeye, a buy boat, one of the last boats built by local boat builder Jim Richardson (described in Chapter 11 on Cambridge), an ancient tug boat, and often visiting tall ships or special sailing vessels. These are at the docks, and sometimes go out on special tours or educational programs.

The museum is always hosting and sponsoring special events. From April through September, there are sometimes Saturday evening concerts by Bay musicians who stroll the grounds. Around mid-May, there is a spring fest which celebrates the arrival of spring through music, boating events, food and entertainment. In later May, there is a Blue Grass Festival. During the last week of June, an antique and classic boat show brings many entries. The Fourth of July brings Big Band night at the Tolchester Beach Bandstand (95) on the premises. Crab Day is held in early August with live music, boat rides, and lots of crabs to eat. In early October, there is the Mid-Atlantic Small Craft Festival with shows and judging. Early November brings Oyster Day. Oystering is a cold weather event. Come to this for oysters prepared many different ways. Learn to shuck and learn something of the oyster industry. One of the regular features held throughout the season are

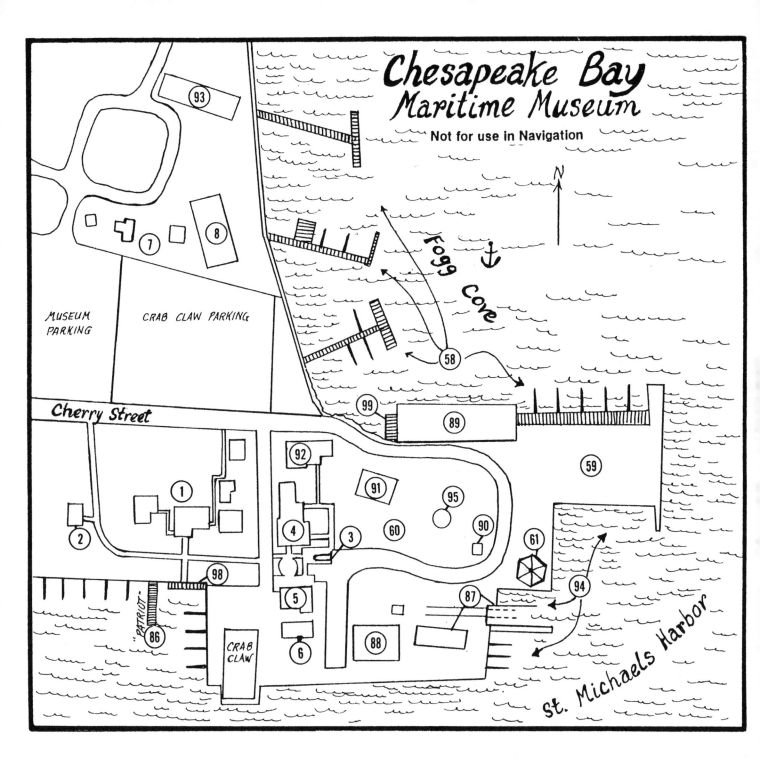

Chesapeake Bay Maritime Museum

Not for use in Navigation

Fogg Cove

St. Michaels Harbor

Cherry Street

MUSEUM PARKING

CRAB CLAW PARKING

CRAB CLAW

"PATRIOT"

Sketch
Chesapeake Bay Maritime
Museum

1. Administration buildings
2. Aquarium
3. Ticket booth
4. Bay of Chesapeake building
5. Museum store
6. Restrooms
7. Historic houses
8. Skipjack building
58. Museum docks
59. Navy Point

60. Chesapeake Bay Maritime Museum
61. Hooper Strait Lighthouse
86. *Patriot*
87. Railway and repair facilities
88. Boat shop
89. Small boat shed
90. Point Lookout Bell Tower
91. Corn Crib
92. Waterfowl building
93. Propulsion building
94. Floating exhibits
95. Tolchester Beach Bandstand
98. Public dinghy dock
99. Dinghy dock for museum members

the famous log canoe races on the Miles River. In mid-September, there is the grand event called "The Bartlett Cup Races" with prestigious trophies and great excitement as the crews hike out high on the boards to balance these precarious craft. In late September are traditional boat races. The events and dates change some, but these are representative of what to expect and when.

Membership in the museum not only helps to preserve the heritage of the Bay, it brings you many special privileges and is a great deal. There are three types of yearly memberships. An individual can join for $25, a family for $35, and a boating membership only costs $50. With a membership you are entitled to unlimited free admission, discounts in the museum store, a magazine, and other privileges depending upon the type of membership. A boating membership entitles you to dockage on a first come first served basis. The docks (58) are nice and right in the middle of the museum and harbor. There is no electricity, but water is available. The dockage fee is considerably less expensive than any of the marinas. There is a daily admission fee for those who do not wish an annual membership, but it makes much more sense to join. The phone number for the museum is (410) 745-2916.

St. Michaels Ashore
Refer to our sketch—"Map of St. Michaels Town & Harbor." Pg. 143

Docked close to the museum, just up from the *Patriot*, the *Odyssey* (97) awaits to take you on nature cruises of the area. She is a custom-built vessel, with air conditioned cabin which has an aquarium. She is equipped to land shore parties and has a swim platform. *Odyssey's* owners, Robert and Alice Jane Lippson, are marine biologists and will take you on an informative tour of the area. They also do custom tours, including overnight trips. Their phone is (410) 745-3255 or 800 344-3255.

A nice feature of St. Michaels is that there is so much within a few blocks walking distance from the harbor. We will not even try to mention everything here, but hopefully this description will give a good overview of what is available. The map has further detail. If you anchor, there is a dinghy dock (98) adjacent west of the Crab Claw. Another dinghy dock (99) within the museum is for members only. Muskrat Park (100) (also known as "Church Cove Park") is at the southwest end of the anchorage (79) and usually there is a free concert on Thursday evenings. You can stroll up and sit on the grass, go up to the shore in your dinghy, or listen from the anchorage.

If you land at the dinghy dock, you will be heading southwesterly up Cherry Street from the Museum, walking past quaint private homes. One constantly recurring problem in this town is that there is such a blend of the historical and present, that often visitors go into private yards by mistake, sometimes even entering the homes. That is why you may notice privacy signs.

Most town explorations start at the corner of Talbot and Cherry Streets because of its location relative to the dinghy dock and Museum. This corner is only a little over a block from the dinghy dock. When you get to this corner, the main section of town is just to your left (south), but first let's take a brief look along the road going in the opposite direction (northwesterly) away from town.

If you turn to your right (northwest), you will immediately find on the northern side of the street (your right as you are walking away from the corner) two light fare restaurants and a High's Ice Cream store (12), which also sells light groceries, deli, and has a copy and fax services. On the same side of the street and a little more than a block down, there is an Evinrude repair shop (16). On the opposite side of Talbot Street, still walking in a northwesterly direction, you will first find Chesapeake Bay Outfitters (10) on the western side of the corner. This store carries a very nice selection of sporting apparel and related items. Continuing on in a northwesterly direc-

Log Canoe Race, St. Michaels

148

Vince's Dock, St. Michaels. Author's *Chez Nous* at right

tion, around two blocks down on the left (western) side of the street, you will see Talbot 208 **(14)**, a more formal restaurant. About a block farther out and on the same side is Big Al's **(15)**, a market carrying fresh seafood, take-out snacks and salads, groceries, package goods, fishing gear, and more. There are other shops and restaurants on this walk, on both sides of the street, all within a few blocks.

A left turn at the corner of Talbot and Cherry first brings you to Justine's Ice Cream Parlor **(9)** on the eastern side of this corner. From here on, walking south, there are many shops, restaurants, and services within a few blocks. These include but are not limited to clothing, antiques, collectibles, candy, hardware, some restaurants, historical places, the post office **(24)**, the town hall, two other grocery stores **(18)** and **(30)** and a welding shop. This is Evans' Foundry **(31)**, a third generation business. They made the iron street signs that you have been reading. Farther on there's a video rental **(29)** with no membership fee which will rent to transient boats, drugstores **(21)**, gourmet shops, package shops, banks **(25)**, a dentist **(33)** and doctor **(32)**, all within several blocks walk.

The Carpenter Street Saloon **(19)** is on the eastern corner of Talbot and Carpenter Street. This was built as a tavern in 1874. It is a real saloon, and one of the best places in town to get information and find out what is going on. There is a family restaurant in the same premises which is very popular locally, and a sports bar upstairs. On weekends, there is usually entertainment.

You will also see on this walk the Christ Episcopal Church **(22)**, the steeple of which rose before you as you entered the harbor. This church was built from stone from the Port Deposit Quarries. The public library **(27)** is on Fremont Street, a block farther away from the waterfront.

A left turn (to the northeast) at Carpenter Street will bring you to "Hell's Crossing" **(35)** at the corner of Locust and Carpenter. It was so named because of the brawls among seamen of old (we don't do that nowadays!) returning to their ships after an evening on the town. For a quieter interlude from the busy main streets, you may wish to visit St. Mary's Square **(34)**, a park deeded for the use of the public forever. It has a museum open on Saturday and Sunday from May through October. Reach this by turning to your left (northeast) at either Mulberry or Chestnut Streets.

This walk takes only a few minutes if you don't stop. You will stop many times. Farther southeast on Talbot are some shopping centers, more grocery stores, and other businesses including Price's Yacht Canvas, Castel Brothers Propeller Shop, and Daffin Marine (engine and general mobile repair work with Mobil service). These are not within walking distance, but are mentioned because you may need these services. A call would arrange whatever you need. Throughout the entire area are many bed and breakfasts. They are far too numerous to mention, and more seem to be coming. For more information, call the Talbot County Chamber of Commerce at (410) 822-4606.

LEEDS CREEK
Refer to Chart #12270-I—"Miles River, St. Michaels, Leeds Creek, Hunting Creek, Long Haul Creek." Pg·141

Leeds Creek is a great place for getting away from the hubbub of St. Michaels. It has a nice beach with many places to anchor in rural settings. However it is very tricky to enter, and the shoal is growing worse according to reports.

Leeds Creek **(1)** is directly across (northeast) from St. Michaels **(30)** and at first glance on the chart looks inviting. A glance into the mouth of the creek often shows a large sailboat tied inside, leading you to believe that access must be easy. A closer look at the chart indicates a narrow entry with shoals on both sides, even worse than the chart shows. The shoal out from Fairview Point **(38)** is moving. According to local people, this shoaling is increasing at other creek entrances in the area. They point out some, such as Woodland Creek **(34)** farther north, that are virtually impassible now to anything but very small boats. These had deep entrances only 20 years ago. Hopefully this will not happen to Leeds Creek. Go in at half tide and rising. It can be done by most boats if they are careful.

First, coming in the river, note R "14" **(2)** off (east-southeast of) Deep Water Point. Though faraway northwest, this is useful, believe it or not, in getting into Leeds Creek. Start in at around 100 feet off (to the south of) G "1" **(3)**. The trick is to round the shoal **(38)** to your left without running into the

149

shoal to the right (4). Once inside Fairview Point, the water is both deep and wide. Before heading in, look in and note some gray rip rap (5) in front of houses on the point to your right on the southeastern shore of the creek. Move your gaze to the left of this rip rap. Just inside (to the left) of it, there is a small beach, which will be partially obscured at high water, and then some marsh with a dock coming off that marsh. Don't confuse this with the larger dock farther up the creek which may have a large sailboat alongside.

You will also see a red nun (6), not on the chart and apparently privately maintained. I did not find this to be helpful or relevant going in, and disregarded it. I found the depths left (west and northwest) of this nun to be less than 5 feet.

Look also down river toward Deep Water Point (7). R "14" will be very conspicuous off that point. This will be useful later for a bearing. Head in from well off G "1" toward the small dock (8). Go carefully.

When you reach the point where your course intersects a line drawn through R "14" to the point of land to your right (south-southeast), you should begin your slow rounding toward your left (northeast) to eventually head toward the beach (9) inside of Fairview Point. If you have trouble with this imaginary line, a bearing of 327°M on R "14" (2) indicates approximately the same line and the point where you start your turn. A third way of determining the area where you begin rounding, is to note when R "14" closes with the trees on the bluff immediately behind it. This also should roughly indicate that you are where you should begin rounding. Then head on up toward the beach which protrudes inside (north of) Fairview Point. As noted earlier, when you are inside Fairview Point, the deep water is much wider. We've drawn a course line for this entry on **Chart # 12270-I**. I found 8 feet minimum on this route. However, the next storm could change this.

Once in, check out the beach behind Fairview Point (9). There is 10 feet very close in, and 5 feet almost up to the beach. There are woods behind, and the area is very pretty for a swim or anchorage.

A very interesting and nice anchorage awaits in the little cove (10) to the left (northwest shore) just upstream from the beach. This is more protected and deep, as the chart shows. It is called locally "Castle Cove" for good reason. Nestled within the trees, with only an intriguing part showing, is Centaur Castle (11). This is a very large castle, painted pink, built this century by Mr. Glen L. Steward and his wife Jacqueline. As you'd expect, there is much talk and fantasy among local folks as to the structure. It is said that Mr. Steward built the castle to be his home in the 1930s after having some obsession with his perceived need for personal security. I understand that it is replete with secret passages, watch towers, and all other things that go with castles. Mr. Steward reportedly slept up in one of the towers, with a gate lowered each night. The perimeters of the estate were closely guarded with fences and dogs. There is a white landing in the cove a little over halfway up and to the left (southwestern side of the cove), as well as one on the opposite side of the peninsula on the Miles River. The castle and surrounding grounds are private and no one should land. If you go up into the cove, past the pink boathouse (12), to the area off the white landing, part of the castle will be visible up in the trees. There is an aerial view of the grounds in the archives in the Chesapeake Bay Maritime Museum's library. I recommend reading the full account of the castle, as well as of the surrounding territory, in the excellent book, "Wye Island," by Boyd Gibbons, published by the Johns Hopkins University Press of Baltimore, copyright 1977.

Proceeding up Leeds Creek past "Castle Cove," you will notice a large white house (13) on the shore to the right (southeastern side) with a creek just upstream (14). Next upstream, there is a two-pronged cove (15) to your left (north shore) which makes another nice anchorage. This is difficult to recognize from the chart. There is a huge yellowish mansion (16) with four white columns on the bank to the right upstream. You won't see it until you round the hump of land on the southeastern bank which faces these two prongs. In the first prong which I prefer, 8 feet carries far enough to tuck up inside. Woods surround you with field behind and a house fairly visible back in the trees.

Continuing on upstream, you soon approach the fixed bridge (17) (vertical clearance 6 feet). Leeds Creek becomes more built up with docks protruding, is much shallower, and not as pretty as an anchorage. The bridge is wooden with a fishing dock built alongside. At the foot of the bridge on your left side (northwest shore) is a ramp (18). The village around the bridge area is called "Tunis Mills" after the Tunis Family who operated the saw mills in the area. Upstream from the bridge, the creek has fewer homes, and grows prettier again. However, this is for very shallow boats. Depths go from 4 feet down to 2 feet, and boats have to clear the bridge.

LONG POINT AND HUNTING CREEK

Heading upriver from Leeds Creek, the Miles River appears to throw a tricky curve between G "5" (19) and Fl G "7" (20). We followed a straight line course just off the markers and found no less than 10 feet. Some boats anchor in the bight (21) before the fixed bridge (22) to the right (south) which crosses the entrance to Oak Creek. This area is pretty wide open, and the bridge noises can be bothersome at night. Also, the shoreline is crowded with homes and other buildings. There is a public concrete ramp (23) just on the south-ern side of the bridge, to your right (west). The channel is marked as is indicated. Vertical clearance for this fixed bridge is 24 feet and there is an overhead power cable with authorized clearance of 40 feet.

We prefer the anchorage (24) just around Long Point (26) and up into the mouth of Hunting Creek (27). This is still a bit open, but not as open as the other anchorage off the bridge, and it is nicer. The piles (28) indicated along the shoreline (northeastern side of the island) are for an old steamboat dock. Some are visible, but should be no bother unless you are too close in. The private markers (29) (green and red) are as indicated, and there should be no problem going in, respecting those markers.

While many anchor in the mouth of the creek southeast of those markers, you can anchor anywhere inside to suit your fancy. The basin (31) east-southeast of the cut (32A) between the island and the mainland is nice, with a beach (32) on the island that is very pretty and deep up close. Inside the beach, a quiet forest awaits. The forest floor is clear and nearly weedless. Deer roam here and often come down to the water. The cut (32A) is wider than the chart indicates, and shallower than the 3 feet shown. The better water is toward the island side, but there are stumps. This island is privately owned and there are some homes on the southern end.

Heading up the creek brings much more civilization with the shore's characteristic mixture of the old and new in homes. At the very head there are very few homes and the area is

Bugeye and Buy Boat on display at Chesapeake Bay Maritime Museum

Carolyn and Melanie Neale, author's daughters, at wooden figurehead,
Chesapeake Bay Maritime Museum, St. Michaels—a great place for kids

beautiful, but the water is shallower than 5 and 6 feet (27A) shown on the chart. Go up as far as your draft permits. The farther up you go, the shallower the water and less reliable the chart.

UPPER MILES RIVER
Refer to Chart #12270-J—"Upper Miles River."

The reaches above Long Point have their share of interesting houses, new and old, and pretty farm scenery. Above the bridge, the river becomes more scenic and less civilized.

As mentioned in this chapter describing St. Michaels, I recommend taking a trip on the *Patriot* cruise boat up this river. Captain Dave will tell you all about it as far as the bridge, and you can judge for yourself whether you wish to explore it further in your boat.

Turning northeast around Long Point (26), the river stretches ahead wide and deep with homes, large, small, old and new farms, and fields ashore. There are really no anchorage coves here, just about anywhere will do if you like mid-river anchoring. There are many trotliners in season, and their markers and operations should be watched. Soon the opening bascule bridge (36) with 18-foot clearance will appear.

Just upriver from the opening to Hunting Creek (27), on the northwestern shore, you may see the small, two-story frame house (37) where the famous opera star John Charles Thomas lived in the 1920s and 30s. Almost across from that on the opposite shore is the Perry Hall (38). The original brick house was built around 1740, but Senator Williams Perry later lived there. This area has been long believed to contain buried treasure. Many have tried to find it to no avail. Most consider the stories to be only fancy. Just upriver from this house, on the same shore, is Kirkham Hall (39), with white columns, formerly part of the Perry estate, now an engineering school. It is rumoured locally that one of the owners once saw the crying ghost of a lady sitting on a bed in this home.

Just before the bridge, a two-pronged creek (40) opens to your right (southeast shore). The entrance is shallow. I could find no more than 3 feet. There is a pretty three-story white house with columned porch and green roof with widow's walk atop, up the creek and to the right as you go up. The creek is very built up with homes, docks, some work boats, and some shallow draft sailboats. Even if your draft allows you in, there is not much privacy here for anchored boats.

As you approach the bridge, if you look carefully at its end on your left, you will see through the trees and vines the ruins of an old Gothic church. Passing through the bridge brings a better view. This was St. Johns Chapel (41), one of the first Gothic revival churches on the Eastern Shore, built in 1835 of granite brought all the way from Port Deposit on the Susquehanna. It was placed on soft ground and began to settle. One Sunday a stone fell and struck a lady worshiping and the church was condemned and has been slowly crumbling since then. Today it sits, ghostly covered with vine and weed, guarding the end of the bridge. Don't go near because of the possibility of falling stones.

The bridge opens sun up to sunset on signal. As might be expected, the river above is less built up. Glebe Creek (42), the first creek to the right (east) above the bridge, has many houses and docks. To the right (south) on the point after the first cove in this creek, is an old house with the remnants of a very old windmill (42A). Continuing up, the banks get higher and the trees hide the fields behind. However, depth is often less than the chart indicates. This is yet another example of the many great gunkholing creeks if you have a light boat that you can push off if you run aground.

Goldsborough Creek (43), next up, is similar in many respects. There are many houses at first, mostly to the right (east shore), but ahead the narrow creeks and the woods and fields close in with quieter beauty. We noticed many mute swans swimming, apparently wild. However, we very early found that the bottom is uneven and much shallower than the chart showed, with stumps and trees ready to do injustice to propellers. This is a nice creek for exploration, but do it in a light boat, and very slowly.

If you pass Goldsborough Creek and head on up the river, very soon a white large house with six thin white columns (44) will come into view on a hill before you, on the bank to your left (west). Passing that house, and coming around the bend, another large mansion confronts the explorer, again straight ahead, and with majestic columns in front. This is called "Ashby 1663" (45) and is a well known inn. This beautiful home was built in the 17th century for the Goldsborough family and at one time was surrounded by a 2,000-acre estate. It would make an excellent place to have guests meet your boat with a place to stay ashore and make day trips in the area. The boat might have to be anchored out off the home, but the river here is fine for this. 'Phone number for the inn is (410) 822-4235.

Rounding to the right (northeast) of the point on which this house presides, the civilization of the river dramatically decreases, as does its depth. Up here woods and field take over again, and you can anchor (46) anywhere in the river, deep in the heart of the Delmarva Peninsula. Proceed very carefully because of shallows. Beware of the possibilities of stumps and submerged logs. Assume only 3-foot depths or less.

Abandoned St. John's chapel at Miles River bridge

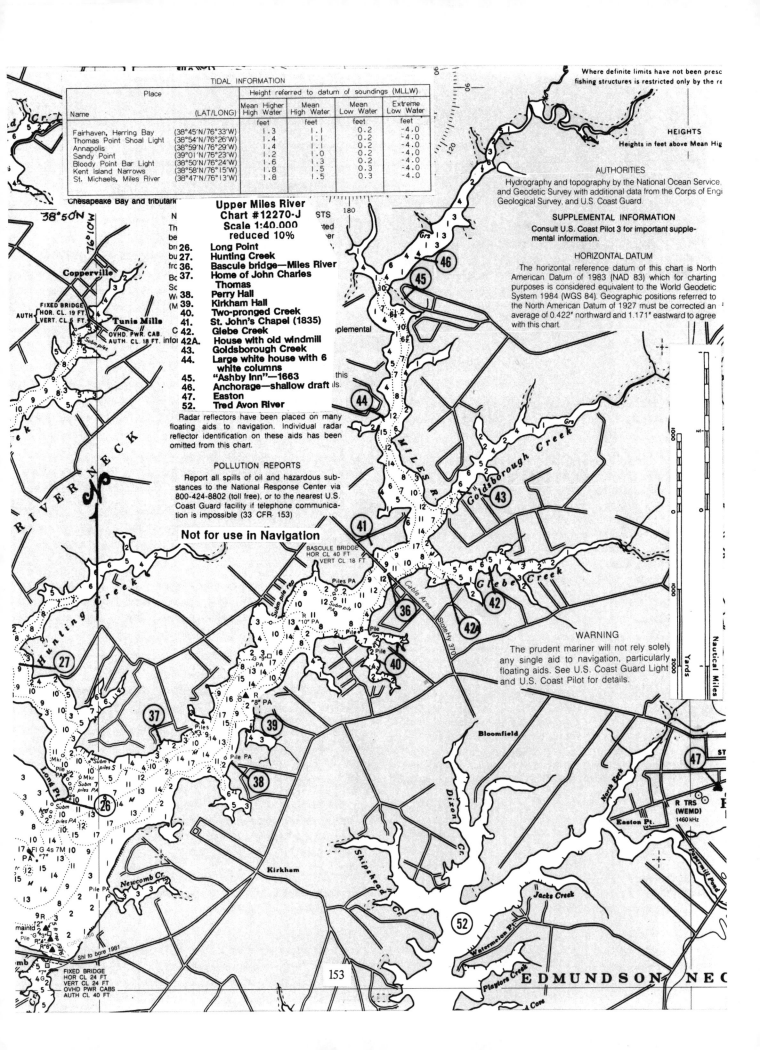

TIDAL INFORMATION

Place		Height referred to datum of soundings (MLLW)			
Name	(LAT/LONG)	Mean Higher High Water	Mean High Water	Mean Low Water	Extreme Low Water
		feet	feet	feet	feet
Fairhaven, Herring Bay	(38°45'N/76°33'W)	1.3	1.1	0.2	-4.0
Thomas Point Shoal Light	(38°54'N/76°26'W)	1.4	1.1	0.2	-4.0
Annapolis	(38°59'N/76°29'W)	1.4	1.1	0.2	-4.0
Sandy Point	(39°01'N/76°23'W)	1.2	1.0	0.2	-4.0
Bloody Point Bar Light	(38°50'N/76°24'W)	1.6	1.3	0.3	-4.0
Kent Island Narrows	(38°58'N/76°15'W)	1.8	1.5	0.3	-4.0
St. Michaels, Miles River	(38°47'N/76°13'W)	1.8	1.5	0.3	-4.0

Chesapeake Bay and tributaries

Upper Miles River
Chart #12270-J
Scale 1:40,000
reduced 10%

26. Long Point
27. Hunting Creek
36. Bascule bridge—Miles River
37. Home of John Charles Thomas
38. Perry Hall
39. Kirkham Hall
40. Two-pronged Creek
41. St. John's Chapel (1835)
42. Glebe Creek
42A. House with old windmill
43. Goldsborough Creek
44. Large white house with 6 white columns
45. "Ashby Inn"—1663
46. Anchorage—shallow draft
47. Easton
52. Tred Avon River

Radar reflectors have been placed on many floating aids to navigation. Individual radar reflector identification on these aids has been omitted from this chart.

POLLUTION REPORTS

Report all spills of oil and hazardous substances to the National Response Center via 800-424-8802 (toll free), or to the nearest U.S. Coast Guard facility if telephone communication is impossible (33 CFR 153)

Not for use in Navigation

AUTHORITIES

Hydrography and topography by the National Ocean Service, and Geodetic Survey with additional data from the Corps of Engi Geological Survey, and U.S. Coast Guard.

SUPPLEMENTAL INFORMATION

Consult U.S. Coast Pilot 3 for important supplemental information.

HORIZONTAL DATUM

The horizontal reference datum of this chart is North American Datum of 1983 (NAD 83) which for charting purposes is considered equivalent to the World Geodetic System 1984 (WGS 84). Geographic positions referred to the North American Datum of 1927 must be corrected an average of 0.422″ northward and 1.171″ eastward to agree with this chart.

HEIGHTS

Heights in feet above Mean Hig

WARNING

The prudent mariner will not rely solely any single aid to navigation, particularly floating aids. See U.S. Coast Guard Light and U.S. Coast Pilot for details.

CHAPTER 11

KNAPPS NARROWS, TILGHMAN ISLAND, AND THE CHOPTANK RIVER

KNAPPS NARROWS

This is a short and important time-saving passage through a narrow neck of land between the Chesapeake Bay and the Choptank River. The passage separates Tilghman Island from the mainland. There are some restaurants and interesting places ashore, but this is not a place where one would normally "hang out" for long while cruising. It is crowded with commercial boats, has swift current, and uncertain entrance depths, although it is dredged from time to time.

Refer to Regional Chart #12263-C—"Choptank River, Northern Shore, Entrance from North"
and
Chart #12266-A—"Knapps Narrows, Tilghman Island." Pg. 156

Last year, Knapps Narrows **(1)** had a depth of 10 feet from end to end and at both entrances. However local people said that it shoals badly and they don't know how long this will last. If you enter from the eastern side while the current is still running from the Chesapeake toward the Choptank, and there is any sea in the Chesapeake, you will see the silt and mud washing through. It does save a great deal of time, and with all the commercial fishing traffic and the skipjacks, you would expect it to maintain at least 5 feet even when nature silts in the latest dredge efforts. Check with marinas in the Narrows as to depth.

Take particular caution entering from the Bay, since shoaling reportedly occurs the worst here. Do not stray from the marked channel, especially Red "2" **(2)**. Note also that the channel heads off to your right (southeast) after you pass R "4" **(3)**. Once inside, the protection and activity of the Narrows compared to the Bay behind you can be breathtaking. Current can run swiftly here, therefore plan carefully for the bridge **(4)** ahead (7 feet clearance) if you have a fair tide. If you are fortunate enough to have it against you, give right of way to those that have the tidal current going their way. The bridge opens on demand with one long and one short. Docking can also require special care because of currents and traffic. The buoys are oriented according to whether you are coming from the Choptank or Bay side. Red is to your right entering from each end.

Refer to our Sketch Chart —"Tilghman Island, Knapps Narrows & Dogwood Harbor." Pg. 157

As soon as you enter from the Chesapeake, there are slips **(5)** with a sign advertising lots for sale to your right (south).

The next facility will be the **Tilghman Inn (6)**. This has lodging and a full restaurant. You can see and taste the flavor of the Bay from here. It is just outside the channel. You can also watch the parade of workboats, including skipjacks, go by. It can be an enjoyable spot to stop. However last year, the slips were silting with no more than 4 feet available at MLW. They are perpendicular to the shore, and docking across the current is normally necessary. They can take a maximum of 40

feet LOA in slips, with longer boats possible alongside, if that area is not occupied. Complimentary dockage is available while dining. There is 30 amp service. Although there are fuel pumps, they have discontinued selling fuel. A large charter boat for day cruises, the *Tilghman Lady*, is based here. They rent bikes and there is entertainment in the lounge on weekends. There is also a tennis court, swimming pool and croquet court. They take Amex, MC, Discover, and Visa.

There are several seafood retail and wholesale houses **(7)** on the south shore. Their signs tell it all. It is possible to dock here and pick up some crabs, oysters or other seafood.

Just before the bridge, to your left (north) going east, is **Knapps Narrows Marina (8)**. This has an inset basin and full service yard with ship's store which includes hardware. There are 127 slips up to 50 feet. They take transients up to 50 feet with electricity up to 220 V/30A. Depth is 7 feet and larger boats can lay alongside the cut. There is a canvas shop on the premises, gas and diesel dock, block and cube ice, pumpout station, laundry, pool, and a 35-ton travelift. They will help with transportation problems. Visa and MC are taken.

Adjacent east of the Marina is the **Bay Hundred (9)** restaurant which is a full menu nice restaurant. There are some docks in front and they will take transients up to 40 feet with depth of 5 feet, and electricity of 15 amps. They sell gas and diesel fuel. There are fishing charters available, including the 46-foot *Nancy Ellen* at 745-6022; and the *Waterdog II*, a 40-foot deadrise. Call 745-2156.

To your right (south) across from the above two establishments is a commercial basin **(10)** which is usually filled with work boats, including some skipjacks. The water is over 6 feet inside and there is a fuel dock at the head. This is connected to a country fishing store. The sign says, "Home of Fairbanks Tackle Information" **(11)**. Mr. Fairbanks said that his father put that up in 1945, and he carries on the tradition. Here you can get snacks, beer and wine, propane, fishing tackle and bait, play pool or pinball, and have nice conversations, especially about fishing.

Coming to Tilghman Island **(35)** by road, this basin is just to your right (west) on the south side of the bridge. There is a public ramp **(12)** in Dogwood Harbor **(13)** just a few miles down the road, on the left (east) after the country store.

Between the basin and the Knapps Narrows Bridge, also to your right (south), is the Bridge Restaurant **(14)**, with a second story room overlooking the activity. On the other side of the bridge, also to your right (south), is **Severn Marine Services (15)** which has another basin with 48 slips, yard and 30-ton lift, a pumpout station and some marine supplies. While there, I noticed a skipjack getting a new bottom.

Now refer back to Chart #12266-A—"Knapps Narrows and Tilghman Island." Pg. 156

Going out into the Choptank is no problem with the markers. The outside eastern channel marker is a 14-foot Fl 4 sec. "1" **(16)** with position of 38°41.4'N by 76°18.8'W. It is usually not honored by boats approaching from the Choptank. They

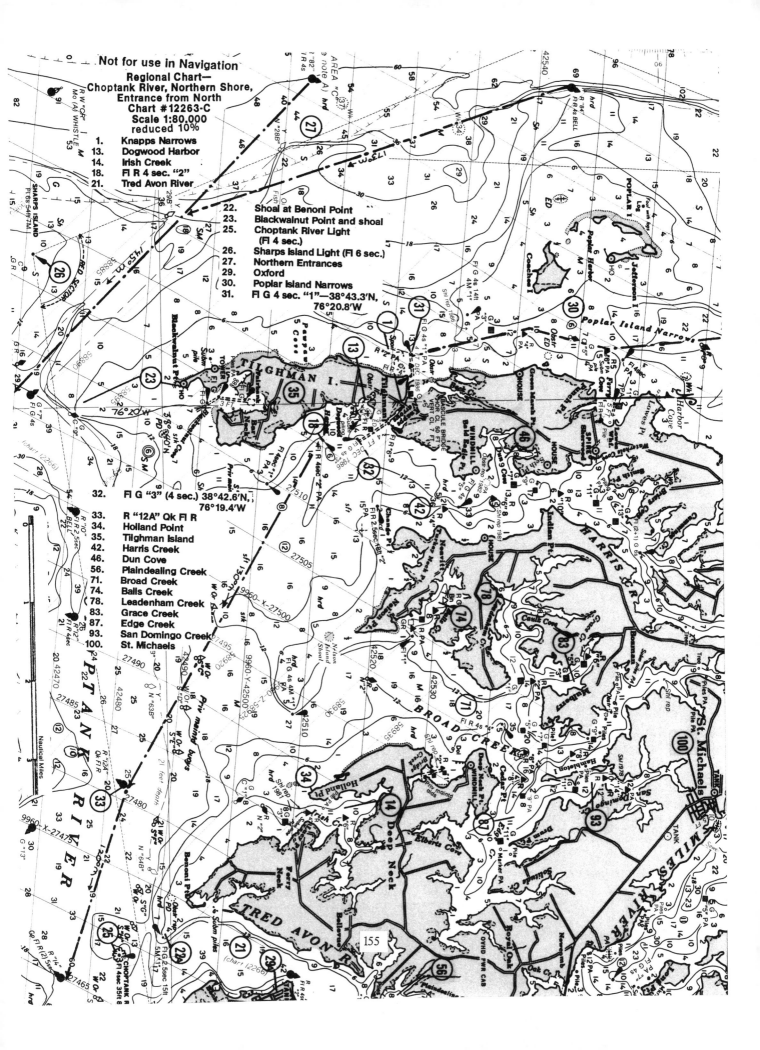

Not for use in Navigation
Regional Chart—
Choptank River, Northern Shore,
Entrance from North
Chart #12263-C
Scale 1:80,000
reduced 10%

1. Knapps Narrows
13. Dogwood Harbor
14. Irish Creek
18. Fl R 4 sec. "2"
21. Tred Avon River

22. Shoal at Benoni Point
23. Blackwalnut Point and shoal
25. Choptank River Light
    (Fl 4 sec.)
26. Sharps Island Light (Fl 6 sec.)
27. Northern Entrances
29. Oxford
30. Poplar Island Narrows
31. Fl G 4 sec. "1"—38°43.3'N,
    76°20.8'W

32. Fl G "3" (4 sec.) 38°42.6'N,
    76°19.4'W
33. R "12A" Qk Fl R
34. Holland Point
35. Tilghman Island
42. Harris Creek
46. Dun Cove
56. Plaindealing Creek
71. Broad Creek
74. Balls Creek
78. Leadenham Creek
83. Grace Creek
87. Edge Creek
93. San Domingo Creek
100. St. Michaels

155

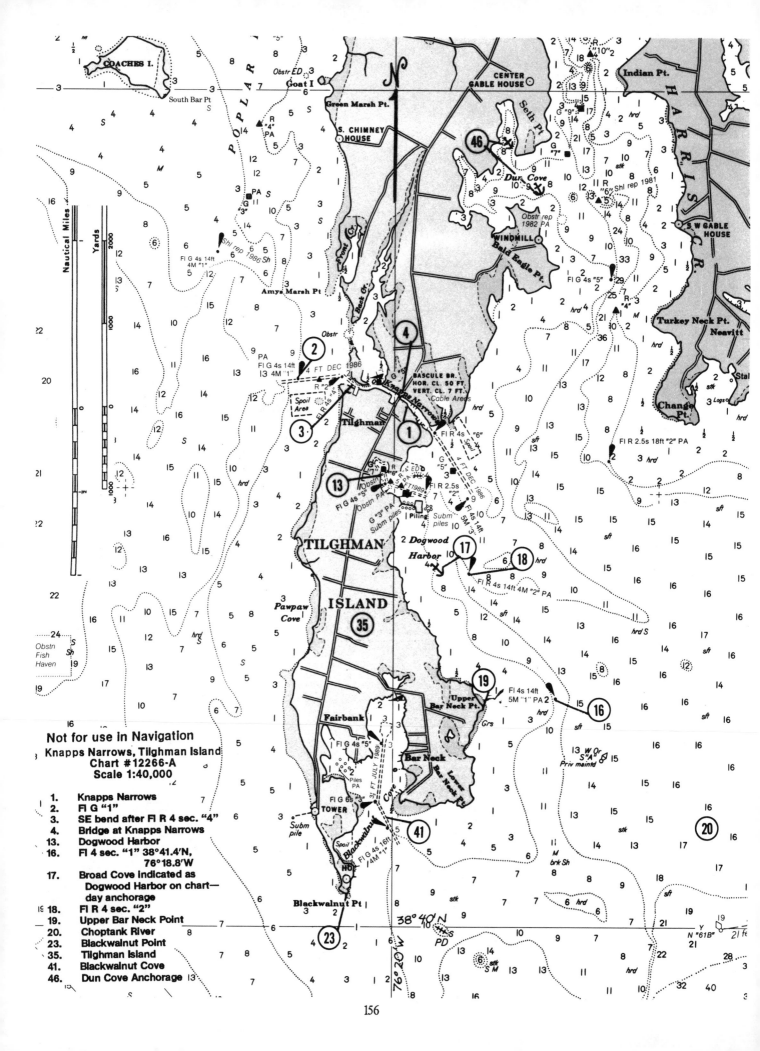

Not for use in Navigation

Knapps Narrows, Tilghman Island
Chart #12266-A
Scale 1:40,000

1. Knapps Narrows
2. Fl G "1"
3. SE bend after Fl R 4 sec. "4"
4. Bridge at Knapps Narrows
13. Dogwood Harbor
16. Fl 4 sec. "1" 38°41.4'N, 76°18.8'W
17. Broad Cove indicated as Dogwood Harbor on chart— day anchorage
18. Fl R 4 sec. "2"
19. Upper Bar Neck Point
20. Choptank River
23. Blackwalnut Point
35. Tilghman Island
41. Blackwalnut Cove
46. Dun Cove Anchorage

156

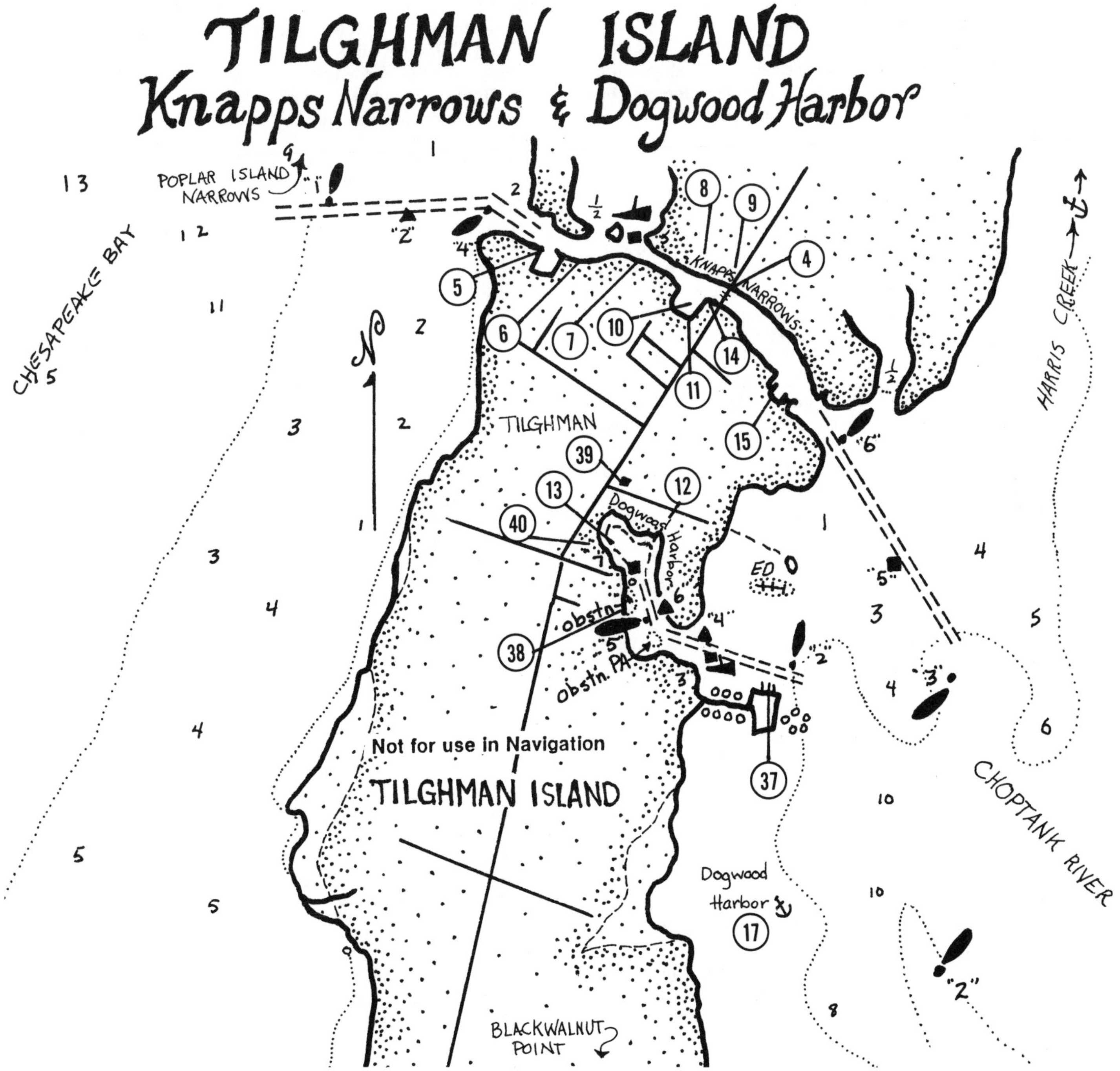

TILGHMAN ISLAND
Knapps Narrows & Dogwood Harbor

POPLAR ISLAND NARROWS

CHESAPEAKE BAY

KNAPPS NARROWS

HARRIS CREEK

TILGHMAN

Dogwood Harbor

ED

Not for use in Navigation

TILGHMAN ISLAND

CHOPTANK RIVER

obstn

obstn PA

Dogwood Harbor

BLACKWALNUT POINT

**Sketch Chart
Tilghman Island, Knapps Narrows
& Dogwood Harbor**

4. Knapps Narrows Bridge
5. Slips with lots for sale
6. Tilghman Inn
7. Seafood—retail & wholesale
8. Knapps Narrows Marina
9. Bay Hundred Restaurant
10. Commercial basin
11. Fuel dock, Fairbanks Tackle
    Information
12. Public ramp—
    Dogwood Harbor
13. Dogwood Harbor—Skipjack
    Fleet dock
14. Bridge Restaurant
15. Severn Marine Services
17. Dogwood Harbor on chart—
    day anchorage
37. Tilghman-on-Chesapeake
    Marina and Yacht Club
38. Harrison's Chesapeake House
39. Tilghman Country Store
40. Lazyjack Inn, Bed & Breakfast,
    sloop *Incredible*

usually go straight in to the 14-foot beacon, Fl R "2" (18) which marks the southern end of a 6-foot shoal. However, when trying to raise the Narrows from the Choptank, the shoreline and misty days can combine to make it sometimes difficult to home into the correct area. This can be a problem because of the shoal just mentioned and because of the shoal extending easterly from Upper Bay Neck Point (19). Therefore, the first (southernmost) outside marker can be important to get your reference.

TILGHMAN ISLAND

Everyone should go here, but there is no protected close anchorage. There is a large commercial Bay fishing fleet here and the largest working skipjack fleet on the Bay. Seeing them lined up at the quay, sometimes two or three abreast, is something that must not be missed. There are marinas, some nice restaurants and inns, and good fishing opportunities.

If you wish to explore Tilghman by dinghy, you can anchor in the broad cove noted as "Dogwood Harbor" (17) on the chart to the east of the island. On a weekend this is very busy, and it can be quite uncomfortable as an anchorage in any wind except right off the shore. If your dinghy is fast enough to make the trip down, there is a great anchorage in Dun Cove (46) just up Harris Creek. This will be described later in this chapter in the "Harris Creek" description.

Refer to Chart #12266-A—"Knapps Narrows, Tilghman Island." PG. 156

Tilghman Island (35) forms the western shore of the large bay that is the mouth of the Choptank (20). If you come in from the north, you will have passed it, and hopefully steered clear of the shoal extending southerly of its Blackwalnut Point (23). Tilghman Island is separated from the mainland by Knapps Narrows (1) which has just been described in this chapter. To get a good flavor of Tilghman, run Knapps Narrows or take a quick glimpse up and down them as you cross the bridge (4) to the island, which passes over the Narrows. Then go into Dogwood Harbor (13) and look around.

Dogwood Harbor

Dogwood Harbor has a well-marked entrance just south of the eastern end of the Narrows. The chart implies that the harbor is the broad cove (17) on the west side of the island. Folks ashore apply the term to the basin which you will find all the way northwest up the channel. I found 6 feet prevailing up to the commercial basin at the end.

Refer to our Sketch Chart—"Tilghman Island, Knapps Narrows & Dogwood Harbor." PG. 157

Going in, a new marina and real estate development greet you to your left (south). This is called Tilghman-On-Chesapeake (37). The marina and its yacht club are on Avalon Island, shown on the chart as the squared tiny island with piles on each side of the strip connecting it to the Tilghman Island. To the north of the strip is the dredged marina basin with power up to 50 amps and nice floating docks. Depth now is 6 feet, but check first. Transients are welcome and receive privileges at the Tilghman-On-Chesapeake Yacht Club. There is a pool on the point overlooking the water. Electricity up to 50 amps is available. The marina does have somewhat of a northerly exposure on high tide. The island began as the oyster

house at the end of a pier in 1897. As years passed, tons of oyster shells thrown over formed what is now the island. At one point, steamboats landed here, and this was a major source of employment in the seafood industry. Now it is a first class marina and development.

Going farther up the channel, the popular Harrison's Chesapeake House (38) appears ahead to the west as the channel curves northerly to your right. It is at Green "5" and has slips in front of a large white house. The controlling depth is 6 feet, although the area coming in is subject to shoaling. They stand by on VHF Channel 88. This is a combination marina, country inn, and sport fishing center. There are 31 slips here with electricity available up to 30 amps, and usually courtesy dockage while dining. There are some groceries and fishing supplies here, beverages, block and cube ice, nice rooms, a swimming pool, a bar, restaurant, sitting and rocking on the front porch relaxing, and charter fishing in the well-known fleet associated with this facility. There is a 15-ton open end lift. Fishing lovers will really appreciate the following policy: if the room is occupied the previous night by fishermen, they will be allowed to shower and change clothes when they come in from their fishing trip before their departure. The post office and St. Michaels bank are a short distance northerly up the main road.

Continuing up the channel, after the turn to the right (northerly), the public ramp (12) appears ahead to the north. To reach the ramp by car, turn left (east) at the Tilghman Country Store (39), which will appear to your left (east) shortly after you cross the bridge. The main attraction of the basin (13) is the fleet of Skipjacks often moored there.

Ashore on this basin is The Lazyjack Inn, Bed and Breakfast (40). This is right at the Skipjack docks, just across the street and to the west of the basin. The owner also charters his own 33-foot sloop, the *Incredible*. In season he will follow the Skipjack fleet as they go out and work, giving the charterers an opportunity to see them in action.

Plan to spend some time in this basin, just sitting in your dinghy and drifting among the majestic Skipjacks tied ashore. Their rigging, long bowsprits, elaborately carved figureheads and name boards, small pushboats on davits astern; all will take you back to a time which few people know today. These boats work in season, dredging under sail. They also race in various Bay events. Do not miss visiting these Chesapeake Bay Skipjacks.

Good times to come here would be in late June when there is a Tilghman Island Seafood Festival, and late October when the folks celebrate Tilghman Island Day. Both of these feature great Bay seafood, Skipjacks, races, parade and games.

Refer to Chart #12266-A. Pg. 156

The chart shows Blackwalnut Cove (41) at the very southern tip of the island. This is now very shallow and is a basin used primarily by local work boats.

CHOPTANK RIVER

Refer to Regional Chart #12263-C—"Choptank River—Northern Shore, Entrance from North" Pg. 155
and
Regional Chart #12263-D—"Western Choptank River (Southern Entrance and Little Choptank River Entrance.)"

This is a huge river, very diverse in its attractions, and with

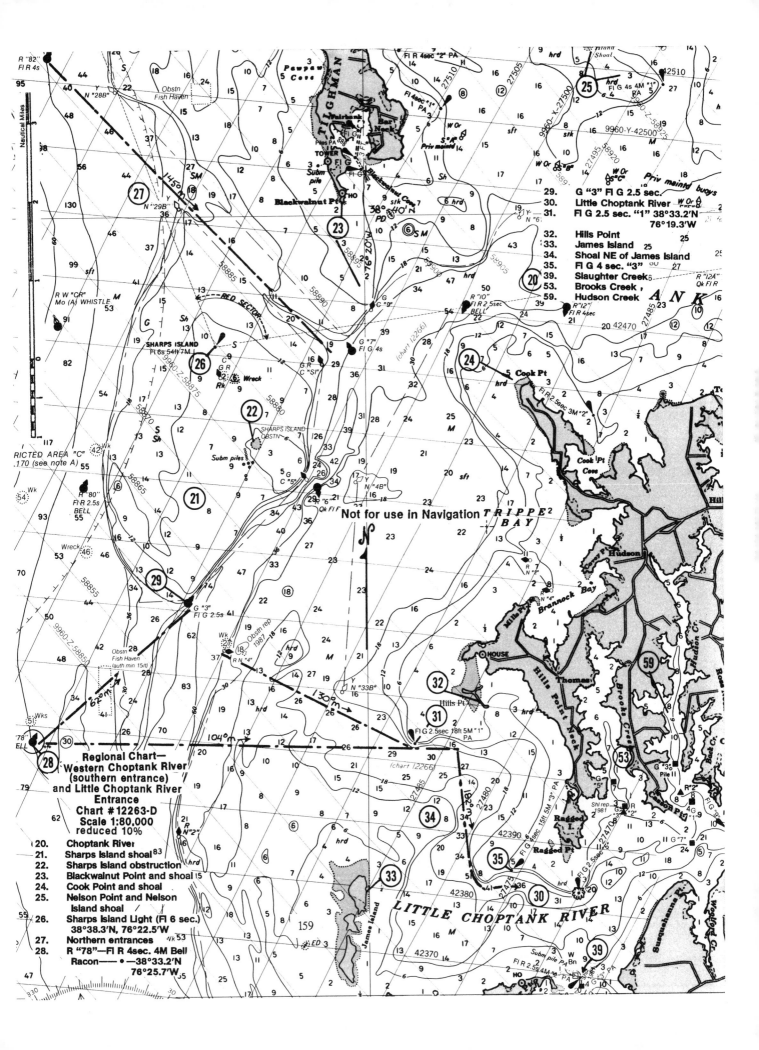

more civilization than the rivers just north and south of it. There are many excellent anchorages, and some very nice places to visit ashore, but not the abundance of supplies and facilities throughout that you will find in other large areas. Cambridge has good facilities and supplies.

Entrance to the Choptank

Gaining entry to the Choptank (20) from the Bay presents no problem if you follow the chart. The main concern is to avoid the huge area of Sharp's Island Shoal (21) which lies west of the mouth of the river. This island used to be inhabited and farmed, but it gradually washed away and now nothing can be seen of it except the markers, designating "Sharp's Island Obstruction" (22). There is debris out there, as well as shallow water, and the area should not be crossed without local knowledge, even in shallow draft vessels.

There is a significant shoal extending in a southerly direction off Blackwalnut Point (23), another extending in a northwesterly direction off Cook Point (24), and another extending well out in a southeasterly direction from Nelson Point (25) once you get inside. These, in addition to the Sharps Island Shoal, make it important to pay attention and honor the buoys even though you are in wide areas of water.

From out in the Bay, heading either straight in or from the north, you should sight Sharps Island Light (26). This marks the northern end of the shoal, but it is set in 11 feet depth. At 54 feet tall with a 6-second flash, it is hard to miss, and it has the distinctive characteristic of leaning way over, having been set that way in 1977 by ice that encased the Bay that winter. It is a brown-red solid cylindrical structure. Its position is 38°38.3'N by 76°22.5'W. Sharps Island Light provides good orientation approaching from any direction.

Refer to Chart #12263-C. Pg. 155

Coming from the north (27), a course of 173°M from Fl R Bell "84" will bring you to N "29B" which is west of the southern end of Tilghman Island. From there, a course of 145°M will bring you to G R "SI" and G "7" which are south of Tilghman Island. If coming in from the Fl R "82" out in the Bay, the course of 145°M will bring you north of N "29B" to G R "SI" and G "7."

Refer to Chart #12263-D. Pg. 159

Entering the Choptank River from the south, pick up Flashing R 4 sec. light buoy "78" (28) in the Chesapeake Channel. Its position is 38°33.2'N by 76°25.7'W. From here a course of 62°M will bring you in the vicinity of Fl G "3" (29) which marks the southern boundary of the shoals. From here, follow the aids in.

Refer to Regional Chart #12263-C—"Choptank River, Northern Shore, Entrance from North." Pg. 155

Many also enter the Choptank through Knapps Narrows (1), especially if they are coming from Eastern Bay and have a shallow enough draft to get through the Poplar Island Narrows (30), as described near the end of Chapter 9. It will help to know here that the outside western marker for Knapps Narrows is Fl G "1" (31) and its position is 38°43.3'N by 76°20.8'W. The east Knapps Narrows Channel marker "3" (32) is a 14-foot flashing beacon and its position is 38°42.6'N by 76°19.4'W. You should also honor the 14-foot Fl R 4 sec. "2" (18) at the east end to avoid the shoal area to its north. A course of 130°M from Fl R "2" will take you to the vicinity of R "17A" (33), well up into the Choptank, well south of Holland Point (34).

Harris Creek

Refer to Chart #12266-B—"Harris Creek, Upper Broad Creek."

This very long and scenic creek is a bit tricky at spots but well worth the effort if you want a beautiful quiet anchorage and complete protection.

Harris Creek (42), like its sister, Broad Creek just to the east, goes inland almost to the shores of the Eastern Bay and the St. Michaels area. At first glance on the chart, it looks easy, but a closer study shows some shoal spots which are of concern for 5 to 6 feet of draft. Like other creeks with long fetches at the entrance, Harris Creek can shoal yearly depending on prevailing winds. I found a minimum of 6 feet up to its fork at the head, although some care was necessary. Strong northerly winds could have left me in the soft friendly mud in several spots at low tide.

Entering is as the chart shows, but we found considerably less water than indicated in the vicinity of R "4" (43), west of Turkey Neck Point (44). I found no special ranges to help here where the channel twists between the shoals off that point and Bald Eagle Point (45). Perhaps it is just as well, because I doubt that the shoals will remain constant because of the exposure. I once saw a local waterman hard aground here just to the west of where he obviously should have been. The best advice is to just go in carefully, watching the charts and depths. There is deep water in the right places, and boats of 6 feet draft take this entrance regularly. I helped the waterman for an hour until the tide got so low that there wasn't enough water for my dinghy!

The first anchorage is the deservedly popular Dun Cove (46) to the left (west) as you enter. I noticed a little less water than shown on the chart, but there is still depth for at least a 7-foot draft. Beware of the shoal (47) to your right (east) as you round off red "6." We avoided the small 6-foot spot in the middle by heading on up toward green "7" (48) (not too close) before beginning the turn to the left (west). Choose your anchorage in Dun Cove according to your pleasure and depths. You will be surrounded by trees, field, and a few homes visible farther in to the west. Holding is good. The north branch (49) around to the right is even prettier with water depths as shown and nice woods close by on the shore to your east. When going in here, be careful to avoid the shoal (50) extending southerly off the point to your north as you round it. There is also a little beach in the woods east of this spot.

Up Harris Creek, the shoal (51) indicated on the chart between G "9" and R "10" (to the west of Indian Point (52)) is there. I found a way around it by preceeding from "9," not directly to "10," but to a point well off the R "10," favoring the green side of the channel, thus leaving R "10" well to my right (east). This compensation can be overdone, so watch the depths. A boat of 4 feet draft would not be concerned. In a boat of greater draft, do this on a half tide and rising, at least the first time you try it.

Anchor in Waterhole Cove (53), Briary Cove (54), or any other place that looks good for you. Both of the coves are simple to enter, and both are very pretty, with farm fields and woods ashore.

As you continue up Harris Creek past these coves, beware of the shoal at (55) Green "13." It is building out a little beyond (east of) the marker. pass well to the east of G "13."

Cummings Creek (56) is another nice spot. Begin turning before you reach the red/green junction marker (57). The duck blind (58) noted on the chart in the southern branch of

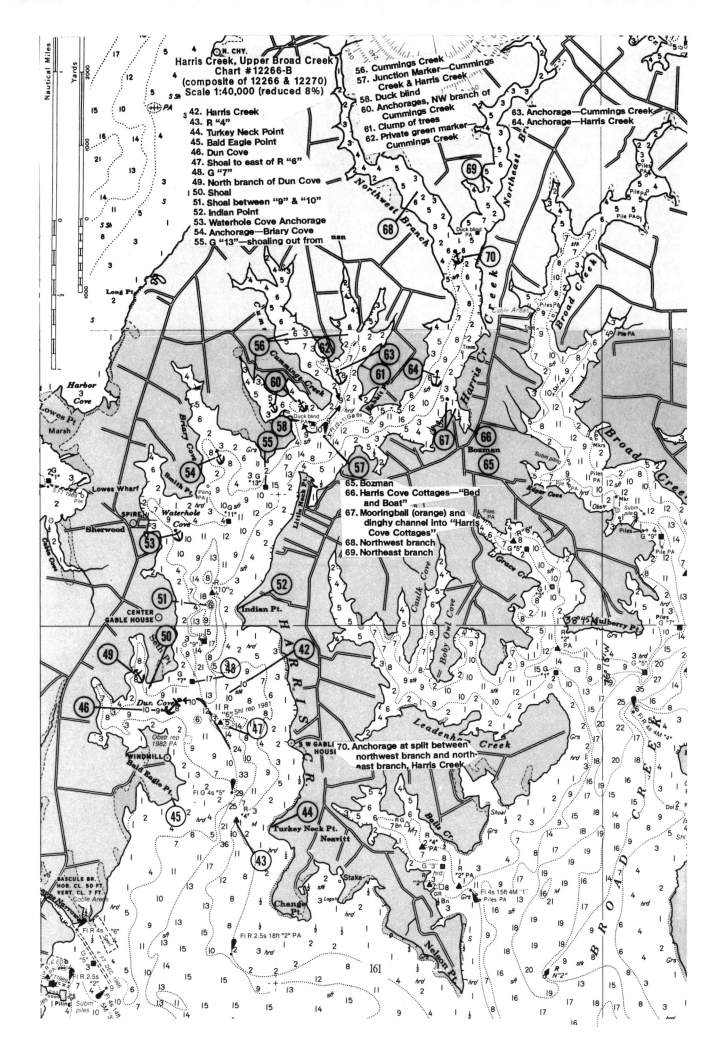

Harris Creek, Upper Broad Creek
Chart #12266-B
(composite of 12266 & 12270)
Scale 1:40,000 (reduced 8%)

42. Harris Creek
43. R "4"
44. Turkey Neck Point
45. Bald Eagle Point
46. Dun Cove
47. Shoal to east of R "6"
48. G "7"
49. North branch of Dun Cove
50. Shoal
51. Shoal between "9" & "10"
52. Indian Point
53. Waterhole Cove Anchorage
54. Anchorage—Briary Cove
55. G "13"—shoaling out from

56. Cummings Creek
57. Junction Marker—Cummings Creek & Harris Creek
58. Duck blind
60. Anchorages, NW branch of Cummings Creek
61. Clump of trees
62. Private green marker— Cummings Creek

63. Anchorage—Cummings Creek
64. Anchorage—Harris Creek

65. Bozman
66. Harris Cove Cottages—"Bed and Boat"
67. Mooringball (orange) and dinghy channel into "Harris Cove Cottages"
68. Northwest branch
69. Northeast branch

70. Anchorage at split between northwest branch and northeast branch, Harris Creek

161

the creek is farther into the point (to the north) than the chart shows. Put it to your right (east) if going into the southern branch. There is a very scenic spot, if your draft allows you to anchor **(60)** where you can see up the little creek to the northwest with its woods and fields. If you can go up there, keeping in the middle, all the better.

I found the main branch of Cummings Creek to the north to carry the water shown. Going in, have the duck blind to your left (west) and head for a rounded large clump of trees **(61)** in the background ashore and ahead to your northeast. This clump of trees is to the left (north) of an area of shore with gray rip rap, and to the left (northwest) of the little cove behind Rabbit Point. There is a private green marker **(62)** to the southwest of these trees. I began rounding to my left (taking a more northerly course) as I neared the green **(62)**. The bottom shoaled up quickly as I approached that northern shore. There is pleasant scenery for an anchorage **(63)** at the split in the creek.

As Harris Creek turns to the northeast, there is less fetch from the south should a hard blow come in from that direction. The creek narrows, and we observed boats anchored in the middle **(64)**. Keep well lit at night if you do this. In the community of Bozman **(65)** is a very interesting "Bed and Boat" called "Harris Cove Cottages" **(66)**. The owners say they don't cook breakfast, but they do rent boats and/or motors. There is a hard surfaced ramp and good crabbing. Guests stay in nice little cottages scattered about the large tree-shaded yard on the cove. This would be a great place for the cruiser to rendezvous with visitors. The boat could anchor off the cove in the Creek, and the visitors could stay ashore in the cottages and visit by skiff and sample the area culture, history, fishing and crabbing. This is located on the eastern side of the creek. It is approximately 1 mile northeast from the Harris Creek/Cummings Creek junction buoy **(57)**. There is a large orange mooring buoy barrel **(67)** at the entrance of the cove, and the shallow dinghy channel in is marked by a row of flags. The southerly shore of the cove has a large brick house.

Farther north, Harris Creek divides and becomes narrower and much more shallow. It is still pretty if you have the draft and temperament to find your way farther. Follow either the northwest branch **(68)** or the northeast branch **(69)** for a beautiful exploration trip into the woods and field of Eastern Shore countryside, interspersed with homes and farms. I would prefer to do this only in a dinghy or outboard, anchoring the main boat out below the split **(70)**, or in the middle. Above the split in either branch, the bottom is uneven and quite shallow in places, with meandering channels. The northeastern branch is the deeper of the two, and a brave and careful gunkholer could do well with a boat of 3 feet draft. The northwestern branch is less civilized, as you would expect with the very shallow water, only 2 feet at the entrance.

BROAD CREEK OFF THE CHOPTANK

Refer to Chart #12266-C—"Broad Creek off the Choptank."

This is not a marina creek. It is for great anchoring. Although much of the creek is very wide with considerable fetch from the south, there are numerous smaller creeks branching off with better protection. The area is very pretty, but fairly built up with rural homes and docks along many banks. You can reach St. Michaels on foot from an anchorage at the head of its San Domingo Creek.

Approach

The approach to Broad Creek **(71)** is not difficult as long as you are not misled by the open water barely covering the shoal **(25)** off Nelson Point **(72)**. Not only is it there, it seems to be building out farther to the south. Stay well east of Fl Gr "1" **(73)**. Its position is 38°41.7'N by 76°14.9'W. We approach it on a northerly course to avoid clipping the end of the Nelson Point shoal. Holland Point shoal **(34)** is ½ NM east of Nelson Point shoal. It is not marked. Once in, you will probably want to proceed on for a while. The creek is well-marked and well-traveled. Side creeks offer many anchoring opportunities.

Balls Creek

Balls Creek **(74)** is not a great choice for anchoring. It is really a bit chancy anchoring outside **(75)** for a dinghy exploration because you will find an oyster shell bottom which may make holding a problem. Inside you will find the first taste of much of the shoreline in the area. There are homes along the banks with many docks. It is pretty, the homes and folks are nice, but you don't get a wilderness feeling in here. Also, unless you have a draft of only 4 feet and can tuck into the long cove **(76)** to your right (north) (on the northern shore), the fetch from the southeast can be a problem. The head of the creek becomes very congested with work boats moored out on stakes and at docks.

Bridge Creek

Bridge Creek **(77)** is very shallow with many private markers inside. The outer area has what appear to be remains of earlier markers which are no longer maintained and deteriorating. I wouldn't consider it as an anchorage.

IDENTIFICATION FOR CHART ON PG. 163

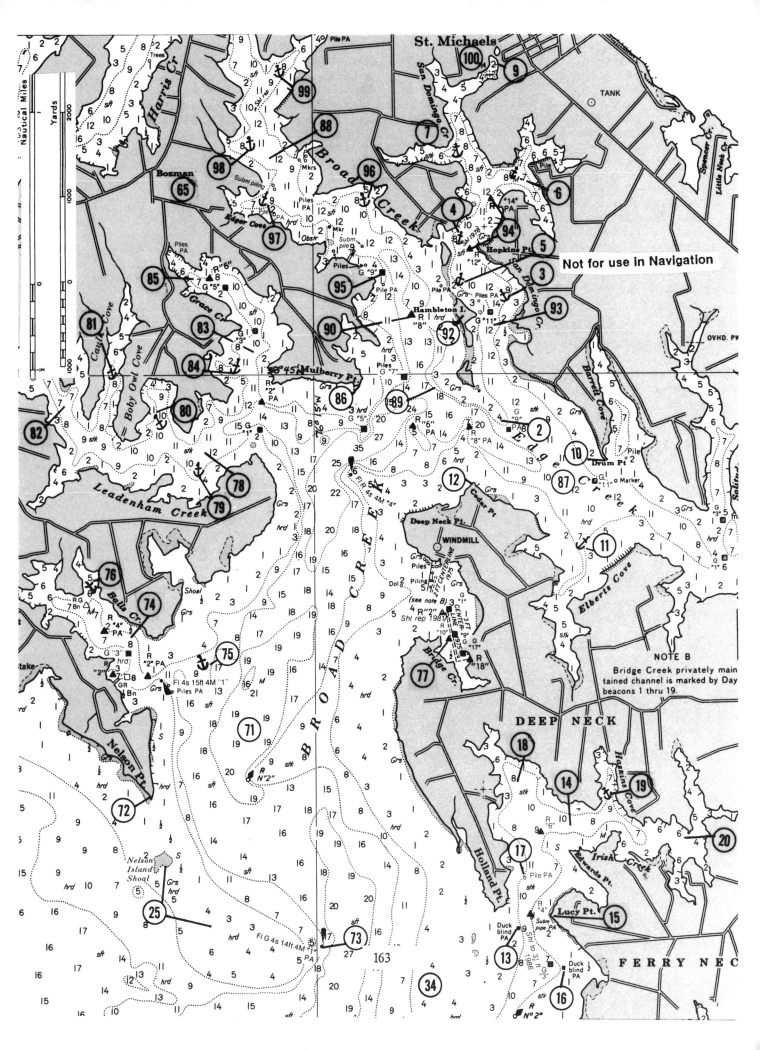

St. Michaels

Not for use in Navigation

NOTE B

Bridge Creek privately maintained channel is marked by Day
beacons 1 thru 19.

DEEP NECK

FERRY NEC

163

Leadenham Creek

There are several very nice anchorages in Leadenham Creek (78), enough for you to take your pick. The entrance is wide and marked, and "middle of the creek navigation" works well inside. The nicest anchorages are in the outer reaches. As you move farther west up Leadenham Creek, there will be homes and docks along the shore until it gets fairly busy.

The wide cove (79) just to the left (the southern shore) after you come in is very pretty. The ground seems higher than normal for the area, with woods and a beautiful rolling field to the south. There may be too much of a fetch to the northwest to suit your tastes, but the next good coves, both on the opposite bank, are close if you are worrying about thunderstorms or a front. Boby Owl Cove (80) and Caulk Cove (81) are both deep enough to tuck well in, and very pretty with woods and field ashore. There are houses inside and with the narrowness of the coves, some cruisers might feel too close. Boby Owl is not as deep, wider, and perhaps better suited for larger boats needing more swinging room. Caulk Cove, long and finger-like, gives you great protection if you don't mind the closeness. Rounding the bend (82) after Caulk Cove and heading up will bring you many more homes and docks until the feeling of congestion begins to set in.

Grace Creek

Sharing the same mouth as Leadenham Creek, Grace Creek (83) also has a fairly populated shoreline with many docks running out from homes.

With the traffic and the southeastern fetch of much of the creek, I would only consider anchoring in the cove to your left (84) (on the western bank) just past the entrance. You must tuck well up into this cove (carefully) in order to avoid the fetch with prevailing southeasterlies.

At the end of Grace Creek (85) are many work boats tied to docks and moored, and a commercial seafood house which buys from the commercial fishermen and crabbers. This is near the village of Bozman (65), where Harris Cove Bed and Boat on Harris Creek is located, just over the neck of land, about ¾ mile away by road.

Upper Broad Creek

Continuing up Broad Creek to Mulberry Point (86), you will have a nice choice of three different branches, Upper Broad Creek (88), San Domingo Creek (93), and Edge Creek (87).

First, we will go into Upper Broad Creek (88). Going in, rounding G "7," I found a hard shallow shoal (89) extending out from the shoaling area just to the southeast of and across the channel from Green "7." This was visible just under the surface at low water. It came up quickly from the deep water of the channel, and was much closer to the deep water than I expected from the chart. There is plenty of deep water to pass, but don't go too far east of the green mark.

Once past the outreaching shoal heading north towards R "8" (90), it is then easy to get confused by the fact that you are looking through the cut north of Hambleton Island (92) into San Domingo Creek (93). The red markers (94) in San Domingo Creek are clearly visible through the cut and appear to be markers for Broad Creek. Local boats sometimes pass through this cut, which can add to the confusion. Once around G "7," just look in a northerly direction for green "9" (95). It is easy to spot up the Broad Creek channel, and will clarify the course and help you to identify the next Broad Creek buoy R "8."

Like many other creeks, this upper branch has fewer homes

and prettier anchorage areas (96) (97) (98) near its lower reaches. Then the shoreline, particularly to the south, becomes congested with homes and docks. However, near the head, the homes thin out and there are quieter anchorages. The upper northeast branch (99), beyond the fork, is protected and nice, with less of the congestion that you passed below. I found less water than charted in this branch, but enough for 6 feet if you are careful.

San Domingo Creek

San Domingo Creek (93) is very nice for its protection and beauty, but is also particularly special because it provides a great quiet back door to St. Michaels (100). There are many homes in the creek, but there is also room to be uncrowded. When going in, be sure to round south of G "9" to avoid the long shoal (2) coming southeasterly off the tip of Hambleton Island (92). The island and its surrounding shoal look like a boot on the chart, and this particular shoal is the toe. The markers are not difficult to spot and the creek is not a difficult one to navigate.

The first nice spot to anchor is the broad cove (3) on the eastern bank of the creek, east of Hambleton Island, and to the northeast of G "11." Here you can tuck in outside the channel in fairly good holding. You'll watch the creek traffic go by, including that of upper Broad Creek through the cut north of the island. Hambleton Island was once much longer, but now it has washed through with several small humps remaining. The main island is wooded with some beach on its eastern shore. Off the northernmost island there is yet another anchorage (4), very pretty, but with only room for one or two boats. Here there is greater depth than charted in the little cove northeast of that island, and south of the mainland. I found 8 feet. The view is nice with the opening through to Upper Broad Creek offering air and a feeling of space, but the bar gives some protection.

You can also anchor farther south, just east of the main opening (5), but local boats scoot through, and it's more exposed to winds from the west or southwest.

There next appears to be a great anchoring spot in the three-pronged fork (6) to your right (on the eastern side) just after you pass R "14." However, this area is very populated with many houses with open yards down to the water. Though this is very well-protected, you will be anchoring in somebody else's backyard. But there are still other anchorages farther up the creek.

Many anchor just off (east of) the cove to your left (7) (on the western bank) or, if your draft is shallow enough, slightly up in that cove. The problem with going very far in is that many private docks line the shore. But there is generally enough room for most boats to anchor just far enough into the mouth of the cove to be out of the mainstream channel. Boats also anchor even farther north, to get closer access to St. Michaels. This is one of the best things about this creek.

St. Michaels is one of the very special villages on the Bay, with all sorts of supplies and provisioning available, as well as the museum and restaurants. And don't forget the ice cream. All of this is described in detail, with a walking map, in Chapter 10. St. Michaels harbor can be very congested and noisy, particularly on weekends or holidays. Many prefer to visit the town from this relatively quiet creek via "Chew Avenue" which ends at a work boat dock (9) in the final northeast fork of the creek. Anchor as close as your draft allows. Then dock your dinghy at the public landing at the very head of the fork. It is easily recognized by many work boats tied and anchored off. It would probably not be a good idea to anchor up in this last fork, although to do so would make for a shorter dinghy ride. The fork is very congested with work boats moored, many docks, and wrecks on the eastern shoal. It not only is too small and congested and busy for an anchorage, but there are many homes right at the water's edge. Though 4 feet is reported up in this fork, I had trouble finding much more than 3½ feet in spots. Most anchor in the main creek and leave their dinghy at the dock for the 5 to 10 minutes walk into town.

Edge Creek

Edge Creek (87) is shallow and can be very tricky. There are also many houses and docks. It certainly is a great place to live ashore, but I don't recommend as a cruising anchorage considering its shoaling difficulties, the often crowded shoreline, and the other nice spots nearby. If I did anchor here, I wouldn't want to go beyond Drum Point (10) and Elberts Cove (11) which is on the south side. This cove is very pretty with a tall hill and beautiful stand of trees on Cedar Point (12). I found deeper water in a wider area than the chart shows. Carefully feel your way in and be sure you have enough swinging room for your draft where you drop anchor. There is a long north and northwest fetch in Elberts Cove, making it hardly ideal for squalls and fronts.

IRISH CREEK
Refer to Chart #12266-C—"Broad Creek off the Choptank."
Pg. 163

The entrance is narrow and curvy, with shoaling in the channel to 3½ feet. The interior contains some pretty areas, but there are enough homes to make Irish Creek not very worthwhile given the risks of entering and other nearby anchoring possibilities.

The chart is very deceiving for the entrance to Irish Creek (14). Whenever there is a creek entrance with wide fetch into open water, beware of shoaling. If there are other entrances for longer creeks with stronger currents nearby, be even more concerned for shoaling. The open water into which the creek empties, and the currents crossing its mouth, make this shoal entrance very tricky and unpredictable.

Don't take more than 3½ feet draft in here, and then on half tide and rising the first time. Don't try it at all with an onshore wind that would set you farther up on the shoals if you bump. Locals maneuver boats of a little deeper draft, but they can keep up with the changes in the shoals. The duck blind (13) off Holland Point is where indicated on the chart, just to the west of Lucy Point (15), and should be kept well to your left (west). Duck blinds are usually built in very shallow water, and they are sometimes changed to suit hunting, not to suit navigators. The duck blind up in the cove (16) just south of Lucy Point will help, if it is still there when you pass through, to judge your position on the chart. The pile (17) is where indicated between Reds "4" and "6" and should also be kept to your left (west). Going in, watch the markers, go slowly, and sound carefully.

The cove (18) in the upper northwestern end of the creek looks fairly inviting as a possible anchorage until you see the long fetch if the wind comes up from a southerly direction. However, this cove is pretty with woods ashore and a large house with a white end and a steeple-like structure.

Haskins Cove (19), in the eastern fork, while more sheltered, is heavily built with many docks coming out from the shore and areas of stone rip rap. There is a large white house with six columns on the point to your left (northwest) coming around into this area. The land is a little higher in here than much of the rest of the creek and there are some woods. The far eastern end (20) of the eastern fork has many homes and docks and is relatively shallow except up close to the docks,

Carolyn Neale showing off her bucket of crabs, La Trappe Creek (pg. 180)

165

and would not make a good anchorage except for boats of less than 4 feet of draft that like a lot of company.

TRED AVON RIVER
Refer to Chart #12266-D—"Tred Avon River Entrance to Oxford and Plaindealing Creek."

This beautiful river winds inland from the historical town of Oxford at its mouth. The town has marina and repair facilities, historic sights, restaurants, and shops. Upriver are miles of scenic countryside, with creeks and coves full of anchorages to suit every taste. Most of it is well-settled, although the homes are not over-crowded.

There are various theories about the origin of the name "Tred Avon." One is that this developed over the ages from the term "third haven," used to describe this third area of refuge in the Choptank. You will notice many old houses on this river, which appear "telescoped" in nature because over the years additions were built to the usually smaller older sections.

Entrance
Entering the Tred Avon (21), note the shoal (22) coming well offshore of Benoni Point (23). Many come this way from Knapps Narrows, (Refer to Chart #12263-C), steering a straight compass course, 127°M, without giving due regard to that shoal or the shoal between Broad and Harris Creeks, and without compensating for the setting wind or current. Stay off both the markers for these shoals. If visibility is poor and you need a course, 130°M from Fl R "2" in the eastern Knapps Narrows approach channel, will take you to the vicinity of R "12A" (33) which is north of Todds Point. 120°M from R "12A" will take you to the vicinity of R "14." Choptank River Light (25), a solid structure 35 feet tall, is not difficult to spot in decent visibility. Benoni Point (23) has a notable house with a tower beside it. Coming in, this looks like an official lighthouse, but it is not. Pass well to the south and southeast of the 15-foot Fl G "1" (26) southeast of Benoni Point.

Rounding northerly into the Tred Avon, you will see to your right (east) the masts of sailboats in the very nice marina at **Bachelor Point Harbor (27).** This dredged basin has good docks and facilities, controlling depth 9 feet. The basin's entrance is jettied and well-marked. Be sure to give enough room to the shoal (28) west of Bachelor's Point. Inside you will find dockage with 80 slips taking boats up to 100 feet alongside, with electricity up to 50 amps, a portable pumpout station that will come to your slip, a nice pool, spacious shower facilities, a sandy beach outside the jetty, a repair and maintenance operation (no haulout), a well-stocked marine store, laundromat, block and cube ice, and Eastern Shore Yacht Charters (30). The distance to Oxford (29) is approximately 1½ miles. This is a nice place to stay unless you want to be right in the hustle and bustle of Oxford. Transportation to town should not be a problem with the friendly help of the marina.

Passing Bachelor Point, you will next see the **Pier Street Marina and Restaurant (31)** to your right (east). This restaurant is modestly priced. There is room at the docks in front for up to 100 feet with 10 feet depth, and complimentary dockage while dining in the restaurant. There are also docks and gas and diesel pumps behind the restaurant. They will take overnight transients with electricity up to 30 amps. Visa, Texaco, and MC are honored. Bulkheads protect the inner docks here, but there is a significant exposure to the west and southwest for the outside docks.

As you proceed on in a northerly direction, you will notice the homes and shops of Oxford off your right (east). There are several possible anchorages, and some nice marinas.

OXFORD AND TOWN CREEK
Refer to Chart #12266-D.

Town Creek goes south into the heart of Oxford. It is well-marked and heavily used. There are several marinas, some with excellent haulout and repair facilities. It is also possible to anchor in the creek, depending on draft and swinging room required. Oxford is a special town, of particular interest to those who like to browse among streets of quaint historical flavor. You can also anchor outside the creek.

Anchorage in the River outside Oxford
Coming in from the Choptank, as you round Fl R "2" and turn to the northeast and east, you will see the **Tred Avon Yacht Club (32)** docks, the ferry docks (33), and a beach (34) on the shore to your right (south) with "The Strand," a row of houses lining the shore above the beach. Many opt to anchor (35) in this area off the beach. The holding is not the best in

Tred Avon Yacht Club, Oxford

166

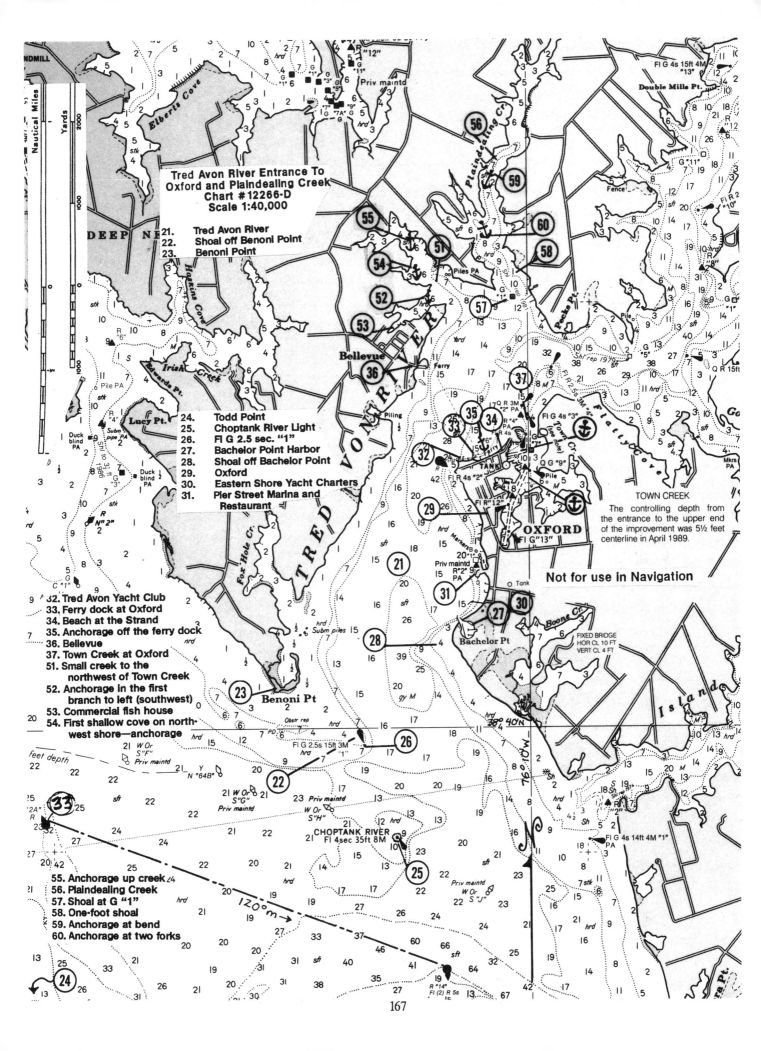

Tred Avon River Entrance To
Oxford and Plaindealing Creek
Chart #12266-D
Scale 1:40,000

21. Tred Avon River
22. Shoal off Benoni Point
23. Benoni Point

24. Todd Point
25. Choptank River Light
26. Fl G 2.5 sec. "1"
27. Bachelor Point Harbor
28. Shoal off Bachelor Point
29. Oxford
30. Eastern Shore Yacht Charters
31. Pier Street Marina and
     Restaurant

32. Tred Avon Yacht Club
33. Ferry dock at Oxford
34. Beach at the Strand
35. Anchorage off the ferry dock
36. Bellevue
37. Town Creek at Oxford
51. Small creek to the
     northwest of Town Creek
52. Anchorage in the first
     branch to left (southwest)
53. Commercial fish house
54. First shallow cove on north-
     west shore—anchorage

55. Anchorage up creek
56. Plaindealing Creek
57. Shoal at G "1"
58. One-foot shoal
59. Anchorage at bend
60. Anchorage at two forks

TOWN CREEK

The controlling depth from
the entrance to the upper end
of the improvement was 5½ feet
centerline in April 1989.

Not for use in Navigation

167

some spots here, with a lot of thin slimy soft mud and a fair amount of junk on the bottom. With care you can get a good bite. Between the ferry line and Town Creek Point, there are areas of good gray clay mixed with firm mud. The ferry that runs between Oxford (29) and Bellevue (36) regularly passes through the area, roughly on the dotted line denoted on the chart. Stay out of his way. You will see him pass if you wait a bit. The ferry has been running continuously here since 1683. This is a busy area. Keep well lit at night.

This area is not as protected as other possible anchorages nearby, but many storms have been survived here. The benefits of stopping at this anchorage are that there is often more breeze than up in Town Creek (37) or the others, and it is less crowded than Town Creek which may be very congested with traffic and anchored boats, and there is a beach here for landing. The sign on the beach, last year was written rather vaguely, but it seemed to indicate that while you could not do many things on the beach, such as launch a boat from the shore or have fires, dinghy landing is permitted. People regularly land here. Other nearby anchorages are described later in this chapter. These include Plaindealing Creek (56) and the cove (51) to its west.

Three hour docking is allowed on the outside of the ferry dock where the sign indicates. Ferry rates are: $1.50 for bikes, $.75 for walkers, and $4.50 for cars plus $.25 for each car passenger; all for one way. The ferry lands at Bellvue across the river, and there is not a great deal to do there except walk inland along the road. But those anchoring in Plaindealing Creek or the cove to its west may wish to take the ferry over to Oxford rather than cross in their dinghy.

Town Creek
Refer to our Sketch Chart—"Town Creek—Oxford"

To enter Town Creek (37), follow the markers, taking care to remain inside the narrow entrance channel. The first marina to your right (west) is **Mears Yacht Haven (38)**.

There is a Mears Point Marina at Kent Narrows, and if you are calling one or the other on VHF Channel 16, it is important that you identify which one you are calling. Mears Yacht Haven is a popular facility and has 96 slips, with dockage for boats to over 100 feet, maximum of 9 feet depth, 110 and 220 electricity, gas and diesel fuel, ice, a swimming pool, laundry and light hardware. Visa and MC are accepted. They advised that they do not have dinghy landing facilities for anchored boats.

The next facility to your right (west) is the **Oxford Boatyard (39)**. They have 82 slips with ability to take transient boats to 10 feet draft (be careful coming into the creek with 10 feet), lengths up to 120 feet, with electricity up to 50 amps at 220 volts. There is a full service yard here with a 75-ton lift with full hull and equipment repair, including rigging and carpentry and some electronics repair. There is a well-stocked marine store and various parts available as well as ice, snacks, and similar items. They are Westerbeke dealers. Visa and MC are honored.

Next up Town Creek to your right (west) is the well-known **Town Creek Restaurant (40)** easily identified by a large sign. They have 25 slips for transients and diners up to 100 feet with up to 50 amps electric, showers, head, and paddle boat rentals. Visa and MC are accepted here. This can be even busier than other facilities on weekends because of the popularity of the restaurant. There is also a place for tenders to dock for restaurant patrons. To the left of the restaurant as you land, is the Chesapeake Motor Yachts (41), a general brokerage agency and selling various new boat lines.

There is also a public launching ramp (42) next door to the restaurant, to its right as you face it from the water.

Many people anchor in the broad area (43) off the cove to the west of G "7" which contains the restaurant and Oxford Boatyard. While there is adequate depth for at least 6 feet of draft and some swinging room, it is very busy and sometimes there is not enough room to anchor here without swinging into other anchored boats or interfering with docking. Weekends

Windsurfer off public beach, The Strand, Oxford. Anchorage off town in background

Town Creek ~ Oxford

Not for use in Navigation

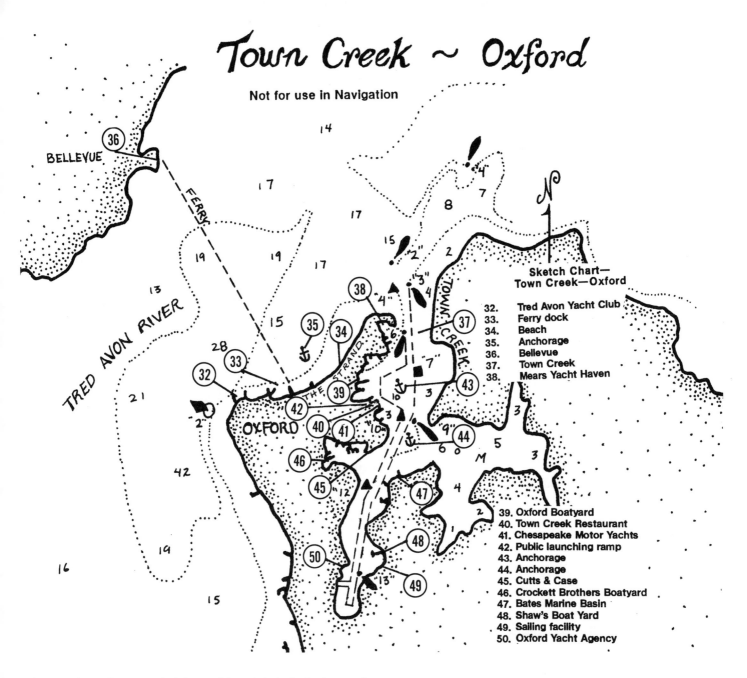

**Sketch Chart—
Town Creek—Oxford**

32. Tred Avon Yacht Club
33. Ferry dock
34. Beach
35. Anchorage
36. Bellevue
37. Town Creek
38. Mears Yacht Haven

39. Oxford Boatyard
40. Town Creek Restaurant
41. Chesapeake Motor Yachts
42. Public launching ramp
43. Anchorage
44. Anchorage
45. Cutts & Case
46. Crockett Brothers Boatyard
47. Bates Marine Basin
48. Shaw's Boat Yard
49. Sailing facility
50. Oxford Yacht Agency

are incredibly crowded here, although it isn't slack even in mid-week. Keep well lit at night.

Proceeding on up the creek, a busy cove will open to your right (west) between G "9" and R "10." Some boats anchor **(44)** off this cove east of the channel and a little to the north of the western cove. This can be fairly tight, since you don't want to swing aground and don't want to be in the channel. The less draft you have, the more you can tuck into the eastern cove and be out of the traffic. Boats of 6 and 7 feet draft may find the area very tight for anchoring.

Rounding just before R "10," to your right (west) into this busy cove, you will see the well-known traditional and modern boat building and repair yard, **Cutts & Case, Inc. (45)** on the northern bank of the cove. There is a small sign on their docks, and a large sign on a red building in the yard. This yard has been building fine wooden yachts for many years, but they are also repair yachts of any material with a very complete yard and shop facilities and skilled craftsman. There is a railway and crane. The yard will take transients if it has a room,

with only around 15 amps generally available on the docks. They invite visitors to see their work, which includes classic yacht building with modern materials. The office is located in an ancient looking small building with a very low ceiling. The sign on the front states: "Byberry House, 1695, oldest house in Oxford."

Inside the cove along its western and northern shore lies **Crockett Brothers Boatyard (46).** There are 64 open slips and 11 covered slips in this large marina with up to 30 amps electric, controlling depth 6 feet. The largest slip is 50 feet but they can handle longer boats alongside. Crockett Brothers Boatyard has been around for a long time. They have a full service haulout and repair service, marina, and well-stocked ship's store including books, clothing, marine hardware and parts, propane and CNG refills, block and cube ice, laundry, a pumpout, and an oil recycling facility. The marina has a very nice floating dinghy dock for its store customers. They sell NOS Charts, Notices to Mariners, and there are bike rentals within walking distance.

The yard has a 30-ton lift with full hull and engine repair, and there is always a mechanic available on weekends in season. Visa, Amex, and Discover are accepted. The post office is about a block's walk up the street, and many other inshore destinations are very close walking from here.

Up the Creek from this cove, and to your left (east), is the **Bates Marine Basin (47)**, identified by a sign. There are transient docks with 8 feet depth, 100 feet alongside, and electricity up to 50 amps. There is a 20-ton lift with yard and repair services, and brokerage. The marina has gas and diesel, laundry, some supplies, and may lend you a bike if one is available. They advise that on weekends they provide transportation to the other side of the creek where the main area of town is to be found. Visa, MC, and Amex are taken.

Next up the creek and also to your left (east) is **Shaw's Boat Yard (48)**, with an obvious sign. It is just to the left of and north of G "13." They have 6 feet depth at the end docks with transient capability of up to 50 feet and up to 30 amps electricity in their 35 slips. There is a small marine store with some hardware, ice, and a laundry. There is a 30-foot 10-ton crane and a 12-ton lift. There is no fuel dock. Daysailers and small boats are available for rent here.

Looking south upstream, you will see to your right the docks and facilities of the **Oxford Yacht Agency, Inc. (50)**. For many years specializing in selling and outfitting Grand Banks, new and used, they now also sell Kadey-Krogen. There are docks available, but they are usually taken by the boats in for work or sale. They have a 50-ton railway and do full yard work on their boats.

History of Oxford

Records indicate that Oxford was founded in 1683, although, as is often the case, there probably existed a village earlier. Originally, it and Annapolis (then called Anne Arundel Town) were the only two official ports of entry for the Maryland Colony. Oxford prospered as a seaport and center of many activities until after the Revolutionary War. British ships regularly stopped here carrying the goods from Europe and the East to supply the needs of the colonists. Many important people lived here and influenced the times. These included Robert Morris, known as the financier of the Revolution, Matthew Tilghman, whom many colonists considered to be the patriarch of Maryland, and Colonel Tench Tilghman, who served as George Washington's aide-de-camp.

After the Revolution, the fortunes of Oxford fell drastically. Without the foreign trade, the town lost much of its prosperity and became a ghost of its former self.

After around 100 years of inactivity, Oxford became prosperous again as the Chesapeake's seafood industry picked up with greater demands and better canning and packing processes. A railroad on the Eastern Shore was of great value.

As the seafood industry dwindled around the early 20th century, so did the fortunes of the town until it once again became a quiet little village. More recently, Oxford has embraced the tourist business and many bed and breakfast inns and historical sights have made it a great attraction for those from the "other side." The opening of the Chesapeake Bay Bridge in 1952 played a major role here, as in the entire area. Today, boats fill the harbor and marinas on weekends, and tourists by car often flood the shops and establishments.

Oxford Ashore

Inland from Town Creek or the beach, within a few blocks walking distance, are numerous buildings of historical interest, collectibles and souvenir shops, and some good restaurants. There isn't really a focal point to begin a walk in Oxford. You

Robert Morris Inn, Oxford

OXFORD

Not for use in Navigation

TRED AVON RIVER

Oxford—Town Sketch Map

1. **Customs House**
   (reconstruction)
2. **Robert Morris Inn**
3. **The Towne Shoppe**
4. **Grapevine House (1798)**
5. **Barnaby House (1770's)**
6. **Academy House**
   (Bratt Mansion)
7. Irish Creek Trading Company
8. 1876 Limosine Servive
9. Town Office
10. Oxford Mews, Bike Boatique
11. Doc's Quick Shop Market
12. Park
13. Oxford Museum & Library
14. Playground & tennis courts
15. Oxford Inn & Pope's Tavern
16. Maryland National Bank
17. Oxford Community Center
18. Fire Department
19. Post Office
20. Yardarm Seafood/Oxford
    Pizza
21. The Masthead (restaurant)
22. The Tender Herb
    (herb & gift shop)
23. Ship's Store—nautical
    supplies and boutique
27. Bachelor Point Harbor Marina
30. Eastern Shore Yacht Charters
31. Pier Street Marina &
    Restaurant
32. Tred Avon Yacht Club
33. Oxford Bellevue Ferry
34. Beach & park
38. Mears Yacht Haven
39. Oxford Boat Yard
40. Town Creek Restaurant
41. Chesapeake Motor Yachts
42. Public Launching Ramp
45. Cutts & Case
    "Byberry House"—(1695)
    "Calico"—cottage—
    (early 1700s)
46. Crockett Brothers Boatyard
47. Bates Marine Basin & Oxford
    Marine, Inc.
48. Shaw's Boat Yard
49. Sailing facility
50. Oxford Yacht Agency

may be starting from one of the marinas or from the beach. Oxford town, in its own way, rambles around within its three shores, with businesses intermixed with private homes.

Refer to our Sketch Map—"Oxford Town Map." Pg. 171

If you land on the beach (34), a southerly walk down N. Morris Street, or a diversion of a few blocks east down Tilghman, Wilson, Market, and High Streets, will bring you to many of the town's attractions. You will first see the old Customs House (1), a replica of the first federal customs house built by the first federal collector of customs. Across the corner, the Robert Morris Inn (2), has long been known for its lodgings and dining. Like many inns of the area, it has some very early style and decoration. Many rooms share baths, and there are neither TVs nor telephones in each room. Walking down one of the hallways upstairs, you notice that the first floor shifts levels slightly. This is because of an ancient addition. The well-known restaurant on the first floor serves on first come, first served basis.

Continuing on brings you to various souvenir, gift, nick-nack, and "everything" shops such as the Towne Shoppe (3), the Tender Herb Shop (22), and the Irish Creek Trading Company (7). Doc's Quick Shop Mart (11) is a small convenience store, and quite handy.

The Oxford Museum (13), on Morris and Market Streets, is open seasonally on weekends or by appointment, and houses artifacts and memorabilia from Oxford's past. This entire area is of historical significance, as you will see and feel while on your walk. The Grapevine House (4) (private residence) at 309 Morris Street built in 1798, has a grapevine in front which was bought over from the Isle of Jersey in early 1890s. The Barnaby House (5) (private residence) at 212 N. Morris St. was built in the 1770s.

The post office (19) is on Wilson and Bank Streets, and the Town Commisioner's Office (9) is at 100 N. Morris Street.

Bike rentals are available in Oxford from the "Oxford Mews, Bike Boatique" (10), 105 Morris Street. Any of the marinas will put you in touch. Eastern Shore Yacht Charters, located at Bachelor Point Harbor south of Oxford (**#27 on Chart 12266-D** earlier in this chapter), charter both sail and power up to 45 feet, bareboat or captained.

You can get good pizzas and seafood at Yardarm Seafood/Oxford Pizza (20), less than a block from the beach on 103 Mill Street. They have carry-out and will deliver to your anchored boat. The 1876 Limousine Service (8), on 110 N Morris Street, will transport you to other points.

There are many other fine businesses in the area. The walking map will give you some ideas. Crockett Brothers has its own very helpful map oriented to the interests of boaters, and the Oxford Business Association publishes a pamphlet which can be obtained at most marinas. One of the great things about Oxford is that it is almost all within a few blocks from the beach or the creek.

OTHER ANCHORAGES IN THE TRED AVON RIVER
Refer to Chart #12266-D—"Tred Avon River Entrance to Oxford and Plaindealing Creek." Pg. 167

Creek Opposite Town Creek

The small creek (51) northwest of Town Creek presents an alternative to anchoring in the hustle and bustle of Oxford. The dinghy ride from here to Oxford is short. There is 4 feet well up the first branch to your left (52) (southwest). With a 5-foot draft, you must anchor nearer the mouth of this southwest branch, but can still get some protection here. Depending on draft, you can anchor inside this branch to avoid altogether the southeasterly fetch. At the head of this branch, there is a commercial fish house (53) with numerous workboats tied and moored off. There is a lot of work boat congestion and traffic up in this branch, and it may be busier than you like. If you get permission to tie the dinghy at the docks at the fish house, the walk to the Bellevue ferry (36) is 10 to 15 minutes. Also the dinghy trip to the actual ferry docks at Bellevue is a short distance down the river, as noted on the chart. The ferry run across to town is a fun trip. There is a park in Bellevue near the ferry dock, with a concrete launching ramp and fishing area.

If the southwest branch is too busy for you, there is 6 feet depth and more swinging room at the mouth of the first shallow cove (54) on the northwest shore of this creek. There are docks on the shore to the east here, and piles to the southwest

Ferry boat Talbot leaving Oxford for Bellevue

of the center bank of the cove. Anchoring just off the middle of the creek should keep the boat clear of these. This gives little protection from the southeast. More protection is available if you draw 5 feet or less and head farther up the creek (55). There are many houses and docks along the shore, especially on the eastern side, but many still prefer this to the crowded anchorages off Oxford.

Plaindealing Creek
Refer to Chart #12266-D. Pg.167

Many anchor in Plaindealing Creek (56) because it is just across from Oxford and not as busy. It is not much farther away from Oxford than the creek described above, but it is easier for larger boats. There is good protection and holding, but with the abundance of houses close to shore, and many docks, I feel a distinct lack of privacy in this relatively narrow creek. When coming in, avoid the shoal coming out to the west of G "1" (57). After passing the marker, there is a tendency to round to the left (northwest) because of the 1-foot shoal (58) on the shore to your right (east). If you round too soon, you will find that the first shoal to the left continues on past G "1." Therefore, proceed slowly and carefully, not turning more northwesterly until well past this outside green marker.

My favorite area in this creek is in the slight bend (59) in the creek just past the two forks to your left (on the western side). Here it is not as crowded ashore as it is closer to the mouth or farther up. I found barely the 7 feet depth indicated. There are houses on the bank to the east but they are set back. The bending bank to the west has trees and woods. Woods predominate the view up the creek, and the town of Oxford with its many sailboat masts presents a nice view in the distance down the creek and across the river. The channel in Plaindealing Creek is narrow, and circling before anchoring may avoid awakening the next morning to an unexpected list. The creek is broader out from the two forks (60) on the west bank just before you come in, but there is less protection here and more houses. Moving slightly up into the basin formed by those forks brings considerably more protection.

Goldsborough Creek
Refer to Chart #12266-E—"Upper Tred Avon, Goldsborough Creek to Easton." Pg.175

After all the houses and shops and marinas of Oxford, it is nice to find a creek where you see and smell woods, marsh and cornfields. Goldsborough Creek (61) is one of the prettiest, least developed creeks on the river. Many avoid it because of the tricky entrance, but it provides good protection in beautiful and natural surroundings.

I find my way in by lining up the cove behind me (62) and a distinctive small house (63) inside Goldsborough Creek. Off the entrance to Goldsborough Creek you will see a cove on the opposite (northwest) side of the river with two large houses (64). The first one is on the point protruding sharply from the western shore of the cove. It is gray and its two stories sit on brick pillars to raise it high above the low ground. There is a rounded section of bay windows in front. The second large house is back in the cove and to the right (east) of the first house as you look in. This also appears grayish and has peaked windows on the second floor and a dock in front with slip and boat lift. The center of the cove is just to the right (east) of these houses as you look into the cove. Use the houses as a frame of reference for the center of the cove (62) as you move away from the cove while heading up into Goldsborough Creek.

Looking into Goldsborough, you will see, far in to the southeast, the triangular roof of a small home nestled in the trees. In the center of this triangle appears one square window. Below the triangle is a sloped roof to a porch, but this is difficult to see until close. To the right (west) of this triangle roof is a field, and the yard from another house appears off to its left (east). I put the center of the cove with the two houses (on the opposite side) on my stern and the triangular roof ahead, and never saw less than 9 feet depth. I did notice that as I passed the little point and crook on the northeastern bank (65) (under the "G" in "Goldsborough" on the chart) that the water was beginning to shoal, and I headed to my right (south) a little here.

Anchoring where the creek turns to the east (66) presents an incredible view, especially looking up the creek. You may wish to continue east, heading up into the main branch. Six feet draft is the maximum to be comfortable here. There is a large boathouse (68) on the northern shore up in a cove. Pass the boathouse and anchor before the split in the creek (69). I found 6 feet almost to the split. The view here is of corn fields, forests, swamps, and the smell is of nature. It is quiet and there is a feeling of isolation. If you have less draft and round the branch (70) to your right (south) at the fork, you will find homes and docks. The chart has private markers (71) noted. These were wooden stakes, and not in good state of repair when I was last there, but were apparently intended to be kept to your right. As usual, the problem with private markers is that they are often not moved as the bottom changes. Unless they look new, I treat them with caution.

The upper reaches of this creek are also pretty but not as nice as the area described above. The number of small homes increase slightly, but the area at the last fork is quite pretty with marshy shores and forest set back behind the lowlands.

Trippe Creek
Entering Trippe Creek (72), pass well around R "6" and head into the creek far enough south of G "1" to avoid the 5-foot shoal (73) to the west of that marker. Most boats "go in the middle" with no problem. The first (74) two coves to your left are nice, the second, "Snug Harbor" (75) being "snugger," but they are both built up with homes and feel crowded when you anchor there.

A conspicuous red brick house with a red seawall in front sits on the far point (76) of Snug Harbor Cove, ahead of you to the northeast as you go in. This will be obvious as you come in the creek. Opposite that, to the right (southern side) of Trippe Creek, is a three-stepped red wall going down to the water on Deepwater Point (77) with a sculpture garden on the point. All of this hides Pirate's Cove until you round the point and see the broad and popular anchorage. It is so named because it was reputed as a hideout for pirates of long ago. Most boats anchor in the open outside area of Pirate's Cove (78). The scenery is pretty, holding is good, there is a lot of room for your neighbor to drag before he snags you! The houses are unobtrusive, and the breezes are better. It is possible to go much farther in up to the mouth of the creek at the head (southern end) of the cove. This brings more protection, but you are closer to the houses and docks ashore. I found 6 feet outside the mouth area of inner Pirate's Cove with 3 feet in the mouth and less inside. Local boats of at least 3 feet were regularly using the inner Pirate's Cove. Straight ahead to the south is a beach (79) with trees behind.

Farther east from Pirate's Cove on the north shore of the

Trippe Creek, is Haskins Cove (80) with a nice surrounding of woods and marsh. There are the ruins of a duck blind (81) on the eastern side of the cove after you enter. Usually these sit in shallower water, near the drop off. I found 5 feet a little past (to the north of) this point. There are a few houses in the area, but overall, if you have a draft to get in, you will love the natural surroundings. The woods and the marsh at the head of the cove are lush and deep, with a hint of wilderness isolation.

Many cruising boats don't proceed much farther up Trippe Creek, but the local folks do regularly, taking in boats of 3 to 4 feet draft close to the end where there are many homes with private docks and pretty scenery. Depending on your draft, it is worthwhile to explore further, at least by dinghy. A huge mansion (82) dominates the hill straight ahead to the east as you round the point across from Haskins Cove (83). The area before (to the west of) this mansion would make a pretty anchorage, with a distinct feeling of the old South with the mansion and rolling green hills and woods around. However I found there to be somewhat less water getting around the point (opposite Haskins Cove) than the chart showed. Usually points are to be well-cleared, and the chart here correctly shows a shallow bar coming out north. There is a duck blind (83) toward the end of the bar. I found it necessary to round well north of the duck blind. The problem occurred just beyond this shoal where the shallow water on the bank to the left (85) (the northern bank) seemed to extend more than indicated. I've shown a dotted line to indicate the limits of this shoal last year. By proceeding cautiously and rounding southeasterly soon after I cleared the point on the southern bank, I found 6 feet in the basin area (86) before the mansion, surrounded by hills, trees, field, and marsh.

Cove Opposite R "8"

In the wide cove on the western bank of the Tred Avon (88), across from R "8," you'll find a nice feeling of privacy, despite the civilization of the river. There is also beautiful scenery at this anchorage. There is a long beach on the western shore, gently U-shaped with the cove. Behind the beach are trees, marsh, and field. Looking across the river one again sees trees. I found 6 feet fairly close to the beach. Two houses are visible upstream, but they are so far away that they don't spoil the feeling of privacy. Some might wish a more protected anchorage, but if you are looking for some open air, great scenery, and a break from all the houses ashore, this could be your spot. On weekends there is a lot of wake here from boats going up and down river.

Cove Northwest of R "10"

This pretty cove, northwest (89) of R "10," has two large houses but they are beautiful. Woods and field predominate making a nice anchorage giving fair protection. Heading straight in, you pass a large white home to your right on the northern bank with a large dock in front. I found 7 feet off this, back inside the opposite point to the south. Farther in, the cove divides into two forks (90). A large home with three sets of double columns graces the point between these forks. The view from the fork up the northern branch is beautiful with trees and marsh. I found 6 feet up to the area off the fork division. A fence blocks off the west fork. There is a beach on the southern shore opposite the first house, but it displayed a posted sign. Trees hide a field behind the beach.

Cove East of R "12"

North past Trippe Creek, there is a small tuck-in cove (91) east of R "12." It provides fair protection if draft allows you to get in far enough and it is a pretty spot. I went in upstream (northeast) of R "12" and headed to the marsh area (92). There is a small creek behind this marsh, just noticeable through binoculars. This is just to the left of a house with dock and covered boat lift and boat house that you will see in an easterly direction as you come in. This took me past the shoal area to east of the marker. To your right on the southwestern point of the cove stands a large two-story gray house with a little steeple or watch tower on the roof and a double boat house. I found 6 feet in past this house, far enough in to afford protection from the south.

Maxmore Creek

Maxmore Creek (93) branching to the north off the Tred Avon River, is very pretty. There's a long shoal extending east off Long Point (94) coming in, and another shoal extending west from the shore shortly after that. Other shoals inside are not as well-defined on the chart. Maxmore Creek has barely over 6 feet in much of its waters at high tide, and is well-settled with pretty homes. Because of the difficulty getting in and because anchoring would be in close proximity to so many back yards, I prefer to anchor in many other easier and more isolated creeks.

Peachblossom Creek

Peachblossom (96) is a fairly popular creek, although it is quite built up ashore, is short on secluded coves, and is a little tricky getting in.

The chart indicates two areas of "obstruction reported" (97). I always hate this when there are no markers on the "obstructions reported." I have read much about going aground entering the creek, and since many people seem to like it, I attempted to find the obstructions and/or shoals. After an hour or so of criss-crossing, I was certain only of shoals. Several routes and ranges fetched up around 6 feet, but the following directions got me at least 7 feet depth all the way to the first anchorage area.

While in the Tred Avon River, look to the western side of the river (behind you as you go in). Over there you will see two houses (98). The upriver (northernmost) house appears mostly single-story with a two-story section on its northern end. There is a porch in front. The second house is downstream of the first (to the south of it) with a brown roof, two chimneys, and a section of V-roof with a window on its southern end. Between these two houses is a very pretty clump of woods. I lined up my stern with the middle of those woods between the houses and headed into Peachblossom Creek to a clump of trees with one tall tree in the middle (99). This clump ahead is on the eastern side of the cove out from the first creek to your right (south). The clump is rather distinctive, with the tall tree in the middle. Many people like to anchor in the cove (100). On this line I found no less than 7 feet. The GPS derived coordinates for my taking off point (1) in the Tred Avon Channel off R "16" is 38°44.25'N by 76°07.32'W.

Up in this cove (100) I found approximately 7 feet depth but it shallowed soon. However, this makes a very pretty anchorage with room for breeze.

In Le Gates Cove (2) on the northern shore, I found 6 feet depths with 8 feet outside. This cove, while more protected, has more houses close to the water than many would like. Soon after entering the Peachblossom Creek, you will see a bridge (3) up ahead with vertical clearance of 6 feet. Go in as far (4) as your draft allows, although the creek continues to be more

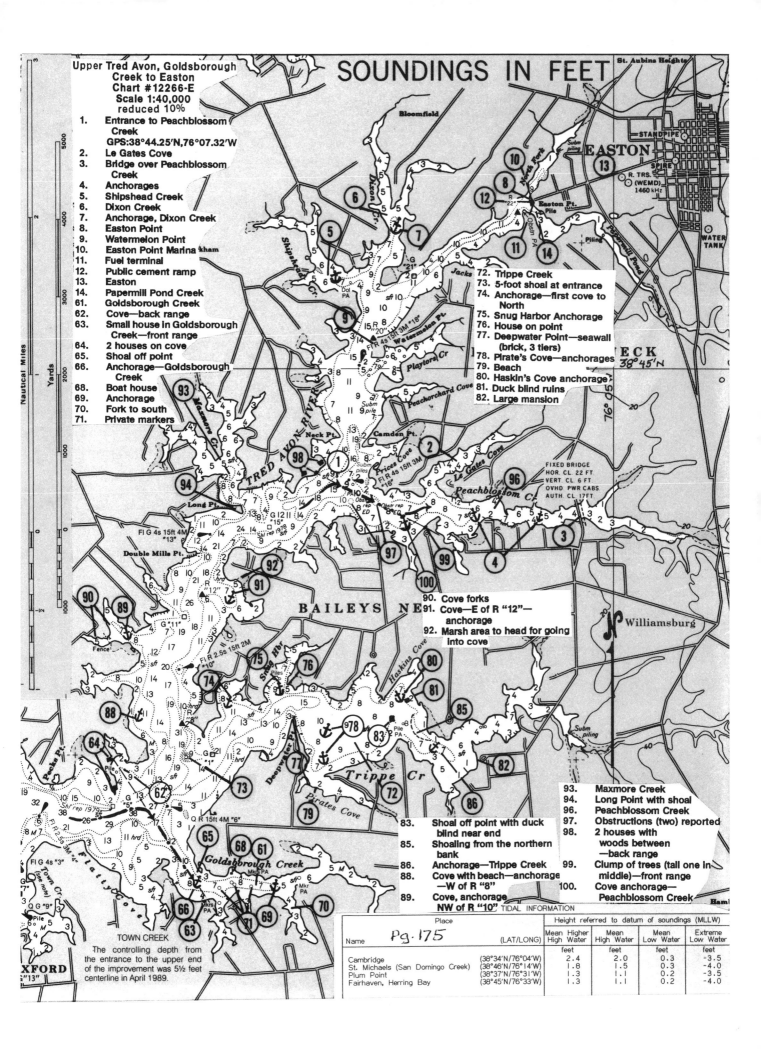

SOUNDINGS IN FEET

Upper Tred Avon, Goldsborough Creek to Easton
Chart #12266-E
Scale 1:40,000
reduced 10%

1. Entrance to Peachblossom Creek
   GPS:38°44.25'N,76°07.32'W
2. Le Gates Cove
3. Bridge over Peachblossom Creek
4. Anchorages
5. Shipshead Creek
6. Dixon Creek
7. Anchorage, Dixon Creek
8. Easton Point
9. Watermelon Point
10. Easton Point Marina
11. Fuel terminal
12. Public cement ramp
13. Easton
14. Papermill Pond Creek
61. Goldsborough Creek
62. Cove—back range
63. Small house in Goldsborough Creek—front range
64. 2 houses on cove
65. Shoal off point
66. Anchorage—Goldsborough Creek
68. Boat house
69. Anchorage
70. Fork to south
71. Private markers

72. Trippe Creek
73. 5-foot shoal at entrance
74. Anchorage—first cove to North
75. Snug Harbor Anchorage
76. House on point
77. Deepwater Point—seawall (brick, 3 tiers)
78. Pirate's Cove—anchorages
79. Beach
80. Haskin's Cove anchorage
81. Duck blind ruins
82. Large mansion

90. Cove forks
91. Cove—E of R "12"— anchorage
92. Marsh area to head for going into cove

83. Shoal off point with duck blind near end
85. Shoaling from the northern bank
86. Anchorage—Trippe Creek
88. Cove with beach—anchorage —W of R "8"
89. Cove, anchorage NW of R "10"

93. Maxmore Creek
94. Long Point with shoal Peachblossom Creek
96. Obstructions (two) reported
97. 2 houses with woods between —back range
99. Clump of trees (tall one in middle)—front range
100. Cove anchorage— Peachblossom Creek

The controlling depth from the entrance to the upper end of the improvement was 5½ feet centerline in April 1989.

FIXED BRIDGE
HOR. CL. 22 FT.
VERT. CL. 6 FT.
OVHD PWR CABS
AUTH. CL. 17 FT.

TIDAL INFORMATION

Place		Height referred to datum of soundings (MLLW)			
Name	(LAT/LONG)	Mean Higher High Water	Mean High Water	Mean Low Water	Extreme Low Water
		feet	feet	feet	feet
Cambridge	(38°34'N/76°04'W)	2.4	2.0	0.3	-3.5
St. Michaels (San Domingo Creek)	(38°46'N/76°14'W)	1.8	1.5	0.3	-4.0
Plum Point	(38°37'N/76°31'W)	1.3	1.1	0.2	-3.5
Fairhaven, Herring Bay	(38°45'N/76°33'W)	1.3	1.1	0.2	-4.0

Pg. 175

populated upstream, is narrow, and not as nice as downstream anchorages.

Shipshead and Dixon Creeks

Shipshead Creek (5) is well-settled with nice homes and docks. Dixon Creek (6) has less housing, is easy and nice, and is around 7 feet deep where it widens just before the fork, making a pretty area to anchor (7). A strong norther will temporarily reduce depth in these two creeks.

Upper Tred Avon

The river up to Easton Point (8) is well-traveled with many nice homes ashore and fields. There is a fair amount of forest, but this area has long been settled to much greater density than other sections in the area, though it is still rural. The river narrows considerably as you head to the right (northeasterly) past Watermelon Point (9), but it is still deep. Tug and barge traffic go to Easton Point regularly. Easton Point contains a fuel terminal and a small but very nice marina by that name.

Easton Point Marina (10) has 25 slips up to 40 feet long, with reasonable rates. Boats drawing more than 6 feet should not go up here because of the shallow spots that seem to snag the unwary downstream. Electrical pedestals on the dock have service up to 50 amps. They have a 12-ton lift, 5-ton forklift, and general repair, and are Seagull dealers. The marine store has a nice assortment of practical hardware, NOS charts, and block and cube ice. The small snack bar has a menu posted on the wall and a community table. The store office has a cast iron stove in the middle, reminiscent of the old days. The marina will help obtain sail and canvas repair and other services available in nearby Easton. They sell bait and tackle, and gas, diesel and K1 kerosene. There is also a launch available here for towing, and they will haul boats over land. Call ahead for a reservation to be assured of space. Visa and MC are honored. They will be helpful in arranging transportations to destinations in Easton.

The fuel terminal (11) is to the east (right) of the marina. They sell gas, diesel, and beverages.

For all practical cruising purposes, the Tred Avon River ends just upstream from the barge docks next to the marina. There is a public cement ramp (12) next to the marina. This is as close as you can get to the town of Easton (13) in a cruis-ing boat. I don't recommend the walk to town, about 1½ miles. Many taking this walk have found that they would rather take their exercise elsewhere. The very helpful and friendly marina can arrange transportation if you wish to explore Easton. The Rustic Inn of Easton restaurant will pick you up. Their entrees are from around $13 to $20 and they enjoy a good reputation. The Historical Society of Talbot County has a walking map of the town. There is also a business map produced by the Downtown Merchant's Association. There is hope that sometime in the future the boating community will have better access to this very nice area. There are other good restaurants, shops, and lodging facilities in this historical town.

The Eastern Shore Limousine Service, Inc. serves Easton and many other Eastern Shore areas. Call (410) 820-8431. There is also a bike rental called Eastern Shore Cycle & Ski on the corner of Dover and Washington Street at 822-4300. This is one block from the well-known and historical Tidewater Inn. The Historical Society of Talbot County, located in Easton at 25 South Washington Street, (822-0733) conducts various tours of the area.

It is possible to anchor just inside Papermill Pond Creek (14) just east of fuel depot, but there is a work boat dock inside and the area could be quite busy. This creek is deeper than the chart indicates up to the basin just beyond these docks, but depth is only 3 feet. The best bet would be to tie up if you want to visit Easton. Anchoring in the narrow river down to Watermelon Point (9) could prove tight if a tug and barge come through.

THE CHOPTANK FROM THE TRED AVON TO CAMBRIDGE
Refer to Chart #12263-E—"Regional Chart—Eastern Choptank River; Eastern Little Choptank River."

Heading southeast up the Choptank after leaving the Tred Avon is an exciting experience. You will have already had such great cruising on this river that you will feel that it must be about "petered out." But as you look up the wide river and realize that there is still to come such an incredible diversity of gunkholes, civilization, and upper river reaches, it becomes breathtaking. The first of many pretty creeks quickly comes up to your left, on the northern bank.

Oxford Boatyard has good repair facilities (pg. 168)

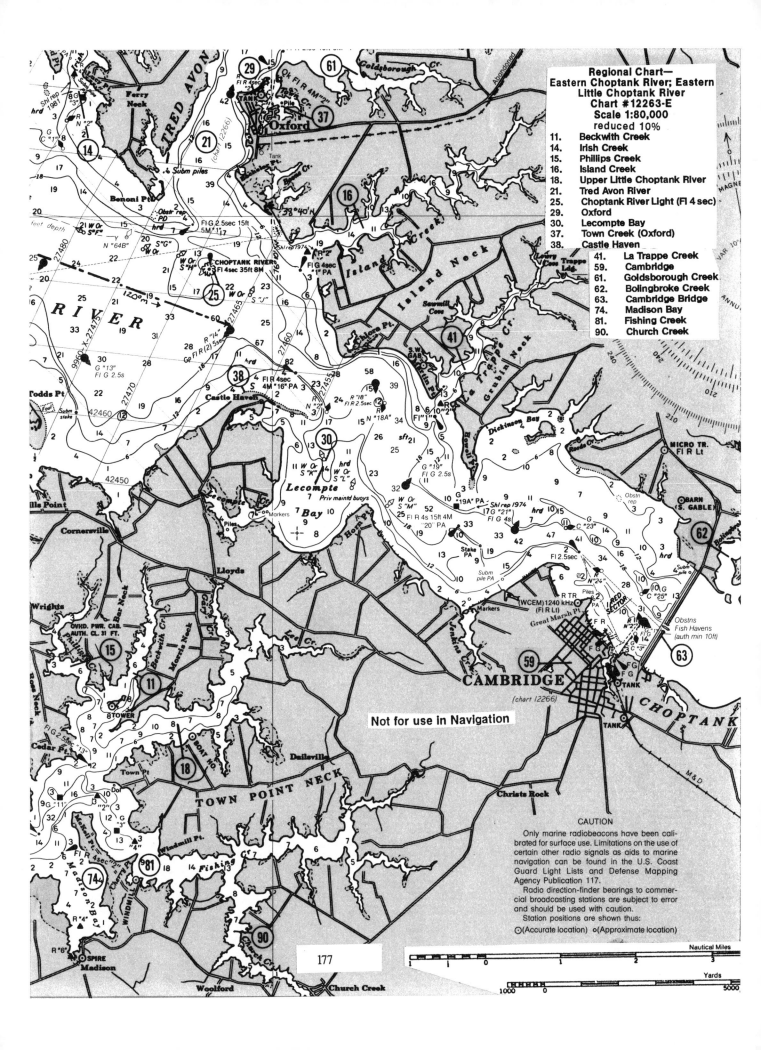

Regional Chart—
Eastern Choptank River; Eastern
Little Choptank River
Chart #12263-E
Scale 1:80,000
reduced 10%

CAMBRIDGE
(chart 12266)

CAUTION

Only marine radiobeacons have been calibrated for surface use. Limitations on the use of
certain other radio signals as aids to marine
navigation can be found in the U.S. Coast
Guard Light Lists and Defense Mapping
Agency Publication 117.

Radio direction-finder bearings to commercial broadcasting stations are subject to error
and should be used with caution.

Station positions are shown thus:

⊙(Accurate location) o(Approximate location)

Nautical Miles

Yards

177

Island Creek
Refer to Chart #12266-F—"Island Creek."

This is a very beautiful creek (16) with deep water, protected coves, and sylvan scenery. The entrance has a shoaling bar, and is subject to changes. Boats drawing 5 feet get in, I recommend that strangers not try it with more than 4 feet draft.

Despite its 14-foot height, finding Island Creek (16) entrance buoy Fl G "1" (15) can be a little difficult, as it blends into the shoreline. The GPS derived coordinates are 38°39.31′N by 76°09.53′W. A course of 60°M from R "14" (17) out in the Choptank channel and to the north of Castle Haven Point (38) will take you to the vicinity of Fl G "1." Castle Haven Point (38) is shown on **Regional Chart #12263-E**.

I spent well over an hour criss-crossing this entrance attempting to find some area of deep water that would enable me to bring in 6-feet draft. What I found convinced me that I would not think of taking in anything over 4 feet on half tide and rising, and with no onshore wind to create swells. This is yet another example of how long fetches can shoal the entrances of otherwise deep creeks. I watched numerous boats with 4½ to 6 feet draft try to go in. The shallower boats made it by following the markers, most others did not. Many tried all sorts of "tricks" that they said they had learned from various sources. None of these worked while I watched. In sounding, I found fingers of shoal reaching into the channel, up and down its course in the critical area between Fl G "1" and R "2" (18). Follow the markers, go carefully, and don't take more than 4 feet in. The creek is beautiful, but don't let it entice you in unless you have a draft for it. The boats going aground all reported that the bottom was hard sand, not soft mud.

The first large cove (19) to your right (on the southern shore) after you enter is nicely tucked in east of a point with a beach (20). A green house with a boathouse also sits on this point. Farther in the cove, the water continues fairly deep almost up to the southern shore, where reigns a pretty brown house high on a hill flanked by green field and woods. Neither of these homes impair your feeling of privacy here, nor do they detract from the pastoral beauty of the place.

Proceeding east up Island Creek, you will soon see more nice anchorages. In the fairly deep small creek (22) to your left (on the northern shore), you can find great shelter far back inside the trees and fields, with some homes and docks. In the cove on the opposite (southern) side (23), water depth continues well into the creek (24), a protected area. The shoreline has woods, marsh, and field with little indication of civilization, although houses on the opposite shore of the main creek are visible. There is no good beach here.

The next nice anchorage upstream (25) doesn't look particularly good on the chart, but the water is deeper closer to the shore than shown. You can tuck in south of the center line of the stream amidst very pretty scenery. Here you are amidst marsh, cattails, woods, and a little bit of beach. There are houses on the other side.

Yet another anchorage lies in the cove to the left (northern bank) (26) with forks at the end. The scenery is beautiful. On the left as you enter (west side of the cove), woods come down to the water, and straight ahead, a white boat house watches you from its white railed dock. Its house is way up in the trees. There is a real feeling of isolation and protection in here. Observe closely the chart. We found the deeper water is to the left (west), especially as you get off the head point at the northern end of the cove where it divides.

Now Island Creek splits. The branch to your left (27) (northern branch) is very built up, with many docks coming far out from shore on both sides to reach the deep water. Toward the end on the eastern side is a very large and interesting house which looks as though it was a huge barn that has been completely and finely rebuilt. There is even a silo on its end.

The right (southern) branch (28) is very different. Here there is very little touch of civilization, with field, wood, marsh, and ferns. Assuming you made it into the creek, don't go in with a boat of more than 4 feet draft, and enter very carefully on half tide and rising. If you have a shallow draft, this branch is well worth the entire trip to the creek.

Lecompte Bay and Creek
Refer to Chart #12266-G—"Choptank River, Castle Haven Point to Hambrooks Bar—Lecompte Bay & LaTrappe Creek."
Pg. 181

Lecompte Bay (30) looks intruiging from the chart, but from the standpoint of anchoring and visiting, it has little to offer most cruisers.

You can anchor in broad places with a lot of protected water. If the wind is blowing from the right direction, you can get all the protection you want. If it is not, this could be a very uncomfortable anchorage. It is broad, the land is fairly low with much clearing and low marsh, and there is a fair scattering of houses around the shore.

Approaching Lecompte Creek (29), you will notice a beautiful long brick wall (31) on the western shore of the bay, surrounding a huge estate with a very large and very long white house. This wall extends far out towards the north along the shore, where it ends with an arched brick bridge over a small marsh-choked creek.

Lecompte Creek is marked with privately maintained markers (32) indicated on the chart. They are obvious and should be followed. Inside depths are as indicated. Here there is a feeling of much width of shallow water and low land.

The land closes in as you reach the western extremities of the creek, but this is shallow. The two branches to the right (33) (north) are prettier than the one you see to the left (34) (south), because the land hasn't been cleared and is full of woods and marsh. The first creek to the right (north) has a power line (35) with the height unmarked. The last branch to the right turns before a headland with an old abandoned wooden house (36), its framing and boards gray and weather-beaten, with two brick chimneys still standing proudly at each end. This is a very pretty branch for dinghy exploration.

The left (southern) branch (34) is very shallow, less than a foot at low water. There is an abandoned boatbuilding and repair facility at the far southern end. The staked channel is obvious, and the machinery is behind the marsh grass up a little cut.

Anchorage South of Castle Haven Point
If you follow the shores northward from Lecompte Creek, Castle Haven Point will be your next exploration point. This looks intruiging on the chart, with its long protective sand spit curling around forming a semi-protected harbor. The brick wall described earlier takes you along the shore toward this point. When I arrived, I was somewhat disappointed because there are several houses and I couldn't find deep water inside the point. Although these homes are nice, they break into the aura of deserted beaches and coves. There is a huge

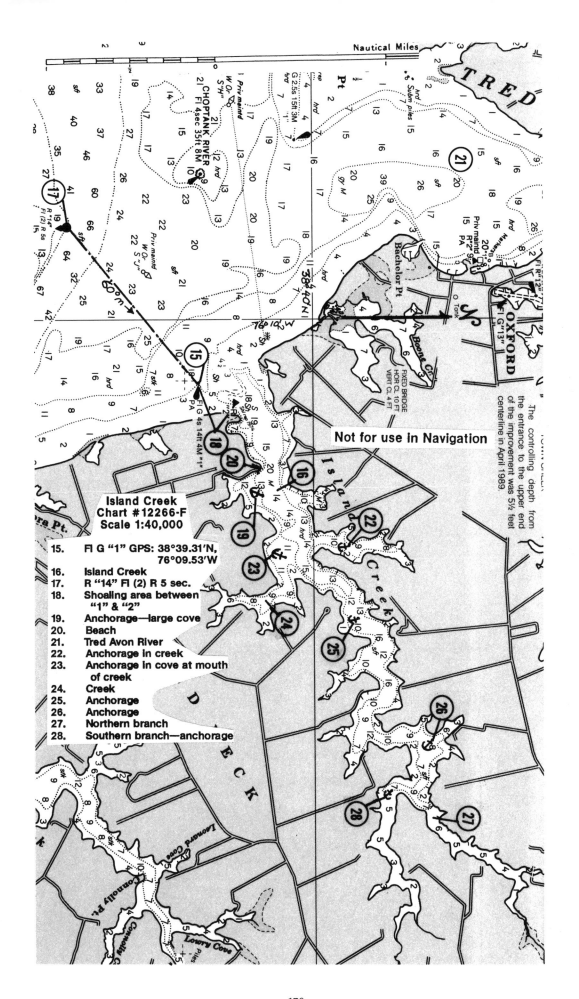

Not for use in Navigation

**Island Creek
Chart #12266-F
Scale 1:40,000**

15. Fl G "1" GPS: 38°39.31'N,
    76°09.53'W
16. Island Creek
17. R "14" Fl (2) R 5 sec.
18. Shoaling area between
    "1" & "2"
19. Anchorage—large cove
20. Beach
21. Tred Avon River
22. Anchorage in creek
23. Anchorage in cove at mouth
    of creek
24. Creek
25. Anchorage
26. Anchorage
27. Northern branch
28. Southern branch—anchorage

The controlling depth from
the entrance to the upper end
of the improvement was 5½ feet
centerline in April 1989.

and very nice house on the point which looks right down onto the beach extending out as a spit. The surrounding land is flat with much of it cleared.

A long and very shallow finger-like shoal (39) extends east from the point, its tip marked by R "2." The chart indicates 7 feet of water in here among the shoals to the west of the point and to the south of the finger shoal. I couldn't find much more than 4 feet (40), often less, even while criss-crossing in the spaces where deep water was indicated. This is not the anchorage it would appear, although it is a pretty spot.

La Trappe Creek

Beautiful anchorages, beaches surrounded by marsh or field, good holding, and excellent protection make La Trappe Creek a must place to go. While there are plenty of homes along the shore, there are many spots to anchor where civilization intrudes very little, some where it is almost not there.

The entrance to La Trappe Creek (41) is distinctive because the two entrance markers (42) are the old fashioned variety with round cylinders with doors and ports, mounted atop of cement caissons, which in turn are surrounded by rocks. The entrance isn't tricky if you just stay between the markers. The one thing to watch is the current. Since the channel line runs diagonally across the mouth of the creek, you may be quickly set to one shoal or another if the tidal current is running strong. It can run strong on full and new moon tides or strong wind conditions.

As soon as you enter, you will see one of the nicest (and most popular) anchorages around, behind (to the north and northwest of) the sand split rounding Martin Point (43). The beach sand spit that you will see protruding northeasterly from Martin Point has deep water up close and is a favorite for local people to land their boats on a weekend and walk the beach. A conspicuous "no tresspassing" sign (44) marks the point above the beach. The anchorage behind the spit has 7 to 8 feet depth, and is wide enough to be cool, yet snug. This will be very crowded on weekends.

Heading farther up La Trappe Creek to the right (on the east side of the creek) is a nice wide cove (45) with areas of good gray clay for great holding. There's room for many boats to anchor and be out of the channel. There are beaches on the shore to the southeast, including one on the southwest point of the cove. The area just off the little unnamed creek (46) has the prettiest view of this anchorage. You are looking up into that creek which is woodsy with marsh and wild field closing in from the banks. This area is closer to the channel because the point opposite comes out toward the creek. However, it is possible to tuck up out of the way. Be sure that you are well lit at night. From here on up, there will be less of an opportunity to walk ashore. There are not as many beaches and the shores are usually private or heavily wooded or have banks and bushes or marsh.

Farther up the creek, there is another very pretty anchoring cove to your right (47) on the eastern side of the creek, just before Sawmill Cove.

The point to the north of this anchorage points into Sawmill Cove (48), another beautiful anchorage if your draft allows you to get up inside. Follow the chart in, staying to the middle, but favoring a little the right (northern side). There is a house and dock to left as you enter. Past this, the bottom comes up and you can't take more than 4 feet in. Even at 4 feet I would expect to find a little mud at times on low water. If you can, go into where it splits showing 5 feet. The right

(north) branch (49) has 5 feet for a short while, and the left (west) branch (50) shallows up much quicker. This is one of the prettiest spots of the Bay. There is almost no sign of civilization except occasional glimpses of fields through the bushes and trees. There are woods, marsh, wild fields with high marsh grass and cattails, and a feeling of isolation. The shallower branch to your left is a very nice area for a dinghy row in the evening. Close to the shore, the forest trees hang over with their large roots kneeling into the water, reminiscent of a swamp.

A little farther up La Trappe Creek, Connolly Cove (51) to the east opposite Leonard Cove (52) is another beautiful place for dinghy exploration. While this and Sawmill Cove would be great anchorages for shallow draft cruising boats, when you start heading up into places like this, you are likely to encounter snags and weeds. This is why I suggest dinghy exploration, although shallow draft cruisers will be well rewarded if they do anchor.

Nearing the main split (53), the creek narrows considerably with trees hanging over the edge of the water. This area has scattered very large houses, some old, and some new with modern design. There are occasional docks. Soon you begin to see outer signs of Trappe Landing in the eastern (main) branch (54) to the east.

Moving into the eastern branch, the water becomes shallower. Don't take more than 5 feet into here, even then with the assumption that you might find a few mud hills. Local boats do take deeper draft. There are some private docks to your left before the landing area, and then the town landing (55) on the northern side, with a ramp and dock for brief stays and loading. Usually work boats are tied here, although there generally is room at the dock for temporary docking. I found less than 5 feet at this dock. Just up from the landing is the home of **Dickerson Boatbuilders, Inc. (56)**. This yard built many well-known Dickerson cruising boats. The marina will take transients, and it offers full repair work, with a 20-ton open end lift. Also the Tuggit Tow and Salvage (57) business makes its home here with hull and engine repairs and rebuilding.

The branch to your left (north), called Lowry Cove (58), has some very large homes and much of the land has been cleared for yards and agriculture. It isn't as pretty for an anchorage as many other sections of La Trappe Creek.

Cambridge
Refer to Chart #12268-A—"Hambrooks Bar to Jamaica Point (including Cambridge)." PG. 182

Cambridge is an old town with a wonderful historical heritage that is changing to a more modern area that will have many things to interest the cruiser. Some commercial places in town and in the creek may not be attractive aesthetically, but among these are places that you should not miss and people whom you will be happy to meet. Do not pass it by.

Approaching Cambridge (59), heading easterly up the Choptank, Hambrooks Bar Light (60) slides by to your left on the southern bank. This looks like a very small white lighthouse on a red base. The bay behind this bar, to the south of the hook, looks enticing as a good weather anchorage on the chart, but the bottom has undergone significant changes lately. The river has eroded through the parts of the bar, and an extension seems to be building out toward the light. Small boats that could formerly pass between the light and the point as a short cut are now often finding the bottom. Many feel that this will have a significant effect on the bottom, per-

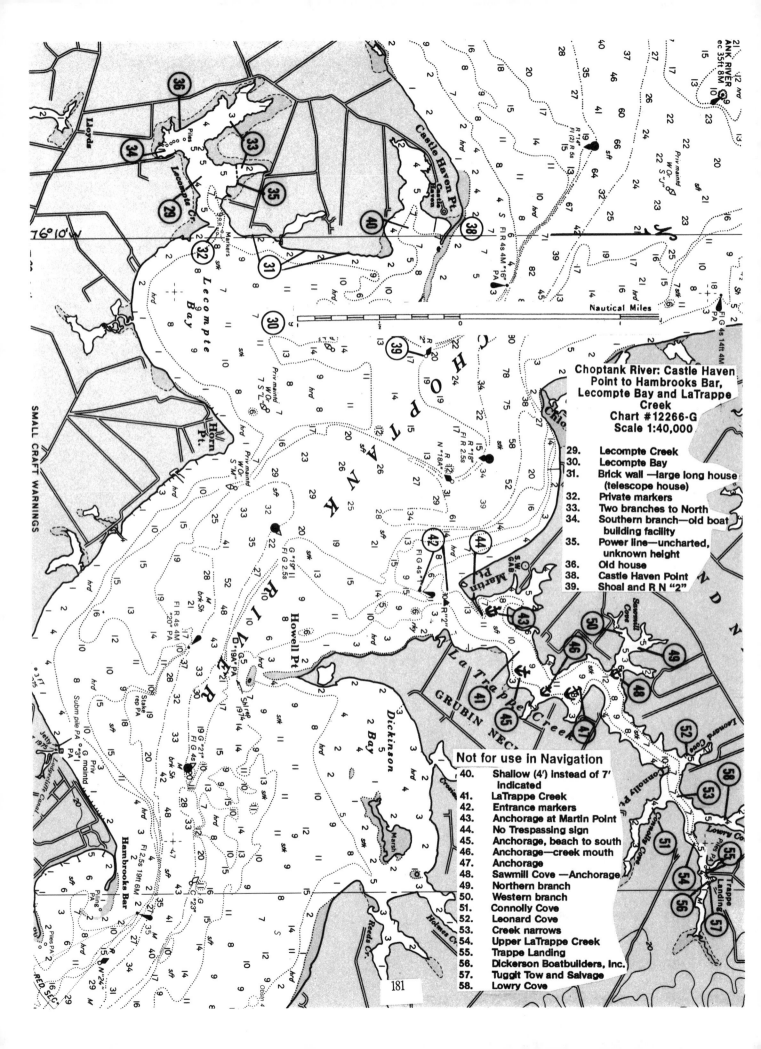

Choptank River: Castle Haven
Point to Hambrooks Bar,
Lecompte Bay and LaTrappe
Creek
Chart #12266-G
Scale 1:40,000

29.	Lecompte Creek
30.	Lecompte Bay
31.	Brick wall —large long house (telescope house)
32.	Private markers
33.	Two branches to North
34.	Southern branch—old boat building facility
35.	Power line—uncharted, unknown height
36.	Old house
38.	Castle Haven Point
39.	Shoal and R N "2"

Not for use in Navigation

40.	Shallow (4') instead of 7' indicated
41.	LaTrappe Creek
42.	Entrance markers
43.	Anchorage at Martin Point
44.	No Trespassing sign
45.	Anchorage, beach to south
46.	Anchorage—creek mouth
47.	Anchorage
48.	Sawmill Cove —Anchorage
49.	Northern branch
50.	Western branch
51.	Connolly Cove
52.	Leonard Cove
53.	Creek narrows
54.	Upper LaTrappe Creek
55.	Trappe Landing
56.	Dickerson Boatbuilders, Inc.
57.	Tuggit Tow and Salvage
58.	Lowry Cove

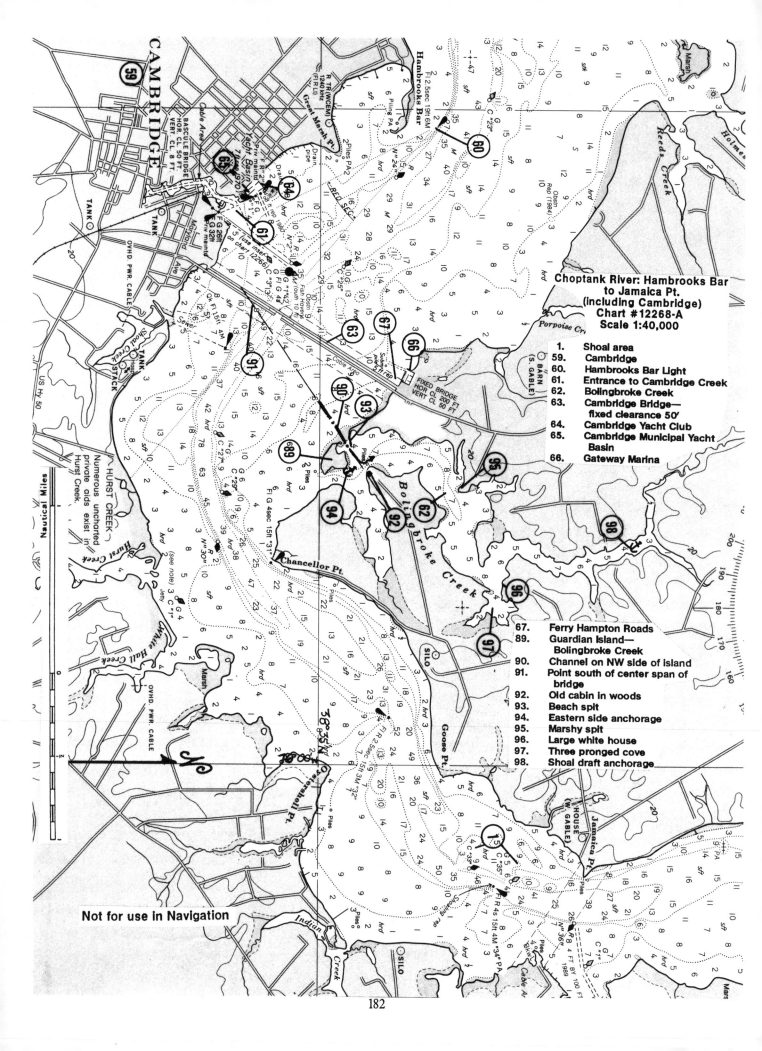

Choptank River: Hambrooks Bar
to Jamaica Pt.
(including Cambridge)
Chart #12268-A
Scale 1:40,000

1. Shoal area
59. Cambridge
60. Hambrooks Bar Light
61. Entrance to Cambridge Creek
62. Bolingbroke Creek
63. Cambridge Bridge—
    fixed clearance 50'
64. Cambridge Yacht Club
65. Cambridge Municipal Yacht
    Basin
66. Gateway Marina

67. Ferry Hampton Roads
89. Guardian Island—
    Bolingbroke Creek
90. Channel on NW side of island
91. Point south of center span of
    bridge
92. Old cabin in woods
93. Beach spit
94. Eastern side anchorage
95. Marshy spit
96. Large white house
97. Three pronged cove
98. Shoal draft anchorage

Not for use in Navigation

Nautical Miles

CAMBRIDGE

182

Crab boat going under bridge, Cambridge Creek

Mr. Charles Wheatley, friendly bridge tender, Cambridge Creek (78) pg. 184

haps as far as the mouth of Bolingbroke Creek (62) on the north shore of the river, east of the bridge. Since the entrance to Cambridge Creek (61) could be subject to shoaling, follow the markers closely. The creek is so heavily used that any channel deviations will probably be marked quickly.

The bridge (63) ahead only has a 50-foot vertical clearance. With the potentially large tide differences, take great care if your masts are anywhere near that height.

Just northwest of Cambridge Creek entrance, the **Cambridge Yacht Club (64)** and the **Cambridge Municipal Yacht Basin (65)** share a bulkheaded basin. You enter in the middle of the bulkhead where it opens. Most who enter this basin head straight for the entrance from R "2" which marks the entrance to the creek. Controlling depth is 6½ feet but check first because of possible shoaling.

The Yacht Club is on the western side of the basin and sells gas and diesel at the entrance. They take transients from other clubs when space is available. The town basin has electricity up to 30 amps, a pumpout, bathroom and showers, laundry, and a dockmaster on duty. They can take vessels up to 70 feet.

On the opposite side of the river from Cambridge Creek, the **Gateway Marina (66)** has a bulkheaded basin with controlling depth of 4 feet. The old ferry *Hampton Roads* (67) sits grounded between the marina and the bridge, a sign on her side advertising "ferry for sale." The marina has 30 amps electricity and can handle up to 50-foot boats. Their yard does engine and hull repairs, and has a 17-ton lift and a crane. The marine store carries a fair assortment of hardware and other items including fishing gear and bait. There is a pumpout and gas and diesel are sold inside the basin. Discover, Visa, and MC cards are honored. The marina is certainly not within walking distance from Cambridge. You would have to traverse the 1½ mile-long bridge. They might be able to help with transportation across the river. Several charter fishing boats operate from here.

Cambridge Creek
Refer to Chart #12266-H (inset)—"Cambridge Harbor & Cambridge Creek."

The entrance to Cambridge Creek is deep and marked. It is very busy and used by deep draft vessels to its far end. The Dorchester County General Hospital (68) dominates the point to your left (southeast) as you head in. The first time in may be a little disconcerting, because the creek doesn't open up until you get into the outer basin. Then it opens to the right at the northwestern corner of the outer basin, and the rest becomes easy.

After you enter the creek to your left (east) is the unmistakable sign for **Yacht Maintenance Co., Inc. (69)**. This is a well established and a very large full service repair, rebuild, and storage yard with some slips and transients welcome. A full size half sailboat is fixed to the side of a main building as a sign. They have depths of 11 feet with transient capability up to 100 feet. Electricity ranges up to 50 amps. There is a 68-ton lift and a 175-ton railway with any type of repair readily available, including stainless and aluminium welding. There is a pumpout station here, but no fuel. They take MC.

Mid-Shore Electronics, Inc. (70) at Yacht Maintenance does sales, service, and installations on commercial and pleasure vessels on the premises. They stand by on VHF Channel 10. They have a high reputation locally. Anytime I find someone who can actually fix a radar, loran, VHF, and other electronic equipment, instead of sending it out, I take good note.

The creek then opens into a basin on the northwest shore which is often used as an anchorage (71). Those ashore and local boaters think of it as an anchorage. Be sure to anchor away from the bridge approaches and the channel area because of traffic, which can include tugs maneuvering. Keep well lit at night.

On the north shore of the anchoring basin, is Clayton Seafood (72), and the Clayton Seafood Restaurant (73). The restaurant has a sign and is easily identified. There is a dinghy dock at the restaurant with 4 feet depth. You are allowed to tie up at the bulkhead while eating, although they do not operate a marina. There is no electricity. The restaurant has a bar, nicely decorated interior, and good food from light fare to dinners costing 5 to 15 dollars.

On the northwest shore of the anchorage is the Dorchester County Building (74), large and with a sign. Inside, the Department of Tourism [(410) 228-1000] will be very helpful during your stay. The County Building has a long bulkhead (75) on the basin, but the signs forbid docking. There are plans to build transient piers off this bulkhead. Across the harbor on the left (eastern) side are some more piers (76), but these belong to the gray condos which come down to the water just before the bridge.

Phillips Oil Co. (77), is the last establishment north of the bridge (78), on the east side of the creek. The sign says "Full Service," but this is for the gas station on the inland side of the building. Phillips Oil is the place to get gas and diesel. I found their prices to be very fair and their personnel to be friendly and very helpful. They will allow you to tie up for a while on their bulkhead as it turns back to the county bulkhead (75) and there is some electricity (20 amps) available. There is 10 feet depth at the fuel docks but if you have to make a long approach to come alongside, it is best to do it from the northern end instead of from the bridge end of the bulkhead. Within the corner between the bridge and the bulkhead (79) there are wrecks near the bulkhead, some of which can't be seen. These do not impair Phillips docks, but a long approach from the bridge and very close to shore could entangle you in those wrecks.

To continue south up the creek, you must pass through the bridge (78). Bridges are often considered to be somewhat of a detriment to boat traffic, but this is not the case in Cambridge. The bascule bridge raises quickly, the bridge tenders are alert and responsive, and very helpful. Call them on Channel 13 or use the horn signal. They open anytime on demand except 12 noon through 1:00 p.m. on weekdays. Our experience with one of the bridge tenders there is not only representative of the bridge, but of the community. My wife and two daughters were regularly crossing the bridge on foot on their various photography missions. They and the bridge tender have always waved. Once when he was getting off watch, they met and the bridge tender volunteered to take us wherever we needed to go in the area, and gave us great information about what was where. When we left, he came to the boat just before we pulled out and presented my children each with a gas filled balloon and an envelope of candy! You'll meet many such nice people on your Eastern Shore cruise.

Passing through the bridge, the view up to the end of the creek opens ahead. To those accustomed to manicured rebuilt waterfronts, this area might seem a bit rough. It is a pleasant mixture of commercial establishments, waterfront under development, and already renewed. To your right on the western shore, new condos (80) have their own docks. To your left, the East Side Pub (81) and light fare restaurant sits right at the foot of the bridge. This establishment has both an up-

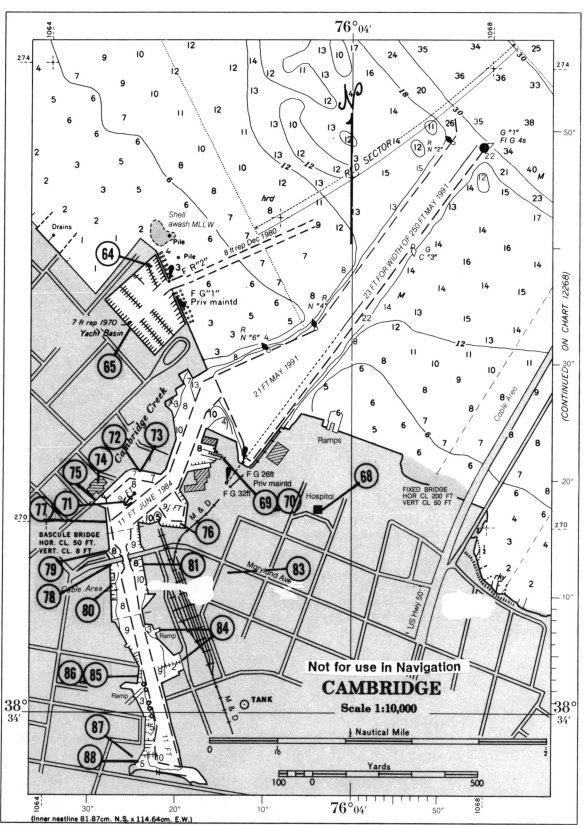

Not for use in Navigation
CAMBRIDGE
Scale 1:10,000

½ Nautical Mile

Yards

(Inner neatline 81.87cm. N.S. x 114.64cm. E.W.)

Cambridge Harbor &	68.	**Dorchester County General**	75.	**Long city bulkhead**	84.	**Park, public ramp, city docks**
Cambridge Creek		**Hospital**	76.	**Docks—condominiums**	85.	**Cambridge Marine, Ltd.**
Chart #12266-H (inset)	69.	**Yacht Maintenance**	77.	**Phillips Oil Co.**	86.	**Eastern Yacht Services**
Scale 1:10,000	70.	**Mid-Shore Electronics, Inc.**	78.	**Cambridge Bridge**	87.	**Cemetery**
	71.	**Anchorage basin**	79.	**Wrecks**	88.	**Generation III Marina**
64.	**Cambridge Yacht Club**	72.	**Clayton Seafood**	80.	**Condominiums**	
65.	**Cambridge Municipal Yacht**	73.	**Clayton Seafood Restaurant**	81.	**East Side Pub**	
	Basin	74.	**Dorchester County Building**	83.	**"Wroten's"—grocery store**	

stairs and downstairs area, with some transient space in front for their customers. The owners also operate Suicide Bridge Restaurant, described in the Upper Choptank section farther on in this chapter, and they will be helpful in getting you out there for dinner. The East Side Pub will also assist in getting you to Kool Ice Seafood (23), (Refer to Cambridge Town Map) which sells most kinds of retail seafood.

The Blue Crab is exemplary of much of Cambridge. The entire family renewed, built, and decorated the premises with their own labor. In the early mornings the owners are there cleaning up, and in the late evening the owners are there helping customers. From the water, the building appears to be plain and still exudes some of the qualities to be expected from a century-old waterfront granary. Inside, the passage of the years has been carefully cleaned from the timbers and floors. Walking about the premises is almost like a museum experience. The family has collected a fascinating assortment of items from the Bay-boats, and Bay life which adorn the inside and outside. You'll enjoy their unusual and historical nautical decor.

Farther up the creek to your left (eastern side) is a park area right down to the bulkhead, a public concrete ramp, and some smaller city docks (84). There is no dockmaster here, and the docks appear to be mostly used by permanent local boats.

Across the creek from these docks a large building with the sign **Cambridge Marine Ltd (85)** identifies this boatyard (formerly Sid Johnson's). There is a marine store which includes a good selection of hardware, and a 30-ton open-end lift. Also at this location is Eastern-Yacht Services (86), which specializes in custom woodworking, painting and varnishing, plexiglass work, fiberglass repairs, and dinghy building. They also work off premises.

Proceeding farther into the creek, you pass a very old cemetry (87) coming almost down to the water's edge on the western shore. Just beyond that is the new **Generation III Marina (88)** and full service boat yard. A short stay in the area will familiarize you with the fact that Jim Richardson was well-recognized as one of the very fine boat builders on the Bay. This yard is run by his grandson. They have up to 10 feet depth, can accomodate up to 120-foot transients, with electric ranging to 50 amps. The lift is 60 tons capability. They can perform both aluminium and stainless welding and other general custom work. There is no marine store here, but they have a very large parts inventory.

Cambridge Ashore
Refer to our Sketch Map—"Cambridge Town Map."

Cambridge is a town where people still swing on the porch in the evenings. You can walk down the streets at supper time and notice the comforting smells of old wooden houses and gravy and potatoes cooking. It is also a place of seafaring heritage and historical palces. Recently the town has begun making a concentrated effort to bring in businesses and attract the boating public.

One of the keys to enjoying Cambridge is to understand that the community is a very old seaport and boatbuilding center, and that it has recently begun a substantial renovation period. Areas around Cambridge Creek, as well as along the creek, are somewhat drab in comparison to other areas that you might visit. This should not discourage your visit. There are also modern and nice facilities for yachts, and the mixture of the different times and traditions, flavored by the

seafaring history of the area is an informative and enjoyable adventure.

West of the creek, shortly after you walk across the bridge and go inland and also to your right a few blocks, is what is commonly known as the historical district with its brick cobbled streets, old buildings, and government offices. This area includes the High Street Historical District (10) (along that street) with nine buildings built in the 1700s and 15 buildings built in the 1800s. Christ Church (9) has gray stone and a steeple towering over the town behind the harbor, and beautiful stained glass windows. There has been a church by this name on that site since 1693, this one built in 1883. Across the street is the Dorchester County Courthouse (8), built in 1852, with a fountain in the park-like front yard. This is called "Spring Valley" and here on a pleasant summer evening you may enjoy a concert.

Also on High Street, there is Cambridge Canvas and Sail Loft (22) between the post office (6) and Locust Street. The Dorchester County Tourism Department has a historical walking tour pamphlet. They are in the County Building (74) at waterside, and can be called at (410) 228-1000. Their pamphlet is found in many stores.

The old downtown section is also on the western side of the bridge, generally to the left of Race Street (11) about three blocks from the bridge. A serious fire in 1910 destroyed much of the commercial district on Race and Muir Streets. Much of the architecture here is from that time period, brick and stone with many tin facades. Many shops are now closed in this section, but there are others open with things you might want

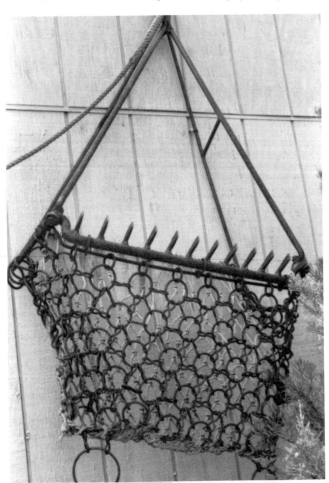

Oyster dredge—type used by oyster sailing fleet
hanging outside Blue Crab restaurant, Cambridge

186

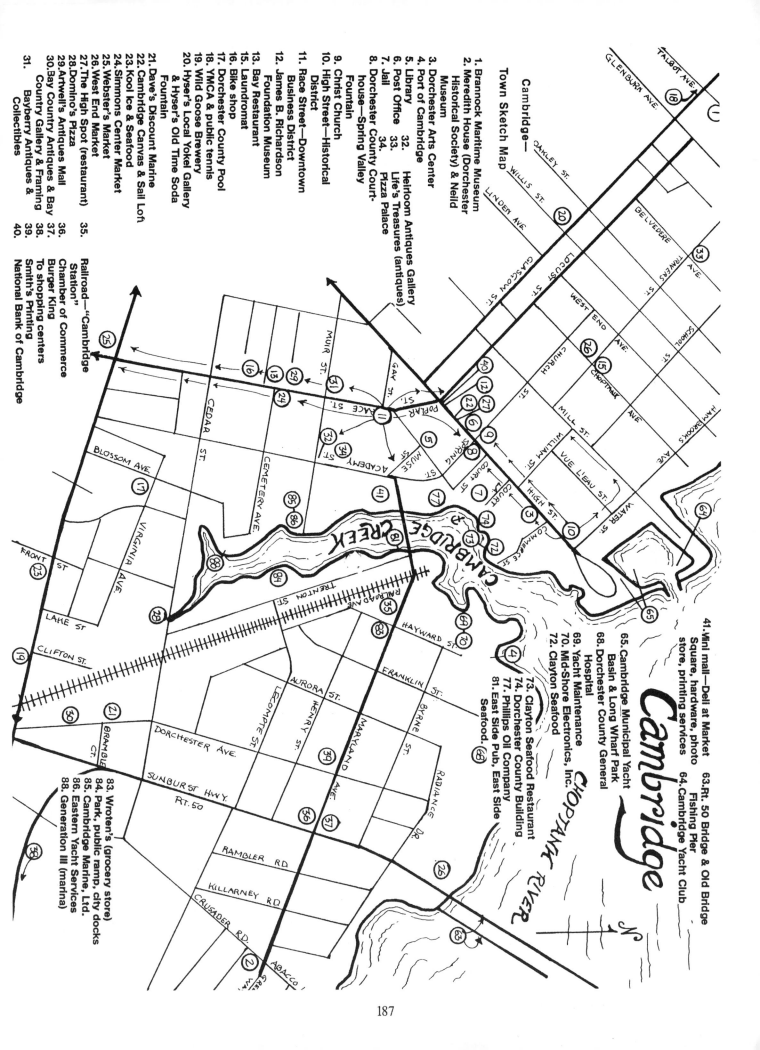

Cambridge—

Town Sketch Map

1. Brannock Maritime Museum
2. Meredith House (Dorchester Historical Society) & Neild Museum
3. Dorchester Arts Center
4. Port of Cambridge
5. Library
6. Post Office
7. Jail
8. Dorchester County Courthouse—Spring Valley Fountain
9. Christ Church
10. High Street—Historical District
11. Race Street—Downtown Business District
12. James B. Richardson Foundation Museum
13. Bay Restaurant
15. Laundromat
16. Bike shop
17. Dorchester County Pool
18. YMCA & public tennis
19. Wild Goose Brewery
20. Hyser's Local Yokel Gallery & Hyser's Old Time Soda Fountain
21. Dave's Discount Marine
22. Cambridge Canvas & Sail Loft
23. Kool Ice & Seafood
24. Simmons Center Market
25. Webster's Market
26. West End Market
27. The High Spot (restaurant)
28. Domino's Pizza
29. Artwell's Antiques Mall
30. Bay Country Antiques & Bay Country Gallery & Framing
31. Bayberry Antiques & Collectibles

32. Heirloom Antiques Gallery
33. Life's Treasures (antiques)
34. Pizza Palace
35. Railroad—"Cambridge Station"
36. Chamber of Commerce
37. Burger King
38. To shopping centers
39. Smith's Printing
40. National Bank of Cambridge

Cambridge

CHOPTANK RIVER

41. Mini mall—Deli at Market Square, hardware, photo store, printing services
63. Rt. 50 Bridge & Old Bridge Fishing Pier
64. Cambridge Yacht Club
65. Cambridge Municipal Yacht Basin & Long Wharf Park
68. Dorchester County General Hospital
69. Yacht Maintenance
70. Mid-Shore Electronics, Inc.
72. Clayton Seafood
73. Clayton Seafood Restaurant
74. Dorchester County Building
77. Phillips Oil Company
81. East Side Pub, East Side Seafood
83. Wroten's (grocery store)
84. Park, public ramp, city docks
85. Cambridge Marine, Ltd.
86. Eastern Yacht Services
88. Generation III (marina)

or need and pleasant folks to help you. Stores include a McCrory's, Woolworth, a bike shop **(16)**, and pharmacies. Immediately to your left (south) as you get off the bridge you will notice a small shopping center **(41)** with a deli and a nice hardware store. There is a Pizza Palace **(34)** on Academy Street, close to this hardware store. Farther out northwest are other points of interest such as the Brannock Maritime Museum **(1)** at 210 Talbot Ave., and the Annie Oakley house where this famous lady of the west retired for a few years. It is said that while living there she was known to take pot shots from her upstairs window at walnuts hanging from her neighbor's tree.

Also on this west side of the creek at the corner of High and Locust streets, you will find the James B. Richardson Foundation Museum **(12)**. This gentleman, now deceased, was one of the deans of Eastern Shore wooden boat building. When you visit Chesapeake Bay Maritime Museum at St. Michaels, you will see the *Mr. Jim*, an example of his work. The museum in Cambridge is dedicated to "Mr. Jim," and other masters like him.

Harriet Ross Tubman, the famous underground railway conductor during the War Between the States, was born in nearby Bucktown, Maryland. A car or ride would be needed. There are guided tours by appointment at (410) 228-0401.

East of the bridge, walking along Maryland Ave. toward Route 50 (which goes across the Choptank bridge), you will find The East Side Pub **(81)**, is to your right (south) on Trenton Street just after you cross the bridge. An old railroad station **(35)** with a red caboose marks that intersection. You will see Yacht Maintenance **(69)** with Midshore Marine Electronics **(70)** to your left (north). Walking on east, you will pass Wroten's Market **(83)** and two convenience stores (one up Hayward Street about a block), and Smith's Printing **(39)** with public fax service, before you reach the Route 50 "main drag." Wroten's Market **(83)** is a very nice grocery store and a butcher shop.

At the Route 50 intersection, immediately to the right (south) will be the Chamber of Commerce Building **(36)**. If you walk farther down the highway, you will find two shopping centers **(38)**. From any marina, these are too far to walk with packages. Stores out here include Sears, hardware stores, Revco, and banks.

At the east end of Maryland Avenue is the Meredith House **(2)**, built in 1760, now the home of Dorchester Historical Society, and also the Neild Museum featuring displays of Dorchester maritime, industrial, farm, and Native American history.

At the head of the creek, near Generation III **(88)**, are several auto parts stores, Dominos Pizza **(28)**, and, within a few blocks, the Wild Goose Brewery **(19)**. This is a local small brewery which brews several quality beers. They will give you a tour if you call ahead. It is a fascinating experience.

Things are rapidly changing in Cambridge. Check with a marina or a Chamber of Commerce or the Department of Tourism for the latest commercial and historical information.

Consider timing your visit to Cambridge to coincide with one of the special events that interest you. These include the Dorchester Art Exhibit on the last weekend in April, a Flower Fair on the first weekend in May, Spocott Windmill Day also that weekend, an antique aircraft fly-in on the third weekend in May, the Cambridge Sail Regatta on the second weekend in July, a seafood festival on the second weekend in August, the Cambridge Classics Powerboat Races on the third weekend in August, Cambridge Seaport Days in September, the Dorchester Showcase on the last weekend in September, and the Cambridge-Dorchester Air Show on the first Sunday in October. Some of these dates vary because of weather and other considerations.

UPPER CHOPTANK RIVER
Refer to Chart #12268-A—"Choptank River: Hambrooks Bar to Jamaica Point including Cambridge." Pg-182

The Cambridge bridge with its 50-foot vertical clearance prohibits many boats from exploring the upper reaches of this beautiful river. If you can get under the bridge and if you like river navigation and love unspoiled lands with forest, swamp, marsh, and just the right spattering of civilization when you need it, this is a great trip.

There is one more typical Bay cruising creek above the Cambridge bridge, before you get into serious up-river explorations. This is Bolingbroke Creek **(62)**. After here, mostly fast boats are seen on the river. Indeed these are more suited to the distances and depths.

The old bridge appears to extend across the river beside the present bridge **(63)**. In fact, this old bridge is a fishing pier extending out from the north and south sides of the river, stopping short of the channel.

Bolingbroke Creek

For gunkholing purposes, this is another great place except that you can barely rely on 3 feet depth at the bar going in, and that is shoaling.

Bolingbroke **(62)** looks enticing even on the chart. I have always felt that there must be some secret way of getting in, and I set out to find it. From that chart, the entrance is obvi-

Anchorage, Cambridge Creek, Cambridge

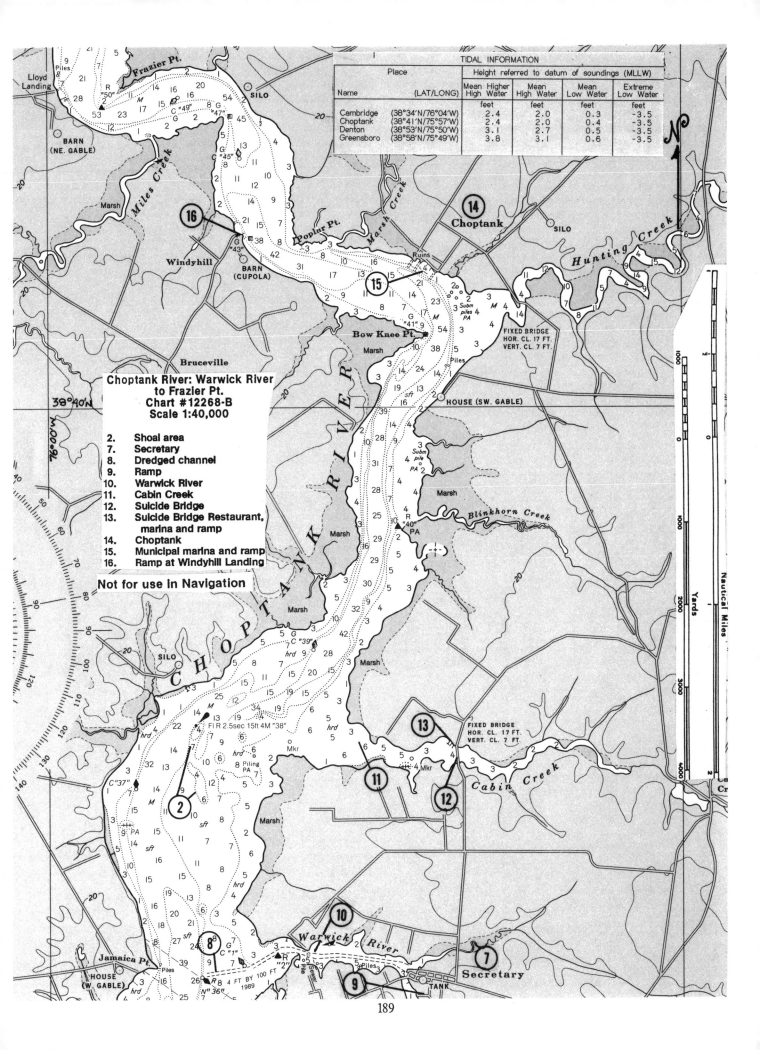

TIDAL INFORMATION

Place		Height referred to datum of soundings (MLLW)			
Name	(LAT/LONG)	Mean Higher High Water	Mean High Water	Mean Low Water	Extreme Low Water
		feet	feet	feet	feet
Cambridge	(38°34'N/76°04'W)	2.4	2.0	0.3	-3.5
Choptank	(38°41'N/75°57'W)	2.4	2.0	0.4	-3.5
Denton	(38°53'N/75°50'W)	3.1	2.7	0.5	-3.5
Greensboro	(38°58'N/75°49'W)	3.8	3.1	0.6	-3.5

Choptank River: Warwick River
to Frazier Pt.
Chart #12268-B
Scale 1:40,000

2.   Shoal area
7.   Secretary
8.   Dredged channel
9.   Ramp
10. Warwick River
11. Cabin Creek
12. Suicide Bridge
13. Suicide Bridge Restaurant,
     marina and ramp
14. Choptank
15. Municipal marina and ramp
16. Ramp at Windyhill Landing

Not for use in Navigation

ously to the east of the guardian island **(89)**. I went in hopefully, as the water remained at 6 feet or so, but very soon it shoaled up to 3 feet and less. Criss-crossing did not reveal any passages. But a short talk with the local expert showed me a better route, although still with no more than 3 feet. This is on the northwest side **(90)** of the island, between it and the mainland, where the chart shows bare at low. The creek now uses this as a major channel for its waters which flow with some speed through here. The cut runs close to the island, but not too close, because there are downed trees near the shore. I used the bridge span **(91)** as one end of a range line (better, a point on the bridge just to the south of the span) and an old cabin **(92)** up in the trees on the point opposite (northeast of) the cut. This cabin is difficult to see, but becomes more visible as you move in. Depths at this entrance area all around the island are not as represented on the chart. This entry bar is very unstable and changing.

The beach spit **(93)** to your left (northwest) coming in is like a finger beckoning on the chart. Actually, this sand spit now extends closer to the island than the chart indicates. Beware the shoal extending from the tip of that finger on up toward that point opposite to the northeast. Because of the shoal area, it is necessary to continue on straight after you pass through the cut. Go in fairly close to the point **(92)** before you come around to your left (northwest). I found 4 feet depth close up to that beach, with 3 feet very close. You can take a shallow draft motor or sailboat right up to the beach in here. The breezes come in across the spit and you can enjoy watching the river or looking upstream into the wooded creek. However, that cut has a lot of current.

There is an eastern side anchorage **(94)** on the northeast side of the island where the old cut used to be. The island is pretty and wooded. From here, you can't see the bridge. There is also beach on the eastern side of the island, and a shallow boat can get pretty close.

Heading up into the creek, you will see high hills and some cliffs and a few nice houses, boathouses, and trees with low lying marsh off the spit to your left (northwest) **(95)**, and woods to your right. Often the water will not be as deep as indicated, but if you got through the entrance, it is deep enough in the channel.

Where the creek turns to your left (northeasterly), you will see a large white house **(96)** with chimneys on each end sitting proudly on a hill with a nice grass yard. A dock extends out in front, and trees frame the house from behind. The three-pronged cove **(97)** to right (to the south of the point with the house) is shallower than indicated, but a great place for a dinghy trip. This is one of those creeks where the forest closes right down to the waters, trees and vines hanging over, casting their shadows into the still creek.

Go on up north beyond this house, where the creek narrows and flows through woods and field with less and less civilization. Depths are generally as indicated on the chart. If your boat can get to where the creek forks for a final time, a wilderness-type anchorage **(98)** awaits in the area marked south of the point of the fork, in 3 feet depth.

Goldsborough House, 200 High St., Cambridge. Circa 1790, unaltered inside and out

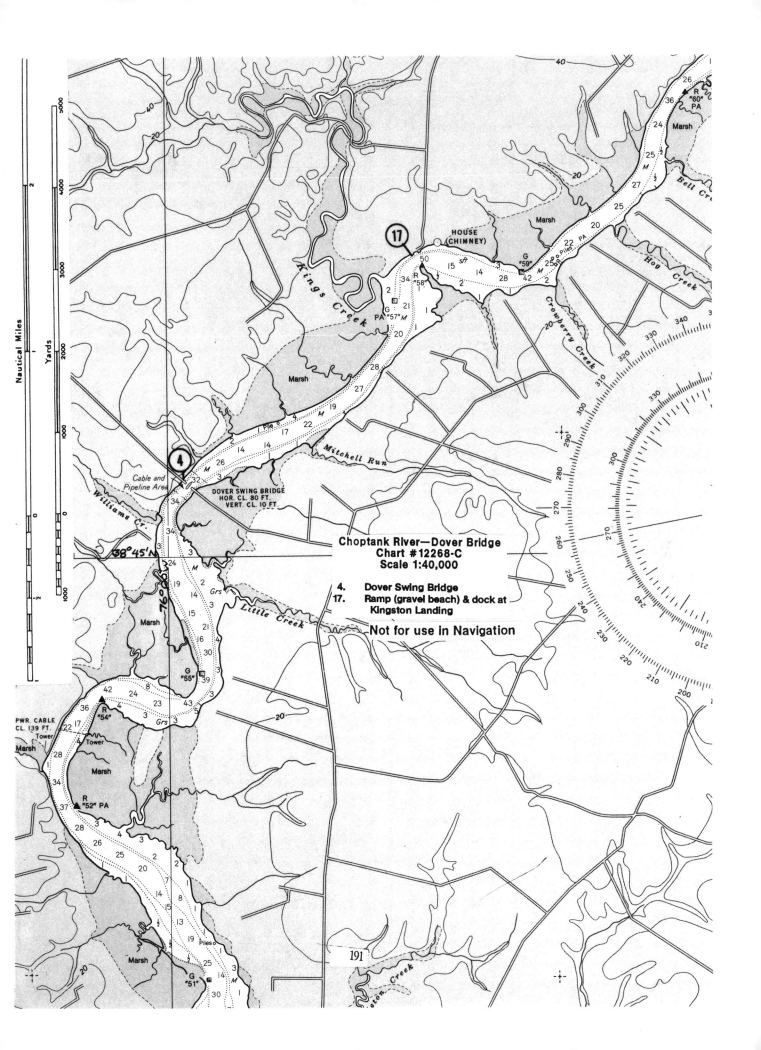

Choptank River—Dover Bridge
Chart #12268-C
Scale 1:40,000

4. Dover Swing Bridge
17. Ramp (gravel beach) & dock at Kingston Landing

Not for use in Navigation

191

Refer to:
Chart #12268-A—"Choptank River: Hambrooks Bar to Jamaica Point (including Cambridge)," PG. 182 and
Chart #12268-B—"Choptank River: Warwick River to Frazier Point," PG. 189 and
Chart #12268-C—"Choptank River: Dover Bridge," PG. 191 and
Chart #12268-D—"Choptank River: Tuckahoe Creek," PG. 193 and
Chart #12268-E—"Choptank River: Denton, Mill Creek to Chapel Branch." PG. 195

Upriver from Bolingbroke Creek (62) (12268-A), the river twists and winds for almost 30 NM to Denton (99) (12268-E). There are few facilities on the stretch, and a supply of fuel for the round trip is advisable. It is possible to get fuel in some places, although not as conveniently as you are accustomed. The general rule for anchorage is that you have to anchor out in the river, in a cove or bend of your choice, taking care to be out of the channel and well lit. Buoys continue all the way up to Denton, but there is still a need for careful river navigation. If you go, you may want to review the description of river navigation in Chapter 1. Many sailboaters may not want to explore the upper Choptank, even if they could get under the bridge, because the distances are so great, and as with any long Bay river, there is much shoaling. The best way to explore this river would be in a small cabin motor boat with no more than a few feet of draft and enough speed to plane. Take along some fishing gear. In the upper reaches above Denton and in Tuckahoe Creek (100) (12268-D) you may be able to run into some good fishing, including bass and crappie.

Shoaling occurs in many areas. Ones that I would especially consider to be notable are just down river from (south of) Jamaica Point in the vicinity of G "33" through Fl R "34" (1) (12268-A), the shoal just down from (south of) Fl R "38" (2) (12268-B) and the Pealiquor Shoal upriver from (north of) R "68" (3) (1268-E). This last was specifically noted by several experienced river navigators as being tricky. The word was, "carefully follow the markers." Local navigators generally consider 6 feet to be the safe maximum up to Denton.

Bridges are also a special consideration. After the fixed bridge at Cambridge, there is the Dover Swing Bridge (4) (12268-C) with a vertical clearance of 10 feet. Check ahead to see if the bridges are operating normally. When we were last there, the Dover Bridge did not have VHF. The next bridges (5) (12268-E) are at Denton where you will find passage upstream from fixed spans controlled by a vertical clearance of 25 feet. There is then a bridge with 10-foot vertical clearance at Greensboro (30) (12268-F). Note the 47-foot power cable just above Denton, with another authorized at 139 feet just after R "52" (6) (12268-E). Never trust what the chart says with regard to overhead cables. They sag, they swing, their clearance can change with heat and storms, and they should be checked before going under.

Warwick River to Frazier Point

Refer to Chart #12268-B—"Choptank River, Warwick River to Frazier Point." PG. 189

Soon after leaving Cambridge, the town of Secretary (7) with its dredged channel (8) and steel mat ramp (9) in the Warwick River (10) comes up to your right, on the east side of the Choptank River. The channel is dredged to 4 feet but don't take more than 3 feet in. Primarily work boats and local runabouts will be found here.

Not far above is Cabin Creek (11), on the east side of the river. This looks like an ordinary creek, but not so. It is the home of the locally well-known suicide bridge (12). When you see it, it will look just like any other creek bridge. It isn't. You will hear in many headquarters that it is haunted.

It began as a wooden bridge, built around 1888. Several bridges have replaced the original, once because it burned, and other times because of wear and tear. Over the years several people have committed suicide on the bridge. Also, may people have reported seeing strange lights and hearing unusual sounds around the bridge.

Some say that it used to be called "Uncle Joe's Bridge," perhaps because of the tavern at its foot, then called "Uncle Joe's Place." Now that tavern is a popular restaurant called, **The Suicide Bridge Restaurant (13)**. The manager reported various strange occurrences in the restaurant such as doors opening without explanation, things falling off shelves, and strange noises. It is the mark of a good restaurant that local people like it. Docks in front of the restaurant have 54 slips and electricity up to 30 amps and transients are welcome. There is complimentary dockage for boaters while eating here. A hard surfaced ramp is also on the premises. The restaurant has handout information giving details of the local legend. The creek is shallow, 3 feet controlling. Follow the chart and stay in the middle. While the restaurant docks weren't operating as a full-time transient marina when we visited, you may be able to tie up here to break up your trip. Call the restaurant at (410) 943-4689.

North from Cabin Creek, you will pass the village of Choptank (14) on the right (eastern shore). There is a **municipal marina (15)** here and a hard-surfaced ramp. It is bulkheaded with mostly motorboats, with available electricity at 15 amps. There is no one permanently on duty here, but a sign

Christ P.E. Church, 1883, Cambridge.
First church on this site built 1693

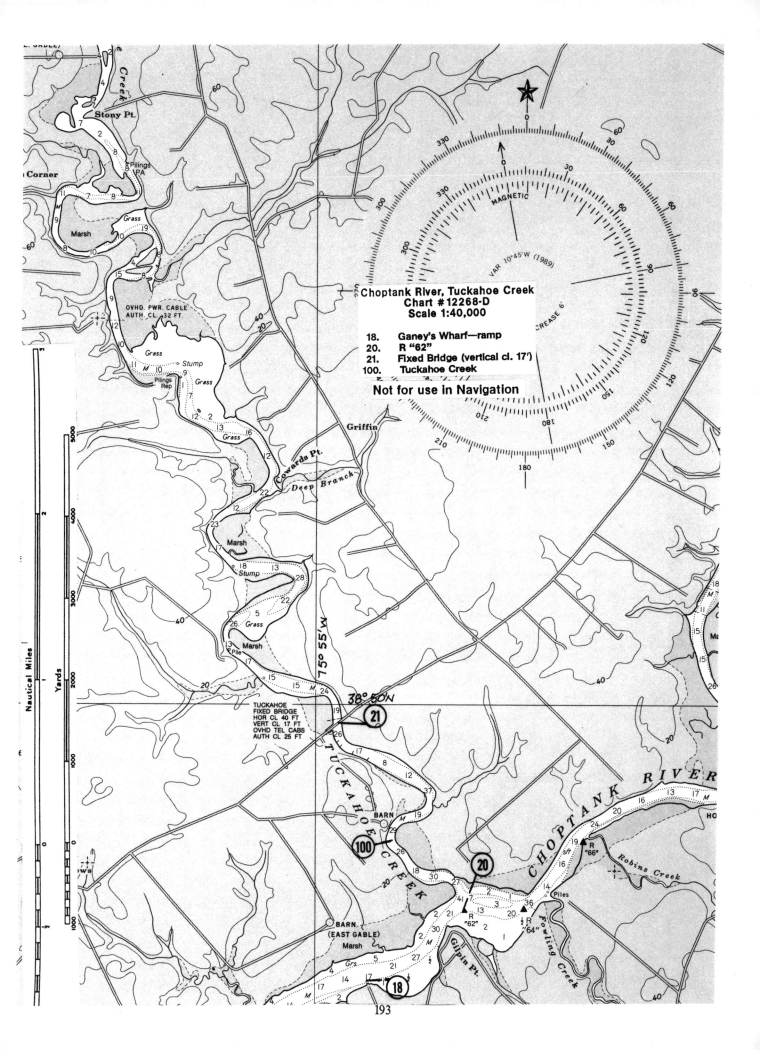

Choptank River, Tuckahoe Creek
Chart #12268-D
Scale 1:40,000

18. Ganey's Wharf—ramp
20. R "62"
21. Fixed Bridge (vertical cl. 17')
100. Tuckahoe Creek

Not for use in Navigation

VAR 10°45'W (1989)

MAGNETIC

OVHD. PWR. CABLE
AUTH. CL. 32 FT.

Stony Pt.

Corner

Marsh

Grass

Stump

Pilings
Rep

Grass

Grass

Grass

Griffin

Cowards Pt.

Deep Branch

Marsh

Stump

Marsh

Grass

Marsh
Pile

TUCKAHOE
FIXED BRIDGE
HOR CL 40 FT
VERT CL 17 FT
OVHD TEL CABS
AUTH CL 25 FT

38°50'N

75°55'W

BARN

BARN
(EAST GABLE)
Marsh

Gipin Pt.

Grs

CHOPTANK RIVER

Robins Creek

Fowling Creek

R "66"

R "62"

R "64"

Nautical Miles

Yards

provides a phone number to call for slips. While they welcome transients, call them in advance at (410) 479-3731. This is primarily a residential village and other than stretching your legs, there are not many things to do or supplies available within walking distance before 1679, there was an Indian settlement at the site. Choptank was named for the settlement and the river.

Launching Ramp

Besides the ramp at Cabin Creek and Choptank, there is another ramp across the river at Windy Hill Landing (16). Kingston Landing (17) (12268-C), much farther up and to the left (west), has a gravel beach ramp and dock. Ganey's Wharf (18) (12268-D), up farther and to the right (east), also has a ramp. Watt's Creek (19) (12268-E), almost at Denton and to the right (east), has a ramp.

Tuckahoe Creek

Refer to Chart #12268-D—"Choptank River: Tuckahoe Creek." Pg. 193

Tuckahoe Creek (100) branches off the Choptank at R "62" (20). It is fascinating and primitively beautiful with swamp and trees from deep forests overhanging the water. It would be nice to do this creek and the Choptank above Denton in a small inboard/outboard with cuddy cabin, and a spare prop or two. This would involve anchoring in a bend of the river for the evening, and not expecting many amenities from shore except the forest sounds of the night, and the forest shade in close. Fishing is good here. A few miles into Tuckahoe Creek, there is a fixed bridge (21) with vertical clearance of 17 feet.

Denton

Refer to Chart #12268-E—"Choptank River: Denton, Mill Creek to Chapel Branch."

Denton (99) is one of those nice quiet small river towns with good people, old houses still well used and lovingly cared for, small shops, and a few restaurants. The first settlement here was established around 1773 on what was then called "Pig Point." The first steam boat, the *Cyrus*, came up the river from Baltimore to Denton in 1850. The town was accidently burned in 1863 by northern troops stationed there, supposedly guarding the town. During their Fourth of July celebration, the accident set fire to a shop building, from whence the flames spread.

Just under (north of) the bridge, on the eastern bank, there is a park with a public hard surfaced launching ramp (22). There is a bulkhead area where you can tie and visit, with better than 6 feet depth. There is no power or water at the bulkhead.

It's a short walk from here to the beautiful old courthouse (23) and nearby town office (24), and the shops (25). The Court Square Corner Grill and Pub (26) at 200 Market Street, has good food for breakfast, lunch and dinner, a pub atmosphere at cocktail time, and take out. At the courthouse there is a farmer's market on Saturdays in the spring and summer.

One of the more scenic views is the jail house (27) which sits on a tall hill just to the north of the town bridges. The view is so pretty that if one were of a mind to misbehave, he might even consider asking the court for a cell with a window over looking the river here, instead of probation!

Across the river on the western bank and north a very short distance is the **Choptank River Yacht Club (28)** (called "the boat club" locally) which has slips available for some boats, a hard ramp, and sells gas. A sign, "CRYC" identifies this facility, and another sign indicates that they can take transients. They appear to be primarily set up to handle smaller motorboats, just the type that I would like to have to explore this river. No one is on duty here except during limited hours, but as in many nice towns like this, you should have no trouble finding someone to help.

Also on the same bank as the club, and just downriver, is a fuel and oil concern called "Crouse, division of Wise Oil and Fuel, Inc." (29). They are across the street from the river, and they are very friendly and knowledgable folks and may be able to help you if you need fuel. Their number is (410) 479-1722. Between the oil company and the yacht club is **Black Dog Boats Works (31)**. These people are well known in the area for rebuild, refit, and repair work, including glass and wood. They have a 25-ton crane. They have some transient slips with electricity up to 30 amps.

Cambridge station. Caboose now a real estate office

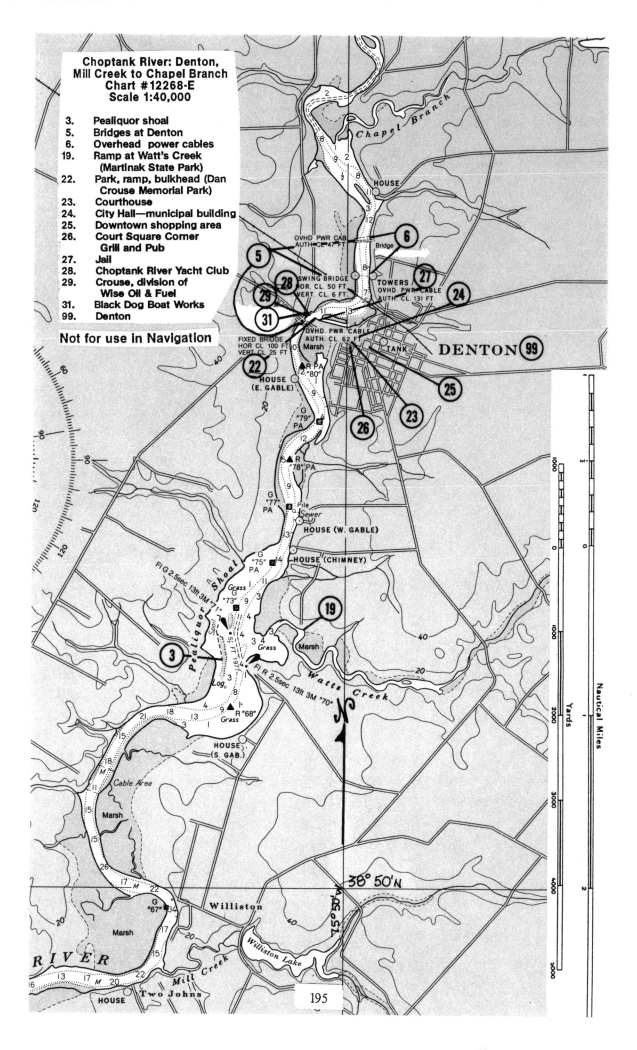

**Choptank River: Denton,
Mill Creek to Chapel Branch
Chart #12268-E
Scale 1:40,000**

3. Pealiquor shoal
5. Bridges at Denton
6. Overhead power cables
19. Ramp at Watt's Creek
     (Martinak State Park)
22. Park, ramp, bulkhead (Dan
     Crouse Memorial Park)
23. Courthouse
24. City Hall—municipal building
25. Downtown shopping area
26. Court Square Corner
     Grill and Pub
27. Jail
28. Choptank River Yacht Club
29. Crouse, division of
     Wise Oil & Fuel
31. Black Dog Boat Works
99. Denton

Not for use in Navigation

Choptank River to Greensboro

Refer to Chart #12268-F—"Choptank River: Continuation to Greensboro."

You could spend months exploring this river and Tuckahoe Creek. It would take a small boat, and a spirit of adventure and some "roughing it" to do this. The area is beautiful, in many cases almost wilderness, and worth the trouble. The Choptank itself continues on to Greensboro (30), and even farther up into the countryside. The controlling depth is reported on the charts at only 2 feet, but the state has recently begun to mark the channel above Denton, summers only, with floating red and green markers. These are replaced every year, occasionally in different positions, and therefore we cannot put them on the chart.

Although the depths will vary, local knowledgable people who fish and run the river advise that it is possible to get close to 6 feet draft to Greensboro if you know where the water is, work the tide, and have a bit of luck. I have not done this, and do not advise attempting it without talking to someone from Denton or Greensboro near the time that you wish to try. You'll need the latest information about this meandering creek-like stream above Denton. Immediately after you leave Denton, you will pass through a railway bridge, normally open, and then shortly thereafter another highway bridge with vertical clearance of 25 feet. There will then be a bridge at Greensboro with 10-foot vertical clearance.

Blue heron statue, Long Wharf Park, Cambridge

Choptank River Yacht Club, Denton (pg. 194)

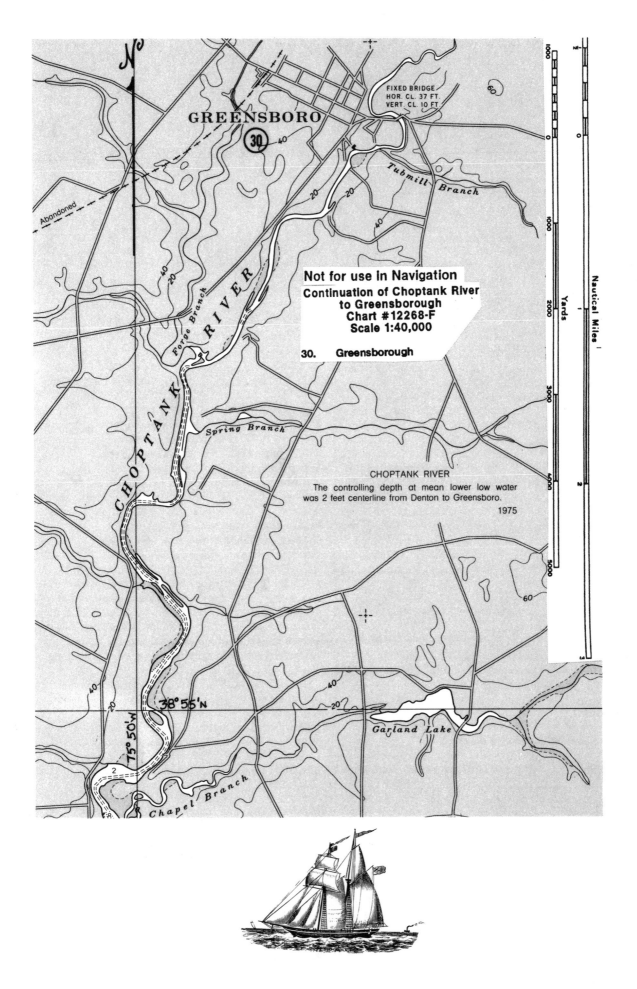

GREENSBORO

FIXED BRIDGE
HOR. CL. 37 FT.
VERT. CL. 10 FT.

Tubmill Branch

Abandoned

CHOPTANK RIVER

Forge Branch

Not for use in Navigation
Continuation of Choptank River
to Greensborough
Chart #12268-F
Scale 1:40,000

30.   Greensborough

Spring Branch

CHOPTANK RIVER
The controlling depth at mean lower low water
was 2 feet centerline from Denton to Greensboro.

1975

38°55'N

75°50'W

Garland Lake

Chapel Branch

Nautical Miles

Yards

1000
0
1000
2000
3000
4000
5000

197

CHAPTER 12

LITTLE CHOPTANK RIVER

This is a very pretty river with only a few boating facilities. There are some very isolated and lonely anchorages until you get up in to the creeks where there is more civilization ashore. The area is less used by cruising boats than the Choptank, but it is a great river for quiet gunkholing.

ENTRANCE

Refer to Chart #12263-D—"Western Choptank River (Southern Entrance) & Little Choptank River Entrance" in Chapter 11 PG 159 and

Chart #12266-I—"Little Choptank Entrance & Brooks Creek." PG 201

The entrance to the Little Choptank (30) (on Chart #12263-D in Chapter 11) is wide and deep, but it winds around shoals and it is important to pay careful attention to your route in. If the air is hazy or there is poor light, there may be some difficulty in orienting yourself as you enter.

The Fl G 2.5 sec. marker "1" (31) off Hills Point (32) is important to locate. It helps you in avoiding the shoal off Hills Point and the shoal (34) off James Island (33). Its position is 38°33.20'N by 76°19.30'W. If you are coming in from out in the Bay, a course of 104°M brings you from Fl R "78" (28) (Chart #12263-D) into the area just south of Fl G "1." (If coming in from the Choptank, steer 130°M from R N "4" to Fl G "1"). Rather than begin your southerly turn when you get off Fl G "1," continue on this course for ½ mile to avoid the shallow water extending in a northeasterly direction off James Island. After clearing this shoal area, head 182°M to bring you to the area west of Fl G "3" (35). Note that a hard shoal (36) extends westerly from Fl G "3," with depths of 8 feet. From here on, the markers are closer together and the spaces are not so wide open.

The scenery as you come into the river will be rather desolate and beautiful. From out here, very few signs of civilization appear. The shorelines are marsh and woods, and the river ahead of you to the east looks wide and lonely.

James Island

Refer to Chart #12264-A—"Little Choptank River, James Island and Slaughter Creek."

James Island (33) lies south of the entrance to the Little Choptank. This island is rapidly eroding, according to local people. I talked with several who remember going out to the island in cars on a corduroy road (road made of slabs of timper placed crossways on the road) before it washed through. The wash between the island and the mainland (37) is deeper than the chart indicates. I found 2½ feet in the middle. Local work boats go through the wash as a short cut, but they know the way. I was told that the water in the wash is around 4 feet deep, but I could not find that much. In any event, it can be done by dinghy or shoal draft boat if you are careful. When going through washes such as this, there is always the danger of stumps or clumps of bottom that have not eroded away.

The island itself is barren and pretty with trees ashore and beach along the water's edge. A pretty sandy (38) beach is in the middle on the northeast side. This is a great place to anchor for the day or visit by dinghy.

SLAUGHTER CREEK

Slaughter Creek has a tricky entrance and is not very good as an anchorage. It does have a marina, country store, a restaurant and a floating Coast Guard Station.

Refer to Chart #12264-A—"Little Choptank River, James Island and Slaughter Creek."

The outside marker for Slaughter Creek (39) Fl R "2" (40) is south of Fl G "5" (41), which is south of Ragged Island (42). The entrance from this marker until markers "6" and "7" (43) is subject to shifting shoals. Last year it had shoaled to 5 feet in places. Don't try to take more than 5 feet draft in there, though the marina inside told me that he could bring in boats up to 6 feet, the maximum draft depending on wind and moon tides. They stand by on Channel 16. If you are going to Slaughter Creek, tie up at this marina since there are not any good anchorages. This marina will be further described below. This entrance has been recently dredged, but seemed to have shoaled since then. Hopefully, the Coast Guard boat up in the creek will keep markers sorted out from the shoals, but they won't be able to stop the shoals from building. Once past these outside markers, the water becomes deeper and "middle of the creek" navigating is the rule.

As you approach the end of this straight and wide creek, you will see the **Taylor's Island Marina (44)** and surrounding facilities to your left (east), a low bridge (45) over the marshy creek straight ahead (in a southerly direction), and the extension of the creek referred to as Chapel Cove (46), turning off to the west. There's a public landing and a country store with a small restaurant in Chapel Cove.

Taylor's Island Marina is hard to miss. It is the only marina on the creek and is on the east shore. Taylor's Island Marina has 80 slips with electricity up to 30 amps. There is a yard facility with a 50-foot 25-ton lift, gas and diesel fuel, MC, Visa, and Shell credit cards are honored. There is a marine store carrying some hardware and other items, including block and cube ice, fishing bait and gear, snacks and beverages. A laundromat is available.

South of the marina are the docks for the Taylor's Island Coast Guard (47). When we last visited they were experimenting with a boat serving as the station house itself, the station's crew living on the boat.

North of the marina stands the Becky Phipps Inn (48), a bed and breakfast. Some say that Becky Phipps was the name of a cannon on ship named the *Dauntless* of Revolutionary War days. Others say that this was the name of the Captain's wife, or that this was the name of a slave aboard. Still others say that *Dauntless* was a British ship involved in the War of 1812, and that a group of watermen went out and captured her as she lay in the creek and brought her cannon, of that

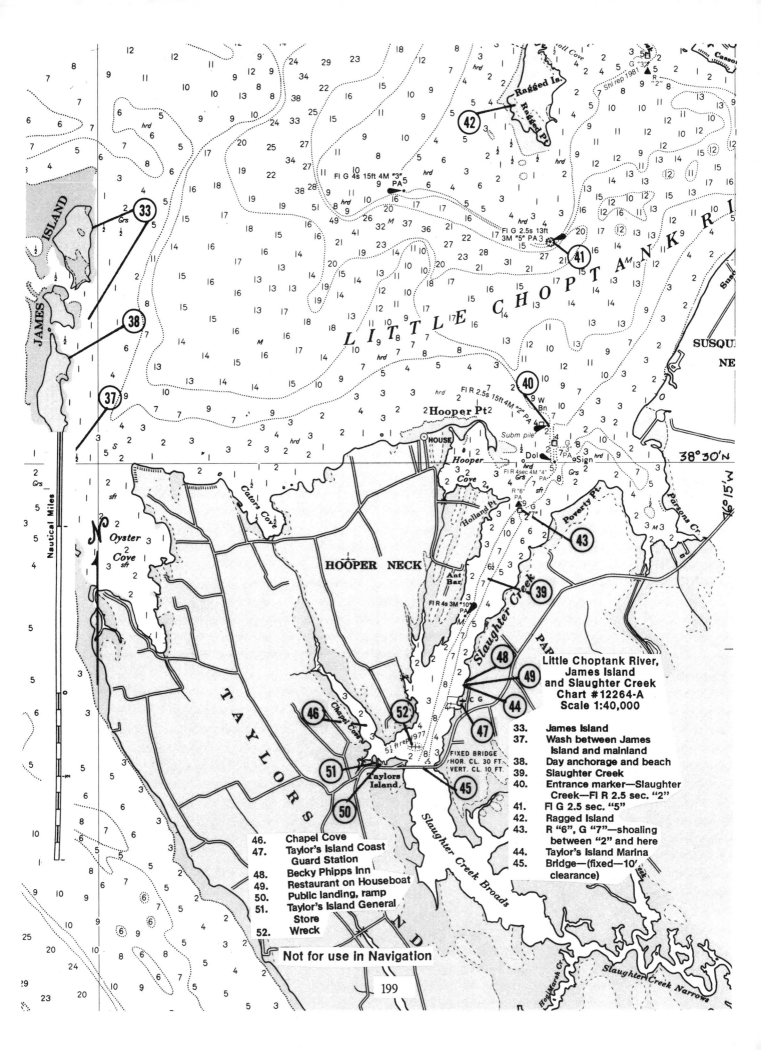

Little Choptank River,
James Island
and Slaughter Creek
Chart #12264-A
Scale 1:40,000

33. James Island
37. Wash between James Island and mainland
38. Day anchorage and beach
39. Slaughter Creek
40. Entrance marker—Slaughter Creek—Fl R 2.5 sec. "2"
41. Fl G 2.5 sec. "5"
42. Ragged Island
43. R "6", G "7"—shoaling between "2" and here
44. Taylor's Island Marina
45. Bridge—(fixed—10' clearance)

46. Chapel Cove
47. Taylor's Island Coast Guard Station
48. Becky Phipps Inn
49. Restaurant on Houseboat
50. Public landing, ramp
51. Taylor's Island General Store
52. Wreck

Not for use in Navigation

199

name, ashore. There is also a restaurant on a houseboat **(49)** tied at the facility. This area will seem remote as you pull in. This is part of what makes it attactive. It is approximately 17 miles from Cambridge.

Chapel Cove **(46)**, the dredged extension to the right (west) at the end of the Slaughter Creek, leads to a bulkheaded public landing with a hard surfaced public ramp **(50)**, clearly visible on the south shore as you turn in. The landing is used by work boats. It is permissible to tie up for a while to go ashore, but this is not an overnight marina. I found 3½ feet depth here.

At the head of the launching ramp parking lot is the Taylor's Island General Store **(51)**, a real country store. Inside you will find many helpful supplies, including clothing items, candies, groceries, and some fresh food. In the back of the store there is a little bar and some tables against the wall. Here you can get beer and beverages, cold cuts and salad and sandwiches, and very good home cooked food. The crab cakes are delicious, and I consider myself to be a crab cake tasting expert. They are happy to cater to boats at the marina or anchored nearby.

The chart notes a wreck **(52)** at the entrance and to the northern side of the channel as it turns to the west. People ashore told me that it had been removed long ago. They did volunteer, however, that many folks around have always thought that there was an old wreck of a pirate ship somewhere out in the creek, still with its cargo. They didn't know of anyone who had actually found any remains, but said that anyone in his right sense wouldn't be talking about it if he did find anything.

BROOKS CREEK
Refer to Chart #12266-I—"Little Choptank—Entrance & Brooks Creek."

This creek is shallow and pretty without any really great anchorages, although there are spots to drop the hook. It is an interesting place to explore, perhaps in a day trip, with a special surprise at the end.

Brooks Creek **(53)** opens to the east of Ragged Island **(42)** on the northern bank of this little Choptank River. It is wide open to the south, very shallow in its upper reaches, and shallow in its lower reaches except for the narrow channel. The entrance is shoaling and unstable. I found only 3½ feet controlling depth at MLW.

It is beautiful going in, with the low island and marsh to the left (west) and a house, apparently a hunting lodge, on the very low land separating the creek from the Bay. As you move farther into the creek, you will see some large homes ashore back in the woods, particularly to the west. Occasionally, in breaks in the trees, you can look westward across the peninsula to the Bay. The one really snug anchorge is in the first cove to the left **(54)** (western side) with 4 feet depth. There are some large houses up within the woods in this cove, and the anchorge would not be as private as you might have expected.

A hard surfaced public ramp **(55)**, farther up Brooks Creek, still on the western shore, lies up inside the marsh bulkheading, with some docks used by local boats. I found only 3 feet depth here. There is a local marina, named **McNamara's Marine (56)** with 18 slips, and a 30-foot railway a little farther up the creek in the cove on the west.

The land continues very low as you proceed north, with beautiful woods and marsh ashore. Soon you will come to a grouping of small houses in the little cove **(57)** to the east. Continue on, carefully, if your boat allows. For most, this is dinghy country. As you get to the end of the creek, you will notice that the ground is flat and marshy. Stand up and look to the northward and you will see the waters of Trippe Bay on the Choptank River **(58)**!

HUDSON CREEK
Refer to Chart #12266-J—"Upper (Eastern) Little Choptank River." PG 203

Hudson Creek has one of our favorite anchorages near its

Taylors Island General Store, Slaughter Creek, Little Choptank R.

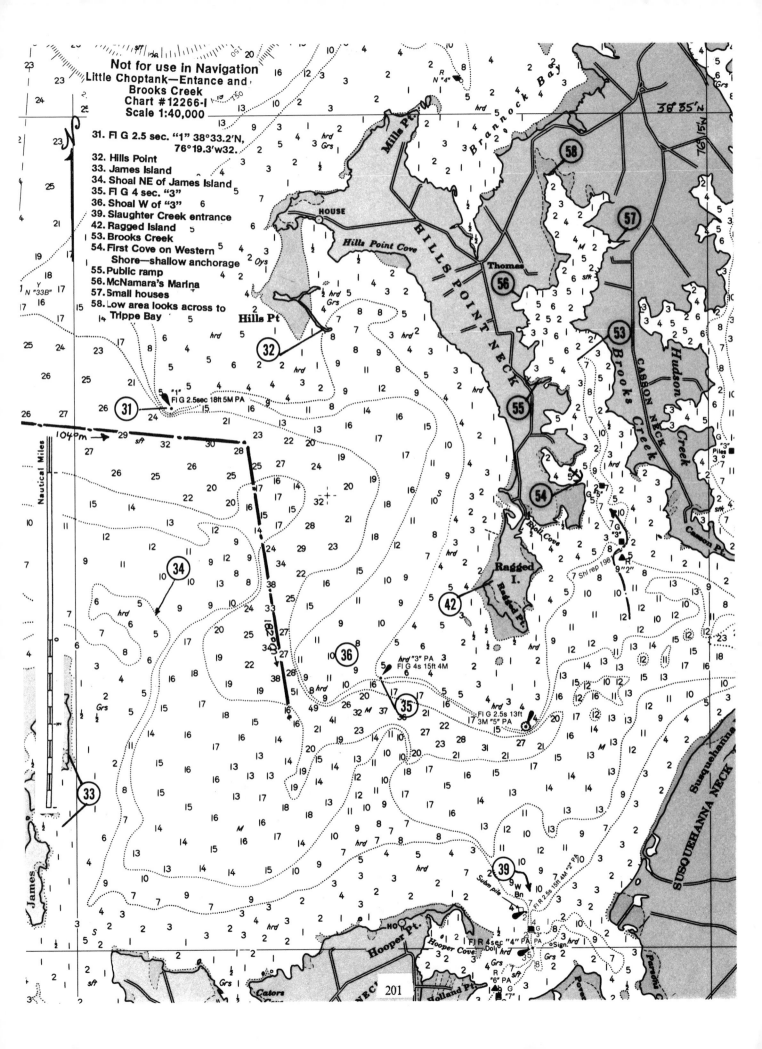

Not for use in Navigation
Little Choptank—Entrance and
Brooks Creek
Chart #12266-I
Scale 1:40,000

31. Fl G 2.5 sec. "1" 38°33.2'N,
    76°19.3'w32.
32. Hills Point
33. James Island
34. Shoal NE of James Island
35. Fl G 4 sec. "3"
36. Shoal W of "3"
39. Slaughter Creek entrance
42. Ragged Island
53. Brooks Creek
54. First Cove on Western
    Shore—shallow anchorage
55. Public ramp
56. McNamara's Marina
57. Small houses
58. Low area looks across to
    Trippe Bay

201

mouth. Farther in, the creek becomes more built up ashore with private homes and docks.

Entering Hudson Creek (59), head in a northerly direction from about half-way (60) between G "7" and Fl G "9,"; rounding the shoal east of Casson Point (61) and avoiding the shoal coming southwesterly off Butter Pot Point (62). Your target as you head in will be G "1" inside, north of Casson Point. Rounding that, you will find a beautiful anchorage (63) back into the southwest of the channel. There is a beach ashore along the neck of Casson Point, with woods behind. There is a bit of a fetch to the southeast, but the shoal behind G "1" helps to block some of the effect of this, and if it gets too bad for your boat, you can always run farther up creek. This anchorage is well-protected from the west and northwest. There is a great feeling of isolation here, with few signs of civilization and usually only an occasional work boat going by in the channel.

For shallower drafted boats, Back Creek (64), just to the north-northeast of the Casson Point anchorage, is beautiful and very snug. Surprisingly, I found the water depths to be what the chart indicates, not shallower, as is so often the case in open creek entrances. I found the deepest entrance water by heading in with R "2" (65) (a Hudson Creek marker) on my right (southeast) and going 35°M. Looking into the creek, there is a small white house (66) ahead, at 37.5°M. I headed just to the left (west) of that house. Continue 35°M until you get to just southeasterly of the point to the left (northwest) (67), then head to the middle. I found 4 feet to be controlling depth.

Inside Back Creek, you'll find mostly dense woods and marsh. Almost anywhere that suits you will be a good anchorge here, as long as your draft permits.

Hudson Creek above the Casson Point anchorge is more civilized, with quite a few small homes ashore. Many of these have docks. The first cove after G "3" (68) has many work boats inside, and several houses. Although it looks as though it would be a nice anchorage, you might feel crowded. The next cove (69) is prettier. It also has houses, but is wider. There is a bulkheaded shore on the northern end.

If you are heading upstream, favor the western side off the point (70). The next cove up (71), on the right (eastern side) has stakes coming out from it to the main channel, on the southern side of the cove. There are now considerably more houses than in the lower section of the creek. These continue on both shores in a pleasant mixture of field, woods, and homes until you reach the fork. The left (western) fork (72) has many houses, but the eastern fork (73) is much prettier for an anchorage. As you turn in, there is a feeling of being in deep countryside, far from the Bay, back in a quieter time, with farms around and only a few modern houses. Farther up this branch where it turns northerly, it becomes crowded again. The prettiest anchorage is near the fork entry.

MADISON BAY

Refer to Chart #12266-K—"Little Choptank River: Madison Bay, Fishing Creek, Church Creek." PG20 5

This is a large open bay with little to attract the cruising boat.

The Madison Bay (74) entrance marker, Fl R "2" (75) indicates a shoal to its west and south. This appears to be extending easterly, and the marker should be passed cautiously.

There is a landing (76) up in the bay, in the dredged area to the southwest. It has a public, concrete launching ramp. **Madison Bay Marine (77)** has 32 slips. They sell gas and diesel. The building behind the marina is a restaurant, open seasonally. I have found 5½ feet controlling depth up to the public

Trinity Episcopal Church, Church Creek

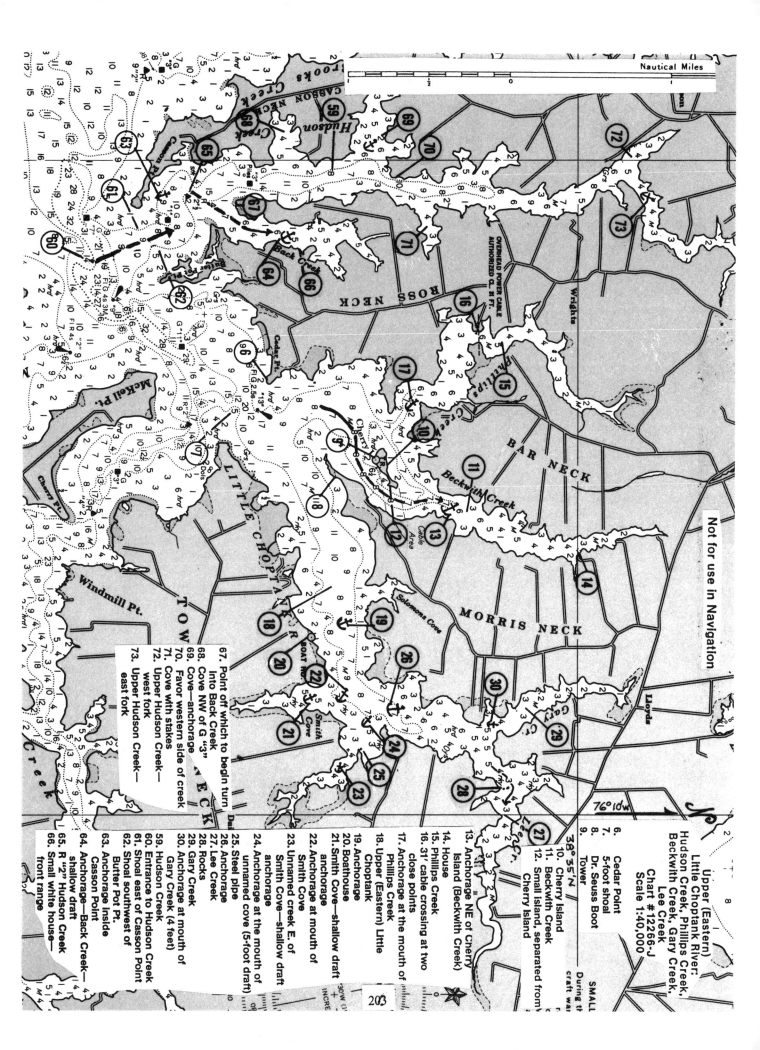

Not for use in Navigation

Nautical Miles

Upper (Eastern)
Little Choptank River:
Hudson Creek, Phillips Creek,
Beckwith Creek, Gary Creek,
Lee Creek
Chart #12266-J
Scale 1:40,000

38°35'N

76°10'W

6. Cedar Point
7. 5-foot shoal
8. Dr. Seuss Boot
9. Tower
10. Cherry Island
11. Beckwith Creek
12. Small Island, separated from
    Cherry Island
13. Anchorage NE of Cherry
    Island (Beckwith Creek)
14. House
15. Phillips Creek
16. 31' cable crossing at two
    close points
17. Anchorage at the mouth of
    Phillips Creek
18. Upper (Eastern) Little
    Choptank
19. Anchorage
20. Boathouse
21. Smith Cove—shallow draft
    anchorage
22. Anchorage at mouth of
    Smith Cove
23. Unnamed creek E. of
    Smith Cove—shallow draft
    anchorage
24. Anchorage at the mouth of
    unnamed cove (5-foot draft)
25. Steel pipe
26. Anchorage
27. Lee Creek
28. Rocks
29. Gary Creek
30. Anchorage at mouth of
    Gary Creek (4 feet)
59. Hudson Creek
60. Entrance to Hudson Creek
61. Shoal east of Hudson Creek
62. Shoal southwest of
    Butter Pot Pt.
63. Anchorage inside
    Casson Point
64. Anchorage—Back Creek—
    shallow draft
65. R "2" Hudson Creek
    front range
66. Small white house—

67. Point off which to begin turn
    into Back Creek
68. Cove NW of G "3"
69. Cove—anchorage
70. Favor western side of creek
71. Cove with stakes
72. Upper Hudson Creek—
    west fork
73. Upper Hudson Creek—
    east fork

203

landing area. The final approach is dredged and marked; stay within the aids.

One pleasant sight coming into the landing is the tall church spire (78), noted on the chart, to the south. This is pointed at the tip, with an open area underneath for the bell.

•

Proceeding up the Little Choptank past the mouth of Madison Bay, beware of the shoal area (79) to the west of McKeil Point. It is reported at 6 feet, but it is in an area where the bottom is likely to drift. There is 16 feet depth between it and the shoal (80) that comes off Butter Pot Point, but the passageway is narrow and deceiving because of the width of the open water here. Fl G "9" is critical, but note that you must round it to avoid the 6-foot shoal to its northeast before heading to G "11" northwest of McKeil Point.

FISHING CREEK AND CHURCH CREEK
Refer to Chart #12266-K.

Fishing Creek is a great place to anchor if your draft permits, and is an ideal area for dinghy exploration. It is settled along most of its banks, but the homes and communities are a natural part of the Eastern Shore Countryside.

Entering Fishing Creek (81) you will want to avoid the 4-foot shoal (82) to the north-northeast of McKeil Point, as you are moving from G "11" in the Little Choptank River Channel to R "2" at the creek entrance. To avoid this shoal (82), head from around 200 feet off (to the south-southeast of) G "11" straight to red "2" and then put R "2" on your right as you near it. The entrance did not seem as tricky as it looked on the chart, but the shoal area is there, as indicated, on both sides.

McKeil Point (83), on your right coming in, has many beautiful pine trees, and a house well up in the trees, barely visible. Looking into the creek from the entrance, you will see mostly forest and marsh, with some houses. As you continue on to G "3" (85), be aware that the shoal which it marks continues on a little past (to the south of) G "3" and refrain from cutting to your left (or rounding to the southeast) too soon.

The windmill shown on the chart appears above tree level to the south as you round Cheery Point. Interestingly, the little finger of Windmill Point, on the left (northeast) side of the creek points across to the windmill on the other side. The shoal extending northeasterly off Cherry Point is marked by a private red marker (87), numbered "6." It is a small float. There is another private floating marker, a G "7" (88) to the southwest of Windmill Point, marking the 5-foot shoal there.

The cove behind (south of) Cherry Point (89) is probably the best anchorage in the creek, because farther up, depths become shallower, the stream becomes narrower, and there are many more houses ashore. There is a farm inside the cove south of Cherry Point, on the north bank, and another house on the southern bank. The wreck noted on the chart, up in the end of the cove is visible, but you don't have to go that far into the cove to anchor.

There are many more houses on the northern bank of the creek above Cherry Point, many with docks. The ground is low on both sides of the creek, as you proceed up toward where Church Creek (90) splits off to the south. There are many houses in this section, and many private docks. As you approach the split, there are even more houses on the southern shore, most of which are small. Straight ahead, to your east, you will see two conspicuous large modern white houses

(91), and a third smaller house, all on the point dividing Church Creek from Fishing Creek.

Church Creek

Rounding into Church Creek, the dense area of small homes continues on the west bank. The first long cove (92) to your left (on the eastern bank) after you enter Church Creek has several houses placed around the shore and is not very private as an anchorage. At the very end there are woods and the cove becomes prettier, and the shallow draft boat of 2½ to 3 feet can anchor in there. The next little cove (93) to the left (east) looks out to small homes on the opposite side of the creek. There is one house up inside the cove, behind the trees on your right (south) after you go in. This again, could be used as an anchorage for a very shallow draft boat of 2½ to 3 feet.

The long cove (94) pointing to the southwest with the village "Woolford" at the end has a highway crossing the end. While up in the cove you can hear the sounds of traffic, and there are still a considerable number of homes around the shore. If you anchor near the mouth, you'll be far away from the road.

Church Creek farther southeast is still densely populated with mid-size homes, many set back in the fields and stands of pines. Depths become much shallower, with several 1-foot areas indicated on the chart. However, I found at least 3 feet controlling depth up to the church described below. It is not marked, but we went carefully and picked our way.

If your draft will allow you, go up to the old church and its graveyard (96) on the southern bank of the creek. At least do this in your dinghy. Note that the chart shows a line of pilings (95) coming out from the southern shore close to the channel. I did not see these, but I passed at high tide. Some remains may still be there. If you stay outside of the two points at each end of the cove from which the piles run, you'll avoid the piling and stay in the channel.

As you approach the church, you first see a graveyard of modern times. However, as you proceed on until you are directly off the point, you will see the church, back within the ancient gnarled trees which have guarded it for centuries. Around the church and close to the water are stones for graves dating back into the 1600s. The tree limbs hang protectively down, casting deep shadows. This is a very beautiful and special place. The church is believed to have been built before 1680 and is Trinity Episcopal Church (96). At one time it possessed a red velvet cushion, presented by Queen Anne. It was said to have been the cushion upon which she kneeled when she was crowned Queen of England. It has long been destroyed in a fire at one of the parsonages where it was stored. It is possible to anchor off the church in the creek, but keep well lit at night. Local residents use the creek often. Upstream from here, the creek becomes even shallower, with a lot more homes, and many mooring stakes for work boats congesting the waters. These work boats generally draw from 2½ to 3 feet, indicating that there is water available for boats of this draft. You can find the deepest water if you proceed slowly keeping an eye on the chart.

Upper Portion of Fishing Creek

Fishing Creek extends far east of Church Creek until it finally divides in to the North (97), (very short) Northeast (98), South (99), and Southeast (100), branches. It is similar to Church Creek and lower Fishing Creek, but is more reminiscent of older Eastern Shore days with old farms and crumbl-

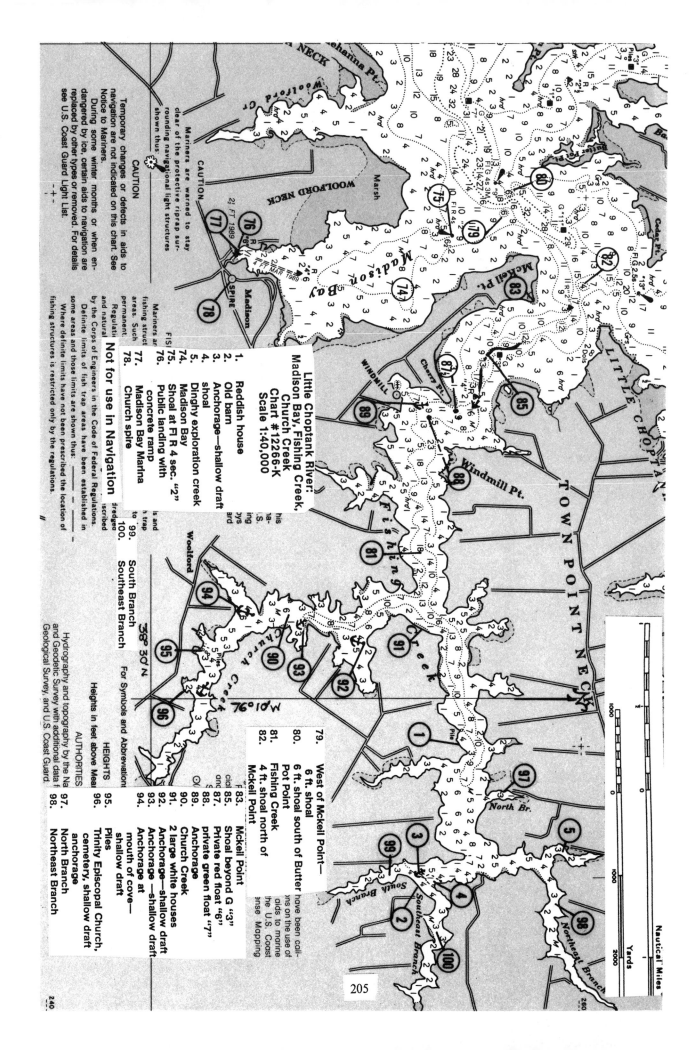

ing barns and silos. A unique conspicuous reddish colored house (1) dominates the point to your south as you proceed east up the creek. This lets you know that you are nearing the final big creek split in this exploration. Looking ahead to the east, you will be impressed with the number of houses, both large and small, which you will see all around you as you reach the area where the three main branches split off. For those whizzing ashore in cars, this is not a great distance from Cambridge. Depths are generally deeper than Church Creek, and a boat drawing 4 feet should find enough water to reach the three major prongs.

In the Southeast Branch (100), although there are woods deep into the creek, you can see structures, apparently tanks, of a factory or a storage facility, way off in the distance over the trees. They are a fitting reminder of the present haunting the quieter past of the area. The South branch is very pretty to explore by dinghy, with less civilization and more woods up to the marshy area at its end.

On the point (2) separating the South from the Southeast Branches stands an old barn, in graceful disrepair, with countryside behind and an aura of old Shore around. There are also modern homes, but not as many as in other sections of this creek. In a boat drawing no more than 3 feet, this would make a lovely anchorage (3). Avoid the 1-foot shoal (4) south-southeasterly coming off the northern point at the entrance to Southeast Branch.

The Northeast Branch (98) has houses on the bank to your right (east) as you enter, and with the low yards and many docks, would not provide a very private anchorage. But very quickly the houses pass behind as the creek continues into a vast expanse of farm field, with the tree line far behind the distances. This would be a beautiful place to wander with corn bowing into the breezes or wheat waving in light air. It is very shallow, only for dinghies, but if you have ever loved walking out in the midst of a growing crop, with nothing to see but the crop around you and nothing to smell but the earth and her fruit, you should go here, and experience this again, in your dinghy.

The unnamed branch which runs off to the north (5), beginning just west of Northeast Branch, is also very beautiful with a few homes and much farmland, great for dinghy exploration.

•

Refer to Chart #12266-J—"Upper (Eastern) Little Choptank River." PG 203
With all of the creeks and coves explored thus far, it seems time to leave the Little Choptank. But not so. What many feel to be the prettiest parts are yet to come in the creeks upriver of Cedar Point (6). There will also be many private homes ashore up here, but there will be easier spots to anchor with more depth and more natural surroundings. As you head northeasterly past Cedar Point, do not pass too far south of Fl G "13." If you do, you may run afoul of the 5-foot shoal (7) to your right (south). Go from G "11" straight to G "13," watching the depth finder. The shoal comes up gradually and you should know it if you are getting too far over to the east. From here your choices are Phillips and Beckwith Creeks to your left, (to the north) or the main branch of the river flowing in a more northeasterly direction to where it splits into Gary and Lee Creeks.

BECKWITH CREEK (11)

Beckwith Creek has a very pretty anchorage near its mouth, guarded by Cherry Island (10).

After rounding Fl G "13," as you look northeast, you will see the tip of the toe of a shoe (8) remarkably resembling a crooked "Dr. Seuss" boot. It is covered with tall forest. Looking toward a north-northeasterly direction, you will see a strange tower (9) on the southern tip of Cherry Island (10) in the middle of the entrance to Beckwith Creek (11). The tower is a square two-story structure which is white on the bottom and red on the top. Cherry Island also has three single-story houses on it, fronted by a bulkhead. Local watermen told me that they believe this to be a private hunting lodge. The tower (9) makes a great landmark as you are sorting things out coming into this area of the river.

If you wish to go on into Beckwith Creek, follow the chart for the deepest water. While the depths of 7 feet are on the northern side of the island, the pass on the south side is wider and easier to follow. The eastern end of Cherry Island has washed through so that it is a second tiny island (12) with a few trees. In the little cove on the south side of the island, you will notice a boathouse and a dock. The dock is indicated on the chart.

Once past the island, Beckwith Creek opens up into a very beautiful vista with trees and field on either side and one lonely house up at the end far to the northeast. Almost any spot just past this island would make a beautiful anchorage (13), with a great feeling of isolation and natural surroundings. Don't bring any more than 6 feet draft up here, and proceed carefully. The deep water is narrow, and there is not much room to circle around up in here. There is a long north-south fetch, but not enough to bother most cruisers in normal weather.

As you continue north into Beckwith Creek, the creek changes, and many more houses come into view. You will see the lonely house that first impressed you as entered, but this house is not now so lonely. It sits on the northwest entrance bank of a small creek (14) running off to the east. When you first saw it, you weren't able to see the other houses frequenting the shores in that section of the creek, The creek continues on through fields and back yards.

PHILLIPS CREEK

Phillips Creek is still very much in ancient times in appearance, and would make a great anchorage for those with the daring and draft to enter.

Refer to Chart # 12266-J. PG 203
Entering Phillips Creek (15), I found the depth as the chart shows, but the channel is very narrow. Once you pass the two guardian points of the entrance area, you see a few old farm buildings and silos around the shore. Nothing in here seems new, and we felt that we were seeing the Shore in olden days. Soon the creek narrows to pass through two very close points (16). I found only 3 feet depth right after I passed through these two points, but I was glad I had come. Here there is deep forest with a narrow band of marsh around the water's edge. The silence of deep woods and pure nature surrounded me. A large area of marsh to the right (east) behind the point on the eastern side has huge thick blackened trunks standing

starkly out of the swaying grasses, like ghosts of the trees that were there generations ago.

You can explore Phillips Creek from your anchorage northeast of Cherry Island in Beckwith Creek, using your dinghy. If you only draw 5 feet, you will find the wide area (17) just inside the narrow entrance of Phillips Creek to be a beautiful place to anchor. You'll be surrounded by farm fields and a few old silos off in the distance. If you are very shallow drafted and are proceeding past the two inner points, beware of stumps which are always at risk in deep woods streams. Also note the authorized 31 feet power cable (16) from point to point. The chart shows depths of 5 and then 4 feet just beyond the points, but don't go in here with more than 3 feet draft, and that on a rising tide . Whichever way you do it, be sure to visit this creek and explore up beyond the two inner points.

UPPER LITTLE CHOPTANK

These upper reaches of the Little Choptank River are very pretty, with mostly forest and field until you get into the extreme upper area which is very settled and lacks privacy in most anchorages. The far upper reaches are so deep into the shore that there are areas of rocky bottom.

As you look northeasterly into the upper Little Choptank (18), you almost see nothing but woods and field. It looks almost like it must have looked before civilization came here. The long point (8) to your left (north) coming in which looks like a boot, is covered with hardwood and pine, with a house up in the arch of the foot. To the right (east) are several houses up in the woods, not very conspicuous from the water. They become more conspicuous as you move abreast of them going east up the river.

As the river broadens past the opening, it also becomes more civilized, although still not as busy as Fishing Creek. Boats drawing more than 4 feet might prefer to anchor here (19) in the wider section of the river, and explore the creeks and coves above by dinghy. This area of the river has mud bottom and the breezes are better. There is a southwest exposure, but if you were expecting such a wind, you could run upriver (26) just a little farther to get a lee. As you proceed farther up, you will be more likely to find rocky or gravel bottom.

Smith Cove

The boat house (20) noted on the chart is an ordinary structure with a V-roof. Smith Cove (21) with its depths of 5, and then 4, and then 3 feet, makes a pretty and snug anchorage for boats with that draft. There is very little to be seen of any civilization up in here, with woods all around. Note the reported area of "rocky bottom" in this cove. This is unusual for the Bay, but more of this type of bottom will be seen ahead in this unusual river. There is some fetch to the north, but it should not be too bad in most weather. Deeper drafted boats can anchor off the entrance to Smith Cove in the middle between the two points. This is also a pleasant anchorage

(22) for drafts of 4 to 6 feet, depending on how far you go in. Be sure to stay in the middle as you approach the two points of the cove because it shoals to either side.

The unnamed creek next upstream from Smith Cove, on your right (west), has an even prettier anchorage (23) for a boat drawing no more than 3 feet. Deeper draft boats of 5 feet can work their way into the outer area between the two outer points (24) of the cove. I found 5 feet about ¾ of the way in. Note here that parts of the bottom are rocky. Be careful when setting your anchor. I found 3½ feet available in an even prettier anchorage (23) a little farther in, behind (southeast of) the finger pointing out into the outer cove. Here you will be surrounded with deep woods and low beautiful marsh. As you round the finger point, you will see a steel pipe (25) out in the water just off (to the west-northwest of) the point. It is noted on the chart as a black dot. If you proceed farther into the creek past this second anchorage, you will soon find some homes and trailers up near the head.

Heading north up the Little Choptank River, you will see many more homes ashore than you would have expected when you first looked into this upper river. But there is not the crowd that existed on Fishing Creek and the river is still pretty. Don't take more than 4 feet draft this far up. More depth is here if you know exactly where to be, but there are no marks or ranges. As you get into Lee and Gary Creeks, 3 feet would be a safer draft, and less as you proceed on.

Lee Creek
Refer to Chart # 12266-J.

Lee Creek is for dinghy exploration for most boats, although a boat of 3 feet could anchor here if he could find a mud spot among the areas of rocky bottom.

In Lee Creek (27) you actually see the rocky bottom that the chart has noted earlier. As you enter the creek, you notice what appears to be an island ahead (in a northeasterly direction). This is the rock area (28) indicated on the chart. These are not huge boulders as you would see in the Susquehanna, but are mounds of smaller rocks mixed with some earth. Bottom such as this would not make good holding. As you come in and first see these islands of large gravel, it appears as though you should put them to your left (north) to pass them and head upstream. As you get closer, you will see that the chart is accurate, and they should go to your right (south). Proceeding around them, you will find depths to be as indicated, with woods and field and some older homes. This is a great area to go into by dinghy.

Gary Creek

Gary Creek (29) ends quickly after you pass the area of its mouth. It gets very shallow as it goes into field and forest. There are homes around the mouth, but you should anchor (30) here to explore upstream by dinghy. If you don't draw more than 4 feet you can tuck up enough into the mouth so that you will be out of the southwest fetch of the river.

207

CHAPTER 13

WESTERN SHORE OF UPPER CHESAPEAKE BAY

BUSH AND GUNPOWDER RIVERS

Refer to Regional Chart #12273-D—"Western Shore Middle River, Gunpowder River, Bush River."

We do not recommend these rivers for cruising because they are a part of the firing range for the United States Army facility, Aberdeen Proving Grounds. This facility serves as a major test and evaluation area for research, development and testing of small arms, artillery, ammunition, tracked and wheeled vehicles, and general military equipment. The channels to these rivers and surrounding waters and creeks and inlets are closed to navigation much of the time. When they are open, navigation allowed is limited, and much of the shoreline is restricted with warnings of unexploded ordinance.

Refer also to Chart #12274-L—"Bush River (Northern Section) PG 211 ↗ and PG 212 ↘
Chart #12274-M—"Upper Gunpowder River, Bird River."

Some marinas are in the upper, open areas of each river. These are used primarily to permanently berth local boats, and some have very good facilities. Locations are marked on our charts of Bush River (upper section) and Upper Gunpowder River and Bird River. If you wish to make arrangements to visit, you will find the marinas friendly and helpful. Phone numbers are in the identification legends on these charts.

The Bush River (3) has a bascule bridge and two overhead power cables, one with 35-feet clearance and the other with 43-feet clearance. The Gunpowder River (2) has two fixed bridges of 11 and 12 feet clearances.

U.S. Army patrol boats are in the area. These can usually be contacted on VHF, although we have personally heard boats attempting to call them unsuccessfully.

Refer to Sketch Chart—"Aberdeen Proving Ground."

Buoys marking restricted lines are can buoys, with orange and white horizontal bands and radar reflectors, and are maintained from June 5 to October 1. They are marked by letters A through L on our sketch chart "Aberdeen Proving Ground Restricted Area."

The restricted area is shown on our sketch chart "Aberdeen Proving Grounds" by dashed lines. Boaters are also advised "not to handle or attempt to remove any remnants from the waters or beaches. These may be extremely dangerous items such as unexploded (dud) ammunition. Violators are subject to prosecution under 18 U.S.C. section 1382 and other applicable statutes." The following is a notice to the boaters published by the Army and contained in a pamphlet disseminated by the facilitiy which shows the restricted area and gives other pertinent information.

IMPORTANT NOTICE TO BOATERS

The adjoining map illustrates the waters, shorelines, and islands within Aberdeen Proving Ground's restricted water zone. Normally, these restricted waters are closed from 7:30 a.m. to 5 p.m. daily except on Saturday, Sunday, and national holidays.

However, the shaded areas on the map which are listed above are closed to the public at all times.

Opening of the restricted water zone is granted for navigational and fishing purposes only.

Navigation includes anchoring a boat within the restricted waters or using the restricted waters for water-skiing provided that no boat or person touches any land (either dry land or underwater land) within the Proving Ground reservation and that no water skier comes closer than 200 meters to any shoreline.

Persons outside of any vessel for any purpose, including, but not limited to, swimming (except for purposes of water skiing as outlined above), scuba diving, or any other purpose are considered in violation of navigation. Violators are subject to prosecution under 18 U.S.C., section 1382, and other applicable statutes.

Landing of boats or personnel on the shorelines or islands within the restricted zone is prohibited at all times.

Entrance to the restricted waters for navigational purposes during periods of firings can be made only by securing a clearance from either the installation's B-Tower Control by telephoning 278-2250/3971, personal or radio contact on ship-shore FM Channel 16 and citizen band Channel 12 with range control (call letters AAAA) or B-Tower AAAA-1, and Worton Point AAAA-2. Loud speakers and flashing red or blue lights as warning signals are installed on all patrol boats.

MIDDLE RIVER

As a typical gunkholing cruising destination, this is not what most people are looking for. Close to Baltimore, its shoreline is heavily populated and cluttered with many docks. There are some marinas used as permanent slips by area people. Some of these have good repair facilities. There are a few restaurants, and there are various parts shops. This is not a good area for food provisioning. Many consider it to be a place for keeping your boat, to cruise away from when the weekend comes, or to visit when you are in the area and need repairs or parts.

Entrance

Refer to Chart #12273-D—"Regional Chart: Western Shore, Middle River, Gunpowder River, Bush River" PG 210
and
Chart #12278-F—"Pooles Island, Middle River Entrance."
PG 213

Thousands of pleasure boats, large and small, enter the Middle River (1) regularly. Be sure that you are not going into the Gunpowder River (2). This would seem hard to do, but local people say that it has been done in error. The Gunpowder

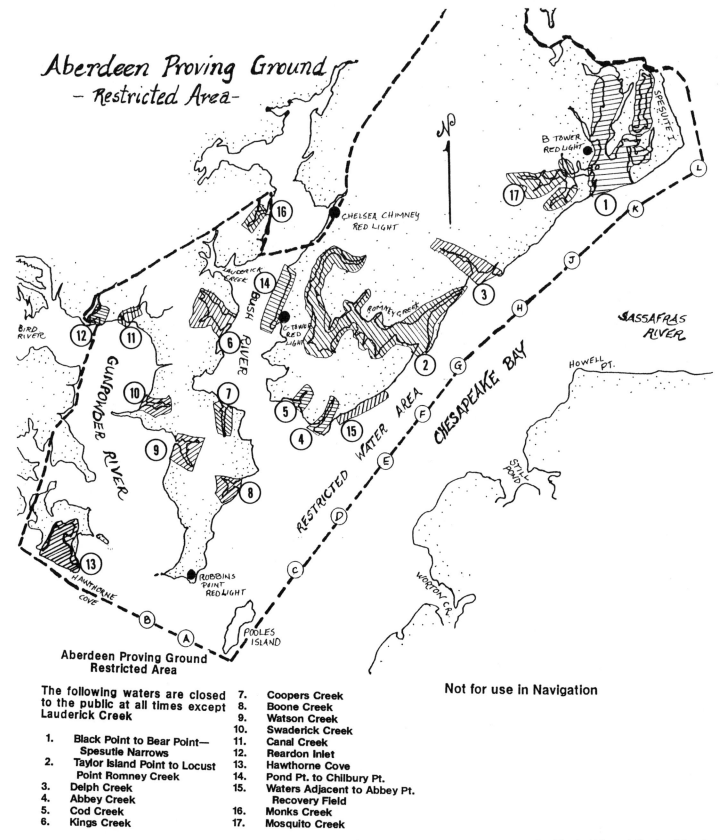

Aberdeen Proving Ground
- Restricted Area-

Aberdeen Proving Ground
Restricted Area

Not for use in Navigation

The following waters are closed to the public at all times except Lauderick Creek

1. Black Point to Bear Point— Spesutie Narrows
2. Taylor Island Point to Locust Point Romney Creek
3. Delph Creek
4. Abbey Creek
5. Cod Creek
6. Kings Creek
7. Coopers Creek
8. Boone Creek
9. Watson Creek
10. Swaderick Creek
11. Canal Creek
12. Reardon Inlet
13. Hawthorne Cove
14. Pond Pt. to Chilbury Pt.
15. Waters Adjacent to Abbey Pt. Recovery Field
16. Monks Creek
17. Mosquito Creek

is part of the Aberdeen Proving Grounds Firing range (86). As such, it is restricted except on weekends, it is "hot" often (you can hear the guns), and even on weekends you cannot land. See the section on the Bush and Gunpowder Rivers at the beginning of this chapter. Probably a patrol boat will approach to warn you off, but it is best to go into the correct river.

Most will be approaching Middle River from the Patapsco or from out in the Bay. There is a great deal of open water in the Bay south of Gunpowder Neck (64) and Pooles Island (65). Looking at this from a boat it seems open and easy. However, much of this is relatively shallow compared to the rest of the Bay.

Coming in from the Bay, be cognizant of Pooles Island Bar Light (4) which is south of Pooles Island. With depths of 7 feet and shoaling reported between it and the island (5) just to its north, you shouldn't pass north of the light. You will

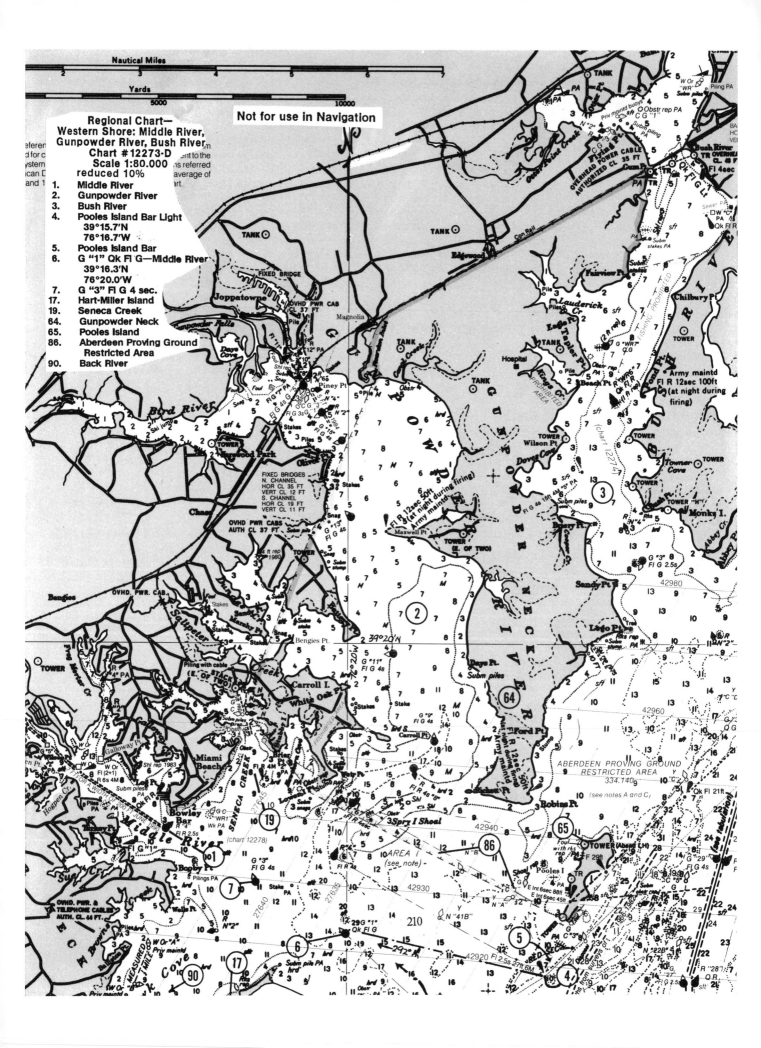

Regional Chart—
Western Shore: Middle River,
Gunpowder River, Bush River
Chart #12273-D
Scale 1:80.000
reduced 10%

1. Middle River
2. Gunpowder River
3. Bush River
4. Pooles Island Bar Light
   39°15.7'N
   76°16.7'W
5. Pooles Island Bar
6. G "1" Qk Fl G—Middle River
   39°16.3'N
   76°20.0'W
7. G "3" Fl G 4 sec.
17. Hart-Miller Island
19. Seneca Creek
64. Gunpowder Neck
65. Pooles Island
86. Aberdeen Proving Ground
    Restricted Area
90. Back River

Not for use in Navigation

Nautical Miles

Yards

ABERDEEN PROVING GROUND
RESTRICTED AREA
334.140
(see notes A and C)

210

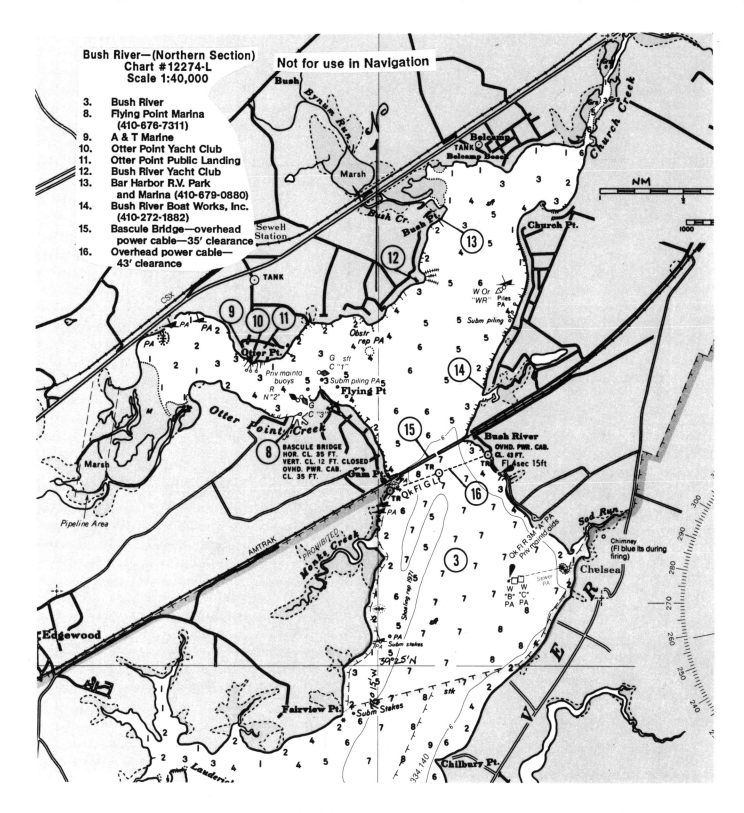

Bush River—(Northern Section)
Chart #12274-L
Scale 1:40,000

3.   Bush River
8.   Flying Point Marina
     (410-676-7311)
9.   A & T Marine
10. Otter Point Yacht Club
11. Otter Point Public Landing
12. Bush River Yacht Club
13. Bar Harbor R.V. Park
     and Marina (410-679-0880)
14. Bush River Boat Works, Inc.
     (410-272-1882)
15. Bascule Bridge—overhead
     power cable—35' clearance
16. Overhead power cable—
     43' clearance

also find it helpful to sight Pooles Island Bar Light (4) for reference. It is 27 feet tall and flashes every 2½". It is a black skeleton tower on a cylindrical base and its position is 39°15.7′N by 76°16.7′W.

Qk Fl G "1" (6), entrance buoy for the Middle River, is 292°M from that light. You should not go up to the light to get this bearing. The position of Qk Fl G "1" is 39°16.3′N by 76°20.0′W.

From the area immediately north of this marker, a course of 308°M takes you into the mouth of Middle River, passing Fl G "3" (7) to your left (to the southwest). Note the shaded line on the chart which comes in a south-southwesterly direc-

tion down the Bay to the east of Pooles Island, then turns west-northwesterly at the southern tip of Pooles Island and heads up into Seneca Creek. That is the boundary (86) of the restricted area over which you should not cross. Within this area there is firing, and there may be unexploded ordinance on the shore. For more information, see the section on the Bush and Gunpowder rivers at the beginning of this chapter.

Refer to Chart 12273-E—"Regional Chart: Western Shore Patapsco River Entrance, Back River, Middle River," in the beginning of Chapter 14, Patapsco River.

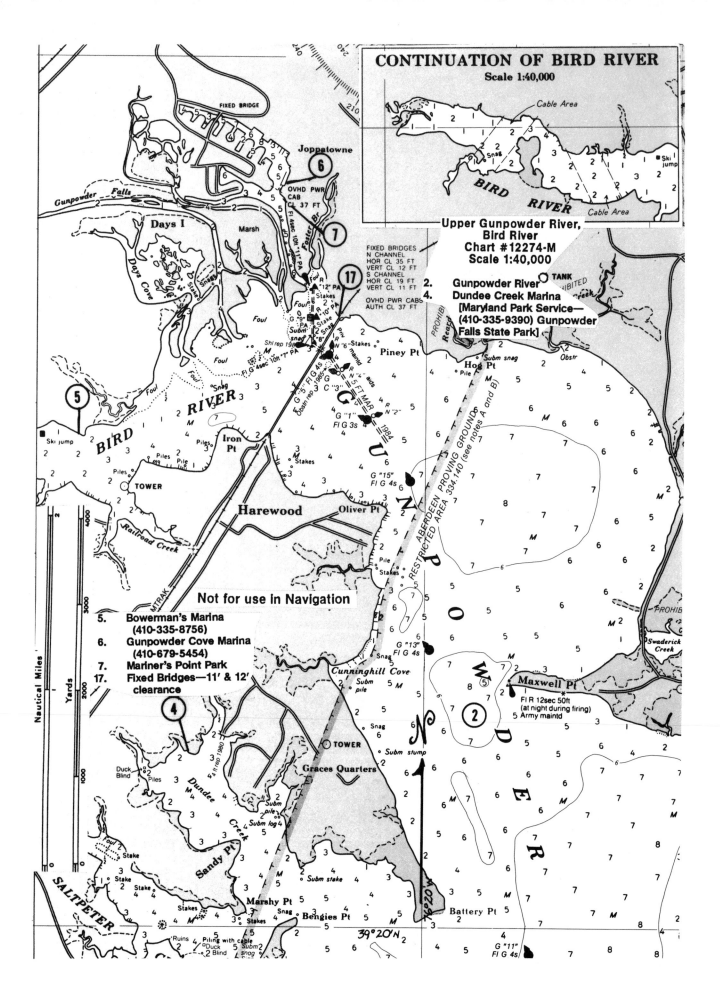

CONTINUATION OF BIRD RIVER
Scale 1:40,000

Upper Gunpowder River,
Bird River
Chart #12274-M
Scale 1:40,000

2. Gunpowder River
4. Dundee Creek Marina
[Maryland Park Service—
(410-335-9390) Gunpowder
Falls State Park]

FIXED BRIDGES
N CHANNEL
HOR CL 35 FT
VERT CL 12 FT
S CHANNEL
HOR CL 19 FT
VERT CL 11 FT
OVHD PWR CABS
AUTH CL 37 FT

OVHD PWR
CAB
CL 37 FT

Not for use in Navigation

5. **Bowerman's Marina**
   (410-335-8756)
6. **Gunpowder Cove Marina**
   (410-679-5454)
7. **Mariner's Point Park**
17. **Fixed Bridges—11' & 12'
   clearance**

39° 20'N

212

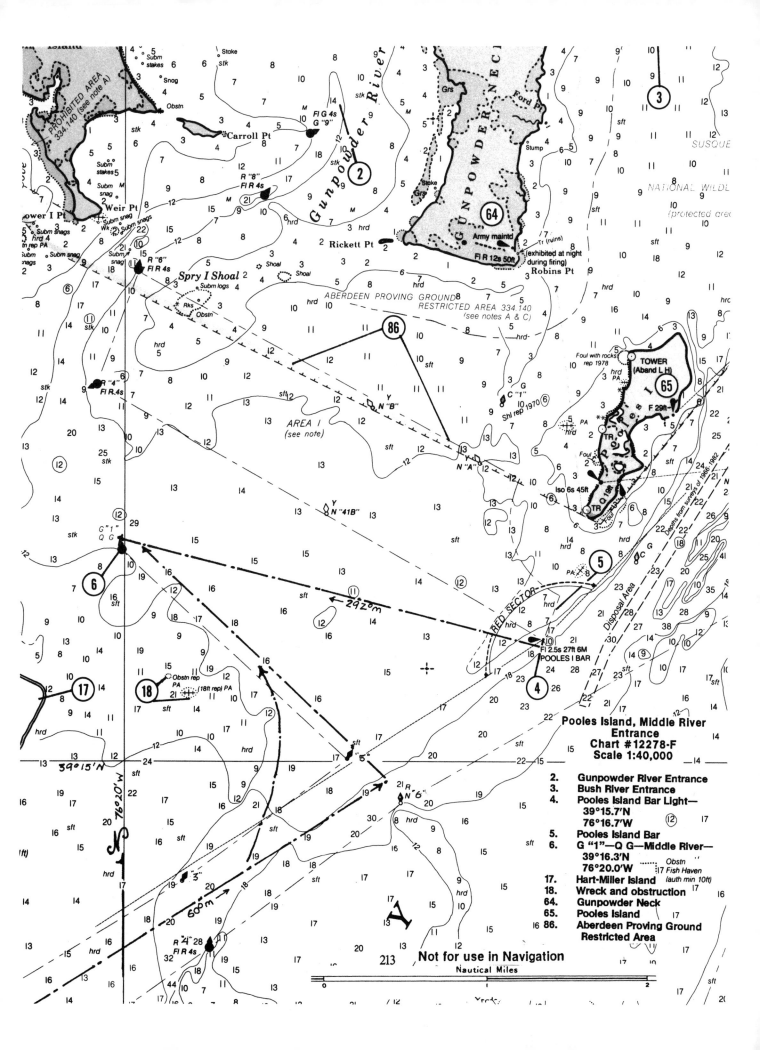

Pooles Island, Middle River Entrance
Chart #12278-F
Scale 1:40,000

Not for use in Navigation
Nautical Miles

213

2. **Gunpowder River Entrance**
3. **Bush River Entrance**
4. **Pooles Island Bar Light—**
   39°15.7'N
   76°16.7'W
5. **Pooles Island Bar**
6. **G "1"—Q G—Middle River—**
   39°16.3'N
   76°20.0'W
17. **Hart-Miller Island**
18. **Wreck and obstruction**
64. **Gunpowder Neck**
65. **Pooles Island**
86. **Aberdeen Proving Ground**
    Restricted Area

When approaching the Middle River from the Patapsco (8), head 60°M from Fl R "4" (9) which is south-southwest of North Point Shoal. When you begin this departure from the Patapsco (Brewerton) Channel (10), you will notice the outer range structure (11) just southwest of North Point. An arrow of land on the shore points to it, as you will see on the chart. This is a bright red light on a 15-foot squat horizontally striped structure. It lines up against the tall white tower (12) on the western shore of Old Road Bay (51). This is for ships coming into the Craighill Channel (13) as they approach Baltimore, but may help to orient you as you head around the point. Soon the markers off Shallow Creek (14) will come up on your left (to the northwest). Next you will see ahead and to your left, just to the south of the southern tip of Pleasure Island (15), the 105-foot tower (16) which is dark on top and white on the bottom with white supports (off the cut going behind Pleasure Island).

Refer to Chart #12278-F. PG 213
Northeast of Pleasure Island is Hart Miller Island (17). This will become a large recreational area after being landfilled. Presently boats land on weekends on the beaches around it. Veering a little to the right (to east of) the course of 60°M to round the shallows off this island, and then rounding the northern end of the island, you should soon intersect the channel going into Middle River. Note that there is a wreck and obstruction (18) reported. We never found either, but they may be there. The 60°M course will avoid these hazards and intersect the channel into Middle River.

Seneca Creek (Northeast of Middle River)
Refer to Chart #12278-G— "Middle River, Seneca Creek."

There are a few marinas in Seneca Creek principally used by shallower draft boats. The area is built up ashore.

Heading into Seneca Creek (19), you will see a large factory-type structure ahead and to the north-northwest. It has two horizontally striped red and white smokestacks (21). You will see the many small homes of "Miami Beach" (22) on the shore to your left (westerly). To find G "3" (23), head for the factory, just to the right of the stacks. Once inside the creek, you will find it heavily built up, with low shorelines, and with no really attractive cruising anchorages. The factory has a bulkheaded channel heading to its right (east) but this quickly ends and is of little interest to pleasure boaters.

Just around the first point to your left (southwest) and up in the first cove lies **Goose Harbor Marina (24)**. I was not able to find much more than 3 feet depths at their docks. Others have reported 6 feet available. There is a gray simulated lighthouse on the fuel dock with a red roof. There are privately placed markers (25) on each side of the entrance channel, as we have noted on the chart. There are many motor boats up to 35 feet, and ice and gasoline and a pumpout station are available. The largest slip is 45 feet with up to 30 amps of electricity, and there is a 45-foot 20-ton boat lift. Some marine supplies are available.

As Seneca Creek veers to the west, you will find **Porter's Seneca Marina (26)**, a full service facility with transient slips. There are 109 slips with the largest up to 50 feet and electricity up to 30 amps. There is a 30-ton open end lift, pumpout station, gas, block and cube ice, a marine store, and Visa and MC are accepted. They are dealers for MerCruiser, and Mercury. If you need a marina here, call them to be sure of their depths at the time. They will answer on Channel 16, and their phone is (410) 335-6563.

Proceeding far up the western end of Seneca Creek brings you to **Beacon Light Marina (27)**. This marina can be identified by its name on a sign and a small white decorative lighthouse in the private yard across the creek. They have 100 slips, accomodating boats up to 30 feet, with 20 to 30 amps of electricity available. They sell gas, and have a marine supply store. MC and Visa are honored. A hard surfaced ramp is available on the premises. Ice is sold in block and cube. There is a lift with a 7-ton capacity. They have 4 feet depth at the deepest area. They are dealers for Johnson, Yamaha, MerCruiser, and Grady White.

Galloway Creek
Refer to Chart #12278-G.

Proceeding into Middle River, you will first notice a large bay, called Galloway Creek (28), opening broadly to your right (north). While affording some protection from northerlies for boats of no more than 5 feet of draft, it is too open to be considered a good anchorage. Note the long shoal (29) extending far out southeasterly from Log Point, the westernmost entrance of this bay (or creek). Favoring the eastern side of the entrance and marina there should keep you clear. Besides the two marinas, the shoreline inside is covered with houses.

The first marina is **Bowley's Quarters Condomarina (30)**. This marina can be identified by its sign. It is behind a large

IDENTS FOR CHART PG 215

Middle River, Seneca Creek Chart #12278-G Scale 1:40,000	
1. Middle River	49. Norman Creek
6. G "1"—Qk Fl G—39°16.3'N 76°20.0'W	50. Crescent Yacht Club
	51. Norman Creek Marina
7. G "3"—Fl G 4 sec.	52. Brown's Cove Marina
19. Seneca Creek	53. Markley's Boat Yard
21. Stacks—red and white horizontal stripe	54. River Watch Marina and Restaurant
22. "Miami Beach"	55. "Kidney Cove"
23. G "3" Can—Seneca Creek	56. Driftwood Inn
24. Goose Harbor Marina	57. Middle River Yacht Club
25. Private Markers	58. Anchor Bay Yacht Sales
26. Porter's Seneca Marina	59. Deckleman's Boat Yard
27. Beacon Light Marina	60. Snug Harbor Boat Yard
28. Galloway Creek	61. Essex Marina Boat Yard
29. Long Shoal off Galloway Creek	62. Hilltop Marine
	63. Anchorage
30. Bowley's Quarters Condomarina	66. Cutter Marine Yacht Basin
31. Galloway Creek Marina	67. Riley's Marina
32. Sue Creek	68. Beudel's Marina & Boat Yard
33. Baltimore Yacht Club	69. 7/11, High's Ice Cream, crab restaurant
34. Anderson Brothers Boat Sales	70. Dark Head Creek
35. Holly Neck Marina	71. Martin Marietta Airport
36. Red Eye Yacht Club	72. Turning Basin
37. Sue Creek Boat Yard	73. Stansbury Yacht Basin
38. Creek north of Red Eye's	74. Stansbury Creek —anchorage—3-4 ft.
39. Anchorage—4 ft. controlling	
40. Sue Haven Yacht Club	75. Glenmar Sailing Association
41. Boating Center of Baltimore	76. Wagus Marina
42. Eastern Yacht Club	77. Private club with docks
43. Private markers—2 stakes— (red & green)	78. Frog Mortar Creek
	79. Moorings—not there
44. Red and green junction marker	80. Long Beach Marina
	81. Anchorage
45. G R Can—junction marker	82. Maryland Marina & Wild Duck Restaurant
46. Anchorage	83. Tradewinds Marina
47. Hopkins Creek	84. Brigadoon Marine Facility
48. Hogpen Creek	85. Edwards Boat Yard
	87. Chesapeake Yachting Center
	88. Carroll Island Mall
	89. Wreck

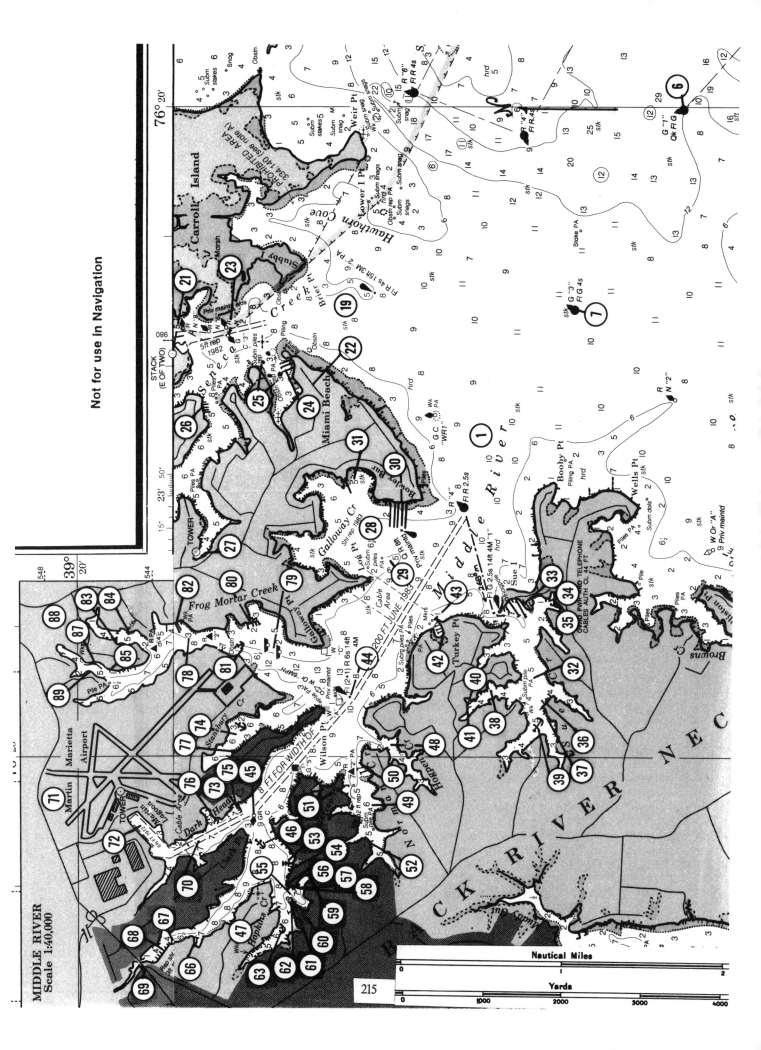

MIDDLE RIVER
Scale 1:40,000

Not for use in Navigation

215

breakwater, to its south. It has 490 slips, with up to 30 amps of electricity available. Both gas and diesel are sold. Ice is sold in block or cube form. There is a lift with a 30-ton capacity. I found 7 feet depth at the deepest area. Other features include a marine store, laundromat, cocktail lounge, and swimming pool.

Galloway Creek Marina (31) appears next, to your east heading in. It has 163 slips with up to 30 amps of electricity available. There is a lift with a 15-ton capacity. They do salvage and towing, and engine and hull repairs.

Sue Creek
Refer to Chart #12278-G. PG 215

This is one of the prettier creeks in Middle River, with some marinas and a nice area to anchor.

As you enter Sue Creek (32), the narrow channel will seem very congested as you approach. On the western point referred to as "Sue Island" on the chart, you will see the very nice **Baltimore Yacht Club (33)** with its buildings up on the shore and a tall flag pole. This is a convenient place to get gas or diesel just as you come in. I found better than 7 feet off these fuel docks. For members of accredited clubs, there are reciprocal privileges. There is a nice restaurant here, and the club is well run and attended.

On the banks opposite the club, to your right coming in (to the west), you will see stakes, as noted on the chart. As you approach the channel, it will open up and not appear so difficult after all. Remember to avoid the shoal to your right making westerly off Turkey Point and also the shoal to your left (east) as you approach. A course of 268°M from Fl R "4" should take you through the deeper water to the vicinity just to the northeast of Fl G "1", where the opening will be clearer to see.

Once you clear the yacht club, the creek opens up into a broad and pretty area. There are numerous homes ashore with many docks; but they do not give the feeling of over crowding that you find elsewhere in this area, and there are still some wooded areas. The creek becomes considerably shallower as you pass beyond the narrow entrance, with 5-foot depths.

As you pass the yacht club, you will see a creek making off to the south behind it. This is shallow, I found only 2 to 3 feet once past the club area. However there are establishments catering to motor boats, up in the creek. Anderson Brothers Boat Sales (34) has sales and dry storage, offering engine and hull repair, and **Holly Neck Marina (35)** has 46 slips and a 15-ton lift with electricity up to 50 amps, and also has engine and hull repairs.

The point of land beyond the next little side creek on the western shore holds an interesting marina called the **Red Eye Yacht Club (36).** This is public marina with a restaurant and bar. It is not related to the bar and restaurant of that name in Kent Narrows, and indeed, is a different type of place. There are 70 slips up to 40 feet with electricity up to 30 amps. I found only 4½ feet depth at the outer docks. The restaurant is informal with good home cooking. A local group of cloggers met there regularly, and there is a country western flair. I was fortunate enough to meet one of the cloggers as he was "messing" with his boat. He was a very helpful gentleman of 76.

West of Red Eye, Sue Creek becomes prettier. **Sue Creek Boat Yard (37)** is just upstream from here, on the same side, with 15 slips and electricity up to 15 amps. On the point of land separating the last two prongs of the creek, at the western end, is a beach with trees behind. The area just off this point, in 5 feet depth (4 feet should be considered to be controlling access), makes a nice anchorage (39).

On the branch to your right (38) (northwest) as you approach this point, all the way its end, you will find first the **Sue Haven Yacht Club (40)** on your right (northeast). The yacht club has a bar for members, but no restaurant. It has a tan house with flag pole and big windows upon the hill just before you get to the Boating Center of Baltimore.

On this same branch (38) is a marina called the **Boating Center of Baltimore..** It has a large area of docks surrounded by woods and homes. It has 60 slips accomodating boats up to 40 feet, with up to 50 amps of electricity available, 4½ feet depth at the deepest. Transients do not regularly come up this far, although they are welcome when there is space. They have gas, block and cube ice, a lift with 12-ton capacity, mechanical work is performed seven days a week, and there is a concrete launching ramp. Their well-stocked marine store supply includes many hard-to-find engine parts for older motors, including Chrysler. They are dealers for MerCruiser, Force, and OMC. They sell new and used boats. They honor Visa and MasterCards.

•

Proceeding farther into Middle River, you will notice a bulkheaded area on the south shore, with boats behind. This snug little cul-de-sac is the home of **Eastern Yacht Club (42).** I did not find more than 2½ to 3 feet depth approaching the bulkheading. There are two stakes (43) at the end of the bulkheading, painted green and red for markers. Inside, the docks have 30 amp service and there is a nice little clubhouse up in the trees to your left (east). There is no room to anchor.

Heading farther upriver, you will soon come to divergent channels at the red and green junction marker (44) to the southeast of Wilson Point. The chart indicates a private marker here. I did not see this, but the junction marker was present. Here there are several choices. We'll describe them clockwise, but if you are looking for a quick and easy anchorage with some nightlife ashore and a good parts and marine supply store as well as a yard and marinas, proceed straight on to the junction buoy (45) off (to the south of) Clark Point and head westerly into the wide area with many 8-foot depth designations. Anchor (46) in the vicinity of the entrance to Hopkins Creek (47). See below under "Hopkins Creek."

Hogpen Creek
Refer to Chart #12278-G. PG 215

Hogpen Creek (48) is a very pretty creek and could make an enjoyable anchorage for small boats with no more than 3 feet draft. The deep water is narrow, and there would not be much swinging room. There are houses ashore on this creek, but they are larger than those in many other areas. There are many trees on the shores, especially on the northwest bank after you round the entrance bend. Though there is deeper water inside, the water is quite shallow at the entrance. If you draw as much as 3 feet, enter carefully, preferably at half tide and rising.

Norman Creek
Norman Creek (49) off the west shore of Middle River, would not be a great place to anchor because of the crowded conditions in the creek and on the shore. There are two marinas and a small yacht club here, but the area seems to be oriented primarily to local business.

As you enter this creek, you will see to your left (on the southern bank) the small brown house of **Crescent Yacht Club (50)** with a few docks. Across from this, on the opposite bank, is a marina which consists of docks along the shore behind which appear to be private homes. This is **Norman Creek Marina (51)**, and they sell gas and block and cube ice.

Farther up the creek is **Brown's Cove Marina (52)**. They did not have room for transients because of their local business. This may not be true when you visit. The marina has 27 slips up to 40 feet with up to 30 amps of electricity. They sell gas and honor Visa, MC, and Discover. There is a concrete ramp and 25-ton lift. They are dealers for OMC, Chrysler, Crusader, Volvo Penta, Westerbeke, and OMC Cobra. There is a marine store.

Hopkins Creek

This is probably the most popular spot for cruisers wishing to anchor and sample this river and also pick up equipment and make a restaurant stop. The main anchorage is actually off the mouth of Hopkins Creek in Middle River. Some of the facilities are not in the creek proper. We're including them here because of the proximity to the creek.

Looking at the chart, the anchorage **(46)** off Hopkins Creek **(47)** will be obvious in the wide area south-southwest of Clark Point. The chart shows a consistent depth of 8 feet, but this could be less with strong northerly winds blowing the water out of the area for a period of several days. The holding is good, and from here there are various opportunities by dinghy. A water taxi operates in season, taking people from the anchorage and other marinas to the popular River Watch Restaurant (and other destinations) which are described below. The major drawback that we found was that the area is heavily traveled, particularly on weekends. This includes a few who have little concern with regard to their wake. See that you are well lit at night, if anchored here. We anchored here on a foggy cold Halloween evening and even then the traffic was impressive.

From this anchorage, looking ashore, you will see on the southern side of the basin the long pier of **Markley's Boat Yard (53)**. This marina can be identified by its large building and sign. It has 85 slips, with up to 50 amps of electricity available. They normally are not a transient marina, their slips being filled by the customers of their full service repair yard. There are lifts with up to 60 tons capacity. They have 6½ feet at the deepest area, an electronics repair shop, a 10-ton crane, and marine hardware.

Next to Markley's, looking around the basin clockwise, is the **River Watch Marina and Restaurant (54)**. This facility is quite prominent on the northwestern side of the point which makes the southern side of the Hopkins Creek entrance. It can be identified by the sign on the restaurant behind the docks. It is a very popular place for boaters in season and year round with its restaurant which features a dockside bar in summer months and a fireplace overlooking the water in the winter. It has 112 slips accomodating boats up to 60 feet long, with more length available on the T's, with up to 50 amps of electricity available. There is both gas and diesel sold and they have a pumpout station. Visa and MC are honored. Ice is sold in block and cube. They have 7½ feet depth at the deepest area. The restaurant is a very popular full menu restaurant and cocktail lounge, with complimentary docking while dining. The restaurant specializes in steak and seafood, and has live entertainment on weekends and other special occasions. As noted above, water taxi service is available for boats anchored out. There are also charter boats sometimes available at their docks, depending upon the season.

The next area to be described resembles a kidney on the south shore of Hopkins Creek. We could not resist calling it "Kidney Cove" **(55)**, although I never heard it called that by

anyone around. It is packed with facilities, and would make a great hurricane hole anchorage except for the congested shore.

The first facility after you leave River Watch is the Driftwood Inn **(56)**, just around the point on its northwest end. This is a smaller restaurant with some docking available in front for diners. Signs there advise 2 hours limit with no overnight. The restaurant has conspicuous dark plate glass windows facing the water, and they advertise speciality nights for different entrees.

Next in, barely distinguishable from the Driftwood, is the **Middle River Yacht Club (57)** with a sign advising dockage for members and guests only. The docks in this area continue around into the cove, and it is hard to determine where one facility leaves off and the other begins.

The next facility is Anchor Bay Yacht Sales **(58)**. The docks for this are connected with the yacht club docks, although the two are separate entities. The yacht sale business has numerous boats on show in the water both outside and inside covered sheds. This is not a transient facility. However, on the premises is an incredibly well-stocked marine supply store with regular stock items and some hard to find things that you would never expect to locate outside of Fort Lauderdale. The prices are competitive. The family that runs this also runs the Anchorage Marina on the Bear Creek off the Patapsco River and the boat supply store under the Rusty Scupper in Baltimore's Inner Harbor. Because of this store, as well as some of the other facilities mentioned, this is a great area to come in for repairs, as well as R and R.

Next in the far southeastern end of the "kidney," is **Deckel man's Boat Yard (59)**. This is primarily a repair and rebuild facility, rather than a regular transient marina, although there are some transient slips up to 60 feet long with electricity up to 50 amps. There is a 40-ton lift and a crane. They advertise that they are one of the oldest licensed and insured marine salvage towing firms in the area. This yard has been in the same family for several generations. I found a little over 6 feet of depth here.

The next facility is **Snug Harbor Boat Yard (60)** with 40 slips and a 12-ton lift.

Essex Marina Boat Yard (61) is on the southeast side of the northwest point separating the "kidney basin" from the rest of Hopkins Creek. There are 88 slips up to 48 feet long with electricity available up to 50 amps, a 30-ton lift, and a 2-ton crane. They sell gas and have a pumpout station, and a marine supply store. Next, **Hilltop Marine (62)** has 33 slips with 15 amp electricity, with private homes ashore behind the docks.

Hopkins Creek is filled with homes and condominiums and many docks on your left (southwest) as you head upstream, but the opposite shore has many trees and is very pretty. I found 5 feet of depth well up into the creek. If you don't mind all the condos looking down on you from the western bank, this is another alternative for anchoring **(63)** within easy dinghy reach for all the facilities around "Kidney Cove."

Upper Middle River

The short run of the Middle River above Hopkins Creek is not a place where most cruising boats would wish to anchor because of its congestion and narrowness, but there are some marinas here, and there is an opportunity to cross the street and reach some fast food and limited grocery shopping. I found depths as indicated on the chart.

The first marina in the upper Middle River is the **Cutter Marine Yacht Basin (66)**. This marina can be identified by its sign and a big cinderblock building with "marine basin" painted white on red. It is on the left (western) side of the river. It has approximately 165 slips accomodating boats up to 70 feet, with up to 30 amps of electricity available. The docks are in an area of the river where there is 6 feet depth, but docks also go up into a little creek where the depth is less. There is a lift with a 25-ton capacity. They honor Visa and MC. They have a marine store with chandlery supplies and ice and beverages, boat sales, and are dealers for MerCruiser, Mariner, Avon, Rinker, and Robalo.

The next marina is on the same side of the river, Riley's Marina (67). This marina can be identified by its sign. It has 100 slips accomodating boats up to 50 feet, with up to 30 amps of electricity available. They sell gas and have a marine supply store. Visa and MC are honored. There are lifts with up to 37-ton capacity and a 5-ton crane. They have 6 feet depth at the deepest area. They are dealers for MerCruiser and Volvo Penta.

The last marina, also on your left, is Beudel's Marina and Boat Yard (68). This marina can be identified by its sign and a big white building on the hill above it with a sign proclaiming "Marine Supplies." It has 150 slips accomodating boats up to 50 feet, with up to 50 amps electricity available. There is gas sold and Visa and MC are honored. There is a lift with a 15-ton capacity. They have 4 feet depth at the deepest area. Other features include propeller reconditioning on the premises, heliarc welding, and propeller shafting in stock. They are dealers for Chrysler engine parts.

Just above Beudel's, you will see a low bridge crossing the river. Just across the bridge street is a 7/11, a High's Ice Cream store, and a small crab speciality restaurant (69), within easy walking from Beudel's. I saw no other area (except for the marinas downstream) to land a dinghy to shop here.

Dark Head Creek

Dark Head Creek (70) has little attraction for a cruising boat. As you enter, you see ahead of you a huge industrial storage center with many white warehouses and hangers related to the Martin Marietta Airport (71) on the shore ahead at the end of the creek. This scene is quite striking and unattractive. The turning basin (72) at the end is just that, with the airport buildings and the sound of the planes and industry around. Also, apartment houses are in sight on your right (south) as you go into the basin. There are many houses on the shores of the creek leading up to this end.

Dark Head Creek does have the Stansbury Yacht Basin (73) on the right (east) with 100 slips accomodating boats up to 45 feet, and a few transient slips when available. Electricity up to 20 amps is on the docks. There is a 35-ton lift, a concrete ramp, and sailing rentals are available. They have a marine supply store. Discover, Visa, and MC are accepted. Gas is sold and both block and cube ice are available. They will assist with transportation, if needed, within a 5-mile radius, when they have a vehicle available. Note the marina is on Dark Head Creek rather than Stansbury Creek (74) nearby. There is 7 feet depth at the outer docks.

The Glenmar Sailing Association (75) at the cove on the right side going in, is a local organization. The Wagus Marina (76) is in the anvil-shaped cove on the left (west side). It is a sailing association with attractive docks and grounds catering to local people.

Stansbury Creek

Stansbury Creek (74) would make a reasonable anchorage for those wishing to escape from some of the hustle and bustle of the other areas, although it is open to the southeast.

There are many private homes and docks on the left bank (western side) and there is a private club with docks (77) at the end on the same side. However, the eastern bank has some pretty woods and there is a relatively pretty place to anchor (74) in 3 to 4 feet depth in the broad cove on the eastern bank. Houses and civilization are certainly in plain sight here on the other bank, but there is a little feeling of privacy. However, airport runways are nearby, and the noise could be bothersome.

Frog Mortar Creek

The creek has some anchorage areas if you can stand the traffic, and several very nice and interesting marinas.

I would not think of beginning a description of Frog Mortar Creek (78) without offering some explanation for the name of this creek. I asked everywhere I stopped along the shores, and was told numerous stories, some best not repeated here. One of the stories is that it is named after frog excrement. The story goes that in the olden days (far olden days) there was so much of it around that folks built houses from it and called it mortar. Another story was that there used to be so many frogs in the creeks making so much noise that it was called "frog motor" and that the passing years changed the pronunciation to "mortar." I am sure that there must be some official reason for this name, well-documented somewhere, I just haven't found it.

The entrance to Frog Mortar Creek is broad and obvious, and you will notice a part of the airport with a large blue building to the northwest of Galloway Point. The chart shows two moorings (79) in the large cove to your right (east). They were not visible last year. We found the depths to be as charted. The upper reaches have been dredged by the large marina here.

The first marina will appear to your right (east) and is the Long Beach Marina (80). This marina can be identified by its extensive docks, still being worked on, and the large work and storage yard behind, as well as its sign. It has 327 slips capable of accomodating boats up to 85 feet, with up to 50 amps of electricity available. There are lifts with up to 20 tons and a railway with 50-foot 20-ton capacity. They have 8 feet depth at the deepest area.

The creek above Long Beach Marina has woods on the left (west) bank, with a runway behind the woods. There are houses, mostly small, on the other bank. This would be a relatively pretty area to anchor (81), except for the traffic.

The next marina is the large and popular Maryland Marina (82). This marina can be identified by its sign. It occupies much of the shore on the east side. In the middle of the marina area, you will notice the Wild Duck Restaurant (82) with its sign and green roof. This marina has 360 slips accomodating boats up to 55 feet with no charge while dining, and with up to 30 amps of electricity available. Discover, Visa, and MC are honored. There is a concrete ramp here also. Ice is sold in block and cube. There is a boat lift capacity of 25 tons. They have 7 feet depths at the deepest area; this can vary with the wind. Other features include sailboat rentals up to 42 feet, a laundry, ability to pull masts up to 50 feet, rigging work, state trailer inspection, and a marine flea market with items taken on consignment. There is also a dry sail launching and storage operation on the premises, with full utilities in this storage area. The marine store is very well stocked with a wide variety of items from serious hardware to entertainment and clothing. The restaurant is popular in the area, and sometimes on weekends or special occasions will have live entertainment. Maryland Marina seemed particularly friendly to the cruising boatmen.

Soon you will come to the fork. Up the branch to the right

(running generally northeasterly) you will find two marinas, and up the left (northwest) branch you will find two more, including a very special place if you love old boats. Both of these branches are too narrow and busy for anchoring. Not only is there a lot of pleasure boat traffic, but many docks line the shores, servicing the homes there.

Proceeding up the right (northeasterly) branch you will come to two marinas on either side of the creek. **Tradewinds (83)** will appear to your left (western) side. This marina can be identified by a big yard with many trees, and a low brown house near the docks with a gray house next to it, and a big blue shed behind. They have 80 slips accomodating boats up to 48 feet, with up to 30 amps of electricity available. Gas is sold. MC and Visa are honored. A small hard surfaced ramp is on the premises. Ice is sold in block and cube. There is a boat lift capacity of 15 tons. Maximum water depth is 5 feet. They are dealers for MerCruiser, Celebrity, Yamaha, Volvo Penta and Fish Hawk. A marine store sells snacks and beverages as well as some hardware. They sell new and used power and sail boats.

Brigadoon Marine Facility (84) is close to Tradewinds, on the opposite side. This marina can be identified by its sign as well as the three-story tan house in its yard and a picnic area which, when I last visited, was covered by a little tent. It has 70 slips, with up to 30 amps of electricity available. Gas and diesel are sold. This marina has an asphalt ramp. Ice is sold in block and cube. There is boat lift capacity of 12 tons. I found 5 feet maximum water depth. They have a marine store, and boat sales.

Above these two marinas you will find a private dock on the right side with many crab pots and some work boats. The creek becomes very shallow and ends amid houses and trees, with a lot of cleared land and yards around its banks.

The left (northwesterly) branch is a little longer with a huge marine facility at the end. First, you will pass **Edwards Boat Yard (85)** on your right (east). This marina can be identified by its sign and a big gray work shed behind the docks, next to a white two-story house which looks like an old country store facing the fuel dock. I had a strange sense of deja vu as I pulled in. It has 110 slips accomodating boats up to 45 feet, with up to 30 amps of electricity available. There is gas sold

on the dock, under the shade, in front of the store. Ice is sold in block or cube. There is a boat lift capacity of 15 tons. This has been a well known repair and building yard for many years. Maximum water depth is 5 feet.

As you pull in you think you have landed somewhere special. As you enter the store, you know you have. There are large windows in front, the floors are old bare wood, and there are long display counters running up and down the length with a counter to the rear. On those shelves and sitting about, are parts and pieces of the boating world which many think to be gone forever. I saw an old round Chris Craft bow hatch, brass manual up-down bilge pumps, ancient exhaust risers still new, and so many other items that I browsed as though I were in a very unique museum. There was even an electric train, too loved to be put away. You can get the usual here, as well as the near antique. You can even buy fishing gear. I would suggest a visit to this "other place in time" up Frog Mortar Creek. Transients don't often find their way in, but if there is room, I am sure you would find a friendly and rewarding stay.

Just up the creek you will enter the dredged channel leading into the very large new facility named **Chesapeake Yachting Center (87)**. This marina can be identified by its sign and large buildings and grounds, which include an indoor work shed capable of housing very large yachts. It has 200 slips accomodating boats up to 80 feet, with up to 50 amps of electricity available. There is regular and hi-test gas and diesel sold. A pumpout is on the premises, free to customers. Visa, MC, Carte Blanche, and Diners are honored. Ice is sold in block and cube. There is a boat lift capacity of 25 tons. Maximum water depth is 6 feet, but I found barely 5 feet to be controlling lower down in the creek before the dredged area. Other features include a very nice laundry, multiple restroom facilities, and a huge service area capable in most areas of work including electronic sales and installation. This marina states that it is a hurricane hole. It is certainly in a very snug and inland position.

Just behind the marina is the Carroll Island Mall **(88)** with a full service drug store, a large grocery store, fast food shops, a video rental, hardware store, and several restaurants.

The chart indicates a wreck **(89)** in the creek where the marina is located. This wreck is there, but it is to the left (westerly) side of the creek, out of the dredged channel, and easily seen. It is the remains of an old wooden boat with other wreckage.

Baltimore Pilot Boat

219

BACK RIVER

While there are a few fair weather anchorages, this is not an ideal spot because of its openness, although there is some pretty scenery on part of the shoreline.

Refer to Charts #12273-D ~~PG 210~~ and
Chart #12273-E CH 14 and
Chart #12278-H— "Back River Entrance, Hart-Miller Island."

For the Back River (90) entrance, see the section on Middle River in this chapter. As you are heading into Middle River, a turn to the southwest just before you reach Fl G "3" will have you heading into the broad mouth of Back River. Note the shoal (91) extending southeasterly off Booby Point and guarded by R Nun "2." Many skippers gradually round the northeastern end of Hart-Miller Island (17), particularly when they are coming from the Patapsco. If you elect to do this, watch your depth closely and take care not to pass too close to the island. With the fill work going on, I would expect the bottom to be unstable for a while, even though there is bulkheading around the project.

Once in the river, go as far up as you wish, depending upon your draft and scenery preferences. You won't find any really pretty anchorages that are also snug in weather. We found that the depths up close to the bridge (92) (Chart #12278-I— Upper Back River) near the end are less than charted. I could find only 2 feet near the bridge. I saw outboards of around 20 feet length buzzing through in seeming confidence, but I couldn't locate any secret channel.

The first and perhaps the most popular attraction of this area is Hart-Miller Island (17). This is now to your left (east) after you have rounded its northern point, having left the entrance channel for Middle River and headed southwesterly into the mouth of Hawk Cove (93). This island, used as a fill area for dredging operations, is now a park, with beautiful shores and calm weather anchorages on its western side. The eastern side is still receiving dredged material and you may see barges and earth moving equipment here. But this work does little to impair the beauty of the western shore. There are coves, beaches, and gently sloping sand for anchoring close in, depending on your draft. Many small local boats will be found here, particularly on weekends. You can go ashore, walk along boardwalks over the marsh, and enjoy the natural setting. There is a dock (94) south of Drum Point, but most people land on the shores. The island has both sections of woods and of marsh on it.

There are several nice areas to anchor behind Hart-Miller Island. Although people anchor all along the western side, some of the better areas are in the coves (95) off the beach areas where indicated on the chart, and in the pretty cove south of Drum Point, just north of the dock there. Those anchorages noted on the northernmost end seem the most popular, with better beaches at this time. The anchorages (96) southwest of Drum Point, on either side of the park dock, are very pretty with a small beach near the point, and woods and marsh ashore. The view out to the bay is nice. On the northern side of Drum Point there is another pretty cove (97) with higher ground and woods. In any of these anchorages, boats of 3 feet draft can get fairly close into shore. The bottom slopes gently. None of this area is good in unsettled weather or with any wind from the wrong direction.

As you approach and pass Fl G "3," the view to the south will seem much more open than what you would expect from the chart, and therefore potentially a bit confusing. This is because the opening (98) between Hart-Miller and Pleasure Island (15) is usually covered with water even over the areas indicated as mud bank, and because the opening (99) between Pleasure Island and northeastern tip of the Patapsco River Neck (100) is broader than you would expect. The position of the 105-foot tower (16) on the southern side of Pleasure Island will help with your orientation. This tower (16) is dark red on top and white on the bottom—the rear range marker for the Craighill Range. There are many small houses and buildings on both sides of Cuckold Point (1). The long dock (2) coming northeasterly off the point is conspicuous.

The cut between Pleasure Island and the Patapsco River Neck is an interesting trip in a dinghy, and is locally used as a short cut between the Patapsco and Back River for boats with no more than 4½ feet draft. This is the type of channel that will probably be subject to serious shoaling, particularly at its two ends. Check before you go through if you have anywhere near that 4½ feet draft. The chart shows a dredged controlling depth of 2½ feet in 1983, but it has apparently been dredged since then. Going in from the north, to orient you, you will have many houses on its western bank and the Craighill Range Tower on the eastern bank at the south end behind the trees and marsh of Pleasure Island. The wide opening that will be the most conspicuous to the east will be the cut between Pleasure Island and Hart-Miller.

The long dock with T protruding northerly from Cuckhold Point is for the Rumrunners Restaurant and Lounge (2) serving light fare including crabs, and full fare. You can also obtain ice here. This is a three-story white building with blue awnings. Don't tie up at the dock unless the weather is very settled. Even then you should secure against possible damaging wakes. As you come out of the cut into the Patapsco, the Bay Bridges loom ahead far down the Bay to the south-southeast. Small cabin cruisers were transiting the cut last year, but the depths may be different when you try it. Half tide and rising is a good idea for the first time.

Inside this cut you will find several small boat fishing docks (3) with skiff rentals available on the west bank, and a restaurant at the southern end of the cove on the western shore of the channel. At the dock in front of the restaurant, I found 3½ feet depth.

Our preferred anchorage (4) for an overnight stay in Back River is off the cove between Cedar Point and Claybank Point. The holding is good here, with a nice new view ashore to the north and enough distance from the crowded shore to the south to afford a feeling of privacy. The shore directly to the south actually has nice woods. There is a park (Rocky Point Park) (6) on the northern shore which means trees and marsh undisturbed by cars and lights. There is a small beach on the shore in this cove. If you expect a northeasterly or easterly, pass on around Witchcoat Point (5) (on Chart #12278-I), described below.

The creek (7) between Rocky and Claybank Points is beautiful as it protrudes into the wooded park. The markers are small red and green stakes. I found 4 feet controlling up to and past the spot where there is * on the chart marking a rock (8). This is actually a beautiful rock ledge protruding from the eastern shore and dropping sharply off into the creek which is over 6 feet deep here. When we passed, there was a picnic table perched on top. Rounding the bend above that, we were jerked out of our revery by two conspicuous sand traps of a large golf course. The creek has hard surfaced public ramps (9) both above and below the rock. I would not sug-

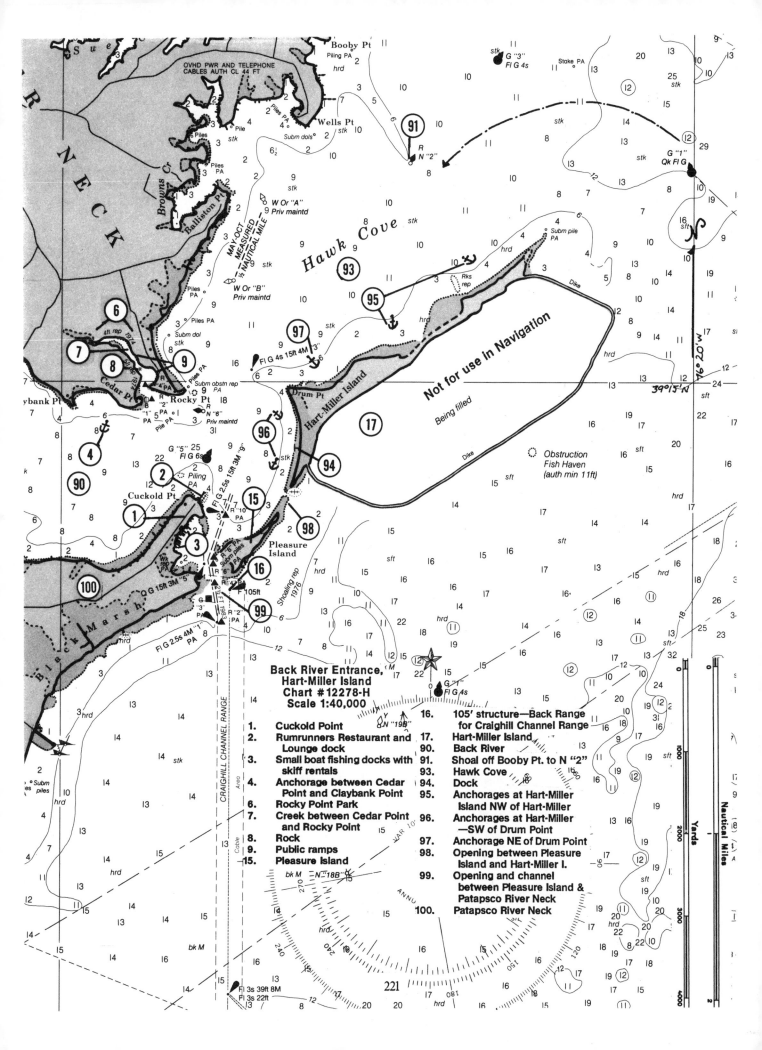

OVHD PWR AND TELEPHONE
CABLES AUTH CL 44 FT

Booby Pt
Piling PA
hrd

Wells Pt

91

R
N "2"

W Or "A"
Priv maintd

W Or "B"
Priv maintd

MAY-OCT
MEASURED
½ NAUTICAL MILE

Hawk Cove

93

95

97

Fl G 4s 15ft 4M "3"

Drum Pt

Hart-Miller Island

Not for use in Navigation

Being filled

17

Dike

Obstruction
Fish Haven
(auth min 11ft)

6

7   **8**   **9**

Cedar Pt

Rocky Pt

96

94

4

90

G "5" 25
Fl G 6s

2

Cuckold Pt

1

3

100

Black Marsh

15

Pleasure
Island

98

16

99

Shoaling rep
1976

105ft

G "1"
Qk Fl G

39°15'N

Subm pile
PA

Rks
rep

39°15'N

CRAIGHILL CHANNEL RANGE

Cable

VAR 10'

bk M   N "18B"

ANNU

221

Fl 3s 39ft 8M
Fl 3s 22ft

Back River Entrance, Hart-Miller Island
Chart #12278-H
Scale 1:40,000

1. **Cuckold Point**
2. **Rumrunners Restaurant and Lounge dock**
3. **Small boat fishing docks with skiff rentals**
4. **Anchorage between Cedar Point and Claybank Point**
6. **Rocky Point Park**
7. **Creek between Cedar Point and Rocky Point**
8. **Rock**
9. **Public ramps**
15. **Pleasure Island**

16. **105' structure—Back Range for Craighill Channel Range**
17. **Hart-Miller Island**
90. **Back River**
91. **Shoal off Booby Pt. to N "2"**
93. **Hawk Cove**
94. **Dock**
95. **Anchorages at Hart-Miller Island NW of Hart-Miller**
96. **Anchorages at Hart-Miller —SW of Drum Point**
97. **Anchorage NE of Drum Point**
98. **Opening between Pleasure Island and Hart-Miller I.**
99. **Opening and channel between Pleasure Island & Patapsco River Neck**
100. **Patapsco River Neck**

G "1"
Fl G 4s

Nautical Miles

Yards
1000
2000
3000
4000

gest anchoring here because of the traffic and narrowness.

Looking up into the Back River from Cedar Point, you will probably be surprised at the natural beauty of this river. There are hills to the north, mostly wooded and areas of housing on the south. Up to the northwestern end of the river, high hills rise behind the low lands at the end of the river. There is considerable civilization around, but the view is pleasing considering what most people expect for this area of the Bay.

Upper Back River
Refer to Chart #12278-I—"Upper Back River."

The cove (10) south of Todd Point is not the anchorage that it may seem from a glance at the chart. It is very built up with a bridge and highway behind it and to its southwest. The shoreline upstream from this cove has many docks. **Rudy's Marina (11)** has 65 slips, 15 amp electricity, a hard surfaced ramp, and lifting capacity up to 15 tons, and ice. These docks, as are many of the docks in this river, are somewhat exposed to the open river. As you round Stansbury Point (12), the shoreline to the south is quite congested, but the view of the tall hills behind the marina is still very pretty.

Witchcoat Point (5) on the right (east bank) has a pretty anchorage on both its upstream and downstream side (13) for boats not exceeding 4 feet draft. On the point is a beautiful stand of deep forest and marsh. On the north (upstream) side of the point, an old boat is sunk upon a beach out of the water. There are stumps around the point. Be careful if going to the shore. On the downstream (south) side, there is also a little beach with marsh and woods. While both of these are pretty, they are also both exposed except from weather coming right off the land.

Key Yacht Club (14) is on the southern shore (to your left going upstream). It has a brown single-story building ashore with dark windows and a porch in front.

On the northern bank, across from Key Yacht Club, and just downstream from the very shallow Muddy Gut (15), is **West Shore Yacht Center (16)** with a few transient slips, offering primarily local service. There is dockage up to 50 feet, 30 amp electricity, 35-ton lift capacity, gas, ice, and some marine supplies. Some repair work is available. As is true generally in this area, this is open to considerable fetch from the river. I found 4 to 5 feet depth at their docks.

Farther upstream still on the right (northern) bank, you will notice Cox Point (17) jutting out into the river just west of the entrance to Deep Creek (18). Here is a hard surfaced launching ramp and a park (17) where you will see people fishing from the shore and the pier. The point has a spit of sand extending southeasterly out into the river. Enter Deep Creek with R "14" on your left (northwest). There are trees and grassy yard on the point and marsh and trees to your right (eastern bank). Beyond those trees is **Essex Yacht Harbor Marina (19)**, an older facility, with 50 slips, lifts up to 20 tons, and a hard surfaced ramp. I found 4 feet depth to be controlling. This marina is set in a very pretty and protected location, snug in the creek with the large surrounding trees. The right branch of the creek passes under a bridge (20) with 10 feet vertical clearance. The left branch terminates against a backdrop of highway, with houses in the middle between the branches. The creek is very shallow above the marina, and you should not stray far to the west of the marina docks.

Upriver from Cox Point, still on the northern side of the river, are two more marinas. First, **Weaver's Marine Service (21)** is identified by its sign on the docks. This is a working and service marina primarily for motor boats. There are 100 slips with electricity up to 50 amps, gas, and lifting capacity up to 25 tons. There is hull and engine repair. They are dealers for MerCruiser, PCM, Marine Air, Sea Breeze, Kohler, Marine Power, and Volvo Penta.

Riverside Marine (22) is next up river on the same side, with a sign identifying itself and "Bayliner" signs on the docks. It has mostly motor boats. There are 140 slips up to 35 feet long with electricity up to 30 amps, and lift capacity up to 20 tons. This marina sells and services Bayliners with an inside showroom. It also sells Capri, Motoryacht, and Trophy boats. They are dealers for Mercury and MerCruiser. There is hull and engine repairs.

The southern shore of this section of the river is heavily settled with conspicuous tank farms up behind Bread and Cheese Creek (23). The bridge (92) has 16 feet vertical clearance. Above it are more bridges, highways, and industry.

Schooner *Harvey Gamage* at "Parade of Sail" Baltimore Inner Harbor
prior to Schooner Race

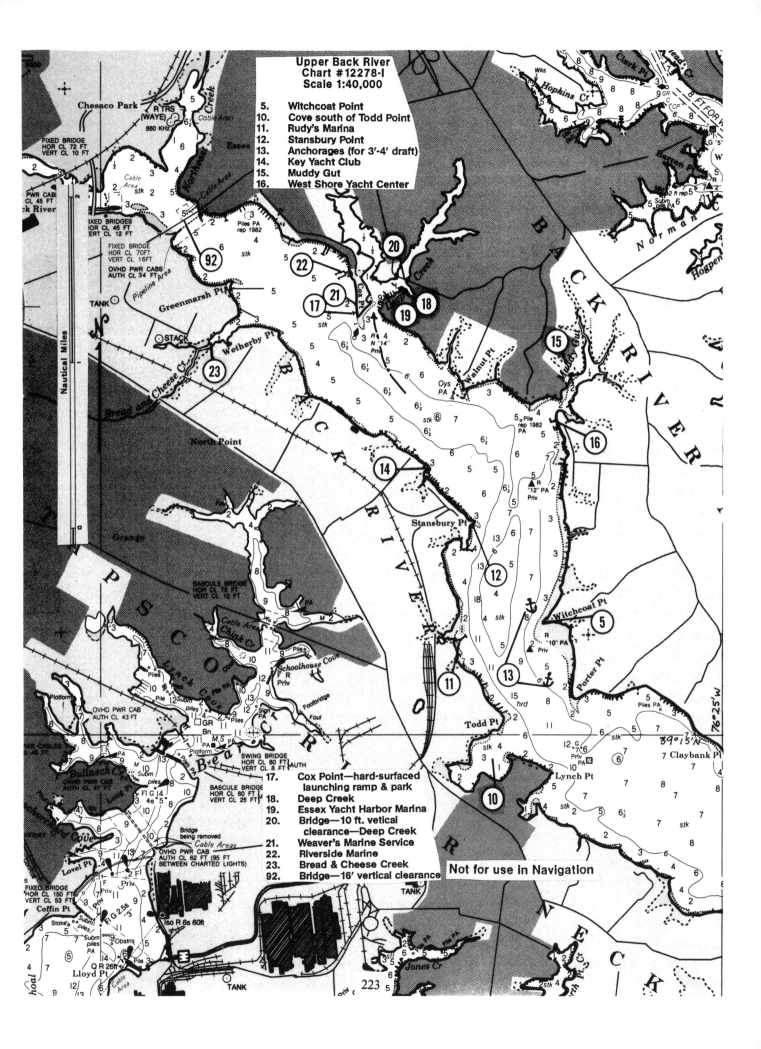

Upper Back River
Chart #12278-I
Scale 1:40,000

5. Witchcoat Point
10. Cove south of Todd Point
11. Rudy's Marina
12. Stansbury Point
13. Anchorages (for 3'-4' draft)
14. Key Yacht Club
15. Muddy Gut
16. West Shore Yacht Center

17. Cox Point—hard-surfaced
    launching ramp & park
18. Deep Creek
19. Essex Yacht Harbor Marina
20. Bridge—10 ft. vetical
    clearance—Deep Creek
21. Weaver's Marine Service
22. Riverside Marine
23. Bread & Cheese Creek
92. Bridge—16' vertical clearance

Not for use in Navigation

223

CHAPTER 14

PATAPSCO RIVER AND BALTIMORE

APPROACH

The Patapsco River is approximately 145 NM north of Hampton Roads and 45 NM from the C&D Canal. The approach to Baltimore is easy. **Chart #12278** covers the entrance from the Bay as well as the river and harbor. **Chart #12273** gives a broader view of the entrance area. This is a huge and heavily used seaport, and the channels into the Patapsco are about as obvious as they come, with markers placed close together and arranged for huge ships to easily enter.

Refer to Regional Chart #12273-E—"Western Shore: Patapsco River Entrance, Back River, Middle River"
and
Regional Chart # 12273-F—"Western Shore: Craighill Channel, Magothy River Entrance." CHAPTER 15

The primary concern of the cruiser is the commercial traffic of all sizes and types. The professionals in these vessels know their jobs, and are often involved in very difficult and critical maneuvering as they cope with heavy traffic. The best advice for the cruiser is to stay out of their way. We should also stand by on VHF 13 as well as 16 to be aware of commercial communications that may be relevant. A 360 degree watch is important because huge vessels steaming in the channel cannot always slow down or turn to avoid traffic ahead. Many of these vessels cannot avoid you if you get in their way, because of their tonnage and momentum. It will take them a very long distance to turn or stop, and if they do turn or stop they might end up aground, at great expense to their owners, and possibly to the owner of the vessel who caused them to go aground. There is plenty of room to have a safe and enjoyable trip up the river if you are careful.

Editor's Note: There is plenty of room for my 5 feet draft ***outside*** *the ship channels. You can parallel these channels without interfering with big ship traffic.*

I'll never forget the day I was on the bridge of a large Chilean freighter coming north up the East River in New York Harbor. He was half-loaded with copper. He had come from Baltimore and was headed for New Haven and points north. He had to wait for mid-tide so he could get under the Brooklyn Bridge. If you clear that one, you'll clear them all. But he also needed half tide for his depth on the leg between the Old Brooklyn Navy Yard and the United Nations Building. Wouldn't you know, right at the critical time, sailboats in the way! This river is so deep most places that some sailboat skippers don't understand why the huge vessels need certain parts of it. We blew our horn and all but one sailboat moved over. This one skipper may have thought that he had the right of way (which he didn't!) or maybe he was day-dreaming. Repeated blasts of our horn finally got his attention, but I think it was our bow wave that moved him over!

I've had peachy times sailing into major harbors—Boston, New York, Baltimore, Miami, Port Everglades and others, but I stay out of the big ship channels, and photograph the *huge vessels as they pass by. Once I came through the Narrows in New York Harbor with the Queen Elizabeth II. I need two frames to get her all in. It was 8 a.m. on a beautiful bright great-to-be-alive morning. All the passengers were on deck with cameras unlimbered for New York's photogenic Upper Bay and they photoed us back!*

There may be rare circumstances where you have the right of way over commercial traffic. But please give way for the laws of mass and momentum! Also pay strict attention to your chart while proceeding out of the channel.

Often these ships have to move fairly rapidly to maintain steerage. This can result in some very large wakes in some of the shallow areas. In the vicinity of Sevenfoot Knoll **(24)** at the northern end of Craighill Channel **(13)**, this swell can cause a very impressive sea. There is a notice on the chart stating that 12-foot seas can be generated here.

To enter, follow the numerous buoys, and stay out of the way of ships. However, a few headings may help the first time, particularly if there is a heavy haze. If you are coming from the south, you will be passing under the Bay Bridges. If you are having trouble doing this, you should not be out in that kind of visibility, but following are the coordinates for the two bridge spans, just in case.

The western span is most always used by large ships. It has a vertical clearance of 186 feet. The position of the center of the span is 38°59.6'N by 76°22.9'W.

The eastern span has vertical clearance of only 58 feet. The center span position is 38°59.3'N by 76°21.5'W.

You should have little trouble sighting Sandy Point Shoal Light **(25)** off the large point of that name on the western shore. This is a large red brick structure which formerly housed a light keeper. It has a white roof and is on a brown cylindrical foundation and is 51 feet tall. Its position is 39°01.0'N by 76°23.1'W.

Heading north from a position to the east of this light or from the Chesapeake Bay Bridge, pick up the southern end of Craighill Channel **(13)**. The position of the entrance green lighted buoy "1 C" **(26)** is 39°01.4'N by 76°22.7'W. Follow this well-marked channel up to where it intersects with the Brewerton Channel **(10)** just to the northwest of the light at Sevenfoot Knoll **(24)**. This light used to be a red round lighthouse but is now of the newer steel girder and platform variety. You will see the older lighthouse ashore as part of the attractions at the Inner Harbor.

Coming down from the north or from the Eastern Shore, it is easy to pick up the Eastern Extension **(83)** of the Brewerton Channel either from the Tolchester Channel on the Eastern Shore or from the marked small boat channel on the eastern side. The beginning mark for the Eastern Extension of Brewerton Channel is a Fl R Bell buoy, "2BE" **(82)**. Its position is 39°08.9'N by 76°20.0'W. This is in a west-northwesterly direction from Swan Point. Note carefully the shallow areas scattered around outside these entrance channels.

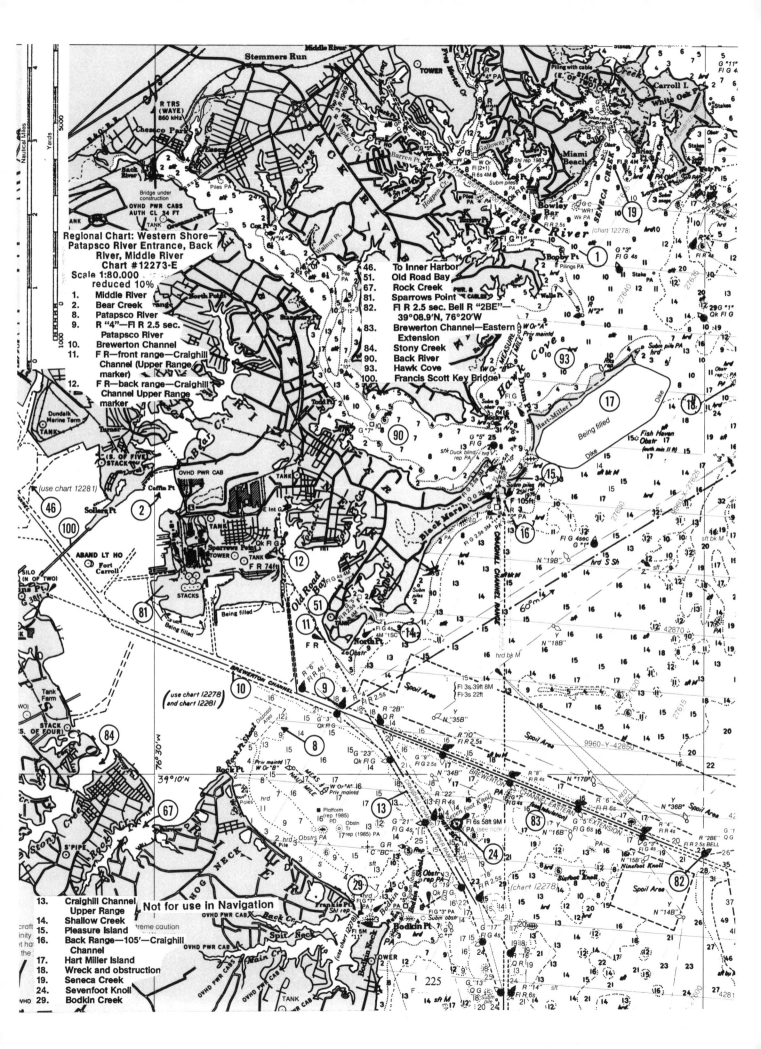

Regional Chart: Western Shore—
Patapsco River Entrance, Back
River, Middle River
Chart #12273-E
Scale 1:80,000
reduced 10%

1. Middle River
2. Bear Creek
8. Patapsco River
9. R "4"—Fl R 2.5 sec.
   Patapsco River
10. Brewerton Channel
11. F R—front range—Craighill
    Channel (Upper Range
    marker)
12. F R—back range—Craighill
    Channel Upper Range
    marker

46. To Inner Harbor
51. Old Road Bay
67. Rock Creek
81. Sparrows Point
82. Fl R 2.5 sec. Bell R "2BE"—
    39°08.9'N, 76°20'W
83. Brewerton Channel—Eastern
    Extension
84. Stony Creek
90. Back River
93. Hawk Cove
100. Francis Scott Key Bridge

Not for use in Navigation

13. Craighill Channel
    Upper Range
14. Shallow Creek
15. Pleasure Island
16. Back Range—105'—Craighill
    Channel
17. Hart Miller Island
18. Wreck and obstruction
19. Seneca Creek
24. Sevenfoot Knoll
29. Bodkin Creek

225

CREEKS OFF THE PATAPSCO RIVER

You will pass heavily industrialized shores, but keep the faith. Numerous creeks with anchorages and marinas will slide by on either side, and we will soon explore each of these in turn. Most cruising boats entering the Patapsco do so for the express purpose of visiting the Inner Harbor of Baltimore. We will describe this later in this chapter, but first you might want to take time to visit or explore some of the creeks branching off the river. Some of these are quite built-up ashore and full of docks and marinas. Others surprisingly offer nice anchorages with woodsy views ashore despite the dense civilization in this part of the world. There are not many things to do ashore outside of the marinas, because there are mostly residential houses and waterfront neighborhoods around these creeks Aside from the views, there is often a very practical reason for anchoring in one of the creeks first.

Many who are planning to visit the Inner Harbor like to first anchor in one of the creeks rather than head right in when they reach the Patapsco. Many feel as I do, that if you are going to check into a marina in the harbor, it is better to do it at the earliest allowable check-in time, and check-out at the latest. This allows you to have more time ashore. For this reason, an anchorage in one of the outlying creeks makes good sense when you arrive late in the day, and after you depart too late to comfortably go very far elsewhere.

Bodkin Creek (29)
Refer to Chart #12278-J—"Bodkin Creek and vicinity."

Bodkin Creek has a few nice marinas and some pleasant anchorages. Although close to Baltimore, it is not a convenient provisioning area.

As is true of most of these entrances, it is important that you follow the markers in from the main channel and not do any wandering around. There are shoal areas here, and some rocks. The area has been settled and busy for a long time and you should take the "obstruction" notices seriously.

To enter Bodkin Creek (29), head to its G "1" from G "17" in the Craighill Channel. G "1" is just northwest of G "17," and very close. From here be sure to follow the markers in to avoid the shoals and obstructions on both sides. The channel is very shallow until you get inside the creek. I found barely 6½ feet to be controlling for this entrance, the shallowest water occurring between G "9" and Fl G "11" (30). This is the type of entrance that could shoal easily because of its exposure and crossing currents. Don't enter the first time in a strong onshore breeze such as a northeaster. The charted rocks and obstructions (31) are close to the channel, and this is no place to be blown astray or pushed aside by the sea.

Some enter from G "21" of the Craighill Channel, picking up GR "BC" (32) which marks a rocky 5-foot shoal. They pass on either side, to intersect with the channel at Fl G "7." They take a 218°M course from G "21" to GR "BC," and then on to the entrance channel. Do not pass closely to GR "BC."

The marinas inside should know channel depths accurately, and you may wish to check with one of them described below. As you enter, you will see a pleasantly natural shoreline, considering the industry of Patapsco. Marsh and woods are abundant in the outer area of the creek, and homes do not destroy the beauty.

As you clear the cut between Old Landen Point and Bodkin Neck, you will see **Geisler's Point Marina (34)** to the right (northwest) behind a bulkhead coming out from the point to protect the docks. The water is shoal out to near the end of this bulkhead, and there is a small private red float (33) just to the east and outside of the bulkhead to mark the shallow water. There are numerous private docks lining the shore before the marina. This marina has 38 slips accommodating boats up to 45 feet, with up to 30 amps of electricity available. There is a hard surfaced ramp.

Heading up Back Creek (35), which opens beyond the bulkhead on the western bank of Bodkin Creek, you find a fair anchorage (36) just to the east of Hickory Point in 8 feet depth. There are woods ashore and the scenery is pretty. Though a few houses are around, they are far enough away to provide enough seclusion. There is a little beach up in the cove. The fetch to the northeast looks out toward the mouth of the creek and the Bay, but the bulkhead gives some protection in most weather. This is the only good anchoring spot in Back Creek in our opinion, because above here, the shores become crowded with houses, almost everyone having a dock, many with boat houses. Many of these homes have small sandy beaches on the water.

Continuing on, you will pass to your right (north) **Shipley's Anchorage (37)**, a small attractive marina which is behind the back yards ashore with 26 slips and 15 amps, and a concrete ramp. There is no marina office. This facility is mostly used by local people with smaller motor boats as a permanent docking.

Nearer the end of this creek is a beautiful small marina, on the southern shore, set in an area of many trees and woods. **Bodkin Marina (38)** has 30 slips with 15 amps. A sign indicates that they sell Carroll gasoline. I found only 4 to 5 feet depth in this area. Instead of the usual clutter of machinery, repair yards, and stored boats above the marina, there are trees with an access road winding up a hill. There are homes here, but most of them have kept the trees in their yards so that the creek up here is very pleasant. Above here, the creek shallows even more, and becomes narrower to eventually peter out among homes.

Back out in Bodkin Creek, you will notice a smaller creek opening to the south. The end of Spit Neck (39) points south to this creek. This creek with its Wharf Creek (40) and Locust Cove (41) extensions is pretty, with homes lining the shores, but not a very good anchorage because of the lack of privacy from all the homes.

In Locust Cove on the right (south) side is **Germershausen's Boat Yard (42)** with a concrete ramp and a 38-foot 15-ton railway. Farther up in the cove, on the other side of the creek, is a facility under construction (43). There were some slips built. I had a difficult time distinguishing this facility from surrounding home docks. There was a sign at the ramp, but nothing was on the sign. I found 3½ feet depth. Wharf Creek is crowded with homes. The chart indicates a "sign" (44) at the junction but I did not see it.

As you round R "12" off (southeast of) Spit Point, you will be approaching a very nice area of Bodkin Creek with several marinas and anchorages. You will notice first **Hammock Island Marina (45)** on the little island extending east from Graveyard Point, connected to the mainland only by a foot bridge. They have 64 slips with electricity up to 30 amps and depths up to 7 feet, but note that there is only 6½ feet at low tide getting into Bodkin Creek. There are no repair facilities here, but these can be found immediately up the creek on the same side. The slips are around the island. There is a recreation and facilities house in the middle of the island with an upstairs room providing a great view, containing a lending li-

brary. The marina is very attractive, quiet, and pleasant. It is a sailboat marina.

Ventnor Marine Service Inc. (46), is at the tip of Graveyard Point. It has an Exxon sign on the dock. They have 127 slips accomodating boats up to 70 feet, with up to 50 amps of electricity available. Gas and diesel are sold. MC and Visa are honored. There is a ramp but it is for private use. Ice is sold in block and cube. There is a boat lift capacity of 10 tons . Maximum water depth is 10 feet, but I only noted around 6½ feet controlling at the entrance to Bodkin Creek. They are dealers for Cobra by OMC, MerCruiser, Volvo Penta, Pleasure Craft, Palmer, Volvo, Chrysler, Coastal, and Crusader. The Maryland Marine Police (46) were operating here from last year.

Before passing the point, I am sure you may be wondering about the origin of the name "Graveyard Point." I am reluctant to tell what I learned, because it may give a negative connotation to the area, but be assured that this is a very pleasant area and great place to visit. I was told that in the very early days of Baltimore, many pigs used to live on this point. Their purpose in life was to consume the garbage delivered there from Baltimore. When that city suffered a cholera epidemic, the pigs took the disease as they dutifully munched away at the garbage and were buried en masse, thus the name. But this long ago event should in no way reflect upon the attractiveness of the area today.

We found two areas here for good anchorages. These are in the cove east of Graveyard Point (47) in 8 feet depth, and between Job Cove and Goose Cove (48) where the chart shows "Stk." Both of these places have homes around on the shore, and the first has the marina in view, but the water is broad enough so that you do not feel too enclosed. The chart shows a submerged pile north of the tip just to the west of Graveyard Point. I did not find this pile. Anchoring or passing well off the point in deep water should avoid this.

If you go farther up the creek, you will find it to be crowded with homes and their docks, with no special coves for anchoring. This continues on, with the creek becoming progressively shallower and narrower until its end.

Just before you reach Perry Cove, on your right (the northern side), you will find **Pleasure Marine Center (49).** This marina can be identified by its sign. They have 109 slips accomodating boats up to 50 feet with up to 30 amps electricity available. Gas is sold. Visa and MC are honored. Ice is sold in block and cube. There is a boat lift capacity of up to 30 tons. Maximum water depth is 6 feet. Other features include brokerage, a picnic area, and some marine hardware available.

Next up the creek, on the same side, and west of Perry Cove, you will find the **Bodkin Yacht Club (50).** This very pretty club is out on the point with slips around the point and a brown club house up on the hill. There is a picnic area with a patio overlooking the river and a children's playground. Depths remain 6 to 7 feet up to Perry Cove, but beyond here, the creek becomes narrow, shallow, and very congested with homes and docks. There are also overhead power cables.

Old Road Bay

Refer to Chart #12278-K—"Old Road Bay, Patapsco River Entrance."

This area is not what a typical cruiser is looking for, and I would pass it by unless I had business with one of the marinas there.

Old Road Bay (51) is a broad open area on the northern shore of the Patapsco River, near its mouth. It has two creeks extending northward, Jones Creek (52) northwest, and North Point Creek (53) extending northeast. Entering Old Road Bay is a matter of following the markers. As you do, you see some heavy industry (Bethlehem Steel's Sparrows Point plant) to your left (west), and many houses on the shore to your right and ahead (north). You will notice the 15 feet tall horizontal red and white striped squat light structure (11) on the point to your right (east) and a water tank (54) which is white and looks like a squashed rain drop. The deep water dredged channel (55) is for the industrial docks on the western shore of the basin, with their huge piles of coal. After you pass those, controlling depth is 4 feet.

Note that there are numerous obstructions charted and that you should be careful to remain in the channel. There is a tendency to continue straight ahead in a northerly direction after you leave the dredged channel and head straight for the creek mouth. Don't do it. Veer to the northeast of R "10" of that dredged channel to pick up the small boat channel in the northeast corner of the basin. The obstructions and wrecks are still there. As you enter Jones Creek, you will see a bulkhead on the point to your right (east) behind R "6." Behind R "6" there is a danger sign (56) noting old pilings where a wharf formerly existed on the point. This creek is full to brim with small houses, private docks, and industry.

Behind (to the north of) the bulkhead on the eastern point guarding the entrance to Jones Creek lies **Old Road Bay Marina (57)** with 84 slips up to 60 feet long and electricity up to 50 amps.

You could anchor (58) in the little bay north of the marina, 4 to 4½ feet depth, but the scenery would be of industry and many small homes crowded close and many old docks, some appearing as though they could easily tumble in with a good blow. The pilings noted in various places around the shore are there, apparently from rotted docks.

On the opposite (north) side of the little bay from the above marina is **Atlantis Marina (59)** with a blue and white gas and diesel sign. There are 80 slips and a 25-ton railway. Just around the point, still on the eastern side, is **Young's Boat Yard (60)** with a 9-ton railway and 4-ton lift, and some slips.

The **North Point Yacht Club (61)** has a white building and some docks on the western shore across from Young's. **Weber Marina (62)** has 45 slips and a 15-ton lift, up in the last cove in the northwest corner of Jones Creek.

North Point Creek (53) is similar to Jones Creek. It has many trailer homes, some of which are sitting very close to the water. The channel is narrow with 6 feet controlling if you are in the right place. There are some private markers. I noticed that there were apparently others which are not now used. If you have business here, I would suggest talking with Markel's Boat Yard (65) about present depths before you enter. **North Point Marina (63)** will come up on your left (west). They have 150 slips, 15 amps electricity, concrete ramp, and a 12-ton lift. They sell gas. **Iman's Boat Yard (64)** is tucked up into the little cove to your right, (east) with 4 feet controlling. I saw many work boats there, and some pleasure boats. They have a 20-ton railway and a 10-ton lift, with 58 slips and 15 amps, engine work and general repairs.

Continuing on up in the narrow channel, **Markel's Boat Yard (65)** is tucked into the first little cove on the left (west). They have 44 slips up to 50 feet, 15 amps of electricity, and gas sold. They honor Visa, Discover and Citgo. You can recognize it by its sign and a Citgo sign. There is also a 15-ton railway and 8-ton lift, with some repairs available. A nice marine store and clean restrooms are up on the hill. They sell

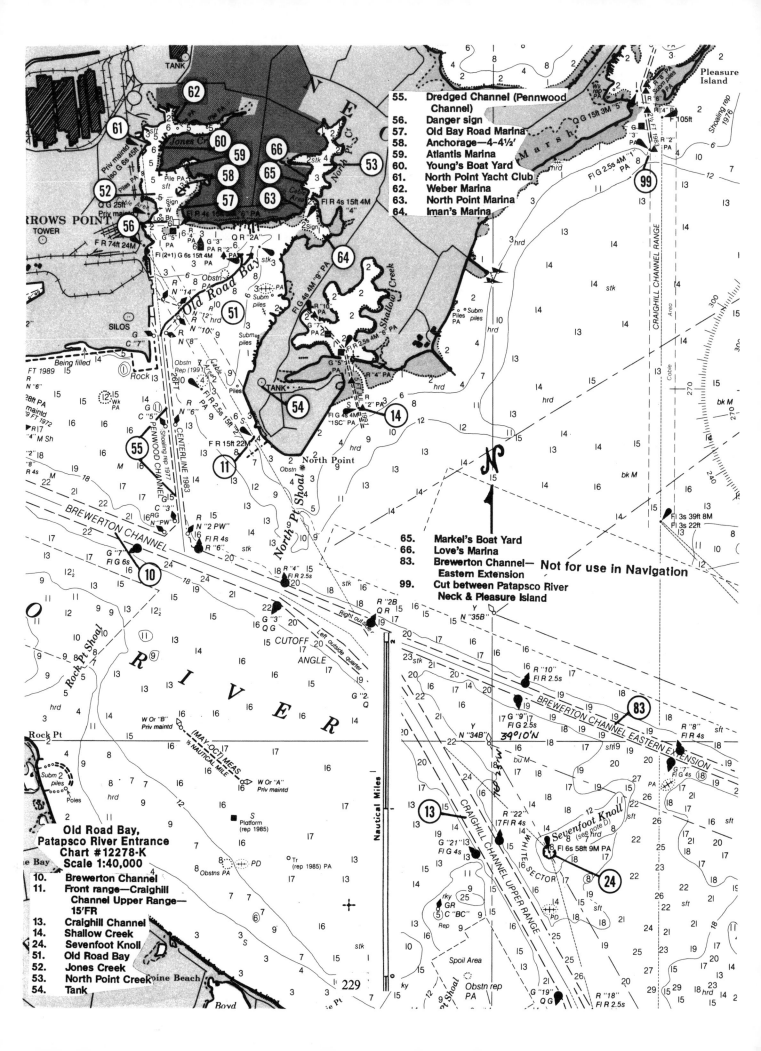

block and cube ice. This is a well-run and cared-for small marina. Capt. Lou Markel would be able to give you the latest on controlling entrance depths if you wished to visit. He has 6 feet maximum depth at his docks.

Love's Marina (66) next appears on your left, with 30 slips with 15 amps electricity, and a 20-ton lift. It is a pleasant looking work place and appears to wrap around a back yard as it goes up into the long cove pointing to westward. I found 4 feet depth in the area, but the creek quickly shoals to 2 feet past this marina.

Rock Creek

Refer to Chart #12278-L—"Rock Creek, Stony Creek and vicinity."

Rock creek is not an ideal cruising creek, but an adequate spot to anchor while waiting to move on or a good spot if you need a nice marina.

It is not quite as easy to find the Rock Creek **(67)** entrance markers from Brewerton Channel in the Patapsco River as it is to find those for Bodkin Creek, because they are farther away from the channel. Head 190°M from G "11". You must avoid White Rocks **(68)** to your east as you proceed to Fl R "2" at Rock Creek entry. You will see "White Rocks" from the Brewerton Channel. They are large, prominent and sinister looking. They normally look rather dark from a distance. As you approach, they begin to appear white or very light gray. The water is deep, as the chart shows, very close to them and often people fish in close. There is a wreck **(69)** noted outside (to the west) of R "2" and R "2A." I did not see it, but it should not be a bother, if it is still there, as long as you are honoring the channel. I found 11 feet to be controlling in this relatively deep entrance.

On the point to your left (east) as you enter the creek, you will see the large and nice facilities of the **Maryland Yacht Club (70)**, with a big sign. There is a beach on the point and a grassy yard around a large club house. It is for members and guests only, though they will sell gas and diesel to the public. The no tresspassing signs are clear and insistent, and I would call them before landing. The docks are noted on the chart on the southwestern side of Fairview Point.

If you look easterly, farther up in the cove behind Fairview Point, you will see Fairview Marine Corporation **(71)** up in Wall Cove **(72)**. They are a full service repair and rebuild facility, and will take transients if space is available, but mostly they don't have space. You won't have trouble finding **Fairview Marine**, nestled on the peninsula where the large docks are indicated on the spot on the northern side of the cove. You'll see their large buildings and sign. They have 117 slips outside and 22 under cover, they can accomodate boats up to very large sizes, with up to 50 amps of electricity available. There is gas and diesel sold, with a large Amoco sign. Visa and Amoco are honored. There is boat lift capacity of up to 100 feet and 100 tons on its railway, with lifts of lesser capacity. I found 8 feet depth. This facility has been in the major repair and rebuild business for many years. They also have a brokerage.

Passing Fairview Point, you cannot miss the very large facility known as **White Rocks Yachting Center (73)**, on your left (southwest) after you pass the point. They have 400 slips accomodating boats up to 50 feet in the slips and much longer alongside with up to 50 amps of electricity available. There was no fuel dock. MC and Visa are honored. They stand by on Channel 72. A ramp is for the private use of their permanent customers. Ice is sold in block and cube. There is

a boat lift capacity of 25 tons with a 3-ton crane. Maximum water depth is 12 feet, although there is only 11 feet at the creek entrance. Other features include several different types of businesses on the premises, offering a very complete place to accomplish any repair and maintenance work such as mast and rigging work, major hull repair, an engine shop specializing in Volvo and Westerbeke and other engines, a surveyor, a very complete marine store with good hardware and parts, and a yacht brokerage and charter service.

Windows on the Bay Restaurant **(74)** is on the bank overlooking White Rocks Yachting Center's docks and the creek. This is full menu restaurant with a relaxed atmosphere. There is often live entertainment on weekends in season, and free dockage is available to customers while dining.

The best anchorage **(75)** area that I found in this creek was in the broad area north of the White Rocks Yachting Center. There is plenty of swinging room and enough wide water so that the residential shoreline and marina don't feel too close. This is a very heavily traveled area. Tuck in as close to the side as you can and keep well lit at night. Going up into Tar Cove **(76)** is also an anchorage possibility, but it would be a tight feeling with homes so close ashore.

Across this broad basin from White Rocks Yachting Center, on the northwestern side, you will see the smaller facility of **Bar Harbor Marina (77)**. They have 50 slips with up to 30 amps of electricity, accomodating boats up to 45 feet, and a 53-foot 35-ton railway with general repairs available. Depths are 10 feet. There is also a yacht transportation truck capable of taking boats up to 30 feet and 10.000 pounds. They do not normally stand by on VHF.

Oak Harbor Marina (78) is very well protected and tucked up in the deep cove on the southeast side of the creek, next up from Tar Cove. This quiet and pretty marina can be identified by its sign. It has 97 slips accomodating boats up to 45 feet, with up to 30 amps of electricity available. There is a boat lift capacity of 30 tons. Water depth is 8 feet, with 10 in some areas. They sell propane, and have an engine repair shop on the premises. They do not stand by on VHF. There is also a canvas specialist here.

Just upstream from Oak Harbor and on the other (northwest) side, the **Pasadena Yacht Yard (79)** has 50 slips up to 50 feet long with electricity up to 30 amps. A large red brick house sits high on a hill overlooking the facility. There is lift capacity up to 35 tons and gas is sold, and Exxon credit cards are accepted. Just upstream from Pasadena Yacht Yard, almost even with the last pole outside of its last dock upstream, there is a marker **(80)** right in the middle of the creek warning of a submerged obstruction and against anchoring.

The creek above this area becomes very crowded with many houses on the shores, and private docks often coming right out to the edge of the channel to find deep water. It is pretty with high hills and many trees among the yards, but there is no room to anchor.

Exiting the creek, you will notice across the river on the northern shore, the well-known shipping terminal and industrial area of Sparrow's Point **(81)**. There is a huge landfill project in progress along its southern shore. The basin **(82)** up inside is for huge commercial vessels.

Stony Creek

Refer to Chart #12278-L.

This is one of the better of the outer Patapsco creeks to anchor while waiting to move on up or down the Bay or to go in-

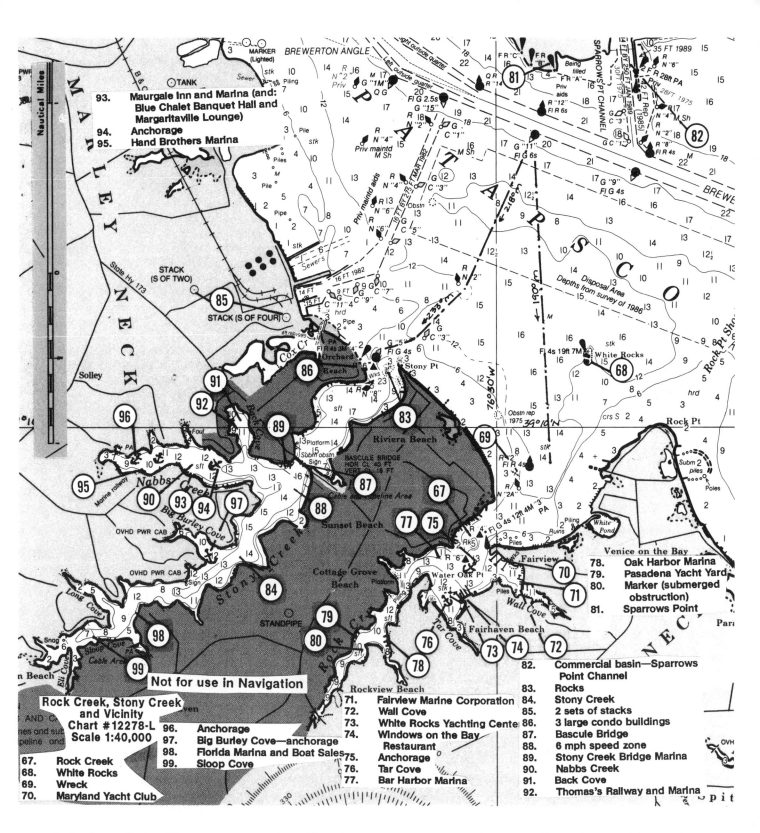

The mouth of Stony Creek **(84)** is a bit difficult to pick out from the shoreline while out in the Brewerton Channel because of the rocks **(83)** between Stony Point and the western shore of the mouth. They make it hard to see an opening. To begin to get your bearings, note the two sets of stacks **(85)** (one set of four and another of two) behind the factory complex on the southwest bank of the Patapsco. These are north-

to the Inner Harbor. There are some marinas. There is an opening bridge just inside the entrance.

west of the creek entrance. Also to the west of the mouth, you will see three large gray-white apartment condos **(86)**. These will be between the stacks and the mouth, and on the western shore of the mouth. It may also help if you can find the large white house back in the trees on the wooded hill on the shore, east of the above landmarks. This will also be to the east of the mouth.

A course of 218°M should bring you from Fl G "11" of the Brewerton Channel to R nun "2," the first Stony Creek marker. From there, a course of 233°M brings you to just west of G "3." This marker may be a bit difficult to pick out from the trees on the hill.

About this time, you may be noticing the large sea monster, with its undulating coils and its long snout pointing to those conspicuous condominiums lined up on the western shore of the creek entrance. The sea monster is actually the rocks charted near the middle of the creek's mouth. When the tide is right, the resemblance is striking. From outside the mouth, it will seem as though your course will put you right up on the western bank as you avoid these rocks, but the narrow channel will become more obvious as you get nearer. You will pass with the sea serpent to your left (east). Follow the markers carefully to avoid the rocks and shoals on each side.

Once inside the tight entrance, you will be surrounded by houses and docks all around, with the factory stacks to your northwest. The bridge (87) is a bascule with 18 feet vertical clearance and some restrictions in opening. Last year these were: from Monday through Friday from 6:30 to 9:00 a.m. and from 3:30 p.m. until 6:30 p.m. it will open at 7:30 a.m. and 5:00 p.m. only, and on Saturdays from 11 a.m. until 7:00 p.m. and on Sundays from 12:00 p.m. until 5:00 p.m., it will be open only on the hour and half hour. It opens on signal on federal and state holidays and other times. So if you have a computer to figure it all out, you can get through this bridge at some time or the other! On the upstream side of the bridge, a 6 mph speed zone (88) begins and lasts the rest of the creek. Don't let the bridge keep you away—it's worth the trouble.

To your right (west), just after going through the bridge, you will find **Stony Creek Bridge Marina (89)**. This marina can be identified by its gas sign. It has 70 slips accomodating boats up to 40 feet, longer alongside, with up to 30 amps of electricity available and state-of-the-art power pedestals, gas, a pumpout, block and cube ice, and a hard surfaced launching ramp. MC and Visa are honored. Water is quite deep at the outer slips. There is a restaurant on the premises and a beach right at the docks.

Nabbs Creek (90) opens to the west just past the marina. This creek is certainly well occupied ashore, but does provide good spots for anchoring. For those wishing a very snug spot, Back Cove (91) looks great, but its shores are extremely crowded with homes. There is also a facility in Back Cove, on its western shore, called **Thomas's Railway and Marina (92)**. There are some docks here and a 75-foot 52-ton railway.

Back out in Nabbs Creek and proceeding farther west, you will find the shores to be covered with trees, particularly on your right (the north side). You will soon notice the large **Maurgale Inn and Marina (93)**. This marina can be identified by its many docks nestled back in the slight cove, its sign, and the restaurant at the head of the docks. They have 132 slips, with up to 50 amps electricity available, pumpout, block and cube ice. Visa and MC are honored. There is boat lift capacity of 20 tons and a 7-ton crane, and some repairs can be made. Maximum water depth available is 10 to 12 feet in the deeper slips. The Blue Chalet Banquet Hall and the Margaritaville Lounge are at the marina, both popular in the area. The restaurant is very nice, elevated and with a good view. Complimentary docking is offered to restaurant patrons.

Nabbs Creek has high hills around its shores, and even on the more populated left (south) side, the homes are often set back in the trees, and the creek is therefore very pretty. Occasionally, you will see tall red cliffs, with reddish beach at the base, particularly on the less populated right side. Pick your spot to anchor (94) here, but be sure to stay well lit at night. It begins to get shallower above Maurgale Marina, depths of 10 and 12 feet becoming 6 and eventually less. But the creek is even prettier up here, and nicer to anchor if you have the draft.

Hand Brothers Marina (95) will appear on the left (southern side) as you approach the end. It has 50 slips, most of which were not occupied when I visited, and a railway. Anchoring (96) above here, you will find woods and quiet reminiscent of the Eastern Shore, if you have the draft. It shoals as the creek goes on, but if you draw less than 6 feet, you can anchor there (96).

Going back out into Stony Creek and heading southwesterly into its upper reaches, you will find more of the high hills, reddish cliffs, and many homes ashore. It isn't as pretty as Nabbs Creek mainly because there are more houses.

The mouth of Big Burley Cove (97) makes a nice and pretty place to anchor. If the wind comes too hard from the northeast or southwest, you can tuck up in far enough to get shelter. Scenery is pleasant and you're not too close to the homes.

There is yet another marina up Stony Creek, named **Florida Marina and Boat Sales (98)**, on your left (southeast) just before (to the east of) Sloop Cove (99). They have 60 slips with electricity up to 15 amps taking boats up to 30 feet with 6 feet controlling depth. Gas is sold and Visa, MC, and Amex are taken. They have a 12-ton lift and do engine repairs including inboard/outboard work, and are dealers for MerCruiser, OMC, Volvo, Mercury, Force, and Chrysler.

Refer to Chart #12278-M—"Patapsco River: Bear Creek."
As you head back out of this creek and turn your sights northwestward up the Patapsco, you will see the majestic Francis Scott Key Bridge (100) spanning the waters ahead, beckoning to the excitement awaiting in Baltimore's Inner Harbor. But first, there are two more creeks that you may wish to consider visiting.

Bear Creek
Refer to Chart #12278-M.
With its heavily settled and industrialized shores and heavy traffic, Bear Creek is not a very good spot to anchor, but there are a few good marinas. Anchor Bay East Marina is one of the best.

The entrance to Bear Creek (2) is easy to find. It bears off to the northeast from QR R "2" of the main Patapsco channel. This is just southeast of the Francis Scott Key Bridge, and just to the southeast of the remains of Ft. Carroll (1). Ft. Carroll still silently guards the river, with an abandoned lighthouse, on an island just southeast of the bridge, and on the right (northeast) side of the main channel. The first buoy, R N "2" is easy to spot. It is close to the channel. From there, follow the markers in the Marine Channel, taking you northeast.

You enter this creek with the roar of the elevated highway to your left (northwest) and cars zooming in a steady stream. To your right, the heavy industry and shipping piers of Sparrows Point predominate the scenery. There are obstructions and piles (3) between Coffin Point and Lloyd Point, and staying in the marked channel is important. Bear Creek illustrates the lesson that in areas where our civilization has been involved with industry, you'll find silent ghosts of the past, in the form of old pilings, wrecks, and foundations, lurking beneath the waters out of the channels. We're certainly not critical of the Baltimore heavy industry. Our country benefitted immensely from the industry of the people there, and they are now a model of clean-up and proper marking.

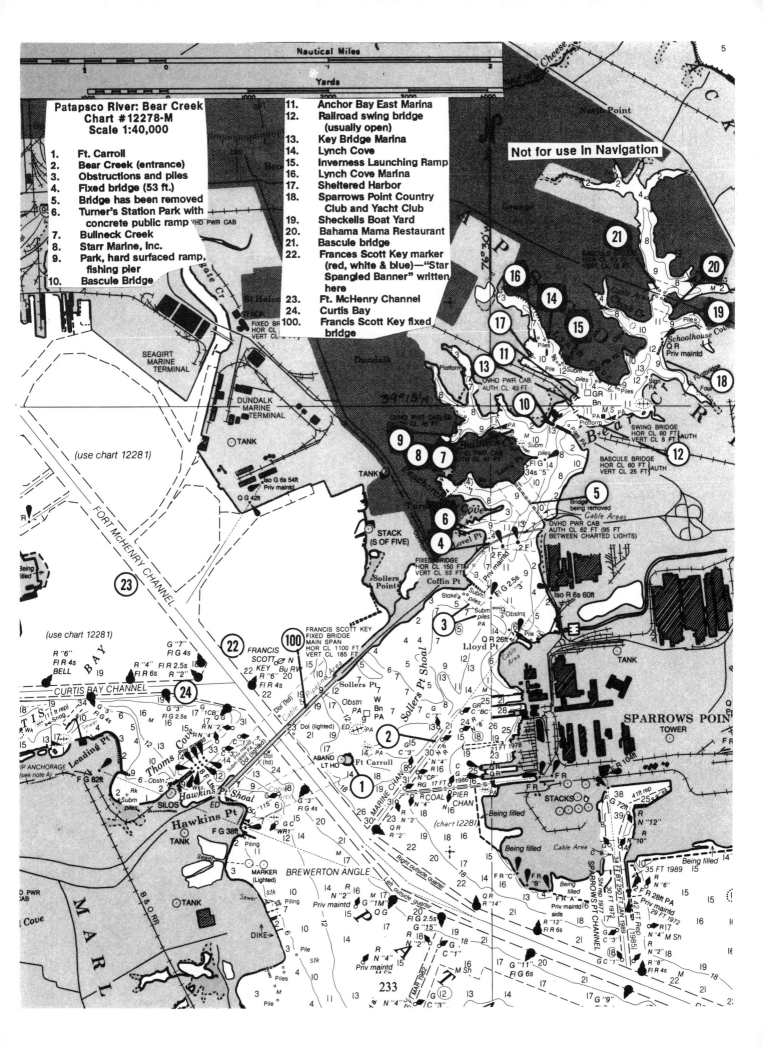

Patapsco River: Bear Creek
Chart #12278-M
Scale 1:40,000

1. Ft. Carroll
2. Bear Creek (entrance)
3. Obstructions and piles
4. Fixed bridge (53 ft.)
5. Bridge has been removed
6. Turner's Station Park with concrete public ramp
7. Bullneck Creek
8. Starr Marine, Inc.
9. Park, hard surfaced ramp, fishing pier
10. Bascule Bridge
11. Anchor Bay East Marina
12. Railroad swing bridge (usually open)
13. Key Bridge Marina
14. Lynch Cove
15. Inverness Launching Ramp
16. Lynch Cove Marina
17. Sheltered Harbor
18. Sparrows Point Country Club and Yacht Club
19. Sheckells Boat Yard
20. Bahama Mama Restaurant
21. Bascule bridge
22. Frances Scott Key marker (red, white & blue)—"Star Spangled Banner" written here
23. Ft. McHenry Channel
24. Curtis Bay
100. Francis Scott Key fixed bridge

Not for use in Navigation

233

Next you will pass under a fixed bridge (4) of only 53 feet vertical clearance. This is less than the normal 65 feet to be found up and down the ICW, and thus will prohibit some sailboats from going farther up. The overhead power cable here has an authorized clearance of 62 feet and 95 feet between the charted lights. Northwest of this fixed bridge, the chart shows a bridge (5) extending southeasterly from Long Point, with a notation that it is being removed. This removal is completed.

Just beyond that first bridge is a little cove on the north side of Lovel Point. I found the water shallowing gradually inside until 4 feet near the end. Inside the cove, on your left (south) is Turner's Station Park and a concrete public ramp (6). The ramp is on the left side. There is more park on the right side also. This cove is a snug anchorage for shallow draft boats but there will be much noise from the park area and surrounding buildings, and much traffic from the ramp. This park is an open recreation area with few trees, and does not present a very scenic view from the water. I saw no indication of the wreck where it is charted in the end of the cove. The whole shoreline has obviously been improved and cleaned up.

Bullneck Creek (7) is not an attractive anchorage because of congestion and many docks. I did not see the wreck noted on the left (south) side of the channel. I found depths to be as charted. Starr Marine Inc. (8) is in the first leg to your left as you reach the branches, on the south shore. They have 60 slips up to 35 feet and 15 amps electricity, a 15-ton crane, and some repair work available. A hard surfaced ramp (9) is on the opposite shore and is part of a grassy park with some picnic tables under shade trees. Note the high tension wire across the creek with an authorized clearance of 43 feet. A fishing pier extends from this park close to that wire, just down stream.

The bascule bridge (10) which you will next encounter has a sign that says to call ahead "whenever possible" and gives the numbers of (410) 284-1880, or 284-0955. If you want the very latest information on this bridge, you will find Anchor Bay East Marina (11) to be very helpful as well as a good place to stop (see below). Above the bridge, a 6 mph speed limit extends to the head of the creek. The railroad swing bridge (12) just upstream is normally in the open position.

As soon as you pass through the railroad bridge, you will see the Key Bridge Marina (13), on the left (west) side right at the bridge. They have 40 slips and a lift.

Next up on the left (west), you will notice the well-kept docks and facilities of Anchor Bay East Marina (11). You will recognize it by its sign and impressive facilities, and the Carroll Fuel sign. They have 67 slips up to 45 feet and 100 feet alongside, up to 50 amps of electricity available, gas and diesel, with discount fuel prices for volume pumping. Visa, MC, and Discover are honored. The full service yard facilities here have a 50-foot 35-ton open end lift. A pumpout is on the docks. Supplies such as block and cube ice, fishing tackle, personal boating items, and beverages are sold here as well as marine parts and hardware. The store has discount prices. There is also a laundromat and a ramp, a nice picnic area, a playground, and they will help with reasonable transportation problems if a vehicle is available. They rent bikes. They also offer fuel recycling, something which many people need but can't find. They are dealers for Onan, Cummings, and Crusader. This is a nice marina with excellent parts and hardware sales on the premises. It is run by members of the same family that run the Anchor Bay over in Middle River, which also has a very impressive marine parts and hardware and supply store.

Lynch Cove (14) extends more like a creek, to the northwest right after you pass Anchor Bay East Marina. Like other coves here, this is not a place to anchor. Inverness Launching Ramp (15) with a park, is located on the north side of the cove with around 100 feet of dock. The ramp is hard surfaced and very wide. On the southern side of Lynch Cove is Lynch Cove Marina (16). They are a permanent slip marina and not interested in transient business. There are 52 slips with 15 amp electricity. Also in this cove is a facility called Sheltered Harbor (17).

Heading farther up Bear Creek brings no improvement in the shoreline, but a few more facilities. The Sparrows Point Country Club and Yacht Club (18) is a nice and large facility with attractive docks and clubhouse. It is a member of the CBCYA.

There is one more bascule bridge on Bear Creek, but before the bridge are a small boatyard in Schoolhouse Cove and a restaurant. Sheckells Boat Yard (19) has 20 slips and a 20-ton railroad and is straight ahead as you turn into the cove. I found 5½ feet of depth up to the docks.

Between Schoolhouse Cove and the bridge is the Bahama Mamma Restaurant (20), on the east side of Bear Creek. There are docks around two sides of the restaurant, since it faces on both the main creek and Schoolhouse Cove. Complimentary docking is available for customers, but most boats over 20 feet would have a difficult time fitting in, although there is up to 10 feet depth available. There was construction at the restaurant last year and there may be room for longer boats now. Here you can get light snacks to full meals, including takeout. There is both an upstairs and downstairs facility, the lower level serving lighter foods and drinks. The upstairs is casual, but with a more complete menu. It also has a bar and pool table, and live entertainment on weekends and special occasions. The view is of the creek and cove. This informal restaurant is popular locally.

The last bridge (21) in Bear Creek has a sign that says "eight hours notice to open, call (410) 284-1815." However, this sign was broken and partly in the water and had obviously been in this condition for a long time. Part of it was obscured, and the "8" could have been "18" or a "48" or a "68" or whatever. The vertical clearance is 12 feet. Perhaps this is a hint, because the creek above is even more congested, and offers little attraction to the cruising boater.

Refer to Chart #12281-B—"Ft. McHenry Channel."

Back out in the Patapsco River, passing the mouth of Bear Creek, you will soon go under the Francis Scott Key Bridge towering overhead. You will have been watching it for some time coming up the river. To us, it is always a beckoning symbol of the spectacular Inner Harbor to come. Just above the bridge to your right (to the north of the center span) there is, in season, a buoy (22) marking the spot where Francis Scott Key wrote the "Star Spangled Banner." He was prisoner on a British vessel involved in the bombardment of Fort McHenry during the War of 1812. After a terrible night of shelling, he looked ashore "in the dawn's early light" and saw the flag still flying over the fort. The buoy has blue, red, and white stripes with a star spangled top. It is in position from June 1 to September 30. After passing under the bridge, you will be in the Fort McHenry Channel (23). On the southern shore, you will see Curtis Bay (24) opening with its busy industrial shoreline. Behind this will be one more creek, this one very nice.

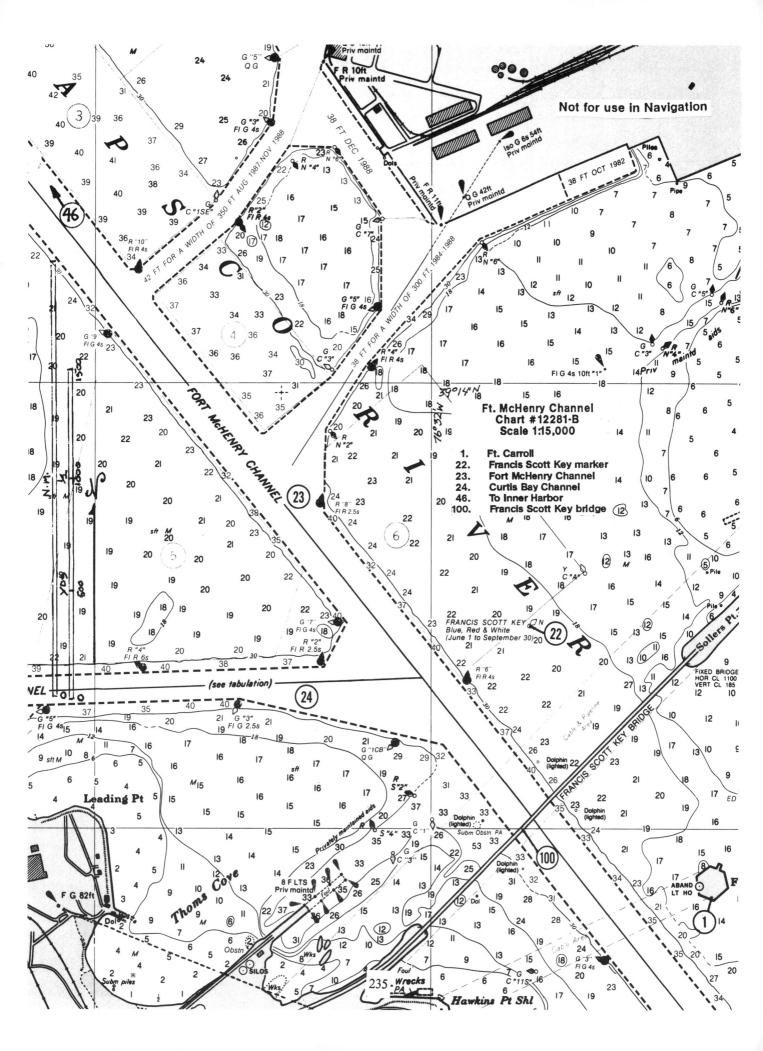

Not for use in Navigation

Ft. McHenry Channel
Chart #12281-B
Scale 1:15,000

1.   Ft. Carroll
22.   Francis Scott Key marker
23.   Fort McHenry Channel
24.   Curtis Bay Channel
46.   To Inner Harbor
100. Francis Scott Key bridge

FRANCIS SCOTT KEY
Blue, Red & White
(June 1 to September 30)

FORT McHENRY CHANNEL

FRANCIS SCOTT KEY BRIDGE

FIXED BRIDGE
HOR CL 1100
VERT CL 185

Sollers Pt

Leading Pt

Thoms Cove

235 · Wrecks
PA

Hawkins Pt Shl

ABAND
LT HO

Curtis Creek

Refer to Chart #12278-N—"Curtis Bay, Curtis Creek"
and
Chart #12281-A—"Curtis Bay."

This deep and easy creek has some nice anchorages worth stopping overnight or a few days, and also a few facilities.

The entrance to Curtis Creek (25) is known as Curtis Bay (24). Do not pre-judge Curtis Creek by what you see in Curtis Bay as you head in. This is an important area for industry and shipping, and is deep and well-marked. Its channel intersects the Ft. McHenry Channel (23) (of the Patapsco River) just northwest of the Francis Scott Key Bridge. Curtis Bay Channel leads off to the west into a shoreline of stacks, coal, loading piers, cranes, tanks, railroads, and commercial docks and buildings. Barges are often moored outside the channel here. The "Dead Ship Anchorage" (26) is to your left (south) as you head in. In days past, this is where many sad derelicts were brought to die and settle to the bottom. This is being cleaned up, but I would not venture out of the channel here, or anywhere else in old and "well used" areas such as this.

Inside Curtis Bay, your channel will veer to your left (south), rounding Sledd's Point. You will see the three bascule bridges (27) ahead, one right after the other. These open on signal and have a vertical clearance of 40 feet. On the west bank just before these bridges (to their north), you will see Smith and Sons Shipyard (28) with railway capability of up to 200 tons and several cranes with capacity up to 60 tons. Industry ashore is still heavy.

Keep the faith and continue on through. It will get better after you pass through the next swing bridge, a railroad bridge (29) usually open, and then pass the well known Curtis Bay Coast Guard Station (30) on your left (on the east bank). This is a repair center for the Coast Guard as well as a large station. Continuing on past Thomas Point on your right (west), you will finally begin to see the promise of this nice creek as industry fades into scenery of trees and a few houses and private docks.

The first several areas where you may wish to anchor lies behind G "1" which guards a little cove (31) on the east bank off the mouth of Furnace Creek. Venture in carefully, north of G "1," until you are far enough in to be safely out of the channel. I found 7 to 8 feet depth here. Beware of submerged pipe and foul area (32) charted in the cove, don't go in very far. An American Legion Hall with its building and grassy yard will be on your left (north) as you enter the cove, with woods and some residences on the right. A pleasant view of marsh and woods lies ahead at the east end of the cove.

Furnace Creek (33) is pretty with deep water as reported on the chart and it would make a good and secure anchorage. You could put your hook down just about any place that you like, but we've marked my favorite spot. There are numerous houses ashore in this creek, but they don't crowd out the pretty scenery like elsewhere in this area.

Just as you go in, you will see in the recess on your left (south), a beach with a dock coming out. This is known as Pt. Pleasant Beach (34) and the building on the shore has a bar inside, a pool table, and light snacks. I found 3 to 4 feet depth at the dock.

Back Creek off Furnace Creek has a little fixed bridge (35) across the mouth, and there is a fence (36) across the next little cove up on the north. But a nice anchorage (37) with 9 feet depth can be found in the next cove There are trees ashore and marshy beaches on either side as you go into that cove. In the end of the cove (northeastern shore), there is a white cliff with a green field on the top. The houses on the south eastern shore on the opposite side of Furnace Creek are distant enough to not interfere with the scenery around you. Continuing on up Furnace Creek, depths become gradually less, and the houses gradually more, until you reach a small fixed bridge near the end.

Proceeding south, back out in Curtis Creek, and you will soon come to a beautiful spot called Tanyard Cove (38), with enough woods and marsh ashore to remind you of many of the rural areas on the Eastern Shore. There is only one readily visible house on the cove, on the left (north side). There are many houses on the other side (western shore) of Curtis Creek, but they do not make unpleasant scenery. You will immediately notice the "wreck" (39) noted on the chart in this cove. It looks as though it is completely blocking the middle, thus rendering the cove unapproachable. I went in carefully looking for it. I proceeded about half way between the two entrance points, and although I didn't find the wreck, several times my depth finder quickly flashed a "7-foot" reading between the two points, slightly to the right (south). I thought that this must be the wreck but wasn't sure, and set out to find someone ashore who might elaborate. I was told that the wreck is toward the northern shore, about 20 yards off shore. It is an old sunken motor yacht 25 to 30 feet long, and is exposed at low water. This is a popular skiing area and many are complaining, attempting to get the wreck removed. I mention all of this because the cove is pretty enough to try out if your draft allows. Hopefully by the time you try Tanyard Cove, the wreck will be removed or marked, but don't count on it.

Above (south of) Tanyard Cove, Curtis Creek blends into Marley Creek (40). This is still a very pretty area, but note the overhead power cables (41) with only 57 feet vertical clearance. This could always be less due to sagging, and even at 57 feet is less than the masts of some sailboats. You will see the huge towers ashore which support the cables. Continuing on up the creek, you will soon find a beautiful small island (42) in the middle, with woods and a house with its dock. I was amazed to find this here in the middle of so much civilization. The creek is beautiful up here. Homes are generally set well back in the trees.

A green marker will tell you to pass the island on its northwestern side. As you do, you will find the C and P Marina (43),

Fort Carroll, Francis Scott Key Bridge in background

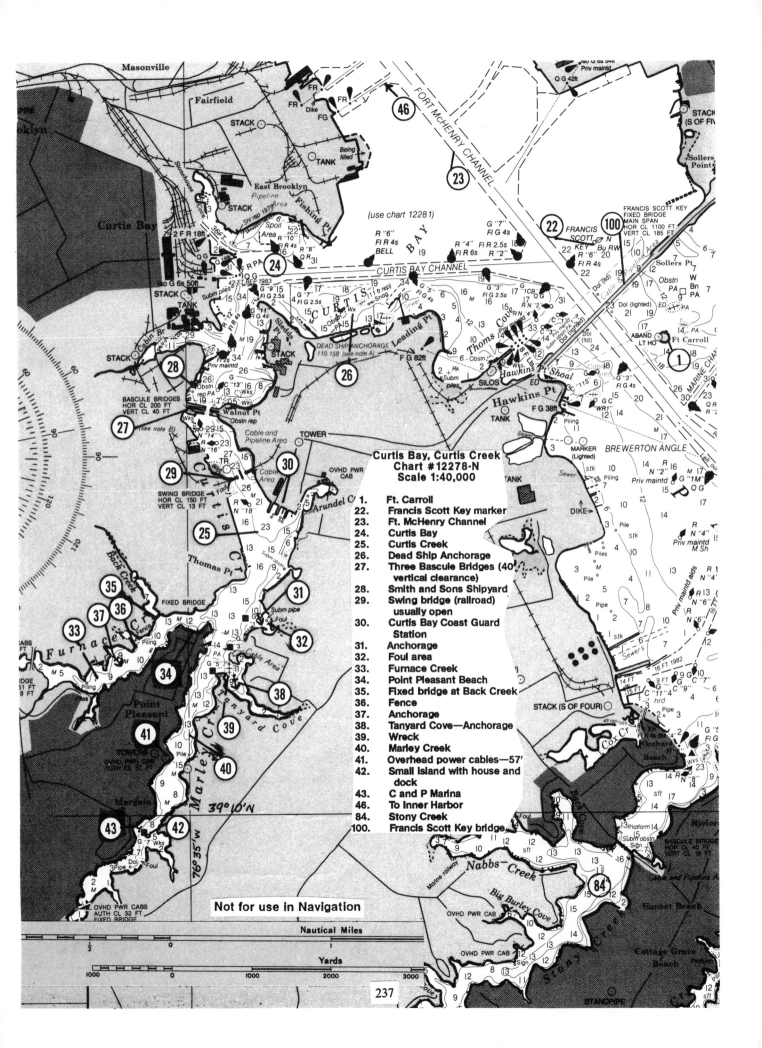

Curtis Bay, Curtis Creek
Chart #12278-N
Scale 1:40,000

1. Ft. Carroll
22. Francis Scott Key marker
23. Ft. McHenry Channel
24. Curtis Bay
25. Curtis Creek
26. Dead Ship Anchorage
27. Three Bascule Bridges (40' vertical clearance)
28. Smith and Sons Shipyard
29. Swing bridge (railroad) usually open
30. Curtis Bay Coast Guard Station
31. Anchorage
32. Foul area
33. Furnace Creek
34. Point Pleasant Beach
35. Fixed bridge at Back Creek
36. Fence
37. Anchorage
38. Tanyard Cove—Anchorage
39. Wreck
40. Marley Creek
41. Overhead power cables—57'
42. Small island with house and dock
43. C and P Marina
46. To Inner Harbor
84. Stony Creek
100. Francis Scott Key bridge

Not for use in Navigation

Nautical Miles

Yards

west of the island. They have 35 slips with electricity up to 15 amps and a cement ramp. There is also a 40-ton railway here. Maximum draft for the railway is 4 feet. They sell gas and honor MC, Visa, Carte Blanche, and Amex. They sell bait but no fishing gear. There are some refreshments available, and both block and cube ice are sold.

The creek just above the island is still very pretty, but it begins to get quite narrow, then shallow. The best anchorages are in the lower reaches. Wherever you anchor, keep well lit at night.

Refer to Chart #12278-O—"Regional Chart: Baltimore (above Key Bridge)."

Back out in the Patapsco River. After going under the bridge and passing Curtis Bay, the river will take you in a northwesterly direction to Ft. McHenry (44). You will pass it to your left (west) heading up the northwest branch (referred to on the charts as "Northwest Harbor") (45) to the Inner Harbor (46), or you will put it to your right (north) if you wish to go to one of the marinas or anchor up the Middle Branch (47). Let's turn first to the Middle Branch (47), saving the delights of the Inner Harbor until last.

MIDDLE BRANCH OF THE PATAPSCO
Refer to Chart #12281-C—"Patapsco River-Ft. McHenry Area." PG 240

The Middle Branch of the Patapsco is largely industrialized but there are several marinas here and an anchorage, although not one of the better ones.

Passing Ft. McHenry (44) to your right (north), you will see the very wide Middle Branch (47) ahead to the west. I have seen people anchored (48) in the area just to the south of Ft. McHenry where there is 7 to 15 feet depth charted with a notation of a 6-foot shoal. I would not suggest this as an anchorage. If you will note the light lines on the chart, you will see that this is where a very large highway tunnel is buried. Curious at seeing other boats anchored there, and having heard that it is sometimes used as an anchorage, I sounded the area and found the bottom to be very uneven with depths fluctuating rapidly. The depths closer in to the shore where the chart shows 8 to 14 feet were sometimes down to around 3 feet.

There is a pipe sticking out of the water, and debris on the bottom. If you anchored here, wakes from passing commercial and pleasure traffic would be uncomfortable, and a wind from almost any direction but the north would have a considerable fetch.

PG 241

Refer to Chart #12281-D—"Patapsco River-Middle Branch."

There is a nicer place to anchor in the cove on the southern side of the river (49), just to the west of Ft. McHenry area. It isn't the prettiest spot on the Patapsco, but it is not bad considering the density of the industry here. This cove is south of Fl G "7" (50). Looking to your south into the cove, you will see old pilings and debris around the shore to your left (the east). There's grass and marsh south of those on the same eastern shore of the cove. On the southern shore, there's a pretty, grassy hill and low woods or brush, with a tall highway bridge in the distance behind. There is marsh and grass on the western shore of the cove. Tugboat and barge moorings (51) are off the eastern point of the cove, as is a lot of debris closer in to that point. Note carefully the wrecks (52) inside. The one charted on the northeastern corner of the eastern point of the cove is visible, the others are not.

With all of the above, you might wonder, "Why bother?" If you need to anchor fairly close to the Inner Harbor but don't want to go inside the Northwestern Branch, this could be your spot. I headed into the cove in a southerly direction from Fl G "7" and saw no less than 6 feet, and that only being in the area where noted on the chart. If you stay off the shores where the wrecks and debris are charted, you will find that the scenery is relatively pleasant and there is fair protection.

Continuing on into the Middle Branch, be sure to follow the well marked channel. As you pass the spoil banks of Ferry Bar (53), you will probably see people fishing from the shore. The Hanover Street Bridge (54) ahead is unique with its impressive gray stone arches. It has a vertical clearance of 38 feet and opens on demand except for rush hours.

In the cove east of the bridge, on the shore to your right (north), you will find **The Baltimore Yacht Basin Marina (55)**. They have 9 feet depth at their docks, 172 slips capable of taking boats up to 70 feet, with up to 50 amp electrical service, a 35-ton lift, with yard work available.

Dead Eyes is a popular restaurant, cocktail lounge, and outside "tiki bar" located at Baltimore Yacht Basin (55). The

Mothball fleet, Baltimore

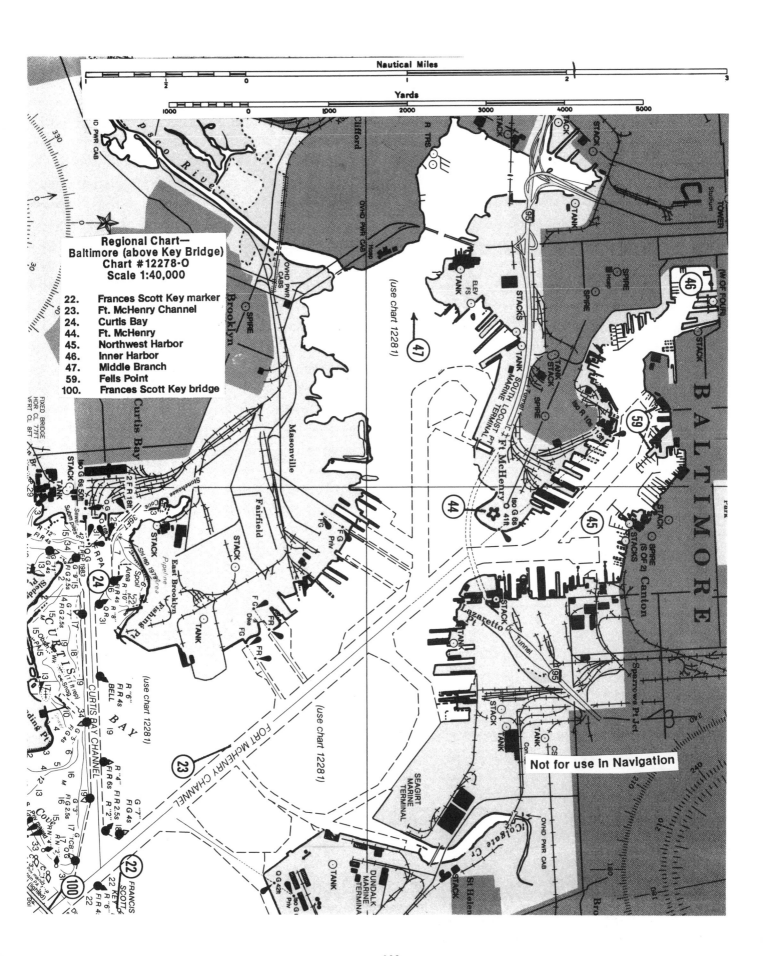

Nautical Miles

Yards

**Regional Chart—
Baltimore (above Key Bridge)
Chart #12278-O
Scale 1:40,000**

22. Frances Scott Key marker
23. Ft. McHenry Channel
24. Curtis Bay
44. Ft. McHenry
45. Northwest Harbor
46. Inner Harbor
47. Middle Branch
59. Fells Point
100. Frances Scott Key bridge

Not for use in Navigation

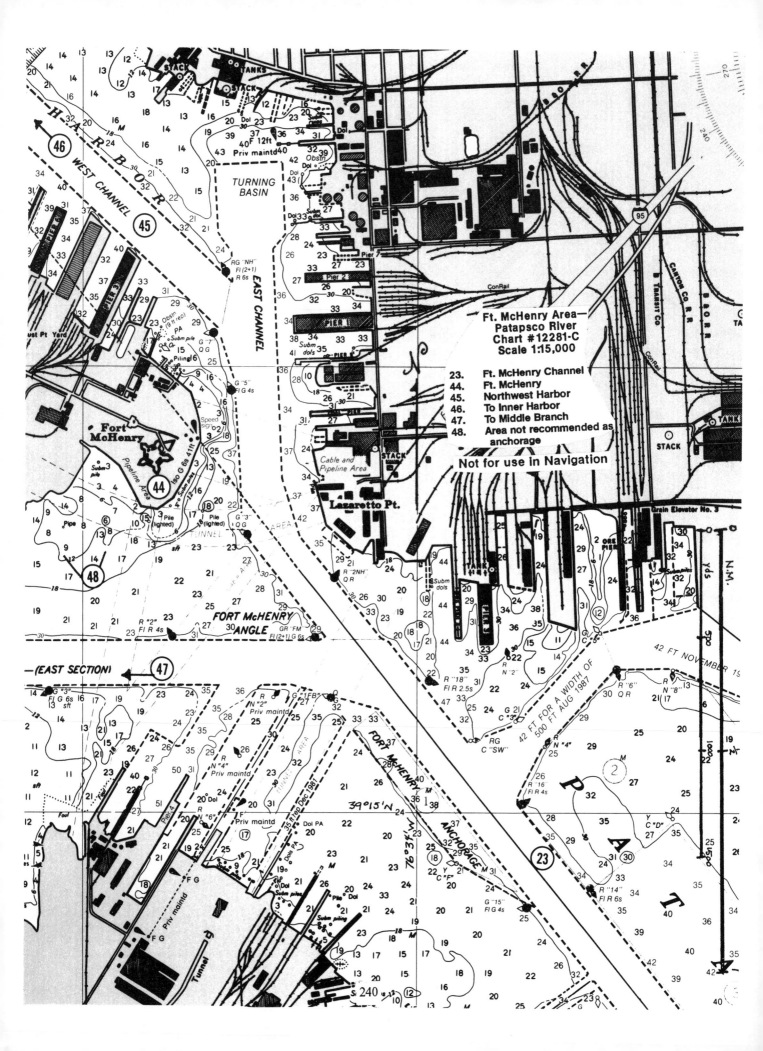

Ft. McHenry Area—
Patapsco River
Chart #12281-C
Scale 1:15,000

23. Ft. McHenry Channel
44. Ft. McHenry
45. Northwest Harbor
46. To Inner Harbor
47. To Middle Branch
48. Area not recommended as
anchorage

Not for use in Navigation

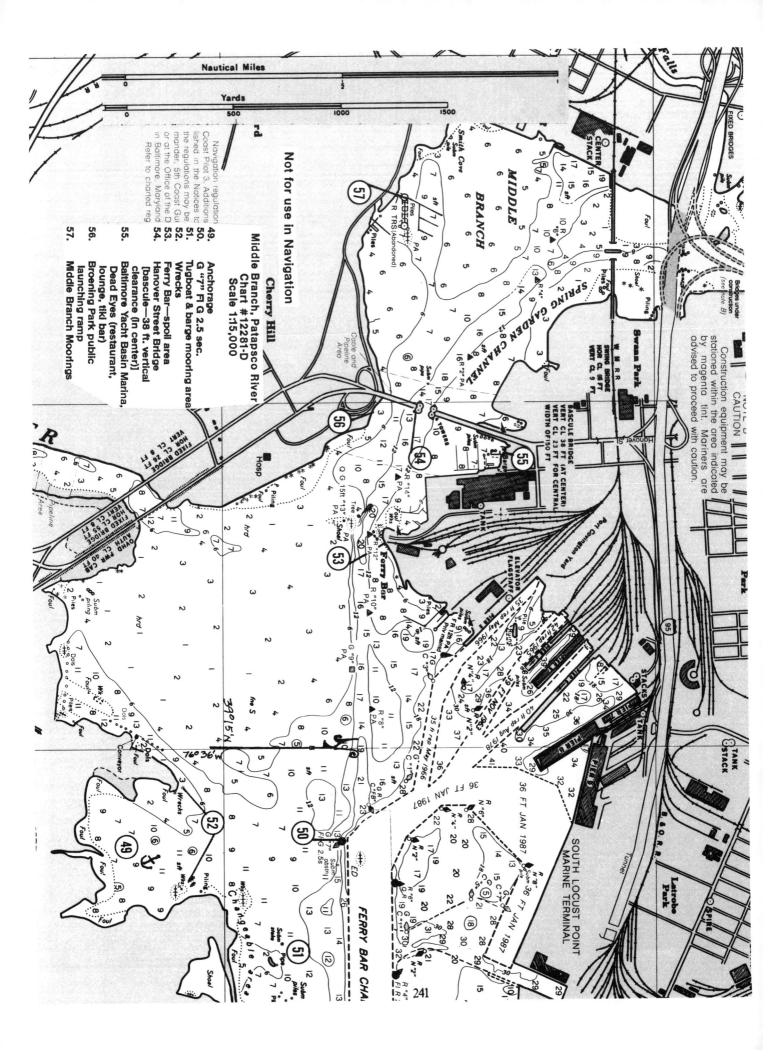

neighborhood behind and around this marina is not one where you would normally expect to find shopping or things to do, but taxi, water taxi, and sometimes help from the marina can probably get you to where you want to go. Across the river from the marina, on the same side of the bridge, is Broening Park Public Launching Ramp (56) with two concrete ramps.

Middle Branch Moorings (57) is on the west side of the Hanover Street Bridge, on the south shore of the river before it heads northerly under yet another bridge. There is not much point in proceeding beyond this marina, because of the industrial development above and the fact that much of the river above the marina is under bridges. The docks and the buildings of Middle Branch Moorings are easy to see just north of the abandoned radio towers noted on the chart. They have 365 slips, servicing boats up to 60 feet with longer space available alongside, electrical service up to 50 amps, a pumpout station, and gas and diesel. They advertise low prices and 93-octane fuel, and give a free pumpout with a fill-up. Visa, Amex, Citgo, and MC are honored here. There's a marine supply store, block and cube ice, snacks and beverages, a laundromat, and a 15-ton lift and general repairs at their yard.

The Inner Harbor is readily accessible from here by the city's Light Rail. The marina will assist you with this. If you draw more than 6 feet, you must be careful coming in, as the 7-foot charted channel between the two shoals is not marked. Marina staff told me that they advise boaters to head from the middle span of the bridge straight into their docks. They monitor Channel 16. Middle Branch Moorings is set in a surrounding park and is a nice place to stop. It is well run with a helpful staff.

NORTHWEST HARBOR
AND
BALTIMORE INNER HARBOR

After days of anchoring in perfect coves surrounded only by woods, field, and marsh, many feel the urge to pamper themselves and indulge in fine restaurants, shopping and sightseeing. When you are ready to do this, or for any other reason, experiencing the Inner City Harbor of Baltimore is, without reservation, one of the finest things you can do for yourself while cruising. It is in the city, and far removed from the sylvan scenes to which you have probably grown to love in Bay cruising, but its attractions more than make up for that. Because it is so special and unique, and because there are so many and varied attractions, we will treat it here somewhat differently than other chapters. The "Inner Harbor" is to be found at the far end of the Northwest Branch of the Patapsco River in the squared off basin. However, surrounding areas in the Northwest Branch are part of the entire experience. Therefore, these will be described here.

Editor's Note: Tom is not exaggerating. Baltimore has done more for visitors who come by boat than nearly any large city. This is a wonderful and exciting place to visit, and should be included on all Chesapeake Bay itineraries. You could spend a week there and not see everything.

Approach to Baltimore Inner Harbor

Refer to Chart #12281-C—"Ft. McHenry area, Patapsco River" PG 240   and

Chart #12281-E—"Baltimore: Inner Harbor and Northwest Harbor."

As you approach the junction where the Middle Branch (47) and the Northwestern Branch (called Northwest Harbor) (45) meet, the scene can be a bit confusing for the first time. Middle Branch will lie straight ahead to the west, wide and obvious. The route to the Inner Harbor (46) in the Northwestern Branch goes to your right (north). It is narrower, and heads into a heavily industrialized area, thus appearing like the wrong route. You will notice Ft. McHenry (44), with its flag, dark stone walls, and surrounding grassy park on the hill in the northwest corner of that junction. (More on this later). You will be putting this to your left (west) to proceed to Northwest Harbor and the Inner Harbor.

On the northeast corner is Lazaretto Point (58). This is industrialized, with tall "Lehigh Cement" silos punctuating the scenery, but there is also a pretty, white lighthouse on the corner. This is not an official installation. It was built privately, and does not have official navigational significance. But it helps to know that you are heading the right way when you see that you are passing between Ft. McHenry and the lighthouse. The shoreline here looks depressing from the viewpoint of a nature-loving cruiser, but keep the faith. It will get much better. Following the wide, deep, and well-marked northwest branch of the Patapsco, you will see the commercial shores begin to give way to renovation, with much still in progress. As you approach the Inner Harbor (46), Fells Point (59) with its marinas passes to starboard.

By this point, the busy channel becomes even busier. Maintain a careful watch all around you. As you approach the Inner Harbor, the sights are going to make it hard to concentrate on navigation, but keep close tabs on all the maritime traffic around you. You can always take a water taxi or other sightseeing boat inexpensively for later sightseeing once you get your boat settled in.

Soon after turning into northwest branch, you will bear to your left (northwest), leaving the turning basin (60) to your

Domino Sugar Plant, Baltimore

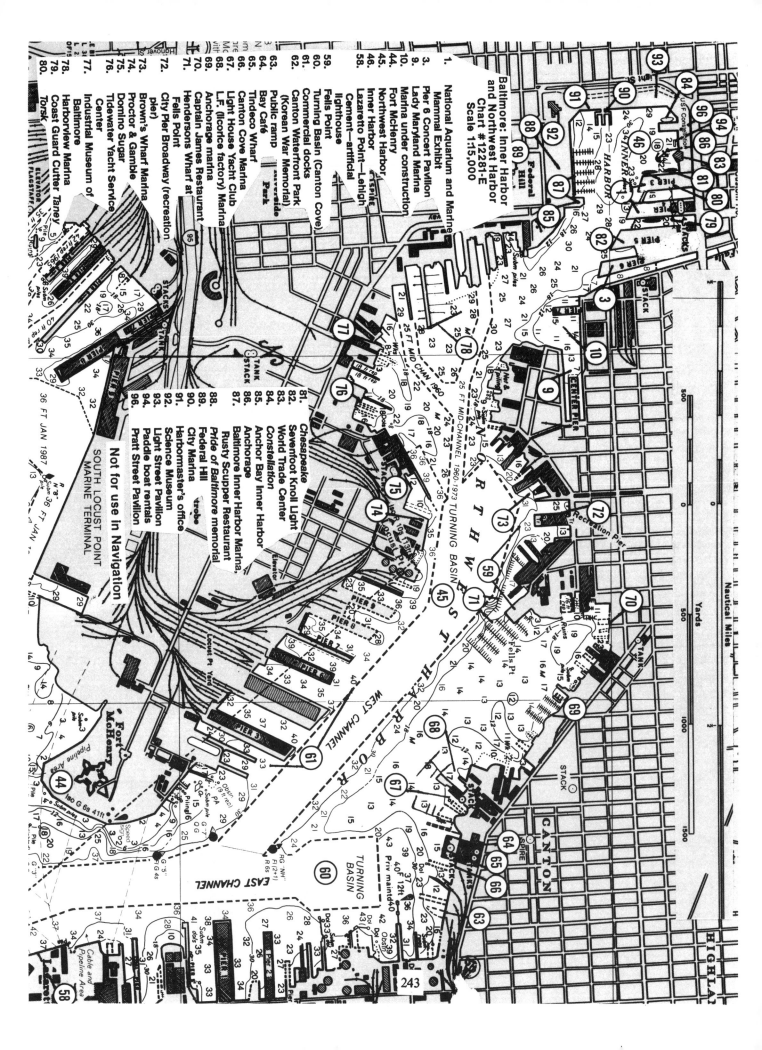

Baltimore: Inner Harbor and Northwest Harbor
Chart #12281-E
Scale 1:15,000

1. National Aquarium and Marine Mammal Exhibit
3. Pier 6 Concert Pavilion
9. Lady Maryland Marina
10. Marina under construction
44. Fort McHenry
45. Northwest Harbor
46. Inner Harbor
58. Lazaretto Point—Lehigh Cement—artificial
59. Lighthouse
60. Fells Point
61. Turning Basin (Canton Cove)
62. Commercial docks
63. Canton Waterfront Park (Korean War Memorial)
64. Public ramp
65. Canton Cove Marina
66. Bay Café
67. Tindeco Wharf
68. Light House Yacht Club
69. L.F. (licorice factory) Marina
70. Anchorage marina
71. Captain James Restaurant
72. Hendersons Wharf at Fells Point
73. City Pier Broadway (recreation pier)
74. Brown's Wharf Marina
75. Proctor & Gamble
76. Domino Sugar
76. Tidewater Yacht Service Center
77. Industrial Museum of Baltimore
78. Harborview Marina
79. Coast Guard Cutter Taney
80. Torsk

81. Chesapeake
82. Seventoot Knoll Light
83. World Trade Center
84. Constellation
85. Anchor Bay Inner Harbor
86. Baltimore Inner Harbor Marina,
87. Rusty Scupper Restaurant
88. Pride of Baltimore memorial
89. Federal Hill
90. City Marina
91. Harbormaster's office
92. Science Museum
93. Light Street Pavilion
94. Paddle boat rentals
96. Pratt Street Pavilion

Not for use in Navigation

SOUTH LOCUST POINT MARINE TERMINAL

243

right (east). There will be numerous commercial shipping docks to your left, but you will begin to see the heavy industry slowly give way to an area which, when you get to the end, will be Baltimore's incredible renaissance. Many consider this to be an ultimate statement of the good things that our civilization can do if we put our minds to it.

The City of Baltimore and various developers have great plans to further renovate the area of the river that we are now describing. Judging from Baltimore's past success in this type of venture, there will probably be substantial and impressive changes in the near future here, all for better boating pleasure. Because of this, some of the names and configuration of the marinas on the right (north) side of the river up to the Inner Harbor may be different by the time you use this book. Do not be surprised to find different alignments and names when you visit. Temporary state of flux is a price we often pay for improvement.

Contact the Baltimore Harbor Maritime Association before you visit, to get the latest on facilities in this area. This active and helpful organization will also give you good and relevant information on many other attractions in the area. They will be happy to mail you a copy of their free booklet, "Baltimore by Boat." Phone them at (410) 276-2600.

Several areas along the waterfront which had distinct boundaries at one time, are now somewhat vague by definition. These include Canton, Fells Point, Hendersons Wharf, and other areas. Opinions differ as to where one specifically left off and the other began. This should not impair your ability to find what you want or tell your transportation driver where you want to go. They all know. These boundaries were initially drawn in relation to waterfront piers and points, but now the neighborhoods extend back from the water.

The turning basin to your right (northwest) is known as Canton Cove (60). Here you will find the Bay Café (64) and a cocktail lounge at Tindeco Wharf (65). This fine restaurant specializes in seafood and steaks. It is a red and brown building with a red smokestack rising behind it. Their sign faces the water. Docks in front are available to customers. A public boat ramp is on the northeastern corner of this cove, with Canton Waterfront Park (63). Also ashore is the Korean War Memorial (62).

Four docking facilities, from the ramp (63) down to the **Anchorage Marina (69)**, are managed by one group whose phone number is (410) 522-1881. They were in a state of development as was the shore behind them. Docks around the restaurant are called the Tindeco Wharf (65). This area features condo apartments, a health club, office and retail space in the reno-

vated buildings behind the wharf. The wharf has very deep water, space for transients up to 35 feet long, electricity up to 50 amps, and it takes MC and Visa. It is close to the Bay Café, and easily accessible, as are all of these establishments, to the attractions which will be described below.

Still in Canton Cove, east of Tindeco Wharf, but before the ramp and park, is the **Canton Cove Marina (66)** with depths of from 5 to 30 feet and transient slips up to 45 feet, with electricity available up to 50 amps. MC and Visa are taken. Block and cube ice are available.

Light House Yacht Club (67) is the last marina to the west at the blue and white lighthouse smokestack. It has deep water with room for transients up to 120 feet long and electric service up to 50 amps. Block and cube ice is available and MC and Visa are accepted.

Just up from the corner of the basin, you will notice what appears to be another lighthouse behind a conspicuous quay with some docks in front. This is actually a smoke stack painted to appear as a lighthouse. There was a sign painted on the large building behind the docks which read "Baltimore Marina Center." This was managed by the same group who managed the above three marina facilities. This marina is **L F Marina (68)** (known as the Licorice Factory to local people). Water depths are 20 feet. Transients up to 120 feet can be accomodated with up to 50 amps of electricity available, Visa and MC are accepted. They have block and cube ice, and gas and diesel fuel.

Farther northwest, you'll find **Anchorage Marina (69)**. It is not managed with the above four. It is a condo-type marina with all floating piers. It has a 1400-foot breakwater to protect boats from wakes in the channel, and the outer dock on the breakwater has a small office in the middle with blue canvas and an American flag above. Depths are 6 to 18 feet and there are over 100 transient spaces capable of taking boats up to 120 feet. Electric service up to 50 amps is available. There is a laundry facility and a take-out deli on the premises, block and cube ice are sold, and both Visa and MC are taken. Another office building is ashore with an active staff and services.

Next upriver northwest is Captain James Restaurant (70) which is a building ashore, modified to look like a ship. There are some docks in front of this for customers, and a gas pump. You will see this up in the basin behind (to the northeast of) Fells Point (59). Coming off Fells Point (59), in a southeasterly direction, are many new and vacant piers, some of which had been damaged and were not yet repaired. They are a part of what is referred to as the "Henderson's Wharf"

Baltimore skyline, Inner Harbor

244

Baltimore Inner Harbor

(71) area and the docks are part of **Fells Point Marina** which is now serving customers with 80 slips open and electricity up to at least 30 amps.

Fells Point was formerly a very famous landing area for the Clipper Ships and other sailing ships that plied the oceans of the world from this seaport. Now it has been renovated and contains a fascinating assortment of shops, restaurants, and sights. The term "Fells Point" today is generally considered to encompass much of the area ashore behind the actual point (59). Next upstream (northwest), you will see a large building with words "City Pier Broadway" (72) conspicuously thereon. This is also locally known as the "recreation pier." An area of free temporary docking (sometimes) is just to its east. This building was being used to film a movie last year.

A water taxi landing is in the cove to the west of the point, at an area called "Brown's Wharf," (73) where you can also find docking. This is a good place to disembark from the taxi and walk around to enjoy the Fells Point area. Shoreside attractions are described farther on in this chapter under "Neighborhoods."

As you have been passing up the river, we have been talking about the sights on the northern shore because this is where you can find some dockage and attractions. The southern shore, to your left, presents a fascinating view of a big city seaport in everyday action, with its loading docks and commercial ships of the world. Of special note is the huge "Proctor and Gamble" sign (74) on Locust Point, designating the manufacturing complex and docks of that company, and then the famous "Domino Sugar" sign (75) over the plant and docks of that company. If there is a large ship offloading as you go by, the sandy-looking material being conveyed ashore will be raw sugar and the molasses-like smell coming from the holds of the ship will be a rare treat.

In the corner west of the Domino sign is **Tidewater Yacht Service Center (76)**, identified by its sign. This is a major and very complete full service repair yard. Its maximum working depth is 20 feet. There are 28 slips and it can handle boats up to 160 feet and has electricity on its docks up to 30 amps. It will take transients if the dock space is not full of boats awaiting work. There's a 60-ton lift, complete engine and hull repair including electronics and sail repair, and a very full parts department. They are dealers for Yanmar, Northern

Lights generators, MerCruiser, gel batteries, and others. They have bathrooms and showers, cube ice, and accept Discover, Visa, and MC. Just upriver of Tidewater, on the same (southern) side, is the Industrial Museum of Baltimore (77), described below under "The Shore at Baltimore Inner Harbor."

Next, still on your left (the south side), is a huge marine resort and business and living complex called Harborview (78). They have 300 slips accomodating yachts up to 250 feet long, with electric service up to 100 amps. Both cable and phone is available at these docks. Gas and diesel are sold, and there is a pumpout facility. The marina includes a floating swimming pool, with bar, an excellent restaurant with catering, a club with privileges for slip holders, state-of-the-art docking for boats of all sizes, and many other amenities. Most major credit cards are honored. There is a very nice service area for yachtsmen, including laundry and multiple bathrooms and showers. This first class marina is the focal point of a huge waterfront development which is designed to create a resort city within the city. There will be condominiums which will complement the area rather than intrude, restaurants, shopping, and complete facilities for boating or those wishing to live on the water. There is a light grocery store, a deli, a marine store, concierge service, and a liquor store. The staff is excellent and thoroughly understand how to make your stay a great experience.

Harborview is so named because it offers a great view into the famous Inner Harbor. It is here that we have been heading. This is an exceptional place, a superb experience, but it is subject to continual change. Therefore as soon as you land (if not before), contact the local information people. The "Baltimore by Boat" booklet mentioned above should be obtained before you leave for a cruise to Baltimore. There are information booths at the foot of the city docks in the inner basin. Take some time to visit these to get the latest, and to maximize your pleasure in whatever time you have available. There is also a ticket office in this same location for most of the attractions that you might wish to visit.

THE INNER HARBOR
AND ITS SURROUNDING ATTRACTIONS
Refer to Chart #12281-E—"Baltimore Inner Harbor and Northwest Harbor." PG 243

I enjoy anchoring in deserted coves of Chesapeake Bay and the Exumas, Bahamas. Therefore the very thought of "inner harbor in a city" would repel me, had I not seen for myself. Like a rose in a thicket, the Inner Harbor is nestled deep within the industrialized waterfront area of the Patapsco River. Once you enter the harbor area, you forget about the factories and commercial docks. Like petals folding away from the center of the rose, this harbor is surrounded with layer upon layer of the finest attractions imaginable.

As you come in, the sights burst upon you. To your starboard, the US Coast Guard Cutter *Taney* **(79)** is berthed alongside one of the piers. She was one of the ships to survive Pearl Harbor and now can be inspected by you from stem to stern. Nearby west lies the submarine USS *Torsk* **(80)**, known as "the galloping ghost of the Japanese Coast." She sank the last two Japanese warships in World War II. A shark's red mouth full of teeth is painted on her bows. A tour gives a rare glimpse into the world of the World War II submariner. This ship is little changed from her days of active duty, and you can almost hear the cries of "dive, dive" or "fire one" as you squeeze between the machinery and living spaces.

North of *Torsk* sits the lightship *Chesapeake* **(81)**, little changed from her days of duty in the Atlantic off the mouth of the Bay. She was built in 1930 and would remain out in terrible storms to guide ships in. She is decommisioned but still operational and a fascinating ship to visit.

The National Aquarium **(1)** rises over the harbor with a living rain forest on top, the plants barely visible in the mist beneath the glass roof and wall. Under that is one of the most fascinating aquariums you will ever see, and a Marine Mammal Pavilion.

You start with surprise as you see the old Sevenfoot Knoll Light **(82)** standing proudly ashore east of the ships and Aquarium on the end of Pier 5. This is the oldest surviving screwpile lighthouse, and the only one employing caisson construction. It was moved ashore in 1988 and placed on the National Register of Historic Places in 1989. A "screw pile" lighthouse was built by literally screwing the main piles into the bottom of the Bay. Today the knoll, which you passed coming into the Patapsco River, is marked by the "newfangled" type of steel girder construction.

Towering on the north shore is the Baltimore World Trade Center **(83)** with other skycrapers behind and to either side. In the northwest corner of the Inner Harbor is the USF *Constellation* **(84)**, the first ship commissioned in the United States Navy. The *Constellation* was launched in 1797 and was active for almost 150 years. Today you can wander about her four decks and see her much as she was in action, talking to guides as you need them. This ship, like the others on display, is still floating. From her silent damp wooden bilges to her towering spars, she breathes history as you walk about.

On the shore around the *Constellation* are two huge pavilions, each full of shops and restaurants of all kinds. Stretching inland five blocks, the sky walk, an elevated sidewalk over the streets, takes you conveniently into hotels and more shops, restaurants, museums and events.

Within the innermost basin are an anchorage **(86)** on the north shore, and two marinas. In busy seasons, reservations are always important for any private marina in the area.

The marina to your left (south) coming into the basin is the **Baltimore Inner Harbor Marina (87)**. You can identify it by its extensive docks and a large two-story building housing the Rusty Scupper Restaurant **(87)** upstairs and the dockmaster's office and a marine supply store downstairs. They will greet you by hailer to arrange for your dockage as you approach. There are 160 slips up to 50 feet, but there is alongside space for boats up to 200 feet. Electricity up to 100 amps is found at the docks as are phone and cable connections. They sell diesel and gas and take Crown, Visa, MC, and Discover for fuel, but require cash or check for dockage. Cube ice is available. There is a pumpout station. The docks are all floating with security fences and gates. The Rusty Scupper Restaurant is a very popular, full menu restaurant overlooking the harbor.

On the downstairs floor under the Rusty Scupper is a very well-stocked marine discount store named Anchor Bay Inner Harbor **(85)**. If this sounds familiar, it is because it is run by members of the same family which runs the Anchor Bay in

Portion of Baltimore Inner Harbor Marina

National Aquarium and USS *Torsk*

the Middle River and the Anchor Bay on Bear Creek. This store specializes in marine hardware, from the common every day items to those hard to get. The owners have a good knowledge of what to buy for what problems, how they work, and will generally have it in stock or can get it fast.

From the south shore facilities, it's a short walk (around two blocks to the pavilions) around the quay to the Inner Harbor main attractions, all of which are clearly in view from these docks.

Before the grassy hill on the south side of the harbor and to the southwest of the Inner Harbor Marina, you will see a ship's tall mast planted in the soil of Rash Field. This is a memorial to the *Pride of Baltimore* (88), an authentically rebuilt Baltimore Clipper which was sponsored by the city and other patrons. She was lost in a storm at sea a few years ago.

South of this, you will notice Federal Hill (89), a tall grassy hill used as a lookout post in the very earliest days of civilization here, because it so well commands views of the river coming in. This will be described further in this chapter under "South Baltimore."

If you wish to go to the **City Marina (90)**, which is closer to the action, call them on VHF Channel 68 for instructions. You will see their finger piers perpendicular to the quay and harbormaster's office (91) ahead of you to the west as you enter the basin. They are between the Science Museum (92) and the Light Street Pavilion (93). But they also have dockage along the quays around the harbor, where you are actually berthed among the attractions. Therefore, yachts of most sizes can be accomodated, including the 200-foot range. Electricity up to 50 amps is available.

This city-run facility operates on a first-come, first-served basis. One of the attractions of tying up here is that you are literally right in the middle of everything that is going on.

There is an excitement that is difficult to describe, with yachts of all sizes and types coming and going, cruise ships with their reveling crowds, constant shows occurring at the amphitheater nearby, and character vessels from all over the Bay. The world is stopping in, often at the next slip, tourists staring in amazement at the sights and show of which you are now a part. The endless shopping and eating, and educational, and cultural experiences are just a short walk over from your decks.

In certain areas around the quay, the city will also let you anchor out and tie your stern to one of the rings in the quay. This is somewhat "med moor" fashion, but you will want your stern well off the quay to avoid damage, and might still have to dinghy in. There is a fee for this. Check with the city dockmaster's office (91) for locations and fee.

The staff of the city marina will assist in any way possible with your dockage at the city facility, and to make your visit successful. They will also help you with information regarding other marinas. Often the city marina is full, and often boaters prefer the quieter but easily accessible docks of other nearby marinas described above. Their patience, professionalism, and courtesy on even the busiest weekends has become known throughout the Bay. The city marina can be reached at (410) 396-3174.

The Inner Harbor anchorage (86) is just under the World Trade Center. It is unique and fun to anchor for a short time in the shadow of skyscrapers and in the center of so much activity, but this buoy-marked anchorage is very small, deep (around 20 feet), usually over-crowded, and has very poor holding in loose slimy black mud. Unfortunately, many try to anchor here without putting out adequate five-to-one scope and without setting their anchors. Thus there is often a general drifting about. Also, the paddle boat rentals (94) on the

247

north shore of the anchorage often spew forth hordes of eager paddle boaters with limited navigational ability and a propensity for bumping anchored yachts! With so much to do ashore, it is better anyway to tie up and not waste time with the dinghy.

The Shore at Baltimore's Inner Harbor
Refer to — "Sketch Chart: Baltimore's Inner Harbor."

Once you step ashore in the Inner Harbor, there is a well-run information center (95) with all the facts you will need to consume a year's stay with hardly a day's repetition. It would be impossible to mention everything to do or all the places to go in this one long chapter. Omissions should not be construed negatively. Start with the information booths (95) on the quay on the west side of the harbor, between the harbormaster's office and pavilions, so that you won't miss any opportunity. After talking with the guides and picking up the brochures, make your plans 27 stories above the street at the top of the World Trade Center (83) where there is a fantastic view of the harbor below, all of the attractions around the harbor, the river coming in, and much of Baltimore. *Editor's Note: Bring your camera!* Also on this floor, a museum shows displays of earlier Baltimore and some industry of the area, and you can look below to see the incredible changes that exist today.

Next, you may wish to visit the Light Street Pavilion (93) on the west side of the Inner Harbor and stop at the fudge shop where they make it as you watch, putting on quite a show, sometimes singing and dancing. Then there are ice cream shops, coffee shops, cheese shops, retail seafood shops, nut shops, pizza houses, raw bars, the famous Phillips Seafood Restaurant, a delicatessen, candy shops and more. At last count, there are 40 food speciality stops, and 13 restaurants in the two pavilions along the quay.

The Pratt Street Pavilion (96), located on the northern side of the harbor, also has restaurants, but it is more oriented to shopping. There are also restaurant and fast food centers and shops and fine stores in the hotels and in the four-story Gallery (97) shopping centers across Pratt Street. You can reach the Gallery via a separate skywalk exiting the second floor of the Pratt Street Pavilion. The restaurant shops are all busy, have strong competition, and are therefore usually very good.

In the shops within just these three malls, you can buy exquisite clothes and jewelry, toys, knives, kites, books, gadgets, socks, perfumes, leather, cameras, maps, software, hats, shoes, and on and on. Just remember that it doesn't stop here. If you want more, take the sky walk farther inland and the experience continues to go on forever. Among the major destinations of this skywalk (98) are the Baltimore Convention Center, the Charles Center, the Baltimore Arena, Old St. Paul's Church, and a Metro entrance. The Baltimore Orioles Stadium at Camden Yards is close to a sky walk exit. The stadium was built with its patrons in mind. It is said that 5,000 seats were given up in order to allow 2 inches wider seats and 4 inches more leg room.

For information about the dining and shopping in the two pavilions and the Gallery, call (410) 332-4191. For general information about shops and services and attractions, call the Office of Promotion and Tourism at (410) 752-8632.

As noted above, at the waterside, The USF *Constellation*, the *Torsk*, and the Lightship *Chesapeake* and the cutter *Taney* are open to visitors, and have been maintained as authentically as possible. Often other ships are tied up alongside for touring. These include Coast Guard cutters, tall ships, and Chesapeake Bay skipjacks.

One example of special Bay boats that you may visit and sail is the skipjack *Minnie V.* (99), in the northwest corner of the Inner Harbor. She's an authentically built oyster dredging boat that will take you on educational cruises for a few hours.

Also there is the *Half Shell* (99), an authentic "buyboat." Buyboats are large deadrise vessels used to buy the oysters from the tongers and dredgers out on the Bay. *Half Shell* has now been modified to take out passengers for a tour.

Also, the *Lady Maryland* (100) is an authentic replica of an 1880's Pungy Schooner, used as a sailing school. These are normally docked in the inner harbor around the quay.

An amphitheater (2) lies under the majestic bow of the *Constellation*, in the corner between the north and west sides of the harbor. Here there is frequent entertainment. Just walk on over and enjoy. If you are docked at the quay next to the *Constellation*, you are almost in the midst of these events. During the spring, summer, and fall, there are many festivals both here and in nearby areas. Usually these celebrate vari-

Crowded quay, Baltimore Inner Harbor

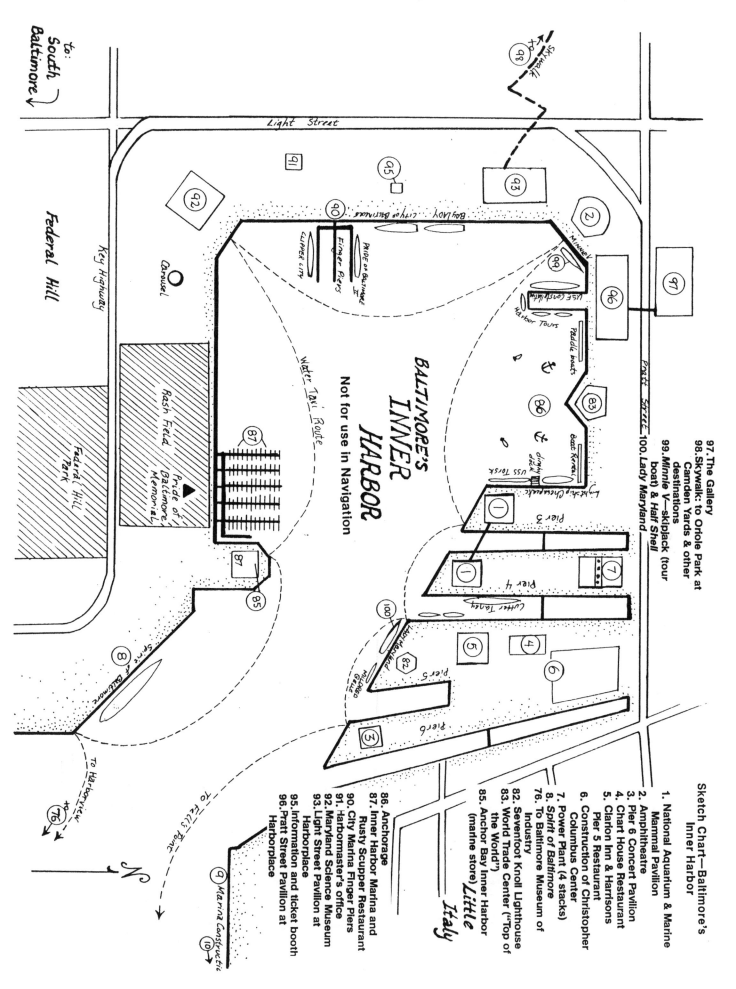

BALTIMORE'S INNER HARBOR

Not for use in Navigation

Sketch Chart—Baltimore's
Inner Harbor

1. National Aquarium & Marine
   Mammal Pavilion
2. Amphitheatre
3. Pier 6 Concert Pavilion
4. Chart House Restaurant
5. Clarion Inn & Harrisons
   Pier 5 Restaurant
6. Construction of Christopher
   Columbus Center
7. Power Plant (4 stacks)
8. Spirit of Baltimore
76. To Baltimore Museum of
    Industry
82. Sevenfoot Knoll Lighthouse
83. World Trade Center ("Top of
    the World")
85. Anchor Bay Inner Harbor
    (marine store) Little
    Italy
86. Anchorage
87. Inner Harbor Marina and
    Rusty Scupper Restaurant
90. City Marina Finger Piers
91. Harbormaster's office
92. Maryland Science Museum
93. Light Street Pavilion at
    Harborplace
95. Information and ticket booth
96. Pratt Street Pavilion at
    Harborplace
97. The Gallery
98. Skywalk: to Oriole Park at
    Camden Yards & other
    destinations
99. *Minnie V*—skipjack (tour
    boat) & *Half Shell*
100. *Lady Maryland*

to: South Baltimore

Light Street

Federal Hill

Key Highway

Federal Hill Park

Rash Field

Pride of Baltimore Memorial

Water Taxi Route

Carousel

Finger Piers

Pride of Baltimore II

Clipper City

City Barricades

Bay Buoy

Pratt Street

Minnie V

USF Constellation

Harbor Tours

Paddle boats

Boat Rental

dinghy dock

USS Torsk

Lightship Chesapeake

Luther Tansey

Pier 3

Pier 4

Pier 5

Pier 6

Lady Maryland

Mildred

Spring of Baltimore

To Harborview

To Fell's Point

Marina Construction

N

249

ous ethnic heritages and they always offer great entertainment, fun, and food.

You can explore beneath the sea in the National Aquarium (1) which is on the northern side, to the east of the Trade Center. Here escalators and moving ramps help to glide you through five levels of exhibits. These include a huge tank several stories high with live creatures including rays, sharks, and tropical fish all swimming in a realistically arranged natural habitat. You descend a ramp in the core of this tank, watching the creatures behind the continuous glass walls as they swim around you. This is one of the most fantastic real-life underwater displays I have ever seen. Topping the Aquarium, five levels over the streets, is a living rain forest so authentic that you quickly forget that you are not in the tropics. This forest shimmers over the boats at anchor in the night, visible through the glass walls surrounding it. The Marine Mammal Pavilion (1) is a separate building that includes a huge mammal tank where there are shows.

East of the Aquarium also on the north shore is a white-domed concert hall called the Pier 6 Concert Pavilion (3). It looks like a strange tent on the end of Pier 6. Here also is The Chart House (4), a nice restaurant, and a great place to take your family. Its menu ranges from light food on up to full meals. It is bright and cheerful and has an outdoor patio. There is also the very nice Harrison's Pier 5 restaurant and a hotel, the Clarion Inn (5).

Under construction on the north shore is a huge center for the study and appreciation of our last earthly frontier, the Ocean. It is to be named the Christopher Columbus Center (6) and will not only contain centers of important research and development projects relating to the sea, but also public viewing and access areas to the work in progress. This world-important facility will be located on Piers 5 and 6. You will also notice a huge building with many smokestacks (7) on Pier 4. This is an old power plant, and is still known by that name. There are plans to redevelop the power plant into a world class sports center with a museum, an entertainment center, and virtual reality display exhibits to simulate different sports.

Also being built is a large new marina facility (9) in the eastern part of this inner area, and adjacent to it and just east of it is the **Lady Maryland Foundation (10)**. (**Refer to Chart**

USF *Constellation*, Baltimore Inner Harbor

Trolley Tour Bus, Baltimore

#12281-E showing exact locations.) This foundation involves local youth in the trade and art of shipbuilding and repair, and Bay culture. One of the themes is the concern for and teaching of black maritime history. You will see worn and battered traditional vessels along some of the docks and ashore. These are being lovingly repaired and renewed by the well-directed skill and efforts of area youth. And in addition to all this, the experience includes practical lessons in commercial enterprise involving the running of a marina. There are very nice docks here, completely protected up in the cove, with brand new top line power pedestals with up to 50 amps electricity, and they take transients. Because this area is a little removed from the innermost hub (there are talks of a waterfront walk extending out this far), the rates are a little less, and your fees contribute to the costs of running this unique and remarkable operation.

At the southwest end of the Inner Harbor is the Maryland Science Center **(92)**. This has many permanent displays and special shows. It includes a planetarium and an IMAX theater with a five-story screen and 38 speakers. In the IMAX are regular shows, some involving fascinating science and nature spectaculars, others involving less esoteric themes. During one of our visits, you could pay the money and see the Rolling Stones in concert in five-story size and 38 speaker sound. This was during evening hours after the regular programming.

In the Baltimore Museum of Industry **(76)** on the southern shore of the branch back toward the Domino sign, you can board the *S.S. Baltimore*, one of the few steam tugs still afloat. The museum also features an early belt-driven machine shop, a transportation exhibit, an industrial power exhibit, and many other displays of early industry.

There are also several large multi-decked cruise and dinner ships that dock at various places around the harbor. These offer weather-protected cruises of several hours duration, some with dining. The *Spirit of Baltimore* **(8)**, docked just to the southeast of the Inner Harbor Marina, is, at this time, the largest, and offers an excellent Broadway-type floor show with singing and dancing after dinner. The stars of the show are your waiters and waitresses, the meals are prepared aboard, and a great time is had by all.

Transportation for Sightseeing

A great feature of this port is that there is much beyond the harbor and the skywalks that can be reached with easy and affordable transportation. This transportation includes trolleys [call (410) 752-2015] with 18 boarding locations, and horse-drawn carriages for the areas close in to the harbor. An excellent way to get an overview of the attractions available is to buy a ticket on the trolley. These run regularly all day, stopping at 18 locations, and you can get on and off as you wish. They pick up every 30 minutes. They each have knowledgeable drivers who keep up a running commentary as you roll along, giving points of interest ranging from the historical, to entertainment, to shopping, and dining. Tickets are $9 per adult per day. They board at various places around the Inner Harbor, including the Inner Harbor west shore behind the city marina dockmaster's office.

For moving around the harbor and outlying areas of the northwest branch, water taxis serve many waterfront areas of major entertainment and attractions. Water taxis cost a little over $3 for a day's ticket. There are also various tour boats, of all sizes, around the harbor.

Baltimore, like any other large city today, has areas which should normally not be walked. These are generally off the "beaten path" and should be obvious. Check when you visit to get the latest information. Touring by trolley or carriage solves this problem.

Historical Perspective

Baltimore was created in 1729 by act of Maryland Governor Benedict Leonard Calvert. This was at the behest of Charles Calvert, who was the 5th Lord Baltimore, and for whom a street and various institutions are named. When Baltimore was founded, it very quickly took over as the major area seaport, having a much deeper and broader harbor than the shipping center of Annapolis to its south. It thrived almost continuously from that point on, being a center for shipping, seafood, industry, shipbuilding, commerce, and culture. As such, it has long dominated the Bay as the Queen City in the minds of many of the Bay's citizens. Even today, talking with the older watermen up and down the Bay, a trip to Baltimore is often considered to be the ultimate adventure.

Others know it as "The Charm City" because of that apt description bestowed upon it by Henry L. Mencken, a native son. When I, long ago, met my first real "Baltimorean," I was amused by his pronunciation of his city, but I soon learned that anyone who is a real native quite properly pronounces it something like "Bawlmr."

As have all major cities, Baltimore has had its good and bad times. These included major fires, plagues, and riots. And of course, as has happened to most seaports of the world, the waterfront within the city became a seriously blighted area. The city of Baltimore began working in the 1950s to rebuild the inner harbor area and make it a world showplace, accessible to all. Unlike so many others, they have succeeded in a way which you must see to believe. Today, cities from around the world send their representatives to Baltimore to see how they did it. But Baltimore did not stop with their astounding success. The renaissance continues. Even as you read this, breath-taking projects are underway, within walking distance from the Inner Harbor, which will make your stay even more incredible and worth repeating year after year. *Editor's note: Baltimore is also one of our country's busiest seaports. You know this from having read Tom's description of the Patapsco River earlier in this chapter. But you'll flip over the huge big ships and their shore facilities as you make your way up the river to the fabulous Inner Harbor. Baltimore is a thriving seaport.*

Seeing the Rest of Baltimore Ashore
Refer to —"Map: Baltimore Inshore"

While we can hardly describe all the attractions of this large city, and while some of them obviously require land transportation and are too far from the water to show on our maps, we will mention a few to give you more idea of the flavor of this special city.

The Baltimore Zoo (too far away for the map) is the third oldest zoo in the nation and covers more than 150 acres. There are over 1,200 creatures there, including the Siberian Tiger, elephants, hippos, camels, rhinos, and giraffes.

Museums within easy distance inshore (some of which are too far away for the map) include the Baltimore Museum of Art with exhibits including painting and sculpture by Matisse, Picasso, Renoir, Cezanne, van Gogh, and Gauguin. If you take the skywalk and get off at St. Paul's Cathedral, you can walk three blocks north and a block west to the renowned Walter's Art Gallery (9). Its collections feature ancient art, medieval art, renaissance and post-renaissance sculpture, old master paintings, 19th century paintings and sculpture, Asian art, manuscripts, and an exhibit of arms and armor.

The Edgar Allan Poe House and Museum (10), too far to walk (north and way west), offers period furniture, exhibits, and special performances. This is where Poe began his writing career. Poe was buried at the Westminster Church (11) at Fayette & Greene Streets. The grave is marked by a large white monument in the yard. Poe's birthday is January 19. Each year for many years, someone has left a partially consumed bottle of Cognac and several roses at his graveside.

Fort McHenry (shown (44) on Chart #12281-C—"Ft. McHenry Area Patapsco River" and on Chart #12278-O— "Regional Chart—Baltimore Above Key Bridge") was mentioned as a navigational reference as we were coming into the northwestern branch of the Patapsco. In the fort, you will find a restored powder magazine, guard rooms, officers' quarters and barracks, and other exhibits. Both water taxi and trolley will take you to the fort from the Inner Harbor.

At the "Flag House and 1812 Museum" (12), one block north and several blocks east of the Inner Harbor, you can visit the original home of Mary Pickersgill who made the flag of which Francis Scott Key wrote as it flew over this fort. The trolley can take you here.

Another interesting museum is "The Shot Tower" (13), northeast of the Inner Harbor, too far to walk. This National Historic Landmark is a 215-foot structure with the appearance of a huge smokestack. Its walls, built of over one million bricks, are 6 feet thick at the bottom and taper to 20 inches at the top. When built in 1828, the tower produced shot by pouring molten lead through perforated pans from the top. The fall of the droplets down the shaft rounded and cooled the shot.

One of the many famous natives of Baltimore, and one of the great jurists of our country, Thurgood Marshall is honored by a bronze statue (14) standing at the northeast corner of Pratt Street and Hopkins Place, a short walk from the skywalk stop on Pratt Street.

To the north of Baltimore (off our map) is the "Cloisters Children's Museum" with very special "hands on" educational displays intended for children from 2 to 12 and their families.

"The Great Blacks in Wax" museum (off our map) is the first wax museum of African-American history in the nation. It contains many life-like, life-size wax figures of important historical and contemporary personalities of African ancestry.

There are numerous historical mansions that can now be visited as museums. These include the 48-room "Evergreen," built in the 1850s, and "Mount Clare" of Georgian architecture and completed in 1760. If you are interested in historical sights and walking, there is an excellent book by Donald T. Fritz entitled "A Walking Tour of Historic and Renaissance Baltimore." It takes you on a walk of about 3 miles, with the Inner Harbor as one place to begin. It not only gives names and locations of places, but interesting narratives of each location.

The Babe Ruth Birthplace and Baseball Center (15) is west of the Inner Harbor. It's obviously a great treat for any baseball fan. It was opened in 1974 as a National Historic Landmark and Shrine. It is the second largest baseball museum in America.

Only ten blocks from the harbor, the B&O Railroad Museum (16) contains, within its 37 acres, five historic buildings and over 120 pieces of full size equipment. This includes an original Roundhouse, historic steam and diesel locomotives, and rare 19th century passenger and freight equipment. If you ever liked trains, come here. It is the greatest chance that you will ever have to see the old locomotives and cars as they were, and never will be again except in this living museum.

Baltimore is also the home of the Calvert School, located in Roland Park. Many families cruising with children use this excellent and well-known correspondence school. If your child is enrolled in Calvert, it can be a very meaningful experience to visit while in the area. If you are in the planning stages of a cruise and home education, a visit would be very helpful. It is necessary to call for an appointment.

Editor's note: There are a dozen correspondence schools that I know of for grade and high school children. Calvert School is one of the most popular. I have met children taking their courses, as I've cruised in many parts of the world. All these kids are learning what they have to know, and most of them are eager and precocious. It's always a pleasure for me to talk to these children—including Tom's delightful daughters!

Neighborhoods and Markets
Refer to Map: —"Baltimore Inshore."

Baltimore has several unique areas which involve a mix of special themes with related attractions and residences. We can only mention a few of the many worthwhile attractions.

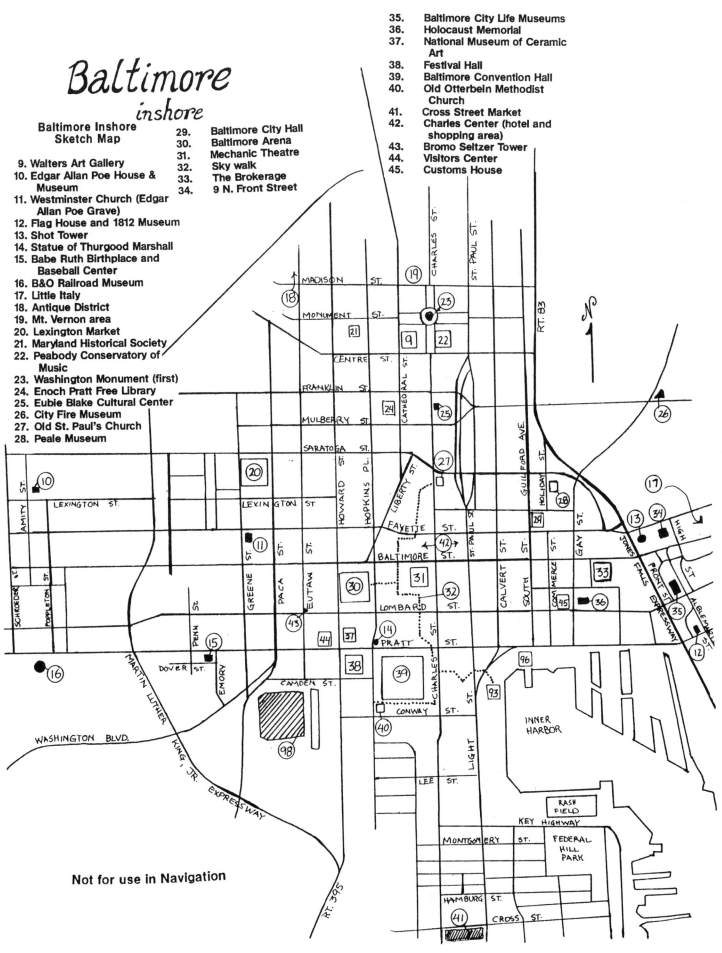

Baltimore
inshore

**Baltimore Inshore
Sketch Map**

9. Walters Art Gallery
10. Edgar Allan Poe House & Museum
11. Westminster Church (Edgar Allan Poe Grave)
12. Flag House and 1812 Museum
13. Shot Tower
14. Statue of Thurgood Marshall
15. Babe Ruth Birthplace and Baseball Center
16. B&O Railroad Museum
17. Little Italy
18. Antique District
19. Mt. Vernon area
20. Lexington Market
21. Maryland Historical Society
22. Peabody Conservatory of Music
23. Washington Monument (first)
24. Enoch Pratt Free Library
25. Eubie Blake Cultural Center
26. City Fire Museum
27. Old St. Paul's Church
28. Peale Museum

29. Baltimore City Hall
30. Baltimore Arena
31. Mechanic Theatre
32. Sky walk
33. The Brokerage
34. 9 N. Front Street

35. Baltimore City Life Museums
36. Holocaust Memorial
37. National Museum of Ceramic Art
38. Festival Hall
39. Baltimore Convention Hall
40. Old Otterbein Methodist Church
41. Cross Street Market
42. Charles Center (hotel and shopping area)
43. Bromo Seltzer Tower
44. Visitors Center
45. Customs House

Not for use in Navigation

253

The information center at the Inner Harbor can provide pamphlets with complete helpful information.

Little Italy **(17)** has over 30 Italian restaurants and many very special homes of its residents who keep the area in a manner reminiscent of the old country. This is just to the east of the Inner Harbor attractions, past the Concert Hall, and lighthouse, a few blocks back from the water. It's also shown on our **"Sketch Chart—Baltimore's Inner Harbor."**

The Historic Antique District **(18)** is too far north and west to walk. It has over 35 antique shops and galleries, an auction house, restaurants, and related businesses. It has been an antique center for over 100 years.

The Mt. Vernon area **(19)**, said to be Baltimore's most historic and elegant neighborhood, contains buildings, museums, and parks open to the public. Many like to stroll through the area and enjoy the ambiance.

Fells Point

Refer to Walking Map—"Baltimore's Fells Point."

Fells Point, mentioned earlier, and readily accessible by water taxi from the Inner Harbor, formerly had 16 shipyards on its shores. For years it was a bustling shipping and ship repair area with seaman's lodgings, pubs, and markets.

Fells Point was named after William Fell who arrived in 1776. He was a shipbuilder from England and was looking for timber. He remained and began building ships here and established quite a reputation in the shipping trade.

Here is where the famous Baltimore Clippers were built. They were notorious for their speed and agility and were quite successful as privateers and war vessels in fighting the British. The *USF Constellation* was also built here, in what was then known as Harris Creek, east of where the Anchorage Marina now lies. Now the area is renovated and contains many historical displays, excellent restaurants, pubs, shops, and other attractions.

One of our favorites is the China Sea Marine Trading Company **(46)**. This is located at a water taxi landing at Fells Point and contains for sale fascinating curiosities of the sea, including diving gear, bridge to engine room telegraphs, cannons, skulls, sailors suits from various navies, pea coats, and just about anything else that the enterprising owners can salvage from around the waterfront.

Francies Restaurant **(47)** is right where the taxi lands at Brown's Wharf. It is a neat little place with a good selection,

Baltimore's Fell's Point

N¹

Not for use in Navigation

Baltimore's Fells Point

17.	Little Italy		Angeline's Art Gallery
46.	China Sea Marine Trading Company	48.	The Deli on Thames St. The Big Iguana (imports) First National Bank of Maryland Eat Bertha's Mussels
47.	Francies Restaurant at Brown's Wharf	49. 50. 71. 72. 73.	Broadway Market Robert Long House Henderson's Wharf Recreation Pier Brown's Wharf Marina (water taxi stop)

Other establishments at Brown's Wharf:
Avante Garde (book store)
Gift Ahoy
Café Madeira

Fells Point, Baltimore

quite popular locally. Not too far away is the Dead End Saloon with the sign describing what it hopes to do for you: "Despair Repair."

You might also want to "Eat Bertha's Mussels" **(48)** and enjoy jazz four nights a week at the establishment with that name, at Broadway and Lancaster. The Broadway Market **(49)** is a well-known local market for the area.

These are just a few representatives of a whole neighborhood of special places. Go ashore, walk around, and see for yourself.

We go into deeper detail with the South Baltimore neighborhood, because this is of particular interest to cruising boaters for supplies and services. But you should not miss Fells Point for its own special brand of attractions. If you are tied at the Lady Maryland Center, or the marina now being constructed next to it, you will find Fells Point area more convenient for walking, but check with local marina personnel for the latest information as to appropriate places to walk to access this area.

South Baltimore
Refer to our Sketch Chart—"South Baltimore." PG 257

South Baltimore is one of the several neighborhoods for which the city is famous. This area presents better shopping for the daily needs of the typical boater, and its shops, compared to those of other more distant neighborhoods, are generally more convenient to boats tied or anchored in the Inner Harbor. The Inner Harbor is primarily oriented as a tourist area, and thus doesn't offer the best in practical day-to-day provisions and services. South Baltimore does, usually at better prices, and also offers much of the "fine life" with great restaurants, pubs, wine and cheese shops, and more. And it is a great place to visit. It is about 5 minutes walk from the Inner Harbor, less if you are docked at the Inner Harbor Marina.

South Baltimore nestles behind Federal Hill Park which overlooks Baltimore Harbor and which was mentioned earlier as a navigational reference. You will have seen the hill to your left as you turned into the Northwest Harbor. It played a major role in the War of 1812. There is a statue here of General Samuel Smith, a Baltimorean hero of that war. When the British landed, led by the very famous battle tactician, General Robert Ross, sharpshooters under General Smith's Command mortally wounded the Redcoat general thus causing disarray among the British ranks. The body of General Ross was taken back to his ship and stored in a barrel of rum until the ship had an opportunity to bury him on British soil in Nova Scotia. During the War Between the States, this hill became quite notorious for many Baltimoreans with Southern sympathies when Union General Benjamin "The Beast" Butler placed cannon at its top to quell any unrest.

There are historical row houses in South Baltimore and ancient cobbled streets, but there is also a great selection of restaurants and pubs and shops and special places. There are also some very fundamental stops for boaters such as the hardware store, a laundry, and a simple grocery store. Below we will mention just a few to give you the general flavor. To list them all will simply take too much room here, and a few minutes walk will introduce most of them to you.

To reach South Baltimore from the Inner Harbor, walk south along Light Street from the southwestern corner of the harbor at the Science Museum. While it is nice to wander around and browse, the most shops and restaurants and services will be found between Light and South Charles Streets to

the east and west, and Montgomery and Ostend Streets to the north and south.

Steve's Supermarket **(51)** at 1000 S. Charles Street at Hamburg Street will take Visa, MC, and Most cards, and will deliver to your boat. They also prepare party trays and bakery and fried chicken.

At Bandaloops Restaurant and Tavern **(52)** at 1024 S. Charles St., you can get carry out. Le Andra's **(53)** at 1016 S Charles St., offers gourmet carry out and catering. They also will deliver to a boat. The Szechuan Restaurant **(54)** at 1125 S Charles St. has Chinese carry-out.

Photo by Mel Neale

Author Tom with daughters Melanie and Carolyn at Columbus' statue, Little Italy, Baltimore

Regis (55) at 1002 Light Street is a true neighborhood pub and restaurant open six nights a week. The local people love it, and there can be no greater recommendation. Sisson's (56) at 36 E. Cross St. has a variety of Cajun menu items and it has its own locally loved micro brewery on the premises. For a really great cafe serving incredible meals and sandwiches, including one of the best Hoagies you will find, try Di Pasquale's (77) on Cross Street adjacent to the Cross Street Market.

Smitty's Discount Liquors (57) at 1044 S. Charles Street and Federal Hill Wine and Spirits (58) at 901 S. Charles Street will both deliver with a reasonable purchase.

There are at least three hardware stores. Collins True Value (59) is at 1105 Light Street, Klein's Hardware (60) is at 912 S. Charles St., and Singers Hardware (61) is at 1129 S. Charles St.

There are at least three laundries. Cross Light Laundry (62) is at 1024 Light Street, Pitilis Dry Cleaners (63) is at 901 Light Street, and Richie Cleaners (64) are at 902 Light Street. There is a shoe repair shop (65) at 1016 Light Street.

Poptronics (67) at 1124 Light Street is an interesting store with an unusual selection of nautical gifts and accessories and marine electronics. Marineland Nautical Sales (68) at 1143 Hull Street has a worldwide selection of charts, a large nautical book selection, instruments, and other navigational resources. If you are running out of money at this point, a Most machine with the Maryland National Bank (69) is at 1046 Light Street.

There are also medical and dental services in this section of the town. Among these are Harbor Health Care Center (70) at 600 Light Street. A full service optometrist, Dr Steven L. Pinson (71), is at 1135 Light Street. There are drug stores with the standard selection of personal items as well as pharmaceutical. These include James Aid Drugs (72) at 1117 Light Street and Rite Aid Pharmacies (73) at 1100 Light Street.

Postal services include Postal Express (79) at 644 E. Fort Ave., South Baltimore Station (74) at 146 W. Ostend, and Mail Boxes, Etc. (75) at 911 S. Charles Street.

Don't miss the Cross Street Market (76). This is one of Baltimore's most popular old-fashioned markets. It has been in operation for many years, and is not only a place where you can find the best of almost anything delicious, but also a place where neighbors come to visit and chat. As soon as you enter the doors of the long hall you know you are in for a treat just by the tantalizing smells mixing and mingling from the stalls. Here you can get cheeses, the best of fresh meats, fruit, seafood, pretzels, ice cream, delicatessen foods, beautiful fresh vegetables, gourmet groceries (even a gourmet vegetable shop). The Cross Street Cheese Shop in the market not only has cheeses, patés, and many other delcacies, it also has some of the best coffee, capuccino, and espresso that you will ever find. They grind the beans for each cup just before it is made, and meticulously follow the very best procedures for the finest brew. And you don't have to buy and leave. You can also eat prepared food in the market, from many of the shops, including a great raw bar. We found better shopping here and better prices than in the food stands in the pavilions at the Inner Harbor.

•

Including Cross Street Market, there are seven regional public markets in Baltimore, some dating back over two centuries. Some are in the "neighborhoods." Call (410) 837-4636 for locations and specifics. One of these, Lexington Market, is the oldest continuously operated market in the United States. It opened in the late 1780s. (It later burned and has been rebuilt.) It houses over 130 merchants. When Oliver Wendell Holmes visited in 1859, he was so impressed with the selection of foods that he declared Baltimore to be "The Gastronomic Capital of the Universe." Today you can purchase from the stalls delicious foods of all kinds.

•

Spend a weekend, or spend years. Baltimore is one of the finest cruising destinations that you will ever visit. Stay a weekend or stay a month. You must see for yourself. Come and enjoy.

Tour boat *Clipper City*, Baltimore Inner Harbor

South Baltimore

51. Steves Supermarket
52. Bandaloops Restaurant and Tavern
53. Le Andra's
54. Szechuan Restaurant (Chinese carry-out)
55. Regis (pub & restaurant)
56. Sisson's
57. Smitty's Discount Liquors
58. Federal Hill Wine & Spirits
59. Collins True Value
60. Klein's Hardware
61. Singer's Hardware
62. Cross Light Laundry
63. Pitilis Dry Cleaners
64. Richie Cleaners
65. Shoe repair shop

Not for use in Navigation

66. Bike shop
67. Poptronics
68. Marineland Nautical Sales
69. Maryland National Bank— Most machine
70. Harbor Health Care Center
71. Dr. Steve Pinson, optometrist
72. James Aid Drugs
73. Rite Aid Pharmacy
74. South Baltimore Station
75. Mail Boxes, Etc.
76. Cross Street Market
77. Di Pasquale's Café
78. Harborview
79. Postal Express
87. Inner Harbor Marina
90. Finger piers—city marina

Siberian tiger, Baltimore Zoo

257

CHAPTER 15

MAGOTHY RIVER AND GIBSON ISLAND

Although the Magothy River contains some beautiful anchorages near its mouth, it runs inland between Baltimore and Annapolis and pierces the heart of a bedroom community. Therefore, the shores are lined with houses and piers once you get into the upper creeks and river areas. The territory is still pretty, but with the crowded shore, it is not what most cruisers desire. The creeks offer excellent protection from severe weather. There are some marinas, but not much convenient opportunity for provisioning.

Entrance
Refer to Regional Chart #12273-F—"Western Shore: Craighill Channel, Magothy River Entrance."

The mouth of the Magothy River (1) is hard to miss with the Bay Bridges just to its south, the industrialized Patapsco to its north, and Baltimore Light House (2) east of the entrance channel. Looking west from the Craighill Channel (13) just north of its G "5" and R "6" (3), you will see the opening (4) between Pavilion Peak and Persimmon Point. Magothy entrance Gr "3" is conspicuous and on a huge caisson. The approach is wide and trouble-free, narrowing only as you near the cut. This entrance is deep and well-marked. There are obstructions on both points outside of the channel, but these are avoided by staying in the channel. You'll have to avoid all of the 6-mile speed buoys scattered everywhere. Very high land with cliffs marks Gibson Island (5) on the northern shore of the entrance.

Approaching from the south, while still out in the Bay, you'll see boats docked at Podickery Creek (6). This is a private facility. Signs proclaim "Private Club, no fuel, no food, no service."

Refer to Chart #12282-A—"Eastern Magothy River, Gibson Island." PG 261

Many homes dot the shore of both sides of the mouth of the Magothy, but those to your right (north) are spectacular. This is the Pavilion Peak (7) area of Gibson Island, a spectacular chunk of nature, and a spectacular chunk of choice and exclusive residential real estate. The huge homes on these high cliffs to the north give the impression of the mountain country of Europe. The bottom off this area is rocky.

Looking ahead into the river, it is easy to get the impression that there is a major fork in the river. Actually, this impression is given by Dobbins Island (8) to the northwest. This high island with brown cliffs and high ground behind, appears to be a division point, but the water around to the north of it is really Sillery Bay (9). This becomes clear as you continue on in. Many sailboat masts appear to the left (south). These are up in Deep Creek (10).

Deep Creek
Refer to Chart #12282-A—"Eastern Magothy River, Gibson Island." PG 261

Heading into Deep Creek (10) gives you a foretaste of what

the area is like farther up the Magothy River. Houses and docks line both shores, with very little space between them. Follow the markers in. Note the shallow shoal coming east off Adams Point to the right (west) between G "1" and Fl G "3." The marina to your left (east) with the Exxon sign is **Fairwinds Marina (11)**. Its sign says "no transients and no overnight mooring." Inside are some community facilities. These are common in many areas of the Bay. When an area is developed, the waterfront will be reserved to serve the development. The docks and ramps will often appear to be marinas. In fact, they are usually for the exclusive use of the home owners, who often have private clubs and other activities.

The Creek feels very narrow continuing on; this is partly because of the many three-story homes high on the hills at the water's edge. The folks in those homes could look right down into your cockpit.

Deep Creek Marina (12) sits on the western bank a short distance in. There is a fuel dock facing the creek, a few piers, and a restaurant on the hill over the docks where you will also see the sign for the marina. The fuel dock pumps gas and diesel from 0800 to 2300 or "until the bar closes." Depth at docks is 6 feet with 45 feet being maximum length for docking alongside. Electricity is 15 to 20 amps. There are no restrooms or showers for the marina. Most people come to enjoy the restaurant. The marina has some permanent slips and also takes transients, but mainly in connection with the restaurant business. This is a nice restaurant, popular locally, with bar and dining overlooking the creek. A lift is immediately before the marina, on the same side. This lift is private and is not related to the marina.

Sillery Bay/Dobbins Island
Refer to Chart #12282-A—"Eastern Magothy River, Gibson Island." PG 261

Most cruisers bypass Deep Creek and head straight for the anchorages on the north side of the river. Sillery Bay (9) is that large area west of Gibson Island (5) and north of Dobbins Island (8). The half moon basin north of Dobbins is an extremely popular anchorage (13). Coming in, do not round Fl G "1" too soon. The shoal behind it carries on north a short distance. The trees on the high hills of Gibson Island to your right (east) are very nice and refreshing to see after a hot day on the Bay.

There is a good protection here from the north and northwest. The shoal line (14) between Dobbins and the mainland appears as open water and gives a feeling of space. This will let westerly winds whistle through, usually without too much sea. The holding is good in thick mud. The surface mud appears to be fairly soft and will slime up your chain, but if you work the hook down to the better stuff underneath, it should be secure.

There is a beach (15) on the northern side of Dobbins Island which is regularly used by local people. I am told that it is private but there are no privacy markers. From this anchor-

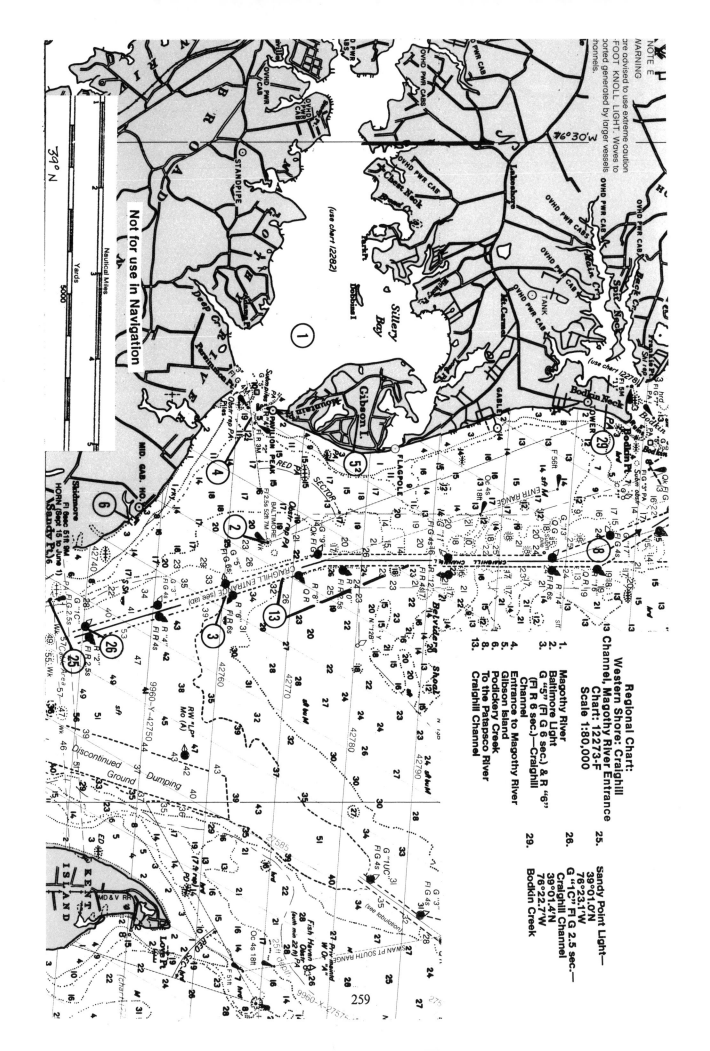

Regional Chart:
Western Shore: Craighill
Channel, Magothy River Entrance
Chart: 12273-F
Scale 1:80,000

1. Magothy River
2. Baltimore Light
3. G "5" (Fl G 6 sec.) & R "6"
   Channel
4. Entrance to Magothy River
5. Gibson Island
6. Podickory Creek
13. Craighill Channel

25. Sandy Point Light—
    39°01.0'N
    76°23.1'W
26. Craighill Channel
    G "1C" Fl G 2.5 sec.—
    39°01.4'N
    76°22.7'W
29. Bodkin Creek

Not for use in Navigation

259

age, you can watch the frequent races out in the river, see the large ships heading up the Craighill Entrance Channel to Baltimore, and enjoy the trees and natural surroundings of the area. The drawback is that everyone comes here. Even on summer week nights, the anchorage can be very crowded, not only with those staying overnight, but also with smaller boats enjoying the evening. It's a popular weekend destination.

Little Island (16) is hard to pick out the first time. It has a small house facing out with a screened porch also facing out. There is a private beach on the northwest side. Some anchor (17) behind Little Island, but the deep water is not wide and you are closer to the private piers on the shore.

Grays Creek (18) is crowded with many small houses and docks, as is typical of the area. The entrance is marked as on the chart, but is narrow and I found a little less than 5 feet depth, particularly between markers "1" and "2." The branch to your right (north) has a marina called Pleasure Cove (19). There is a sign and a structure appearing as a red barn behind it. It has 52 slips, 15 amp electricity, cube ice, gas and diesel, and a boatel with fork lift and 30-ton travelift.

GIBSON ISLAND
Refer to Chart #12282-A.

As mentioned earlier, Gibson Island (5) is a private residential area. Its high hills, spectacular bluffs, and very nice homes are quite impressive as you glide by. The island also gives good shelter, not only in Sillery Bay, but also up inside its two harbors, both of which you access from Sillery Bay.

Follow the markers carefully while heading in toward Holland Point (20). There is plenty of deep water, but there is also plenty of shoal water outside the channel. With all the space around and the nice scenery, it is easy to wander astray. Up in Tar Cove (21) to your left heading in (north), you will notice a small privately marked channel (22) leading into a shallow basin with some boats inside. To the east is the narrow passage (23) between Long Point and Holland Point. It looks tricky on the chart, with obstructions to your left (north) and the shoal off Long Point to your left. However many large boats do this every day, as you will see when you get inside.

Cornfield Creek (24) opens up to the left (north) behind Long Point. It is very narrow, with depths as charted. Inside are many houses, often small, crowded around the shores. Many have docks. There is a dock with fuel pumps (25) behind a house to the left, and some short slips. A sign said that the facility is closed. Cornfield Creek isn't a good anchorage with all of the homes. There's a much nicer anchorage nearby.

Just around Holland Point, you will see a beautiful and very protected spot to anchor (26) and relax. This is in the cove between Holland Point and Purdy Point, on the south side of the channel. The shore of Gibson Island is high hill, woods, and marsh. There is a nice beach inside Purdy Point. On the mainland stands a very beautiful and very old mansion with six thin white columns and a white stone fence. This is a place to stop, moving into the cove to the right, well out of the busy channel. The protection is great and the scenery beautiful. The channel has a 6 mph limit, which should control the wake fairly well. The chart indicates another very inviting anchorage around Purdy Point in the Inner Harbor (27) but there isn't much room to anchor there.

Inner Harbor (27) is the home of **Gibson Island Yacht Club** (28). Follow the chart and respect the private markers. From

Inner Harbor, you can see Chesapeake Bay over the isthmus connecting Gibson to the mainland. There are so many boats on moorings here that there is hardly a space to anchor. It can be done, but carefully. Gibson Island Yacht Club may have a guest mooring or dock space for members of other recognized clubs. It's best to reserve ahead if you qualify.

In Redhouse Cove (29) more masts are visible. This is the home of the **White Boat Works (30)**. They are a full service yard with a 25-ton lift, railway, and crane. There is dock space and moorings for boats being serviced, with dry storage available.

Carolyn Neale enjoying her perch
in the rigging

LEGEND FOR CHART ON PG 261

Eastern Magothy River, Gibson Island Chart #12282-A Scale 1:25,000		
1. Magothy River	16.	Little Island
4. Entrance Markers	17.	Anchorage—Little Island
5. Gibson Island	18.	Grays Creek
7. Pavilion Peak	19.	Pleasure Cove
8. Dobbins Island	20.	Holland Point
9. Sillery Bay	21.	Tar Cove
10. Deep Creek	22.	Private Channel, shallow basin
11. Fairwinds Marina	23.	Narrow passage between Holland Point & Long Point
12. Deep Creek Marina	24.	Cornfield Creek
13. Anchorage—Dobbins Island	25.	Dock & fuel pumps (sign said closed)
14. Shoal	26.	Anchorage
15. Beach	27.	Inner Harbor
	28.	Gibson Island Yacht Club
	29.	Redhouse Cove
	30.	White Boat Works

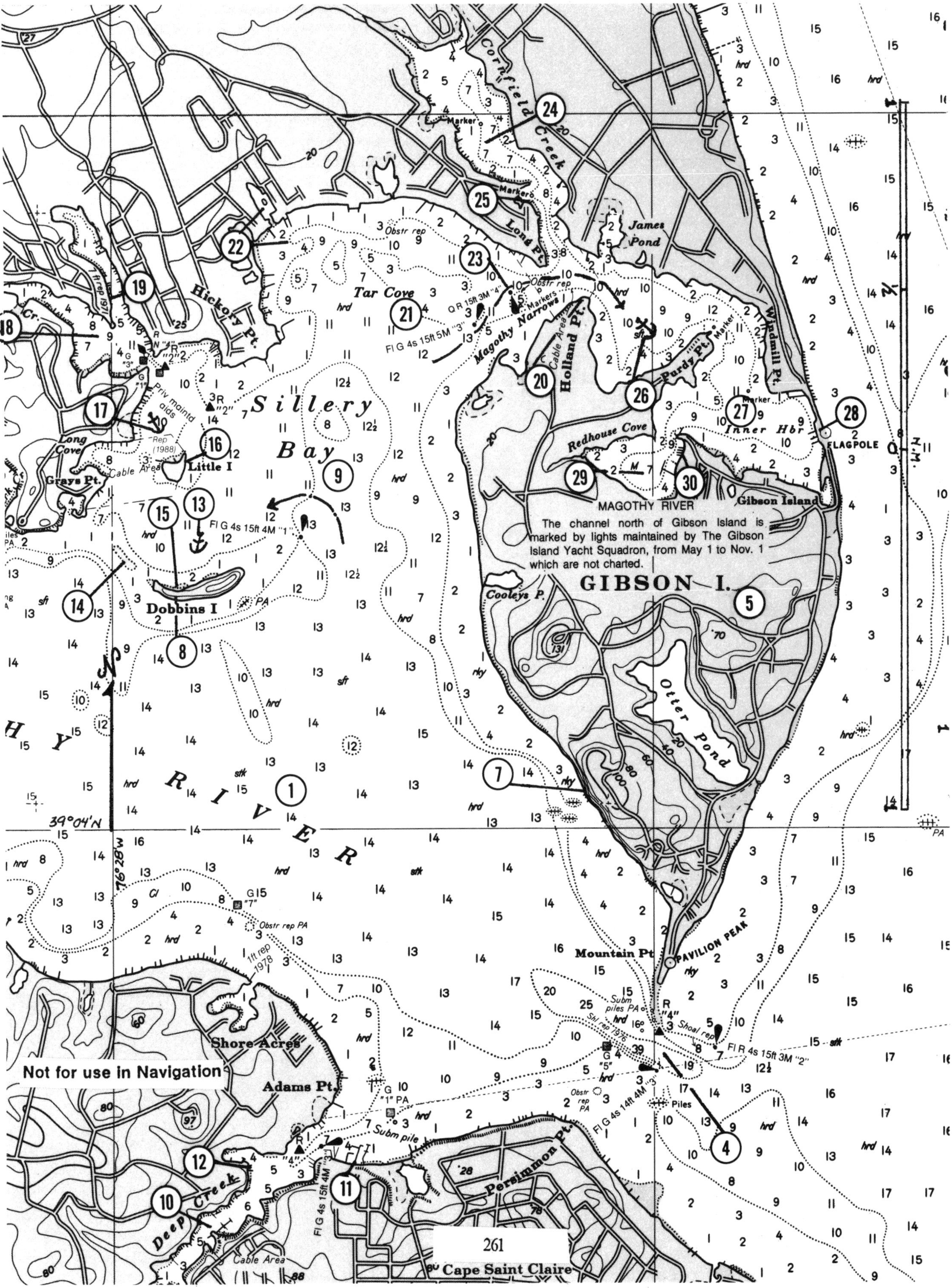
MAGOTHY RIVER
The channel north of Gibson Island is marked by lights maintained by The Gibson Island Yacht Squadron, from May 1 to Nov. 1 which are not charted.
GIBSON I.
Gibson Island
Sillery Bay
Magothy Narrows
Tar Cove
Hickory Pt.
Cornfield Creek
Long Pt.
James Pond
Holland Pt.
Purdy Pt.
Windmill Pt.
Inner Hbr
FLAGPOLE
Redhouse Cove
Cooleys P.
Otter Pond
Mountain Pt
PAVILION PEAK
Little I
Dobbins I
Long Cove
Grays Pt.
Shore Acres
Adams Pt.
Deep Creek
Persimmon Pt.
Cape Saint Claire
Cable Area
Not for use in Navigation
39°04'N
76°28'W

WESTERN MAGOTHY RIVER

Broad Creek
Refer to Chart #12282-B—"Western Magothy River."

There is yet another very nice anchorage area farther west in Broad Creek (31). The entrance markers G "3" and R "2" are easy to spot. Note that the rocky shoal (32) extends out into the channel from G "3." This should cause no difficulty because there is plenty of water to move over a little to your right (east). To the right (east), on Park Point (33) sits a very interesting multiple-storied glass house with a white horizontal support structure. The hill around the house with its woods and field is very pretty. Looking ahead into the creek, the prettiest anchorage (34) is between Rock Point and the 2-foot shoal coming out from the western shore to the north. Here there are high hills and trees, a beach, and the opening to the Magothy to the south. This could create more of a fetch than would be comfortable to some. It is possible to move up into the vicinity of the little island (35), rounding the 2-foot shoal. Depths can very quickly change in here, and the area is very built up ashore with houses high on hills looking down. There are tiny white floating shoal markers (36) lining the shoal which must be observed. The little island (35) has a beach on its north end. The north shore of the creek has a series of docks.

Forked Creek
Back out in the Magothy River, you will see Forked Creek (37) on the southern shore. It is well built up and narrow for anchoring. Most of it is exposed to the north. **Belvedere Yacht Club, Inc. (46)** is on the shore to your left. They don't have any guest moorings or slips.

•

Heading deeper into the Magothy, take note of the position of Fl R "10" (38) out in the middle, south of Chest Neck. Because of its distance from the shore, it is easy to miss, but the shoal north of it is there. On South Ferry Point, behind G "11" stands two rows of very conspicuous gray three-story condos (39). These can help in getting your bearings.

Mill & Dividing Creeks
The entrance to these two creeks is wide and deep, but typically crowded. Passing the mouth of Mill Creek (40) to your left (southeast) is an old jetty and an Exxon sign (41). They don't sell fuel. Red and green poles mark the water through the jetty. Inside to the left (northeast) is **Ferry Point Yacht Basin, Inc. (42)**. There are 100 slips up to 50 feet long with up to 30 amps of electricity, a cement ramp, and an open-end boat lift which will handle 40 feet at 20 tons. There is storage and a repair yard. Up Dividing Creek (43) at its fork, **Thompson and Langville (44)** is a facility with 5 slips, railway up to 40 tons and hull repairs.

Magothy Marina
After rounding G "11," **Magothy Marina (45)** will become obvious to left (west-southwest) within the cove there, and between Dividing and Cypress Creeks (47). A large sign identifies this nice and immaculately maintained marina. The fuel dock with a pumpout station is easy access and sells gas and diesel. Depth is 8 feet. Visa and MC are accepted. The 182 slips have electricity up to 220V/50 amp, there are laundry facilities and a swimming pool. The showers are private individual shower/head units with shower, toilet, and sink in each. The bulkhead dock can take up to 120 feet alongside. There is a ramp but it is for the permanent customers. This is a "Westrec" managed facility.

Cypress Creek
On the shores of Cypress Creek (47) you will see once again, wall-to-wall housing and docks. Leaving Magothy Marina, the entrance is easy enough to the left (southwest) up in the cove. Just before the split in the creek, on your left (the southeastern bank) is a full service yard and repair facility, called **Cypress Marine (48)** with 39 slips up to 80 feet. Electricity is available up to 50 amps, and there is a laundromat as well as cube ice and other supplies. There are a 50-ton lift and a crane, full service boat and engine repair, including the building and rebuilding of wooden and fiberglass boats. This area is very close by car to the Gov. Ritchie Highway (49) and Annapolis. The right fork of Cypress Creek has a small facility called **Struble's Marina (50)** with 25 slips up to 40 feet.

UPPER MAGOTHY

There is a G/R junction buoy (51) off Focal Point for Cattail Creek (52) and the upper Magothy (53), just before R "2." South of the junction buoy an attractive facility appears to left. This is **Whitehurst Yacht Club (54)**, a private community club. Proceeding on past this junction and up the Magothy, a totem pole (55) guards the point to your right (east) and north of G "15."

Just upstream from R "16" and to the left (on the southwestern shore) is **Hamilton Harbour Marina (56)**. A sign and fuel dock (gas and diesel) and lift identify the facility. Depth is 10 feet with 22 slips to handle up to 40-foot boats. Electricity is 30 amps and there is a pumpout. The marine store has some supplies and block and cube ice. There is a 20-ton lift and 1500 pound forklift. There is also a large boatel here.

The river remains deep and pretty with the usual heavy density of homes on the shore. If you continue exploring and don't draw more than 5 feet, you will be rewarded by the Riverdale Restaurant (57) with cocktail lounge and cube ice on the left (western shore). The restaurant is red with two white-bricked terraces in front with tables. There are docks for customers, up to 200 feet, with no charge while dining. I found 5 feet depths here, although there is 6½ feet depth controlling downstream. Deeper drafted boats could anchor (59) and go by dinghy. This is a popular place locally.

The water continues to shoal here as you approach the head of the river. Many would prefer to anchor downstream and come here by dinghy. Beyond the restaurant, the water shallows considerably and eventually a fixed bridge (60) with 9-foot vertical clearance crosses near the head.

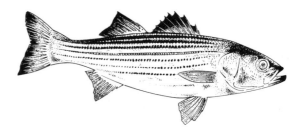

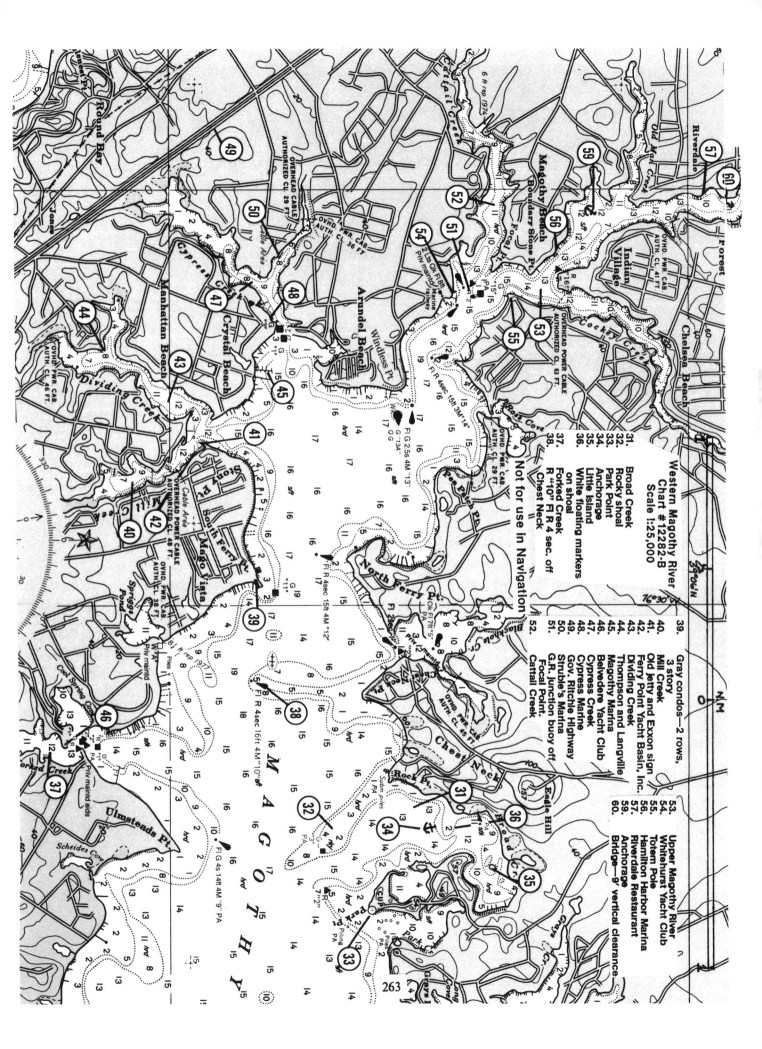

Western Magothy River
Chart #12282-B
Scale 1:25,000

31. Broad Creek
32. Rocky shoal
33. Park Point
34. Anchorage
35. Little Island
36. White floating markers on shoal
37. Forked Creek
38. Chest Neck

39. Gray condos—2 rows, 3 story
40. Mill Creek
41. Old jetty and Exxon sign
42. Ferry Point Yacht Basin, Inc.
43. Dividing Creek
44. Thompson and Langville
45. Magothy Marina
46. Belvedere Yacht Club
47. Cypress Creek
48. Cypress Marine
49. Gov. Ritchie Highway
50. Struble's Marina
51. G.R. Junction buoy off Focal Point.
52. Cattail Creek

53. Upper Magothy River
54. Whitehurst Yacht Club
55. Totem Pole
56. Hamilton Harbor Marina
57. Riverdale Restaurant
59. Anchorage
60. Bridge—9' vertical clearance

Not for use in Navigation

263

CHAPTER 16

SANDY POINT STATE PARK, WHITEHALL BAY, MEREDITH CREEK, WHITEHALL CREEK, MILL CREEK

SANDY POINT STATE PARK

Refer to Regional Chart #12263-E—"Western Shore: West River to Sandy Point"   and

Chart #12282-C—"Sandy Point State Park & Whitehall Bay." PG 267

Sandy Point State Park is nice, but it is primarily oriented to land visitors or temporary boating stopovers, and is not a good place to visit as a destination for most cruising boats. It does have nice launching ramps.

Sandy Point State Park (1) was built by the state of Maryland in the 1950s. The park has been rebuilt. This includes major landscaping as well as a structure modification.

Entrance to the park from the Bay is via the channel (2) parallel to the Bay Bridges (3), on the north side of the bridges on the western shore. The channel is buoyed and jettied. Although the depth was dredged to 8 feet, shoaling has occured, and 6 feet is questionable. This is to be corrected. Because of all of these changes in progress, call the park at (410) 974-2772 to get the latest.

Once you are inside, a large pond opens up. Inside are docks for daytime visitation, and small boat (with outboard) rentals. Boaters can come in from the Bay and dock, but they are not supposed to remain overnight except in emergencies. Ashore you can get gas, ice and beverages, light snacks, camping items such as sun glasses and sun tan lotion, and bait and some tackle. There are 22 cement launching ramps and a pumpout. They honor Visa, MC, and Amoco. There is a nice beach, walking trails, a playground, and picnic areas. In the plans are a special wind-surfing area and a sailboat catamaran launching area.

For boats of shallow draft, this should certainly be considered as a storm refuge when needed. The pond and docks are landlocked and very secure. I don't consider this to be a good hurricane hole, however, because the land is so low between the pond and the Bay.

In late October, a large festival called "Chesapeake Bay Appreciation Days" is conducted at the park and surrounding areas. One of the main events is skipjack races offshore.

WHITEHALL BAY

Refer to Regional Chart #12263-E—"Western Shore, West River to Sandy Point"   and

Chart #12282-C—"Sandy Point State Park and Whitehall Bay." PG 267

Many cruising boats pass up Whitehall Bay and its creeks as they pass them while heading south into the more popular Severn River. If you can get in, Meredith Creek provides great protection and beauty, while the busier Whitehall and Mill Creeks provide more anchorages and some services.

Approach

Approaching Whitehall Bay (4) can be a bit of a puzzle on a misty day because it is so wide and you must avoid Whitehall Flats (5) and North Shoals (6). A northerly course from Fl R bell "2" (45) (southeast of the mouth of the Severn) takes you to Fl R "2" (7) in the entrance to Whitehall Bay. The position of Fl R "2" (7) is 38°59.2'N by 76°26.3'W. Don't go right up to this marker, because it is at the tip of the shoal. Looking in, you will see to the west of the entrance, the red and white radio towers on the peninsula north of Greenbury Point (8). Northeast of the entrance, you will find a small white water tower (9) back behind the trees, and to the east of that, the Chesapeake Bay Bridges (3). As you head into Whitehall Bay, you will enjoy the beautiful wooded shore of Hackett Point (10) to your right (east), although the antennae forest to your left (west) will mar the scenery a bit.

Anchorage North of Hackett Point (10)

We have found that in calm or winds from the northwest, north, through the northeast, there is a nice anchorage (11) for those preferring open spaces. There is a thick forest ashore, civilization seems far in the background to the west, and it is very pretty. This can get very rolly in the wrong kind of wind.

On the neck between Whitehall Creek and Meredith Creek, you will see the majestic columns of the old Whitehall Mansion (12), facing southerly, back from the water and among the trees.

IDENTIFICATIONS FOR CHART ON PG 265

**Regional Chart—
Western Shore: West River
to Sandy Point** (West River, Rhode River, South River, Severn River, Whitehall Bay)
Chart #12263-E
Scale 1:80,000
reduced 10%

1.	Sandy Point State Park
2.	Coast Guard Annapolis
3.	Bay Bridge—(William P. Lane, Jr. Memorial Bridges)
4.	Whitehall Bay
6.	Galesville
7.	Kent Island
8.	Greensbury Point (red & white radio towers)
11.	Ramsay Lake
13.	Meredith Creek
20.	Parish Creek
21.	Harness Creek
23.	Whitehall Creek
28.	Glebe Bay & Glebe Creek
29.	Mill Creek
35.	Aberdeen Creek
40.	Severn River
41.	U.S. Naval Academy Buildings
42.	Thomas Point Light— 38°53.9'N, 76°26.2'W
43.	"1 AH"
44.	GRC "SR"
45.	R "2" (entrance channel to Severn River)
46.	Greenbury shoal light Fl W 4 sec. 40', 38°58.1'N, 76°27.3'W
47.	Bloody Point Light
47A.	Crab Creek
48.	Lake Ogleton
53.	Almshouse Creek
55.	Church Creek
57.	Back Creek
58.	Spa Creek
59.	Annapolis
62.	Weems Creek
65.	Eastport
84.	West River
85.	Rhode River
91.	South River
95.	Duvall Creek
98.	Selby Bay

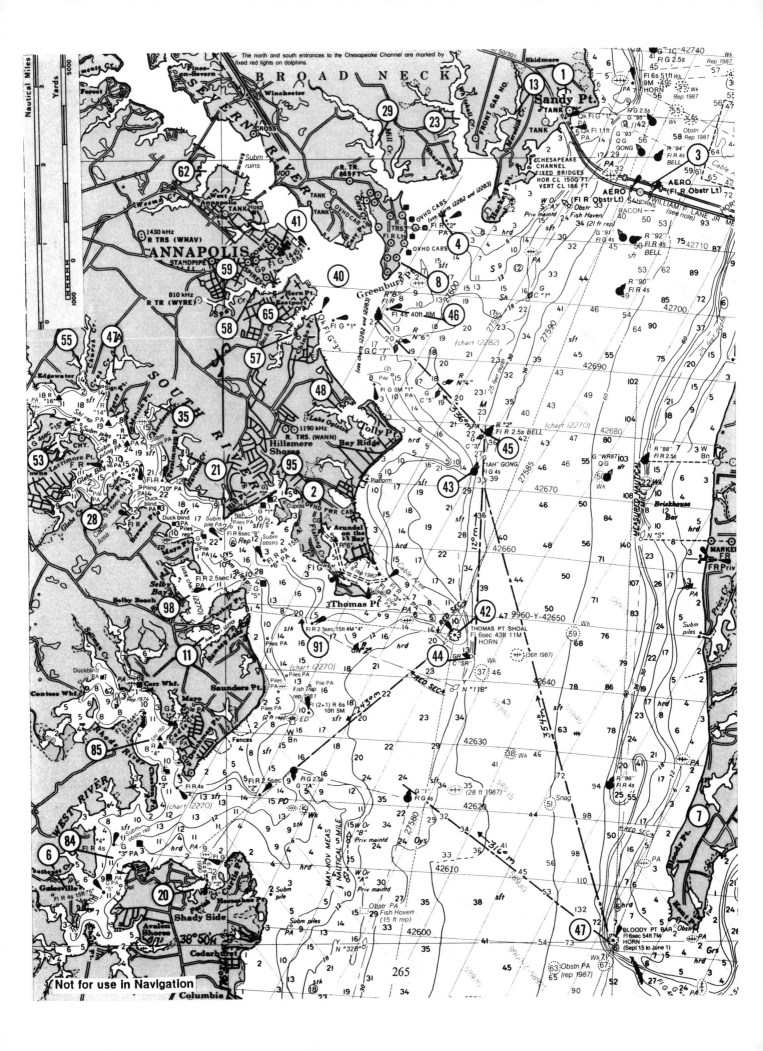

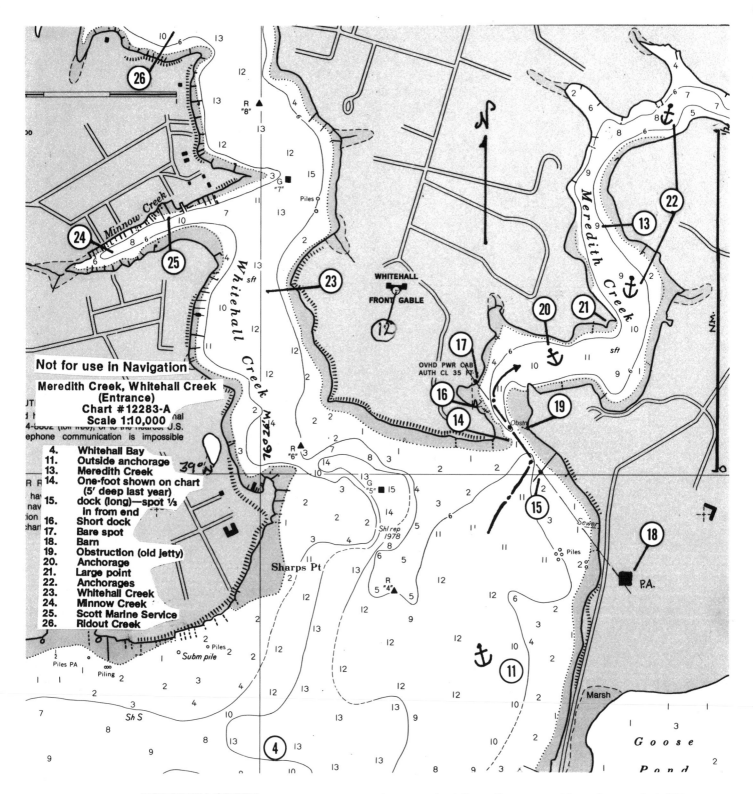

Not for use in Navigation

Meredith Creek, Whitehall Creek
(Entrance)
Chart #12283-A
Scale 1:10,000

4. Whitehall Bay
11. Outside anchorage
13. Meredith Creek
14. One-foot shown on chart
    (5' deep last year)
15. dock (long)—spot ⅓
    in from end
16. Short dock
17. Bare spot
18. Barn
19. Obstruction (old jetty)
20. Anchorage
21. Large point
22. Anchorages
23. Whitehall Creek
24. Minnow Creek
25. Scott Marine Service
26. Ridout Creek

MEREDITH CREEK

Refer to Chart #12283-A—"Meredith Creek, Whitehall Creek (Entrance)."

If you have the draft, you will find one of the nicest anchorages in the Bay in Meredith Creek **(13)**. The chart shows 1-foot controlling **(14)** at the mouth, but last year 5 feet or more could be taken in at low tide. Two things allow this. First, the creek has been dredged. The entrance may fill in, but there are some sailboats drawing close to 6 feet permanently moored inside. I suspect that the entrance will be maintained

to some extent. Secondly, you must know how to do it. What follows is how we found the water, hopefully it will do the trick for you when you arrive.

As you approach the entrance, you will see to your right (northeast) a long pier **(15)** coming out in a southwesterly direction. Behind this pier, up in the yard, is a beautiful two-story brick mansion with a tall flag pole in the front yard. Proceed up to the end of this pier, on its northern side, and parallel that northern side of the pier as though you were to go ashore. About one-third of the way in from the end of the pier, we saw a white mark painted on the wood underneath.

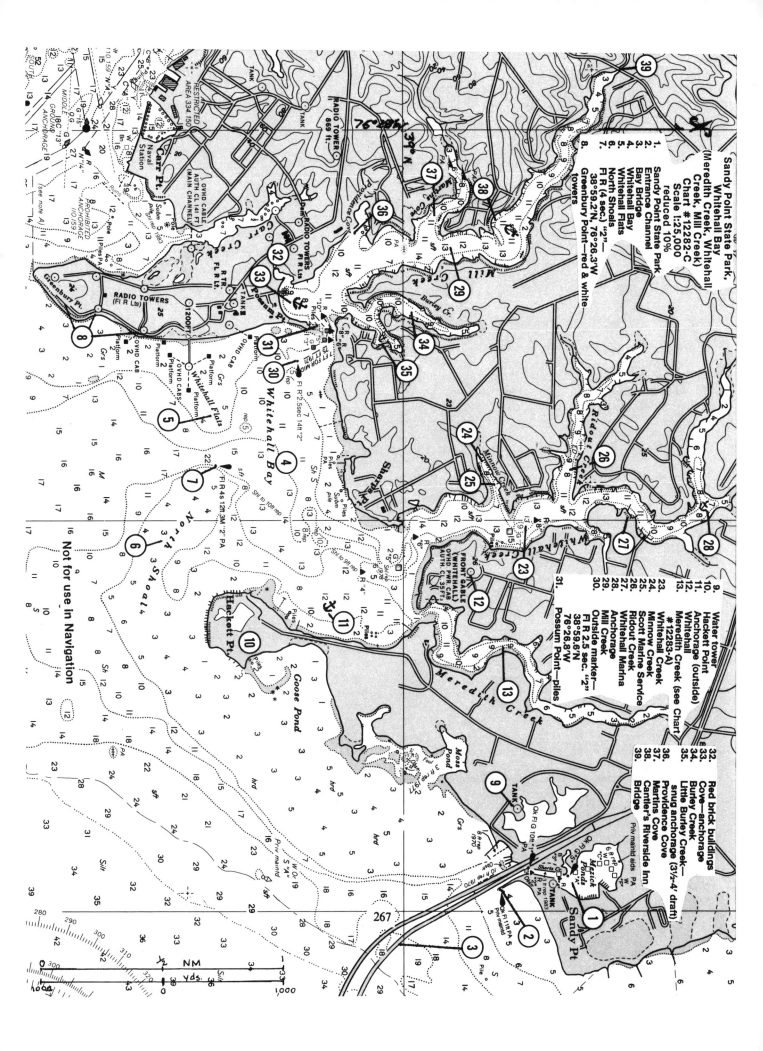

This was faded and may not last for long. When you are off this mark (around ⅓ in from the end of the pier), turn to your left (north-northwesterly) and head along the northeastern shore toward the entrance. If you look inside the entrance, you will see a pier coming in a north-northeasterly direction off the bank (16) ahead and to the left of the creek (north-northwesterly). To the right (east) of this, you should notice a bare spot (17) on the bank ahead. Behind you, ashore on the grounds of the mansion, there is a barn (18). The best water was on a course on a range between this barn and the bare spot, going in through the cut. The channel is very narrow, but once you get in, you will probably feel it to be worth the effort. Note well the obstruction (19) marked coming out in a westerly direction from the eastern entrance point. This is an old wood jetty, not visible at high water, and dangerous if you run upon it. It was not marked last year.

Once in, the best anchorage (20) is behind (to the north of) the right (eastern) entrance point with its little beach on the spit. Here you can take a boat of 5 feet draft almost up to the beach, anchoring on the shore, and a 7-foot draft boat almost that close. Looking over the beach you will see the open waters of Whitehall Bay and the Chesapeake to your south. All around is woods and quietness.

If you proceed farther up the creek, you will find homes as you round the large point (21) to your left (west). Many of them are quite large, set back from the water, with hills. You can take your pick to anchor (22) in one beautiful area or another. The most secluded anchorage is (20), behind the entrance spit. As you near the headwaters, you will begin seeing the white dome of a water tower behind the trees.

WHITEHALL CREEK
Refer to Chart #12282-C—"Sandy Point State Park & Whitehall Bay" PG 267 and Chart #12283-A—"Meredith Creek, Whitehall Creek (Entrance)." PG 266

The entrance to Whitehall Creek is tricky and it is mostly residential with a few services and a nice marina.

The best advice for the approach to Whitehall Creek (23) is to study the chart and follow it and the markers, rounding where the shoals are indicated, according to your draft. I didn't find a range that really worked. Sailboats of 4 to 5 feet do this regularly. The chart shows deeper water if you are in the right place.

After you get inside, the navigation is more straightforward. At first you will see woods to your right (east) and sparse population to your left (west). The estate of Whitehall Mansion (12) has kept that point to the east unsettled. As you proceed farther up the creek, there will be considerably more houses and docks. Minnow Creek (24), to your left (west) is very heavily built. **Scott Marine Service**, is a small yard, (25), with 14 slips, a 15-ton lift, and 20 amp electricity. Rideout Creek (26) also has many homes, on both sides. It's too narrow with all the docks to make a good anchorage. At its head the civilization decreases, but so do depths. Boats of 2½ to 3 feet draft may enjoy the quietness here as the creek turns into marsh.

Refer to Chart #12282-C. PG 267
Proceeding up the main creek, **Whitehall Marina (27)** will appear on the right (eastern bank) just before the creek turns to your left (the northwest and west). This has 134 "condo-minium" slips taking boats, including transients, up to 75 feet long with up to 50 amp electric service, moorings, and a marine store, with CNG available and block and cube ice. There is a full service yard with lift capacity up to 50 tons. This is a quiet and very pretty marina with many trees and grassy yards. Most boats there are sailboats. No fuel is sold.

As you round the bend to the northwest and west beyond the marina, you will find yourself in a very pretty area to anchor (28), with homes more tucked up into the trees and hills.

MILL CREEK
Refer to Chart #12282-C—"Sandy Point State Park & Whitehall Bay" PG 267 and Chart #12283-B—"Mill Creek Entrance."

Mill Creek is pretty, but heavily built up as it winds back toward the Annapolis outskirts. A popular restaurant and crab house bring many boats up this creek.

The approach to Mill Creek (29) isn't difficult to find once you are in Whitehall Bay. However the outside marker, Fl R "2" (30) can be a little difficult to see because it is against the shoreline. Its position is 38° 59.6′N by 76°26.8′W. From this marker, follow the channel in carefully. It is dredged but narrow. Don't bring in a boat deeper than 6 feet. If there is shoaling, you'd need half tide and rising to take 6 feet in there.

After you clear the narrow marked channel, the scenery greeting you is pretty, with many homes and trees, behind a shore still often lined with marsh. But you will find as you go up that the houses increase in number and that there really aren't any secluded places to anchor. You could "set her down" just about anywhere that suits you if you are out of the traffic and don't mind the wakes and homes ashore.

Rounding Possum Point (31), you should see heavy old pilings marching out from the point to the channel. These do not come into the channel, but would be dangerous if you were out of the channel and had not already been stopped by running aground. As you clear Possum Point, you will notice red brick buildings (32) at the base of the radio towers to your left (south), and government piers up in the cove behind (to the west of) that point. These all make the cove unattractive for anchoring (33), although it would certainly do if you don't mind the scenery.

To the north of the Possum Point Cove (immediately to your right after you clear the entrance channel), you will see Burley Creek (34) and Little Burley Creek (35) opening up. There are so many houses in here with docks that I was reminded of being on a town residential street. Little Burley does thin out some near its end and a boat of no more than around 30 feet length and of no more than 3½ to 4 feet draft could find a nice anchorage here. There is not much swinging room anywhere in the creek because of its narrowness and the docks.

Providence Cove (36) next on the western shore has many homes with private docks extending out.

Martins Cove (37), the next to come up on your left (west) is full of houses and traffic, and has a work boat landing dock on its northern shore.

Refer to Chart #12282-C. PG 267
Back out in Mill Creek just around the bend, you will see Cantler's Riverside Inn (38). This is a restaurant specializing in crabs and other seafood, as well as regular fare. It is large and open inside with a bar and atmosphere suited for eating

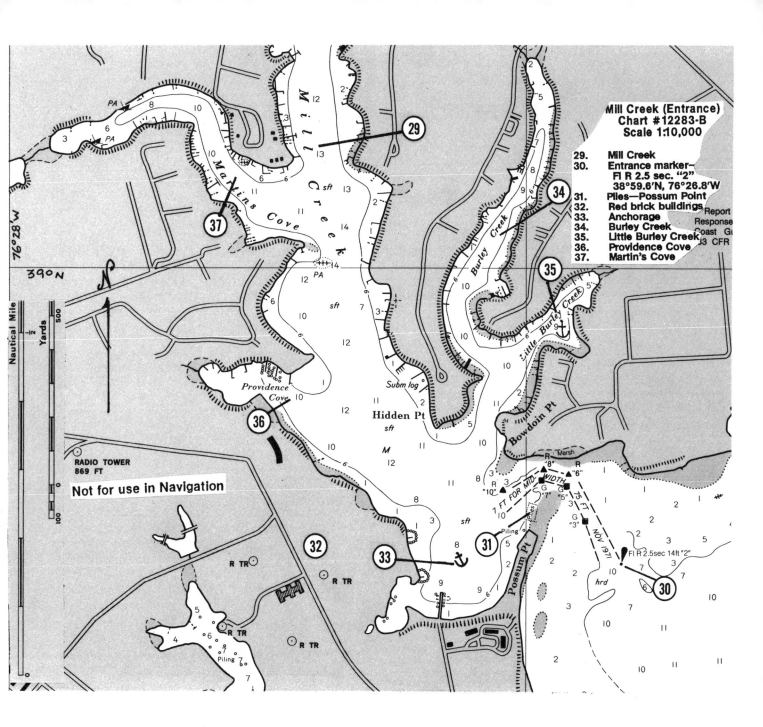

Mill Creek (Entrance)
Chart #12283-B
Scale 1:10,000

29. Mill Creek
30. Entrance marker—
    Fl R 2.5 sec. "2"
    38°59.6'N, 76°26.8'W
31. Piles—Possum Point
32. Red brick buildings
33. Anchorage
34. Burley Creek
35. Little Burley Creek
36. Providence Cove
37. Martin's Cove

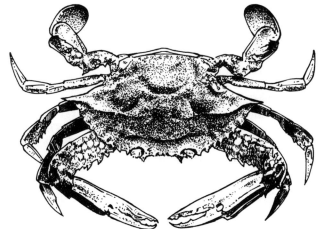

crabs. It also has a nice outside eating area overlooking the water. The entire restaurant, sitting up on the hill, has nice water views. The menu goes from light fare up to $16. The dock in the front sells gas and provides a space for patrons to land. As you walk up the dock, you will pass a large soft crab shedding operation and can watch them working. You can buy these soft shell crabs here, live or frozen, to take with you. Ice is also available, and charter fishing boats. Work boats come and go here, offloading their catch.

From here on up to the bridge **(39)** at the end, the creek continues with many homes on either side, but retaining trees and marsh. The bridge at the end has only 10 feet vertical clearance. Above that is marsh.

CHAPTER 17

SEVERN RIVER AND ANNAPOLIS

Refer to Regional Chart #12263-E—"Western Shore—West River to Sandy Point" at the beginning of Chapter 16. PG265

The Severn River has many excellent anchorages in both town and country surroundings. It also has Annapolis, probably one of the primary provisioning and maintenance stops on the East Coast, as well as an area of special entertainment and historical significance to the cruiser.

APPROACH

The Severn River (40) entrance is hard to miss. It is just to the south of Bay Bridges (3), on the western shore, with the gray buildings of the Naval Academy (41) visible up inside to the west, and a forest of tall slender radio towers (8) on the shore to the north of the entrance channel. If you are coming in from the south, you will first notice Thomas Point Light (42) on the western shore. Its position is 38°53.9′N by 76°26.2′W. This was built in 1875 and is one of the few remaining screwpile lighthouses in the Bay. Then take care to round Tolly Point Shoal with its lighted 4 sec. flashing gong "1AH" (43), 12°M from the GR marker (44) southeast of Thomas Point Light. From here you will pick up Fl R "2" (45) of the entrance channel. Follow the buoys in on a course of 336°M. Be sure to avoid the long Greenbury Point Shoal protruding southwesterly from that point. There is a Greenbury Shoal Light (46), flashing white every 4 sec., 40 feet tall, on a skeletal tower. Its position is 38°58.1′N by 76°27.3′W. However, the shoal extends just beyond this light to its northwest and southwesterly into the channel. Honor Fl R "8."

If you are coming in from the north, follow the shoreline around after passing through the Bay Bridges. Coming from the Eastern Shore, Gong "1AH" is 354°M from Bloody Point Light (47). From far offshore, you will see the radio towers on the shore, south of the Bay Bridges, and then the Academy.

LAKE OGLETON

Lake Ogleton is west of Tolly Point on the south shore of the Severn River, at the entrance. This is a nice anchorage for weather but the marinas are for local homeowners and the shoreline is mostly private.

Refer to Chart #12283-C—"Lake Ogleton."
The outside marker (47) for Lake Ogleton (48) is a 15-foot Fl G "1" on a pile. Its position is 38°57.1′N by 76°27.5′W. Follow the narrow marked channel in. I found 5½ feet to be controlling at the entrance, but this is a dredged channel that can quickly change because of the northeastern exposure.

Once you get into the lake, it will open up around you with much deeper water than the 5½ feet depth in the entrance channel. Ashore, you will see both homes and woods, in a pleasant mixture of scenery. There are many docks, some in groups, but these are not public marinas. The main attraction of this lake from the viewpoint of most cruisers is that it provides an attractive anchorage (49), virtually landlocked when you are expecting severe weather.

The first group of docks you will encounter to your left (south) are those of Bay Ridge Civic Association (50), at the far end. There are then other private docks around the shore. The Cove (51) to the northwest of Oak Point has many houses with docks around its shore, but is not unattractive and may provide the snugger anchorage that some would want. As you enter the western branch (52), you will find hills around you, the high ground being a preview of what you will find in the upper Severn. There are also numerous moorings scattered about. Homes are generally set back from the water and the area is pretty. As you reach the west end, you will see docks wrapped around the shore. These are also community piers.

CHESAPEAKE HARBOUR
Refer to Chart #12283-D—"Annapolis: Eastport, Back Creek & Chesapeake Harbour."

Chesapeake Harbour is a nice landlocked marina surrounded by condominiums. To identify Chesapeake Harbour (53) from the mouth of the Severn, look for a large area of gray condominium buildings (54) on the shore in a westerly direction from G "7." The outside entrance marker is a privately maintained 14-foot Fl R "2" (55) on a pile. Its position is 38°57.6′N by 76°28.0′W. This is a well-maintained facility, and the entrance channel is kept at 8 feet controlling.

As soon as you get inside the cut, you will find a very nice marina packed with well laid out slips and nice boats. There is no place to anchor in this privately dredged basin. The dockmaster's office (56) is on the second story of the red building at the end of the thorofare which turns directly to your left (south) after you enter, passing between the docks. Before entering, a call first on VHF would be appropriate to make arrangements for docking.

There are 200 slips, and boats up to 90 feet will find room, with longer spaces available alongside. Electricity up to 100 amps is available, as are phone and TV hook-ups and a pumpout station. A long beach and fishing pier are bayside. Visa and MC are taken. There is a small marine store, two pools, and tennis and golf nearby. Sam's Waterfront Café (56) (not connected with another restaurant of similar name in Annapolis) is a very nice restaurant and lounge overlooking the harbor with rounded dining room and wrap around windows. Sam's has a full course menu up to around $22 for entrees, as well as entertainment and light fare outside on weekends. Water taxi to Annapolis town docks is available.

THE ANNAPOLIS AREA

We rate the anchorage only fair for protection because during a major storm, there are too many boats and piers

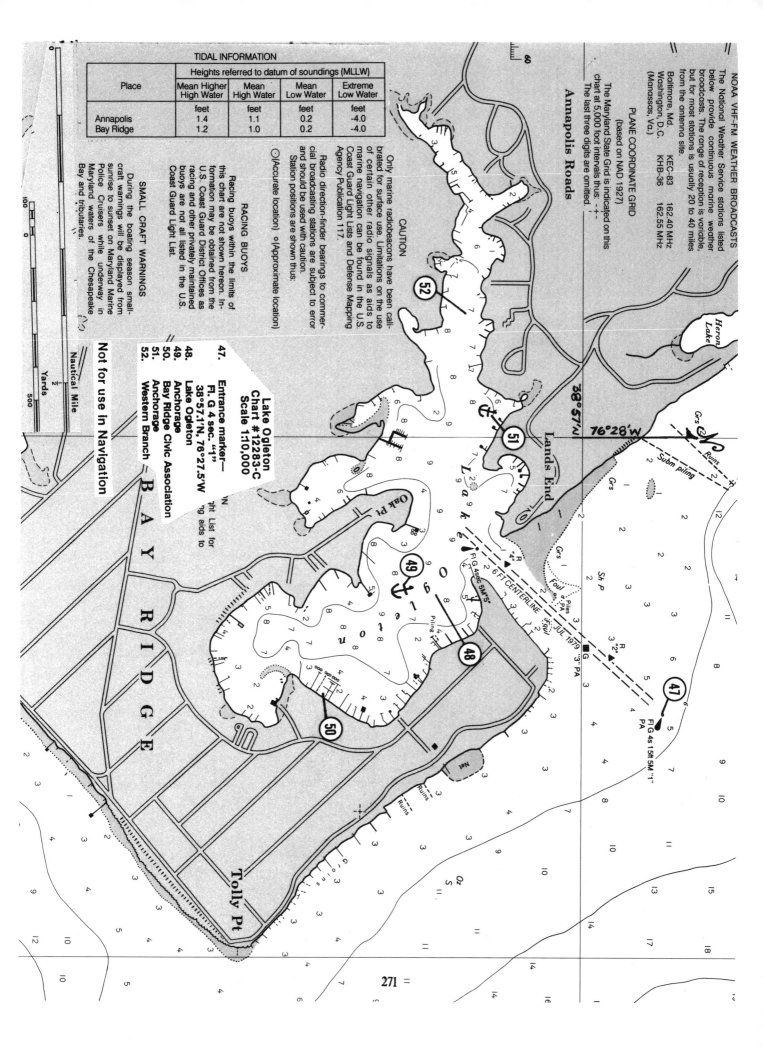

NOAA VHF-FM WEATHER BROADCASTS

The National Weather Service stations listed below provide continuous marine weather broadcasts. The range of reception is variable, but for most stations is usually 20 to 40 miles from the antenna site.

Baltimore, Md.	KEC-83 162.40 MHz
Washington, D.C.	KHB-36 162.55 MHz
(Manassas, Va.)	

PLANE COORDINATE GRID
(based on NAD 1927)

The Maryland State Grid is indicated on this chart at 5,000 foot intervals thus: ⊢+
The last three digits are omitted.

Annapolis Roads

TIDAL INFORMATION

Place	Heights referred to datum of soundings (MLLW)			
	Mean Higher High Water	Mean High Water	Mean Low Water	Extreme Low Water
	feet	feet	feet	feet
Annapolis	1.4	1.1	0.2	-4.0
Bay Ridge	1.2	1.0	0.2	-4.0

CAUTION

Only marine radiobeacons have been calibrated for surface use. Limitations on the use of certain other radio signals as aids to marine navigation can be found in the U.S. Coast Guard Light Lists and Defense Mapping Agency Publication 117.

Radio direction-finder bearings to commercial broadcasting stations are subject to error and should be used with caution. Station positions are shown thus:

⊙(Accurate location) ○(Approximate location)

RACING BUOYS

Racing buoys within the limits of this chart are not shown hereon. Information may be obtained from the U.S. Coast Guard District Offices as racing and other privately maintained buoys are not all listed in the U.S. Coast Guard Light List.

SMALL CRAFT WARNINGS

During the boating season small-craft warnings will be displayed from sunrise to sunset on Maryland Marine Police Cruisers while underway in Maryland waters of the Chesapeake Bay and tributaries.

Lake Ogleton
Chart #12283-C
Scale 1:10,000

47. Entrance marker—
Fl. G 4 sec. "1"
38°57.1'N, 76°27.5'W
48. Lake Ogleton
49. Anchorage
50. Anchorage
51. Bay Ridge Civic Association
52. Western Branch

Not for use in Navigation

B A Y   R I D G E

Heron Lake

Lands End

Tolly Pt

38°57'N

76°28'W

271

around. The surroundings around the central area contains some of the east coast's prime yacht repair and provisioning facilities and opportunities, and thus cannot be covered with trees and flowers. Much of the scenery, as in and around Annapolis town docks and Market Slip, is very attractive by anyone's standards, particularly from the historical perspective and architectural interest.

Refer to Chart #12282-D—"Severn River: Annapolis and Vicinity."

The general area of Back Creek (57), Spa Creek (58), and Annapolis (59) are interwoven, and often considered to be a part of the same experience. Most consider the central attraction to be the waterfront area of Annapolis on Spa Creek and the City Dock at Market Slip (60) (now known as "Ego Alley"). Back Creek and the opposite side of Spa Creek are considered working areas, although they also have many pleasurable attractions, with various anchorages interspersed. Most points of reference for the visitor begin with the area immediately around Market Slip (60), referred to locally as "City Dock" or "Market Space" when referring to the area at the far end of the Slip with its "Market House" (61). Actually, the city has around 17 miles of waterfront, and includes three peninsulas formed by four creeks. Back, Spa, and Weems Creeks (62) all offer anchorages or moorings. College Creek (63) is spanned by fixed low bridges and goes into Naval Academy (41) grounds.

Annapolis has many dinghy landings, so the boater need not feel restricted. Almost every street that ends on the water has a landing, with a sign placed by the Harbormaster's office. These are designated on our detail charts as L1, L2, etc. (not on Chart #12282-D). These dinghy landing areas are shown on Chart #12283-E—"Annapolis: Spa Creek" and sketch chart of Eastport.

The section of Annapolis around and north of Market Slip is known as the "historical area" (64), and has been so designated. This small city lives and works within a wealth of old and famous buildings and scenes. Most visitors make this their primary destination for sightseeing, shopping, and restaurants, although the Eastport (65) and other areas should not be overlooked.

When you arrive in the Annapolis area, you will constantly hear people refer to "Eastport." This is technically a part of Annapolis, but is the unique area between Spa and Back Creeks. It is important to the boater because it is full of marine facilities and services, most on one of the creeks, but some back from the shore. It also has some nice restaurants and areas of historical interest. Actually, a walk of only a few blocks will take you across the Eastport peninsula from one creek to the other. Most marinas allow you to land your dinghy if you ask first.

The Annapolis Harbormaster, Rick Dahlgren, is an experienced boater (over 30 years), has a 100-ton master's license, and is dedicated to seeing that boaters enjoy their visit. His office (66) can be reached on Channel 16, and they have a patrol boat marked with the city seal.

Various rules have been designed to avoid problems which could otherwise occur because of the huge amount of boating traffic. Many areas have 6 mph speed limits. All of the downtown Annapolis area does. These are usually well-marked by buoys. No rafting is allowed at city moorings (67) or docks (68) (owned by the city). Anchoring is not allowed within the mooring area. Barbecuing is not allowed at city docks. Dumpsters are at various locations, including the city docks.

Additional help is found in a marine services guide called the "Portbook" which covers that area and Galesville, Deale, Solomons, and areas on the Eastern Shore. There is also a very good pamphlet entitled "Welcome to Annapolis, a Mariner's Guide to Capital City." These are full of valuable information regarding businesses and services and boating needs. They are well organized, include maps, and are available free at most marinas and information centers, and other places. There is an information booth (66) in front of the Harbormaster's office on the eastern side of the Market Slip, which will have these and many other pamphlets.

There is a very active "Jiffy" water taxi service, with numerous boats, which will pick up and deliver to most convenient places. They stand by on VHF Channel 68. You will generally find their drivers to be helpful with information. The company and Annapolis Landing Marina and Up the Creek, a gourmet waterfront café at the marina, have published a pamphlet especially relevant to the needs of the boaters, based upon the questions their captains usually get. You can pick this up for free from the water taxis or most marinas, or the information booth.

Seasonal events include an Annapolis Spring Boat Show (not to be confused with the later Boat Shows in October), an Annapolis Waterfront Festival in April, the Chesapeake Bay Bridge Walk and Bayfest in May at nearby Sandy Point State Park, the Mid-Atlantic Wine Festival, Fourth of July Celebration, and Annapolis Rotary Crab Feast in July, the Maryland Seafood Festival and the Kunta Kinte Heritage Festival in September, and the United States Sailboat Show and United States Powerboat show, as well as Chesapeake Appreciation Days, in October. There are various important games at the Naval Academy.

State House, Annapolis

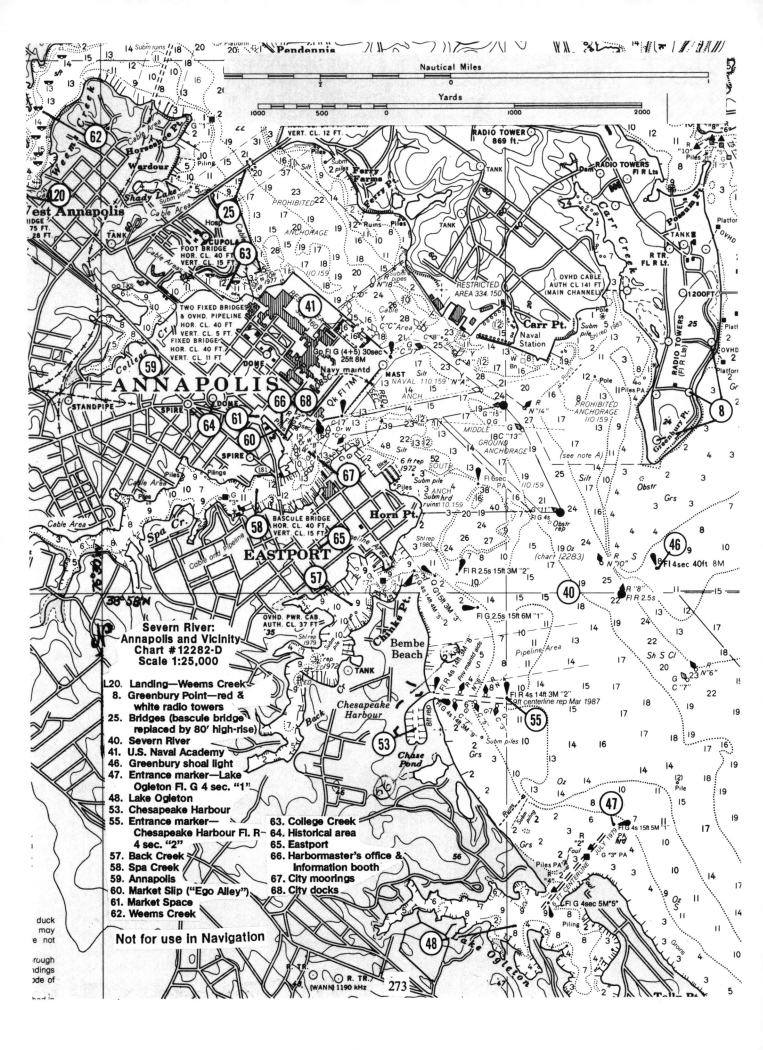

Severn River:
Annapolis and Vicinity
Chart #12282-D
Scale 1:25,000

L20. Landing—Weems Creek
  8. Greenbury Point—red &
      white radio towers
 25. Bridges (bascule bridge
      replaced by 80' high-rise)
 40. Severn River
 41. U.S. Naval Academy
 46. Greenbury shoal light
 47. Entrance marker—Lake
      Ogleton Fl. G 4 sec. "1"
 48. Lake Ogleton
 53. Chesapeake Harbour
 55. Entrance marker—
      Chesapeake Harbour Fl. R
      4 sec. "2"
 57. Back Creek
 58. Spa Creek
 59. Annapolis
 60. Market Slip ("Ego Alley")
 61. Market Space
 62. Weems Creek

 63. College Creek
 64. Historical area
 65. Eastport
 66. Harbormaster's office &
      Information booth
 67. City moorings
 68. City docks

Not for use in Navigation

273

Back Creek

On or near the banks of Back Creek and Spa Creek, you can get just about any marine service or commodity that you may want or need. We will attempt to give a representative sample of the businesses. Omission of any should not be construed negatively.

Refer to Chart #12283-D—"Annapolis: Eastport, Back Creek & Chesapeake Harbour"
and
our "Sketch Map of Eastport." PG 277

When entering Back Creek (57), it is important to realize that the actual channel is much narrower than the broad entrance area. The shoal off Horn Point (69) extends not only easterly toward the Severn River Channel, but also southeasterly towards the channel into Back Creek. It will be important to follow the channel markers in. These begin just south of the opening. You can easily identify the opening from out in the Severn by spotting the whitish-blue onion-shaped water tower (70) just to the left (southwest) of that opening. To the right (northwest) of the opening are the red-roofed two-story condominiums of Horn Point Harbor (71). There are often many sailboats moored just inside the entrance and to the right (south) side of the channel. These belong to the sailing school there.

The first marina to your right (north) after you enter the creek is **Horn Point Harbor Marina (71)**. It sits behind a steel bulkhead to protect its docks from an otherwise northeast exposure. Behind the marina are the red-roofed condominiums which you noticed coming in. Horn Point Harbor Marina has 60 slips up to 60 feet in length, and electricity up to 50 amps. There is a full service repair and custom yacht-building business here with a 15-ton crane.

Next to your right (north) is the well-known Maryland Waterman's Cooperative (72). This sells wholesale and retail seafood as well as beverages and ice and other supplies. Next to this, although not very noticeable from the water, is the Barge House Museum (73) with exhibits to show the waterman's life and history.

When you came in, you noticed the many sailboats moored out on the left (southern) side of the channel. These belong to the Annapolis Sailing School (74), whose three-story building and floating docks you will see as the first facility on that side. They claim to be the oldest sailing school in the U.S. They are famous and popular with two additional locations in Florida and another in St. Croix, U.S. Virgin Islands. Their 'phone number is 1-800-638-9192. Womanship is another Annapolis sailing school that teaches women, couples, or families, located at 410 Severn Ave, Annapolis MD 21403. Womanship also has branches in Florida, the Virgin Islands, New England, and the Pacific Northwest. Their 'phone number is (410) 267-6661.

Next to the right (northern) side is **Bert Jabin's Yacht Yard, Eastport (75)**. Bert Jabin has several locations, another huge one up the creek. These include marina spaces and services from many different contractors, all on the yard premises. The one here has 90 slips up to 50 feet with electricity up to 50 amps, and lift capacity up to 30 tons. The facility is on a peninsula, and there are more services and shops in the area than the eye initially sees, until you head around behind the docks.

Next on the same side is **Muller Marine (76)** with 40 slips capable of taking boats up to 45 feet, electricity up to 30 amps, and repair work available. The sign is on a crane; painted on the building is "Eastport Marina" and "Hood." Next, at the end of the dock on the same side, you will see the North Sails (77) sign. Here you can drop off sails for repair or get new ones fitted. Transient slips are usually available at Muller Marine.

Mears Marina (78) will then be conspicuous to your right (west) with its large sign and wooden bulkheading. There are 300 slips taking boats up to 70 feet long with electricity up to 50 amps, laundromat, air-conditioned rest rooms, an olympic-sized pool, seven tennis courts with a pro shop, playground and poolside snack bar, charcoal pit picnic area, the **Severn River Yacht Club (79)**, and a repair and maintenance facility.

On the left (eastern) side, after you pass the Annapolis Sail-

**Chesapeake Bay skipjack *Stanley Norman* tour boat has no engine. Here she's pushed
into her berth by her yawl boat to return passengers in "Ego Alley," Annapolis**

274

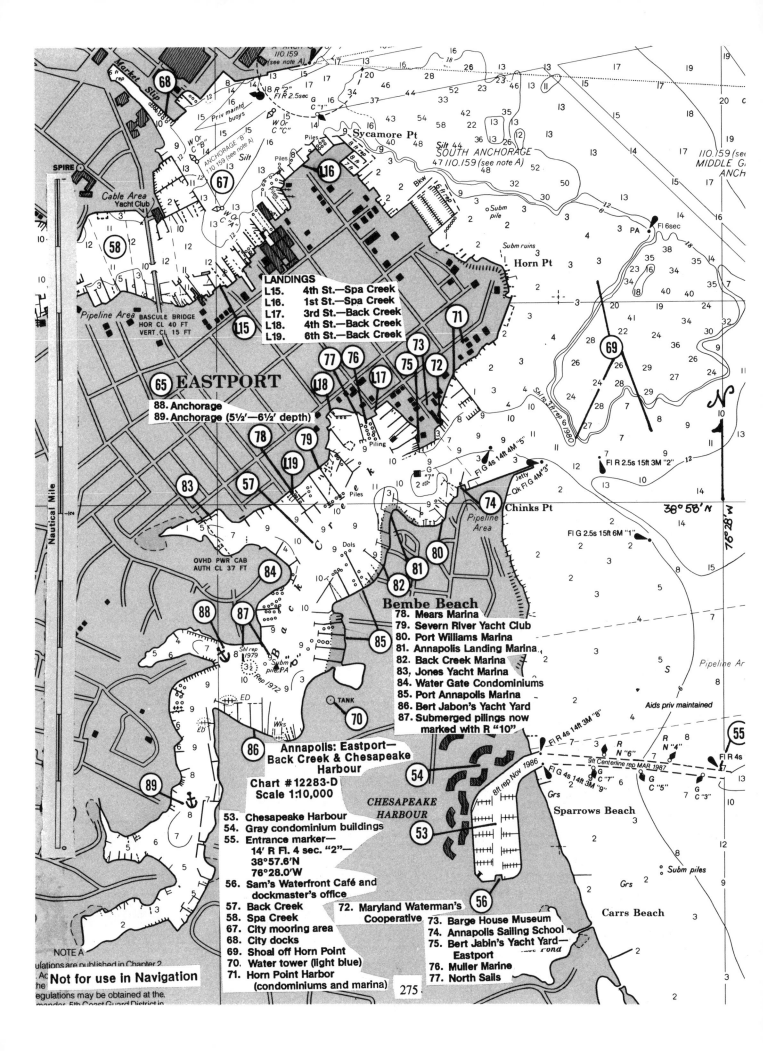

LANDINGS
L15. 4th St.—Spa Creek
L16. 1st St.—Spa Creek
L17. 3rd St.—Back Creek
L18. 4th St.—Back Creek
L19. 6th St.—Back Creek

EASTPORT

88. Anchorage
89. Anchorage (5½'–6½' depth)

Bembe Beach

78. Mears Marina
79. Severn River Yacht Club
80. Port Williams Marina
81. Annapolis Landing Marina
82. Back Creek Marina
83. Jones Yacht Marina
84. Water Gate Condominiums
85. Port Annapolis Marina
86. Bert Jabon's Yacht Yard
87. Submerged pilings now marked with R "10"

Annapolis: Eastport—Back Creek & Chesapeake Harbour

Chart #12283-D
Scale 1:10,000

53. Chesapeake Harbour
54. Gray condominium buildings
55. Entrance marker—
    14' R Fl. 4 sec. "2"—
    38°57.6'N
    76°28.0'W
56. Sam's Waterfront Café and dockmaster's office
57. Back Creek
58. Spa Creek
67. City mooring area
68. City docks
69. Shoal off Horn Point
70. Water tower (light blue)
71. Horn Point Harbor (condominiums and marina)
72. Maryland Waterman's Cooperative
73. Barge House Museum
74. Annapolis Sailing School
75. Bert Jabin's Yacht Yard—Eastport
76. Muller Marine
77. North Sails

Cable Area Yacht Club

BASCULE BRIDGE
HOR CL 40 FT
VERT. CL 15 FT

OVHD PWR CAB
AUTH CL 37 FT

Sycamore Pt

SOUTH ANCHORAGE
47 110.159 (see note A)

Horn Pt

Chinks Pt

CHESAPEAKE HARBOUR

Sparrows Beach

Carrs Beach

38° 58' N

SPIRE

Nautical Mile

Pipeline Area

TANK

Not for use in Navigation

275

ing School, you will see a cove which has some docks in it with the sign **Port Williams Marina (80)** and some work boats.

Around the next point coming out on this side will be the very nice **Annapolis Landing Marina (81)** with its Amoco sign and a red-roofed gray building on a hill. They have 100 slips taking boats up to 60 feet (up to 130 feet alongside) offering electricity to 50 amps, with cable TV and phone hook-ups. They sell gas and diesel and have pumpout with easy access. They offer a discount for slip holders for the water taxi which docks there. Within its nicely landscaped grounds, the marina has a volley ball and picnic area, laundromat, block and cube ice, a small "Gourmet to Go" shop, a bed and breakfast, and boat, canvas, and engine repair. When available, they have a courtesy car for slip holders who need nearby shopping. An engine repair shop here are dealers for Volvo Penta, Yamaha, Kohler, and others.

Annapolis Landing also has a unique "Boat & Breakfast." You rent one of the "Berthed Boats" for the night and are served breakfast aboard in the morning. Enrolled boats range from ordinary sailboats to a huge refitted former European canal barge.

Next up on the same side is **Back Creek Marina (82)** with 25 slips up to 50 feet and 30 amp electricity, and some repair work.

The creek has a short branch making off to the west. Inside on the northern side is the small **Jones Yacht Marina (83)** with 15 slips primarily used locally. As you approach the point that separates this branch and the main creek, you will probably be impressed by the huge number of light gray condominiums belonging to the Water Gate Condominium **(84)** complex. They extend well back on this point, well up the creek, with docks coming out all along the shore. They continue on up and around the shores of the next cove to the right (west). With the marina docks on the other side of the creek, this entire area is all business with little room for anchoring.

Just before you get to that first westerly branch and "condo point," you will see the very fine **Port Annapolis Marina (85)** on your left (east side) with its sign which includes a seagull

sitting on three pilings with the sun behind. There are 240 slips here with space available for boats of 50 feet plus alongside, electricity up to 50 amps, and a pumpout. There is also a waterside deli, a marine store, block and cube ice, a laundromat, a pool, picnic area, a full service yard with hauling capacity up to 35 tons and a sailing school. Boat charters are available. Unlike many other areas on this creek, this marina has maintained a great many trees and natural beauty around its facilities.

Next up on the same side is the second **Bert Jabin's Yacht Yard (86)** that you find on the creek, again with very large collection of boat repair and refitting specialists on the premises. There is a large sign over the buildings, and the docks spread around the point. There are 200 slips, with electricity up to 50 amps, lifting capacity up to 35 tons and a 14-ton crane, laundromat, block and cube ice, marine store, and power and sail charters.

The chart shows submerged pilings **(87)** to the southeast of the point as noted. There is now a red beacon "10" there, and, honoring that beacon, I did not find any pilings. The 3½-foot shoal reported to the south of the point can be avoided, if it is still there, by favoring the eastern side with the Bert Jabin docks. Some boats anchor **(88)** in the mouth of the cove here, but it is a very congested place.

The only relatively quiet place to anchor **(89)** in the creek is above this point in the area just before (to the north of) where the creek makes its final split before it dies in a gentler bed of marsh and not so many buildings. Here there is 5½ to 6½ feet of depth and room to swing.

Spa Creek Waterfront before the Bridge
Refer to Chart #12283-E—"Annapolis: Spa Creek." PG 279

Spa Creek is what most people consider to be "Annapolis" when they come here for the first time. There are moorings, anchorages, marinas and service areas, and the shoreside attractions of old Annapolis.

Jiffy Taxi in "Ego Alley" gets you around Annapolis waterfront.
Note bow unloading pulpit and step

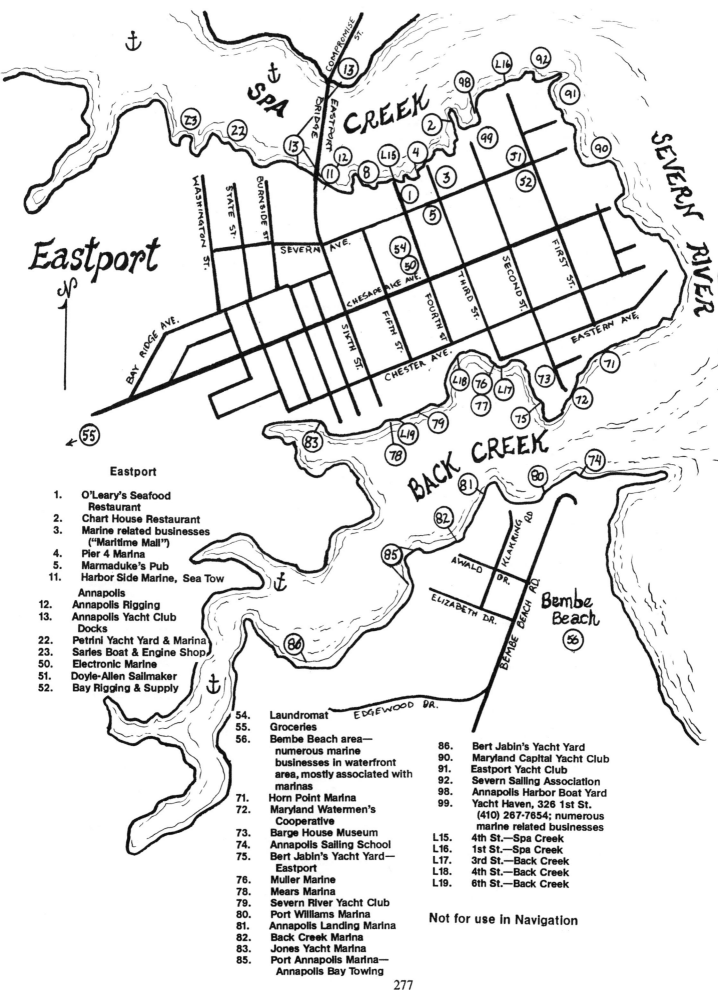

Eastport

1. O'Leary's Seafood
   Restaurant
2. Chart House Restaurant
3. Marine related businesses
   ("Maritime Mall")
4. Pier 4 Marina
5. Marmaduke's Pub
11. Harbor Side Marine, Sea Tow

Annapolis

12. Annapolis Rigging
13. Annapolis Yacht Club
    Docks
22. Petrini Yacht Yard & Marina
23. Sarles Boat & Engine Shop
50. Electronic Marine
51. Doyle-Allen Sailmaker
52. Bay Rigging & Supply

54. Laundromat
55. Groceries
56. Bembe Beach area—
    numerous marine
    businesses in waterfront
    area, mostly associated with
    marinas
71. Horn Point Marina
72. Maryland Watermen's
    Cooperative
73. Barge House Museum
74. Annapolis Sailing School
75. Bert Jabin's Yacht Yard—
    Eastport
76. Muller Marine
78. Mears Marina
79. Severn River Yacht Club
80. Port Williams Marina
81. Annapolis Landing Marina
82. Back Creek Marina
83. Jones Yacht Marina
85. Port Annapolis Marina—
    Annapolis Bay Towing

86. Bert Jabin's Yacht Yard
90. Maryland Capital Yacht Club
91. Eastport Yacht Club
92. Severn Sailing Association
98. Annapolis Harbor Boat Yard
99. Yacht Haven, 326 1st St.
    (410) 267-7654; numerous
    marine related businesses
L15. 4th St.—Spa Creek
L16. 1st St.—Spa Creek
L17. 3rd St.—Back Creek
L18. 4th St.—Back Creek
L19. 6th St.—Back Creek

Not for use in Navigation

When you approach Spa Creek from the Severn, you are impressed by the majesty of the U.S. Naval Academy (41) which predominates your senses, its gray buildings stretching around the shore ahead on both sides of the river. As you round the peninsula of Eastport, you will be greeted by a smorgasbord of boating activities. First you see to your left (southwest) the docks of the **Maryland Capital Yacht Club (90)**, then the **Eastport Yacht Club (91)**, and then the Severn Sailing Association (92). To your left in the outer Spa Creek (southern bank) and on the Eastport side, will be an incredible collection of marinas, docks, and services, more of what we call the "maritime mall." Straight ahead you will see the bridge (93), more docks, the "Market Slip" (60), and then to your right, the Naval Academy grounds. Everywhere there will be boats. Many hundreds of boats of all kinds anchored, moored, and docked impress upon you that this is a special place for boaters.

As you turn westerly into the creek, you will see a mooring area (67) marked by buoys in the middle of the basin. The moorings have white conical plastic buoys, and the mooring area is denoted by small floating red and green navigational buoys. The navigational channels run around that area. These moorings are maintained and rented by the city of Annapolis through the Harbormaster's Office (66). Last year, mooring fee was $15 per night, considerably more than what is normally charged in this section of the country and farther south. There are heads and shower facilities ashore under the Harbormaster's Office. Use of showers is included with dockage and mooring. A $1 fee is charged for all others. An attraction for these moorings is that the bottom is not good holding in that area. With the large number of boats always trying to anchor within the protection of the creek, many consider the moorings to be of benefit. Moorings and the slips in Market Slip (68), which are also rented by the city, are on a first come first served basis. The slips are generally around 12 feet wide, with one at 16 feet. Some have electricity at 20 and at 30 amps. There is also bulkhead docking available from the city in the Slip for longer boats. No rafting at City Dock or the moorings is permitted. If you wish to moor or dock at the city facilities, call the Harbormaster on VHF Channel 16 and they will assist you.

If you wish to anchor, you may do so (94) & (25) above the bridges (more on this later) or, if you don't mind the wakes and sea, you can anchor off (southeast of) the seawall of the Naval Academy (95), keeping out of the channel. If you do this, it is important to be sure that your anchor is set well. Some boats don't, and drag down on the rocks and cement of the wall, doing great damage to themselves. A strong easterly wind can come up suddenly and cause quite a bit of sea here.

There is a "South Anchorage" (96) noted on the chart, but we seldom see anyone (except some very large vessels) use this because it is also very exposed and generally too deep. If you anchor here, note the steep shoal, from 30 to 40 feet to around 3 feet, close to the shore.

From these moorings or anchorages, you can watch the Naval Academy cadets drill and march. On Thursday evenings and at other times, concerts are given by the Academy band, or sections thereof. If you anchor close to the bulkhead after mid-August, you will be awakened in the early hours of the morning and afforded a severe guilt trip as you watch the plebes run and exercise together.

Going around this basin east of the bridge in a clockwise fashion, we will end up at Market Slip. First on your left (south) after you pass the Severn Sailing Association (92), you will see condominiums (97) with a private area in front.

Next is **Annapolis Harbor Boat Yard (98)**. In addition to its full service yard facility, it has 52 slips with dockage for small and very large vessels alongside, with electricity up to 50 amps. This is a large working yard, and much of the premises are taken up by this nature of business. There is a 70-foot crane for tall mast pulling, and a 35-ton lift. Behind this is a brown building, several stories high, which is part of Yacht Haven (99), with innumerable services.

Of particular interest to many is the Outfitters USA (100) shop which you will find behind the brown private condos which are just to the north of Annapolis Harbor Boat Yard. These people specialize in inflatables and life-saving equipment, including serious off-shore equipment. They are certified to repack and repair all of the major brands of survival rafts. They also handle other lines such as Johnson and Suzuki and foul weather gear.

O'Leary's Seafood Restaurant (1) is very popular and has a small white single-story building with red roof and a few docks for free tie-up while dining.

The Chart House Restaurant (2) is a large brown building out over the water with an A-frame roof and glass walls facing the water. This is a popular full menu restaurant. If you think it looks like a huge enclosed boat house, you are correct. This used to be the Trumpy boat house when that famous boatbuilder was turning out some of the finest yachts ever built. Behind this restaurant are more marine-related businesses (3) of every description.

Pier 4 Marina (4) has 36 slips with electricity up to 30 amps and a full assembly of marine businesses behind it in a six-story gray building.

IDENTIFICATIONS FOR CHART ON PG 279

Annapolis: Spa Creek

Chart #12283-E
Scale 1:10,000
reduced 10%

1.	O'Leary's Seafood Restaurant	66.	Harbormaster's office, showers, information
2.	Chart House Restaurant	67.	City mooring area
3.	Marine related businesses	68.	City Docks
4.	Pier 4 Marina	90.	Maryland Capital Yacht Club
5.	Marmaduke's Pub	91.	Eastport Yacht Club
8.	Annapolis City Marina (Womanship, Carroll's Creek Café)	92.	Severn Sailing Association
		93.	Spa Creek Bridge
		94.	Anchorage—above bridge
11.	Harbor Side Marine	95.	Anchorage—off sea wall
12.	Annapolis Rigging	96.	South Anchorage
13.	Annapolis Yacht Club	97.	Condominiums with docks
14.	Annapolis Yacht Basin	98.	Annapolis Harbor Boat Yard
15.	Marriott Hotel, Pusser's	99.	Yacht Haven
16.	Water Activities Center (Northeast Wind Yacht Group)	100.	Outfitters U.S.A.
17.	Fleet Reserve Club		**PUBLIC LANDINGS**
18.	Chesapeake Marine Tours	L1.	Prince George St. (Boat show only)
19.	Fawcett Boat Supplies	L2.	Market Slip (under 17')
20.	St. Mary's Catholic Church	L3.	Shipwright
21.	Carroll House	L4.	Revell St.
22.	Petrini Marina	L5.	Market St.
23.	Sarles Boat and Engine Shop	L6.	Conduit St.
24.	Arnold Gay Yacht Yard	L7.	Charles St.
25.	Anchorages—upper Spa Creek	L8.	Southgate Ave.
		L9.	Taney St.
41.	U.S. Naval Academy	L10.	Cheston St.
60.	Market Slip ("Ego Alley")	L11.	Lafayette Park
61.	Market Space, Kunta Kinte plaque	L12.	Monticello
		L13.	Amos Garret
63.	College Creek	L14.	Truxton Park
		L15.	4th St. Spa Creek
		L16.	1st St. Spa Creek
		L17.	3rd St. Back Creek
		L18.	4th St. Back Creek
		L19.	6th St. Back Creek

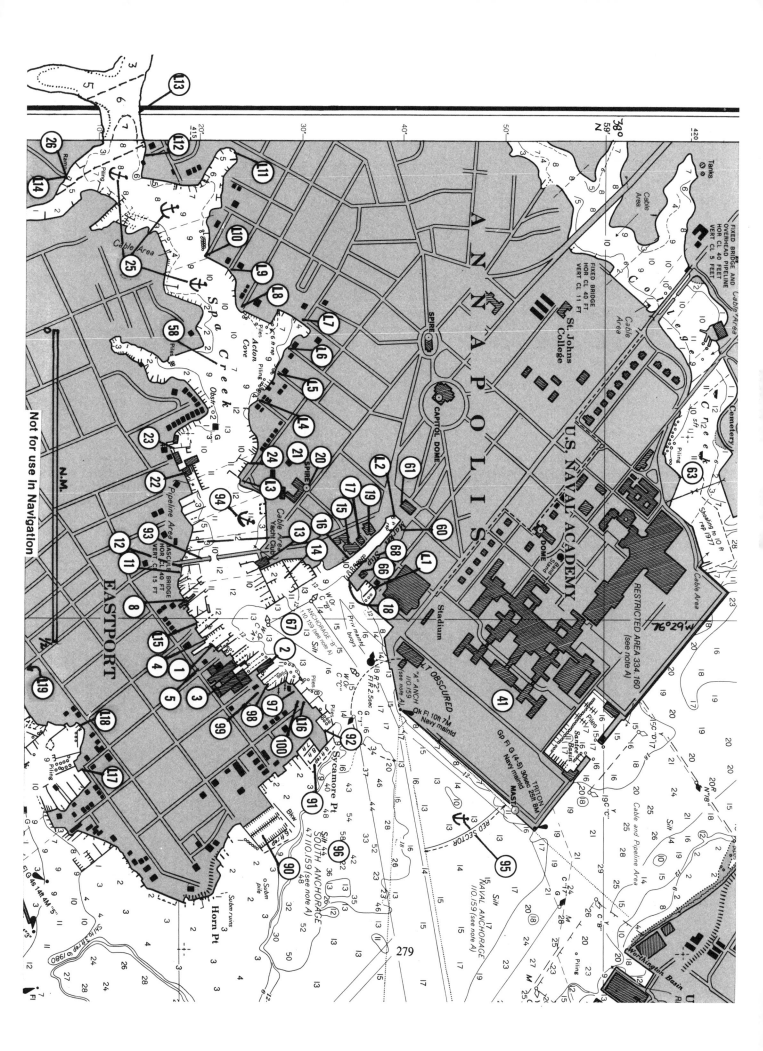

A block back from the water, you will find the popular Marmaduke's Pub (5) at 301 Severn Ave. There is a nice pub atmosphere as you enter, but with a distinct sailing flavor. This includes sailing and racing events played from a video over the bar, and a regular clientele involved with and interested in sailing. There is a piano bar upstairs with regular sing-alongs, and also a quiet dining room with entrees up to around $18.

In one of the buildings behind these docks, you will find one of the larger management and ownership companies on the Bay, Coastal Properties and Management, Inc. It either owns or manages a large assortment of facilities which you may wish to use as you cruise around the Bay. You can make reservations and arrangements here at this central office. It has an impressive record of well-run facilities. These include the **Lady Maryland Marina** at the Inner Harbor of Baltimore (see Chapter 14 for more discussion of this interesting marina and concept), Pier 4 (4) in Annapolis, **Piney Narrows Yacht Haven**, Kent Narrows Yacht Services, **Oxford Boat Yard**, Dickerson Boat Builders, Fort Washington on the Potomac (near Washington D.C.), and the **Town Center Marina** in Solomons on the Patuxent. You can contact the facilities individually or at this central number (410) 269-0933.

Also behind the Pier 4 (4) area is Northeast Wind Yacht Group, an organization that owns or manages various charter and marine interests around the Bay. These include the charter opportunities at the Marriott Dock such as the 74-foot *Woodwind*, a bed and breakfast called Green Street, approximately a half block's walk from City Dock, bare boat motor and sail charter operations in the Bay and other areas such as Mystic, CT and Naples, FL, the Steamboat Landing Restaurant and Marina in Galesville on the West River (see Chapter 19 for detailed description), and various marina accomodations around the Bay. You can call here at 800-638-5139 to arrange for their services all around the Bay.

Annapolis City Marina (8) has 90 slips up to 75 feet with electricity up to 50 amps, has a laundromat and marine store and block and cube ice, sells gas and diesel at an easy access dock with white painted pilings and red tops. There is a large five-story gray building (parking on street level) with numerous marine-related services, including the Womanship Sailing School for Women. Carroll's Creek Café is located on the second floor. This is a very popular restaurant serving lunch, dinner, and Sunday brunch. It will also deliver to boats.

Harbor Side Marine (11), has 45 slips and electricity up to 30 amps, lifting capacity up to 60 tons, and full service yard. Annapolis Rigging (12) can be found here.

With your gaze passing along the bridge to the north side of the creek, you will see **Annapolis Yacht Club (13)**, with its dock on the corner extending around almost to the bridge, and its impressive three-story building behind the docks.

Annapolis Yacht Basin (14) lies on the western side of the outer creek basin, just to the north of Annapolis Yacht Club docks, and to the south of the tall red brick Marriott Hotel (15). The Yacht Basin has a big Amoco sign over its dock house and 110 bulkheaded slips running up to 100 feet with longer space available alongside and electricity up to 50 amps, TV connections, laundromat, an easy access gas and diesel and pumpout dock.

Market Slip

Market Slip (60) was so named many years ago because it was here that commercial fishing boats came to sell from their docks to wholesalers and individuals alike. Around this Slip was a market area where they could get not only seafood, but groceries and other supplies. The fact that this is now known as "Ego Alley" does not mean that it no longer possesses these older characteristics. Very recently, we have seen commercial seafood boats selling crabs to individuals ashore, and there are still great marketing opportunities around the slip, described below. Up until a few years ago, there were parking meters around the quay, not for cars but for boats. Now you pay at the Harbormaster's office (66), by the hour or for the night. At the head of the Slip, a plaque (61) commemorates the arrival of Kunta Kinte in 1767. This was the African slave now so well known from the book "Roots" by Alex Haley.

Market Slip is called "Ego Alley" because of the number of boaters who love to parade their vessels up and down the slip to look at the other boats and sights, and to be looked at themselves. On any pretty evening you are apt to get a taste of the ego parade, but Wednesday evenings the parade picks up quite a bit. Friday evenings, and all day and much of the night Saturday, there is a constant stream of boats of all types and sizes coming into the Slip, turning around (hopefully) at the end, and steaming back out again. Sunday afternoons are perhaps the finest of the parade times. If you are tied to the city piers on the right (northeast) side, be prepared for the show, and you might also wish to have your fenders ready!

As you head into Market Slip, you will notice on your right (east) the two-story brick building of the Welcome Center and Harbormaster's office (66) on the second floor behind the large dark windows. Downstairs are the restrooms and showers for those at the city slips or moorings. The information center is in a brick booth between the building and the Slip. The city slips are all on that side of the Market Slip.

Annapolis Marriott Waterfront Hotel (15), on the outer southwestern side of Market Slip is six stories tall, and has dockage alongside at the quay at the entrance to Market Slip for boats up to 100 feet and more, with electricity up to 50 amps. There are 150 guest rooms and one suite, an exercise room, and most usual hotel services. The proximity of the Marriott makes Annapolis a good crew change port.

At the hotel's waterfront is the first East Coast "Pusser's Rum" facility, with a store, lounge and restaurant. It is extensively decorated in the tradition of old England and its ships, and is already very popular.

Also located here is the "Water Activities Center" (16) operated by the Northeast Wind Yacht Group, described above. This includes daysail charters, charter fishing, cruises on the 60-foot motor yacht the *Happy Daze VI*, electric paddle boat rentals, sport motor boat rentals, and sails on the beautiful 74-foot schooner *Woodwind* which you will normally find docked here.

Next in, on the same side as the Marriot, is the private Fleet Reserve Club (17). On the outer northeastern edge of Market Slip, you will notice several cruise boats of varying sizes. These belong to Chesapeake Marine Tours (18) They offer cruises of different types, durations, and destinations. Details can be obtained there.

On the southwestern side of the Slip is Fawcett Boat Supplies (19) and its 170 feet of bulkheading on the Slip for docking by its customers while they are in the store. This is an institution in the Bay, for years being one of the major suppliers of about anything that you could possibly want or need for your boat, from serious hardware, to clothing, to books, to gear and equipment, to dishes and cocktail napkins, and anything else. They are staffed by knowledgable boaters, often by experienced cruisers and liveaboards, who are very helpful with questions as to what you need and how to use it, and are knowledgeable about the services available in the surrounding area. Pricing here is very competitive, and you can see and study what you get, often finding on the shelves what you have desperately needed for years, but haven't even known how to look for. *Editor's Note: Fawcett has charts to everywhere, and one of the Bay's best nautical book shelves.*

Ashore all around Market Slip ("Ego Alley") are shopping and historical sights. The space immediately at the head of the Slip, where you may tie your tender, has a Market House and other marketing opportunities around it, and is called, appropriately, "Market Space" **(61)**.

At the very end of Market Slip is a popular dinghy landing **(L-2)** for tenders under 17 feet, Here you can land in the middle of downtown Annapolis with the convenience of all of the shops around the Slip within a few minutes walk. These are described below under "Annapolis Ashore."

Spa Creek Above (West of) the Bridge

Spa Creek above the bridge still has some marinas and services on its shore, but as soon as you pass through the bridge it begins to be quieter and more relaxed. This is where many people go to anchor, returning to the downtown area by dinghy, or landing at one of the many dinghy landing areas on the upper creek, **(L-4)** to **(L-12)**. Be sure that you anchor close to where we have drawn an anchor on our **chart #12283-E**. There's a cable area both sides of the bridge, and a pipeline area to the west of the anchorage. The anchorage is between the cable area and the pipeline area. Both these areas are shown on the chart.

Spa Creek Bridge **(93)** is very busy and very important to the community because of vehicular, pedestrian, and water traffic that it handles. It is one of the most walked across vehicular bridges that I have encountered. As a cruiser remaining for any time in that area, you will probably find yourself going under and over it as you go up and down the creek and walk between Eastport and the Market Slip area. The bridgetender's phone is (410) 974-3840. It has a large sign with an opening schedule long enough to fill a page and nearly impossible to read if there is any wind or tide which you must deal with. The schedule changes upon season, and there are rush hour restrictions. For the latest and the detailed schedule deviations, call the bridge tender on VHF Channel 13. Last year, the schedule was as follows: May 1 to October 31, Monday through Friday: opens on the hour and half hour, except from 7:30 a.m. to 9:00 a.m. and 4:30 p.m. to 7:30 p.m. it will be closed, except that it will open at 6:00 p.m. to 7:00 p.m. for waiting traffic. From November 1 to April 30, Monday through Friday: Opens on the hour and half hour except from 7:30 a.m. to 9:00 a.m. and from 4:30 p.m. to 6:00 p.m. On holidays and weekends year round, it opens on signal on the hour and half hour.

Editor's note: During our Chesapeake Bay cruise in the 1950s, Art Webber and I were tied at a slip at the Annapolis Yacht Club. just east of the bascule bridge. I had 'phoned my brother, Irve, who then worked for the U.S. Agriculture Department and lived in Silver Springs, MD. He and his wife would come down after work, have Happy Hour with us on my boat, then we'd all go to dinner ashore, and stay overnight at his house. He'd bring us back to the Yacht Club in the morning.

He showed up two hours late. The bridge opened for boat traffic, and some stupid hurried driver tried to beat the opening. He didn't make it. His front wheels hung over the opening, and they couldn't close the bridge! Art and I could see what was happening, and started our own Happy Hour. Irve

Harbormaster's Office (left) and Visitor Information (right)

281

never knew why he was hung up in traffic for two hours. It took forever for a tow truck with a crane to lift the car off the bridge. I hope that's a rare happening. but this is one busy bridge!

When you pass through the bridge, you will immediately encounter boats anchored (94), to be close to the central area. Note that there is a cable area to both sides of the bridge. No one would want to anchor this close to the bridge, but it is also important that anchors not be dragged across the bottom in this area, as can sometimes happen when setting or retrieving an anchor. As mentioned above, there is also a pipeline area west of the anchorage (94). Both are shown on the chart. The anchorage is between them.

The first set of docks to your left (south) after you pass through the bridge now belongs to the Annapolis Yacht Club (13). To your right (north), the tall spire of St. Mary's Catholic Church (20) graces the skyline ashore; next to it is Carroll House (21). Both are described below in the section on Annapolis Ashore.

Petrini Marina (22) and facilities, up farther on the left (south), has a blue and white sign with 60 slips with electricity up to 50 amps, and a 50-ton lift with a full service yard.

Next up on the same side is **Sarles Boat and Engine Shop (23)** with a large Amoco sign for gas and diesel. Here there are 50 slips, both opened and covered, railway with capacity up to 20 tons, and a smaller lift, and a full service yard. This yard has been in business since 1907.

Arnold Gay Yacht Yard (24) with 35 slips, some capable of taking boats up to 80 feet, with electricity up to 50 amps, is on the opposite shore. This is only several blocks from the downtown area. Arnold Gay's business is another long-established Annapolis shipyard.

Proceeding up the creek, you will find houses and condominiums on both sides, with boats anchored and moored almost the length of the creek. You should avoid the cable areas noted on the chart. These are generally marked on both sides of the creek with slender vertical signs denoting the crossing. Interpret these liberally and give the areas between the signs a wide berth.

At its head, the creek splits into two forks, each of which has fewer houses and becomes marshy. The anchorages (25) in the upper creek are less crowded, but a longer dinghy ride to the downtown area. One particularly nice spot up here is in the long cove pointing off to the south, on the southern bank, just before you reach the split. On the western banks of this cove is a very nice city park with a public ramp (26). Because of the trees and park, the area at the mouth of the cove is very attractive. Again, avoid the cable area. The ramp can make this busy on weekends, but the entire area is busy.

Annapolis History

The area around Annapolis was first settled in 1649 by Puritans who came up from Virginia and built on the northern bank of the Severn, naming their settlement "Providence." Lord Baltimore was busily engaged in establishing Catholic holdings in the area, and established a strong settlement down the Bay at St. Mary's. When he began settling the Severn, the Puritans resisted. Finally, Lord Baltimore's governor, William Stone, sailed up the Severn in 1655 to assert authority. The two sides fought on Horn Point on Spa Creek, and the Puritans won, killing many of the Catholics and capturing Stone. For several years thereafter, the Puritans held authority in the area, finally losing it to the wealthy and politically powerful Calverts.

In 1660, the first surveying was performed on the southern bank for a town to be called "Anne Arundel Town" after Lady Anne Arundel, wife of Cecil Calvert. In 1694, it was renamed, after England's Queen Anne when it became the capital of the colony of Maryland, thus "Annapolis." Because of its central location, excellent harbor, and early development, it became a center of shipping, commerce, government and culture by the mid-1700s, with many fine homes built around that time.

Our country's third-oldest college, now called St. John's, was founded here in 1696. On this campus stands the "Liberty Tree" (46), a 400-year-old tulip tree, which was a rallying place for the local Sons of Liberty of the Revolutionary War. The four Maryland signers of the Declaration of Independence had homes here, which you can see today. This period became known as the "golden age of Annapolis." Many at this time considered the town to have been the "Athens" of the colonies. Many of the homes and other buildings of the time are still in use and well-preserved. They can be visited today within a short walk of the waterfront.

Three Centuries Tours, phone (410) 263-5401, conducts excellent tours guided by knowledgable and entertaining citizens dressed in period costumes.

Annapolis was one of the many centers of discontent in the period leading to the American Revolution. After the Boston Tea Party of 1773, citizens of Annapolis, in 1774, forced the sinking of a merchant ship which had carried tea and been forced to pay taxes to off-load the tea, and numerous indentured servants. In 1772 the State House was built. This is still operating and is said to be the oldest continuously operating State Capitol building. In December, 1783, George Washington resigned his Commision as Commander-in-Chief of the Continental Army in this building, which was then being used as the temporary capitol of the new country. A short time later, the Treaty of Paris was ratified in this building.

During the War of 1812, two forts which had been built at the mouth of the Severn were manned, in expectation of British attack by sea. The British fleet sailed up the Patuxent, to the south, and landed, eventually marching to take and burn Washington. They then proceeded up the Bay, by-passing Annapolis, although lookouts were able to count and evaluate the British ships and pass on this helpful information to defenders of Ft. McHenry in Baltimore, where the British eventually unsuccessfully attacked as Francis Scott Key watched.

After the Revolutionary War, the town's prominence as a seaport diminished somewhat, as was characteristic of other towns on the Bay. In 1845, the U.S. Naval Academy was founded here, and since then has played a significant role in the community's development and character. A guided tour should be a must. A visitor's center has a souvenir shop and excellent tours.

During the War Between the States, the town had a great deal of Southern sympathy. Lincoln had received only three votes from the county. But Union troops under Benjamin Butler (called "Benjamin the Beast" by some unhappy with his occupation) and the forces at the Naval Academy helped to keep the area within the Union fold.

The area's history was quieter after that, with agricultural and seafood businesses growing around the shores.

Today, a walk up the narrow brick paved streets between the old buildings provides a unique taste of the early history of our country and one of its finer cities, preserved in working form by the people who live their daily lives there. Several tours and historical pamphlets are available through the Information Center (66).

ANNAPOLIS ASHORE
Refer to our Sketch Map, "Annapolis—Historic Area."
PG 285

There is a plethora of very helpful guide pamphlets (most of which are free), and tours to allow you to exhaust your desires for shoreside forays, either for shopping or historical study. *Editor's note: A tour is always a good idea in a strange city, to orient you, and provide an overall view. You can then go back to the areas that interest you the most. In Annapolis, these are walking tours because everything is so close together that a walking tour is practical.*

The pamphlets and guide information can be obtained at the Information Center in front of the Harbormaster's office (66), or by calling the Annapolis and Anne Arundel County Conference and Visitors Bureau at (410) 268-TOUR. This very helpful organization should be contacted prior to your visit so that you will have time to study what they have to offer and savor your plans. You may also wish to contact the Chamber of Commerce at (410) 268-7676. Shuttle bus information can be obtained at (410) 263-7964. There are at least three guided tours available. Information on these is available at the information booth.

You can begin from anywhere you have your boat. The water taxi service, the dinghy landings, the close proximity even to Back Creek of much of the area, makes this quite feasible. If you want to shop for anything imaginable, simply pick up one of the pamphlets described earlier for detailed information.

Around City Dock

Around the waterfront at City Dock, you will find much of what you may need. Fawcett's (19) at the inside southwestern corner of the Slip has already been mentioned.

In the Market House, originally built in 1858, in the center of the Market Space (61) at the head of the Slip, you will find prepared and raw fresh seafood, pizza, bakery goods, yogurt, poultry, a coffee shop, sandwiches, deli food, and various other items.

Stevens Hardware (2) is located on the northeastern side of the Slip, on Dock Street, facing the water. This is an old-fashioned hardware store which also sells items of interest to boaters. Bay Country Electronics (3) at 4 Dock Street, behind the Harbormaster's Building, has a wide assortment of marine electronics, experienced repair service, knowledgeable assistance, and competitive prices.

On the corner of Prince George Street and Randall (about a half block east from Market Space) is Rainbow Cleaners (4), offering one day service. Also, on Dock Street (5) east of the Slip, is a bike shop and a sports clothing shop. There is an ice cream shop here, and there are some very nice ones within around two blocks walk up Main Street (6).

Several nice restaurants are also in this immediate area around the Slip. These include the Harborhouse (7) behind the dockmaster's building; Armadillo's, featuring Mexican and American cuisine and often live entertainment, with entrees up to around $17; the historical Middleton's Tavern (9) (at City Dock and Randall Street), which was opened as an inn for seafaring men in 1750, and now serves both light and full fare in an authentic historical setting inside (entrees ranging up to around $40) as well as a sidewalk café; Maria's Sicillian Ristorante (10) at 12 Market Space with authentic Italian cuisine including freshly-cut veal dishes and fresh seafood; and McGarvey's (11) on Dock Street, also locally popular. Above the Banana Republic store on 100 Main Street, and overlooking the City Dock, is Buddy's Crabs and Ribs (22). This is a must restaurant for crabs. They take special care to assure that your crabs have both claws and are full of meat. At Cornhill Street and Market Place, Riordan's Saloon and Restaurant (23) has a raw bar, fresh seafood and ribs, in an early 1900s atmosphere. Griffins offers quiet atmosphere and fine dining.

On the corner of Compromise and Main Streets, in the northwest corner of the Slip area, is the Annapolis Summer Garden Theater (25). The shows are varied, including Broadway hits. The actors are usually local talent. The audience sits "under the stars" in what is believed to have been the stable area where George Washington's horses were kept when he came to town. The Theater building is the "Old Shaw Blacksmith Shop" which was there as early as the 1690s.

Just around the corner and up Main Street is the Victualling Warehouse Maritime Museum (26). The original building on the site was built in 1740 and was a food supply center for the Continental Army. Now the museum contains displays depicting aspects of the area's maritime history.

Inshore from City Dock

A stroll up Cornhill Street (in a northwesterly direction) provides a quick and interesting view into the antiquity of the

Author's *Chez Nous* at Fawcett's, a large marine supply store with an excellent selection of charts and nautical books. Capitol dome in right background

area around you. Gaily painted houses crowd close together over the quiet brick street. Residences and small shops remind you of what this area was like in the early days of its civilization. Cornhill and Fleet Street intersect in a V, and here you will find a building built within the "V" and opening back onto each street. Looking uphill on Cornhill Street, you will see the State House (27) on the hill in State Circle.

If you head in a northwesterly direction up the brick paved Main Street (6), you will find a great many shops. stores, services and restaurants as you walk uphill. Here are clothing stores, liquor and wine shops, a bath and home store, galleries, jewelers, one-hour photo stores, pharmacies, a very nice ice cream shop, a gourmet coffee shop, a sushi bar, all within about three blocks. You can also find a Burger King (29) just north on the other side of Conduit Street, although you may not recognize it, because its building conforms to the local historical guideline codes.

Continuing on up Main will bring you to Church Circle. The tall spire of St. Anne's Church (30) will have been your beacon ahead during this walk. The original church was build here in 1692. King William presented a silver communion service to the church in 1695, and it is still in use today. There is a U.S. Post Office (31) on the northern side of the circle. From the circle, the streets fan out like spokes of a wheel, School Street being the quickest link to State Circle, less than a block away.

The Maryland Inn (32), in the V corner and spreading out between Main and Duke of Gloucester Streets, is on the site of the "Drummer's Lot." From 1712 and many years after, a drummer boy would stand here and give news to residents through various combinations of beats, somewhat like a town crier. Among other duties, he called the General Assembly to session and kept the town gate closed to keep out the cows.

As in all good systems, there were a few flaws. Occasionally the drummers, with a little extra spirits from local taverns, were said to have drummed late in the night with messages not quite appropriate. Shortly after 1772, an elegant home was built here. Today, with additions, this is the Maryland Inn. It has enjoyed a long history as an important inn. As an example of its past, Spanish admirals who were being held as prisoners of war were quartered here.

You can stay as a guest overnight, or just dine in its prestigious fine restaurant, The Treaty of Paris (32). The entrance is down the Duke of Gloucester Street. Entrees here range over $50 in this formal restaurant, located just below street level. There is also the popular King of France (32) tavern here, which often features well-known entertainers.

If you continue away from Church Circle and down Duke of Gloucester Street, you will eventually reach the Spa Creek Bridge to Eastport, unless you turn left (easterly) on Green Street to get back to Market Space. On this walk you will be passing through quiet historical homes, and also pass the Town Hall (33) on the eastern side of the street. On the western side of the street where Newman Street intersects, you'll see St. Mary's Catholic Church (20) built in 1858. Over this is the beautiful white steeple that you will see on the northern bank just after you pass through the Spa Creek bridge and anchor in the upper reaches of that creek. Behind the Church is the Carroll House (21), the birthplace of Charles Carroll, the only Catholic to sign the Declaration of Independence.

If you leave Church Circle at Franklin Street, walking in a westerly direction, you will find the Bannecker-Douglass Museum (34) at 84 Franklin Street. This contains exhibits and displays of African-American culture and arts. There are lectures, films and changing exhibits. This is located in the Vic-torian-Gothic structure which used to be the Old Mount Moriah African Methodist Episcopal Church.

If you leave Church Circle by turning in an easterly direction and walking out on School Street, you'll see the white dome of the Maryland Statehouse (27) ahead in State Circle. This was built in 1772 through 1779, and served as the Capitol of the U.S. from November 26, 1783 through August 1784. This building has a beautiful lawn and brick-paved road encircling it. It is surrounded by many other buildings of historical interest, still in use today as government offices, inns, restaurants, and other uses. From here, looking easterly, you can see the green dome with gold top of the Naval Academy Chapel (35).

State Circle and Maryland Avenue (36) running east from it toward the Naval Academy, are considered by Annapolitans to be a unique and very special area within the rest of the historical district. In 1696, when the town was laid out, this highest point was chosen for the State House. Roads were laid out from it as spokes in a wheel. By the 18th century, Maryland Avenue (36) was considered to be the most fashionable street, upon which many fine homes were built. Now the shops and restaurants around the circle and down this avenue are favored by many because of their special service and merchandise. Also in this circle is the Governor's Mansion (37), with an offspring of the Wye oak planted here in 1987. See Chapter 10 on the Wye River.

A walk of around two blocks in an easterly direction out Randall Street from City Market brings you to Gate 1, the visitor's entrance to the United States Naval Academy (41) which can be toured through its Visitor's Center (41) just inside Gate 1. The phone is (410) 263-6933. Among areas of special interest is the Chapel with Tiffany windows. The Chapel was built in 1904 with its cornerstone laid by Admiral Dewey. Here is the crypt of naval hero John Paul Jones. There is also

IDENTIFICATIONS FOR MAP ON PG 285

Annapolis—Historic Area

L1.	Dinghy landing (during boat show only)	30.	St. Anne's Church
L2.	Dinghy landing—Market Slip	31.	Post Office
2.	Stevens Hardware	32.	Maryland Inn and Treaty of Paris Restaurant, King of France Tavern
3.	Bay Country Electronics		
4.	Rainbow Cleaners	33.	Town Hall
5.	Shops (bike, ice cream, sports clothing, imports)	34.	Banneker-Douglass Museum
		35.	U.S. Naval Academy Chapel
6.	Main Street shopping district	36.	Maryland Avenue (business district)
7.	Harborhouse Restaurant		
8.	Armadillo's	37.	Governor's Mansion
9.	Middleton's Tavern	38.	Hospital—Anne Arundel Medical Center (410) 267-1000
10.	Maria's Sicilian Ristorante		
11.	McGarvey's		
13.	Annapolis Yacht Club	39.	Reynold's Tavern
14.	Annapolis Yacht Basin	41.	U.S. Naval Academy Visitor's Center
15.	Annapolis Marriott Hotel, Pusser's		
		42.	William Paca House and Gardens
16.	Northeast Wind Yacht Group	43.	Brice House
17.	Fleet Reserve Club	44.	Hammond-Harwood House
18.	Chesapeake Marine Tours	45.	Chase—Lloyd House
19.	Fawcett Boat Supplies	46.	St. John's College and Liberty Tree
20.	St. Mary's Catholic Church		
21.	Charles Carroll Mansion	47.	Anne Arundel County Courthouse
22.	Buddy's Crabs and Ribs		
23.	Riordan's	48.	Shiplap House
24.	Arnold Gay Yacht Yard	49.	Ogle Hall—Alumni House
25.	Annapolis Summer Garden Theater	61.	Market house, market space
		66.	Harbormaster, restrooms, visitor information
26.	Victualling Warehouse Maritime Museum		
		67.	City moorings
27.	State House and Old Treasury	68.	City docks
29.	Burger King	93.	Eastport Bridge

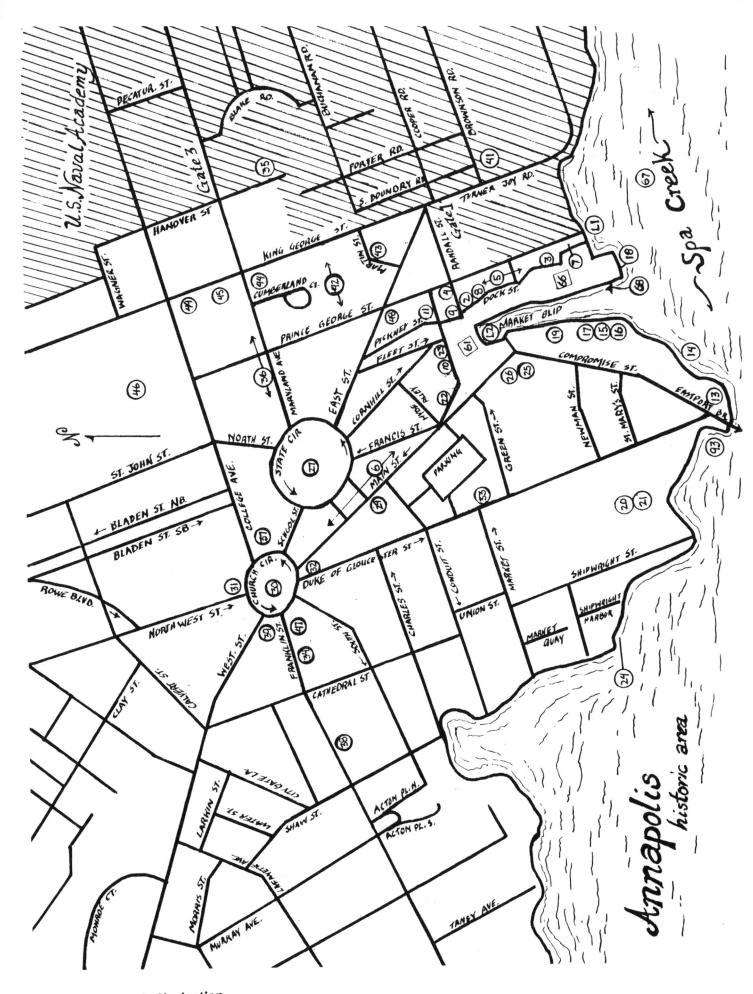

a Naval Academy Museum, and the foremast of the battleship Maine, destroyed in Cuba before the Spanish-American War, and many other items of interest. Foremost is the insight into the daily living and training of the future officers of the Unites States Navy.

Instead of walking up into the town from the City Dock if you wish to walk over to Eastport from the head of Market Slip, walk south down Compromise Street. After a little over two blocks, you will find the Spa Creek Bridge (93). In 1781, General Lafayette encamped on the shore of the creek on the Eastport side of the Bridge. Take Severn Avenue, the first street to your left (northeast) just after you reach the other side, and walk northeasterly to find the land entrances to the many businesses described earlier in this chapter on the Eastport side of Spa Creek east of the bridge. The shore of the Back Creek with its facilities is just a few blocks away.

SEVERN RIVER ABOVE ANNAPOLIS THROUGH ROUND BAY

Refer to Chart #12282-E—"Severn River—from Bridges to below Round Bay."

Above Annapolis, the Severn River is beautiful, with high banks and many nice spots for anchoring. Opportunities ashore are limited unless you go into Annapolis.

Most people visit Annapolis and then leave this beautiful area, but the Severn above Annapolis is a great place to gunkhole, hide from serious weather, or park while doing business in town if you have a fast dinghy, or can arrange land transportation. .

As you head past the mouth of Spa Creek, you will see buildings and roads and a bridge ahead, but these are not a prelude of things to come. The bridges (25) and (34) are fixed and have an 80-clearance. The old bascule bridge (25) shown on the chart has been replaced by a fixed high-rise bridge, 80 feet clearance. The way ahead is relatively easy as long as you stay off the points, and watch the chart and aids to navigation. The chart shows a line of "submerged ruins" and "submerged piles" (26) running in a northeasterly direction off the southwest bank of the Severn just upstream from Horseshoe Point between the bridges. We remained in the middle of the river and saw no sign of this.

The bustle of Annapolis and the Naval Academy quickly gives way northwest of the bridges to a quiet river of high hills. There are many homes, but much of the river was built in planned communities, with the result that most of the homes are back in the trees. Most of the spots that look like landings, beaches, or marinas are actually private community facilities with no public landing.

As you approach the mouth of Weems Creek (62), you will see the large white mansion of Manresa (27) high on the hill opposite (north of) the southern bank of the creek, and tall red cliffs on the same bank just upstream. There will be many more impressive large homes set within high hills and cliffs as you travel upriver.

Weems Creek

Weems Creek (62) has many moorings and homes, with West Annapolis along its eastern bank. However, there is usually room to anchor and there is a landing (L-20) between the bridges on the eastern bank. Many of the moorings, both in this creek and others in the vicinity, belong to the Naval

Academy and are so marked on their large white floats. They are primarily used during hurricane warnings.

This creek is easily identified because it is the first major creek on your left (southwest) after you pass the first bridge (25). There is a "WC" marker (28) to the east northeast off the point to your right (northwest point) as you enter. The shoal comes up abruptly and should be given wide berth.

The first cove to your right (northwest), behind that outside point on the creek is a very pretty anchorage (29), although too exposed for some. There are woods up on the shore, enough fetch for a breeze on a hot night, and the houses on the southeastern shore are not overbearing. As you go farther up, the creek will become more sheltered, also more congested.

Most boats anchor in the basin (30) before the first bridge. There are also many boats here on private moorings and many houses ashore with docks. Many tenders land on the southeastern shore (21), just downstream of the bridge, on a beach with a big oak tree where they tie their tenders. This may be curtailed in the future, check for signs. This is within a neighborhood and those using the landing here should be careful not to inadvertently tresspass or interfere with private property. This is near the foot of Annapolis Street. A walk toward Annapolis of about two blocks down Ridgley Road (the road that passes over the bridge and which is about one block southwest from Annapolis Street) will bring you to the Northwoods Restaurant, at 609 Melvin Avenue. This has a very high local reputation and specializes in fine Italian cuisine and fresh seafood. The atmosphere within the restaurant is quite nice, but informal dress is acceptable. There is also a supermarket, and a small shopping center which includes a drugstore, all within a few blocks. The Annapolis downtown Market Slip area is over 1½ miles away, walking out Annapolis Street along some roads that become quite busy with traffic in places.

The drawbridge (31) opens on demand from sunrise to sunset, May 1 to October 31; after that, and on all evenings, you must call (410) 841-5466 and give 3 hours notice. Once you do this, they will not wait for more than 15 minutes from the time for which you must request an opening. The bridgetender's house is under the bridge, up against the southern bank of the river. Annie has been the tender for some time, and can be very helpful with local information when she has time to talk. People frequently drive their tenders up to her "front door" and stop to chat.

The area between the two bridges is not as congested with moorings and other boats, and also makes a snug anchorage (32). Sirens and horns and sound of the roadways are noticeable in this part of the creek. The next bridge (33) is fixed with a vertical clearance of only 28 feet. Above it there are fewer anchored boats, and also less congestion on the shore with high hills and trees.

Luce Creek

Luce Creek (35) has many moorings, including Navy moorings. In the branch to your right (36) (west) at the end, there is a pretty cove with 8½ feet of depth just above the last mooring, but note the 4 feet controlling depth at the Luce Creek entrance. On the shore in the cove (36) is a very pretty older house almost at water level with slender white columns supporting a second story front porch, brick chimneys on each end, and a beautiful weeping willow tree in front. The house was built at the base of a ravine, with hills all around, and reminds me of what real working country farm homes were all about when I was young. This makes a pretty anchorage.

TIDAL INFORMATION

Place		Height referred to datum of soundings (MLLW)			
Name	(LAT/LONG)	Mean Higher High Water	Mean High Water	Mean Low Water	Extreme Low Water
		feet	feet	feet	feet
Annapolis	(38°59'N/76°29'W)	1.4	1.1	0.2	-4.0
Mountain Point, Gibson Island	(39°04'N/76°26'W)	1.2	1.0	0.2	-4.5

(589)

Not for use in Navigation

Severn River—from Bridges to
Below Round Bay
Chart #12282-E
Scale 1:25,000

L20. Public Landing
25. Bascule bridge replaced by
    80' vertical clearance
    high-rise
26. Submerged piles and ruins
27. Manresa
28. "WC" with long shoal
29. Anchorage
30. Anchorage
31. Swing bridge
    ("Annie's house")
32. Anchorage between bridges
33. Fixed bridge
34. High-rise fixed bridge—80'
    vertical clearance
35. Luce Creek
36. Fixed bridge (28' vertical
    clearance)

37. Cool Spring Cove—
    anchorage
38. 6 mph speed limit sign—treat
    as red marker
39. 120' red cliff
40. Chase Creek
41. Shoal at "2A"—(extends
    beyond "2A")
42. Northern branch—
    private moorings
43. Eastern branch—anchorage
44. Saltworks Creek
45. Shoal at entrance
46. Clements Creek
47. Anchorage

48. Brewer Creek
49. Brewer Pond
62. Weems Creek

287

Looking back out of the creek, you see the red cliffs all the way across the Severn.

Cool Spring Cove

Cool Spring Cove (37) on the northeastern shore has a name that surely invites, but it is guarded by a difficult shoal coming off the point to your right (south) after you enter. Stay well off this point, almost into the left (northwest) bank. The shoal is very shallow and there is a cement bulkhead just below the water at high tide running out on the shoal. There is a 6 MPH speed sign (38) just off the point, and it is necessary to treat that as a red buoy, keeping it to your right going in. The location of this buoy (38) may be changed when you enter. We found controlling depth in this narrow entrance to be almost 10 feet when we were in the right place.

Once inside there is a nice cove, but with many houses up on the hills, many docks coming out into the water, and a feeling of a lack of privacy for anchoring, although this is very snug for weather once you get in. The surrounding ground is very high. Note the 120-foot red cliffs (39) on the northwestern bank as you enter.

Chase Creek

Chase Creek (40) also has high red cliffs guarding its western bank. Guarding its entrance is the shoal extending from the western outer point. This shoal extends beyond the Red Marker "2A" (41), making downstream toward the bridge. Stay well south of that marker. Inside there are almost shore-to-shore private moorings in the northern branch (42), with more open water and less congestion in the eastern branch (43) which is narrower.

Saltworks Creek

The entrance to Saltworks Creek (44) has a tricky shoal (45) extending easterly off its western bank. If you come in from the downriver side, favoring the south, you should miss it. Inside the creek, the hills are very high and steep right at the water's edge and covered with homes. Many of these homes sit close enough to the water to look down into your cockpit. There are also many moorings, including Naval Academy moorings. The homes in this pretty creek continue on right up to the end.

Clements Creek

Clements Creek (46) has a wide entrance and many moorings inside, both private and Navy. There are many houses ashore with both individual docks and community docking areas along the creek. We felt that the nicest spot for anchoring was just upstream (westerly) of where the plotted moorings stop (47). Here there are fewer homes, park-like docking areas ashore, and much wood and marsh on both sides.

Brewer Creek

Brewer Creek (48) is deep and pretty with very high shores on either side, but it is very crowded, too much so to make a pleasant anchorage for most people. On the right (north) the high sides have four tiers of houses rising up from the water's edge, one over the other, each tier set back and above the lower one, ascending up the hill. The left (south) bank only has one row of houses, but it is all along the upper reaches of the bank, all the homes having a great view down into the creek. Boat docks line the creek on both sides, and there are many boats on private moorings.

U.S. Naval Academy Midshipmen sailing in the Severn River

Fleet Street Shops, Annapolis

McGarvey's Saloon, Annapolis

Brewer Pond

Refer to Chart #12282-F—"Severn River—Round Bay to the Narrows."

Brewer Pond (49) is of interest primarily as a gunkholer dinghy explorer's delight. It looks impossible on the chart, and the entry is very shallow. I suggest dinghy only, but its very pretty and rewarding inside. It is separated from the river by a high cliff-finger of land with trees atop, but this is narrow and has washed away in the middle so that you can see through inside from the river. There is a beach (50) along its shore and on this point. The entrance is just upstream (to the west of) a very impressive pier (51) coming out north from the southwestern bank of the Severn, north of "Sherwood Forest." This pier has a green roof over the end and part of the dock, with a netted swimming area on its eastern side. It is private and is a part of a local community club. Across the river (on the northeastern bank) there is a huge and beautiful home high up in the trees on Arnold Point (52).

I could find no more than 2 feet at the entrance. I had to finally give up looking for a deeper cut because my dinghy outboard propeller kept digging at the bottom. It may be there somewhere where I wasn't. There is a stump (53) that could be submerged at high water, to the west of the dock, about half way down the length of the dock, toward the spit of sand to the north of the entrance. I would go in favoring the dock if I could not see the stump.

ROUND BAY AND VICINITY

As you pass between Brewer and Arnold Points, Round Bay (54) opens up with its wide spaces, high tree-covered hills, and St. Helena Island (55). There are many homes around in this pleasant area. Many choose to anchor (56) behind St. Helena, picking their spot to suit the breezes, or up in the creeks to the southwest of the island.

As you begin your turn to the northwest toward St. Helena Island, you will love the high, wooded, seemingly unpopulated hill (57) on the outer southern shore of Little Round Bay (58). We did not find any wreck (59) as indicated on the chart to the east of the island, nor was there any marked. St. Helena's has some interesting homes tucked up behind the trees, and bunkers built back into the hill just above the water on the southern side. Note well the underwater cable area (60) on the western side of the island. There are slender vertical cable markers on each end. The marker on the island is easy to spot, but the western one is up in Brown's Cove (61) and more difficult to pick out. It is in front of a small white house that you will see on the northern bank of the cove, as you look in.

If you don't want to anchor in the open spaces around the island, there are two great creeks for snug anchoring enjoyment.

Editor's note: We anchored once in the bight on the north shore to visit a friend who lived there. Round Bay is one of the most beautiful anchorages in the beautiful Severn River.

Hopkins and Maynadier Creeks (off Round Bay)

Hopkins Creek (62) has an intriguing entrance in deep water passing close to the tip of the finger point beckoning you in. Unlike many guardian finger points which have deeper water behind them allowing anchorage close to a beach, we found the water behind this to be shallow as indicated (63).

This is a very pretty creek, with some homes but also a great deal of woods and natural shoreline. The first cove (64) to your left (southeast) is very pretty and affords a beautiful, snug anchorage with high wooded hills all around. There is a house noticeable within the trees on its northeastern bank, but nearly hidden. Proceeding farther up into the creek in a southwesterly direction, you will find more homes at first, then a relaxation back to nature toward the end. Anchor anywhere in here to suit your draft.

Maynadier Creek (66) provides great protection after you pass Mathiers Point to your north and the next little point to your south. When you approach the entrance, be sure to keep G "3" to your left (south). The shoal (67) that it guards comes well off the shore, and there is a tendency to pass the green on the wrong side. There is a pretty beach on Mathiers Point. This creek is amply populated, but the basin at the end makes a nice anchorage (68) with enough space available to be far enough from the homes, most of which are set back in the woods. Within the basin, you will notice mostly trees ashore and some marsh before the hills rise from the creek. I found a little less depth than the chart indicated, but enough for a 6½-foot draft boat. The deeper water is along the northwest side. This may be a popular skiing area on weekends.

Browns Cove (off Round Bay)

Brown's Cove (61), to the west of St. Helena Island, is too busy and full of boats and docks to provide good anchorage. Smith's Marina (69) there has Amoco gas (Visa, Amoco, MC are taken), 60 slips up to 40 feet and 15 amp electric, and a little store with some snacks and beverages, a few marine supplies, and block and cube ice. This marina could be a handy place to pick up such items if you are anchored nearby. There is also a 35-ton lift and a hard surfaced ramp. They specialize in inboard, stern drive, and outboard repairs as well as other full service repair work. If entering the cove, you will see a small red float and a green float (70) between the two points guarding the cove. I found controlling depths to be 5 feet at the marina area, with greater depths coming in.

SEVERN RIVER ABOVE ROUND BAY

Many cruising boats stop with Round Bay, but the Severn River offers many more scenic anchorages. Heading upriver from Round Bay, you will see a generous scattering of docks and homes among the trees on the high hills.

Plum and Valentine Creeks

Plum (71) and Valentine Creeks (72) are both very pretty with hills and woods, the nice homes set back into the trees. Either branch is fine for anchoring. We prefer the branch to your left (southern) because it is a bit prettier. There are docks serving the homes almost everywhere. This branch is particularly nice, with more natural surroundings at its end in the little basin. Depths here are shallow, and if you draw more than 3½ feet, feel your way carefully in this basin. Take care to avoid a cable area here. The cable area is marked with the usual vertical white signs. If they are gone when you visit or you can't find them, go elsewhere rather than take a chance.

Yantz Creek

Yantz Creek (73) is another intruiging-looking entrance

Severn River—Round Bay
to the Narrows
Chart #12282-F
Scale 1:25,000

49. Brewer Pond
50. Beach
51. Pier at Sherwood Forest
52. Arnold Point
53. Stump
54. Round Bay

55. St. Helena Island
56. Anchorages
57. High hill
58. Little Round Bay
59. Wreck
60. Cable area
61. Brown's Cove
62. Hopkins Creek
63. Shallow area inside spit
64. Anchorages
66. Maynadier Creek
67. Shoal at entrance to creeks
68. Anchorage (ski area on weekends)
69. Smith's Marina
70. Private red and green markers
71. Plum Creek
72. Valentine Creek—Anchorage

73. Yantz Creek (2½ feet controlling depth at entrance)
74. Sign (private) at Sandy Spit
75. Anchorage—shoal draft (2½')
76. Forked Creek
77. Anchorage
78. Sappington's Yacht Yard
79. Low fixed bridge
80. Large estate on bluff, "no tresspassing" sign
81. Rock Cove

Not for use in Navigation

problem on the chart, but there is a shallow channel in, between the tip and the spit and the land to its north. As you approach, it seems as though the sandy spit goes all the way across, but the channel will open as you get close. A sign on the sandy spit (74) proclaims that it is a private community beach. I found 2½ feet to be the controlling depth just inside the cut, although there was more depth in the cut itself. The chart notes a wreck (position doubtful) in the area. We did not find one in the channel.

Once you get inside, you will find a nice wide landlocked pond surrounded by hills and houses, with many docks and boats moored. Anchoring in the middle of the basin (75) affords some privacy, allows you to see all over the spit into the Severn, and gives the protection of the hills on all sides but the southwest.

Forked Creek

You can go right past Forked Creek (76) without seeing its entrance, but it will open up after you get close to the tip of the 40-foot high bluff and look back north. This creek is not as attractive as others because of the number of homes ashore and the boating congestion. It is a good snug anchorage (77) and there's a marina inside. As you head up to the entrance you will see inside a large gray corrugated metal boathouse (78) on the point where it forks. The entrance point on your right (east) has a beach and trees. There are fine homes on the high land to your left (west). The right (eastern) fork winds up into the hills lined with docks with homes above. Most of the homes have plentiful trees around. This fork ends in a little cul-de-sac with two huge white-columned mansions up on the hill to the north. One of these had a fast boat lifted on hoists and a blue canopy over it. We found 7½ feet depth here.

The left (northwest) branch dies quickly for boaters because of a very low fixed solid bridge (79) crossing. The big boat house on the split belongs to **Sappington's Yacht Yard (78)**. They have moorings, 130 open and covered slips with electricity up to 30 amps, and a 50-ton railway and smaller lift. There are a few rowboats for rent here also. A MerCruiser sign is over one of the docks. We found 8 feet depth up to the marina.

Rock Cove

Passing by the mouth of Forked Creek, you will see a rather spectacular estate on the 40-foot bluff (80) on the northern side of the river. The tip of this is a pretty rocky beach. When we passed it, was guarded with a very serious "no tresspassing" sign. Rock Cove (81) to the west of this point has a pretty view to its eastern bank with tall red cliffs, and a view of many homes along the shore of the creek to its west.

UPPER SEVERN RIVER
Refer to Chart #12282-G—"Upper Severn River (above Round Bay)."

Proceeding on, you will see the docks and house of "Fairwinds on the Severn" (82) on the northern bank of the Severn, just before Stevens Creek (83), which ends quickly inside with homes and docks. The southern shore in this section is sparsely built with mostly deep looking woods on its hills.

As you pass the narrow opening to the south of Mathews Point (84) with its large beige colored brick house and manicured lawn, you will see another bay opening (85), complete with islands and beautiful surroundings.

A little island in the middle (86) has a tiny clump of trees on its highest part with beach around its shore. When we last passed through on a hot August day, it was literally covered with boys and dogs, all gleefully playing on the island and in the waters around. It is possible to anchor (87) fairly close to the northeast side of the island in 7 feet depth. You can anchor farther north in this cove to get more protection from northerly weather.

There is a larger island (88) toward the southern shore, with more trees. Behind this, many boats are moored and there is a community area dock. We found 5½ feet controlling depths in going around behind this island (88), between it and the mainland. This is not a good place to anchor because of the moored boats and docks.

Just around the "Indian Landing" point is a marina apparently used primarily by inboard/outboards lifted out. There is a Mercury sign on the head of the dock. This is **Indian Landing Marina (89)** and has 30 slips with a 10-ton forklift and electricity up to 15 amps.

There is yet another island (90), in the western end of the next basin up river. This has stumps around it and should be approached very cautiously. It has a reddish dirt beach with gravel and is not as attractive as the island (86) out in the middle of the last basin. An anchorage here would not be as pretty. Looking straight up the river above that island you see more high wooded hills, the theme of the Severn River.

Osprey with nest on piling

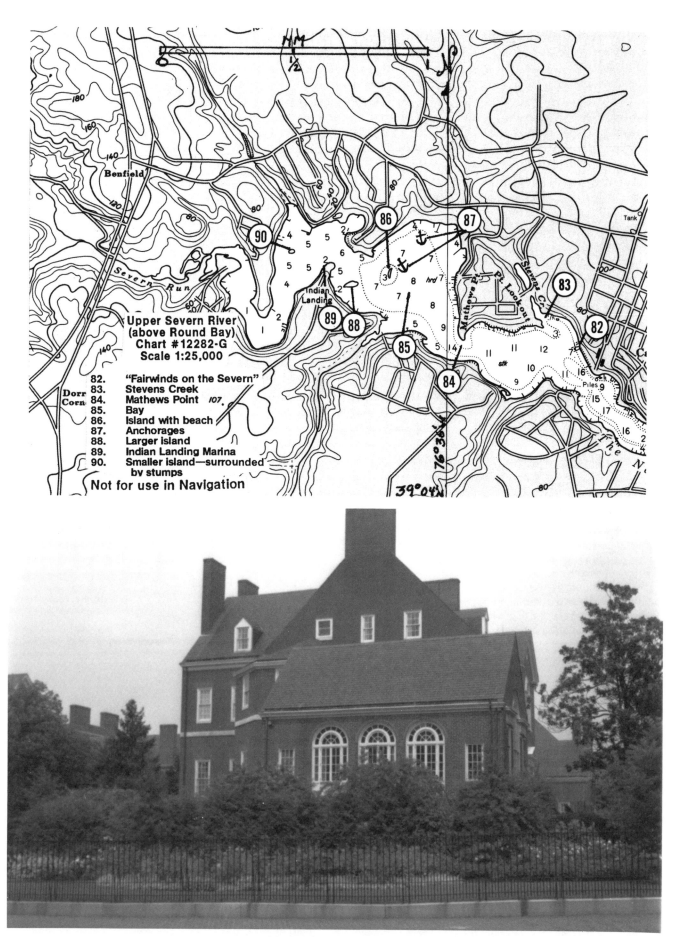

Upper Severn River
(above Round Bay)
Chart #12282-G
Scale 1:25,000

82.   "Fairwinds on the Severn"
83.   Stevens Creek
84.   Mathews Point
85.   Bay
86.   Island with beach
87.   Anchorages
88.   Larger island
89.   Indian Landing Marina
90.   Smaller island—surrounded
      by stumps

Not for use in Navigation

Governor's Mansion, Annapolis

CHAPTER 18

SOUTH RIVER

SOUTH RIVER

Refer to Regional Chart #12263-E—"Western Shore West River to Sandy Point" at the beginning of Chapter 16
and
Chart #12270-K—"South River—Entrance and Eastern Section."

Just south of the Severn, South River presents some beautiful and very protected anchorages and a few marinas that are close to Annapolis by land. This gives South River greater interest ashore and better access to facilities because it is close to Annapolis.

South River has developed a local reputation of having an unusually high incidence of fast-running high-powered motor boats racing up and down its long reach, particularly on weekends. While we noticed that this certainly occurs, it isn't as common as with other areas. Unfortunately, many other locations also have this race track phenomen. Slower moving motorboats and sailboats should be aware, but there are many areas of enforced 6 mph speed limits on South River, and there are many very nice places to anchor far outside of the rush.

Entry

The entrance to the South River (91) is just south of Thomas Point Light (42), and is hard to miss if you have located that light, position 38°53.9'N by 76°26.2'W. It is south of the Severn River (40) entrance area, and far enough out in the Bay to sight easily.

This river mouth is wide and easy although the markers should be honored. As you come in, you will see a river of much forest and homes, previewing another example of the Bay's delightful mixture of nature and civilization.

Cherrytree Cove

Refer to Chart #12270-K—"South River—Entrance and Eastern Section."

Cherrytree Cove (92), on the northern shore just inside the mouth of the river, is a pretty cove for anchoring a boat of no more than 3½ feet draft if you are careful. Head in from several hundred feet upstream (northwest) of Fl R "6." I found 4 feet to prevail all the way up to the anchoring spot, although the chart shows less. There were ripples of sand crossing the bottom, lessening the depth in places and indicating that possible shifting could occur in severe weather. Once inside the cove, the depths of 4 feet were more consistent. I found no sign of submerged obstructions on this route, but there is a danger sign on a white float with orange stripes (93), to which a finger of land is conveniently pointing. This sign marks the remains of what appear to have been old pilings which would be just under the surface at high tide. They are west of the route into this cove.

Looking in, you will see a beach on the right (eastern) side of the cove and a black wooden bulkhead on the northwest-

ern side of the entrance. In the distance are the slender radio towers on the northern entrance bank of the Severn. There are tall trees and marsh around the shore, with a few impressive houses built well back behind the grassy and wooded shores. Straight ahead is a large home with turret-like windows and two tall brick chimneys at either end.

As you get into Cherrytree Cove, you will find a pretty beach on your right (east) forming a spit curving back up northerly into the cove. There is marsh around the beach, and trees behind the marsh. There is 3½ to 4 feet of depth behind this spit and it makes a great spot for a boat drawing no more than that. There is a wide open fetch to the south, but a boat tucked behind the spit could find protection and have the view without exposure. The shallower your draft, the more protection you can get here. From studying the surroundings, I would expect this bottom to be likely to change and shift during a severe storm from the southeast. Your approach should be made carefully.

Duvall Creek

Duvall Creek (95) next to your right (northeast bank) has a heavily populated community around its shores, particularly on its west bank. Community docks are just behind the rock breakwall on the thin point of land protruding northeasterly from that bank. There are also many moorings in the creek. With the crowded conditions and southwestern exposure, it would not be an anchorage of choice. Other better spots are close by.

Selby Bay and Ramsay Lake

This area has a nice anchorage and several marinas primarily used by motor boats.

Refer to Chart #12270-K—"South River"
and
Inset Chart #12270-L—"Selby Bay." PG 297

As you round Turkey Point (96), take special care to keep G"5" to your south, staying well off it. The submerged pilings charted as coming northeasterly off Turkey Point are still there, and visible at low tide. Going into Selby Bay (98), there will be houses and a beach on Turkey Point. You'll see woods on Mayo Point (99) to your northwest, with the beautiful marsh of Long Point (100) extending southeasterly from the point. Fl R "2" can be spotted to the southeast of the tip of Long Point.

Touring Selby Bay in a clockwise fashion, you will first spot the **Selby Bay Yacht Club (1)**. This is just inside and before you get to the inside R "2" which is the second marker into the cut through the bridge. There is a white clubhouse with rounded windows and roof, and a swimming pool behind the docks. Next up the shore and just to the west, you will see a large boathouse extending out over the water. This is **Burr Yacht Sales (2)** with over 20 slips.

Behind Burr Yacht Sales, you will see a sign announcing Turkey Point Marina. This appears at first to be at or next to

2. Coast Guard Annapolis
11. Ramsay Lake
21. Harness Creek
22. Persimmon Point
    (with duck blind)
23. Park
24. Anchorages
25. South branch of cove in
    Harness Creek
26. North branch of cove in
    Harness Creek
27. Cove
28. Glebe Bay
29. 2-foot shoal
30. Brewer Creek
31. Pocahontas Creek
32. Private markers at Fl R "2"
33. Pocahontas Creek
    Yacht Club
34. Hardy Marine
35. Aberdeen Creek

Not for use in Navigation

36. Cove behind Melvin Point
    Gr "1"
37. Snug anchorage (3½' draft)
38. Gunkhole anchorage
39. (4' controlling depth)
40. Severn River entrance
41. Submerged piles
42. Thomas Point Light
43. Londontowne Marina
44. Glebe Creek anchorage
45. Shallow branch
    of Glebe Creek
46. Anchorage Cove in
    northerly wind
47. Crab Creek
48. Anchorage
49. Private markers
    at tip of point
50. Light brown house
51. Anchorages
52. Branches at end of Crab
    Creek (snug, shallow
    anchorages)
53. Almshouse Creek
54. Condominium complex
55. Church Creek

56. 2-ft. shoal at entrance
57. Anchorage cove
91. South River
92. Cherrytree Cove—shoal
    draft anchorage (3½')
93. Submerged obstructions
    (marked with white
    & orange float)

95. Duvall Creek
96. Turkey Point (with
    submerged pilings)
98. Selby Bay
99. Mayo Point
100. Long Point

295

the yacht sales premises, but actually the sign and marina are across the road. By water, it's in Ramsay Lake on the other side of the fixed bridge (3) to your right (east) immediately after you pass through. Ramsay Lake is described later in this chapter.

Anchor Yacht Basin (4) is on the west shore of Selby Bay near the south end. There is a large Texaco sign on the dock and they have gas and diesel, block and cube ice, 100 slips with up to 50 amp electricity, taking boats up to 55 feet, with a lift capacity up to 35 tons, and general repair, marine store, and restaurant. They are dealers for Chrysler Marine, MerCruiser and Westerbeke. There are beverage machines.

Holiday Point Marina (5) is on the northwestern side of the cove with three piers and a gray building ashore. There are 150 slips with electricity up to 50 amps and repair facilities.

Proceeding clockwise around Selby Bay, you will next see a private swimming club (6) with a pier and net to keep nettles out, and then Selby Bay Yacht Basin (7), just beyond (east of) Fl R "4." Here there is a big gray boat house with a gas and diesel dock. This has 100 slips open and covered up to 60 feet with electricity up to 50 amps. There is some repair work available.

The remainder of the western shoreline is houses and docks, but there is a very nice anchorage (8) in the far northwestern end of the bay. To reach this, you must proceed in on a northwesterly direction, putting FL R "4" to your left (southwest). We found deep water by going 150 yards beyond (southwesterly of) R "2." Then head on a course of 323°M for the trees (9) that are just to the right (northeast) of the mouth of the little creek at the northwest end of Selby Bay. The farther in you go, the prettier it gets, and I have seen some very busy weekends with very few boats here. The wakes are not as bad as might be expected because of the long distance from the channel, and the 6 mph speed limit.

A boat of 3 feet draft could tuck up in the little cove (10) to get better protection. We found more depth here than charted, unless you get too close in to the shore. This cove, and the entire area is very pretty, with the woods and marsh nearby overshadowing the civilization from the homes and marinas on the other shores. It could get rough in a strong southeasterly.

Ramsay Lake

Ramsay Lake (11) appears somewhat inaccessible from a cursory glance at the chart, but quite a few motor boats go in, and some small ones even come in directly from the river on the east of Turkey Point. The fixed bridge (3) with 10 feet vertical clearance was being rebuilt last year. The "lake" is a nice wide bay with a pleasant mixture of woods and homes ashore. Local boats do go through the cut at the opposite (northeastern) end (12). Controlling depth through this pass is 2½ feet. Because of the 10 feet bridge clearance and the shallow entry, most boats inside are motor boats, not drawing more than 4 feet.

Turkey Point Marina (13), the first marina to your left (east) immediately after you come through the bridge, has a little over 100 slips with electricity up to 30 amps, and a maximum slip length of 40 feet with longer spaces available. They have Amoco gasoline, block and cube ice, a boat lift, a hard surfaced ramp, marine store, and repair work. Amoco, MC, and Visa are accepted. We observed primarily motor boats under 40 feet here.

On the opposite side of the lake, immediately to your right (west) after you come through the bridge, is Bay View Marina (14) identified by a sign on a two-story house. They have 150

slips up to 50 feet long with electricity up to 30 amps and a pumpout, gas, and some charter fishing boats. Lift capacity is up to 15 tons with repairs available.

South River Marina (15), with a big gas sign and a dock house by its pumps, is next on the same side. They take Visa and MC. There are 30 slips with electricity up to 30 amps, a marine store, and repairs available.

Just around the corner from Turkey Point Marina, to the southeast, the dock of Little Island Marina (16) with a pineapple sign on the end comes out from a green yard. There are 40 slips with electricity up to 30 amps, a laundromat, and wet and dry storage.

Across the lake, on the southwestern shore, is Mayo Ridge Marina (17) with a little white house in a grassy yard behind some boat docks with up to 20 amps electricity. There is a hard surfaced ramp.

The small creek (18) pointing southerly at the southeast corner of this lake, has 3 feet controlling depth. There are many homes and docks inside, with a high shore and many trees. It would be of little interest to a cruiser except a smaller motor boat looking for a very snug hole. Last year, the tight entrance was marked with stakes with red and green markers on them. They are at the two sharp outside guardian points.

Heading out Ramsay Lake, there is a very shallow shoal (19) on the northern side. The tip of this is marked with a small private red float. Be sure to stay south of that shoal. Continuing on northeastward, Ramsay Bay Marina (20) with a T dock can be found in the cove to the east in the Shoreham Beach area.

Despite what the chart indicates, it is possible for small shallow boats to pass through between Turkey Point and the point north of Shoreham Beach (12). I observed local boats drawing around 3 feet doing this, and I set out to find the route. It wasn't difficult to find because there were locally placed PVC stakes with red and green painted tops marking the way. These are only stakes, and I would not depend on their accuracy. Don't take this route without first talking with someone local, or watching someone else go in, or trying it first with your dinghy. The shoals here are in an area prone to shifting and the local people may not have had an opportunity to change the stakes with each shift. I found 2½ feet to be controlling here. The bottom was mostly sandy.

Harness Creek

Refer to Chart #12270-K—"South River—Entrance and Eastern Section." PG 295

Harness Creek goes north off the northeast shore of South River. It is one of the prettiest anchorages on the Bay, and very secure. There is some beach area and a park on the eastern shore. Anchorages in the creek are very crowded on weekends and many other times.

The entrance to Harness Creek is straightforward, with a duck blind off Persimmon Point (22) on your left (west) and high wooded hills on the right (east) with a park area and benches. Stay well to the east of Persimmon Point with its shoal making south and southeasterly. The entrance is wide, and few boats get into trouble here.

The eastern bank of this creek is a state park (23) and thus the natural beauty of the deep forest there is relatively undisturbed, making a welcome retreat back into wilderness in this very civilized area. Most of the creek has acceptable holding bottom of mud, but care is required in backing down and setting the hook. If you get deep into some of the wooded coves

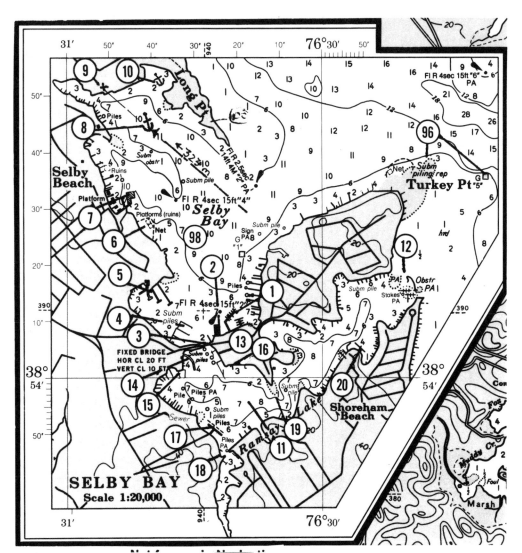

Not for use in Navigation

Melanie Neale sailing author's *Chez Nous*

297

where there is little current, you will be more likely to find mud slime and poor holding.

The first of many "favorite anchorages" (24) is just behind the spit of sand to your right (east) as you enter. There is a beach here and deep water, at least 8 feet, up very close to the inside of the spit. Boats anchored here have the benefit of the beach, some pulling right up to the sand. They can look over the spit out into South River and get the southerly breezes, yet have the protection and woods of the cove. On weekends, this can develop into a serious party spot.

Many other boats anchor just upstream (24) into the first cove to the right (east). This has high woods all around on the eastern side, and a pretty scene of woods and a few quiet homes with nice lawns back on the western side. Most anchor in the outer reaches of this cove, but for the true nature lovers who have boats not requiring a lot of room to maneuver, the inner sanctum of the cove is exquisite. The chart shows two forks at the head of the cove, each with very shallow water. In fact, these are perhaps the best that Harness Creek has to offer. Head straight into the cove. You'll see a cliff with a log fence ahead of you. Before you get to the cliff, you will see the forks opening to either side.

The southern fork (25) has 7 to 8 feet depths. Inside, you are surrounded by tall hills with trees towering over the quiet water. You see nothing but woods, water, and sky and hear the sounds of the forest as though you were camping out. Stay in the middle to get in, and be forewarned that while there is plenty of depth for most boats, there is not much room to maneuver. Also it is best not to venture too close to the shores because the overhanging trees sometimes fall in, leaving logs just under the surface near the shore. There is a shoal coming westerly off the last point to your left (east) just before you reach the end of this fork. The bottom is loose mud. Make sure you are set because there is not much room to drag.

The left (north) fork (26) has a nice anchorage for boats drawing no more than 3½ to 4 feet, depending upon where you settle. This also is beautiful, surrounded by high wooded hills. There is more room than the south fork, but it is shallower, and a little tricky getting in. Stay to your left (northwest) and off the tip of the marshy point coming out from the right (southeastern) entrance bank. Often these tips are very deep at the end, but this shoals gradually. It is marshy, indicating a settled state and therefore less of a drop-off at its tip and behind it than you would expect from a clean sandy point. Once in, you will find depths to be 3½ to 4 feet, depending on how close you are to the shore. This is a beautiful spot, and not as likely to be crowded because it is shallower and more difficult to enter.

Proceeding up Harness Creek, you will round the next point to your right (east) and find a set of docks on the eastern shore with paddle boat rentals. These belong to the park, and landing by boaters is not encouraged. There is a pay phone at the head of this dock. The area off these docks makes another beautiful anchorage (24), often less crowded than the ones mentioned above. Adequate depths extend in to the cove deeper than the chart indicates, with 6 feet carrying well up into the cove, and 3½ feet close to the end. I found the best depths by favoring the right (southern) side as I worked up into the cove.

Above (to the north of) this cove is a broad cove (24) on the eastern side, with high hill and deep water up to 6 feet fairly close into the eastern bank. Many people like to anchor here, nestled near the eastern bank, for a more open feeling. I kept detecting very uneven bottom here, perhaps logs, or perhaps just ripples.

The creek continues to be very pretty as you move upstream, with the park on the eastern bank. However, the private homes on the western bank become more obvious here as the creek narrows and the number of homes increases. This continues to be the case all the way up to the marshy end. The best anchorages are behind, closer to the mouth of the creek.

•

Back out in the South River, you will pass a deep and wide cove to your left (southwest) (27) on the northwestern side of Mayo Point. This may look intriguing for boats enjoying the wide open spaces, but it has a long northern exposure. The docks at its head are private, and the beach along its southeastern shore is posted. The charted duck blind is still there.

Brewer and Pocahontas Creeks

These creeks are congested and there are other nicer anchorages nearby off South River.

When entering Brewer Creek (30), be sure to round northwest of the 4-foot shoal extending northwesterly off the point to your left (southeast). It is not marked.

Pocahontas Creek (31) at first looks interesting to the gunkholer, but then you notice the many docks coming out from the shore. The entrance is marked by an official looking Fl R "2," but this seems almost irrelevant when you see the rest of the privately placed small markers. There are three closely-placed red markers, and two greens, all clustered around the Fl R "2" (32) as though guarding it. When we passed the shoal, it extended well beyond that Fl R "2," and the actual end was marked by a small red nun. The distances between the markers seemed no more than 10 to 15 feet. This is too close to indicate on our chart, but note that they are there and follow them closely. I found 4 feet depth to be controlling in this area.

After you get through this cut, up in the cove to the right (west), you will find **Pocahontas Creek Yacht Club and Marina (33)** with a green painted lift and house with green top and cinder block bottom. It has a large garage door and a solar panel on the roof. This is pretty, tucked away with weeping willow trees. There are 50 slips here with electricity up to 30 amps and there is a closed end lift and a 17-ton railway. Continuing up the creek will reveal **Hardy Marine (34)**, on the right (southwest) with a concrete ramp, some slips, and some repairs.

Aberdeen Creek

This is another pretty creek, north off South River. There is a moderate covering of homes ashore, and a snug anchorage near the end for shallower boats.

Entering Aberdeen Creek (35), beware of the shoals on both sides and stay in the middle, watching the depths. These shoals were not marked last year, but the channel is wide enough to make this easier than it seems. The cove (36) immediately to your left (west) behind Melvin Point is pretty, but fairly exposed as an anchorage. There is a large home up on the point with white columns, and other homes scattered around.

You could anchor anywhere in the creek, but the right (eastern) fork has a snug and pretty area for boats drawing 3½ to 4 feet. As you follow this branch, it will turn to your left (north) at a Gr "1" (37) marker which seems to be out of place up here in the hitherto unmarked creek. This marks a shoal extending out from the point to the northeast as the creek turns. Stay south of it. Homes are ashore behind and around this point. If you proceed on, you will find the snug anchorage (38) with many vine-covered trees on the hilly shores, and a few quiet unobtrusive homes around.

A gunkholer's delight awaits in the left (western) fork (39), which at first glance, appears to be closed off. In fact it is not, and there are several shallow draft sailboats at the docks of some of the nice homes nestled around the shores inside. Their masts visible over the rounded guardian spit gave away the almost-secret entrance. Approach the spit, and proceed on through the narrow cut, with the spit on your right (east), keeping to the middle. We found 4½ feet in the cut, but only 4 feet inside. Here is a landlocked hole snug in any storm. The homes all around the shore with wide yards down to the water would impair the feeling of privacy, but what complete protection!

Glebe Bay

Glebe Bay opens wide off the southwest shore of South River. This broad bay has a few marinas, but it is not attractive for anchoring because of its open expanses and the crowded homes ahore in the creek. There is a good anchorage in Glebe Creek.

Entering Glebe Bay (28) is simple enough. However, I saw no markers for the submerged piles (41) indicated east of Larrimore Point. These are up on the shoal which extends out easterly from the point. Favor the southeastern side upon entering. Another problem comes if you forget the 2-foot shoal (29) in the middle of Glebe Bay, and the shallow water extending southeasterly off the western shore. This is not marked. Stay toward the eastern side proceeding up into the bay. **Londontowne Marina (43)** is nestled in the cove to your right (northwest) just after you enter the bay. They have gas, block and cube ice, some transient slips, a large indoor and outside dry storage area, and lift for inboard/outboard boats and some repair and parts for I/O boats.

If you proceed on up into Glebe Creek, you will find a nice small anchorage (44) behind (southwest) of the point extending out from its southeastern entrance shore. You can take 8 feet of draft up behind the point far enough to be protected from the northeasterly fetch into Glebe Bay, anchoring close to the trees along the shore. Except for an old dock coming out from the curve of the shore, there is just woods, marsh, and beach here. Homes on the opposite bank are in the distance.

The creek above here is congested with homes and docks, but the long branch pointing southwesterly with a 2-foot depth indicated, is very pretty. Favor your right (northeast) and remain well off the point to your southwest as you come in, in order to find the deeper water. I found 2½ to 3 feet in much of this branch. Once you get inside (45) around the bend, there is little to be seen except woods and marsh.

•

Continuing up South River, you will notice a narrow and long little cove between Melvin and Ferry Points on the northern side of the river across from Glebe Bay. While offering a snug anchorage (46) from northers, this cove is very built up with houses ashore and their docks and boats.

Crab Creek

Crab Creek (47), also on the northern shore, is not as cluttered as the cove just to its southeast described above, and it has some nicer spots to anchor. As soon as you enter, you can swing around behind the guardian entrance point (48) to your left (west) where there is 12 feet depth. If you anchor there, you'll look over the spit at the river, or up into the creek with nice homes and wide yards around the shore.

Many people head farther up the creek and pass through the very narrow channel northwest of the little finger of land coming out from the eastern shore. We found at least 6½ feet to be controlling last year, as described below. There are red and green privately placed floating markers (49) at the tip of the finger. We found the best water by approaching the point on the right (east) side of the creek, and then running out along the finger, rounding to come through between those markers. As you pass through the cut and around the finger tip, your bow should be pointing to a light brown house on the hill (50) on the bank now ahead of you (the northeastern bank inside). Head towards this house, remaining close to the marshy point to your left (north), because the finger is partly submerged, more so at higher tides. Soon the water will deepen into the nice basin. The deep channel between the points is narrow, and if you have a 6-foot draft and the tide is not rising, you may want to check it out first by dinghy, but local people frequently come in here.

In this first basin (51), many boats anchor, with open spaces around them and the houses on the wooded hills. The next basin (51), farther north, is also pretty as an anchorage. This also has nice homes on the surrounding hilly shores. The two branches at the end (52) of this creek are both crowded with homes and docks, but still pretty and more snug. You can't go very far into the northern branch if you have a tall mast. The overhead power cable there has an authorized clearance of 43 feet. Most people prefer the anchorages in the lower part of the creek.

Almshouse Creek

Almshouse Creek (53) is on the southern bank of South River, across from Crab Creek. It is very congested inside with low shores, houses crowding the water, and many private individual docks and private community docks. The northwestern entrance bank is marked by a huge condominium development (54), with large mutiple-story reddish wood buildings and surrounding yards mostly barren of trees.

If you go into this creek to visit or perhaps for temporary refuge, you should approach from the downstream (eastern) side, rounding the southeastern entrance point, to avoid the large shoal extending northeasterly and easterly off the northwestern point with the condos. These shoals are marked as to the river channel by Fl G "15." Note the submerged piles indicated on the chart.

Church Creek

Church Creek (55) goes straight north off South River. It is a long and beautiful creek, heading straight back into the high hills of the forest. It's fiord-like, but with very gentle "mountains" and a few homes among the trees. It is deep as the chart shows. Go in and cruise up and down between the hills and pick your favorite spot to anchor. The 2-foot shoal (56) extending out southeasterly from the entrance point on the left (west) must be avoided by approaching the creek from the southeast. If you try to come in straight from the middle of the river, heading straight for the middle of the mouth, you will find yourself aground.

As you glide up the creek, you will notice a cove with two forks (57) to your left (west) soon after you enter. This looks intriguing for anyone looking for an anchorage without the long north-south fetch of the creek, but it is more than that. As you nose into the cove, you can anchor anywhere among the hills, the few houses barely noticeable back in the trees. If you go just beyond the little finger point protruding in a southerly direction from the northern side of the cove, and look to your north, you will notice that it separates the main creek from an even snugger and prettier spot behind it. Carefully go up inside, putting the point to your east, and take a deep breath. It is very pretty. A light-colored house sits upon the woods, hardly noticeable, on the point to the east. There is a small dock on the shore under the house, but it blends in. You can go almost to the northern end of the cove and find 4 to 5 feet depths, less at the end. Avoid the entrance point to your left (west) favoring the eastern side.

At the far upper extreme of Church Creek, there are more homes and the magic of the creek seems to become diffused by the subtle additional signs of civilization.

•

Refer to Chart #12270-M—"South River—Western Section."

The area which we are now describing in South River has 6 mph speed limits (58). These are well-noted with marked floats, and it extends at this time above the first bridge, resuming from time to time upriver for areas of more congestion. These limits may be changed, and it is always wise to keep a watch for notices. The speed limits are taken quite seriously by much of the local populace and the patrolling law enforcement officers.

Warehouse Creek

Warehouse Creek (59) is another very congested creek with homes crowding the shore and many docks coming out to the channel. Like creeks of similar nature, it is pretty and a nice place to live ashore, but of little interest for the typical cruiser looking for secluded anchorages or shoreside attractions. Warehouse Creek Boatyard (60) is on the right (western) side with some slips and haul and repair service, generally used by boats of small to moderate size.

Wrecks

We saw no markings for the wreck (61) charted at the northwestern side of the mouth of Warehouse Creek on the shoal. Chesapeake Bay charts are full of wreck reports, because at one time or another, many boats were abandoned or lost in the waters and on the shores. Often these wrecks have long since oozed into the mud or been removed, but the symbols remain, seemingly forever. When we see a symbol, we look for the wreck, and we inquire for someone who knows, but usually there is no report. If we don't see it, we so report, but some trace of it may be there, and we must proceed cautiously.

•

On the southern bank of South River, just downstream (east) of the first bridge, is Pier 7 Marina (62). This is conspicuous with its large two-story gray building and sign on top. There is a grassy yard on the hill behind the building. There are 200 slips up to 60 feet with electricity up to 30 amps and a hard surfaced ramp. South River Café and Lounge (63) is a restaurant with dockside bar, back from the marina on its upriver side, between it and the bridge. There is complimentary docking while eating at the restaurant. Many of the piers are somewhat exposed to a fetch from up and down river, as is true of other marinas on South River.

On the northern bank of the river, also just downstream from the bridge, is the very nice Liberty Yacht Club and Marina (64). Transients are welcome and receive yacht club privileges while they are there. There are over 300 slips up to 50 feet, with longer spaces available alongside up to 100 feet, and

electricity up to 50 amps and phone hookups available. Gas and diesel are sold from an easily accessed floating pier with a nice fender system. There is block and cube ice, a nice swimming pool, fireplace, lounge, grill and TV area in the club, laundromat, charter boats, a good marine store, a 25-ton lift and a 10-ton forklift with indoor storage, and general repair services. The docks and premises are well-maintained. This marina is only a few minutes drive from downtown Annapolis. It is also within walking distance from the restaurant across the bridge at Pier 7, and with the one at the Oak Grove Marine Center (which you can get to by walking under the bridge) and within a few minutes drive by car from several very complete shopping centers and grocery stores. The staff is very helpful with transportation. There are some moorings in the cove just to the east of the marina, and it is possible to anchor (65) here if you can find room and do not mind the southeastern exposure down the river.

The first bridge (66) in South River is fixed with a vertical clearance of 53 feet. Immediately above it on the northern bank, you will see more marine facilities.

Immediately to your right (north) after you come through the bridge, you will see the docks and small beach of Suntime Boat Rental (67), where you can rent boats from jet skis to 90 horsepower center console speed boats. The next docks, on the same side, belong to the large Oak Grove Marine Center (68) with over 130 slips with electricity up to 30 amps, taking boats up to 60 feet, selling Amoco gas and diesel. There is a hard surfaced ramp and marine store, ice, and a forklift. Fergie's Restaurant there has a cocktail lounge in a light tan two-story building with black windows on the second story. These premises extend upriver to a large cement building with the Oak Grove Marine Center sign.

Next, and around in the cove, still on the north side of the river, is the large Wilkens Yacht Sales (69) facility selling Hatteras and other vessels. This has some slips up to 70 feet long, and a large repair facility with lift capacity up to 60 tons.

Gingerville Creek

Gingerville Creek (70) on the north side of South River begins with the bustle and congestion of Oak Grove Marine Center and Wilkens Yacht Sales, and quiets down to nice homes, mostly set back into the land. It is a very pretty place for boats to anchor anywhere that may look pleasing. Gingerville Creek ends in marsh and shallow water. We did not see the wreck (71) portrayed on the chart, but proceed carefully.

Beards Creek

Beards Creek (72), first on the southern shore above the first bridge, offers more nice anchorage spots. Its entrance can catch the unwary because of the long 1-foot shoal (73) extending much of the way across its mouth from its western entrance shore. The end of this shoal is supposedly marked by a junction buoy which is green on top and red on the bottom. However, the shoal extends at least 10 feet southwest beyond this buoy, so give it a wide berth passing well south of it.

As you first look into the creek, there will be many high hills with woods, but also houses and private piers. The scenery is prettier after the creek makes its first bend to the left (southeasterly) around a point with a large wreck symbol (74) noted. We found no indication of the wreck in the channel, but there may be still something there. Proceed cautiously.

In the area around this bend, we found the nicest scenery for anchoring (75). with fewer sightings of civilization among

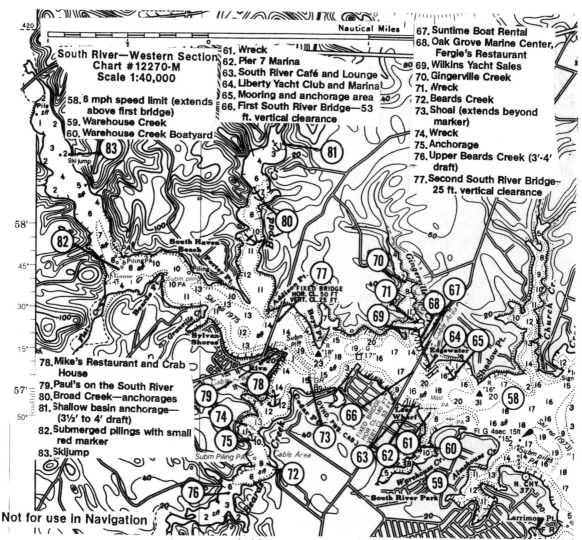

South River—Western Section
Chart #12270-M
Scale 1:40,000

58. 6 mph speed limit (extends above first bridge)
59. Warehouse Creek
60. Warehouse Creek Boatyard
61. Wreck
62. Pier 7 Marina
63. South River Café and Lounge
64. Liberty Yacht Club and Marina
65. Mooring and anchorage area
66. First South River Bridge—53 ft. vertical clearance
67. Suntime Boat Rental
68. Oak Grove Marine Center, Fergie's Restaurant
69. Wilkins Yacht Sales
70. Gingerville Creek
71. Wreck
72. Beards Creek
73. Shoal (extends beyond marker)
74. Wreck
75. Anchorage
76. Upper Beards Creek (3'-4' draft)
77. Second South River Bridge—25 ft. vertical clearance
78. Mike's Restaurant and Crab House
79. Paul's on the South River
80. Broad Creek—anchorages
81. Shallow basin anchorage—(3½' to 4' draft)
82. Submerged pilings with small red marker
83. Skijump

Not for use in Navigation

the wooded hills. Note the cable crossing area, marked by a vertical sign on each side. In much of this area, you can anchor close up to the trees in water 7 to 8 feet deep. Avoid the area where there is a submerged pile charted.

Farther up Beard Creek, the shoreline at first becomes somewhat more settled, but then the creek ends, typically in marsh and shallow water with forest in the background. A boat with 3 or 4 feet draft can reach this pretty upper creek area (76).

•

In the tight corner between the western side of the Beards Creek entrance and the second South River Bridge (77), there are two establishments of interest to the boater. The first is Mike's Restaurant and Crab House (78), recognizable by its sign. There are docks in front and on the side, and the crab house itself is one story with large windows on the water. You can tie up at the crab house docks and eat steamed crabs and shrimp as well as other fare, in typical crab house tradition. There is a bar and lounge here. In back of the restaurant is a "country store" which is more like a convenience store, yet with a country store flavor both in decor and goods. Here you can get normal convenience store items as well as fishing gear and bait, block and cube ice, subs and sandwiches, cheeses, suntan lotion, and other helpful items for the boater.

Between Mike's and the bridge, and set back more from the water, is Paul's on the South River (79), a much more formal restaurant with full entree menu and quieter atmosphere.

There is a T dock in front of this restaurant for courtesy docking while dining. The two establishments are concerned that you tie up at the proper dock for the business that you are visiting.

Broad Creek

The second bridge (77) has only 25 feet vertical clearance. Above the bridge, the river appears to split into two vertical branches. The right (northern) branch is actually Broad Creek (80). This creek is straight and unremarkable for special coves or spots. Anywhere that you may wish to anchor would be pretty. If you have only 3½ to 4 feet draft, you will find the basin (81) at the head of the creek to be particularly nice with marsh at the end and trees far in the background, unfortunately punctuated by a tall antenna far in the distance.

•

Continuing on up the river, the chart shows pilings above and to the west of Beards Point (82), on the north side of the river. These were not visible last year, but there is a small red marker off the point to steer the boater clear of the area where the piles would be located. As you round the bend and head northwesterly upriver, you are again looking deep into beautiful Maryland countryside with rolling hills and woods back from the marshy shore into which this river eventually recedes. As a final shout from civilization, there is a ski ramp and ski area (83) thus rendering this otherwise very nice anchorage area noisy on weekends.

CHAPTER 19

WEST AND RHODE RIVERS

Refer to Regional Chart #12263-E at the beginning of
Chapter 16   and
Chart #12270-N—"West River and Rhode River."

These two rivers are often thought of as being one cruising area, the Rhode opening from just within the mouth of the West River. They offer both a beautiful and sparsely populated anchorage area and the nice small village of Galesville, which has several large full service marinas and restaurants. In the village, you can tie up or anchor.

Entering the West (84) and Rhode (85) Rivers from the Bay presents little difficulty. Coming in from the north, a landmark is Thomas Point Light (42). Its position is 38°53.9′N by 76°26.2′W. A course of 243°M will bring you from that light to Fl G "1A" (86) in the entrance to these rivers. You must pass east of the light and northwest of Fl G "1A." Coming in from the Eastern Bay area, a course of 316°M will bring you from Bloody Point Bar light to G "1." In approaching from the southeaast or south, care should be taken to avoid the shoal extending well out into the Bay east of Curtis Point (88). The shoreline greeting you from these rivers is mostly wooded, with homes scattered around and some areas of heavier settlement.

RHODE RIVER

First, let's head into the Rhode River (85) with its great anchorages and beautiful surroundings. The entrance is on your right (north) between Dutchman (89) and Cheston (90) Points as you come into the West River. Dutchman Point is mostly wooded, but it has a large white building at its southern tip. There are heavy docks and a gray rock jetty on the southwestern side of the point. One of the most "uptown" duck blinds I have ever seen sat to the west of the point last year, very sturdily built and appearing quite commodious. Cheston Point, west of Dutchman Point, has clay banks with forest, and no houses visible. Curtis Point (88) is lower and more settled.

As you head northerly into the Rhode and pass G "3," you will see nice beach beneath the high banks on the southern side of the cove to your west. While some anchor here (91), it is rather exposed. There are better anchorages farther up Rhode River, and those anchorages are what attracts most cruisers to this river.

Cadle Creek

Cadle Creek (92) is to your right (east) as you head into the Rhode River. It is of little interest to most cruising boats, unless they need work or docking from one of the marinas inside. This is a well-settled creek with many docks protruding from the shore and a few marinas. The land is much flatter than other creeks in the vicinity, and most would prefer to anchor in some of the other places described further on in this chapter.

Entering Cadle Creek, follow the markers. It may appear at first that G "1" and R "2" are in the wrong place as you begin to enter. However, the channel bends to your left (northerly) and they will line up correctly as you approach them. G "1" has a big corrugated box on four pilings beside it, apparently used for monitoring of tidal or other data. When you get into the creek, you will immediately see the boats moored out and the many docks.

As you enter the creek, you will notice sailboat masts and other signs of a marina on the opposite (southeastern) side of a little spit separating the main creek from the cove on its southeastern side. This is a community club (93).

The first marina on the left (western bank) is Cadle Creek Marina (94) with 50 slips and electricity up to 30 amps, gas and diesel, some marine supplies and repair work. It has a big "Coastal" fuel sign, with red letters on white background. There is a sign also that advertises railway service, fiberglass

IDENTIFICATIONS FOR CHART PG 303

West River & Rhode River		40.	**Public dock and park**
Chart #12270-N		41.	**West River Market and**
Scale 1:40.000			**Trading Company**
reduced 10%		42.	**Thomas Point Light—**
1.	**Flat Island**		**38°53.9′N, 76°26.2′W**
2.	**Contee's Wharf**	43.	**Small park overlooking West**
3.	**Anchorage southwest of Big**		**River**
	Island (shallow draft)	44.	**West River Sailing Club**
4.	**Cut south of Big Island—3½′**	45.	**Woodfield Fish and Oyster**
	controlling depth		**Co., Inc.**
5.	**Steamboat Landing—**	46.	**Cox Creek, Tenthouse**
	Restaurant and Marina		**Creek—(temporary**
6.	**Galesville**		**anchorages)**
7.	**Sellman Creek—shallow draft**	47.	**Chesapeake Yacht Club**
	anchorage	48.	**Private red markers—3′**
8.	**3′ shoal**		**controlling depth**
11.	**Entrance to Bear Neck Creek**	49.	**Anchorage—shallow draft**
12.	**Carr Wharf**		**(3′ controlling depth)**
13.	**Blue Water Marina**	50.	**Chalk Point Marine**
14.	**Rhode River Marina**	51.	**Hartge Yacht Yard**
15.	**Anchorage (5′ draft)**	52.	**Lerch Creek (shallow draft**
16.	**Anchorage (4′ draft)**		**—2½′)**
17.	**Whitemarsh Creek**	53.	**Private marker at point**
19.	**Holiday Hill Marina**	54.	**Shady Oaks Marina**
20.	**Parish Creek**	55.	**Private marker into Shady**
21.	**Dredged channel to Parish**		**Oaks Marina (5′ controlling**
	Creek—3½′ controlling		**depth)**
22.	**Parish Creek Marina and**	56.	**Topside Inn and Topside**
	Boatyard		**Groceries**
23.	**Commercial Seafood**	84.	**West River**
	Landing	85.	**Rhode River**
24.	**Wood's Wharf**	86.	**Fl G 2.5 sec. G "1A"**
25.	**Jerry's Boatyard**	87.	**Fl (2+1) R 6 sec. at Saunders**
26.	**Backyard Boats—Shadyside**		**Point—38°52.9′N,**
27.	**Cheston Creek**		**76°28.6′W**
28.	**Wreck**	88.	**Curtis Point with shoal**
29.	**Ski course marked with floats**	89.	**Dutchman Point**
30.	**Scaffold Creek (3½′ draft)**	90.	**Cheston Point**
31.	**Little Island**	91.	**Anchorage—Rhode River**
32.	**Popham Creek (shallow draft**	92.	**Cadle Creek**
	anchorage—2½′ feet)	93.	**Community docks**
34.	**Stump**	94.	**Cadle Creek Marina**
35.	**South Creek**	95.	**West River Yacht Club**
36.	**Anchorage—Galesville**	96.	**Casa Rio Marina**
37.	**Anchorage—S. of Chalk Point**	97.	**Anchorages in Rhode River at**
38.	**Galesville Yacht Yard**		**Islands**
39.	**Pirate's Cove Restaurant &**	98.	**Shoal at Fl G "7"**
	Marina, Big Mary's Patio Bar,	99.	**High Island**
	Motel	100.	**Big Island**

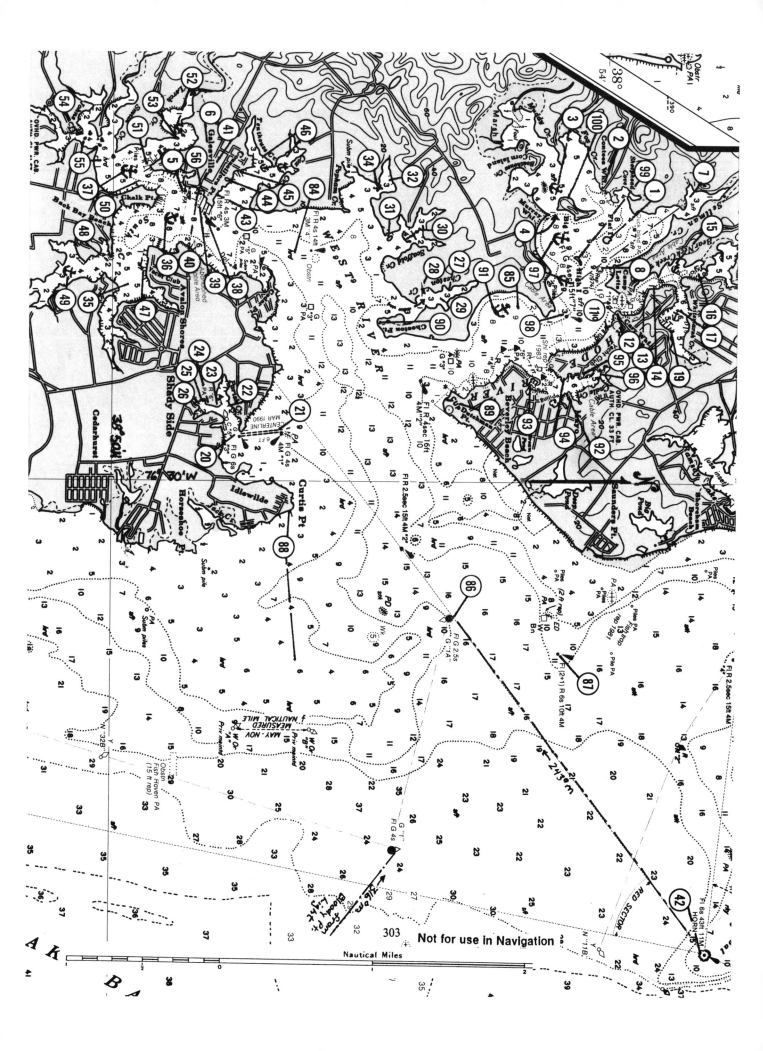

303

Not for use in Navigation

and wood repair, ice, and bait. We found 6½ feet depth at the fuel dock.

Up a little farther on the left (western) bank is the **West River Yacht Club (95)** with its white house up on the hill behind the docks. If you are a member of a recognized club, you may be able to arrange dockage here. The shore here is lined with docks, and it is difficult to distinguish one set from another.

The next commercial set of docks belongs to **Casa Rio Marina (96)**. Here there are 50 slips around the shoreline which bends into a cove. They are up to 40 feet long, with electricity up to 30 amps. There is lifting capacity up to 15 tons and a ramp. We found only 5 feet controlling up to the lift area, which is up in the cove. This is a full service yard with a huge work shed. The work area runs along and behind the docking area and is separated from it by a line of trees. They are dealers for Awlgrip, Crusader, Chrysler, Universal and Westerbeke.

•

Back out in the Rhode River, you will find that the basin around High Island **(99)** to the west of F G "7" **(98)** is one of the Bay's nicest anchorages **(97)**, with several different areas from which to choose. There are crowds here on weekends and holidays. Many are so eager to get settled here that they don't notice the shoal extending east and northeasterly from the point to the southwest of Fl G "7" **(98)**. This shoal actually extends out a little to the east and to the north of the marker, which should be given wide berth. Once around, there are many choices to anchor among the islands according to your preference for the scenery and fetches, and your depth. Most prefer to anchor close to High Island **(99)** and to its southeast, or up between High and Big Islands **(100)** in the nice cove.

Although it appears from the chart that orientation in this basin is simple, the islands are a bit confusing at first because High Island is very small and Big Island **(100)** looks as though it is the highest. Actually, if you look closely at High Island, you will see that it is the victim of serious erosion from the waves of the centuries and is mostly washed away to a flat shadow of its former self, with a nice little beach on its southeastern side. However, there still remains a very high although slender section with a few scrub trees, which explains its name. Big Island is less exposed to wave action and is less eroded, thus retaining most of its height and a nice stand of forest with some buildings to be seen on the north side. As you enter, Flat Island **(1)** looks like part of the mainland. It doesn't clearly separate itself until you explore around to the northeast or southwest of it.

Contees Wharf **(2)**, on the northern shore of the basin has numerous "no trespassing" signs, and the brightly painted buildings with docks to the east of the wharf are private.

The cove **(97)** to the south of Big and High Islands has a beautiful clay bank with thick trees above and a nice beach on the shore. There are no trespassing signs along the beach. The islands also have beaches.

If your draft allows you to get in the area to the southwest of Big Island **(3)**, you will be rewarded with an even more isolated feeling, although as the chart shows, the creeks and areas close to the shore are very shallow. I found 3½ feet controlling depth between Big Island and the mainland **(4)**. The bottom is uneven, and I would expect stumps or at least ridges to remain and I recommend the safe route around the northern end of Big Island.

Last year, the enterprising owners of **Steamboat Landing Restaurant and Marina (5)** in Galesville **(6)** up the West River 3 miles to the south, were coming regularly by boat to the an-

chorage on Saturdays to pick up orders for Sunday morning bagels, coffee, newspapers, milk, ice, and other items. They will also come here to taxi people wishing to dine at the restaurant. There are a few other places around the Bay where this type of service exists, but none that we have found yet where it exists in such a relatively remote and beautiful anchorage. Such luxury in paradise!

Sellman Creek

If you are a bit more daring, draw no more than 4 feet and want an even prettier and more secure anchorage, feel your way into Sellman Creek **(7)** for one of the most pristine anchorages on the Bay. We were concerned about entering because of the 3-foot shoal **(8)** indicated to the south of the docks of Camp Letts. A small white two-story building with a white bannister around a second floor front porch is behind these docks. From here, you will occasionally see small sailboats, canoes, and outboards venture forth.

From a position about midway between Fl G "7" and High Island, sight the eastern end of the point of land which is just to the southwest of Fl G "7." Then look north-northwesterly up into the entrance of the creek. The entrance will be to the left (west) of the camp building and docks. Note Flat Island, which you will pass to your left (southwest) as you go in. Inside the mouth of the creek will be a deep area of marsh grass up on the shore on the point on the western side of the creek. Keep the trees on the point to the southwest of Fl G "7" on your stern and head for the middle of the marshy point in the creek (it will appear as marsh ahead).

Doing this, we found no less than 8 feet going past the shoal area, but we also found that the deep water is very narrow. A line on the chart between these range points will pass over land or shoal, depending upon exactly how you place it, but the actual sighting worked for us. We found nothing else remarkable upon which to take bearings that worked. If the duck blind is still in the creek when you enter, that will be to your left (west). There is not much point in going into Sellman Creek with more than 4 feet draft, because the pretty area is no deeper than this.

Once you get into the creek, you will find one of the prettiest and seemingly untouched areas of the Bay. There is a camp dock on the eastern shore up behind the first point on the eastern shore and a house is barely visible up in the trees in the high land behind the dock. Other than this and occasional camp activity (sometimes skiing), you are in the midst of trees and marsh and Chesapeake Bay countryside floating in the mists of another time. Anchor where your draft allows.

Bear Neck Creek

Bear Neck Creek **(11)** has a few nice marinas with repair yards and some pleasant anchorages.

The entrance to this creek is just to the north of a large public wharf at Carr Wharf **(12)**, where you will often see people fishing. We found no wreck obstructing the entrance although it may be there to the side. Boats pass through the entrance daily in the marked channel.

Blue Water Marina (13) is the first marina on your right (northeast) after you enter the creek. It is across from G "3" which has a square corrugated metal box beside it, apparently used for tidal or other data collecting. The docks of the marina are set at the base of a hill with tall trees and pleasant surroundings. At the top of the hill is a blue house set back up in the trees. The buildings of the marina around the water are red. There are 60 slips and two railways capable of hauling at least 20 tons, and a large workshed.

Proceeding farther into the creek, you will find the shore to your right (northeast) to have many houses while the opposite shore is mostly very pretty woods, a part of the park on Bear Neck. The next marina on this creek is **Rhode River Marina (14)** with a gray boathouse and docks on either side. There are 100 slips and electricity up to 50 amps, lifting capacity up to 15 tons, and gas and diesel are at a convenient dock. They are dealers for MerCruiser, OMC, and Westerbeke. They have morning coffee, donuts, and newspapers on weekends, and hot sandwiches and soft drinks and cube or block ice. We found 6½ feet depth at the fuel dock.

Our favorite anchorage in this creek is the cove **(15)** to your left (west) where, with no more than 5 feet of draft, you can anchor well out of the channel close to the beautiful forest hanging over the water.

There is another special place **(16)** in Bear Neck Creek for boats drawing no more than 4 feet. Near the end and on the left (western) side you will see a small clump of hard ground with a few cedar trees growing, with marsh between it and the mainland. A ribbon of marsh comes out on the upstream side of the clump and extends well back from the shores up to deep forest. Before this clump, you can anchor close to the shore, depending on your draft. This shore has deep forest, a nice little low tide beach under the trees, and wild flowers in season. The view from this spot is lovely. If you go farther upstream around the "Cedar Tree Island" **(16)** (my name), you will be disappointed to find many boats moored and many houses, and the area not as pretty.

Whitemarsh Creek

Because of the number of homes and docks on the shore, Whitemarsh Creek **(17)** is not an attractive anchorage for those looking for seclusion, although the basin in the middle of the creek is certainly secure in a blow. **Holiday Hill Marina (19)** with its tree-covered grounds, stained wooden bath house, and convenience building is here. They have 130 slips up to 60 feet and electricity up to 30 amps, some phone outlets, a laundromat, and a cement ramp. This is a quiet place to keep your boat. I found no offices on the premises, but there is a phone number posted, and someone on a boat at the docks is always available.

Parish Creek in Shadyside

Parish Creek **(20)**, once thriving with the seafood industry, is now quiet with many unused commercial docks and buildings alongside. It would not make an attractive anchorage, and the entrance is very shallow.

The dredged channel **(21)** into the creek is subject to serious shoaling with the vast northeast fetch and shallow sandy bottom all around. Although the chart shows a dredged 6-foot centerline entrance depth, we found 3½ feet to be controlling, with some difficulty in finding even that between the markers. I asked one of the watermen about the depths, and he said "you find it if you're lucky." If you enter, follow the markers closely, and try to get recent local advice. A good source to call would be Backyard Boats, described below. Work boats still use Parish Creek.

As you come into the creek, you will see large brick buildings to your left (east) and empty docks. There are old, mostly frame houses back on the shore around the creek, many with crab pots in the yards. Parish Creek branches to your right (west) shortly after you enter; we found the deepest water to be on the southern side of the entrance to this branch, where you will see commercial boats docked. Along the right (northern) shore of the side creek is **Parish Creek Marina and Boat Yard (22)**. There are 100 slips lining the shore with electricity up to 30 amps, a concrete ramp, and boat lifts up to 25 tons.

The southwest junction corner between the two branches of Parish Creek has a working seafood landing area for commercial boats **(23)**. Next is **Wood's Wharf (24)**, also on the right (western) side of the southern extension of the creek, with a concrete ramp and a few slips. **Jerry's Boatyard (25)** comes next on this side, with a few docks for rent and a telephone number to call.

The last marina down on the western side, and the only one selling gas and diesel, is **Backyard Boats-Shadyside (26)**. Here there are 50 slips up to almost 30 feet long, 15 amp electricity, a 25-ton lift, and a full service boat yard. They are dealers for Catalina, Mercury, MerCruiser, Mach 1, Thompson and Universal. There is a large Coastal fuel sign over their outer docks and they honor Discover, Visa and MC.

Anchorage, Rhode River

Cheston Creek

Cheston Creek (27) lies hidden behind Cheston Point (90) on the northern shore. It will open up as you round that point. It is for shallow draft boats only, but it is one of the prettiest creeks on the Bay. We found 2½ feet to be controlling, although the chart indicates less. I have spoken with local people who say that they can get in with around 3 feet at low tide. The creek is very worthwhile if you have a shallow boat. We found the deepest water to be toward the right (east) side of the outer entrance area where there is 5 feet reported against the marsh. As we approached the guardian point protruding easterly form the western shore, we found the deeper water to be on the left (west) side of the creek, closer to that point. Once past the point and the 1-foot area at which it seems to point, depths remain more evenly around 3 feet.

Inside this creek, the view and aura is surely like what must have enchanted Captain John Smith as he explored these waters. There is nothing to be seen except deep woods down to the water, rising back up gentle hills, with fringes of marsh grass in the quiet shallow coves. We couldn't even find the "wreck" (28) noted on the western side. Even looking out the mouth of the creek to the river, the atmosphere is saved by the fact that, except for an occasional boat passing by, all you will see are woods on the southern bank of the river.

But it is not perfect. There is a ski course marked by floats (29) in the middle of the creek, and there are U.S. Government "no trespassing" signs on the shore. The signs are small and very hard to see from the water and most of the time there is no one here skiing.

Scaffold Creek

Scaffold Creek (30) has a nice anchorage for northerlies, and provides what is probably a less populous spot on weekends. The chart shows 4 feet but I found only 3½ feet going in. A nice place to anchor is off the point to your left (west) with a road coming down and a small dock coming out. There is a large two-story gray stone house here. The scenery is nice, particularly as you look up either of the two shallow branches. There are a few private moorings around, and the possibility of some wake coming from outside as the larger boats speed by out in the river. The little island (31) noted on the left (west) at the entrance is just a small outlying stand of marsh.

Popham Creek

In Popham Creek (32) we are reminded of ancient farmland Chesapeake countryside. If you have no more than 3 feet of draft, go in carefully up to the "Dr. Suess foot" where the two little docks are sticking into the arch. Last year there was a very large, permanent-looking stump (34) off the front of the "ankle" (to the east of the point), toward the western side of the creek. This was visible but the branches will soon rot and the log will probably remain here beneath the surface for some time. This is a typical hazard of exploring these shallow less-travelled beautiful spots. Here are old farm houses out in field and a two rut country road. This is the way it used to be, and often around the Chesapeake, still is, where fields are for farming and not condominiums. Unfortunately, this area is exposed to the river and the south and southeast. If you draw no more than 2½ feet, you can carefully get up into the "toe" of the foot to your west. There you will find beautiful scenery and good protection.

Tenthouse Creek

Heading south up the West River past the pretty creeks on the northern bank and the hills and home on the southern bank, you soon begin to see the Galesville area open up with its large anchoring basin (36) surrounded by small village conveniences for the boater. There is yet one more interesting creek that you pass before you reach Galesville.

Tenthouse Creek (46) is to your right (northwest) around Councillors Point before you reach the Galesville marinas. Tenthouse Creek was so named because in the early colonial days, so many people attended the annual Quaker meetings, that they had to erect many tents to house them during the meetings.

As you move up this creek, first on the shore to your left (west), before you actually reach the small creek, will be the docks, small sailing boats ashore, and club house of the West River Sailing Club (44).

Woodfield Fish and Oyster Co. Inc. (45), founded by Captain John Henry Woodfield, is Galesville's largest "industry." It's a seafood packing and landing facility and ice house. There are some docks here mostly used by local work boats, and a ramp. Retail seafood is available as well as ice. They are farther up in the creek, with docks and various commercial vessels both at the docks and moorings. There are some old commercial vessel wrecks just upstream of the seafood house, on the left (southern) shore.

Small shoal draft boats wishing to escape from a norther would find Tenthouse Creek or Cox Creek (46) just to its northwest, to be an acceptable temporary anchorage. In addition to the seafood house, there are some other commercial docks and also homes on the shores. The bottom off the seafood house likely has some debris from its use over the centuries, but the upper reaches of each little creek would be nicer if you have no more than 3 feet draft.

GALESVILLE

The area to the east of Galesville, where the river meets the mouth of South Creek (35), is an excellent anchorage (36) for enjoying the restaurants, shops, supply and repair facilities, and sights of this nice town. Generally, the bottom is of gray mud and will hold well if you first work to set your anchor down beneath the surface and if you use a good amount of chain. The anchorage is too open for some people, but there are other smaller spots nearby (described below), although not as convenient. In a strong northerly, this anchorage (36) can get rough, and on a northeasterly, the waves often wrap around the point into South Creek, thus causing a beam roll. On winds such as these, you can move farther up into South Creek or around Chalk Point into the basin there (37).

The first facility to your right (west) as you enter what I will refer to as the "Galesville Basin" is the Galesville Yacht Yard (38). There are over 150 slips including some covered, the largest 50 feet with room for longer vessels alongside, and electricity up to 50 amps and a 30-ton lift, marine store, and pool. A very convenient fuel dock for both gas and diesel fronts the basin. There are a few supplies and cube and block ice in the dock house. The block ice is not the ice that was crushed and refrozen that you so often find today. This is solid ice in up to 20-pound blocks and it lasts a long time. The ice house supplier is around the corner up Tenthouse Creek. Local people say that it's one of the oldest ice houses in Maryland. Galesville Yacht Yard are dealers for Cummings, Volvo Penta, and Westerbeke. This large facility has complete hull and engine repair, rigging, brokerage and sales, general mechanical repairs, a carpentry shop, and a ships store.

Next up from Galesville Yacht Yard, on the same side of the river, is the **Pirate's Cove Restaurant and Marina (39)**. This well known restaurant began some time ago as primarily a restaurant facility. Now there are almost 90 slips with regular marina service and electricity up to 30 amps, an outside bar, "Big Mary's Patio Bar," and small motel. Docking is complimentary while dining. The restaurant fare ranges from full menu to light snacks in different settings both inside and outside. There is a raw bar and often live entertainment at the lounge. They will pick up from the anchorage. Call them on VHF Channel 16.

Passing Pirate's Cove, you will then see the public dock **(40)**, but this is used principally for fishing. There is a very small park area with porta-potties just above the dock.

Steamboat Landing

The next facility, still to your right (on the west shore) is the **Steamboat Landing Restaurant and Marina (5)**. This is a very fine restaurant out on a pier at a historical spot. They have 25 slips up to 50 feet with much longer spaces available alongside, with electricity up to 50 amps, and block and cube ice. The Northeast Winds Charter operations keep a fleet at these docks. They have charter boats both power and sail up to 40 feet in length, and chartered cruises on a large motor yacht, as well as fishing charters. The restaurant has excellent food with a menu that ranges from light fare to full entrees, in a very nice but comfortable atmosphere. It sits out on the old landing pier, slightly above and in the midst of the boats tied

around it, and it has three glass sides so that the diners can look out over the harbor and the boats. In the center of the restaurant is an attractive fireplace which provides a great atmosphere as well as additional warmth when the northers blow through. There are also tables outside in front of the restaurant at the marina docks, but slightly elevated. It is this restaurant that operates the shuttle and "take-out" service to the Rhode River anchorage described earlier in this chapter. This restaurant will also pick up from the closer anchorages.

From time to time, there are various special activities at Steamboat Landing. These include special theme nights at the restaurant, when different types of cuisine are featured, a "dockbuster party" once a month, with live bands, an Octoberfest, a Cajun festival, and a seafood festival. Also, a Draketail is usually docked here for inspection and tour. This is an authentically rebuilt Chesapeake Bay work boat, built by the "Draketail Society."

Steamboat Landing was originally named because of the Chesapeake Bay steamers which landed here regularly from the 1850s to the 1930s. Perhaps the best remembered was the elegant *Emma Giles*, built in 1887. Her hull was wooden planking over iron frames. She had an unusual round wheelhouse, and beehives carved over her paddle wheel boxes instead of the customary eagle. You will find many pictures of this lady, and there's a great model in the Country Store described below. The known use of this spot dates back far beyond the steamboat age to early European settlement. In 1684, it was officially designated as a port of entry to serve the surrounding settlers. In more recent times, there have been traditional "crab shacks" here, where people come and eat

West River Sailing Club. Optimist Class sailing dinghies are used world-wide for children beginers sailing lessons

crab in somewhat rough surroundings. The present establishment capitalizes on the historical theme, but don't be misled by the "crabhouse" description. While you can have really great raw bar and crab house enjoyment here, the inside restaurant is very nice and far from rough.

Galesville History

The certificate of survey for the land now including the Galesville area was granted to the Clarkes and the Browns in 1652. They were Quakers who had come to the area from the lower Bay because of the unfriendly treatment they had received from the Virginia settlements. Galesville was at first called "Browntown." Almost immediately, it became a shipping point for the surrounding colonialists. It had a wide protected anchorage and was central to the area. It also became a meeting area for the surrounding Quakers, having large meetings lasting for several days. The tent encampments set up to accomodate the visitors gave name to "Tenthouse Creek." In the Revolutionary War, a British raiding party silenced a cannon at Chalk Point and attacked a boatyard upstream. The name Galesville did not come until 1924, when the village was renamed in honor of John Gale, a planter of the colonial days.

Galesville Ashore

A walk around Galesville will not take long. What you will find will be a few knick-knack shopping opportunities, many supplies and services for boating, a few restaurants and a great country store, and many very nice people who are glad to see you. The waterfront street, Riverside Drive, runs by the marinas mentioned above. Most of the establishments are on this street or very close. Main Street intersects Riverside Drive just north of Steamboat Landing. There is a natural inclination to walk out Main Street, thinking that this is where the "main" things will be. However, other than the Post Office, you will probably find most of what you need along Riverside Drive and on Main within less than a block's walk to the west.

Begin your tour with a visit to the West River Market Trading Company (41) on the north side of Main Street, less than a block from Riverside Drive. This is, in all of the best connotations of the words, a "genuine country store," but it is also much more. Inside you will find a genuine "Cinderella" wood-burning stove built in 1914. It sits in the center of the middle and only aisle, toward the back. Around the stove are benches, an early 1900s barber's chair, an old checker board which you may use, and a cracker barrel with some old magazines on top. They include editions from "Motorboating" from as far back as 1940 and "Rudder" from at least as far back as 1947. And they are there for the same reasons they were there in 1940—for you to have a seat by the stove and pick them up and read them. In this store are also an ancient National cash register, authentic ceiling fans, a very large locally-made model of the steamboat *Emma Giles* who formerly served the area, a "Mercury Athletic Scale" where you put in a penny, twist the grip and test your strength, a nickel scale, and early 1950s Coca Cola chest, a Kentucky rifle and a gunpowder tin, and an electric train, which blows its whistle, smokes, and runs around on tracks hung from the ceiling.

In this store you can also find groceries, some hardware, hand-dipped ice cream and fresh meats. Attached to the side in a different section is a newer deli with delicious foods of all sorts, including sandwiches and salads and cheeses and plates and platters to go or eat there. They make their own barbecue,

and you will never find any better. They will deliver to boats if you wish. The owner, John Whitman, can help you with most of your questions about the area, and he also has a charter fishing boat.

The location of this store was formerly the site of the Kolb's General Merchandise Store which was the second-oldest structure in the village. Across the street was a blacksmith shop in former days.

There are several art and antique shops in the area, including one next to the Country Store, which is owned by the same people.

Still on Main and near the corner is Topside Groceries (56) with bait and block and cube ice and a large supply of spirits, and the Topside Inn (56) with a piano bar and a brick chimney fireplace in the middle, nice wood paneling and blue shutters. If you turn southerly down Riverside Drive, you will find Steamboat Landing (5) less than half a block away.

Walking a little over a block northerly from Main along Riverside Drive will bring you a few other establishments, including the Pirate's Cove (40) and the marinas. At the very end is a small park (43) for sitting and looking out over the West River and watching the sun set. On the stone as you leave the street and step into the grass, is a lovely poem entitled "Sunset on West River" by Elizabeth T. Dixon, a former schoolteacher in the community, for whom the park is named. Riverside Drive ends here, but a turn to your left (west) takes you out to the West River Sailing Club (44) and the ice and seafood house.

South Creek

South Creek (35) runs in a southeast direction opposite the Galesville shoreline, its mouth forming part of the large anchoring basin. It has a cons;derable number of homes with extending docks, the prettiest areas being in the upper reaches of its branches where depths of only 2½ to 3 feet prevail.

As you head toward South Creek, you will see the large and impressive facilities of the **Chesapeake Yacht Club (47)** on the northeastern corner of its entrance. There is a large single-story tan clubhouse with darker brown roof, and swimming pool behind the docks. If you are a member of a recognized yacht club, you may be able to arrange docking.

Heading up the southern branch, you will notice two small privately placed red markers (48) (the first a small float and the second a little red triangle on a PVC pipe) off the point to warn you of the shoal there, and then a second set of reds just upstream (southerly). These markers are to get you through the shallow area all marked with 2 feet depth off that point. Carefully following the markers, we found 3 feet to be controlling. Looking ahead, you will enjoy a very pretty creek of woods and marsh, with a big red boathouse with green shutters on the point to your right (west). Above the boathouse the depths are from 3 to 5 feet, depending on how far up the creek you go. This is a pretty spot for anchoring (49) with 3 feet draft.

We found less than 3 feet entering the creek branch bending around to the east and many homes inside. The branch bending back up to the north is also very populated ashore. It is a little deeper but narrow. It would be difficult to anchor there because of the docks protruding out from the shore.

Creeks South of Galesville, West of Chalk Point

Proceeding up the West River west of Chalk Point, you will find three more marina facilities, and other anchorages if you don't mind a bit of company. As you pass Chalk Point, keep it well to your east because the long dock charted extending to the north was seriously decayed last year. You don't want to run over any piling stumps, although with the boating traffic in the area, I would expect that this will be marked if it becomes hazardous.

The facility on your left (east) inside Chalk Point is **Chalk Point Marine (50)** with 30 slips, an 80-ton railway, and a large work building.

As you headed upriver from Steamboat Landing, you will have noticed the bulkhead and sign of the large facilities of **Hartge Yacht Yard (51)** on the point of land pointing southerly into the basin upstream of Chalk Point. This facility can accomodate most vessels at its docks or in its yard, up to 75 feet in its slips with longer possible alongside. There are over 200 slips, some covered, with electricity up to 50 amps. Many moorings are rented in the basin to their south and in Lerch Creek (52). They sell Amoco gas and diesel, have a pumpout, block and cube ice, CNG, and have a large marine and supply parts operation and have new and used boat sales and charters. There are three railways up to 60 tons and 75 feet and heated sheds. Most marine trades are represented. They are dealers for Awlgrip and Imron, Quadrant Spars, Adler-Barbour, Westerbeke, Volvo, Lehman, Universal, Yanmar, Harken, and others. The business has been in the same family since 1865.

It is possible to anchor in the basin to the south of Hartge's (37), but it is full of moorings and crowded. On the south side of this basin is a church camp with a pretty church and grounds along the shore. Lerch Creek also has moorings in its outer deeper mouth, leaving only a little room for additional anchoring. This creek quickly shallows above the moorings and marina docks, but it is quite pretty above the docks if you have the 2 to 3 feet draft to get into there. The point extending out from the southern side has a bar at the tip (marked by a private buoy) (53) which makes great anchorage (52) to its west for very shallow draft boats of 2 to 2½ feet.

The West River south of Hartge's quickly divides into shallow creeks as it ends, none making very good anchorages because of their shallow depths, all with some homes along the shores, all growing quickly shallow as they reach their marshy conclusions.

There is yet one more marina, the large gray boathouse that you will see as you head upstream. This is **Shady Oaks Marina (54)** with over 40 slips, some covered, taking boats up to 60 feet with longer alongside, and electricity up to 50 amps and a large 100-ton railway capable of hauling vessels over 100 feet long and a full service yard. It has a few moorings in the creek off its docks. The entrance to this marina is very carefully marked with many privately placed markers (55) beginning in the area off the mouth of Smith Creek. It is important to follow these markers. Boats use the channel all the time, and I would assume that the markers will be maintained. We found 5 feet to be controlling to this marina, although the chart indicates four. If you draw more than 4 feet, check with the marina for the latest information. They monitor VHF Channel 16.

West River Market and Trading Post

CHAPTER 20

HERRING BAY TO COVE POINT

Refer to Regional Chart #12263-F—"Western Shore: Herring Bay to Plum Point."

This chapter includes the huge marina facility at Rose Haven in the south end of Herring Bay as well as the creeks and facilities at the north end. There are no natural deep indentations or rivers in this shore, though several harbors have been dredged into the shores. This is not a heavily populated shore.

HERRING BAY

History

The first recorded discovery by European civilization came in 1608, when Captain John Smith visited and was impressed by the fishing. In 1663, Francis and Margaret Holland, both Quakers, had surveyed the area then called "Holland Hills," thus the name "Holland Point." In 1671, Quakers began meeting in the settlement called "Herring Creek Hundred." They built what was probably the first schoolhouse in the area near Herring Creek. In 1698, Richard Harrison purchased a portion of this tract and built for himself a home inland named "Holly Hill."

As is true of many other areas of the Bay, there is much said about Blackbeard burying treasure in the area, but no known proof. The area remained little changed until 1947, when Joseph Rose purchased the land at the south end, which he developed into "Rose Haven." This is now Herrington Harbour, but you will see reminders of the name in the area today. The chart still refers to the area as "Rose Haven."

Approach to Herring Bay

The approach to Herring Bay (57) is straightforward. The channels are well-marked. Because this is a relatively exposed shore that can have quite a sea rolling from the northeast through the southeast, I am giving some GPS positions, in the event that you are doing this in bad weather or at night.

Refer to Chart #12270-O—"Herring Bay." ᛊᚴ ᛉᛁᛉ

From out in the Bay, if you look in a westerly direction from Fl G "83" (58) (Chart #12263-F) of the ship channel, you will be looking into Herring Bay. There is a small group of houses called "Fairhaven" (59) in the middle of Herring Bay. South of Fairhaven (60), you'll see white cliffs with wooded tops. The two creeks and Herrington Harbour Marina are north and south of Fairhaven, respectively. There is a privately maintained lighthouse at Herrington Harbour (62), which can help if you are trying to get the general location at night. It is 65 feet tall and flashes white every 9 seconds. It is maintained from April 1 to October 30. Its position is 38°43.5'N by 76°32.4'W. This is on land inside Herrington Harbour.

The first marker into Herrington Bay is 2.5 sec. Fl G (63). Its position is 38°44.4'N by 76°30.9'W. The second Herring Bay marker is a Fl R "2" (64), and it guards the southern tip

of the Long Bar Shoal extending southerly from the northern end of Herring Bay. Don't try to cut across this nearly 2 NM long bar across unless you have very shallow draft, and **never** in heavy weather.

Herrington Harbour Approach

The **Herrington Harbour Marina (62)** maintains a well-marked channel **(65)** which is easy to see from the Herring Bay channel. It is approximately 80 feet wide with regular dredging. Sailing in is not allowed. Last year controlling depth was 7 feet. They will be happy to advise you of the latest depth if you call them on VHF Channel 16 or 9. The chart refers to the dredged basin area of Herrington Harbour as Rose Haven, as you will understand from its history above. Before you get to the privately maintained Herrington Harbour marker, there is an official marker designated as the Rose Haven Channel light "1," QG **(66)**. It is 30 feet outside the channel limit. Its position is 38°44.1'N by 76°32.3'W. The entrance to the channel is next marked by the privately maintained entrance daybeacon "1A" **(65)**. Its position is 38°43.9'N by 76°32.4'W. There is also a lighted range **(68)** into the marina. Its front range marker, a quick green flash 15 feet tall, is 38°43.5'N by 76°32.6'W. This is an orange daymark with black and white stripes on a white post. The rear entrance range marker is 150 yards back in a south-southeasterly direction from the front light. It is a flashing green 23 feet tall, and is an orange daymark with black and white stripes on a white post.

Rose Haven/Herrington Harbour

Although Herrington Harbour is somewhat "all by itself" in this area of the Bay, it is conveniently located in relation to other favorite destinations. It is approximately 17 NM from the Annapolis City Dock, 22 NM from St. Michaels, 9 NM from Knapps Narrows, 21 NM from Oxford, and 31 NM from Solomons.

Herrington Harbour is an excellent facility. The marina is "out in the country," although the facility itself, in comparison to others, has great attractions. The marina completely fills this privately dredged basin, and there is no place to anchor here. The two creeks **(69)** & **(70)** on the northern end of Herring Bay do not make good anchorages either, because they have wall-to-wall docks ashore and are extremely busy.

Yet another unusual aspect of this destination is that there is another very large facility under the same ownership in Tracys Creek **(69)** at the north end of Herring Bay. This marina also has many slips, but is primarily their work facility, with very impressive repair and rebuild capacity. It is called **Herrington Harbour North (71)**, and works with its sister facility. Herrington Harbour North **(71)** has a boat lift capacity of 35 tons.

As you approach Herrington Harbour South, you'll see the tall white "lighthouse building" on the shore, the pink single-story buildings of the inn on the beach immediately south of the entrance, and the huge number of masts and motorboats behind the beach, within the basin. They have 631 open slips

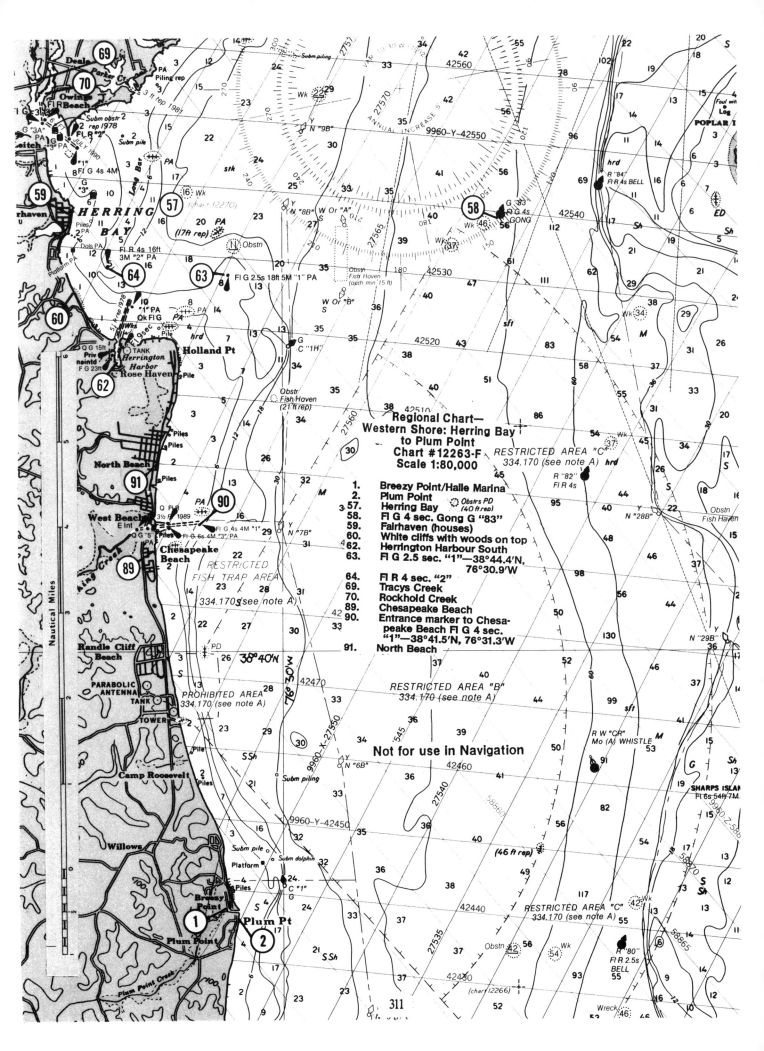

and 12 covered, accomodating boats up to 100 feet, with up to 50 amps of electricity available, gas and diesel, a pumpout, and block and cube ice. Maximum water depth available is 7 feet. MC, Visa, Amoco, and AMEX are honored.

Herrington Harbour is one of the finest marinas on the Bay. This huge basin is full of slips, but the shoreline is so well-maintained that you have a feeling of being in natural surroundings, as indeed you are. Natural marshes are carefully maintained around the basin, with forest to the west. Banana and palm trees are everywhere, giving a definite island flavor. This is heightened by the thatched roofs on the beach, and the Carribbean decor of the restaurant and inn.

The marina boasts an excellent restaurant including Caribbean decor, menu selection, food preparation, atmosphere, and management. It is under the square "lighthouse." From within, you can overlook the pool or the harbor and Bay while dining. There are three different dining areas, including an area downstairs where casual dining is the norm; a lounge and light fare area beside the pool; and an upstairs area that features crab feasts and other lighter menu items. The restaurant also grills hamburgers and prepares ligh¹ food and sells outdoors beside the pool. There is live entertainment on weekends and special occasions. This establishment is owned and managed by the same family that owns the marina. This enables the restaurant to be consistent in its excellence, even during mid-week periods when there are fewer crowds.

Also on the premises is an inn, recently remodeled. These pink-painted units are just back from the beach and south of the inlet. They are also adjacent to the pool and a children's playground. Across the street from the marina offices are a deli serving take-out and light lunches and breakfasts, a food store, a used boat sales office which also runs a van to various nearby locations, and which rents both sail and power boats usually up to 40 feet long. Fishing charter boats are available at the marina, as is bait and some tackle.

The area covered by the slips is huge. Therefore, there are three widely separated shower and restroom areas. The main area is centrally located and contains eight full private air-conditioned units each containing shower, sink, toilet, and dressing area.

Other recreation includes tennis, shuffleboard, windsurfing, volleyball, a huge pool, bike rentals, and a popular golf range approximately 5 miles away. The old resort towns of North Beach and Chesapeake Beach are approximately 3 miles to the south.

The marina offers club discounts to boats traveling in groups of five or more if they register and pay at the same time and through their fleet captain.

Environmental concerns are obvious here, with great care being taken in all aspects. For example, the shoreline under and around the docks is maintained carefully with marsh and natural growth rather than simple bulkheads. "Bat Mansions" are found all over the grounds. The flying residents keep the mosquito population under control without the need for spraying. Free pumpouts during weekdays are offered to permanent slip holders. The marina has also built special nesting platforms above its private markers so that ospreys can build nests on a secure platform that is high enough so as to not obscure the marker.

Special events are scheduled here, including fireworks on the Fourth of July and Wednesday races.

Most types of in-the-water maintenance work can be done here, but in **Herrington Harbour North** you will find one of the most complete repair and maintenance facilities on the Bay.

Even though it is miles north in Tracys Creek, I will describe it here because it is part of the same facility and under the same overall management, and it is where you will probably go if you needed work done nearby. The approach will be described in the section on Tracys Creek.

Herrington Harbour North has speciality shops covering all trades. One of the many interesting things I saw there was a new building designed especially for the blister and other indoor work on sailboats. This building had a sailboat mast sticking out of its roof. It was built with a slit in the top of its roof so that sailboats can be rolled in without being dismasted. The door is closed behind, the slit is closed over, leaving the top of the mast sticking out, and the rest of the boat in a climate-controlled area. There is an even larger building for motorboats. Both of these have radiant heating from the floor for winter work when the humidity is at its lowest and the blister victims don't use their boats anyway. This facility can handle boats up to 65 feet long and 25 feet wide indoors.

There are also 625 permanent and some transient slips, up to 50 feet at this marina, but I suggest going to Herrington Harbour South for slips, because that is where the best "creature attractions" are located.

Environmental concerns are evident here, as they are at Herrington Harbour South. There are debris traps at the work areas and hauling areas; oil, fuel, and aluminum recycling are practiced, as are water and shoreline management.

ROCKHOLD AND TRACYS CREEKS (NORTH END OF HERRING BAY)

These two creeks have shorelines almost completely lined with docks, some private. There are some marinas and some "semi-private" docks. With the notable exception of Herrington Harbour North and its maintenance facilities and a few other smaller marinas, there is not much here to attract the visiting cruiser.

Herrington Harbor North.
Covered shed for working on sailboats

312

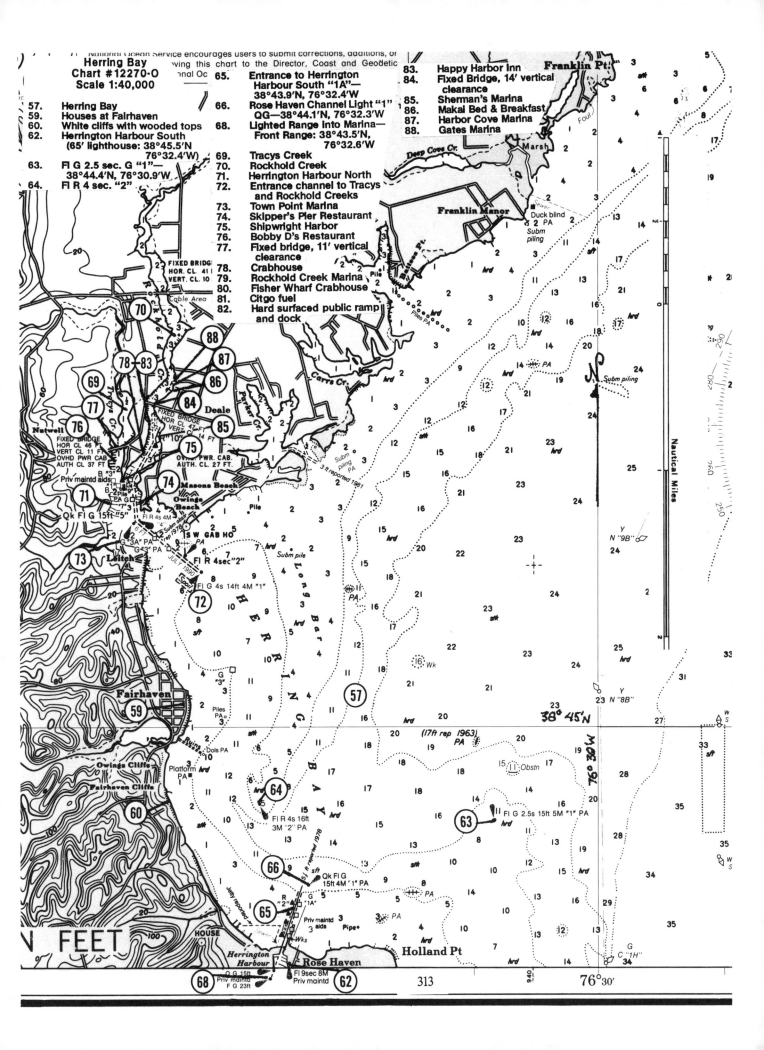

Herring Bay
Chart #12270-O
Scale 1:40,000

57. Herring Bay
59. Houses at Fairhaven
60. White cliffs with wooded tops
62. Herrington Harbour South (65' lighthouse: 38°45.5'N 76°32.4'W)
63. Fl G 2.5 sec. G "1"— 38°44.4'N, 76°30.9'W
64. Fl R 4 sec. "2"
65. Entrance to Herrington Harbour South "1A"— 38°43.9'N, 76°32.4'W
66. Rose Haven Channel Light "1" QG—38°44.1'N, 76°32.3'W
68. Lighted Range Into Marina— Front Range: 38°43.5'N, 76°32.6'W
69. Tracys Creek
70. Rockhold Creek
71. Herrington Harbour North
72. Entrance channel to Tracys and Rockhold Creeks
73. Town Point Marina
74. Skipper's Pier Restaurant
75. Shipwright Harbor
76. Bobby D's Restaurant
77. Fixed bridge, 11' vertical clearance
78. Crabhouse
79. Rockhold Creek Marina
80. Fisher Wharf Crabhouse
81. Citgo fuel
82. Hard surfaced public ramp and dock
83. Happy Harbor Inn
84. Fixed Bridge, 14' vertical clearance
85. Sherman's Marina
86. Makai Bed & Breakfast
87. Harbor Cove Marina
88. Gates Marina

313

The approach to Rockhold **(70)** and Tracys Creeks **(69)** is the same as for the lower end of Herring Bay. After you reach Fl R "2," (position given above), continue on in a northerly direction, honoring G "3" and the other markers. Avoid Long Bar Shoal and the shoal extending out from the western shore to the west of G "3." You will see a jetty to the north, extending out in a southerly direction from the point at Owings Beach. It ends on the northern side of the channel into the creeks. Follow the creek buoys **(72)** in, taking care to stay within their channel.

The first marina to the left (south) after you enter the mouth of Rockhold Creek, is **Town Point Marina (73)** with 50 slips and electricity up to 50 amps.

To your right (on the northern shore) is **Skipper's Pier Restaurant (74)** and docks. Skipper's Pier can be identified by an Amoco sign and a brown roof over the end of its dock. It has 10 slips, free while dining, and gas and diesel. There is also a cocktail lounge here.

As soon as you enter the creek, you will see the huge docking and repair facilities of **Herrington Harbour North (71)**, all described above under Herrington Harbour Marina. There is an Amoco sign at their gas and fuel dock, as well as their name sign. If entering here, you should turn to your left (west) at Gr "5" and head westerly for the markers at their docks, because there is a shoal west of Gr "7." Call them before entering, because there was talk of removing this shoal last year. In any event, it does not keep you from getting to the marina.

Straight ahead (to your north) you will see other docks, seeming to be in the middle of the creek. These are a part of **Shipwright Harbor (75)**, a marina and repair yard that is on the point between Tracys and Rockhold Creeks. Their docks line both sides of that point, and are in both creeks.

Shipwright Harbour Marina can be identified by its location at the creek split and a sign. They have 250 slips, with up to 30 amps of electricity available, gas and diesel, block and cube ice, boat lift capacity of 15 tons and a 12-ton crane, a laundromat and pool. Maximum water depth is 7 feet. Other features include boat sales and brokerage. They take MC and Visa.

Refer to Sketch Chart—"Junction—Tracys Creek-Rockhold Creek."

You will reach the junction of Tracys Creek and Rockhold Creek while still off Herrington Harbour North, with the slips of Shipwright ahead to your north. There is no junction buoy here. Instead, if you are to proceed up Tracys Creek, you must pick up the first of its markers, numbers "1" and "2" after G "7" of Rockhold Creek. You will pass G "7" to your left (west) and then see G "1" and R "2" both to your left ahead. Pass between them to go into Tracys Creek. If you wish to continue proceeding up Rockhold Channel, head on to G "9" of that channel. We are including a sketch chart because this is somewhat confusing, particularly when there is a lot of traffic in the creek.

Tracys Creek

If you go up Tracys Creek, you will see Herrington Harbour North continuing on the shore to the left (west). Soon you will reach **Bobby D's Restaurant (76)** on the left (west) with slips for customers, just before the fixed bridge **(77)** that crosses the vertical clearance of 11 feet. On the right (eastern) side of the creek is pier after pier, many private homes, and some maritime businesses. Above the bridge, the creek becomes very shallow, although pretty.

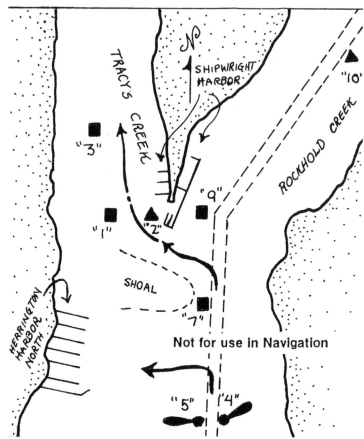

~ JUNCTION ~
TRACY'S CREEK — ROCKHOLD CREEK

Not for use in Navigation

Rockhold Creek

If you continue up Rockhold Creek, you will first see the continuation of Shipwright's docks as they wrap around the point and continue on up this creek. You will also find a jumble of dock after dock lining the shoreline, with some marinas and many private homes. Seven feet of depth is reported in the dredged channel, but no more than 4 feet after Gates Marina described below.

Shortly after you pass Shipwright's, there is a small crabhouse **(78)** on the left (west side) advertising both hard and soft shell crabs. You can land a small boat here to make a purchase. Next up on the left (west) is **Rockhold Creek Marina (79)** with a 20-ton lift and yard, mobile marine service and charterboat fishing. Still on the same side of the creek, opposite R "10," is the Fisher Wharf Crabhouse **(80)** with tables out on the dock and approximately 40 feet of dock space on the creek.

Just upstream from this crabhouse is a **Citgo** sign over a few docks **(81)** with a gas and diesel pump. You will also see a public hard surfaced **ramp and dock (82)**, with no overnight docking allowed, on the left (west) side of the creek. Then you will come to the **Happy Harbor Inn (83)**, which is a locally popular fishing center with 22 slips and 15 amp electricity, many charter fishing boats, and a restaurant. Fishing tackle and bait is available here, as are block and cube ice. This is the last facility on the left (west) before the fixed bridge **(84)** with its 14-foot vertical clearance. On the right (east) side of the creek is **Sherman's Marina (85)** selling both gas and diesel. Sherman's has a hard surfaced ramp.

After you pass through the bridge, you will notice the mod-

314

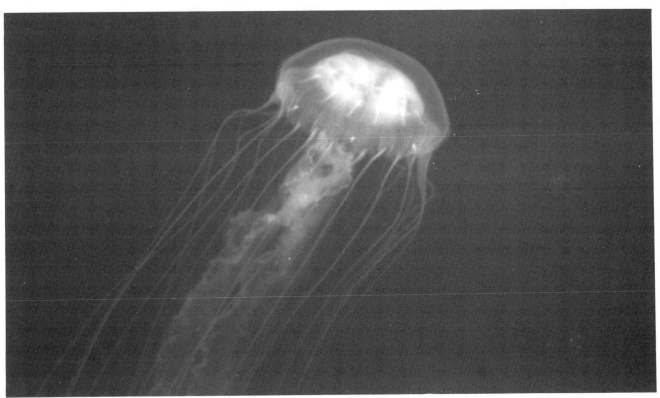

Stinging nettle

Photo by Mel Neale

Tom and Melanie coming back to *Chez Nous*

ern-looking brown two-story Makai Bed and Breakfast (86) to your right (east). Next you will see Harbor Cove Marina (87), also on the right (east) with its large blue building and a smaller building with blue and white awnings. They have 87 slips with electricity up to 50 amps, Amoco gas, lift capacity up to 25 tons, and a hard ramp.

Next up, on the east side, is Gates Marina (88) with a Sea Ray sign, 130 slips up to 50 feet, 30 amp electric, gas, honoring MC and Visa, and with a lift capacity up to 25 tons. Gates Marina has 6 feet depths. Beyond here the creek becomes prettier. It maintains around 4 feet depth for a while, and then becomes very shallow.

WESTERN SHORE BETWEEN HERRING BAY AND PATUXENT

The western shoreline between Herring Bay and the Patuxent River appears to be without harbors as you pass by offshore, but there are a few places to enter, particularly if you do not draw more than 5 feet.

Refer to Regional Chart #12263-F—"Western Shore: Herring Bay to Plum Point" PG 311
and
Regional Chart #12263-G—"Western Shore: R "78" to Cove Point."

Passing south of Herring Bay (57), you will see many homes ashore interspersed with cliffs and trees and beaches. Much of this is resort area for those living around Washington and other points inland.

Chesapeake Beach

Refer to Chart #12266-L—"Chesapeake Beach." PG 318

Soon you will see the resort town of Chesapeake Beach (89). This reminds me of an ocean fishing village with an inlet cutting into the shoreline. Inside is a fair collection of seafood restaurants and fishing establishments, and docks full of fishing boats, many for charter.

Looking to westward from the Bay, you will first notice three aqua blue water tanks on the shore. The middle one may be a bit difficult to see without binoculars because of surrounding trees. If you notice a conspicuous checked red and white tank, this will be to the south of the three. Between the southernmost and the middle aqua blue tower you should see the buoys marking the channel (90) into Chesapeake Beach Harbor. On the southern side of the channel will be a conspicuous two-story dark brick building with dark windows. Just to the north of this entrance and its village, you will see the houses of the village of "North Beach" (91). A boardwalk along the shore goes, almost without interruption, from one town to the other.

Follow the markers in, but check with a local establishment for depth if you draw more than 3 feet. Call them on Channels 9 or 16. Like all entrances on an open shore, this area could shoal very quickly. It is heavily used by the local fleet, primarily fishing boats. The outside marker, Fl G 4 sec "1" (90) is 50 feet south of the channel limit. Its position is 38°41.5'N by 76°31.3'W. There is a quick white flashing front light range (92) and a 6-second white behind it in a westerly direction.

As you come into the jetties, you will see within the jetties, a dock coming perpendicularly out from the shore to the east

of the Rod and Reel Restaurant (93). The dock is protected by a bulkhead. Boats are kept at this dock, and it can be a little confusing the first time. There are 79 slips with 100 feet maximum length available and electricity up to 50 amps. Dockage is free while dining. Gas, diesel, fishing bait and tackle, block and cube ice and snacks are sold. MC and Visa are taken. Fishing charter boats operate from here.

The creek channel passes to the right (north) of this dock. A small railroad museum (94) with a car is just in from the beach to the left (south) of the entrance. This commemorates the time when this village used to be a major resort center with its hotels, gambling, amusement park and, of course, a railroad.

Before you reach the bridge (95), you will find Abner's Ribs (96), a restaurant and marina on the left (south side) of the creek. There are 91 slips with up to 40 feet length available, 15 amp electricity, lifting capacity up to 15 tons, some repairs available, and ice, bait and charter boats.

The fixed bridge (95) has vertical clearance of only 10 feet. If you have a slip east of the bridge, it's a short walk to facilities west of the bridge.

Passing through the bridge brings you to a Subway (97) fast food restaurant, visible from the water on the left (south side) of the creek just inside the bridge. Also to the west of the bridge you will find Kellam's Marina (98), involving both sides of the creek. It has 140 slips with up to 30 amps electricity, gas, a 30-ton railway, 12-ton lift, hard surfaced ramps, and general repair work, Visa and MC are taken. There is also a crab house, on the south side.

The Harbor House and Marina (99) is to the west of the bridge, all the way in on the south side of the creek. There are 44 slips here with 15 amp electricity and many charter fishing boats.

Crabbing on dock pilings

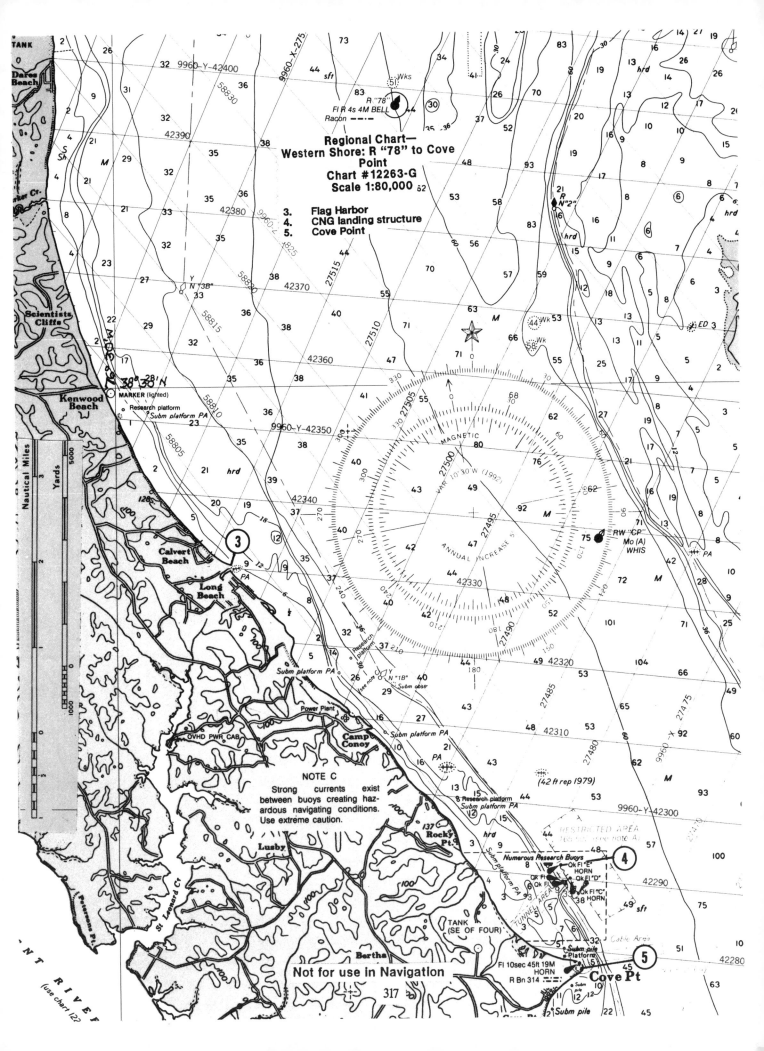

Regional Chart—
Western Shore: R "78" to Cove Point
Chart #12263-G
Scale 1:80,000

3. Flag Harbor
4. CNG landing structure
5. Cove Point

NOTE C
Strong currents exist
between buoys creating hazardous navigating conditions.
Use extreme caution.

Not for use in Navigation

317

Breezy Point

Refer to Chart #12266-M—"Breezy Point."

Heading down the Bay, the next harbor of any size is a basin containing **Breezy Point/Halle Marina (1)**, just to the north of Plum Point **(2)**. This has many trailers set up along the beach, and a channel with controlling depth of only 3 feet. There are 230 slips with electricity up to 30 amps, hard surfaced ramps, boat lifting capacity up to 17.5 tons, and a store selling bait and tackle, snacks, block and cube ice, hardware, some food items, beverages, gasoline, and miscellaneous other items. Visa and MC are honored.

The harbor is a basin with docks around the parimeters and work area around much of that. There are numerous charter fishing boats here. The entrance has an old cement quay on the sides.

Flag Harbor

Refer to Regional Chart #12263-G—"Western Shore: R"78" to Cove Point." PG 317 and
Chart #12264-B—"Flag Harbor."

Next of interest south down the Bay is **Flag Harbor Yacht Haven (3)**. This is a very pleasant marina tucked in between two hills. This marina has 170 slips with electricity up to 30 amps, gas and diesel, a pool, a pumpout, lifting up to 20 tons, and general repair work. Depths are subject to shoaling because of the location. Don't take in more than 4 feet without first checking present conditions by calling them on VHF Channels 9 or 16.

You can recognize this marina by a tall white column-like structure on the shore immediately to the north of the entrance, and a double-layered area of houses to the south. Jetties extend out on either side of the entrance, and privately maintained lights are on the ends. It is to the north of a huge compressed natural gas landing structure **(4)**. This is a man-made island of steel and concrete, cranes and buildings, sitting high on pilings out in the Bay. It will be readily apparent east of the western shore just north of Cove Point **(5)**. Cove Point is around 6 miles to the south of Flag Harbor.

We found no nearby attractions or stores. Flag Harbor is deep in an exclusive residential area. Two large very high hills, with nice homes nestled in the trees, swoop down to what was formerly a ravine. In this low point between the hills lies the marina, dredged out long ago. The hills rise on either side when you enter, with a feeling of complete security. There are many signs around advising no trespassing into the surrounding community.

97. Subway fast food restaurant
98. Kellam's Marina
99. Harbor House and Marina

Chesapeake Beach
Chart #12266-L
Scale 1:40,000

89. Chesapeake Beach
90. Fl G 4 sec. "1"—
    38°41.5'N, 76°31.3'W—
    entrance marker
91. North Beach
92. Range lights
93. Rod & Reel Restaurant
94. Railroad Museum
95. Fixed Bridge—vertical cl. 10'
96. Abner's Ribs restaurant & marina

Not for use in Navigation

Duck resting

318

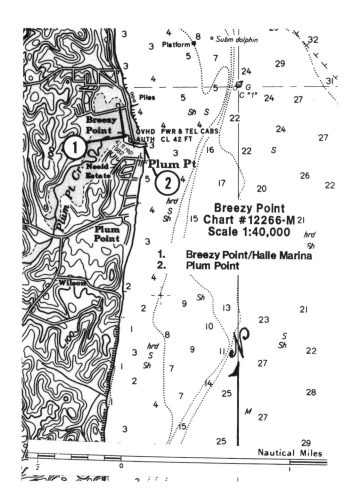

Breezy Point
Chart #12266-M
Scale 1:40,000

1. Breezy Point/Halle Marina
2. Plum Point

Not for use in Navigation

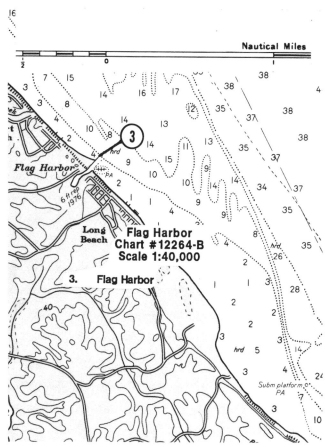

Flag Harbor
Chart #12264-B
Scale 1:40,000

3. Flag Harbor

Not for use in Navigation

Flag Harbor Marina

319

CHAPTER 21

PATUXENT RIVER

The Patuxent River runs deep back into rural southern Maryland, without any large cities. The small boating-oriented village of Solomons Island is near its mouth. Very beautiful and protected anchorages are in many creeks.

ENTRANCE

Refer to Chart #12264-C—"Cove Point & Patuxent River Entrance."

Approaching the Patuxent River (3) from the north, you will see to your west the remarkable shoreline of Calvert Cliffs (6). They are light reddish brown in color, run for around 30 miles to the north of the Patuxent, and make an unmistakable landmark. Against this backdrop you will see the large, now unused offshore CNG loading dock (4), standing starkly on huge steel legs. Just to the south of that, in mute contrast, is the beautiful Cove Point Lighthouse (5) with its quaint white cylindrical tower and the small white lightkeepers' buildings beside it. Rounding Cove Point, many just follow the shoreline in, leaving Little Cove Point (7) a safe distance to the west. If you do "follow the shoreline," beware of the many crab pot floats usually in the area.

If approaching from the south, you will see the weather devastated remains of Cedar Point Light (8), with the old three-story brick building (the third story consists of its V roof) standing in the water just to the east of the point. This was built on solid land in the late 1800s. Now, with vacant windows staring like mad eyes, it stubbornly resists the storms that are taking its foundation back to the sea. Pass it well to your west, rounding Fl G "1PR" (9) to avoid the shoal. The position of "1PR" is 38°18.24'N by 76°21.20'W.

Heading into the Patuxent is primarily a matter of following the buoys and avoiding the sailing and fishing boats. The entrance funnels into the narrower space between Drum Point (14) on the northern bank and Fl G "3" (15) off Hog Point on the southern bank. The southern bank is part of the Patuxent Naval Air Station and you will see its buildings behind the trees. The northern bank is high and has nice homes and woods. Drum Point Light was built around 1883 in 10 feet of water, and by 1918 was on land at low tide.

West of the two points (16) mentioned above, we often see boats anchored in various locations to the east of the Solomons entrance, usually for an overnight stop while heading up or down the Bay. Obviously, this area can get quite rough, and there are many boats transitting back and forth and up and down. Many of these are sport fishing boats leaving rapidly in the wee hours of the dawn, and work boats leaving before dawn. Occasionally, large navy vessels pass up or down river in the channel. It is not advisable to anchor here overnight, particularly with some good creeks so nearby.

Patuxent Naval Air Station

Most of the land ashore behind Cedar Point, and much of the southern bank of the lower Patuxent, belongs to the Patuxent Naval Air Station (10). You will notice some of its buildings, and you will certainly be aware of its planes, even when you are down in the southern Chesapeake, as they make their approaches. There is a visitors center for this important Naval installation, but you must arrange for ground transportation to reach it.

This naval air station has a firing target (11) out in the Bay that is potentially very hazardous to boats not taking care to avoid its vicinity. Although it is not within the geographical boundaries of this "Northern Bay" volume, I mention it because it is directly in the route that many pleasure boats take when they are coming up the Bay and approaching the Patuxent from the south. Most boats simply travel from Point No Point Light on a course of 355°M on up the coast until they reach the G "1PR" off Cedar Point. However, the target area is on this general heading, just under 5 miles north of No Point Light and 5 miles south of Cedar Point. The range is marked by buoys and it has targets on steel piles. The GPS derived position 1 mile to its west is 38°12.59'N by 76°19.28'W. Usually there are Navy patrol boats out when firing is in progress, but this should not be relied upon. The area should be given a wide berth. We have seen planes shooting at the targets. The preferred route up the Bay is out in the well-marked large ship channel, but most do not use this because of the ships and the extra time it requires. You can head into the river after clearing and rounding G "1PR" off Cedar Point.

Calvert Cliffs

The entrance to the Patuxent River should not be described without some mention of the remarkable "Calvert Cliffs" (6), which are very conspicuous from any approach to the river. These appear as very high reddish brown dirt cliffs lining the western shore of the Bay, north of the entrance to the Patuxent. These 30-mile long cliffs are not merely conspicuous and pretty, they are very famous for the fossils that have been found there over the years. Captain John Smith was amazed when he saw them, and named them "Rickard's Cliffs." The Calverts, so dominant in the vicinity in later times, gave many places their name.

These cliffs were formed by the natural erosion of the Bay after the last of the ice age when this section of the continent lifted up and the sea level fell. This allowed the currents of the Susquehanna and the waves of the forming Bay to cut into what had once been a sea bed where thousands of years of plant and creature remains had settled and been buried. As you look at the cliffs, you see different layers of sea floor, sliced as though it were a huge cake, with fossils buried within, and sometimes tumbling to the beach below.

There is now a Calvert Cliffs State Park (13) at this site. You may walk the beaches and pick up fossils yourself, as long as they come from the beach and you do not take anything from (or do anything to increase the erosion of) the cliffs. Over 600 species of fossils have been identified from the cliffs. These include teeth from many species of shark.

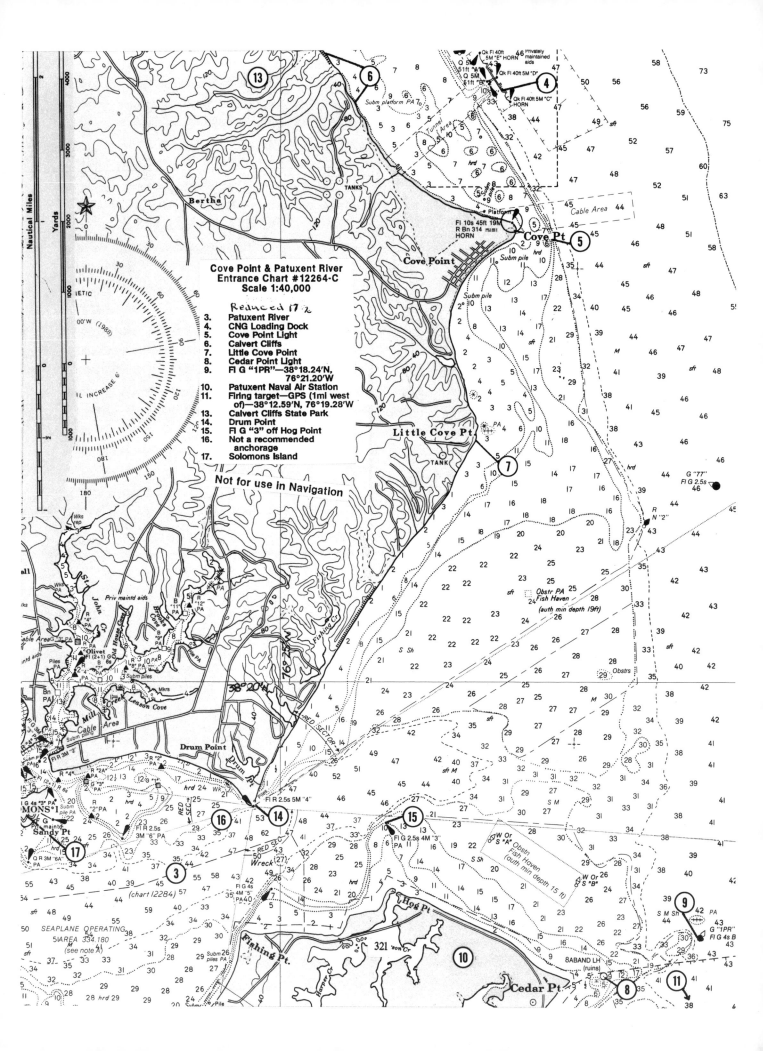

**Cove Point & Patuxent River
Entrance Chart #12264-C
Scale 1:40,000**

Reduced 17 ½

3. Patuxent River
4. CNG Loading Dock
5. Cove Point Light
6. Calvert Cliffs
7. Little Cove Point
8. Cedar Point Light
9. Fl G "1PR"—38°18.24'N, 76°21.20'W
10. Patuxent Naval Air Station
11. Firing target—GPS (1mi west of)—38°12.59'N, 76°19.28'W
13. Calvert Cliffs State Park
14. Drum Point
15. Fl G "3" off Hog Point
16. Not a recommended anchorage
17. Solomons Island

Not for use in Navigation

Some of these may also be seen in the Calvert Marine Museum in Solomons Island, described below.

Thirteen miles of marked foot trails are open for walking as well as the beach. There are also fishing and picnic areas. The park is regularly accessed from land. You would have to arrange transportation from Solomons Island or some other nearby stop.

SOLOMONS ISLAND AREA

Solomons Island is actually a small peninsula village joined by a man-made causeway of many years. However, most cruisers, when they use the term, think of not only that village, but also of the three creeks around it, at least Back Creek which borders the village.

The area has many pretty and snug anchorages, and the quaint village has many attractions for the boater and some excellent marinas. While some of the anchorages are beautiful, other parts of the area have been built up considerably recently. Aside from the good opportunities for marine supplies, there are not very convenient grocery or other shopping opportunities except a small shopping mall a few blocks' walk from Hospitality Harbor, at the end of Back Creek.

Entrance to Solomons Island
Refer to Chart #12264-D—"Lower Patuxent River: Solomons" and
Chart #12284-A—"Solomons: Entrance and Back Creek" and PG 325
Chart #12284-B—"Back Creek Continuation." PG 324

There are two channels into Solomons Island (17) and Back Creek (18). The route close to the northern shore (19) is used extensively by local boaters. Twelve feet is controlling depth, but if you miss the marks, you will find a very shallow shoal (20) of 2 to 3 feet. Most deep draft cruising boats use the main route (21) between Fl R "6" on the eastern side of the entrance, and QR "6A" off Sandy Point (22) on the western side. As you turn in to the north between these markers, you will see ahead the bulkheading around the northeastern tip of Solomons Island. This belongs to the University of Maryland Research Center (23).

The 6 mph speed limit is rigidly enforced from here on in. I once asked a very helpful officer of the DNR Marine Police how dinghies were supposed to keep track of their exact speed. He explained that any wake was too much, regardless of speed, because your wake could cause people to lose their balance while getting on or off a boat at a marina dock.

As soon as you pass the northeasterly tip of Solomons Island, you will see huge opportunities awaiting both ashore and along the shores. Depending upon your preferences, you may wish to go up Mill Creek (25) to your right (northeast) with its numerous quiet anchorages, or you may wish to head into Back Creek for a marina or more crowded anchorage. If you want convenient access to the village, you should choose Back Creek.

Immediately confronting the navigator is the bulkheaded triangular island seemingly in the middle of the channel. This is called "Molly's Leg" (26). I have heard several stories about the source of this name. One, is that the leg of a pirate named "Moll" was buried or found there many years ago when it was a natural island. It is now a dredge fill island. The charts indicate very scarce water (27) to the north of the island, between it and the southern docks of Calvert Marina (28). In fact, we

found at least 8 feet depth here, including up to the fuel and other docks of this marina, even where the charts report 2 and 3 feet. Obviously, it has been dredged and you can pass on either side of the island. Most, coming in for the first time, follow the main channel and put the island on their right (northeast) in order to check out the town.

Solomons Island
The basin (29), southwest of Molly's Leg, is a very popular anchorage for many reasons. It is convenient if you are just passing through and stopping for the night. It is close to the restaurants and attractions on the shores surrounding it. There is a certain excitement here as boats come and go and the establishments ashore liven up for weekends. There are some problems with this anchorage however. The loose mud bottom is not the best holding. With the 5:1 scope needed, it can get crowded fast. Unfortunately, many just come for the fun ashore, leave their boats without properly setting their anchor or letting out scope, to give others the pleasure of fending off their boats when they start dragging!

As mentioned earlier, the first set of docks and buildings to your left (south) as you round the point is the University of Maryland Research facility (23) with its research boats. Continuing around the point in a clockwise circle, the next facility, with conspicuous four-story open dry storage racks, and next to the research center, is **Solomons Point Marina (30)**, selling gas and diesel, and displaying a sign on the dock. They have 25 slips taking boats up to 50 feet and longer alongside, with electricity up to 50 amps, a yard with closed end lift capacity up to 20 tons, some marine supplies, a laundromat nearby, and a small but helpful convenience store.

Next is **Harbor Island Marina (31)** with 100 slips and alongside space for boats up to 175 feet, electricity up to 50 amps, selling Chevron diesel and gas, marine supplies, repair yard with a 25-ton lift and machine shop and welding capability, laundromat nearby, and a nice restaurant and lounge on the premises, in a blue-gray two-story building. They are dealers for OMC and Volvo Penta.

You will then see a collection of small docks (32), some of which are for dinghy landing for the restaurants ashore and some of which are for fishing boat charters. All along the western shore of this basin you will see one dock after another. Some are private.

One of the most impressive structures on the shore, and indeed, one of the most impressive establishments in the area, is the tall two-story V-roofed building of the **Lighthouse Inn (33)**, patterned in many respects after Cedar Point Lighthouse. They have glass walls looking out both on this creek and the river on the west side of the peninsula. There are slips here in two piers capable of accomodating 10 boats with electricity up to 30 amps. Water depths range up to 15 feet at the end of the docks, and alongside capacity is at least 60 feet.

There is complimentary docking while dining. Lighthouse Inn is one of the finest restaurants that you will find, as to food preparation and excellence, service, decor, and atmosphere. It also exudes the historical flavor of the area and contains fascinating artifacts and decor. There are authentic photographs of the Solomons Island area taken in the late 1800s and early 1900s spread tastefully on all the walls. You can look out the surrounding windows and see the harbor as it is today, and then look up at the pictures and see it as it was. The owner and builder of this restaurant is particularly well-versed in local history and lore, and has personally taken great pains to see that his customers appreciate and enjoy

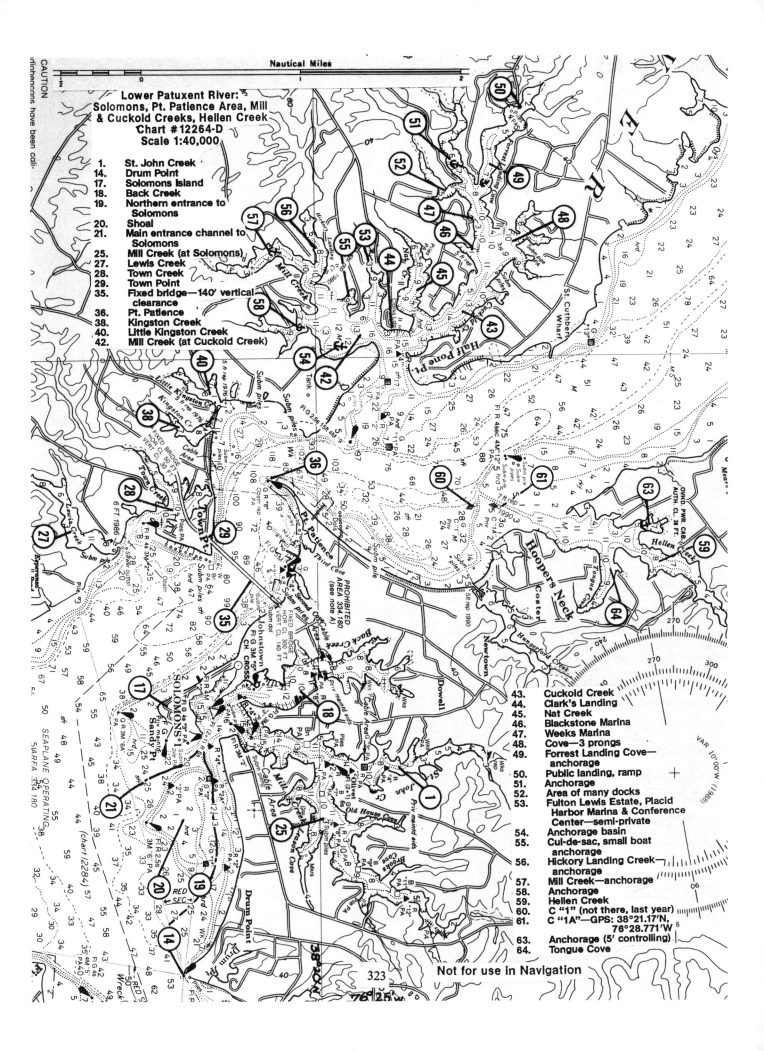

Lower Patuxent River:
Solomons, Pt. Patience Area, Mill
& Cuckold Creeks, Hellen Creek
Chart #12264-D
Scale 1:40,000

1. St. John Creek
14. Drum Point
17. Solomons Island
18. Back Creek
19. Northern entrance to Solomons
20. Shoal
21. Main entrance channel to Solomons
25. Mill Creek (at Solomons)
27. Lewis Creek
28. Town Creek
29. Town Point
35. Fixed bridge—140' vertical clearance
36. Pt. Patience
38. Kingston Creek
40. Little Kingston Creek
42. Mill Creek (at Cuckold Creek)

43. Cuckold Creek
44. Clark's Landing
45. Nat Creek
46. Blackstone Marina
47. Weeks Marina
48. Cove—3 prongs
49. Forrest Landing Cove—anchorage
50. Public landing, ramp
51. Anchorage
52. Area of many docks
53. Fulton Lewis Estate, Placid Harbor Marina & Conference Center—semi-private
54. Anchorage basin
55. Cul-de-sac, small boat anchorage
56. Hickory Landing Creek—anchorage
57. Mill Creek—anchorage
58. Anchorage
59. Hellen Creek
60. C "1" (not there, last year)
61. C "1A"—GPS: 38°21.17'N, 76°28.771'W [5]
63. Anchorage (5' controlling)
64. Tongue Cove

Not for use in Navigation

the unique heritage surrounding them as they dine. The buildings to the south of the restaurant are luxury suites, also with docks in front, making this an excellent place to have guests come who would not wish to stay aboard. Reservations are usually needed.

The bar in the Lighthouse Inn is an authentically built "⅓ scale skipjack," complete and accurate in every detail except the modifications needed to allow it to serve as a bar. This is not the type of cheap imitation that you so often see in restaurants. It was built by local shipbuilding craftsmen with loving attention to authentic detail. Some of those responsible for the carvings work as Master Carvers in the wood-carving section of the Calvert Marine Museum, just upstream. I was told somewhat apologetically, that the hand-carved blocks on the vessel are "only" Black Oak instead of the traditional Lignum Vitae, because of the difficulty in obtaining that wood. Pull up your stool to the decks of the *Spirit of Solomons* and look out the broad windows at the harbor where boats like this formerly worked. There is also a bar and tables outside over the docks and the water, where you can order light fare. On weekends and many other times, there is very tasteful and enjoyable live entertainment.

Next, and just to the north of the Lighthouse, is **Bowen's Inn and Restaurant (34)** with a few slips. The **Solomons Island Yacht Club (35)** appears next, with its very nice two-story clubhouse with white columns and a comfortable front porch and numerous docks and a dinghy dock. This is private with reciprocation privileges for members of other recognized clubs. There is a sign on its dock (SIYS).

To the north next are the docks of Hurricane Alley Dock Bay and Eatery **(36)**. This has a light fare bar and grill with a small convenience shop behind. There was formerly a grocery store here. We are now moving into what is referred to as "The Narrows" **(37)**, a narrow slip between the peninsula and Janes Point. No anchoring is allowed here. The docks and yard facilities that you see on your right (east) belong to **Town Center Marina (38)**, and most of the docks on your left (west) belong to establishments which do a lot of business relating to sport fishing, including charter boats.

The docks of **O'Berry Marine Service (39)** have 15 slips primarily for small outboard or I/O boats. There is a well-stocked marine store here, particularly suited to the needs of this type of boater. Outboard and other types of repair are done here. Their services include repair for Johnson and MerCruiser.

Proceeding deeper into The Narrows, the buildings and docks of Rhumb Line Inn **(40)** are near the end. This is a full menu

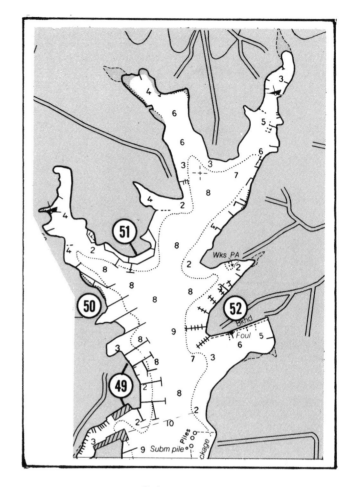

Solomons:
Continuation of Back Creek
Chart #12284-B
Scale 1:10,000

49.   Spring Cove Marina
50.   Hospitality Harbor Marina, Holiday Inn, dinghy landing for shopping center
51.   Solomons Landing—housing and private dock area
52.   Oyster Bay condo and dock area

Not for use in Navigation

Calvert Marine Museum, Solomons

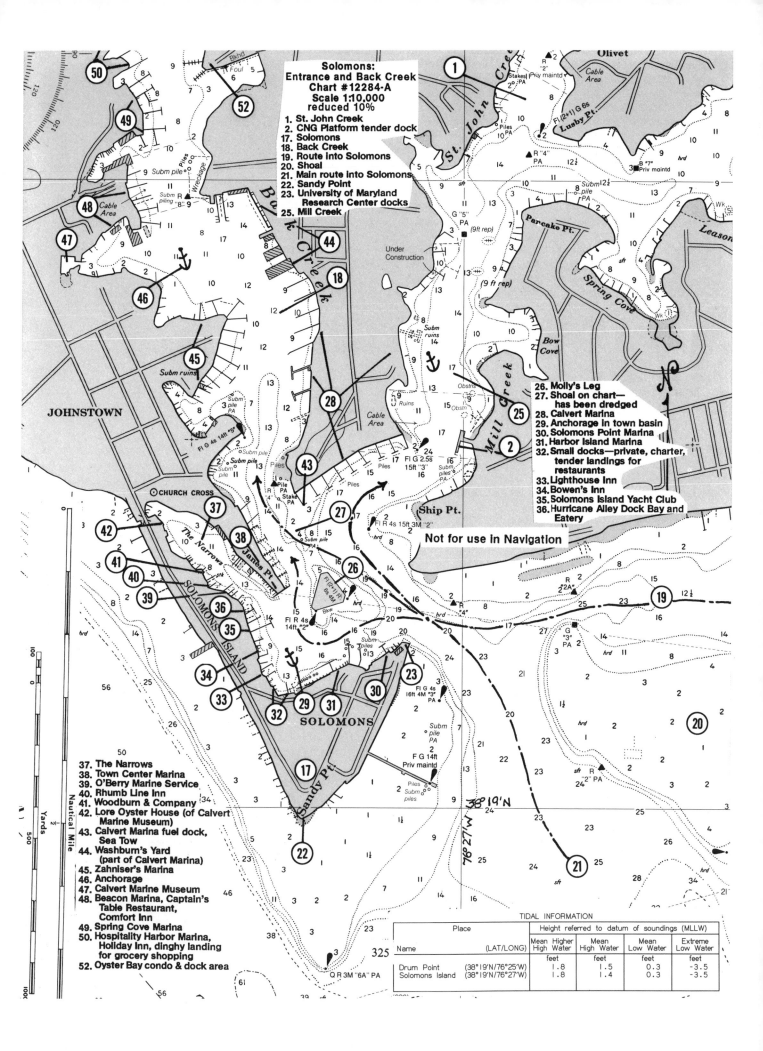

Solomons:
Entrance and Back Creek
Chart #12284-A
Scale 1:10,000
reduced 10%
1. St. John Creek
2. CNG Platform tender dock
17. Solomons
18. Back Creek
19. Route into Solomons
20. Shoal
21. Main route into Solomons
22. Sandy Point
23. University of Maryland
    Research Center docks
25. Mill Creek

26. Molly's Leg
27. Shoal on chart—
    has been dredged
28. Calvert Marina
29. Anchorage in town basin
30. Solomons Point Marina
31. Harbor Island Marina
32. Small docks—private, charter,
    tender landings for
    restaurants
33. Lighthouse Inn
34. Bowen's Inn
35. Solomons Island Yacht Club
36. Hurricane Alley Dock Bay and
    Eatery

Not for use in Navigation

37. The Narrows
38. Town Center Marina
39. O'Berry Marine Service
40. Rhumb Line Inn
41. Woodburn & Company
42. Lore Oyster House (of Calvert
    Marine Museum)
43. Calvert Marina fuel dock,
    Sea Tow
44. Washburn's Yard
    (part of Calvert Marina)
45. Zahniser's Marina
46. Anchorage
47. Calvert Marine Museum
48. Beacon Marina, Captain's
    Table Restaurant,
    Comfort Inn
49. Spring Cove Marina
50. Hospitality Harbor Marina,
    Holiday Inn, dinghy landing
    for grocery shopping
52. Oyster Bay condo & dock area

JOHNSTOWN

SOLOMONS ISLAND

SOLOMONS

325

TIDAL INFORMATION

Place		Height referred to datum of soundings (MLLW)			
Name	(LAT/LONG)	Mean Higher High Water	Mean High Water	Mean Low Water	Extreme Low Water
		feet	feet	feet	feet
Drum Point	(38°19'N/76°25'W)	1.8	1.5	0.3	-3.5
Solomons Island	(38°19'N/76°27'W)	1.8	1.4	0.3	-3.5

restaurant and there are some docks for complimentary docking while dining. There is a great deal of fishing charter boat activity around this center, with many of these boats waiting and ready to take you out to the best spots. This can be an exciting place to be when they come in after a good day. The next facility up, **Woodburn & Company (41)**, has a few slips sometimes available and sells gas and diesel and hosts a whole fleet of fishing charter boats at its docks.

All the way at the end, still on the west side, are the old buildings of the Lore Oyster House (42), now associated with the Calvert Marine Museum.

Most of Janes Point is occupied by the large facilities of **Town Center Marina (38)**. You will see it straight ahead to your north as you round Molly's Leg. There are over 100 slips here up to 50 feet long, with electricity up to 100 amps and capacity for very large vessels to lay alongside. Gas and diesel are sold on the flat tip of the point facing southward. The large full service work yard has a lift capacity up to 50 tons. They have CNG gas, and block and cube ice. This marina is somewhat removed from the attractions of Solomons Island if you don't like walking, but they provide courtesy transportation when available.

Solomons Island Ashore
Refer to Town Map— "Solomons Island."

As mentioned earlier, many people refer to the three creeks when they use the term "Solomons Island" (17), but when people go ashore, they usually do so in the village of that name on the peninsula connected to the mainland by a causeway (53). This village is now receiving quite a bit of tourist traffic by car in addition to the boating population, and has added many facilities in the last few years.

The area with most attractions lies on the island. Our walk begins with the causeway connecting the island with the mainland, and will head south down Main Street which extends down the length of the island to its southern tip. At the causeway, you can look into The Narrows to your east, or the Patuxent River to your west. However, before heading south, we will mention some of the points of interest north up this road, not only because they are there, but also because Back Creek, with several marinas from which you may begin your exploration, extends well north of the causeway.

If you head north, you would find Solomons Boat Rental (54) just to your left (west side of the road), on the Patuxent River. They rent small skiffs and jet ski type vessels. Most of what you will see will be quaint private homes with a few interspersed notion and similar shops. C Street, on the way, takes you to **Zahniser's Marina (45)**. After a little over four blocks, you will find the very helpful Tourist Information Center (55) with staff, maps, and pamphlets. This is just west of the Calvert Marine Museum (47). Just beyond the Information Center, Lore Street, running off to your right (east), will bring you to **Comfort Inn and Beacon Marina (48)** and **Spring Cove Marina (49)**, described under Back Creek below. On the northeast corner of this intersection is a putt putt golf range (56). About two more blocks will bring you to Roy Rogers (57) and the Patuxent Plaza (58), the shopping center described below. For your creek reference, this shopping center is west of the Spring Cove and Hospitality Harbor (50) area.

Walking south now, beginning at the causeway, you will first come upon the white two-story Lore Oyster House (42), a very old seafood packing building now a part of the Calvert Marine Museum. This seafood business began here in 1888.

There is then the Rhumb Line Inn (40) with charter boats on the docks around and the Woodburn and Company (41) and Bunky's Charters (59) with their fishing charter operations.

Across the street on the western side is a county park (60) with grassy yard overlooking the Patuxent River, benches, and a historical plaque about Solomons. A short walk farther south, on the left (eastern) side of the street, is another small park with public restrooms (61). Just down from this, you will find O'Berry Marine Service (39) mentioned above. Continuing down will take you by various small restaurants, bed and breakfasts, and notion shops. The Seahorses Restaurant (62), night club and inn has several eating areas. One on the porch facing the street has sand on the floor with shells and other beach decor.

Proceeding farther south, you will see on your right the large Solomons Pier Restaurant and Lounge (63) overlooking the Patuxent, with docks for complimentary docking while dining, if you have a shoal draft boat and are not concerned about possible wake or wave action from the Patuxent. You can walk to any of these places from secure anchorages or marina slips inside (east of) Solomons Island. Solomons Pier has a full fare menu as well as light fare such as pizza, subs, and ice cream.

Next to your left (east), you will notice a sign for "Thomas Crabs" (64). This is a private home on Back Creek where they shed and sell soft crabs. A visit should be informative and enjoyable. Just south from that, on the same side, is the historical and pretty St. Peters Episcopal Church (65), built in 1889.

After you pass Lighthouse Inn Restaurant (33) (described above), you will find a one hour film developer (66), again on the eastern side of the road, just as it curves in a more easterly direction. Around the turn you will find China Harbor Restaurant (67), on the southern side of the street, and also a motel. A Tiki bar and restaurant (68) is next door. These establishments are across the street from the water front where there are some piers for small boat docking for some of the businesses. Just a little farther down, behind the area of Solomons Point Marina (30), you will find the Solomons Island Laundry (69) and the new buildings of Chesapeake Biological Laboratory (70). The laundry is self-service.

Patuxent River Pilot Boats, Solomons

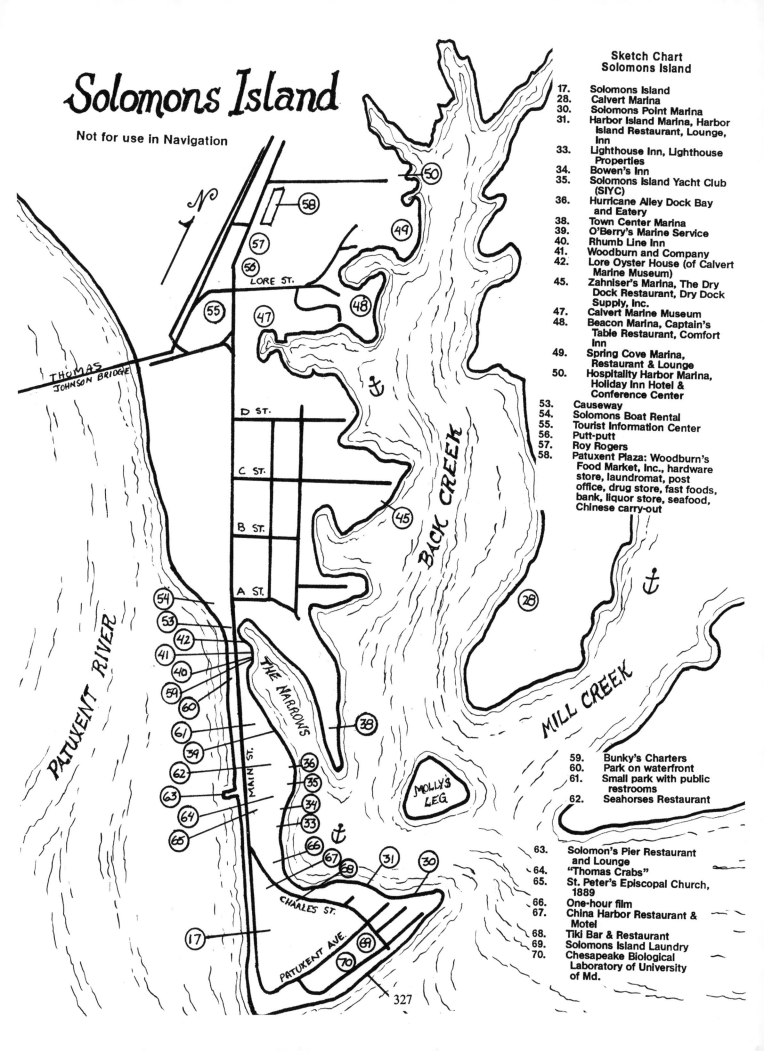

Solomons Island

Not for use in Navigation

Sketch Chart
Solomons Island

17. Solomons Island
28. Calvert Marina
30. Solomons Point Marina
31. Harbor Island Marina, Harbor
    Island Restaurant, Lounge,
    Inn
33. Lighthouse Inn, Lighthouse
    Properties
34. Bowen's Inn
35. Solomons Island Yacht Club
    (SIYC)
36. Hurricane Alley Dock Bay
    and Eatery
38. Town Center Marina
39. O'Berry's Marine Service
40. Rhumb Line Inn
41. Woodburn and Company
42. Lore Oyster House (of Calvert
    Marine Museum)
45. Zahniser's Marina, The Dry
    Dock Restaurant, Dry Dock
    Supply, Inc.
47. Calvert Marine Museum
48. Beacon Marina, Captain's
    Table Restaurant, Comfort
    Inn
49. Spring Cove Marina,
    Restaurant & Lounge
50. Hospitality Harbor Marina,
    Holiday Inn Hotel &
    Conference Center
53. Causeway
54. Solomons Boat Rental
55. Tourist Information Center
56. Putt-putt
57. Roy Rogers
58. Patuxent Plaza: Woodburn's
    Food Market, Inc., hardware
    store, laundromat, post
    office, drug store, fast foods,
    bank, liquor store, seafood,
    Chinese carry-out

59. Bunky's Charters
60. Park on waterfront
61. Small park with public
    restrooms
62. Seahorses Restaurant

63. Solomon's Pier Restaurant
    and Lounge
64. "Thomas Crabs"
65. St. Peter's Episcopal Church,
    1889
66. One-hour film
67. China Harbor Restaurant &
    Motel
68. Tiki Bar & Restaurant
69. Solomons Island Laundry
70. Chesapeake Biological
    Laboratory of University
    of Md.

327

Proceeding up Back Creek

Refer to Chart #12284-A—"Solomons: Entrance and Back Creek" PG 325 and
Chart #12284-B—"Back Creek Continuation." PG 323

Proceeding up Back Creek, you will see the fuel docks (gas and diesel) of the well-known **Calvert Marina (43)** to your right (east). There are 400 slips here with capacity for the largest of pleasure vessels as well as the smallest, and electricity up to 100 amps. The well-established full service yard has lift capacity up to 70 tons with most trades represented. There is a marine store, laundromat, cocktail lounge and restaurant, block and cube ice, NOS charts, and pool. The fuel docks down at the end of the peninsula are where the charts indicate around 2 to 3 feet depths. This has all been dredged and we found 8 feet here. If you come into the fuel docks, keep R "4" to your north. There is shoal to the east of that mark, but this does not interfere with docking at the fuel dock. Approach from either side of Molly's Leg. MC and Visa are both honored.

Calvert Marina extends all the way up Back Creek on this peninsula to and including the area locally known as **"Washburn's Yard" (44)**. The old name is still on the roof of the building. It also includes new slips on the south side of the point of the peninsula, and the slips belonging to the condominium development on the eastern side of the peninsula, on Mill Creek. Much of the premises are pleasant yard and trees down near the point.

Continuing northerly up the creek, with Calvert Marina and facilities still to your right (east) as you pass FL G "5," you will begin to see to the left (west side) the docks of another huge and very well known marina and full service yard. This is **Zahniser's Marina (45)**, owned by the same family for many years, with over 300 slips up to 55 feet and longer spaces alongside, electricity up to 50 amps, a gas and diesel dock alongside the channel, pumpout station, a full service yard including electronics service and sail loft and mast and rigging work, with haulout capacity up to 60 tons. A very well stocked marine store carries many parts commonly needed, as well as general marine items, clothing, hardware, CNG, and more. There is a small restaurant and cocktail lounge on the premises, laundromat, and pool. They assist with transportation when able and loan bikes. There is a convenient dinghy dock on the northern side of the peninsula upon which Zahniser's is located, and this therefore makes a good place to get parts and marine supplies when anchored. They are dealers for Awlgrip, Imron, Perkins, Onan, Adler-Barbour, Volvo Penta, Westerbeke, IMI, Universal, and Yanmar, among others.

The cove **(46)** immediately to the north of Zahniser's, still on the west side, is the anchorage of choice for many boats who visit this area. There is not as much traffic as out in the Solomons Island basin, the holding is better, the depths are better (9 to 11 feet), and it is close to the supplies at Zahniser's and Calvert and right out from the Calvert Marine Museum **(47)**. There is a "no anchorage" sign in the passage into the museum. It is also closer to a spot where you may land for access to groceries and a small shopping center, described below.

Deep in the anchoring cove, you will see an old screw pile lighthouse sitting up on the shore as though cast adrift and lost. Not lost at all but quite at home, this is the old Drum Point Lighthouse, now a landmark of the Calvert Marine Museum. You can land by dinghy at the docks marked for this purpose up in this cove. There are many interesting displays here, including models, hands-on exhibits, live fish tanks, fossils, wetland displays, Bay boats, and the *Wm. B. Tennison*, built as a bugeye in 1899, converted later to a buyboat, and now the oldest Coast Guard licensed passenger vessel on the Chesapeake. She takes out tours around the harbor and into the river.

The next facility up, on the left (west) begins on the northern bank on the cove just mentioned and extends northerly and around into the next cove. The is the **Beacon Marina (48)** facility, now encompassing several entities that were formerly independently owned. This large facility has over 200 slips with alongside space for over 100 feet, electricity up to 50 amps, pool, block and cube ice, a full service yard with 35-ton lift and a railway and mast crane, and the Captain's Table restaurant offering waterfront dining. Here also is the large Comfort Inn Hotel, the lobby of which maintains VHF Channel 16 watch for the marina facilities 24 hours a day.

North of the next cove up, still on the western side, is the very pretty **Spring Cove Marina (49)**. There are 250 slips, some covered, up to 50 feet long with greater lengths available alongside, electricity up to 50 amps, gas and diesel, a pumpout, laundromat, pool, block and cube ice, and a very nice store with boating supplies, related items such as sun lotion and some clothing, light groceries and souvenir items. A full service yard has lift capacity up to 30 tons. The yard is well back inland from the waterfront area and does not interfere with the park-like atmosphere around the docks. The docks, pool, and store are in an area of many trees, pretty lawn, and grounds covered with pine needles. There is a restaurant with cocktail lounge on the premises.

The last public facility up the creek is still on the west side. (All of the facilities that you will have been passing on the eastern side will be those of the multi-faceted Calvert Marina). This is the **Hospitality Harbor Marina (50)**, at the base of tree-covered hills, behind which you will see a tastefully blended large brown brick Holiday Inn Hotel. Hospitality Harbor has 75 slips with alongside space for very large vessels and electricity up to 50 amps, a pumpout, laundromat, pool, and many of the facilities that you would expect at a Holiday Inn, such as restaurant, lounge, conference center, and rooms.

An important feature of Hospitality Harbor Marina is that its docks are just a few blocks away from the Patuxent Plaza shopping center. This has a good grocery store, hardware store, laundromat, post office, drug store, some fast food and other restaurants (including pizza), clothing store, a seafood market, a liquor store, a local bank, a Chinese carry-out, ice cream parlor, and other facilities. If you are anchored (the anchorage north of Zahniser's is not far by dinghy), you may use the dinghy dock at the Hospitality Harbor, a floating dock along the shore, for a reasonable charge per day, and accomplish a great deal of shopping.

Above the Hospitality Harbor, the creek divides into three branches, each rather narrow and shallow as the charts indicate. Looking up the creek, you'll see pretty woods ashore, but there are many homes within the trees and docks extending out into the deep water. As branches begin to split, you will find many docks to your right (east) belonging to the Oyster Bay **(52)** condominium development. Just beyond the first branch to the west, there are many piers belonging to a private housing development, Solomons Landing **(51)**. Because of the piers in what are narrow waters in the first place, there is not room for many boats to anchor here.

•

Special events in Solomons include the Patuxent River

328

Discovery Day in early May, a waterside music festival on Memorial Day, a fishing tournament in June, Fourth of July fireworks, the Yachting Magazine Yacht Racing Week in August, an arts and crafts festival on Labor Day weekend, and Patuxent River Appreciation Days in mid-October.

MILL AND ST. JOHN CREEKS

These creeks offer several beautiful and protected anchorages, but have only one full service marina, and little to do ashore. The attractions of Solomons Island are accessible from some of the anchorages if you have a fast dinghy, but watch the speed limits.

Refer to Chart #12284-A—"Solomons: Entrance and Back Creek." PG 325

Mill (25) and St. John Creeks (1) are overlooked by many cruisers because of the attractions on Solomons Island. They often anchor in the Back Creek, enjoy the area, and then pass on. These two creeks are quiet and very pretty, and offer nice places to gunkhole regardless of their busy neighbor.

Heading in, east of Molly's Leg (26), you get an early view of what much of the rest of the creeks are like. To your left (north) are the southern docks of **Calvert Marina (28)**, and on the eastern shore there is an industrial type of landing (2) originally for tenders to the CNG landing platform offshore in the Bay. However the scenery looking up Mill Creek is one of green trees and marsh, with quiet homes in the background.

Refer to Chart #12284-C—"Solomons: Mill Creek, St. John Creek." PG 331

Many boats like to anchor (3) along the western side of Mill Creek in the area opposite and to the south of Bow Cove (4). We saw no indication of the submerged ruins noted, but most do not anchor that close to the shore. This western shore is pretty with deep trees. The industrial landing dock (2) downstream mars the view only to a small extent.

Just upstream on the western side are the new docks for a housing development called "Harbour at Solomons" (5). There is a privately maintained yellow flashing marker guarding those docks. The chart notes wrecks (7) off the docks. We saw no evidence of these and boats of 6 feet draft and more regularly pass the area.

St. John Creek

Dodson's Boatyard (8) has a boathouse with some docks for repair work and occasionally a tug or other commercial equipment nearby. They have a 50-foot 25-ton railway.

If you proceed up St. John Creek (1), you will see pretty nice homes with docks and boathouses surrounded by woods and hills. Lusby Cove (9) to the east of Gr "3" is a nice anchorage but is surrounded by homes and docks and affords little privacy. Beware the shoal (10) extending out from (south and to the east of) Gr "3." This shoal extends beyond the marker. Hutchins Cove (11) is very built up and crowded with homes and docks.

Proceeding on up St. John Creek, you will soon forget about the hustle and bustle of the Solomons. The banks have high hills, at times almost looking like foothills, covered with trees. There are nice homes, but they are usually set well back into the trees, and the docks and boats don't impinge too heavily on the natural beauty of the creek. This is an excellent place to anchor anywhere (12) that you enjoy the scenery most, going up as far as you wish, depending upon your draft.

Mill Creek

If you follow Mill Creek around Pancake Point (13) to the east, you will see a well-populated shoreline on both sides, but this is still a pretty creek. The junction buoy (14) to the southwest of Lusby Point is green on top. When we last passed, it appeared to have been red on the bottom, much faded.

While in Mill Creek, don't miss a visit to Dodson's Country Store (15) on the northern shore. You will see a long dock coming out from the shore, an old boathouse with gas pump by its side, and a very authentic old country store. It has a green front and red sides and an old Coca Cola sign (and the faded name of the store) on the hill just up from the dock. If you are fortunate, you may find Mr. James Dodson, who has run this store for over 50 years. He will tell you that the store has been there for over 100 years. There has been little bow-

Dawn Piper anchored in Mill Creek

ing to newfangledness here. From the long aisle or beneath the glass-covered shelves along each side of the aisle, you can get a soda, some crackers, some light groceries or lots of other things that country stores are good for. You may like to sit on the chairs on the front porch, talking and enjoying the view.

Spring (16) and Leason Coves (17) are both very crowded with homes and docks. Old House Cove (19) is not quite so crowded but has enough homes which, coupled with its narrowness, results in scant privacy for any boat anchoring. The large black block on the chart of its western shore is a huge green painted boat house.

Another great anchorage (20), though somewhat open, is just upstream from Old House Cove. The area is wide enough, and the homes set far enough back from the shore among many trees, that this is indeed a very pleasant place to anchor. The bottom is thick mud and gray clay, both good holding once you get your anchor dug in. The northern point of that basin on the northwest side of the creek has submerged pilings noted (21). A house has been constructed ashore with a new dock, and probably those piles are no longer there. I saw no sign of them. If you keep green private marker numbered "9" to your north, you will be clear of the area.

Another pretty anchorage, with a snugger lee from the east or west, lies in Brooks Cove area (22). You may prefer to anchor up into the mouth of that cove if you have the draft and don't mind the limited swinging room. Above G "11," the docks and homes on the shore noticeably increase, the houses often built back up on the hills rising above the creek. This area is quite pretty, but with a feeling of much more civilization than the lower reaches.

Near the head of the creek is Pine Cove Marina (23) with over 100 slips up to 40 feet, electricity up to 30 amps, a 15-ton lift and cement ramp. I found the controlling approach depth to be 3 feet. I did not see the wreck (24) reported, but it is or was probably in the area marked by a pole. There is a marine store and they do general repair work, including aluminum welding.

PATUXENT RIVER

Editor's Note: Solomons Island and surrounding creeks are every bit as worthwhile your visits as Tom has described. Don't leave Chesapeake Bay without stopping there. But if you have time and enjoy exploration of new places, go on up the Patuxent River, for some prime gunkholing. Tom Neale explored it all, and his description follows.

Carolyn Neale in her favorite perch aboard *Chez Nous*

Dodson's Store, Mill Creek

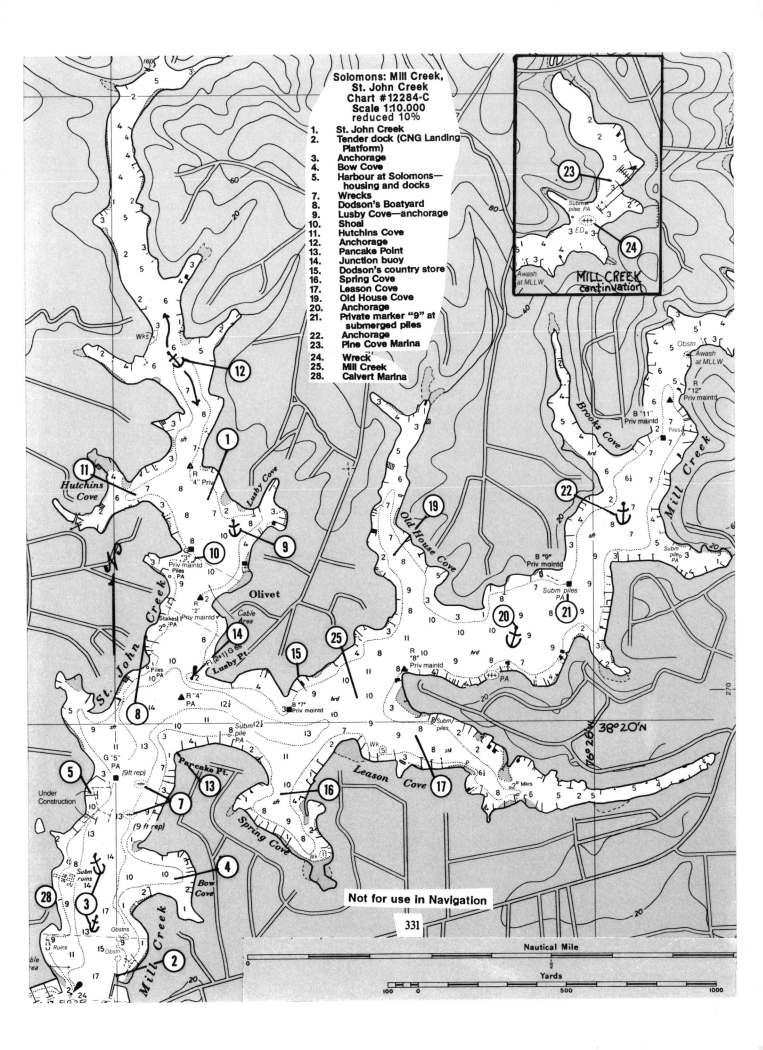

Solomons: Mill Creek,
St. John Creek
Chart #12284-C
Scale 1:10,000
reduced 10%

1. St. John Creek
2. Tender dock (CNG Landing Platform)
3. Anchorage
4. Bow Cove
5. Harbour at Solomons—housing and docks
7. Wrecks
8. Dodson's Boatyard
9. Lusby Cove—anchorage
10. Shoal
11. Hutchins Cove
12. Anchorage
13. Pancake Point
14. Junction buoy
15. Dodson's country store
16. Spring Cove
17. Leason Cove
19. Old House Cove
20. Anchorage
21. Private marker "9" at submerged piles
22. Anchorage
23. Pine Cove Marina
24. Wreck
25. Mill Creek
28. Calvert Marina

MILL CREEK
continuation

Not for use in Navigation

Nautical Mile

Yards

Lewis Creek
Refer to Chart #12284-D—"Lewis Creek."

Back out in the Patuxent River and on the southwest shore before the bridge, Lewis Creek (27), is considered by many in the area to be a great hurricane hole. It is exceptionally snug, as well as pretty. It is so snug that it takes a great act of faith to find and then attempt its narrow entrance, but we found just under 7 feet controlling getting in. Because of the approach and entrance, it is not often used by cruising boats, but you should definitely consider it if you are looking for a very snug and pretty anchorage not too far from civlization.

The entrance to this creek is just to the southeast of the much larger entrance of Town Creek (28) on the southwestern side of the river. If you look into the western shore from out in the Patuxent, downstream of the opening into Town Creek, you will see a beach (30) south of that entrance. To the right (north) of the beach is a large two-story mansion with eight white columns. Just to the right (northwest) of that, you will see entrance R "2" against the shore. The red and green floats marking the entrance are noted as privately maintained and normally only there from March to September. As you approach from a northeasterly direction, you should see that the actual entrance into the creek is just to the left (east) of the beach. Between the creek entrance and the beach is a brown two-story house (32) with the beach in front.

We found the best depths by approaching toward the northeastern point and passing close to the green float and then heading toward the left (southeastern) end of the brown house (32) which took us up close to the red float. Before reaching the red float, make a sharp turn to your left (southerly direction) and head on into the creek, passing the shoreside beach to your west, and the beach at the tip of the point on your east. Though we found almost 7 feet here, you have to be in exactly the right place. At times of high flow, the current can be fairly swift in this very narrow opening. Remember that floats sometimes drift, and that on low tides when their mooring lines have more scope, they may be a little off station because of the current and wind. If your draft exceeds 5 feet, I recommend a half tide and rising entrance for your first try.

Once inside, the creek opens up into very pretty land-locked anchorages (33) with nice high hills, woods and homes. You can continue on up into the creek as your draft allows, picking the spot of your choice. It is all beautiful and protected. As the creek turns to your right (westerly), it becomes smaller, thus offering less fetch depending upon where you settle, and it's even prettier.

Town Creek
Refer to Chart #12284-E—"Patuxent River: Town Creek, Point Patience, Kingston Creek, Little Kingston Creek."
PG 334

In our opinion, Town Creek (28) is not of much interest for the cruising boater. There are some marinas inside, primarily for local motor boats with some emphasis on the inboard/outboard type. Most transients desiring a marina would rather tie up over in Solomons with its attractions. Anchoring is possible in Town Creek but not very attractive because of the close homes and structures ashore. Also, busy State Highway #4 crosses the center of the creek with a vertical clearance of 30 feet, roaring to the Thomas Johnson Memorial Bridge over the Patuxent. The Bridge of the Patuxent River has 140 feet vertical clearance.

What appeared to be the primary going marina last year was the **Boatel California (34)** in the northern end of the northern branch of Town Creek. Its large tan building can be seen both from this creek and the Patuxent on the north side of the little neck of land separating Town Point from the mainland. They have storage and some facilities for boats, mostly inboard/outboards, a forklift, gas and diesel, and a marine shop.

PATUXENT ABOVE TOWN CREEK
Refer to Chart #12264-D—"Lower Patuxent River: Solomons, Point Patience Area, Mill & Cuckold Creeks, Hellen Creek" PG 323 and
Chart #12284-E—"Patuxent River: Town Creek, Point Patience, Kingston Creek, Little Kingston Creek." PG 334

After you pass under the Thomas Johnson Memorial Bridge (35) with its 140 feet of vertical clearance, the river becomes less congested ashore with several very pretty creeks, a few marinas, and miles of river exploration opportunity far up into the rural southern Maryland western shore countryside. If you require more than 3½ feet depth, don't count on easy fueling above St. Leonard's Creek.

As you approach the bridge, you will find depths under your keel of around 100 feet, tumbling down to around 120 feet in places close to the bridge and then off Point Patience (36). This point has a long beach at its tip, but it is not open to the public, being a part of the U.S. Navy grounds which will be obvious from the signs and naval vessels docked on the northern shore to the east of the point. All of the basin area (37) and even Second Cove are considered off limits to the public because of the official activities. Second Cove has a private military marina. When rounding Patience Point, beware that its shoal extends well beyond (south of) the Fl G "8" marker near its tip.

Kingston and Little Kingston Creeks
Refer to Chart #12284-E—"Patuxent River: Town Creek, Point Patience, Kingston Creek, Little Kingston Creek."

We found 5 feet depths to be controlling within the jettied entrance to Kingston Creek (38). The current of the Patuxent River sweeps up and down, and shoaling is to be expected. Last year, we found the deepest water to be in the middle of the jetties. Once inside, you will find high hills with some houses and docks, and pretty anchorages (39), especially after the creek bends around to the southwest.

Little Kingston Creek (40), just upstream and west of Kingston Creek, has an entrance jetty (41) on the left (east) as you enter, and the same concern for shoaling is pertinent here. This is much shallower. We found 3 feet right up against the bulkhead on the left (east) as we came in. The sand from the marshy beach to the right (west) extends almost to that bulkhead, thus making a very narrow entrance. The chart shows 1-foot inside the entrance. We found a little more than that, but judging from local boats permanently moored there, there must be some area of deeper water that I was not able to discover. This is a pretty creek, but hardly worth the trouble for anchoring, considering the other nice and easier places nearby.

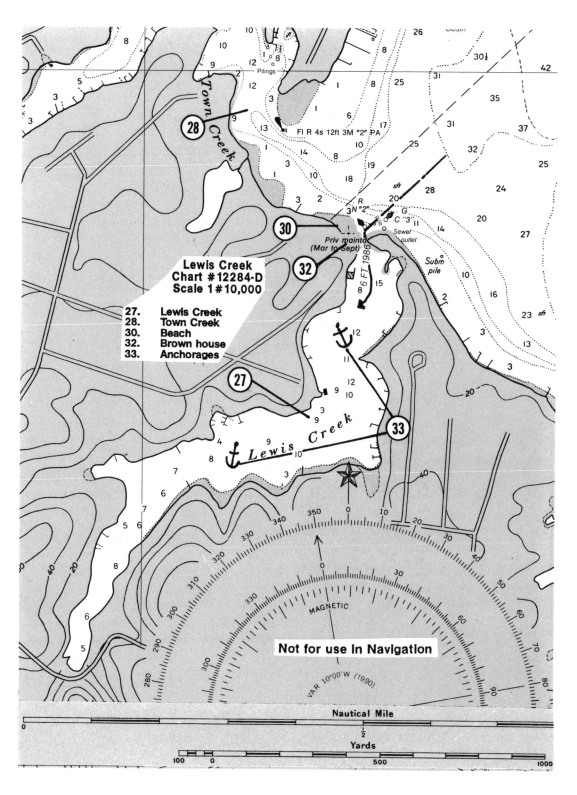

Lewis Creek
Chart #12284-D
Scale 1 # 10,000

27.	Lewis Creek
28.	Town Creek
30.	Beach
32.	Brown house
33.	Anchorages

Town Creek

28

30

32

27

Lewis Creek

33

Fl R 4s 12ft 3M "2" PA

Pilings

Priv maintd
(Mar to Sept)

R
3N"2"

G
C "3" 11

Sewer
outlet

Subm
pile

6 FT 1986

sft

MAGNETIC

Not for use in Navigation

VAR 10°00'W (1990)

	Nautical Mile		
0		½	

		Yards		
100	0		500	1000

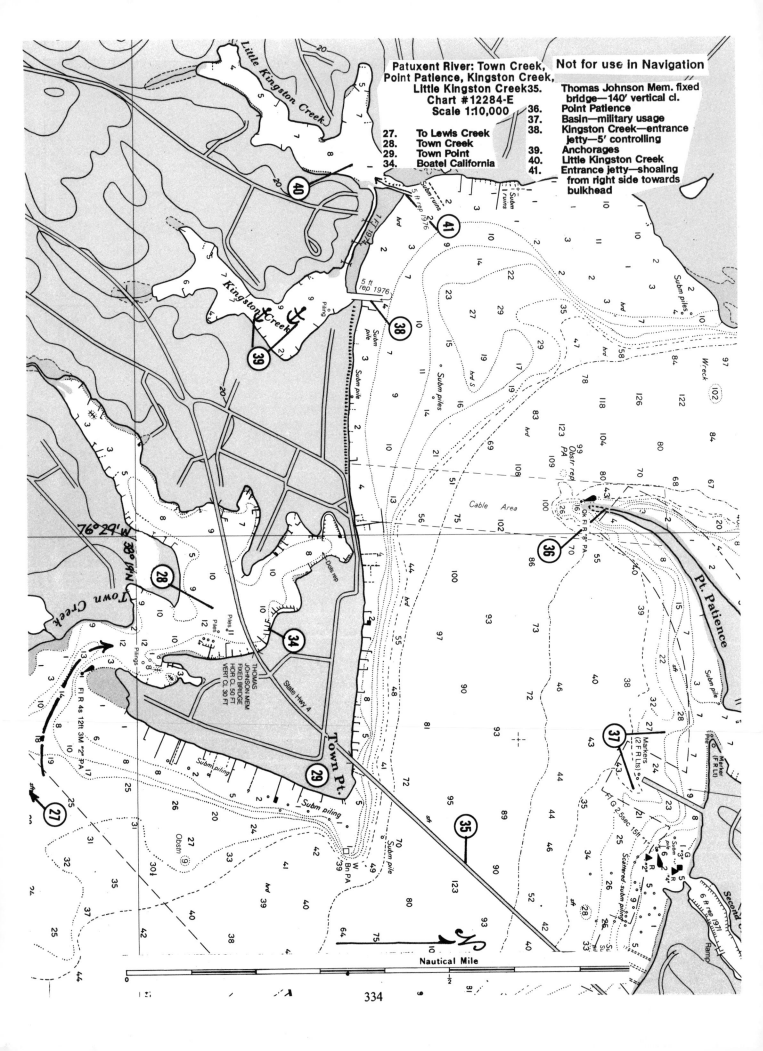

Patuxent River: Town Creek,
Point Patience, Kingston Creek,
Little Kingston Creek35.
Chart #12284-E
Scale 1:10,000

27.   **To Lewis Creek**
28.   **Town Creek**
29.   **Town Point**
34.   **Boatel California**

Not for use in Navigation

35.   **Thomas Johnson Mem. fixed**
      bridge—140' vertical cl.
36.   **Point Patience**
37.   **Basin—military usage**
38.   **Kingston Creek—entrance**
      jetty—5' controlling
39.   **Anchorages**
40.   **Little Kingston Creek**
41.   **Entrance jetty—shoaling**
      from right side towards
      bulkhead

Nautical Mile

Mill and Cuckold Creeks

Refer to Chart #12264-D—"Lower Patuxent River: Solomons, Point Patience Area, Mill and Cuckold Creeks, Hellen Creek." *PG 323*

Mill **(42)** and Cuckhold Creeks **(43)** are pretty, with a few very nice anchorages. The common approach is wide, well-buoyed, and easy. On Half Pone Point, north of the entrance channel, you will see a clump of trees on the end, and then inside, a few houses with wide yard and grass coming down to the water. The shoreline to the left (south) as you enter is heavily wooded.

Looking straight into the entrance (to the west), you will see **Clarks Landing (44)** between the fork of the two creeks. There is a small white building with a screened-in front porch and a Chevron sign. A hard surfaced ramp is to the left (south) of the building and a work dock in front. The building is a light fare restaurant with cocktail lounge, and there is some docking space in front of it for customers.

Cuckold Creek to the north and west, has pretty branches. **Nat Creek (45)**, the first that you will encounter to your left (west) after you turn north off Clarks Landing, is pretty but narrow with numerous houses and docks. While it would make a snug anchorage in the area of 9-foot depths, some might consider it too tight or not private enough because of its narrowness.

Continuing on up Cuckold Creek, you may still find many houses and docks, but also many trees and a very pretty area to choose your favorite anchorage. Soon you will see **Blackstone Marina (46)** on your left (southwest) shortly after rounding the bend, on the northwest corner of the little creek. It has a two-story blue and white house with 60 slips, some covered, taking boats up to 50 feet, with electricity up to 50 amps, a crane and a 20-ton lift, block and cube ice, boat supplies, and some repair work available.

Weeks Marina (47), next up Cuckold Creek and on the same side, has a two-story white house and over 50 slips taking boats up to 50 feet with 15 amp electricity, a 50-ton railway which can haul up to 85 feet, block and cube ice, some hardware, and a pumpout. Weeks Marina has mostly sailboats.

The cove to the north **(48)** has three prongs, mostly built up with houses and docks. The prong on the right (east) is the prettiest, with 6½ feet depth near the entrance and less as you go in. There are nicer places to anchor in the creek. Note the submerged pipe indicated in the middle prong, sufficient reason not to anchor there.

Proceeding farther, Forest Landing Cove **(49)** is pretty with trees and houses. At its head is a nice **public landing (50)** at the foot of a high sloping hill with launching ramp. This can be quite busy for an anchorage. The branch to its south **(51)** is prettier with woods, field, and houses with deep yards. The branch opposite **(52)** the mouth of Forest Landing Cove has docks running almost out to the middle.

Most folks head into Mill Creek **(42)** because of a very popular anchorage there. Before reaching this anchorage, you will pass a creek on your right **(53)** (west) after passing Clarks Landing as you head southwest into Mill Creek. Looking in reveals a startling sight because of a huge building area near the head with extensive bulkheading and other construction. This is Placid Harbor, once the private home of World War II news correspondent Fulton Lewis, Jr., later a resort, and now privately-owned. The creek **(53)** is not a recommended anchorage.

The anchorage of choice for many is in the large basin **(54)** to the southeast where 11 feet of depth can be carried close to shore. The shore around this basin has large hills with red cliffs and deep woods on top. Although the chart doesn't really indicate it, there is a marshy area at the head of the cove, separating the water from the trees. An onion-shaped green water tower can be seen in the background behind the trees as you approach. You can anchor close to the shore and be close to the natural scenery.

One drawback that we have found with this anchorage is that there is a fair fetch to the northwest, and the holding is not the best. Therefore it is important to be sure your hook is in tight and set from the northwest if you are expecting any thunderstorms or cold fronts. The little cul-de-sac **(55)** with 9 feet depth to the northwest of the basin would make a snug anchorage for small boats expecting a blow, but there are many docks here coming well out toward the deeper water.

Hickory Landing Creek **(56)** is also well-settled, but many of the homes are older, more traditional "southern Maryland" in nature, making the creek quite pleasant, particularly up near the end as it reaches marsh in 6 feet depth. Our favorite spot was the 8-foot spot half-way up. Entering this creek, stay well off the point to the north guarding the entrance, particularly if you draw more than 3½ feet.

The main branch of Mill Creek is also very pretty, anywhere that you may prefer. Our favorite area **(57)** was between the bend to the southwest and the bend to the south. Depths here are no more than 7 feet, and the channel is rather narrow. This south end of Mill Creek is very protected.

One of the nicest anchorages **(58)** in this area is often missed by most cruisers because the chart really doesn't do it justice. Just south of the main Mill Creek anchorage, you will see a creek running southerly with several branches. Its mouth is separated from the main anchorage by a 3-foot shoal. There is a little crooked point guarding the eastern shore of its entrance. The chart indicates shoal out to beyond the tip of the crooked point. Actually, you can snuggle behind that point in water up to 7 to 8 feet, looking securely out over the point into the wider water, yet protected from the northerly fetch, surrounded by beautiful woods and marsh. The point has a nice beach at low water. We found 7 to 8 feet depths up close to the woods. There are houses on the other side of the creek, but they don't really impair the quiet enjoyment here. If you go farther up this creek, you will find its branches to be very full of homes, boathouses, and docks.

Hellen Creek

Hellen Creek **(59)** is on the east shore of the Patuxent River, north of Hoopers Neck. Hellen Creek **(59)** is rather cluttered but there are a few nice spots to anchor. The entrance to the creek is a narrow, dredged channel through very shallow water. We found 5 feet to be controlling in the channel. This is one of those areas where you can expect shoaling. There are other nice anchorages around that have easier entries. If you go in, ask a local boat or take the soundings from your dink for prevailing depths.

The entrance comes in from the southwest, down river and southeast of FL R "12." When we entered, the green floats were difficult to see. G "1" **(60)** was no longer there, the first marker being floating G "1A" **(61)**. Its GPS derived position is 38°21.17'N by 76°28.771'W. When looking for this from out in the river, you'll find the marker offshore of a small one-story redwood house partially behind the trees on the eastern entrance bank. This house is just to the left of a large two-story gray house with black roof and white windows.

Once inside, we found the little cove **(63)** on the northwest shore opposite Tongue Cove to offer one of the better spots to anchor in the creek, up where 7 feet of depth is noted in its northern end. However, there was only 5 feet controlling depth into this cove. There are houses around, many with obviously seafood and crabbing as one of the family jobs, but there is enough field and wood to make the spot pleasant. Tongue Cove (64) is very cluttered and not attractive from the viewpoint of most cruisers. As you travel farther into the main creek, there are more houses on either side and depths gradually lessen.

ST. LEONARD CREEK

St. Leonard Creek is well worth your visit for its beautiful anchorages. It's one of Chesapeake Bay's prettier creeks. It also is home to Vera's White Sands, a place so unique and special that it draws visitors from the entire region.

Refer to Chart #12264-E—"Lower Central Patuxent River: St. Leonard Creek, Island Creek."
St. Leonard Creek (65) has a wide and easy entrance. Be sure to honor the markers because the shoal, particularly off Petersons Point (62), extends out south ¼NM. Note that FL R "14" (66), south of Peterson Point, is a Patuxent River marker, not a marker for St. Leonard Creek. Go in to the right (east of) G "1" to avoid the shoal. We'll describe a few of our favorite anchorages, but you should explore the creek and anchor anywhere that you like. Most of it is very pretty.

Jefferson Patterson Park and Museum
Petersons Point is the home of Jefferson Patterson Park and Museum (62). This is listed in the national register of Historical Landmarks. It was the scene of a significant naval battle in the War of 1812. A small fleet of U.S. boats under the command of Commodore Joshua Barney (most were essentially barges) was bottled up here by the much larger British fleet. In a daring surprise attack, the U.S. fleet drove them off and escaped upriver to Benedict. However, the British were soon reinforced and landed troops which proceeded on to Washington. The phone for the park is (410) 586-0050. The Calvert Marine Museum in Solomons contains displays and more information about the battle.

Mackall Anchorage
The first great spot to anchor will open up to your west soon after you enter, in the Mackall area (67). The point to your right (north) as you enter this cove has a grassy lawn with a beach at its base and a pier with white-topped pilings at its tip. This is marked "private." We found the deeper water to be on this side. We found 8 to 9 feet depth well up into the end of the cove, deep into the woods. We could not find any indications of the wreck. The chart shows it off the northern point up inside (under the "AC" in Mackall). We did find that the bottom shoals off this point. It should be given a wide berth. Anchor anywhere in here that pleases you. All of it is surrounded by woods, marshy shoreline, and quiet.

Anchorages in Sollers Area
The first cove on your right (68) as you head up the creek, in the Sollers area to the northeast of Rodney Point, has many houses on the hills above the cove and many docks.
There is a nice creek (69) just upstream from that on the same side, with a gray rock jetty on the point to the left (north) as you enter and a beach with a marsh point on the

right. The rocks may extend out a bit. It is advisable to leave the left (north) point some room as you pass. The point to the left points to the beach, the point to the right is a little bit inside the point to the left. Just inside the point to the left and just outside the point to the right is a private Gr "1" on a stick. We found the best water about halfway between the green marker and the southern point. Controlling depth in the entrance is 5½ feet. Inside, you will find a beautiful basin, 7 feet or more deep, with woods on the right (south) side and in the interior, and houses to the left. These are nice homes, set well back up the high hills. On the bank to the south, there's a very picturesque wreck and decaying old work boats a little inside the point.

Coves Farther North
Another beautiful spot is in the next creek (70) up, still on right (eastern) shore. We found 4½ feet controlling in the entrance. Inside you will find a few houses, but mostly deep woods with a little marsh ringing the shore and trees overhanging the water, giving the anchored boat a feeling of quiet seclusion amidst nature. Most like to anchor just inside behind (to the east of) the spit, although you can go farther in as your draft allows. To enter, favor the left (northern side), passing fairly close to the dock (71) that is noted on the chart there. As you approach the guardian point to your right (south), stay about two-thirds of the distance between it and the north shore, thus still favoring that northern shore. We found the chart to be a little misleading in that a shoal comes off the southern guardian point in a more **northerly direction** than you would expect, since the chart shows it wrapping more easterly. After passing the dock, we found it best to continue heading for the left (northern) point until you clear the right (southern) point before rounding that right point into the basin.
An attractive possibility next appears on the chart in the next cove (72) up the creek on the west shore, with 7 feet depth well up inside. However, this is very built up with many docks well out into the deep water, and thus not a very good anchorage.
The little cove (73) on the east shore, between "Leonard" and "Creek" on the chart, is also very pretty. There are some houses up on the hill as you enter, but these give way to solitude and high wooded hills up inside. The tiny island noted on the right (south) side is just a clump of marsh with a shallow but pretty basin behind it, trees overshadowing from the forested shore.

Rollins Cove (75)
Rollins Cove (75), also on the east shore, just below (to the south of) Breedens Point, is yet another beautiful spot to stay. It is hard to see from St. Leonard Creek. The high dirt cliff on Breedens Point makes it stand out. Just in from that, there is then a break in the cliff and a beach. These are just to the north of the mouth of Rollins Cove. We proceeded in carefully, staying generally to the middle, but rounding the guardian finger on the right (south) of the entrance. This has marsh with a little beach that may be a few inches under water at very high tide. We found 5½ feet depth right up to the backside of the spit and beach and also close to the woods ashore. Don't take in more than 7 feet, and this very carefully. Overall, we found depths to be shallower than the chart indicated. This is a beautiful spot. There is also rather deep water, as the chart shows, close to the trees throughout much of this creek. Be sure to watch for stumps as you nestle close to trees in any of the waters of Chesapeake Bay. There are a few houses

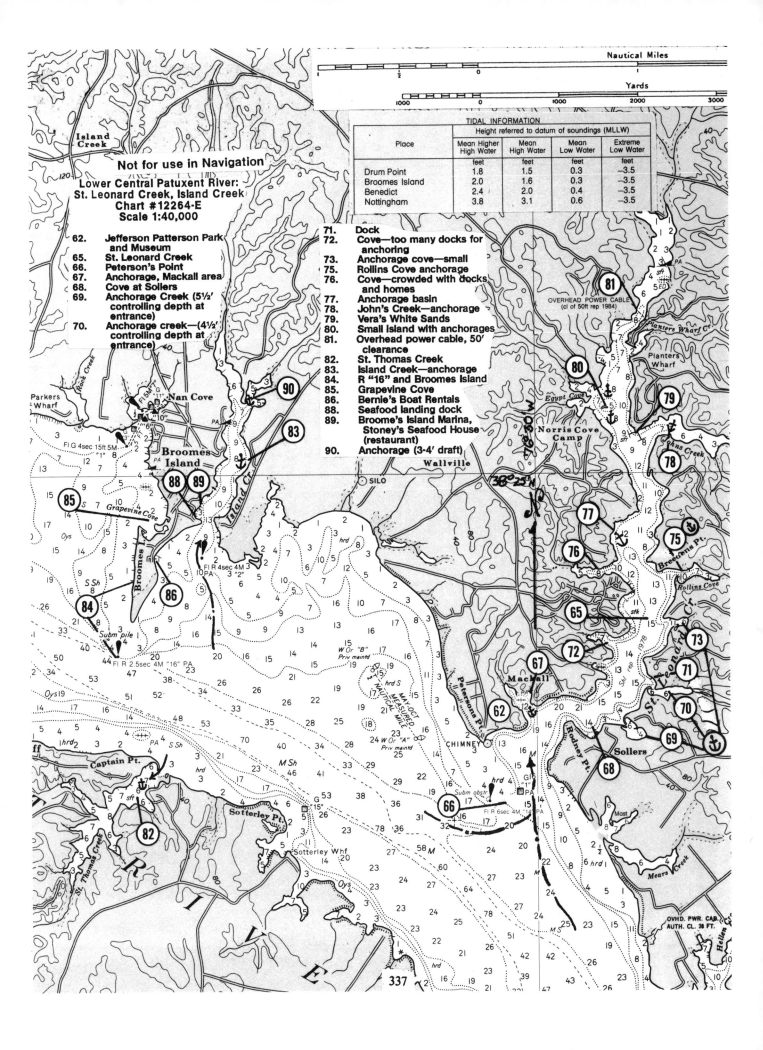

Not for use in Navigation

Lower Central Patuxent River:
St. Leonard Creek, Island Creek
Chart #12264-E
Scale 1:40,000

Nautical Miles

Yards

TIDAL INFORMATION

Height referred to datum of soundings (MLLW)

Place	Mean Higher High Water	Mean High Water	Mean Low Water	Extreme Low Water
	feet	feet	feet	feet
Drum Point	1.8	1.5	0.3	−3.5
Broomes Island	2.0	1.6	0.3	−3.5
Benedict	2.4	2.0	0.4	−3.5
Nottingham	3.8	3.1	0.6	−3.5

62. Jefferson Patterson Park and Museum
65. St. Leonard Creek
66. Peterson's Point
67. Anchorage, Mackall area
68. Cove at Sollers
69. Anchorage Creek (5½' controlling depth at entrance)
70. Anchorage creek—(4½' controlling depth at entrance)
71. Dock
72. Cove—too many docks for anchoring
73. Anchorage cove—small
75. Rollins Cove anchorage
76. Cove—crowded with docks and homes
77. Anchorage basin
78. John's Creek—anchorage
79. Vera's White Sands
80. Small island with anchorages
81. Overhead power cable, 50' clearance
82. St. Thomas Creek
83. Island Creek—anchorage
84. R "16" and Broomes Island
85. Grapevine Cove
86. Bernie's Boat Rentals
88. Seafood landing dock
89. Broome's Island Marina, Stoney's Seafood House (restaurant)
90. Anchorage (3-4' draft)

337

in this creek, but you will hardly notice them in the overpowering majesty of quiet natural surroundings.

West Shore Anchorages North of Rollins Cove

Breedens Point points to a deep cove (76) on the west shore of St. Leonards Creek. This looks very nice, but there are many conspicuous homes with docks coming so far out to the deep water that there is little room for relaxed anchoring. Just upstream from this cove is a broad basin (77) in the main creek. There's 12 feet depth to the west. This makes a very pleasant anchorage. The trees grow right down to the water. There is a little bit of beach among the stumps and marsh grass at the water's edge. You can go very close in to the forest, or anchor farther out where there are fewer bugs and more breeze.

Vera's White Sands (79)

Farther north, St. Leonard Creek divides into its main branch and Johns Creek (78), which runs off to the east. On the tip of the broad peninsula between the two branches is one of Chesapeake Bay's more unique destinations, **Vera's White Sands (79)**. Vera's is famous far and wide, not only among boaters, but from all who seek fine dining in an exotic atmosphere. It is not at all unusual for people to drive all the way out from Washington for the experience of an evening here. You will see their docks and buildings on the shore ahead as you approach. This is a special place. Vera's has over 100 slips available with space alongside for very large boats, electricity up to 50 amps, gas and diesel, pool, snacks, small beach with thatched grass umbrellas, cocktail lounge and restaurant, all within the carefully cultured atmosphere of a tropical island paradise.

To understand and fully appreciate the establishment, it is important to know something about Vera Freeman, who is not merely the owner, but a now almost legendary queen of finery. Her special quality of being able to create and live a fantasy island, realistically and in the middle of the "other world" gives the place its real meaning.

Vera, daughter of an Indian mother, grew up on a Crow reservation in Montana. Her age is ageless. An unusually attractive girl, she went to Hollywood with her mother around 1950 to seek stardom and fame. There she met Dr. Effrus Freeman, a very popular Hollywood eye specialist. He was comfortable financially. They married and began a luxurious life, traveling around the world and enjoying the very finest that the various countries had to offer. This included yachting excursions, as well as steamship cruises. Dr. Freeman purchased many acres of property in Calvert County. He and Vera fashioned this resort along the lines of a tropical paradise, a south seas fantasy, both inside and out. They established a first class restaurant within this setting, offering island and international dishes as well as local specialities, not to mention their famous selection of exotic drinks. Dr. Freeman passed away some time ago, but Vera still lives here in her dream house and oversees the operation.

Inside and around the grounds are Vera's collections from her many world travels. Others have sometimes implied that these are imitative plastic, but much of the fascinating decor

Entrance to "Vera's White Sands" restaurant, a live fantasy island
deep in the heart of the Patuxent's back country

is authentic, with tales that can be told by Vera if you are fortunate enough to meet her and talk. She still travels widely, with special trips on *Queen Elizabeth II*, her first she said, around 28 years ago.

When not travelling, she can usually be seen making a grand entrance from her home every afternoon around six to preside over the evening. She is always elegantly dressed in long flowing gowns with many jewels and rings, her white hair flowing beneath a crown-like head band that, to some, is perhaps reminiscent of both her Indian heritage and her queenly life. She loves many places—thinks that "Bombay is exotic, like living in a fairy-tale: Rome is romantic, Paris is beautiful—but no, then they all are." Then she says, "but if you stay right here it is easy because it is dreamy, but I would like to make it even more so." And mostly, she says, she likes the people who come. Then she insists that we see the incredible sunset from the western windows overlooking the water.

This resort has been visited by the rich and famous as well as the everyday boater. It has been the subject of national magazine and television coverage. It is worth a visit to experience this singular, totally different Chesapeake Bay institution. Because of experiences with people coming to "just look" and impinging upon the atmosphere and the privacy of the guests, there are signs suggesting that sight-seeing and loitering is not appropriate. However, a cocktail hour or evening meal is worth the fare while Vera is there.

Vera Freeman comes to the restaurant dressed like this whenever she's home

Johns Creek

Passing Vera's White Sands to your left (north) and turning up into Johns Creek, you will see her 10,000-square foot private white dream home with its Byzantine architectural concepts, turrets, and golden onion dome on top, as well as her private landing dock with its gilded gates.

Soon the creek returns to the more typical Bay landscape, with homes, many quite large, on the northern shore and primarily deep woods on the southern shore. Take your choice of anchorages in Johns Creek. If you have a draft of 2½ to 3 feet, you can find even quieter surroundings where the creek turns into a tiny marsh-bordered stream at its end.

Upstream from Vera's

To head upstream above White Sands on the main branch of St. Leonard Creek, you will pass the docks and beach with thatched umbrellas. As though nature had conspired with Vera, there's a small island **(80)** upstream, possibly enchanted given the other surroundings. Egypt Cove lies behind it to the west. This island has substantially eroded in the last few years, but there is still beach on the northern side. You can anchor off its shores, depending upon your draft. We found 6½ feet depth on the western side and 4 feet on the northern side several 100 feet out. South of the island, we found 7 feet up to 200 feet out. The island has a few trees and bushes, but is smaller than what you may expect from the chart. Egypt Cove is substantially built with homes and docks. If you pass the island by, it is better to go east of it to head upstream.

Beware of the overhead power cable **(81)** of 50 feet reported vertical clearance. Never trust those reported clearances with electrical wires because they sometimes sag or change for other reasons. This one is marked well with red balls on the lowest cable and white vertical warning floats both above and below the lines. The creek is much more civilized ashore up here and not as attractive, or as secluded, as St. Leonard Creek's lower reaches. There are some interesting homes, such as the very large one to the east of the first charted wreck, high on hill, which has three stories of brown stone with many windows, looking like a tower. We did not see evidence of any wrecks.

Proceeding farther up the creek, if you have 2½ feet of draft or less, you can experience passing of yet another spectacular Chesapeake creek into the countryside, winding up in the marsh and melting within its low bed nestled between high forest-covered hills.

ST. THOMAS CREEK
Refer to Chart #12264-E—"Lower Central Patuxent River: St. Leonard Creek, Island Creek." PG 337

St. Thomas Creek **(82)** is off the south shore of the Patuxent River. It is a bit tricky getting in but your reward will be a beautiful anchorage just inside the entrance spit or anywhere upstream.

The chart shows 3 feet controlling of the entrance to this creek, and that was all we could find. This is unfortunate, because of the deeper water inside and pretty surroundings. As we went in, we found the deep water by favoring the western side and the tip of the spit that curves around from that shore. However, don't favor the spit too closely for the bottom abruptly comes up to around 1 foot of depth just off the spit. Last year, a stake marked the end of this shoal extending out from the spit.

As you look up the creek, you will see high hills and beautiful woods, with not many homes visible. The basin behind the spit has 6 feet of depth close to the sandy shore of the spit and is a great place to drop the hook. On the eastern shore of the creek, the beach is private but pretty. If you wish to go upstream, take your pick anywhere in this creek.

ISLAND CREEK

Island Creek (83) goes north into the north shore of Patuxent River. There is a small store inside, a marina for smaller boats, and some very nice spots to anchor.

The creek is identifiable by its position relative to FL R "16" off the tip of Broomes Island (84), which is really a long finger of land pointing southerly into the Patuxent River. The finger is low with field and marsh and a few houses, and if your boat is high enough, you can see over it into Grapevine Cove (85) as you pass to its east while heading into Island Creek. Looking up to the north into the background behind the spit, you will see beautiful high hills. There was a duck blind at the tip of the point last year.

We went in heading straight for the mouth of the creek. There is a 5-foot shoal indicated just to the south of Fl R "2." I found no reliable way of getting around this area, and I understand that it shifts, so I would not recommend taking in a boat with more draft than that.

In the crook of the shore to your left (west), you will notice the docks and structures of **Bernie's Boat Rentals (86)** with small boats available for fishing and a hard ramp. Mobil gas is sold as are beverages, fishing supplies, ice and smaller items. There are some docks, very exposed to the river. This would be a convenient spot to get gas if you are running the river and didn't wish to detour much.

As you pass through the two entrance points to the creek, you will notice the only other commercial activity here. There is a seafood landing dock (88) just inside the point to your left (west). **Broomes Island Marina (89)**, just north, has 50 slips, electricity up to 30 amps, a pumpout, a laundromat, and block and cube ice. Stoney's Seafood House is a restaurant at the head of the marina docks. Across the road from the marina is a small market with some groceries and beverages and other items.

If you continue on up the creek, you will find a nice spot to anchor in the little cove (83) to the right (east). Here the scenery is of woods and field with older country homes scattered around. When you reach the area where the creek splits, you will think that you are looking at a little island when you see the peninsula. The branch to the right (east) has high hills, a few houses, trees and marsh. This is another scenic spot to anchor (90) if your draft is no more than 3 feet. The branch to the west is more populated, though depths are greater.

BATTLE CREEK

Refer to Chart #12264-F—"Central Patuxent River: Battle Creek."

Battle Creek (91) extends north of the northeast shore of the Patuxent River. It is so named for the battles there during the War of 1812 when the British bottled up a small portion of the U.S. fleet inside. Prison Point (92), on its western bank, is named for the same reasons.

As we reached approximately the half way point between Fr R "18" and R "20," we headed in a northeasterly direction

to pick up the entrance markers. They may be a bit hard to see at first, but they will emerge from the background as you approach. R "2" at first is obscured by the red cliffs behind it, but it will appear, to the right (east) of the cliffs. Give both G "1" and R "2" a wide berth as you round each. There is a shoal coming southeasterly off Prison Point behind G "1" and extending out to the channel between that mark and R "2." Proceed slowly and carefully here.

Battle Creek is more of a farming creek than many of the others. You will notice farmhouses and silos as you enter. As you pass Prison Point, you will see a nice beach behind its crook, west of R "2." This should not make a very good anchorage, however, because of its exposure to the Patuxent River. The first good anchorage is the first cove (94) to the left (west). Here there is pretty farmland with much low land around, a few farm houses, and some trees.

The second cove (95) to the left is even prettier, especially at its northern end, where there are high hills with woods. Just to the right (north) of the marsh is a little beach which goes up into the overhanging trees. There is a house set back in the trees at the southern end of the cove.

Long Cove (96), on the opposite (eastern) side of the creek, has several houses on both sides as you enter, and even a private community dock on its northern bank just inside the entrance point on that side. But then civilization becomes less evident as you proceed. For a draft of not much more than 3 feet, this is a snug spot.

The next special place in Battle Creek is in the inconspicuous-looking little cove (98) on the western side, if you don't draw more than 3 feet. Carefully go into here as far as your draft allows. You will be surrounded by beautiful forest with little sign of civilization close by. There is one dock coming out from the northern shore of the cove, but we could not see the house to which it belonged.

SANDGATES

For those getting hungry, there are two restaurants back out on the Patuxent at Sandgates which is on the southern bank and just down stream of the entrance of Cat Creek. Seabreeze (99) is the easternmost of the two. It is a brown house with the name on the A frame on top. It has a brown roof and docks in front and woods behind. A sign advertises food and drinks and crabs.

Just upstream of that is the Sandgates Inn (100), a brick building with its front wall painted tan and a tan roof. This also has a dock in front. We found 4½ feet at the outside docks.

CAT CREEK

To the south of the Patuxent River marker Fl R "18," you will see the entrance marker to Cat Creek (1) at the end of the jetties. There are two jetties with a Chevron sign on the end of the right (north) jetty. A flashing light is over the sign. Inside is **Cape St. Mary's Marina (2)**, but not any good spot to anchor unless your draft is very shallow and you like a crowd. It is a handy place to stop for fuel or snacks or beverages if you are running the river in a small boat.

Inside behind the jetties, you will see the clutter of buildings, a high-rise boat storage structure, and activity. To the left (south) of the entrance is a group of houses on a tall bank

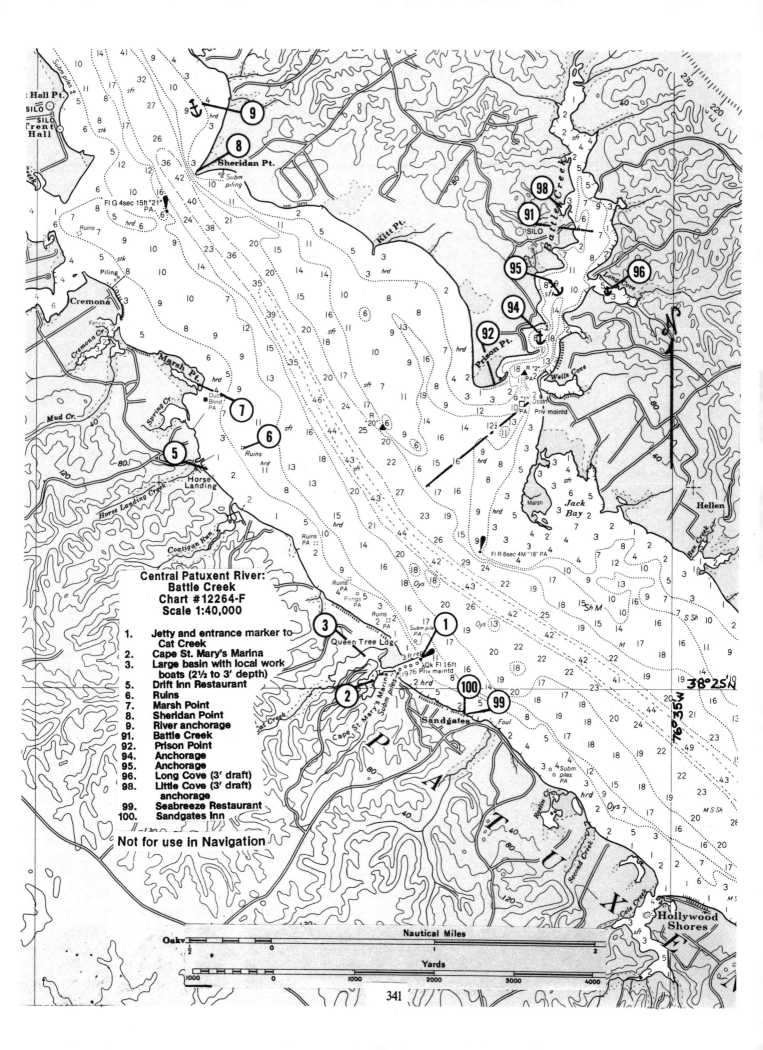

Central Patuxent River:
Battle Creek
Chart #12264-F
Scale 1:40,000

1. Jetty and entrance marker to Cat Creek
2. Cape St. Mary's Marina
3. Large basin with local work boats (2½ to 3' depth)
5. Drift Inn Restaurant
6. Ruins
7. Marsh Point
8. Sheridan Point
9. River anchorage
91. Battle Creek
92. Prison Point
94. Anchorage
95. Anchorage
96. Long Cove (3' draft)
98. Little Cove (3' draft) anchorage
99. Seabreeze Restaurant
100. Sandgates Inn

Not for use in Navigation

341

which gives way to a cliff as it comes around into the entrance area.

Last year, there were very temporary white floats, most lying over on their sides to mark the way up to the jetty. This course ran on an approach from an east-northeasterly direction over the shallows. The channel in the jettied entrance was badly shoaled. We found the best water by staying in the middle. There is quite a bit of work boat and small motorboat activity in this channel, and if you need to come in, you will probably be able to get some good current information as to the vagaries of the shifting and filling from the marina on VHF. Call them on VHF channel 9 or 16. From the size of the boats inside, I would guess that the channel will be maintained for at least 3 to 3½ feet depths. The much larger basin (3) to the west of the docking area is full of moored local boats. We found only 2½ to 3 feet controlling depths there and thus the basin would not be conducive to anchoring for most. It is pretty ashore, with many houses.

As you come to the end of the entrance channel, you will see the shore bulkhead to your left (on the eastern side of the creek) and the docks of **Cape St. Marys Marina** and other buildings. They have over 100 slips here up to 45 feet in length, with electricity up to 30 amps, repair work and lifting capacity for up to 10 tons, a hard ramp, and gas and diesel. There is also a small restaurant, and a small marine supply store where you can also get snacks, beverages, and ice and fishing supplies.

FARTHER UPSTREAM

Proceeding on up the Patuxent River you can either relax and enjoy the scenery, or stop here or there for brief shoreside visits. West of R "20," near Horse Landing, you will find the Drift Inn Restaurant (5). It has white walls, a blue awning, and light brown roof. There are small houses around the restaurant and an oyster shell beach in front. There is a pier for landing, but it is exposed to the river. We found 3 feet depth at the dock. We saw no signs of the "ruins" (6) noted off the dock, but noticed many stakes in the water. Avoid the area around these stakes. Drift Inn is popular locally, with full menu, but very informal setting.

Just upriver, still on the western side of the river, you will see a beach on the downstream side of Marsh Point (7). As you round the point, you will see the two huge power company stacks ahead to your northwest far in the background, creating a startling break in the pleasant countryside. But the land ashore is still very pretty with red cliffs and farmland, old barns and silos. A good example of this is Sheridan Point (8) on the eastern side, with a beach along the shore and marsh, the land rolling up in hillside to an old farm house with red roof and white columns. For those who don't mind exposed river anchorages, the bay (9) on the upstream side of this point is quite pretty, offering protection from the northeast and east. Here again there are woods and fields surrounding the bay, and another old house with white columns and green lawn descending through the trees.

Indian Creek

Refer to Chart #12264-G—"Upper Central Patuxent River: Benedict."

Long Point (10), west of G "23" has another pretty beach with low land ashore and quiet homes. The platform (11) indicated on the chart is clearly visible. The platform is atop substantial concrete pilings connected with beams. Around this point, you will see the bridge and the small settlement of Benedict.

South of Benedict, you may wish to consider Indian Creek (12) for an anchorage. We headed straight in and found a great spot behind the spit on the northern side with 3½ feet depth. It is beautiful here with marsh and sand on the spit, woods ashore, and low countryside all around. There are homes in the distance, but they don't overly intrude on your privacy in this spot.

BENEDICT

Before actually reaching the village of Benedict (13), you will find **Benedict Marina (14)** tucked into its southern shore. A jetty is on the right (east) and a white marker is on the left (west). We found an orange flasher, resembling those found marking construction scenes on highways, on the end of the jetty. Inside are buildings and docks with 40 slips and a hard ramp. A small restaurant is located at the docks. It's a short walk north from Benedict Marina to town.

When you reach Benedict, you will see a clutter of docks along the shore, all exposed to any weather and wave from the river. Many of the buildings behind the docks relate to the seafood industry. There are many old pilings and stakes along the shore, remnants of older docks and moorings. Approach carefully.

Chappelear's Place (15) is a shoreside restaurant with cocktail lounge, and long dock for customers extending out from the white building. We found 4 feet depth at the end. Next, **Shorter's Place (16)** has some slips, gas, and a restaurant and cocktail lounge, in a red building. They serve seafood and other fare including carry-out. There are some tables on the dock outside.

Closer to the bridge is the long and well-maintained dock of **De Soto's Landing (17)** with a long dock coming out from the yard around a two-story brown building and a high-rise rack behind, a few slips up to 45 feet, Chevron gas, lifting up to 7½ tons, a nice concrete ramp, and they are dealers for MerCruiser, and OMC. There is also a marine store geared to motorboats.

Next upstream, is **Ray's Pier (18)** with a friendly full menu restaurant, cocktail lounge, snack bar, and complimentary docking.

If you stop at Ray's Pier or De Soto's landing, a short walk will bring you to a post office and a nice convenience store where they will make good fresh sandwiches-to-go. Go out, (south) to the tar road, turn left, and less than 5 minutes' walk will bring you there.

Directly across the river from Benedict is **Hallowing Point Landing (20)** with hard surfaced ramp.

To proceed farther into the Southern Maryland countryside, you must pass the Benedict Swing Bridge (19) with 16 feet vertical clearance. It swings open at the middle and clears the way to mile upon mile upon mile of typical upriver meandering to your heart's content.

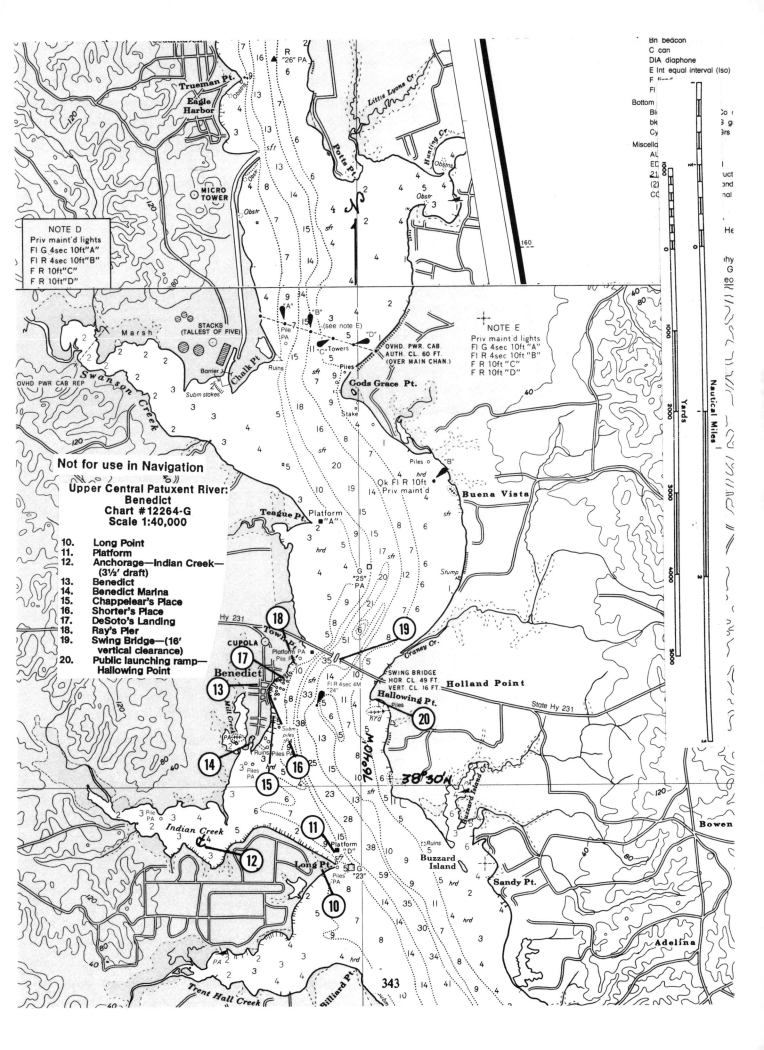

Not for use in Navigation

Upper Central Patuxent River: Benedict
Chart #12264-G
Scale 1:40,000

10. Long Point
11. Platform
12. Anchorage—Indian Creek—(3½' draft)
13. Benedict
14. Benedict Marina
15. Chappelear's Place
16. Shorter's Place
17. DeSoto's Landing
18. Ray's Pier
19. Swing Bridge—(16' vertical clearance)
20. Public launching ramp—Hallowing Point

NOTE D
Priv maint'd lights
Fl G 4sec 10ft "A"
Fl R 4sec 10ft "B"
F R 10ft "C"
F R 10ft "D"

NOTE E
Priv maint'd lights
Fl G 4sec 10ft "A"
Fl R 4sec 10ft "B"
F R 10ft "C"
F R 10ft "D"

343

Refer to Chart #12264-H—"Upper Patuxent River: Above Benedict to Nottingham."

The shoreline is much of what you will already have seen with variations along the way. Most will chose not to proceed farther. Carry whatever fuel and water you will need to return and don't count on any anchorages other than out in the river, unless you are a shallow creek boat that can go anywhere. The best way to enjoy this section of the river would be in a small, fast motorboat with ample fuel and speed to return to the lower river by dusk.

Cedar Point Lighthouse ruins, Patuxent River

If you go this far up the Patuxent River (chart on pg. 345), marinas are nonexistent. If you need help anywhere in the river or the nearby Chesapeake Bay, Sea Tow, standing by at Calvert Marina, Solomons, can come to your rescue

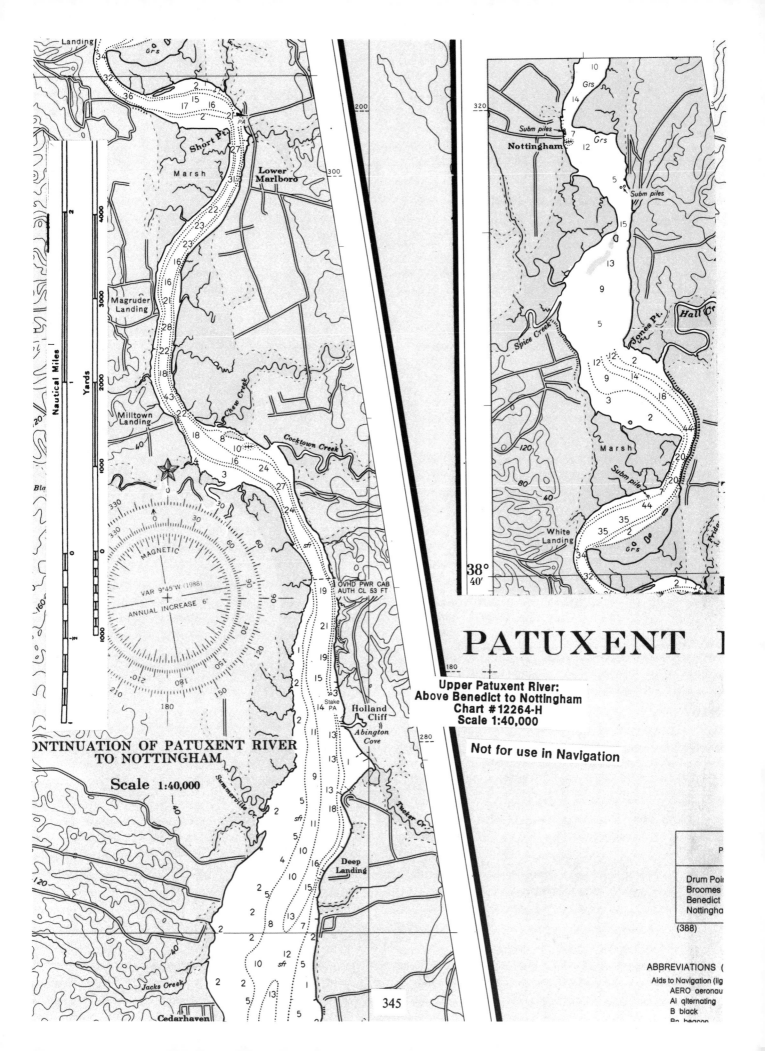

PATUXENT

Upper Patuxent River:
Above Benedict to Nottingham
Chart #12264-H
Scale 1:40,000

Not for use in Navigation

CONTINUATION OF PATUXENT RIVER
TO NOTTINGHAM

Scale 1:40,000

OVHD PWR CAB
AUTH CL 53 FT

MAGNETIC

VAR 9°45'W (1988)

ANNUAL INCREASE 6'

Landing

Short Pt

Lower
Marlboro

Marsh

Magruder
Landing

Milltown
Landing

Chew Creek

Cocktown Creek

Holland
Cliff

Abington
Cove

Summerville Cr.

Deep
Landing

Tucker Cr.

Jacks Creek

Cedarhaven

Stake
PA

Nottingham

Spice Creek

Jones Pt.

Hall Cr

Marsh

White
Landing

Subm piles

Grs

345

(388)

Drum Poi
Broomes
Benedict
Nottingha

ABBREVIATIONS (

Aids to Navigation (lig
AERO aeronau
Al alternating
B black
Bn beacon

38°
40'

APPENDIX I

BOOKS AND MUSIC

When you take your cruise, you will enjoy it more if you have good reference books aboard. All of those mentioned in the text are good examples. I would also suggest reading, if you have not already done so, the novel "Chesapeake" by James A. Michener, published by Random House. This fine work of fiction sweeps through much of the history of the Bay, but in a thoroughly researched and realistic manner. It will help to provide an understanding of the waters, shores, and people. "Boating Almanac, Volume IV," by Peter A. Geis is updated annually and has a good list of marina statuses, "Cruising the Chesapeake" by Shellenberger, published by International Marine Publishing Company provides background information for many different cruising areas. "Chesapeake Bay Country" by Swepson Earle, published by Weathervane, although somewhat outdated, provides informative reading for those interested in the many old homes and farms around the shores. It also gives historical and cultural information. Also interesting is, "Rivers of the Eastern Shore" by Hulbert Footner, published by Tidewater. This gives history, lore, and interesting stories of the land around these rivers, interspersed with interesting descriptions of daily life of the inhabitants of early days. The book entitled "Wye Island" by Boyd Gibbons, published by Johns Hopkins University Press gives humorous and fascinating insight into the earlier days of the Wye River and its surrounding country. "Adventuring in the Chesapeake Bay Area," a Sierra Club travel guide to the tidewater country around the Bay gives helpful information for those traveling by land.

The music of the Chesapeake is as varied as the Bay itself, and at festivals everywhere you will hear different parts of it, performed by many groups, both professional and spontaneous. We strongly suggest that you buy some of this to take along, perhaps also to listen to before you go and after you return.

Among our favorites are "Chesapeake Born," and "Come Full Circle" by Tom Wisner and his group. These tape albums feature songs of Tom (and some by his son Mark) done with native love, feeling and incredible beauty. These songs are about such things as oyster dredge boats, Bay lands and rivers, storms, watermen, tall tales, and sailing. I have cruised the Bay with delight for almost 50 years, and have never found any collection of songs that better represent and characterize the Bay, its culture and people. His song "Chesapeake Born" was used as the title song for the National Geographic special, "Chesapeake Born." His albums are included in the National Museum as part of the Smithsonian Folkways Collection. Among other awards for his promotion of the Bay, Tom Wisner was the recipient of the Maryland Governor's Citation in 1986 for his work to preserve the Bay, using his songs and stories. He now teaches near Solomon's Island. Order tapes from him at: Tom Wisner Studio, Box 7, California, Maryland 20619.

BIBLIOGRAPHY

See also List of Charts, Publications and Sources near the front of this book.

Bowen, John, *Adventuring in the Chesapeake Bay Area*, a Sierra Club travel guide, 400 pages, (1989) $12.95; published by Sierra Books, P.O. Box 5853, Pasadena, CA 91117-0853.

Brown, Alexander Crosby, *Steam Packets on the Chesapeake: A History of Old Bay Line Since 1840*, 207 pages, (1961) $12.95; published by Tidewater Publications, P.O. Box 456, Centreville, MD 21617.

Burgess, Robert, H., *Chesapeake Bay Sailing Craft*, 300 pages, (1975), $12.50. Out of print since 1984. Available in some libraries. Published by Tidewater Publications, P.O. Box 456, Centreville, MD 21617.

Burgess, Robert, H., *This Was The Chesapeake*; 223 pages, (1963), $24.95, published by Tidewater Publications, P.O. Box 456, Centreville, MD 21617.

Earle, Swepson, "The Chesapeake Bay Country," 512 pages, (1923), Weathervane Books, a division of Imprint Society, Inc., Distributed by Crown Publishers, Inc.

Fishing in Maryland, $6. Published annually by Fishing in Maryland, Inc., Box 201, 10 Shanney Brook Court, Phoenix, MD 21131-0201. Phone: (301) 243-3413. Editor: Pete Barrett.

Footner, Hulbert, *Rivers of the Eastern Shore*, 318 pages, (1979). Reprint of 1944 edition, $19.95; published by Tidewater Publications, P.O. Box 456, Centreville, MD 21617.

Geis, Peter A., *Boating Almanac, Vol. IV*; $12.50, published annually by Boating Almanac Co. Inc., 203 McKinsey Road, Severna Park, MD 21146. Phone: (310) 647-0084; Fax: (310) 647-0440.

Gibbons, Boyd, *Wye Island—Outsiders, Insiders and Resistance to Change*, 248 pages, (1977) $20.95. Paperback (1987), $12.95. Published by Resources for the Future, Box 4852, Hampden Station, Baltimore, MD 21211.

Gillmer, Thomas C., *Pride of Baltimore: The Story of the Baltimore Clippers*, 226 pages, paperback (1994), $15.95. Published by International Marine Publishing Company, P.O. Box 220, Camden, ME 04843.

Jacoby, Mark E., *Working the Chesapeake: Watermen on the Bay*, 155 pages, $24.95. Paperback edition (1991), $14.95, University of Maryland publication, Maryland Sea Grant College, 0112 Skinners Hall, College Park, MD 20742.

Michener, James A., *Chesapeake*, 865 pages, (1991) $45, Random House, 201 E. 50 M St., 22nd Floor, New York, NY 10022.

Shellenberger, William H., *Cruising the Chesapeake: A Gunkholer's Guide*, 448 pages, (1990), $34.95. Published by the International Marine Publishing Company, P.O. Box 220, Camden, ME 04843.

Snediker, Quentin, and Jensen, Ann, *Chesapeake Bay Schooners*, 252 pages, (1992) $44.95. Published by Tidewater Publications, P.O. Box 456, Centreville, MD 21617.

Warner, William W., *Beautiful Swimmers: Watermen, Crabs and the Chesapeake*, 320 pages, (1976), $22.50, published by Atlantic-Little Brown & Co., Atlantic Monthly, 19 Union Square, 11th Floor, New York, NY 10003.

—(1977) Penguin Books, paperback $6.95, Viking Penguin, 375 Hudson St., NY, NY 10014-3657.

Whitehead III, John H., *Watermen of the Chesapeake Bay*, (1979), $19.95. Published by Whitehead Photo, Fousbee Street, Richmond, VA 23220.

Wisner, Tom and his group, *Chesapeake Born* and *Come Full Circle*; tapes available from: Tom Wisner Studio, Box 7, California, MD 20619.

APPENDIX II

FESTIVALS

It seems that almost every town, village, county, and city has a festival of some sort at some time or another during the year. Some have many, some have only one, but more pop up each season. That is one of the reasons why we often refer you to county and city publicity offices, chambers of commerce, and similar agencies when you are planning a cruise. The following is a representative listing of some of the more well-known festivals. But the entire Bay experience is a festival and the people living around it know that, so that they think nothing of coming up with a new one to suit a mood or occasion. Always ask when you pull into port, and prepare to join in the fun.

Dates change, sometimes yearly, in the constant juggle to avoid conflicts with other festivals and to get good weather. Sometimes events are cancelled for the year because the weather will not cooperate. We arrange this list according to the months when the events usually occur. Some events, such as the Fourth of July Celebrations, the Chestertown Tea Party, and the Annapolis Boat Shows, always occur at a certain time.

MAY

Duck Decoy Festival at Harve de Grace where the Bay begins, enjoy an art unique to the Bay in this town that considers itself to be the Duck Decoy Capital of the World. Other towns also sometimes make this claim—go and judge them all. You will not only see and be able to purchase beautiful examples of this rare art, but enjoy displays of related crafts, and good food.

The Chestertown Tea Party Festival in Chestertown, takes place way up the Chester River. The trip up this beautiful river is pleasure enough, but when you reach the fine old historical town, you will relish walks through its tree-shaded streets, visits to its historical landmark homes, and revel in the reenactment of the Tea Party of May 23, 1774 when the British taxes were protested by a certain unscheduled offloading of British tea. Local people dress in clothing from the period and reenact the event. There are also parades, bands, historical displays, and good food.

Springfest of St. Michaels. One of the many events in this town, there are art shows, craft displays, music, concerts, and food in a celebration of the arrival of Spring, centering in the Chesapeake Bay Maritime Museum.

Celebrations of the Arts Festival at Easton and the Chesapeake Bay Maritime Museum of St. Michaels. This features Smithsonian programs, regional and national entertainment, bluegrass, jazz, and arts and crafts booths.

Oxford Fine Arts Fair. An invitational show with the environment of Chesapeake Bay featured.

A combination of Solomons Island festivals revolving around the Calvert Marine Museum celebrating awareness of the Bay music along the waterfront, and family enjoyment of the Bay.

JUNE

Boat Show in the Water in Baltimore's Inner Harbor. See and board craft, and visit displays of boating equipment.

National Flag Day celebration at Baltimore. Although many of the events are around the Inner Harbor, there is special emphasis on Ft. Mc Henry where the words of the "Star Spangled Banner" were written as Francis Scott Key, from his prison ship anchored in the Patapsco River, saw to his delight and amazement, the flag still flying after the terrible cannon bombardment of the fort. A red, white and blue buoy marks where this ship was anchored. You may tour the fort, preserved to show you the way it was then.

Tilghman Island Seafood Festival. This island has been home of many of the beautiful skipjack fleet for generations, as well as many more of the Bay's working watermen. Come for games, rides, a parade and contests, and some real down home Bay seafood cooking and eating. It is also great to meet the people who bring it from the waters to you.

Harbor Expo, in the Canton section of Baltimore's harbor. You will pass Canton on your right as you head into the Inner Harbor. This was formerly a shipbuilding and seaport area where clipper ships docked. Now it is a unique neighborhood with shops and homes, and this festival allows you to enjoy some of the best of Canton in one weekend.

Antique and Classic Boat Show at the Chesapeake Maritime Museum at St. Michaels. These are primarily power boats and runabouts, but also include some sailboats. There are contests for the boats.

JULY

Almost everywhere you go, there will be fireworks displays on the Fourth. Every year there are more; some put on by governmental agencies, some by private concerns. To mention a few: Havre de Grace (also a carnival and Independence Day Festival), Rock Hall (Parades, food, waterman sports, displays, music—an old Bay tradition), Baltimore Inner Harbor, Annapolis, Cambridge, North East in the town park on the water, Chestertown, Chesapeake Beach, Herrington Harbour South, Solomons Island, St. Michaels, Galesville.

Big Band Night at Chesapeake Bay Maritime Museum in St. Michaels, featuring big band era swing and music.

Cambridge Sail Regatta, at Cambridge on the Choptank. Here are races, parties, displays, and fun.

AUGUST

Kent Narrows Power Boat Races. Fast and powerful boats, hydroplanes and other types featuring internationally known racers as well as local racers, compete in this exciting event centered in the exciting Kent Narrows.

Governor's Cup Log Canoe Race, sponsored by the Miles River Yacht Club near St. Michaels. These graceful authentic log canoes can be seen racing, either formally or for fun, throughout the year. But this is the grand event and great fun to watch while anchored out in the Miles River. Boats built prior to and after 1917 compete for different awards. There are also special related events ashore.

Harve de Grace Arts and Crafts Show. It is as the name implies, with booths and stalls throughout the town and especially in the waterfront park. This includes concerts and good food.

Betterton Day. On the southern shore of the entrance to the Sassafras River, this small quiet town was formerly a widely visited beach and recreational area. Seeking a revival, with nice beach and public docks and ramp, the town offers arts, crafts, good food, and fun on its special day.

Crab Day in St. Michaels. Steeped in the Bay's tradition, and with the Bay-famous Crab Claw restaurant in the center, what better place to celebrate the Bay's most famous feisty denizen of the deep with crab races, eating, lore, educational displays, fun and music. But, as with any visit to this town, the Museum and the rest of the area will widely broaden your enjoyment.

Party on the Bay. This event is celebrated throughout the waterfront community of Maryland in many different ways, and most places of major population will be involved in some way. Sandy Point State Park on the western shore at the foot (north side) of the Bay Bridges is one center of celebration.

Governor's Cup Race from Annapolis to St. Mary's City. A grand sailing event with parties and celebrations at each end.

Governor's Cup Fishing Tournament. This is state-wide and also includes Virginia. There are different areas all over the Bay for registration and weighing in, one probably wherever you will be. Just ask.

Seafood Festival of Harford County in Havre de Grace. While seafood is the main theme, with booths and kitchens all over the town, concerts, crafts and lore are also featured under the trees and along the streets.

Hydroplane Races at Havre de Grace on the Susquehanna. Watch these fast and daring boats from the marinas or the shores of the town.

Seafood Festival of Dorchester County at Cambridge. Dock in the basin or the municipal marina and enjoy not only the good food, but all the other things that go with these festivals on the Bay. Crafts, arts, music, and entertainment.

Bayfest of North Beach. Just north of Chesapeake Beach, this small community once enjoyed a reputation as a very popular vacation resort. Now it is seeking a revival and this festival, on the shores of the Chesapeake, seeks to celebrate various aspects of Bay culture. Many will visit by car.

Classic Powerboat Regatta of Cambridge. See many of the old beauties, mahogany and leather gleaming, both in competition and display.

SEPTEMBER

Bartlett Cup Log Canoe Race. Yet another of these exciting sailing events, off Navy Point in St. Michaels.

Museum Day in St. Michaels. The purpose of this is to both enjoy and support the Chesapeake Bay Maritime Museum. There are concerts, shows, displays, arts and crafts, boat races, and fundraising opportunities for the museum.

Seafood Festival at Annapolis. Revel in more of the best of Bay seafood eating at the state's capital.

Chestertown Candlelight Walking Tour. Most of the town

within walking distance of the waterfront (where you can anchor or dock) is a designated national historical landmark area. The old homes and businesses, sheltered by ancient towering trees, set back in quiet lanes, make a very special setting for this walk into the shadows of the past.

Havre de Grace Fall Harvest. In celebration of the harvest, once again this old but vibrant town hosts food booths, arts, crafts, concerts, and shows, with more of an emphasis on the surrounding rural countryside, as well as the Bay.

Deal Island Skipjack Races. A festival ashore compliments the grande event as the skipjacks race across the waters and time. Enjoy seafood, arts, crafts, music, and most importantly, a celebration and support of these marvelous craft and their heritage.

Cambridge Seaport Days. Cambridge has a history as a seaport, and this as well as its re-emergence into a present day boating center, are celebrated around the changing waterfront.

St. Michaels Traditional Sailboat Races. Beautiful boats carefully restored and maintained sail as if from the past on the waters of the Miles River.

OCTOBER

U.S. Sailboat Show and U.S. Power Boat Show at Annapolis, Maryland. Both of these are in-the-water shows where you can board the boat of your dreams. "Ego Alley" is transformed into a floating show of docks, booths, and boats. The grounds and docks around the slips are covered with huge tents full of displays of every sort of boating accessory and equipment. The shows are alternated each year, so that one or the other falls on the Columbus Day weekend, lasting from Trade Day on Thursday, to the following Monday.

Baltimore On the Bay. This is a weekend of events of all kinds and themes involving appreciation of the Bay. The best spot to enjoy in the Inner Harbor.

Fells Point Festival in Baltimore. Fells Point, a neighbor of Canton, was a shipbuilding and port area, of particular fame for such vessels as clipper ships, and even the USF *Constellation*. Now it is a unique neighborhood of shops, homes, pubs and restaurants. This festival features arts and crafts, street displays, concerts, jugglers, food such as seafood and pit beef, and more.

Decoy Festival at North East. In the museum, on the park grounds next to the water, and throughout the town, are displays not only of beautiful locally carved duck decoys, but all the related culture. Included, of course, are food booths, concerts, and arts and crafts.

Mid Atlantic Small Craft Festival, at St. Michaels in the Chesapeake Bay Maritime Museum. Participants from near and far bring crafts that they have lovingly made or preserved, and show them in rare display. There are also lectures, seminars, racing and boat competition.

Tilghman Island Day. The local watermen and the Fire Department celebrate the Bay and the island as only they could with food, arts and crafts, displays of Bay culture, concerts, entertainment and skipjack and work boat races.

Patuxent River Appreciation Days at Solomons Island. The Calvert Marine Museum plays a major role in this event, but also the entire community participates with music, arts and crafts, seafood booths and other special events.

The Great Chesapeake Bay Schooner Race begins at Baltimore and ends at Waterside in Norfolk. Many beautiful and authentic schooners, some very old, some carefully reconstructed replicas, join in this race down the Bay.

Chesapeake Appreciation Days at Sandy Point State Park. This is usually the weekend before the beginning of oyster season, or the last of October. Sandy Point State Park is the focal point for a festival designed to attract the attention of those ashore and inland to the Bay and its heritage. It has all of the displays and attractions that you might expect of an event so named, but our favorite is the skipjack races in the Bay waters off the park. They will be fresh from summer repairs and maintenance, and ready to begin a winter of hard work in the Bay. It is great to watch these from your boat.

NOVEMBER

Waterfowl Festival at Easton. usually in mid-November, this features renowned wildlife artists, decoys, carvings and paintings, goose calling and retriever demonstrating, seafood, and shopping. Proceeds are donated to the preservation of waterfowl environment. There is also a Waterfowl Hunting demonstration at the Chesapeake Bay Maritime Museum in St. Michaels, in conjunction with this event. There are live demonstrations of past and present forms of waterfowl hunting.

Oyster Day at the Chesapeake Bay Maritime Museum in St. Michaels. Includes demonstrations of tonging and nippering, a shell skipping contest and good food.

APPENDIX III

HISTORY

EARLIEST EXPLORATIONS

In 1573 Sir Ralph Lane explored northward from Sir Walter Raleigh's colony, Roanoke, near what is now Cape Hatteras, North Carolina. He came upon a vast inland sea near which dwelled an Indian tribe called "Chesepiuc." According to some accounts, Lane named the Bay "Chesapeake," which reportedly meant "Mother of the Waters." ("Chesapeake Bay A Pictorial Maritime History," by M.V. Brewington, Crown Publishers, Inc. by arrangement with Tidewater Publishers, Cornell Maritime Press, 1956, page 1.) But Lane and the people from his colony did not settle the Bay. They had their own difficulties, culminating in the forever mysterious vanishing of the Lost Colony of Roanoke, around 1590. These Englishmen had actually been preceded by the Spanish, as early as the 1500s. The Spaniards had marveled at the water and land, but they too withdrew without any lasting settlement. The first permanent English-speaking settlement began at Jamestown where one of the Bay's most avid cruisers began his Bay explorations.

JAMESTOWN

Captain John Smith, born in England in 1580, embarked with the colonists on the three ships, *Susan Constant, Godspede, and Discovery,* after a life already full of adventure. Exact replicas of these tiny ships are in the water at Jamestown on the James River in the lower Bay. Walking about the decks and envisioning their trip across the Atlantic, with the conditions of the trip and number of souls aboard, will make your cruise seem like a luxury liner, no matter how small your boat.

While crossing the Atlantic, Smith was accused by others aboard of conspiracy, and he was imprisoned. When the ships reached land, it was discovered that Smith was intended to be one of the leaders by the London Company, and he was freed. He then led the Jamestown colonists to survival. It is quite clear, that but for this wily, feisty, and brave leader, the "gentlemen" of that colony would have never made it through the first winters. He made an ironclad rule, to which some of the dandies were not accustomed. "He who will not work shall not eat."

Although this first settlement was in Jamestown on the James on the lower Bay, Captain John Smith found time to launch numerous exploration trips up the Bay and its tributaries, looking for the ever-elusive westward passage to the riches of the East. This persistent explorer and leader very carefully charted much of the Bay. He explored many tributaries in launches and smaller sailing craft. Some accounts say that Smith named the Bay from the Indian word "Che sep ack" meaning "country on a great river." Smith was conquered by some of the Indian nations ashore, and negotiated with and became friends with others. The story of young Pocahontas, daughter of Chief Powhatan, who stood in the way of Smith's execution is one of the many treasures from this period. According to Smith, she stood before him as he was to be executed, and pled for his life to her father, who granted his daughter's wish. She later was taken to England and treated royally, but died, it is told, missing her home.

Captain John Smith's Journals

Much of our knowledge of what the early Bay was like, and many of the names we still use around the Bay come from Captain John Smith's journals of his adventures. Smith's description of the Bay in 1608 is still accurate today.

"The country is not mountainous not yet low but such pleasant plaine, hils and fertile valleys, one prettily crossing on other, and watered so conveniently with their sweete brooks and cristall springs, as if art itselfe had devised them . . .

The mildness of the aire, the fertilitie of the soile, and the situation of the rivers are so propitious to the nature and use of man as no place is more convenient for pleasure, profit, and man's sustenance . . .

The waters, Isles, and shoals are full of safe harbours for ships of warre or marchandize, for boats of all sortes, for transportation or fishing."

Captain John Smith's journeys took him throughout the Bay, both north and south. And from that time, the history of the Bay has been an interwoven story. We can't just discuss the northern or southern area histories, because the story can only be told as a whole.

INDIAN TRIBES

The land was already populated well before the Europeans arrived. There were several major Indian tribes around the Bay, even aligned as confederations from time to time. The ill-prepared and sometimes lazy Jamestown colonists would not have survived without the help of the Indians. When the white men first tried to settle the lower Bay in 1607, this tribe was governed by Chief Powhatan who ruled his large confederation. Captain John Smith early realized that this nation would play an important role in the success of the colonies. The Indians taught the first settlers many lessons that enabled them to survive in the difficult environment.

After Chief Powhatan, his brother Opitchapan led the confederation. Soon however, the more aggressive Opechancanough, another brother, became chief. Opechancanough was fearful of the growing threat of the colonists, for just cause. Disputes followed, often the fault of the colonists. In March of 1622, the Jamestown settlement was attacked by members of the Powhatan tribe under Chief Openchancanough.

Almost 350 settlers, men. women, and children were killed. From here on, numerous fights broke out. Peace was on and off, until in 1644 Openchancanough again swept down, killing almost 500 settlers. Soon thereafter he was killed, and a more stable peace began in that area.

In the upper Bay, Susquehannocks controlled much of the area, occasionally attacking other weaker tribes, including those of the lower Bay. They also resisted the settlers, but were eventually defeated and pushed into the area north of the Bay.

Today, there may still be found the descendants of these first settlers around the shores. One such place is on the upper reaches of the Mattaponi and Pamunkey Rivers. These rivers are born far back in the Virginia countryside. If you are traveling Route 95 between Richmond and Washington, you will pass over their beginnings. They then flow down from the farm and forest covered hills until they come together to form the York River, which empties into the lower Bay. On the shores of these two rivers, well above their junction, there still exist two tribes. Their names are the same as the rivers beside which their reservations are located. These are the direct descendants of the Powhatans and they still revere Chief Opechancanough for his intelligence, wisdom, and able leadership. Chief Custalow of the Mattaponi Tribe has told me that a primary camping site for Chief Opechancanough was in the area between the two rivers.

Indian Reservations

As early as 1658 the Mattaponi and Pamunkey reservations were confirmed to those tribes by the Governor, the Council, and the Grand Assembly of Virginia [1 Henning's Statutes-at-Large 466-468 (1657-1658)]. In 1677 the King of England, through the Governor of Virginia, made a treaty with several Indian tribes in the area, including the Pamunkey and the Mattaponi. This treaty states in part,

"... The said Indian Kings and Queens and their Subjects shall hold their lands, and have the same confirmed to them and their posterity by Patent under the Seale of this his Majesties Colony, without any fee gratuity or Reward for ye same, in such sort, and in as free and firme manner as others his Majesties Liege Subjects, have and enjoye their lands, and possessions, paying onely yearly for, and in lieu of a Quitrent or acknowledgement for the same three Indian Arrowes."

(14 Virginia Magazine of History and Biography, pg. 289-296 at pg. 290-291, July 1906-April 1907).

Since the time of the early colonists, the Bay has continuously played a critical role in the development of the nation. The first session of representative government in America occurred in Jamestown in 1619. The European settlers continued to pour in, carving towns and farms and plantations out of the rich forests. Civilization spread all around the shores and up the tributaries; sometimes peacefully, and sometimes involving fights with the displaced Indian Nations, and also sometimes involving fights among themselves.

NORTHERN BAY SETTLEMENTS

In 1631, Kent Island was settled by Virginia colonist William Claiborne. He began a successful trading and farming operation on the island, expanding as time passed. But his influence in what is now Maryland was short lived. In England, the powerful and energetic Lord Baltimore was anxious to establish a haven for Roman Catholics, having felt the pinch of intolerance himself in those troubled times for England. He sought a grant in the new world from the King, but died before it could be fulfilled. His son received from the King a large tract of land including what is now Maryland, as well as a territory to the north. In 1633, Leonard Calvert, another of the family, came over with 200 colonists, founding St. Marys City.

In the later 1630s, there was a series of skirmishes between the settlers at St. Marys under the leadership of Governor Calvert, and William Claiborne who had earlier settled on Kent Island under the auspices of the Virginia Charter. Both of these charters had been presented by the King, but there were understandable conflicts considering the nature of the grants and the lack of knowledge about the geography of the area. Ultimately Governor Calvert's forces succeeded in securing that upper Bay area for the Maryland colony.

The Calverts were very concerned with religious freedom, and attempted to insure tolerance within their lands. In 1649, the first religious tolerance act in the Americas was passed in this colony. In 1655 and ensuing years, there were battles again, this time between Calvert's forces and the Puritans who settled on the Severn near what is now Annapolis. Accounts differ as to who was at fault.

The first of the 13 colonies began to organize themselves along the shores of the Bay, forming governments at first loyal to the King of England, gradually developing loyalties to their own destinies and the slowly emerging ideas of a new nation to "turn the world upside down." Areas of high civilization and culture grew on the Bay shores, among these, the Williamsburg area near the James, and Annapolis, Chestertown, and then Baltimore in the upper Bay. Smaller towns such as Havre de Grace, Oxford, and Georgetown supported surrounding farms and served as shipping centers to the large cities, and sometimes to Europe itself.

BIRTH OF OUR NATION

The idea of a new nation grew slowly and almost painfully, many of the loyalists resisting to the end the idea of disloyalty to the King and the Mother Country, which had brought stability and a degree of civilized comfort to these shores. In numerous petitions, the colonists asked the King for relief and fairness, but with no resolution of the growing differences involving issues such as taxation, trade restrictions, and self-goverment. In 1765, the notorious Stamp Act was passed. Tempers grew shorter and events quickened. Patrick Henry demanded "Give me Liberty or give me Death" in Williamsburg in 1775, and in Chestertown the colonists destroyed a shipment of tea in their own Tea Party on May 23, 1774. In Annapolis, a similar event occurred during the same year.

When war broke out, the British Naval presence was strong throughout the Bay, the American Navy puny in comparison. But the French joined the Colonists, and their naval forces were very helpful in the Bay, as was their infantry ashore. When the British surrendered to the American forces and their French allies, it was on the shores of one of the major tributaries, the York River at Yorktown, on October 18, 1781. In December 1783, George Washington resigned his commision as Commander-in-Chief of the Continental Army in the statehouse of Annapolis, which was then being used as the temporary capitol of the new country. A short time later, the Treaty of Paris was ratified in this building.

Washington D.C.
In 1793, the cornerstone of the nation's permanent capitol building was laid on the shores of the Potomac, hithertofore a river of plantations and tobacco trade. The site, chosen after some bickering and much bargaining, was picked by George Washington and the city was planned by that gentleman, Thomas Jefferson, and Pierre L'Enfant. In 1800 the government moved from the high civilization of Philadelphia to the relative "wilderness" of the new city of Washington, D.C.

WAR OF 1812

Times of hostility along the Bay's shores came again in the War of 1812 during which Admiral Cockburn sailed the waters, bombing and burning many a village and town. Almost any village that you will visit will have stories of this time. These include Havre de Grace, Georgetown, Oxford, St. Michaels, Annapolis, Galesville, and many others. It was off Baltimore, while imprisoned on a British ship, that Francis Scott Key wrote the words to the "Star Spangled Banner," seeing it gloriously wave over Ft. McHenry after a night of grueling shelling by the British fleet. When you visit Baltimore, you will see, in season, a red, white, and blue buoy marking the spot where the prison ship was anchored.

PIRATES

As would be expected, throughout all of the early growth of civilization, pirates sailed the Bay from time to time. These were particularly numerous during times of war when various governments sanctioned the actions. In the disputes between Maryland and Virginia settlers, acts of piracy or "loyalty to the cause" (depending upon one's perspective) were frequent. The famous Baltimore Clippers, sanctioned by the American Government during the War of 1812, were certainly considered pirates by the British. Perhaps the most notorious pirate of all times operated along the Carolina coast and to the south, but Blackbeard legends persist around the Bay. It was Lieutenant Governor Alexander Spotswood of Virginia, who finally sent out a fleet to capture this ferocious menace. Under the leadership of Lt. Robert Maynard, Blackbeard was killed, and the story has it that his head was bought back to the Chesapeake on the bow of a ship, to be impaled on a stake in Hampton in the lower Bay for all to see. One story has it that the huge skull was later fashioned into a drinking cup.

POST-WAR PROSPERITY

After the War of 1812, the waves of commerce and civilization rolled on unhampered, and the shores of the Bay became more densely populated. The waters were full of sailing ships taking passengers and cargo from the countryside up the tributaries to the cities and overseas. Soon came steamships, and then railroads that ended some of the shipping lines.

The Civil War (War Between the States)
The War Between the States saw the Bay primarily under control of the Union, with major battles throughout the countryside along its shores. McClellan tried, seemingly forever, to march inland along the York-James River peninsula to conquer Richmond. The Confederacy attempted to break the blockade with its ironclad *Merrimac* in Hampton Roads. When the Union hastily sent the ironclad *Monitor* to engage this threat, there ensued on March 8, 1862, the first naval battle between ironclad steamships, which changed forever the course of naval warfare.

Commerce
Throughout all of this development, and long before, the Bay has been a source of abundant seafood for its citizens. The Indians fished and relished oysters, clams, and crabs.

In his writings, Captain John Smith marveled continuously at the abundance of fish. And the settlers brought new ways to harvest them, the new ways improving over the years until modern machinery and method have seriously jeopardized this once overwhelming abundance. Along the way, beautiful seaworthy and functional vessels were developed that are unique to the Bay's heritage. These are described in Chapter 1. Today, cruising around the Bay, you can still see them working. For example, the Skipjack fleet is one of the few fleets of working sailing fishing vessels left in the world.

CRADLE OF THE NATION

Today as you cruise the Bay, you are truly cruising the cradle of the Nation. History overflows from the shores all around you. Anywhere you choose to land, you can find local residents, historical societies, and governmental agencies ready to tell you stories of the past and show you where they happened. This text attempts to set out some of the interesting historical notes as they relate to the areas described. Follow the suggestions and delve into the past yourself. Each harbor holds treasures enough for many visits.

PLACES TO VISIT OF HISTORICAL SIGNIFICANCE

The entire Bay is one fascinating experience in history. Throughout the descriptions of different places, we have tried to give historical background and point out special places. Following are a few of the highlights. More details and many other interesting places will be found in our harbor descriptions.

Almost anywhere you go in the Bay you will hear stories about an attack of some sort by Admiral Cockburn, who led a British fleet during the War of 1812. In Georgetown, on the Sassafras, you can visit the Kitty Knight House, now an inn. This survived the Admiral's attack when he ordered that it be spared out of respect for the daring and daunting defense of the home by its then owner, Miss Knight.

In Havre de Grace across the Bay and on the Susqhehanna, you will hear stories of and see the spot where their hero of the war fired the town's sole cannon at the passing British fleet.

In Charlestown on the Northeast River, you will hear of the breastworks hastily constructed to defend the area, to be washed away by a rain storm before the British arrived.

In St. Michaels, on the Miles River, you will hear the stories of the "town that fooled the British" referring to placements of lanterns in the trees to misdirect British cannon fire.

During the War of 1812, Frances Scott Key wrote the words to the "Star Spangled Banner" while in an anchored prison ship downstream of Ft. McHenry. A buoy marks the spot where the prison ship lay, and you can take tours of the fort. Baltimore, being an area of major concentration of civilization from the very early days, has many other places of interest. Some of these include a shot tower, the grave site of Edgar Allan Poe, a museum tracing the history of the nation's railroads with many well-maintained locomotives and cars. You can tour them all in relative ease from the water, after visiting the information booths at the Inner Harbor.

In Chestertown, far up the Chester River, you can visit many houses, now designated as Historical Landmarks, from the Colonial age. See the waterfront area where they had their own Tea Party in the times leading up to the Revolution, and the College that George Washington founded (it bears his name) in part with money raised from a lottery.

In Annapolis, you will visit the State House, built in 1772. It served briefly as the center of government for the new nation. Here also is a large area designated as a Historical Landmark, with buildings of rich heritage.

At Steamboat Landing in Galesville, visit and dine where beautiful steamboats such as the *Emma Giles* regularly loaded cargo and passengers in the days of steam and travel by water.

In Oxford on the Tred Avon are many Historical Landmark buildings, including a colonial customs house and the Robert Morris Inn, still operating.

Informative historical references that you may wish to bring include "This Was the Chesapeake" by Robert H. Burgess, published by Tidewater Publishers. This gives a great deal of background about many of the homes that you will pass ashore. "Rivers on the Eastern Shore," by Hulbert Footner, published by Tidewater Publishers, will also be good background reading. Also refer to bibliography, Appendix I.

Working on rigging *Pride of Baltimore* topsail schooner,
Baltimore Inner Harbor. Chapter 14

APPENDIX IV

POSITION FIXES

The following positions are derived either from the Light List or by use of a Magellan GPS. Please read about and beware of GPS limitations, as discussed in Chapter 1. Even positions given in the Light List are designated as approximate. Never rely on any one source. Always use your own observations, a set of currently corrected NOS charts, and prudent seamanship.

These positions are arranged according to general locations, listed alphabetically. Positions given are the ones we found to be particularly helpful for that area.

Bohemia River

Flashing red "2" off Long Point. This is difficult to spot on hazy summer days. My GPS derived position for this is 39°28.54' by 75°53.18'. This is a point just inside (to the left of) the marker.

Chesapeake Beach

The outside marker, Fl G 4 sec. "1" is 50 feet outside of the channel limit. Its position is 38°41.5'N by 76°31.3'W.

Chester River

Flashing Red Bell "2BE" marks the eastern end of the eastern extension of Brewerton Channel. Its position is 39°08.9'N by 76°20.0'W.

Red Nun "2" marks the end of the Love Point Shoal. Its positions is 39°04.0'N by 76°16.4'W.

Love Point Light has a bell and is on a 35-foot skeleton structure. Its position is 39°03.4'N by 76°17.0'W.

Choptank River

Sharps Island Light. This marks the northern end of the shoal, but it is set in 11 feet of water. At 54 feet tall with a 6 sec. flash, it is hard to miss, and it has the distinctive characteristic of leaning way over. It was set that way in 1977 by the ice that encased the Bay that winter. It is a brown-red solid cylindrical structure. Its position is 38°38.3'N by 76°22.5'W.

Flashing R 4 sec. lighted buoy "78" in the Chesapeake Channel. Its position is 38°33.2'N by 76°25.7'W.

Outside western marker for Knapps Narrows is Fl G "1" and its position is 38°43.3'N by 76°20.8'W.

East Knapps Narrows Channel marker "3" is a 14-foot flashing beacon. Its position is 38°42.6'N by 76°19.4'W. Broad Creek Fl Gr "1." Its position is 38°41.7'N by 76°14.9'W.

Tred Avon River turning point for Peach Blossom Creek. GPS derived coordinates for my taking-off point in the Tred Avon channel off R "16" is 38°44.25'N by 76°07.32'W.

Island Creek entrance buoy Fl G "1," despite its 14-foot height, can be a little difficult as it tends to blend into the shoreline. The GPS derived coordinates are 38°39.31'N by 76°09.53'W.

Eastern Bay and Tributaries

Bloody Point Bar Light, a 54-foot circular brown structure appearing reddish, on a cylindrical foundation, is easy to see against Kent Point. Its position is 38°50'N by 76°23.5'W.

Fl G bell G "1" which is south of Kent Point. Its position is 38°49.1'N by 76°22.2'W.

Kent Narrow southern approach Fl G "1" is 38°57.3'N by 76°14.6'W.

Herring Bay

The privately maintained lighthouse at Herrington Harbour can help if you are trying to get the general location at night. It is 65 feet tall and flashes every 9 sec. Its characteristics may be changed soon. It is maintained from April 1 to October 30. Its position is 38°43.5'N by 76°32.4'W.

First marker into Herring Bay is a 2.5 sec. Fl G, 18 feet tall. Its position is 38°44.4'N by 76°30.9'W.

Rose Haven Channel light "1," QG. It is approximately 30 feet outside the channel limit. Its position is 38°44.1'N by 76°32.3'W.

Herrington Harbor South entrance is marked by the privately maintained daybeacon "1A." Its position is 38°43.9'N by 76°32.4'W.

Herrington Harbor South front range marker is a quick green flash 15 feet tall. Its position is 38°43.5'N by 76°32.6'W.

Knapps Narrows

Knapps Narrows outside eastern channel marker is a 14-foot Fl 4 sec. "1." Its position is 38°41.4'N by 76°18.8'W.

Little Choptank River

Fl G 2.5 sec. marker "1" off Hills Point is important to locate. It helps you avoid the shoal off Hills Point and the shoal off James Island. Its position is 38°33.20'N by 76°19.30'W.

Middle River

Pooles Island Bar Light south of Pooles Island, is 27 feet tall and flashes every 2.5 sec. It is a black skeleton tower on a cylindrical base. Its position is 39°15.7'N by 76°16.7'W.

Middle River Entrance Buoy Qk Fl G "1" is 39°16.3'N by 76°20.0'W.

Bay Bridge

Bay Bridges center of the span position is 38°59.6'N by 76°22.9'W.

Bay Bridges eastern span, with a vertical clearance of only 58 feet, has a center of span position of 38°59.3'N by 76°21.5'W.

Patapsco River

Sandy Point Shoal Light has a white roof and is on a brown cylindrical foundation and is 51 feet tall. Its position is 39°01.0'N by 76°23.1'W.

Southern end of Craighill Channel. The position of the entrance green lighted buoy "1C" is 39°01.4'N by 76°22.7'W.

Eastern Extension of Brewerton Channel has a Fl R Bell buoy, "2BE." Its position is 39°08.9'N by 76°20.0'W.

Patuxent River

About 1-mile west of Target Area the GPS derived position, is 38°12.59'N by 76°19.28'W.

G "1PR" off Cedar Point. Its position is 38°18.24'N by 76°21.20'W.

Helen Creek G "1A." Its GPS derived position is 38°21.170'N by 76°28.771'W.

Sassafras River

Ordinary Point Anchorage. I found 6 feet up to the area of the GPS derived position of 39°22.38'N and 75°58.70'W.

Knight Island shoal in the Back Creek entrance ends in the vicinity of 39°22.79'N and 75°56.87'W.

Severn River

Thomas Point Light on the western shore. Its position is 38°53.9'N by 76°26.2'W.

Greenbury Shoal Light, flashing white every 4 sec. 40 feet tall, on a skeletal tower. Its position is 38°58.1'N by 76°27.3'W.

Lake Ogleton outside marker is a 15-foot Fl G on a pile. Its position is 38°57.1'N by 76°27.5'W.

Chesapeake Harbour outside entrance marker is a privately maintained 14-foot Fl R on a pile. Its position is 38°57.6'N by 76°28.0'W.

Still Pond

Still Pond entrance Fl R "2." The GPS derived position is 39°20.20'N by 76°08.20'W.

Susquehanna

RG "A" which marks the junction for the Susquehanna channel and the North East River Channel. On a misty day this may be hard to pick up. We took GPS coordinates of 39°26.50'N by 76°02.10'W for this mark, and this is what the Light list shows.

West River

Sanders Point Shoal Junction light, Fl (2+1) which is to the east of Sanders Point. Its position is 38°52.9'N by 76°28.6'W.

Whitehall Bay

Fl R bell "2" (southeast of the mouth of the Severn) takes you to Fl R "2" in the entrance to Whitehall Bay. The position of this marker is 38°59.2'N by 76°26.3'W.

Mill Creek outside marker can be a little difficult to see because it is against the shoreline. Its position is 38°59.6'N by 76°26.8'W.

APPENDIX V

U.S. COAST GUARD STATIONS OF UPPER BAY

The upper Bay is covered by four U.S. Coast Guard Stations. It is important to be able to tell them exactly where you are when you call.

Still Pond

This station is just inside the entrance to Still Pond Creek on the northern shore, behind (to the east of) the spit of sand guarding the entrance to the creek. You will see its radio towers and the tops of its buildings as you approach Still Pond Bay.

Curtis Bay

This is located up the Curtis Creek which is up the Patapsco River. After you pass through three bridges you will see it on the left (eastern) shore. This is a very large facility with sections performing both search and rescue operations and repair work for Coast Guard vessels.

Annapolis

Contrary to what you might expect, this is not in the city of Annapolis. It is located more strategically in Fishing Creek in Thomas Point. The entrance to the creek is north-westerly from Thomas Point Light.

Taylors Island

This is no longer considered a "Station" within the normal use of that word, because most of the shore facility has been closed and major parts of operation moved to a 50-foot Cutter. This was an experimental operation at the time of this writing. It allows the crew to be in a better state of readiness to respond, and allows mobility of the station. The base, when the boat was there, was Slaughters Creek in the Little Choptank, at the southern end of the creek on the eastern side with the marina. However the boat is not there at all times, and may be stationed in various locations as the need requires. When the boat is not in this location, other Coast Guard locations will respond to your call, and if you still need assistance in that vicinity, it is still appropriate to call "U.S. Coast Guard Taylors Island."

APPENDIX VI

SOME HELPFUL PHONE NUMBERS

This list includes a few phone numbers that might be helpful. We list a few bridge phone numbers which we felt there may be special need to call because of, for example, a requirement for advance opening arrangements. We also list some public information numbers when the offices are not near the water. If you desire a yearly updated list of marine-related Chesapeake Bay phone numbers, you should obtain the "Chesapeake Bay Edition Boaters Directory" published by Marine Publications Company, 325 N. Newport Blvd., Newport Beach, CA 92663.

"Ashby 1663" (410) 822-4235
Aberdeen Proving Grounds Military Range Safety Office (410) 278-2792
Annapolis shuttle bus information (410) 263-7964
Annapolis Area Chamber of Commerce (410) 268-7676
Anne Arundel County Conference and Visitors Bureau (410) 268-TOUR
Baltimore Harbor Maritime Association (410) 276-2600
Baltimore, The Office of Promotion and Tourism (410) 752-8632.
Baltimore City Dockmaster's Office (410) 396-3174
Baltimore Gallery and Inner Harbor Pavilions (malls) (410) 332-4191
Baltimore Neighborhood Markets information (410) 837-4636
Baltimore Trolleys (410) 752-2015
Bay Bridge Airport near Stevensvile (410) 643-4363
Bear Creek Bascule Bridge (410) 284-1880; 284-0955
Bear Creek, last bridge, (410) 284-1815
Bogle's Wharf Public Landing (410) 778-4600
Chesapeake Village Shopping Mall (410) 827-8699
Chesapeake Bay Maritime Museum (410) 745-2916
Chestertown Area Chamber of Commerce (410) 778-0416
Chestertown Bridge 800-787-9439 or (410) 829-3008
Choptank Municipal Marina (410) 479-3731
Church Hill Theater in Church Hill (410) 758-1331
Coastal Properties and Management, Inc. (410) 269-0933
Conowingo Dam Authority (410) 457-2409

Cove House near Queenstown (410) 827-6300
Crab Alley Marina (410) 643-7339
Crouse Oil at Denton (410) 479-1722
Dorchester County Department of Tourism (410) 228-1000
Eastern Shore Limousine Service, Inc. serves Easton and many other eastern shore areas. Call (410) 820-8431
Eastern Neck Wildlife Refuge (410) 639-7056
Elk Neck State Park (410) 287-5333
Harriet Ross Tubman Birthplace, for tours call (410) 228-0401
Havre de Grace Area Chamber of Commerce (410) 939-3303
Hill Holidays Travel Agency (410) 885-2797; 800 874-4558
Historical Society of Kent County (410) 778-3499
Jefferson Patterson Park and Museum at St. Leonard Creek (410) 586-0050
Kennersly Point Marina (410) 758-2394
Kent and Queen Anne's Hospital (410) 778-3300
Kent County Chamber of Commerce in Chestertown (410) 778-0416
Kent Harbour Marina (410) 643-2445
Kent County public ramps and fee information: County Department of Parks and Recreation (410) 778-1948
Marine Electronics Service in Elkton (410) 398-0471
Mount Harmon on the Sassafras (410) 275-8819
Multi dealers antiques market near Queenstown (410) 827-6640
Public transportation system utilizing busses for area around Kent Narrows (410) 758-0848
Queen Annes County Visitors Center near Kent Narrows (410) 643-8908
Ramp Information for Queen Annes County (410) 758 0835; 778-4430
Sandy Point State Park (410) 974-2772
Spa Creek Bridge (410) 974-3840
Suicide Bridge Restaurant (410) 943-4689
Talbot County Chamber of Commerce (410) 822-4606
United States Naval Academy Visitor's Center (410) 263-6933
Weems Creek Drawbridge (410) 841-5466
Wildfowl Trust of North America near Kent Narrows (410) 827-6694

Steamboat Landing Restaurant. Author's *Chez Nous* at far left. Chapter 19

APPENDIX VII

MAJOR LIGHTS & MARKERS:

(FROM LIGHT LIST, VOL. II OR G.P.S. DERIVED)

Sandy Point to Susquehanna River
Chart #12273
Scale 1:80,000

1. Arnold Point Light, Fl W 4 sec., 39°27.8′N, 75°58.0′W
2. Bohemia River, Fl R 4 sec., "2," GPS: 39°28.54′N, 75°53.18′W
3. Susquehanna River, North East River, RG "A," GPS: 39°26.5′N, 76°02.10′W
4. Elk River, "1 ER," Fl G 2.5 sec., 39°23.8′N, 76°03.3′W
5. Howell Point Light, Fl W 4 sec., 39°22.3′N, 76°06.7′W
6. Still Pond Entrance, Fl R "2" GPS: 39°20.20′N, 76°08.20′W
7. Worton Point Light, Fl W 6 sec., 39°19.1′N, 76°11.2′W
8. Pooles Island Bar light, Fl 2.5 sec., 39°15.7′N, 76°16.7′W
9. Middle River Entrance, QG "1," 39°16.3′N, 76°20.0′W
10. Sevenfoot Knoll Light, Fl W 6 sec., 39°09.3′N, 76°24.5′W
11. Brewerton Channel, QG "3," 39°10.9′N, 76°26.7′W
12. Love Point Light, Fl 6 sec., 39°03.4′N, 76°17.0′W
13. Love Point Shoal, R N "2," 39°04.0′N, 76°16.4′W
14. Fl G 4 sec., "1 UC," 39°04.8′N, 76°18.9′W
15. Brewerton Channel, Eastern Extension, Fl R 2.5 sec., Bell "2BE" 39°08.9′N, 76°20.0′W
16. Craighill Channel Entrance, Fl G 2.5 sec., "1C," 39°01.4′N, 76°22.7′W
17. Baltimore Light, Fl 2.5 sec., 39°03.5′N, 76°24.0′W
18. Sandy Point Shoal Light, Fl 6 sec., 39°01.0′N, 76°23.1′W

Patuxent River Entrance to Sandy Point
Composite Chart #12263 & #12230
Scale 1:80,000

16. Craighill Channel Entrance, Fl G 2.5 sec., "1C" 39°01.4′N, 76°22.7′W
18. Sandy Point Shoal Light, Fl 6 sec., 39°01.0′N, 76°23.1′W
19. Bay Bridges, Center Span, 38°59.6′N, 76°22.9′W
20. Bay Bridges, Eastern Span, 38°59.3′N, 76°21.5′W
21. Chesapeake Bay "#88," Fl R 2.5 sec., 38°56.1′N, 76°22.9′W
22. Whitehall Bay, Fl R "2," 38°59.2′N, 76°26.3′W
23. Greenbury Shoal Light, Fl W 4 sec., 38°58.1′N, 76°27.3′W
24. Lake Ogleton Entrance, Fl G "1," 38°57.1′N, 76°27.5′W
25. Thomas Point Shoal Light, Fl W 6 sec. (2 red sectors), 38°53.9′N, 76°26.2′W

26. Bloody Point Light, Fl W 6 sec. (2 red sectors), 38°50.0′N, 76°23.5′W
27. Eastern Bay, Fl G 4 sec., Bell "1," 38°49.1′N, 76°22.2′W
28. Wye River, Buoy "1," 38°50.0′N, 76°12.6′W
29. Kent Narrows, Southern approach, Fl G 4 sec., "1," 38°57.3′N, 76°14.6′W
30. South River Entrance Buoy, "2," 38°53.7′N, 76°27.9′W
31. Sanders Point Shoal Junction Light, Fl (2+1) R 6 sec., 38°52.9′N, 76°28.6′W
32. Poplar Island Narrows Light, "1" Fl G 4 sec., 38°44.0′N, 76°21.4′W
33. Knapps Narrows Western Side, "1" Fl G 4 sec., 38°43.3′N, 76°20.8′W
34. Knapps Narrows Eastern Side, "3" Fl G 4 sec., 38°42.6′N, 76°19.4′W
35. Lighted Whistle, "CR," 38°38.6′N, 76°25.2′W
36. Sharps Island Light, Fl W 6.5 sec. (red sector), 38°38.3′N, 76°22.5′W
37. Chesapeake Bay "#78," Fl R. 4 sec., 38°33.2′N, 76°25.7′W
38. Broad Creek, Fl G 4 sec., "1" 38°41.7′N, 76°14.9′W
39. Island Creek, Fl G 4 sec., "1," GPS: 38°39.31′N, 76°09.53′W
40. Choptank River Light, Fl W 4 sec., 38°39.4′N, 76°11.1′W
41. Tred Avon River, "1" Fl G 2.5 sec., 38°39.9′N, 76°11.3′W
42. Little Choptank River, Fl G 2.5 sec., "1" 38°33.2′N, 76°19.3′W
43. Herring Bay, Fl G 2.5 sec., "1," 38° 44.4′N, 76°30.9′W
44. Rose Haven Channel Light, QG "1,"38°44.1′N, 76°32.3′W
45. Chesapeake Beach, Fl G 4 sec., "1," 38°41.5′N, 76°31.3′W
46. Cove Point Platform Light, A QW 38°24.1′N, 76°23.2′W
47. Cove Point Light, Fl W 10 sec., 38°23.2′N, 76°22.9′W
48. GR "1 PR"   GPS: 38°18.24′N, Fl G 4 sec., Bell   76°21.20′W
49. Drum Point Light, "4," Fl R 2.5 sec., 38°19.1′N, 76°25.3′W
50. Target area, 1 NM west of, GPS: 38°12.59′N, 76°19.28′W
51. Hooper Island Light, Fl W 6 sec., 38°15.4′N, 76°15.0′W

Other Helpful Lights — South of Chart Coverage:

1. Point No Point Light: Fl W 6 sec., 38°07.7′N, 76°17.4′W
2. Point Lookout Light: Fl (2) W 5 sec., 38°01.6′N, 76°19.3′W
3. Smith Point Light (in VA), Fl W 10 sec. (red sector), 37°52.8′N, 76°11.0′W

Container ship. This one's leaving Baltimore, but you'll encounter freighters in deep water channels all over Chesapeake Bay. Give them right of way.

APPENDIX VIII

TIDAL DIFFERENCES AND OTHER CONSTANTS

The VHF weather channel gives daily high and low tides for Baltimore Harbor at Fort McHenry.

Following are differentials for predictions on Baltimore Harbor at Fort McHenry, for points covered by this book. Please note that Time Differentials are given in hours and minutes, but Height Differentials are all ratios, to be multiplied by daily height predictions for Baltimore Harbor. For instance, the daily height predictions for Baltimore for July 1, 1995 are:

    0211 first low, height 0.6 feet above MLW
    0847 first high, height 1.8 feet above MLW
    1531 2nd low, height 0.6 feet above MLW
    2126 2nd high, height 1.4 feet above MLW

To determine times of high and low water at Taylor Island, Slaughter Creek, you subtract the differentials given in the table below.

    0211 first low time
    −0315
    ————
    2256 that puts you into June 30 late in the day

    0847 first high time
    −305
    ————
    0542

Because many of Chesapeake Bay's harbors and anchorages are shallow, the times of high and low tides are very important. These examples above make calculations easy enough if you have daily predictions for Baltimore, given on the VHF weather channel.

Equally important are heights of these daily predictions. To get these, you have to multiply the ratios shown in our Height Differentials by the heights given for Baltimore. Using July 1, 1995 as an example:

    First low = 0.6 feet, multiply by 1.2 = 0.72 feet above MLW
    First high = 1.8 feet, multiply by 1.2 = 2.16 feet above MLW

These differentials are taken from NOAA "Tide Tables for the East Coast of North and South America." We strongly recommend that you carry the current year's predictions aboard. This table is intended to be a helpful reference if you don't have them.

PLACE	DIFFERENCES				RANGES	
	Time		Height			
	High Water hrs. min.	Low water hrs. min.	High Water All of the figures for heights are ratios to be multiplied by the daily height predictions for Baltimore	Low water	Mean Ft.	Spring Ft.
Eastern Shore						
Little Choptonk River						
Taylors I., Slaughter Creek	−3 05	−3 15	1.08	1.08	1.2	1.4
Woolford, Church Creek	−3 21	−3 00	1.27	1.29	1.4	1.6
Cherry Island, Beckwiths Creek	−3 17	−3 01	1.17	1.17	1.3	1.5
Hudson Creek	−3 45	−3 21	1.27	1.29	1.4	1.6
Sharps Island Light	−3 47	−3 50	1.18	1.17	1.3	1.5
Choptank River						
Choptank River Light	−3 13	−3 08	1.27	1.29	1.4	1.6
Cambridge	−2 44	−2 41	1.47	1.42	1.6	1.7
Choptank	−2 09	−1 48	1.46	1.46	1.6	1.8
Dover Bridge	−0 34	−0 43	1.54	1.54	1.7	1.9
Denton	+0 17	+0 32	1.98	2.00	2.2	2.5
Greensboro	+1 22	+1 18	2.27	2.29	2.5	2.9
Wayman Wharf, Tuckahoe Creek	+0 57	+0 35	2.17	2.17	2.4	2.8
Tred Avon River						
Oxford	−3 01	−2 50	1.27	1.29	1.4	1.6
Easton Point	−2 55	−2 40	1.46	1.46	1.6	1.8

Deep Neck Point, Broad Creek	-3	06	-2	51	1.29	1.29	1.4	1.6
St. Michaels, San Domingo Creek	-3	04	-2	56	1.27	1.29	1.4	1.6
Avalon, Dogwood Harbor	-3	04	-2	53	1.14	1.17	1.3	1.5
Poplar Island	-3	08	-3	08	1.09	1.09	1.2	1.3
Ferry Cove, Eastern Bay	-2	57	-2	54	0.90	0.92	1.0	1.2
Claiborne, Eastern Bay	-2	36	-2	33	1.00	1.00	1.1	1.3
St. Michaels, Miles River	-2	14	-1	58	1.08	1.08	1.2	1.4
Wye Landing, Wye East River	-2	01	-1	41	1.18	1.16	1.3	1.5
Kent Island Narrows	-1	40	-1	28	1.08	1.08	1.2	1.4
Matapeake, Kent Island	-1	29	-1	48	0.89	0.89	1.0	1.1
Bloody Point Bar Light	-2	42	-2	44	1.00	1.00	1.1	1.3

Chester River

Love Point	-0	20	-0	36	1.00	1.00	1.1	1.3
Queenstown	-0	04	-0	14	1.18	1.17	1.3	1.5
Shipyard Landing, Langford Creek	+0	18	+0	15	1.35	1.33	1.5	1.7
Centreville Landing, Corsica R.	+0	10	+0	09	1.46	1.46	1.6	1.8
Cliffs Point	+0	02	-0	07	1.36	1.38	1.5	1.7
Cliffs Wharf	+0	02	-0	04	1.36	1.38	1.5	1.7
Chestertown	+0	47	+0	34	1.63	1.63	1.8	2.1
Crumpton	+1	22	+1	23	2.17	2.17	2.4	2.8
Millington	+2	07	+2	40	1.80	1.79	2.0	2.3
Deep Landing, Swan Creek	-0	08	-0	09	1.00	1.00	1.1	1.3
Tolchester	+0	28	+0	23	1.08	1.08	1.2	1.4
Worton Creek entrance	+1	11	+1	13	1.18	1.17	1.3	1.5

Sassafras River

Betterton	+2	31	+2	18	1.45	1.45	1.6	1.8
Georgetown	+2	05	+2	05	1.83	1.83	2.0	2.3

Elk River

Town Point Wharf	+3	17	+3	00	1.86	1.88	2.1	2.4
Courthouse Point	+2	53	+2	48	2.00	2.00	2.2	2.5
Old Frenchtown Wharf	+3	04	+2	55	2.08	2.08	2.3	2.6
Charlestown, Northeast River	+3	42	+3	58	1.71	1.71	1.9	2.2

Chesapeake Bay, western shore
Susquehanna River

Havre de Grace	+3	11	+3	30	1.59	1.59	1.8	1.9
Port Deposit	+4	04	+4	58	1.90	1.92	2.1	2.4
Fishing Battery Light	+2	33	+2	41	1.90	1.92	2.1	2.4
Pond Light	+1	37	+1	42	1.27	1.29	1.4	1.6
Pooles Island	+0	55	+0	49	1.09	1.08	1.2	1.4
Battery Point, Gunpowder River	+1	04	+1	10	1.08	1.08	1.2	1.4
Bowley Bar, Middle River	+0	51	+0	43	1.08	1.08	1.2	1.4
Rocky Point, Back River	+0	46	+0	38	1.00	1.00	1.1	1.2
Sevenfoot Knoll Light	-0	06	-0	10	0.82	0.83	0.9	1.1

Patapsco River

North Point	+0	02	-0	01	0.94	1.00	1.0	1.2
Fort Carroll	+0	03	+0	11	1.00	1.00	1.1	1.3
Baltimore, Fort McHenry			Daily Predictions				1.1	1.3
Fells Point, Baltimore Harbor	+0	09	+0	16	1.08	1.08	1.2	1.3
Middle Branch, Baltimore Harbor	+0	26	+0	28	0.90	0.92	1.0	1.2
Mountain Point, Magothy River	-0	14	-0	09	0.71	0.71	0.8	1.0
Sandy Point	-1	21	-1	25	0.71	0.71	0.8	0.9
Greenbury Point Shoal Light	-1	46	-1	50	0.72	0.71	0.8	0.9

Severn River

Cedar Point	-0	47	-0	49	0.62	0.62	0.7	0.8
Brewer Point	-1	00	-1	00	0.71	0.71	0.8	0.9
Annapolis	-1	38	-1	49	0.81	0.83	0.9	1.1
Bay Ridge	-2	01	-2	05	0.74	0.70	0.8	1.0
Thomas Point Shoal Light	-2	04	-2	16	0.81	0.83	0.9	1.0
Edgewater, South River	-2	01	-2	12	0.81	0.83	0.9	1.0
Gingerville Creek, South River	-2	09	-2	00	0.90	0.92	1.0	1.1
Rhode River (County Wharf)	-2	04	-2	14	0.91	0.92	1.0	1.1

Shady Side, West River	-1	58	-1 48	0.81	0.83	0.9	1.0
Galesville, West River	-1	48	-1 38	0.81	0.83	0.9	1.0
Fairhaven, Herring Bay	-2	55	-3 01	0.81	0.83	0.9	1.0
Rose Haven	-2	47	-2 49	0.81	0.83	0.9	1.0
Chesapeake Beach	-2	52	-3 04	0.91	0.92	1.0	1.1
Plum Point	-3	30	-3 33	0.82	0.83	0.9	1.0
Long Beach	-4	10	-4 12	0.90	0.92	1.0	1.2
Cove Point	-4	05	-4 27	1.17	1.17	1.3	1.5
Patuxent River							
Drum Point	-4	51	-5 01	1.11	1.08	1.2	1.4
Solomons Island	-4	45	-4 52	1.07	1.08	1.2	1.3
Broomes Island	-4	29	-4 21	1.17	1.17	1.3	1.5
Benedict	-4	10	-3 56	1.45	1.45	1.6	1.9
Lower Marlboro	-2	59	-2 55	1.62	1.63	1.8	2.0
Nottingham	-2	47	-2 29	2.29	2.29	2.5	2.9
Hills Bridge (Route 4)	-1	07	-0 38	2.17	2.17	2.4	2.8
Cedar Point	-4	54	-5 02	1.08	1.08	1.2	1.4
Point No Point	-5	27	-5 39	1.18	1.17	1.3	1.5
Point Lookout	-5	26	-5 36	1.11	1.08	1.2	1.4

Kids playing in waterfront park, Galesville.   Chapter 19

APPENDIX IX

CHESAPEAKE BAY CHARTER LIST

Fortunately for those who live in other parts of the country, there are thriving charter fleets in Chesapeake Bay, any kind of boat you could want.

Most of the boats are chartered bareboat, though several of the charter companies will put a skipper aboard for those who want them. We have included a list of charter brokers, who may be able to put you aboard a completely crewed boat, where you will be a passenger. You won't find a fleet of luxury yachts for charter with crew, like summers in New England or the Mediterranean, or winters in Florida or the Carribbean, but these charter brokers may be able to find something for you. At this time, there are no windjammers in Chesapeake Bay, such as you find in New England.

Consider the bareboat fleet even if your boat is in Long Island Sound or North Carolina. Working people have limited amounts of time. I've sailed my own boat to Chesapeake Bay from Stamford, CT four times. While I enjoyed sails down and back, it limited my cruising time in the Bay. I'm an inveterate charterer to far away places and next time I'll charter in the Bay. Charter the boat of your choice, and enjoy a leisurely cruise for all the time you have. Chapter I gives you Tom's suggested itineraries for one, two and three week cruises.

We are not including prices or detailed descriptions of boats, because these change rapidly. Prices generally are competitive with other popular areas. Consider early and late season sailing when charter boats are less in demand and prices may be lower. Chesapeake Bay has a long cruising season, about four to six weeks longer than Long Island Sound. October is a great cruising month on Chesapeake Bay.

Try to make arrangements well in advance. Most of the choice boats are booked for the season, months ahead, though you may get someone's last minute cancellation. Six months is not too much lead time for reserving a charter boat. Tom Neale's guide will make it easy for you. He assumes basic cruising skills on your part, especially good navigational skills. You'll enjoy this lovely Bay, as thousands of other charterers have done.

BAREBOAT CHARTERS

Allied Yacht Charters
326 1st Street, Suite 29
Annapolis, MD 21403
(800) 922-4820; (410) 280-1522
12 sailboats

Annapolis Bay Charters
7310 Edgewood Road
P.O. Box 4604
Annapolis, MD 21403
(410) 269-1776; (800) 292-1119
40 sailboats, all sizes many makes.

**Annapolis Yacht Sales &
Charters (AYS)**
7416 Edgewood Road
Annapolis, MD 21403
(410) 267-8181; (800) 382-8181
Fax: (410) 267-7409
Fleet has 28 boats including catamarans, sailing school. Captains available.

Blue Goose Enterprises
P.O. Box 433
Severn, MD 21144
(800) 874-6673
Fleet has 7 boats, all power.

C&C Charters Maryland
506 Kent Narrows Way North
Grasonville, MD 21638
(800) 733-7245; (410) 827-7888
Fleet has 26 boats, power and sail, can provide skipper.

Carolina Wind Yachting Center
P. O. Box 967, 411 West Main Street
Washington, NC 27889
(800) 334-7671; (919) 946-4653
10 sailboats

Chesapeake Sailing Association
1525 Bayville Street
Norfolk, VA 23503
(800) 296-7245; (804) 588-2022

**Chesapeake Sailing School &
Yacht Charters**
7074 Bembe Beach Road
Annapolis, MD 21403
(800) 966-0032; (410) 269-1594;
(301) 261-2810 (DC)
16 sailboats

Eastern Shore Yacht Charters
P. O. Box 88
202 Bank Street
Oxford, MD 21654
(410) 226-5000
Fleet has 17 boats, power and sail, can provide skipper.

Free State Yachts, Inc.
64 Old South River
Edgewater, MD 21037
(410) 266-9060
14 sailboats

Gratitude Yachting Sales
Spring Cove Marina on Swan Creek
5990 Lawton Ave
Rock Hall, MD 21661
(410) 639-7111
Fax: (410) 639-7345
22 sailboats

Gratitude Yachting Center
Route 33, P. O. Box 969
Deltaville, VA   23043
5 sailboats

Hartge Chesapeake Charters
4881 Church Lane
P.O. Box 134
Galesville, MD 20765
(410) 867-7240; (301) 261-9040
15 sailboats

Haven Charters
20846 Rock Hall Avenue
Rock Hall, MD 21661
(410) 639-7140
13 sailboats

Havre de Grace Sailing Services
P.O. Box 441
Tidewater Marina
Havre de Grace, MD 21078
(800) 526-1528; (410) 939-2869
12 sailboats

Julyan Chesapeake Charters
Box 98
Oxford, MD 21654
(410) 226-5777; (410) 226-5450

La Vida Yachts, Inc.
22174 Great Oak Landing Road
Chestertown, MD 21620
(410) 778-6330
14 sailboats

North East Wind Yacht Group
Box 4220
Annapolis, MD 21403
(800) 638-5139; (301) 267-6333
Fleet has more than 20 boats,
power and sail, can provide skipper.

Paradise Bay Yacht Charters
Annapolis Landing Marina
980 Awald Drive
Annapolis, MD 21403
(800) 877-9330; (410) 268-9330
25 sailboats

Pelorus Marina
P.O. Box 479
20927 Bayside Avenue
Rock Hall, MD 21661
(410) 639-2151

The Sailing Emporium
P. O. Box 597
21144 Green Lane
Rock Hall, MD 21661
(410) 778-1342
14 sailboats

The Sailing Place
612 Atlantic Beach Cswy.
Atlantic Beach, NC 28512
(919) 726-5664
6 sailboats

Sassafras Charters
P.O. Box 267
Galena, MD 21635
(800) 548-1358; (301) 648-5827
Fleet has 2 boats, both power,
can provide skipper.

Spar Charters
1525 Bayville Street
Norfolk, VA   23503
(800) 296-7245; (804) 588-2022
13 sailboats

Sunsail Annapolis Landing Marina
980 Awald Road
P.O. Box 3515
Annapolis, MD 21403
(410) 280-2553; (800) 327-2276
Fax: (410) 280-2406
Fleet has 6 Hunter 336's

Sunsail
115 East Broward Blvd.
Ft. Lauderdale, FL   33301
(800) 327-2276
13 sailboats

Whittaker Creek Charters
P. O. Box 357
Oriental, NC   28571
(919) 249-0666
10 sailboats

BROKERS FOR CREWED BOATS

Free State Yachts
P.O. Box 6529
Annapolis, MD 21401
(800) 394-6484
Sail and power, sailing lessons.

Annapolis Bay Charters, Inc.
Box 4604.
Annapolis, MD 21403
(410) 269-1776; (301) 261-1815
Fax: (410) 280-5644
Chesapeake, Annapolis and
Solomons Island. Power and sail,
30'-65'.

Aventura Yacht Charters & Sales
P.O. Box 80-0202
Aventura, FL 33280
(305) 933-1963
Fax: (305) 936-8007
Power and sail, 50'-250'.

Bartram & Brakenhoff, Inc.
Two Marina Plaza
Goat Island
Newport, RI 02840
(401) 846-7355
Fax: (401) 847-6329
Power and sail, 50'-250'.

Camper & Nicholsons USA, Inc.
450 Royal Palm Way
Palm Beach, FL 33480
(407) 655-2121
Fax: (407) 655-2202
Power and sail, 60'+.

Fraser Yachts
2230 SE 17th Street
Ft. Lauderdale, FL 33316
(305) 463-0640
Fax: (305) 462-1028
Power and sail, 60'-300'.

Lynn Jachney Charters, Inc.
Box 302
Marblehead, MA 01945
(800) 223-2050; (617) 639-0787
Fax: (617) 639-0216
Power and sail, 43'-200'.

Nicholson Yacht Charters, Inc.
432 Colombia Street, Suite 21A
Cambridge, MA 02141
(800) 662-6066; (617) 225-0555
Fax: (617) 225-0190
Power and sail, 40'-200'.

North East Wind Yacht Group
P.O. Box 4220
Pier 4
301 Fourth Street
Annapolis, MD 21403
(800) 638-5139; (410) 267-6333
Fax: (410) 263-2881
Power and sail, 30'-47'.

Northrop & Johnson
1901 SE 4th Avenue
Ft. Lauderdale, FL 33316
(305) 522-3344
Fax: (305) 522-9500
Power and sail, 60'-200'.

Russell Yacht Charters
404 Hulls Highway, Suite 85
Southport, CT 06490
(800) 635-8895; (203) 255-2783
Fax: (203) 255-3426
Power and sail, 41'-401'.

Sparkman & Stephens, Inc.
529 Fifth Avenue, 14th Floor
New York, NY 10017
(212) 661-6170
Fax: (212) 661-1235
Power and sail, 50'-446'.

United/Derecktor-Gunnell Yachts
901 SE 17th Street, Suite 205
Ft. Lauderdale, FL 33316
(305) 524-4616; (305) 949-3415
Fax: (305) 524-4621
Power and sail, 50'+.

Ann Wallis White Charter Yacht Consultants
P.O. Box 4100
Horn Point Marina
Annapolis, MD 21403
(800) 732-3861; (410) 263-6366
Fax: (410) 263-0399
Power and sail. 49'-243'.

Whitney Yacht Charters, Inc.
4065 Crockers Lake Blvd.,
Suite 2722
Sarasota, FL 34238
(800) 223-1426; (813)-927-0108
Fax: (813)-922-7819
Power and sail, 38'-125'.

Topside Inn Restaurant, Chapter 19

Sailboat leaving anchorage, Rhode River, Chapter 19

Traditional tour boats, Baltimore Harbor, Chapter 14

Melanie Neale, author's daughter in barber's chair
among antiques at West River Market, Chapter 19

Stone steps leading to second level of homes
above Main St., Port Deposit, Chapter 2

Character boat at Penn's Beach Marina,
Havre de Grace, Chapter 2

Catfish float, North East, MD, Chapter 3

Thursday night races, Tidewater Marina, Havre de Grace, Chapter 2

Bayou Hotel, Havre de Grace, Chapter 2

One of many carved wood sculptures, Rock Hall, Chapter 7

Rogers Tavern, Perryville, MD, Chapter 2

Lockhouse Museum, Havre de Grace, Chapter 2

TIDAL CURRENT CHARTS

The following pages show Tidal Currents, taken from the NOAA Tidal Current Charts, one for each hour of a complete tidal cycle (12 hours). We strongly recommend that you carry "Current Tables for the East Coast," published annually by NOAA. These give many more points than the following charts, and should be carried aboard on your Chesapeake Bay cruise. Price and sources are listed near the front of the book under Charts, Publications, Sources.

The Tidal Current charts on the following pages are only intended to give you an overall view of what the current will be doing at a given time. Strong winds can affect times and velocity of tidal currents. The ebb will be reinforced by a strong norther, and will be lessened in velocity by a strong southerly. Conversely the flood will be stronger in a strong southerly, and lessened by a strong norther. Times of change may also be delayed in strong winds. Because tidal current flows generally north and south in Chesapeake Bay, north or south winds will have greatest effect. Because so much fresh water flows into the Bay, currents can be increased by heavy rains or spring freshets.

The speeds given with most arrows are in knots at spring tides, which occur at new or full moons, when tidal currents are stronger than average. Where "weak" is noted on the charts, velocities are less than 1/10 of a knot.

To get the actual velocity for any given day, you need the Tidal Current Tables (price and sources near front of the book under Charts, Publications, Sources), but we have found these charts to be helpful, and are therefore reproducing them.

Hand tonging for oysters, Chester River, Chapter 8

Unloading oysters, Rock Hall, Chapter 7

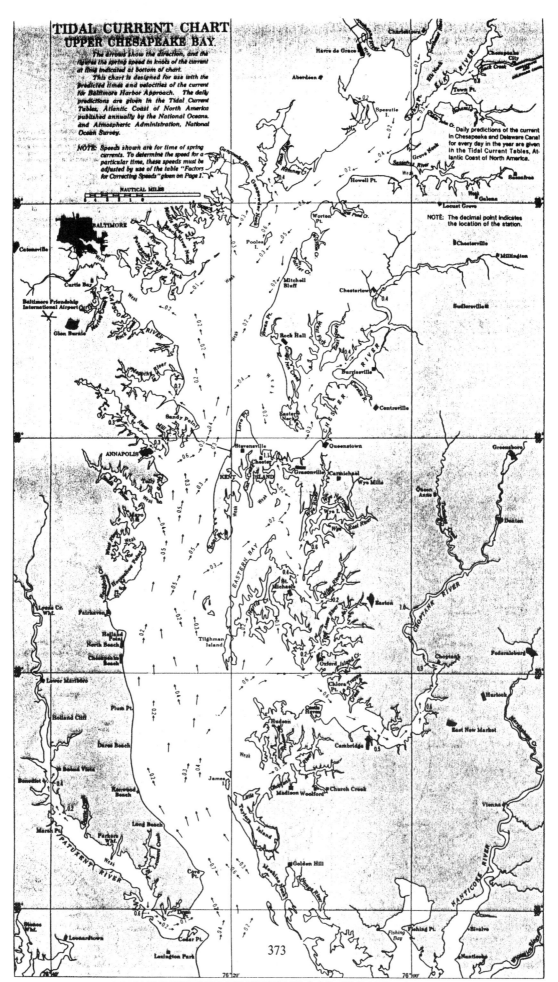

TWO HOURS BEFORE MAXIMUM FLOOD AT BALTIMORE hARBOR APPROACH

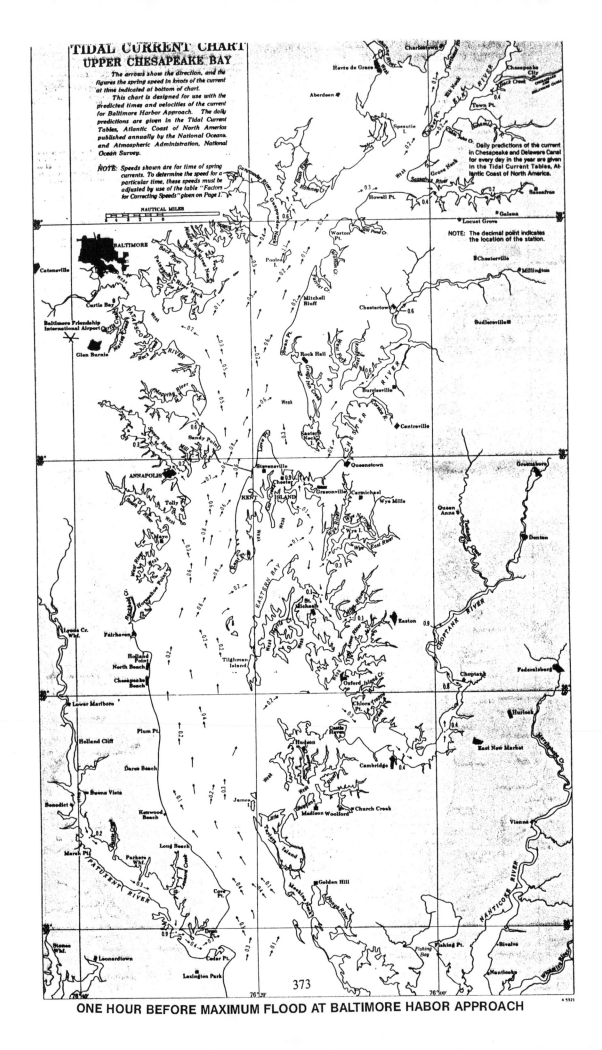

ONE HOUR BEFORE MAXIMUM FLOOD AT BALTIMORE HABOR APPROACH

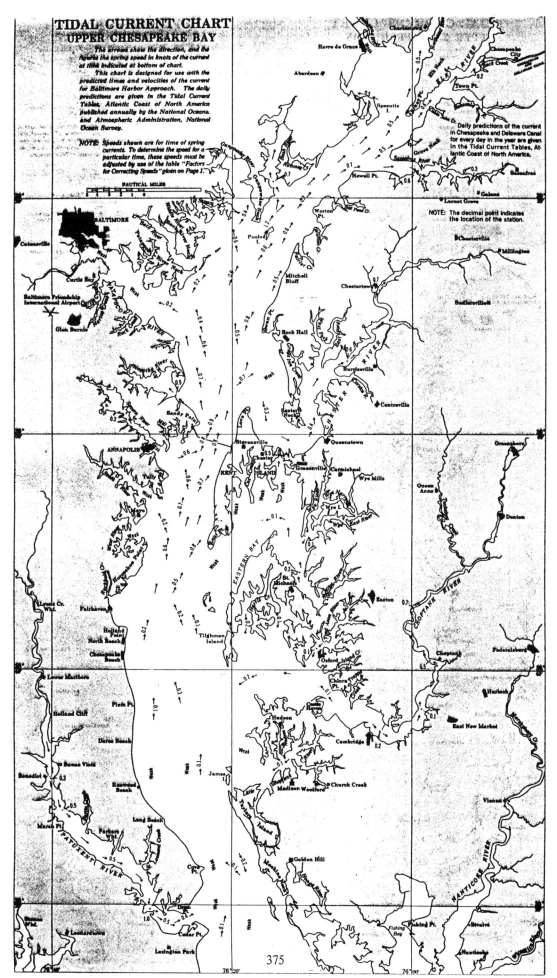

MAXIMUM FLOOD AT BALTIMORE HARBOR APPROACH

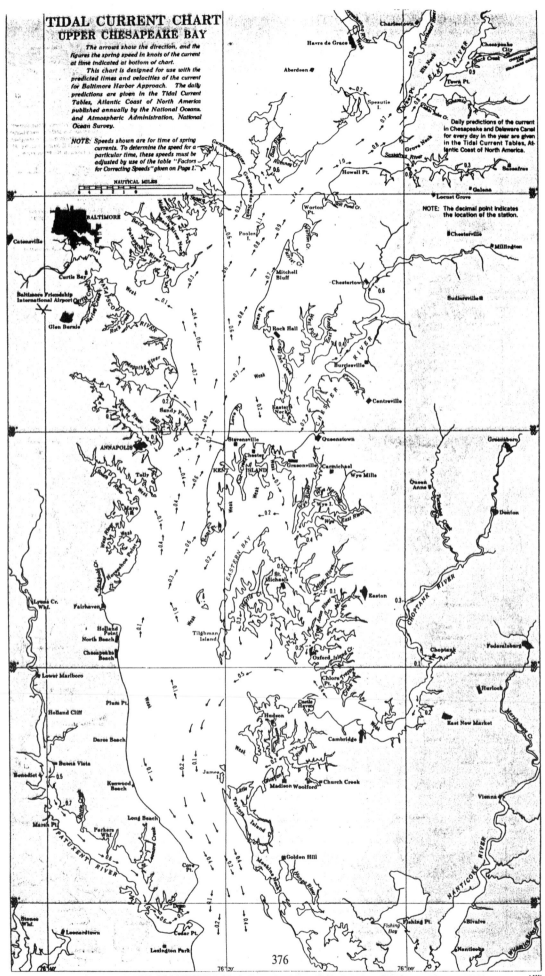

ONE HOUR AFTER MAXIMUM FLOOD AT BALTIMORE HARBOR APPROACH

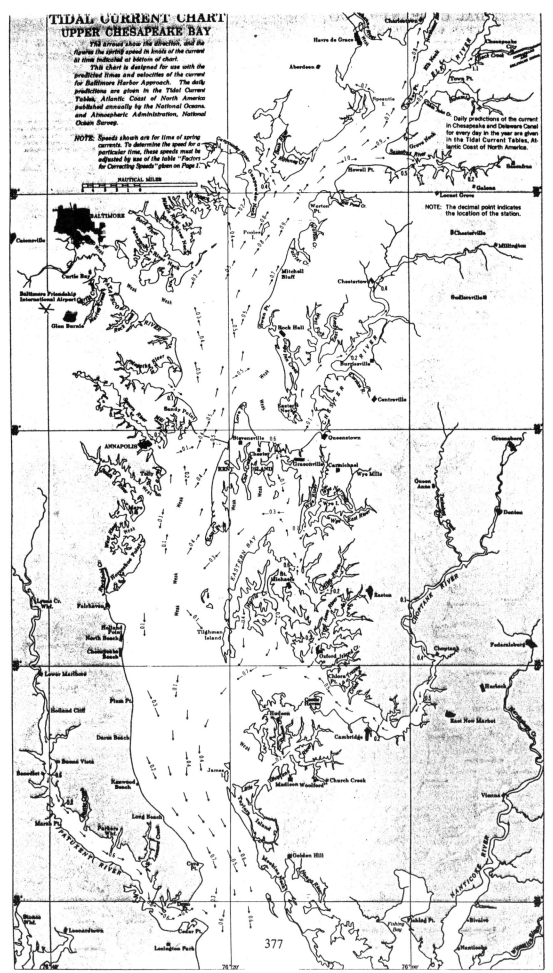

TWO HOURS AFTER MAXIMUM FLOOD AT BALTIMORE HARBOR APPROACH

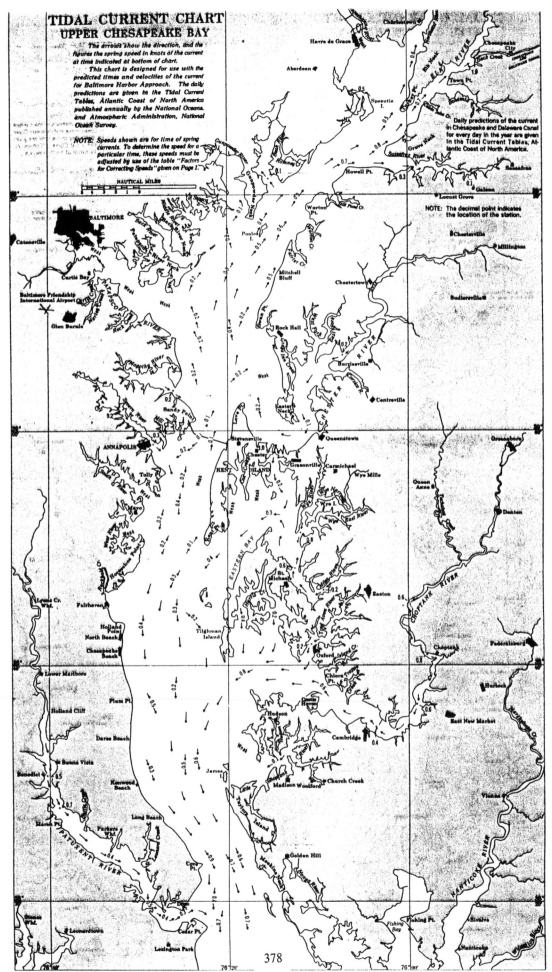

TIDAL CURRENT CHART
UPPER CHESAPEAKE BAY

The arrows show the direction, and the figures the spring speed in knots of the current at time indicated at bottom of chart.

This chart is designed for use with the predicted times and velocities of the current for Baltimore Harbor Approach. The daily predictions are given in the Tidal Current Tables, Atlantic Coast of North America published annually by the National Oceans and Atmospheric Administration, National Ocean Survey.

NOTE: Speeds shown are for time of spring currents. To determine the speed for a particular time, these speeds must be adjusted by use of the table "Factors for Correcting Speeds" given on Page 1.

NAUTICAL MILES

Daily predictions of the current in Chesapeake and Delaware Canal for every day in the year are given in the Tidal Current Tables, Atlantic Coast of North America.

NOTE: The decimal point indicates the location of the station.

378

THREE HOURS AFTER MAXIMUM FLOOD AT BALTIMORE HARBOR APPROACH

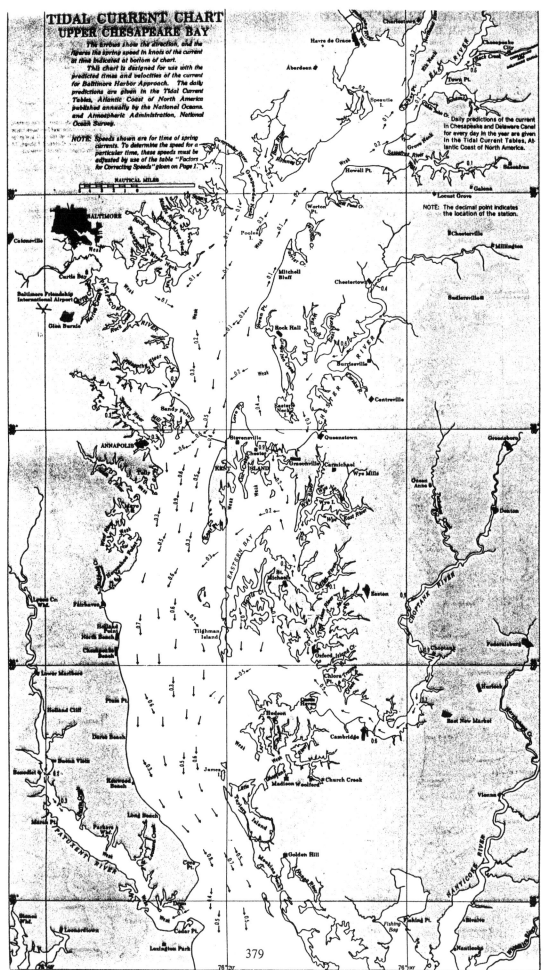

TWO HOURS BEFORE MAXIMUM EBB AT BALTIMORE HARBOR APPORACH

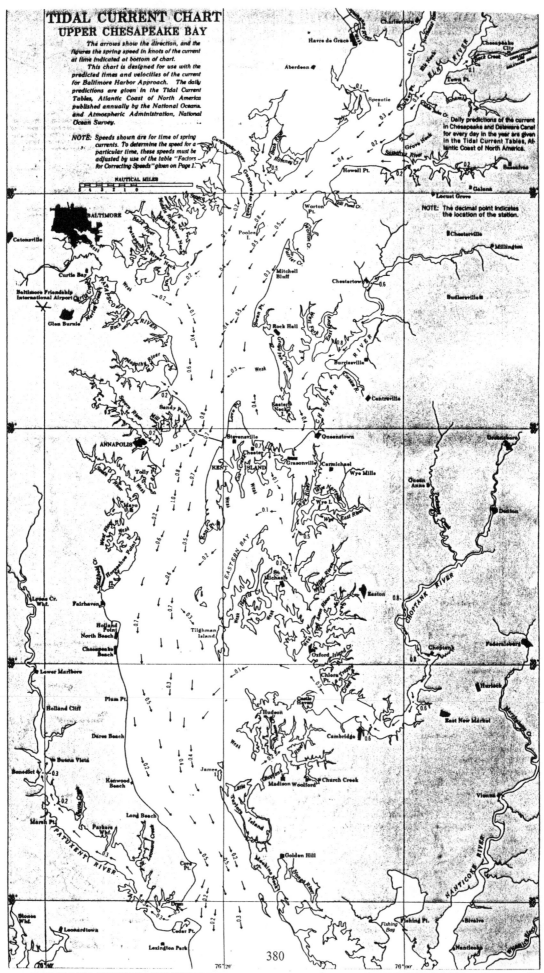

TIDAL CURRENT CHART
UPPER CHESAPEAKE BAY

The arrows show the direction, and the figures the spring speed in knots of the current at time indicated at bottom of chart.

This chart is designed for use with the predicted times and velocities of the current for Baltimore Harbor Approach. The daily predictions are given in the Tidal Current Tables, Atlantic Coast of North America published annually by the National Oceanic and Atmospheric Administration, National Ocean Survey.

NOTE: Speeds shown are for time of spring currents. To determine the speed for a particular time, these speeds must be adjusted by use of the table "Factors for Correcting Speeds" given on Page 1.

NAUTICAL MILES

Daily predictions of the current in Chesapeake and Delaware Canal for every day in the year are given in the Tidal Current Tables, Atlantic Coast of North America.

NOTE: The decimal point indicates the location of the station.

380

ONE HOUR BEFORE MAXIMUM EBB AT BALTIMORE HARBOR APPROACH

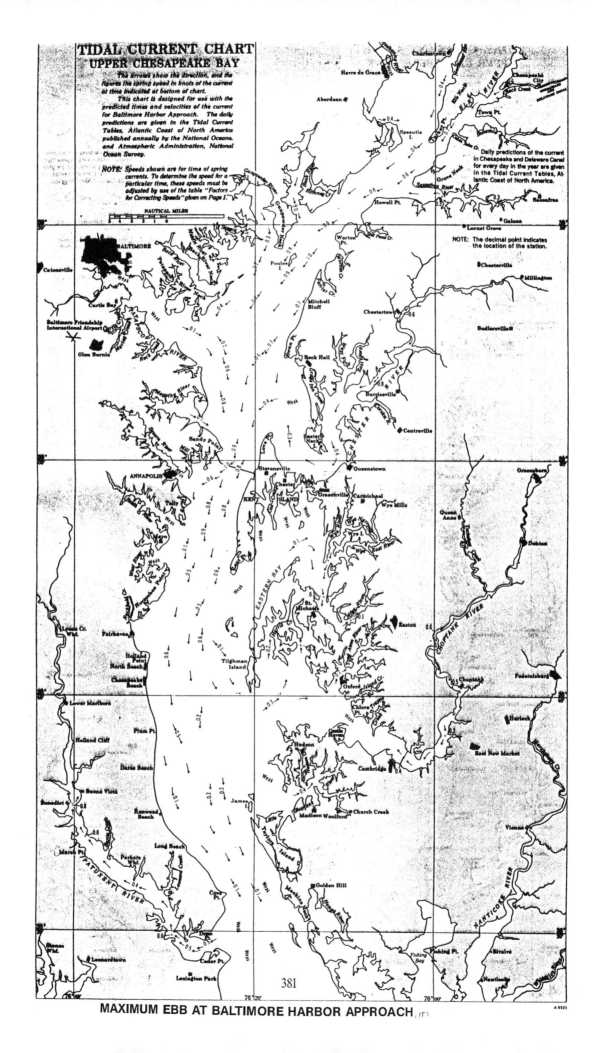

TIDAL CURRENT CHART
UPPER CHESAPEAKE BAY

The arrows show the direction, and the figures the spring speed in knots of the current at time indicated at bottom of chart.

This chart is designed for use with the predicted times and velocities of the current for Baltimore Harbor Approach. The daily predictions are given in the Tidal Current Tables, Atlantic Coast of North America published annually by the National Oceanic and Atmospheric Administration, National Ocean Survey.

NOTE: Speeds shown are for time of spring currents. To determine the speed for a particular time, these speeds must be adjusted by use of the table "Factors for Correcting Speeds" given on Page 1.

NAUTICAL MILES

Daily predictions of the current in Chesapeake and Delaware Canal for every day in the year are given in the Tidal Current Tables, Atlantic Coast of North America.

NOTE: The decimal point indicates the location of the station.

MAXIMUM EBB AT BALTIMORE HARBOR APPROACH (E)

A 5321

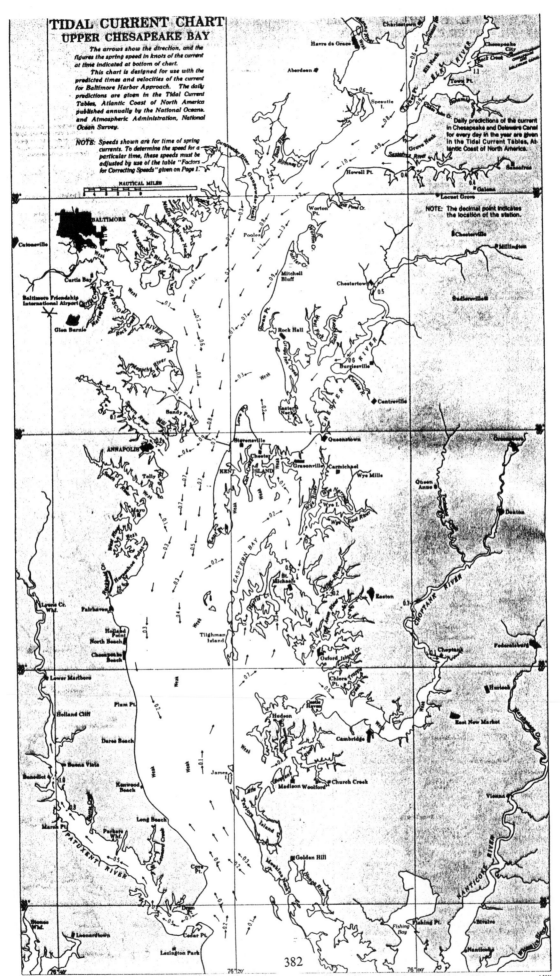

ONE HOUR AFTER MAXIMUM EBB AT BALTIMORE HARBOR APPROACH

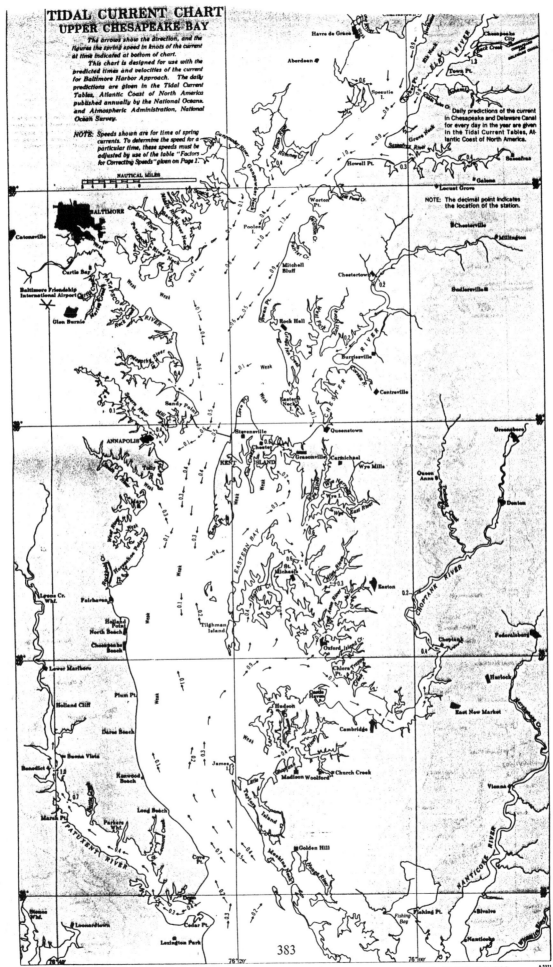

TIDAL CURRENT CHART
UPPER CHESAPEAKE BAY

The arrows show the direction, and the figures the spring speed in knots of the current at time indicated at bottom of chart.

This chart is designed for use with the predicted times and velocities of the current for Baltimore Harbor Approach. The daily predictions are given in the Tidal Current Tables, Atlantic Coast of North America published annually by the National Oceanic and Atmospheric Administration, National Ocean Survey.

NOTE: Speeds shown are for time of spring currents. To determine the speed for a particular time, these speeds must be adjusted by use of the table "Factors for Correcting Speeds" given on Page 1.

NAUTICAL MILES

Daily predictions of the current in Chesapeake and Delaware Canal for every day in the year are given in the Tidal Current Tables, Atlantic Coast of North America.

NOTE: The decimal point indicates the location of the station.

A 5371

TWO HOURS AFTER MAXIMUM EBB AT BALTIMORE HARBOR APPROACH

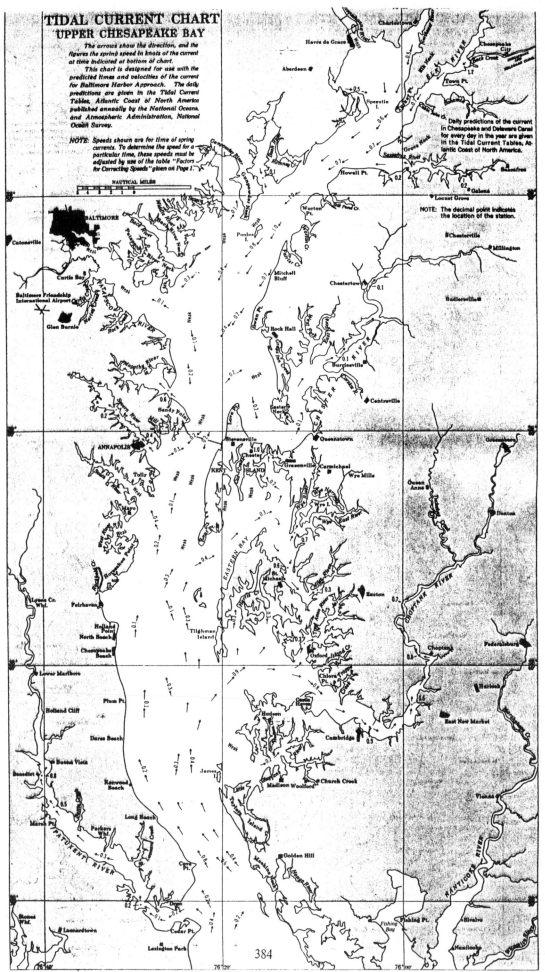

TIDAL CURRENT CHART
UPPER CHESAPEAKE BAY

The arrows show the direction, and the figures the spring speed in knots of the current at time indicated at bottom of chart.

This chart is designed for use with the predicted times and velocities of the current for Baltimore Harbor Approach. The daily predictions are given in the Tidal Current Tables, Atlantic Coast of North America published annually by the National Oceanic and Atmospheric Administration, National Ocean Survey.

NOTE: Speeds shown are for time of spring currents. To determine the speed for a particular time, these speeds must be adjusted by use of the table "Factors for Correcting Speeds" given on Page 1.

NAUTICAL MILES

Daily predictions of the current in Chesapeake and Delaware Canal for every day in the year are given in the Tidal Current Tables, Atlantic Coast of North America.

NOTE: The decimal point indicates the location of the station.

384

THREE HOURS AFTER MAXIMUM EBB AT BALTIMORE HARBOR APPROACH

A-5121